THE BOOK OF A THOUSAND JUDGEMENTS

(A SASANIAN LAW-BOOK)

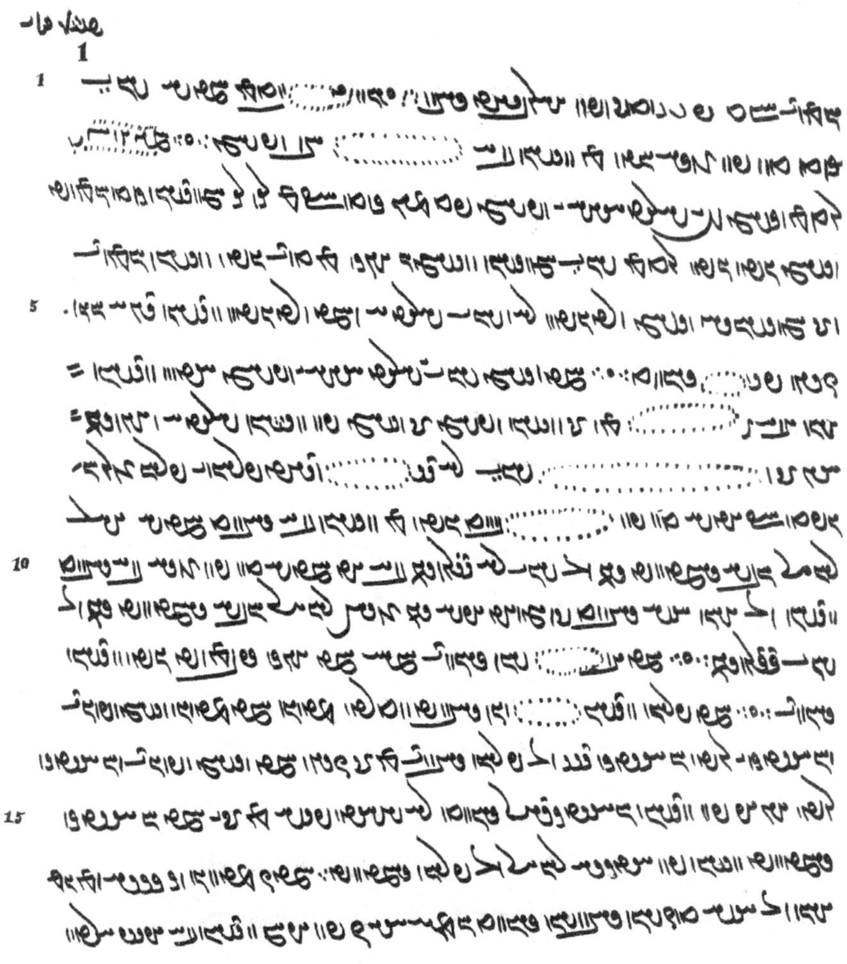

Source: Ervad Tehmuras Dinshaw Anklesaria, *The Madigan-i-Hazar Dadistan,* Part II, with an Introduction by Jivanji Jamshedji Modi, The Fort Printing Press, Bombay, 1901, page 1.

Persian Heritage Foundation
Bibliotheca Persica Reprints

THE BOOK OF A THOUSAND JUDGEMENTS
(A SASANIAN LAW-BOOK)

Introduction, Transcription and Translation of the Pahlavi Text,
Notes, Glossary and Indexes by

Anahit Perikhanian
(St. Petersburg Branch of the Institute of Oriental Studies, Russian Academy of Sciences)

Translated from Russian by

Nina Garsoian
(Columbia University)

Since 1980
Mazda Publishers
Costa Mesa, California 2026

Publication of this book was made possible by a grant from
The A. K. Jabbari Trust

Mazda Publishers, Inc.
Academic publishers since 1980
A. K. Jabbari, publisher
www.mazdapublishers.com

First published in hardcover edition in 1994 by Mazda Publishers
in association with Bibliotheca Persica

Library of Congress Control Number: 2024946213

Softcover (alk. paper)
ISBN 10: 1-56859-409-7
ISBN 13: 978-1-56859-409-5

CONTENTS

GENERAL EDITOR'S NOTE

The *Sasanian Law-Book* or *The Book of A Thousand Judgments* is a unique document about the Sasanian legal system. Prior to being converted to Islam in the second half of the 7th century, Zoroastrian Persia had developed a sophisticated legal system under Sasanian rule (226-651 C. E.); it possessed, however, no formal legal code but, rather, collections of legal cases and decisions that could serve as guides to judges and others. The *Sasanian Law-Book* is the sole example of such a collection that has reached us and, thus, it is the most important source for our knowledge of the laws of Sasanian Persia. It is important not only for the study of Sasanian society and institutions, but also for the comparative study of Judaic and Islamic laws, as both have in certain periods been influenced by Sasanian law.

Dr. Anahit Perikhanian, a foremost scholar in the field of Iranian philology as well as social and administrative institutions of Persia and Armenia in the Parthian and Sasanian periods, published an edition and a translation into Russian of the *Sasanian Law-Book* in 1973. As she explains in her Preface, Dr. Perikhanian has now incorporated further research on the *Law-Book* into this new version with a view of providing the students in the field with as reliable a text, translation and commentary as our present knowledge of Middle Persian and Sasanian life and culture permits. The translation into English has been expertly prepared and edited for the Persian Heritage Series by Professor Nina Garsoïan, Avedissian Professor Emerita of Armenian History at Columbia University.

In 1995 Dr. Perikhanian was invited by the Center for Iranian Studies, Columbia University to deliver a series of lectures on "Iranian Law of Property during the Sasanian Period" based on the *Sasanian Law-Book*. As the content of the lectures will be found in more elaborate form in this volume, it also serves as No. 9 in the Columbia Lectures in Iranian Studies Series.

The publication of this book follows an agreement between the Center for Iranian Studies, Columbia University, and the St. Petersburg branch of the Institute of Oriental Studies of the Russian Academy of Sciences, where Dr. Perikhanian is a Senior Research Fellow.

E. Yarshater

PREFACE TO THE ENGLISH EDITION

The first scholarly edition of this Pahlavi text with an Introduction, a Russian translation and an indexed Glossary was published in Erevan in 1973. Immediately after it came out, I received an offer to publish — within the Persian Heritage Series — an English version of it with a view of making available to a wider group of scholars the valuable material on Sasanian legal, administrative and social institutions contained in this unique document. My English being inadequate to the purpose, Professor Nina Garsoïan (Columbia University, New York) kindly consented to provide an English translation of the Russian text in the Erevan edition. The English version — with a number of corrections and structural changes — was ready for the press in 1976. Its publication, however, has been long delayed for reasons that are of no interest here.

During the period of over twenty years that have elapsed since 1973 my interest for this text and its problems, both legal and philological, has never lessened and, as a result, several articles and a monograph on Iranian Society and Law under Arsacids and Sasanians have been published by me in the interval. Consequently it has become inevitable to introduce important changes in practically every part of the work; in the Glossary, many entries have had to be written afresh.

Here — as in the Russian edition — the system used by Chr.Bartholomae and his school, as well as by H. S. Nyberg, H. W. Bailey and E.Benveniste, has been chosen for the presentation of the Pahlavi text. Despite its many inconsequencies and its remoteness from the phonological state of the Late Sasanian Middle Persian, this system of transcription seems preferable to me for it is much closer to traditional Pahlavi spellings.

As in the Russian edition, here too for the translation of Pahlavi legal terms the terminology of the non-receptioned Roman Law is used, following the common practice in European works on comparative Law. But some specifically Iranian technical terms (*e. g. stūr, čakar, magupat*) have been transcribed in italics rather than translated into English. In certain cases, technical terms with several meanings (*e. g. dastaβar*) have been given varying translations suited to particular contexts. In all such cases and many others, the technical terminology has been elucidated further in the Glossary. Reconstructed or conjectural entries in the Glossary have invariably been marked with an asterisk.

The following symbols have been used:

( ) — parentheses indicate restorations of the missing words in the text and editorial clarifications;

[ ] — square brackets indicate the reconstruction of *lacunae*;

⟨ ⟩ — pointed brackets indicate *errata*, repetitions and redundant *iẓāfa*'s. They are also used for intrusive characters, as well as in the case of ⟨k⟩ in Pahlavi rendering of |ō| in Avestan compounds;

/ — the dash indicates variants;

+ — a cross at the right end of a word marks an incorrect spelling in the ms.

The underlined k̲, t̲, s̲ denote Av. γ, δ, ϑ in the Pahlavi renderings of Avestan terms.

Because of the greater inflexibility of the English sentence structure, it has, unfortunately, proved impossible to preserve in the English translation the linear parallelism maintained between the text of the facsimile edition and the Russian translation.

I owe a great deal to my teacher Professor Igor Diakonoff: to him, the godfather of the Russian edition of this text, my thanks are reiterated here. My thanks are likewise due to the *Persian Heritage Series* and to Professor E. Yarshater for accepting the sponsorship of this work. It is a pleasant duty to express my gratitude to my friend Professor Nina Garsoïan for having kindly given a lot of her time to the hard task of translating my work into English. Since her English translation has been thoroughly checked and corrected by me, I am solely responsible for every error the users of the present edition will find in it. Finally, my thanks are due to Mr Oleg Shakirov (St. Petersburg) for his great care in the type-setting of this book.

Anahit Perikhanian

Institute of Oriental Studies, St. Petersburg

INTRODUCTION

The Manuscript

European scholars first learned of the existence of a manuscript of the *Book of A Thousand Judgments* or *Sasanian Law-Book* from the notices of J. Darmesteter and E. West [1]. The text of this document has reached us in a single, defective, and relatively late manuscript copied in Iran in the XVIIth century. In 1872, the Parsi scholar, T. D. Anklesaria purchased twenty folios of this manuscript in Iran and took them to Bombay. After Anklesaria had prepared a copy of these folios for a facsimile edition, it became known that fifty-five additional folios of the same manuscript had been purchased by M. L. Hataria and were preserved in his library. These included the initial folio giving the title of the work and the author's name. This portion of the manuscript was taken to Bombay, together with the rest of Hataria's library, and a facsimile edition with an Introduction by the well-known Parsi scholar, J. J. Modi, was brought out in Poona in 1901 [2]. The facsimile edition of the twenty folios collected by T. D. Anklesaria was finally published in 1912 — likewise with an Introduction by J. J. Modi [3].

As is evident from a number of formal indications, all seventy-five folios — the 55 of the former Hataria collection (= Part I) and the 20 of the Anklesaria collection (= Part II) — belong to the same manuscript: they are written in the same hand, on the same paper, and normally contain seventeen lines on a side. An indication of the date is to be found in a Persian gloss in the margin of one of the folios (p. 98 of the Facsimile edition) which reads as follows,

> This book was given by the daughter of Asfandyār Nōširvān to her ... (one word illegible) Rustam Nōširvān Bamānyār in exchange for the book of *Yašts* (and) of the *Visparad*, and the sum of one thousand dinars was also conveyed to him in full settlement of the account. Written on the day *Gōš* of the month *Adar*, in the year 1006 of Yazdkart.

Consequently, the year 1006 of Yazdkart (= A.D. 1637) must be taken as the *terminus ad quem* for this manuscript.The other notes added by various owners of the manuscripts (pp. 103, 109) are devoid of interest.

The facsimile editions of both parts of the manuscript reproduce the sequential order assigned to the folios during the second half of the last century at the time when they became part of the private collections of M. L. Hataria and T. D. Anklesaria. Page numbers were the only addition made for publication. As J. Modi already noted in his Introduction, however, this sequence did not correspond to the original order of the folios in the text. Thus, owing to the confusion in the sequence of the folios in Part I (= the Hataria ms.) the beginning of the *Law-Book* appears on page 79, *i. e.* on folio 40a of the sewn manuscript. The prior Persian numbering still appears on the majority of the folios, but several have torn-off corners so that this indication is now lost. The original sequence of folios was preserved only in Part II (= the Anklesaria ms.) despite occasional errors in numbering (*e. g.* two pairs of folios are marked 84 and 89 respectively). A number of folios are missing altogether; these add up to no less than fifty folios or some forty percent of the original text. Finally, the surviving portion of the manuscript contains folios in a very poor state of preservation and numerous sections are riddled with worm holes.

Throughout the *Law-Book*, except in the Prologue of the author or rather the compiler, the material is set out in "articles" containing legal cases and their decisions. The "articles" are grouped in chapters bearing titles which reflect the main subject treated in them [4]. Rarer are cases where the title corresponds to some formal unifying criterion determining the selection of articles grouped in the given chapter [5]. It must be noted, however, that the content of an article does not always correspond to the title of the chapter in which it is found. Moreover the legal aspects subsumed in a single article of a particular chapter are unquestionably far richer and broader than the set of problems specified in the title of the chapter. Next to each title, an *abǰad* number indicates the position of the chapter within the order of chapters in the complete manuscript of the *Law-Book*. In a few cases (four in all) this sequential number has been left out. No general rule governs the position of this number which appears indiscriminately before or after, above or below the title of the chapter. This lack of uniformity is an indication that the numbering of the chapters did not take place at the time when the manuscript was copied, but was added subsequently. Nevertheless, insofar as this numbering was intended for the complete text before the alteration in the order of the folios, it gives the possibility of restoring the initial sequence of chapters and of gaining a clearer idea of the original size of the document.

In his Introduction to the facsimile edition of the Hataria collection, J. J. Modi gave considerable attention to the restoration of the correct sequence of folios in both parts of the manuscript. The copy of this edition formerly belonging to Carl H. Salemann (now in the library of the Oriental Institute of the Russian Academy of Sciences in St. Petersburg) contains a manuscript table, in Salemann's own hand, giving the original order of the folios. This table has been included in the present edition together with a few additional precisions and a translation of Salemann's German indications. The table also gives a clear picture of the position of the Anklesaria folios within the complete manuscript.

Both parts of the *Sasanian Law-Book* are now in the keeping of the K. R. Cama Oriental Institute in Bombay.

SEQUENCE OF FOLIOS

(According to the Table of Carl H. Salemann)

Number of Missing Folios	Persian Numbering of the Ms.	Pagination of the Facsimile Edition	Numbering of the Chapters
	Hataria manuscript		
	(1)	79—80	(Incipit)
17 folios	—	75—76	VII
	20—25	1—12	[XVI]—XXII
	(26)	83—84	
1 folio			
	28—29	13—16	XXIII
1 folio			
	31—34	17—24	XXV—XXVI
1 folio			
	36—41	25—36	XXVII—XXX
2 folios			
	44—45	37—40	XXXIII
	(46)	85—86	XXXIV
1 folio			
	48—51	41—48	
2 folios			
	54	49—50	
2 folios			
	57	51—52	
1 folio			
	59—61	53—58	XXXVIII—XL
	62—63	59—62	XLI
	64	63—64	XLII
1 folio			
	66—67	65—68	XLIII
1 folio			
	70	69—70	
1 folio			

Number of Missing Folios	Persian Numbering of the Ms.	Pagination of the Facsimile Edition	Numbering of the Chapters
	72	71—72	XLV—XLVI
1 folio			
	—	73—74	Numberless
	—	75—76	XLVII
at least 1 folio	Anklesaria manuscript		
	74—75	1—4	from (XLVII bis) +
	76—84	5—22	XLVIII
	84 bis	23—24	to LI
	85—89	25—34	LII—(LIII)
	89 bis—91	35—40	(LIV)
	Hataria manuscript		
	93—94	99—102	
at least 1 folio			
	—	103—110	
	Out of sequence		
		77—78	
		81—82	
		87—88	
		89—90	
		91—92 + 97—98	

The Author and Date of the Text

In his Prologue to the *Law-Book* (see **79**, 3—13) the compiler records both his own name: Farraxvmart son of Vahrām (*Farraxvmart ī Vahrāmān*) and the title of his work: "*The Book of A Thousand Judgements*" (*Mātakdān ī Hazār Dātastān*). The compiler gives no further information about himself or his period; at least, none is to be found in the surviving folios. Soon after the discovery of the manuscript, J. Darmesteter (see note 1) suggested a ninth century date for the text. This conclusion was based on the identification of the name *Yuvān-Yam*, one of the authorities cited by the compiler of the *Law-Book*, with that of the father of the two well-known Zoroastrian figures of the ninth century, Manuščihr and Zātspram. More recently, however, Mary Boyce [6] rightly observed that the coincidence of names does not necessarily imply the identification of the two personages. This conclusion is supported by the fact that in the entire *Law-Book* there is not a single piece of direct or indirect evidence pointing to a period beyond the limits of the Sasanian era; not a single fact is characteristic of Post-Sasanian Iran. There is, moreover, good reason to believe that the text was composed before the fall of the Sasanian state. Thus, all the titles found in the "Chapter regarding the Competence of Officials" [LII], as well as in other chapters, belong to the Sasanian milieu. The same is true of all the terminology pertaining to administrative-territorial divisions. Furthermore, the compiler of the *Law-Book* refers to a series of Sasanian official regulations as to still operative norms; these could obviously not have remained in force after the fall of the Sasanian empire. He cites royal decrees of Kavāt and Xusrav I Anōšakruvān regarding official seals, *i. e.*, the regulations set down in official instructions which were sent out to the *šahrs* for the information of judicial authorities; decrees issued by administrative bodies are also mentioned. The compiler apparently lived in Pārs — as is obvious from the toponyms found in the text, the majority of which are located in this province — and his principal residence seems to have been the city of Gōr (modern Fīrūzābād). References to historical figures, especially to rulers, as well as to dated documents preserved in the archives of the city of Gōr and in its court records make it possible to determine the period in which he was working and in which the *Law-Book* was compiled. The latest document mentioned in the surviving portion of the text is dated in the twenty-sixth year of *Xusrav ī Ōhrmizdān* (=A.D. 615). Consequently, the *Book of A Thousand Judgements* must have been composed *ca.* A.D. 620, and its compiler, Farraxvmart son of Vahrām, a resident of the city of Gōr in the province of Artaxšahr-Xvarreh, was a contemporary of Xusrav II Parvēz (A.D. 591—628).

The Character of the Text and its Sources

Sasanian Iran had no codified law. Consequently, the *Book of A Thousand Judgements* is not a law-code; nor is it a legal treatise. It is the only surviving Pahlavi example of a genre common in the Sasanian period: a collection of legal cases. Such compilations were made to serve as manuals of judicial proce-

This purpose determined not only the selection of problems for which solutions were provided, but also the sources consulted by the compilers, since such manuals obviously had to be based on authoritative sources enjoying particular prestige in legal proceedings. Two basic groups of sources can be identified from the text of the *Sasanian Law-Book*.

The first group reflects the traditional regulations set down in the legal *nask*s of the *Avesta* and especially the Pahlavi commentaries on these *nask*s called *čāštak*s ("teachings, precepts"). The authority of the *Avesta* in legal proceedings rests on a historical foundation. Ancient law in general formed a part of religious ethics and social ethics were similarly sanctified by religion. In Zoroastrian Iran, with its dogmatic faith, this bond between religion and law was particularly close and it survived side by side with a highly developed state and a broad range of secular legal institutions. Nevertheless, by the beginning of the Parthian period, the regulations set down in the five strictly legal *nask*s (*Nīkā-ṯum, ZLB' slnčt, Huspāram, Sakāṯum, Vīdēvdāt*) composing the legal section (*dātīk*) of the *Avesta* canon [7] were no longer satisfactory for the stage of development reached by Iranian society. This circumstance, as well as the language barrier presented by the *Avesta*, made imperative an extensive commentary upon these *nask*s in the light of the new legal and procedural regulations developed by social practice during the centuries that followed their composition. We have no evidence allowing us to determine the precise period in which written commentaries first appeared (oral exegeses on the Avestan *nask*s may even have been made under the Achaemenids). Their appearance need not have been directly connected with the setting down of the *Avesta*, although the existence of a written text would obviously have provided additional stimulus for its commentary. Whatever may have been the circumstances, it was this Pahlavi commentary on the text of the *Avesta* that came to exert a practical influence on legal procedure [8].

In his reference to the authorities of the commentators (*dastaβarān*), the compiler of the *Sasanian Law-Book* cites some forty names. Most of these are also found in the Pahlavi *Avesta* (*Zand*) set down in the reign of Xusrav I Anōšakruvān [9]. Among the citations from the *čāštak*s occurring in the *Law-Book* we find cases where one commentator refers to the opinion of another, evidently his predecessor, while the latter, in another context, relies on the *čāštak* of yet a third commentator who lived still earlier. These references make it possible to determine the relative chronology of some of the commentaries and to postulate the existence of this genre in Pahlavi literature as early as the IVth century A.D. This question will be considered in greater detail elsewhere. It will suffice here to note that a similar observation was made by J. C. Tavadia on the basis of the information found in one of the paragraphs of the *Šāyast nē-šāyast* (see *ŠnŠ* pp. 28—29, note). Tavadia distinguished two groups of commentators and established the following internal chronology for each of these groups:

group *A*: Ātur-Ōhrmizd → Gōgušnasp → Mētō⟨k⟩māh;

group *B*: Ātur-Farnbaγ ī Narsēyān → Sōšyans → Aparak.

These two groups represent independent traditions. In one of them Aparak figures as the disciple of Sōšyans, and Sōšyans as that of Ātur-Farnbaγ; while in the other, Mēṯō⟨k⟩māh is the follower of Gōgušnasp, who was in turn a follower of Ātur-Ōhrmizd. This division is confirmed by the Pahlavi commentary on the *Vīdēvdāt* in which the opinions of these representatives of the two traditions show corresponding divergencies. The compiler of the *Sasanian Law-Book* clearly distinguished the two traditions or schools of commentators each of which was identified by the name of its leading proponent: *aparakīkān*, "the followers of Aparak", and *mēṯō⟨k⟩māhīkān*, "the followers of *Mēṯō⟨k⟩māh*" (see **50**, 13, 15; **52**, 15). The names of a number of commentators (Zamasp, Rāt-Ohrmizd, Vahrām-šāt, Farraxv-Zurvān, and others) occur for the first time in this text. Hence, the information of the *Law-Book* allows us to enlarge our knowledge of the wealth of exegetical literature existing in Sasanian times and to increase the accuracy of a series of details [10].

The authority and practical value of the *čāštak*s was so great that the *magupatān magupat* Veh-Šāhpuhr, president of the commission that set down the official canon of the *Avesta* under Xusrav I, had a general commentary composed for each of the *nask*s on the basis of the *čāštak*s already in existence. This commentary became a part of the new canon [11].

Farraxvmart usually cites a specific commentator to whom he refers by name, or name and patronymic. But he also gives general references such as: "it has been written by commentators", "it is stated in the *čāštak*s", or "according to (the teaching of) the *čāštak*s" (*pat čāštak*). In the text of the *Law-Book* such references to commentaries are often given side by side — and in formal opposition — with equally general references to existing norms and regulations (*kartak*, lit. "procedure") for legal procedure (see, *e. g.* **A13**, 7—8; **A15**, 12—15; **A35**, 13—14), that had either been adopted as the result of long legal practice, or had been officially promulgated. No strict division existed between the "spheres" of the *čāštak*s and the *kartak*, since "canonic" precepts as well as official regulations embraced both private law and the norms of judicial procedure. However, many of the precepts of the *čāštak*s had been intended for a long vanished society and no longer had any practical application; while, on the other hand, the massive influx of new norms and official regulations intended for the guidance of judicial bodies could not find adequate reflection in commentaries on the legal *nask*s. Consequently, Farraxvmart's extensive use of the *kartak* makes of his *Law-Book* a repository of information on this second source of legal procedure.

One of the chapters in the *Law-Book* (**A12**, 10—**A16**, 6) is entitled: "Chapter concerning regulations which, it is said, must be adhered to in judicial proceedings and which are also set down in the *Dātastān-nāmak*, the '*Book of Judgements*'". The regulations in this chapter are given without any references to sources. In this case, the compiler took his material at second hand, specifically from the *Dātastān-nāmak*, a collection apparently compiled under Xusrav I and enjoying a wide reputation, since it is also cited in the *Law-Book* of Īšō'bōxt. References to official texts and instructions are also common in other sections of the *Sasanian Law-Book*. Thus, we find frequent references to the

Memorial [*Aβyātkār*] of the *magupatān magupat* Veh-Šāhpuhr, of whom we have already spoken above. This treatise demonstrates the active participation of the *magupatān magupat* in the realm of legal procedure. More specifically, Veh-Šāhpuhr's *Memorial* laid down the obligation of keeping court records during the trial of a series of crimes, especially in the case of capital offenses, and of attaching these records to the document containing the text of the sentence. The *Memorial* of Veh-Šāhpuhr was reproduced, and copies authenticated with his seal were distributed to the *šahrs*. The compiler of the *Sasanian Law-Book* is obviously referring to such a copy, bearing Veh-Šāhpuhr's seal, which must have been preserved in the archives of the judicial department of the city of Gōr (see **A34**, 6—9; **A34**, 10—13; **A34**, 13—16; **A38**, 6—12). The "*Precepts*" or "*Testament*" [*Handarz*] of Veh-Šāhpuhr are also cited in the *Law-Book*. Judging from the quotations (**A35**, 14—16; **A36**, 16—37, 1), this was not a private document, but rather a didactic work that had acquired a semi-official status from the prestige of its author.

In the second half of the Sasanian era special collections were compiled for the guidance of administrative bodies and judicial departments. In addition to general information of the competencies and duties of various departments, ranks, and officials, these collections contained extracts from official decrees and decisions. The *Sasanian Law-Book* cites from such a collection, known as the *Xvēškārīh-nāmak ī kārfrāmānān* ("*The Book regarding the Duties of Officials*"), a decree or regulation concerning the confiscation by the royal treasury of the property of Manichaeans or of persons spreading the Manichaean doctrine. The text of this decree had been circulated to all the *šahrs* of the empire by the *rat* Mahraspand (**A38**, 16—**A39**, 1). The *Law-Book* also refers (**A26**, 15) to another collection of similar type, the *Xvēškārīh-nāmak ī magupatān*, ("*The Book regarding the Duties of Magupats*"). The utility of these collections for judicial practice was not restricted to the citations of extracts from official documents to be found in them: regulations on the rights and duties of officials and of the clergy were also taken into consideration in judicial proceedings. This is attested by the inclusion in the *Law-Book* of a special "Chapter concerning the Competence of Officials" (**A25**, 15—**A30**, 5), dealing with the competence of such officials as the *ōstāndār* or the *hamārkar*, despite the fact that they were not directly concerned with legal proceedings. Familiarity with the categories of documents or information that various officials were empowered to give out, the types of cases in which they might appear as representatives of juridical persons, etc., was indispensable for judges in the performance of their professional functions.

Numerous regulations regarding legal procedure emanated from the heads of the clergy, so that the already mentioned example of this type of activity attributed to the *magupatān magupāt* Veh-Šāhpuhr is not the only one found in the *Law-Book*. The text also contains a reference to a section of instructions drawn up by the chancellery of the *magupat* of the province of Artaxšahr-Xvarreh (**A40**, 9—11), as well as indications of the participation of the *ēhrpats* in the development of various aspects of legal procedure (**5**, 9—**6**, 2). The *Regulation of the Order of Appeals*, *Mustaβar-nāmak* (**A5**, 10), seems to have been composed in the same milieu. The *Law-Book* likewise mentions a document called *Nipištak*; this evidently was a collection of instructions or precepts composed at various times by judicial authorities. It contained, in particular, the precepts of the *rat* Mahraspand on the oath to be taken at trials dealing with the recovery of a debt from the debtor's heirs (**13**, 4—5; **59**, 6—10).

Certain royal decrees are also cited in the *Law-Book*, among them, the decrees of Kavāt and Xusrav I on the use of official seals by the *magupat*s, by financial officials — such as the *hamārkar*s, and by the judges (**93**, 4—9; *cf.* **100**, 5—7; **A12**, 13—17; and the Glossary *s. v. driyōš*). Still more interesting is an enactment by the *rat*s and other officials regulating legal procedure in the province of Artaxšahr-Xvarreh, which dates from the reign of Xusrav I (**78**, 2—11). This enactment contains some administrative clauses, such as the setting up of judicial offices having a secretariat staffed with four scribes in each *rōtastāk* of the province; but judging from the extant version, the main stress lay on the dealing with the general revision of court decisions and judicial process which was to be rigorously observed. Although the enactment cited in the *Law-Book* concerns only the province of Artaxšahr-Xvarreh, there seems to be little doubt that it was inspired by the general legal reform of Xusrav I Anōšakruvān, and that we have here an isolated example of the ratification of this reform by the *rat*s and administrators of a particular province. Its requirements for the review of judicial sentences, as well as for the drawing up of new records of interrogations and other documents can easily be connected with the situation in Iran during the period of the active repression of the Mazdakite movement [12].

Finally, for the compilation of his *Law-Book*, Farraxvmart also had recourse to court records that he had seen in the archives of the city of Gōr (see, *e. g.*, **100**, 7—11), and to private documents, copies of which were apparently preserved in the same archives.

The Content and Significance of the Law-Book

The judicial cases and decisions collected in the *Law-Book* cover for the most part the field of private law. In the surviving portion of the compilation points dealing with administrative or public law are met only sporadically and even these are mostly details of administrative law closely linked with legal proceedings such as the competencies of officials mentioned above. This is altogether natural for a legal collection compiled as a practical manual intended for judges, and it is reasonable to suppose that the same was true in the lost sections of the original text. The multitude of facts contained in the *Law-Book* reveals to the investigator an area almost unknown from other sources: property and contractual relationships, social forms and institutions, criminal law, the system of legal proceedings, as well as details of judicial procedure and of the formal drawing up of official documents. The incredible wealth of information supplied by the *Law-Book* on all of these points makes it possible to reconstruct in its main lines the whole of the Iranian legal system. Moreover, it provides invaluable assistance for the understanding of other Pahlavi texts, in particular, the *Dēnkart*, the *Dātastān-ī dēnik*, the *Handarz*s and the Pahlavi *rivāyat*s, as well as of Middle Persian and Parthian inscriptions. The *Law-Book* is of major importance for the study of the legal regulations of the Christian communities of Sasanian Iran set out in the *Law-Book of Išō'bōxt*, which has come down to us in a Syriac translation, and of the *Babylonian Talmud*, which reflects the legal system of the Jewish communities living in the Sasanian state. Furthermore, it helps us to understand a number of terms and realia in early Armenian historical and canonical literature. What has already been said above concerning the sources used by Farraxvmart for the compilation of his *Law-Book* gives us some indication of the importance of this work for the history of Iranian legal tradition and literature. The sociologist or historian meeting this text for the first time will unquestionably note the high level reached by Iranian law in this period: the strictness and clarity of the system of succession and of the classification of real rights, the elaborate treatment of judicial procedure and of other categories.

The text of the *Law-Book* greatly increases our knowledge or Middle Persian vocabulary (especially of legal terminology) and phraseology; it contains a series of Avestan forms some of which are missing from the surviving portions of the *Avesta*, and a number of new heterograms. Nor is the linguistic interest of the *Law-Book* limited to its vocabulary: the specific nature of a juridical text makes of this *Law-Book* an excellent instrument for the study of Middle Persian syntax, since every nuance in formulation carries a legal implication, and the accuracy of the translation can in most cases be checked by a confrontation of parallel contexts as well as through the existing system of legal *realia*.

The Studies of the Text

Soon after the publication of the facsimile edition of the Hataria manuscript in 1901, Christian Bartholomae began his study of the *Law-Book* with the publication in 1910 of an article "On the Sasanian *Law-Book*". This article was followed by several more, likewise dedicated to this text [13]. In these articles, Bartholomae gave full or partial transcriptions and translations of a considerable number of articles in the *Law-Book* together with a philological and substantive commentary. Although the interpretation proposed for a number of terms — including crucial ones — was incorrect and most of Bartholomae's translations require rectifications of either their entirety or of details, we must acknowledge with thanks the great importance of his work which laid the foundation for the scientific study of this exceedingly interesting and valuable but very difficult document.

The first Iranist to concern himself with the *Law-Book* after Bartholomae's death was his pupil A.Pagliaro who published several articles on separate legal terms and *realia* found in it. The most important of these was his extensive study of "Antichresis Security in Sasanian Law" [14].

Increasing interest in the text has been displayed during the past decades. Almost all the articles of the *Law-Book* dealing with private endowments of fire-temples and foundations "for the soul" have been transcribed and translated in the study of the French Iranist J.-P. de Menasce, who also devoted six other articles to material found in the text [15]. The articles relating to fire-temples and pious, "soul", foundations were likewise edited and studied by Mary Boyce [16] and myself [17]. The information on certain institutions of family law and terminology associated with them have been investigated in two articles by G.Klingenschmitt [18]. Problems connected with the text and with Iranian legal institutions have been investigated in some of my other articles [19], and I have also published (in Russian) a detailed study of Ancient Iranian law and society. A brief outline (in English) of the Iranian legal system in the Parthian and Sasanian period has been offered by me in the third volume of the *Cambridge History of Iran* [20].

The Russian edition of the *Law-Book* [21] is the first attempt at a transcription and translation of the entire manuscript [22]. Since the original manuscript was not accessible to me and the attempt to obtain a microfilm copy proved unsuccessful, the textual work had to be done from the published facsimile editions, whose technical execution was unfortunately not beyond criticism. The translation of articles has been commented only where this seemed indispensable for the understanding of the text.

Brief descriptions of legal terms will be found in the "Glossary" given at the end of the present volume. This is a selective list of juridical terms and of words of particular interest in a legal context; it is not intended as a complete listing of the vocabulary found in the text. Numerical references to the articles of the text have also been included in the "Glossary" in order to assist the reader in tracing all the contexts in which a particular term or institution appears. Other "Indices" and "Abbreviations" will also be found at the end of the volume. Finally, a list of the *Law-Book's* chapter headings in the order of their appearance in the manuscript follows the Notes to the Introduction. While the revised English edition of the *Law-Book* was in preparation, an edition of both parts of the manuscript prepared by M. Macuch [23] appeared in Germany. A detailed review of her work will be published by me presently.

Anahit Perikhanian

Notes to the Introduction

1. J. Darmesteter, *Revue critique d'histoire et de littérature*, nouv. sér., XXIV/49 (1887), pp. 425—427; E. W. West, "Pahlavi Literature", *Grundriss der iranischen Philologie*, II (Strasburg, 1896), pp. 116—117.

2. *Mâdigân-i Hazâr Dâdistân*. A Photozincographed Facsimile of a Ms. belonging to the M. L. Hoshang Hâtariâ Library in the Zarthoshti Anjuman Atashbeharam, with an Introduction by J. J. Modi (Poona, 1901).

3. *The Social Code of the Parsees in Sassanian Times or the Mâdigân-i-hazār Dâdistân*, part II, by T. D. Anklesaria with an Introduction by J. J. Modi (Bombay, 1912).

4. *E. g.* the "Chapter concerning divorce" [= Chapter XIX] and the "Chapter concerning the settlement of a debt with partners (= co-heirs) and joint-debtors (= *correi*)" [= Chapter XXXVIII].

5. *E. g.* titles such as the following. "Chapter concerning some judicial decisions by the authorities (*i. e.*, the commentators of the Avestan *nasks* — *A. P.*) written down exactly by those who heard them", "Chapter in which one opinion follows another". (This chapter includes articles beginning with the words "Moreover it is said", "In addition, it is said", etc.).

6. M. Boyce, "Middle Persian Literature", *Handbuch der Orientalistik*, Pt I, IV/2 (Leiden—Cologne, 1968), p. 62 and No. I.

7. Two more *nasks*: *Čihrdāt* (historical in content) and *Bayān-yašt* (liturgical) were apparently added to this section during the IVth or even the VIth century A.D. by classifiers who strove to give a symmetrical structure — with seven *nasks* per section — to all parts of the canonical text. Only one of the legal *nasks* of the *Avesta* canon, the *Vidēvdāt* [*Vd*] "Law driving away the *daēvas*", has survived, see E. Benveniste, "Que signifie Vidēvdāt?", *Henning Memorial Volume*, M. Boyce and I. Gershevitch edd. (London, 1970), pp. 37—42 for the precise meaning of the title. Nevertheless, we can obtain some idea of their entire content from the summary given in the eighth book of the *Dēnkart* and from occasional references to them in other Pahlavi texts.

8. Ritual prescriptions predominate over legal ones in the *Vidēvdāt*, which has reached us both in the Avestan original and in the Zand redaction. This balance was reversed in the other four legal *nasks*, which have not survived and whose summary in the *Dēnkart* had to be made from the Zand since their Avestan text was already lost in the IXth century A.D. Furthermore, the *Dēnkart* summary was drawn not from the — more or less equivalent — translation of the original *Avesta* but from the "expanded" redaction of the translation, since this summary mixes archaic features obviously traceable to the original *Avesta* with legal forms absolutely irreconcilable with the primitive stage of development reflected in other sections of the *Avesta*, among them the *Vidēvdāt*. Thus, for example, the summary of the *Nīkāṯum nask* speaks of the equality of a citizen and an alien before the law (*DkM*, 699, 7—8), of the right of a slave to bring suit against a citizen in certain real action (*DkM*, 708, 10—12), of judicial representative (*DkM*, 700, 6—9; 708, 16—17), of a woman's right to appear as plaintiff before a court as her husband's judicial representative and to testify as a witness (*DkM*, 706, 16—18; 708, 18—20), of junior and senior judicial boards and of courts of appeal (*DkM*, 708, 1—2), as well as of the rights of the *magupatān magupat* — a title first met in the IVth century A.D. — to annul a judicial decision (*DkM*, 711, 12—13).

9. For instance, the commentator Aparak is cited 32 times in the Pahlavi *Vīdēvdāt*, 57 times in the *Nīrangistān*, once in the Pahlavi *Yasna*. He is also mentioned in the later texts. 29 times in the *Nāmakīhā i Manuščihr*, and 8 times in the *Šāyast nē-šāyast*.

10. Thus, there is a reference to a certain *Dipīr* (lit. "scribe, secretary") in the late treatise *Šāyast nē-šāyast* (2, 44); E. W. West (*SBE*, V (1880), p. 257 No. 7) mistook him for the author of this treatise, but it is evident from the *Law-Book* (*MHD* **2**, 5) that *Dipīr* is the surname of the Sasanian commentator whose actual name was Xvatāybūt.

11. See the *Nāmakīhā ī Manuščihr*, I, iv, 14—18. Subsequently, the general commentary gradually supplanted the *čāštaks* of individual authors because of its particular prestige. Nevertheless, even in such a late text as the *Šāyast nē-šāyast*, we find the reference (*ŠnŠ*, **2**, 1) to a commentary of Mēṯō⟨k⟩māh on the *Vīdēvdāt* (*Vīdēvdāt ī Mēṯō⟨k⟩māh*) and more particularly to its third *fargard* next to frequent references to the general commentary in Veh-Šahpuhr's redaction. Hence, we must conclude that some of the early commentaries were still in existence in the IXth century A.D. It is interesting to note that *fargard* three of the *Vīdēvdāt ī Mēṯō⟨k⟩māh* corresponded to *fargard* seven of the surviving (canonical) Pahlavi *Vidēvdāt*. According to J. C. Tavadia who noted this detail (*ŠnŠ*, p. 30 n.), the subdivision of chapters in the *Vīdēvdāt ī Mēṯō⟨k⟩māh* differed from the one in the canonical redaction of this *nask*.

12. In large part this repression was also carried out through legal channels in the form of the prosecution of "heresy" and of ideological-religious tendencies hostile to orthodox Zoroas-

trianism (*cf.* "Glossary", *s. v. ahramōγīh, zandīkīh*). According to the *Law-Book*, these were among the offences subject to penalties ranging up to the total loss of legal capacity. The abuse of judicial procedure in these cases must have led to serious disorders in the functioning of the courts. It spread to trials of other types and apparently provoked the reform of Xusrav I.

13. Chr.Bartholomae, "Uber ein sasanidisches Rechtsbuch", *SHAW* (1910, Abh. 11), pp. 3—25; "Beitrage zur Kenntnis des sasanidischen Rechts", *WZKM*, 27 (1913), pp. 347—374; "Der Verbalkontrakt im sasanidischen Recht", *SHAW* (1917 Abh. 11), pp. 3—15; "Zum sasanidischen Recht, I—V", *SHAW* (1918, Abh. 5), pp. 3—50; (1918, Abh. 14); pp. 3—50 (1920, Abh. 18), pp. 3—66; (1922, Abh. 5), pp. 3—57; (1923, Abh. 9), pp. 3—56; "Die Frau im sasanidischen Recht", *Kultur und Sprache*, 5 (Heidelberg, 1925).

14. A. Pagliaro, "L'anticresi nel diritto sāsānidico", *RSO*, XV (1935), pp. 275—315; "Note di lessicografia pahlavica", *RSO*, XXIII (1948), pp. 52—68; "Aspetti del diritto sasanidico: *hačašmānd 'interdictum'*", RSO, XXIV (1949), pp. 120—130. "Notes on Pahlavi Lexicography", *Jackson Mem. Vol.*, Bombay 1954, pp. 72—83.

J-P. de Menasce, "Le protecteur des pauvres dans l'Iran sassanide", *Mélanges H. Massé*, Téhéran, 1963, pp. 282—287; "Some Pahlavi Words in the Original and in the Syriac Translation of Išōbōxt Corpus Iuris", *J. M. Unvala Mem. Vol.*, Bombay, 1964, pp. 6—11; *Feux et fondations pieuses dans le droit sassanide* (Paris, 1964); "Les données géographiques dans le *Mātigān ī Hazār Dātistān*", *Indo-Iranica. Mélanges présentés à G. Morgenstierne* (Wiesbaden, 1964), pp. 149—154; "Textes pehlevis sur les qanats", *Acta Orientalia*, XXX (Copenhagen, 1966), pp. 168—175. Formules juridiques et syntaxe pehlevie, *Bulletin of the Iranian Culture Foundation*, I/1 (1969), pp. 11—20.

16. M. Boyce, "On Sacred Fires of the Zoroastrians", *BSOAS*, XXXI/1 (1968), pp. 52—68; "The Pious Foundations of the Zoroastrians", *BSOAS*, XXXI/2 (1968), pp. 270—289.

17. A. G. Perixanjan, "*Chastnye tselevye fondy v drevnem Irane i problema proisxoždenija vakfa* [Private Foundations in Ancient Iran and the origin of the *waqf*]", *VDI* (1973/1), pp. 3—24.

18. G. Klingenschmitt, "Die Erbtochter im sassanidischen Recht", *MSS*, XXI (1967), pp. 59—70; "Neue Avesta-Fragmente", *MSS*, XXIX (1971), pp. 111—174.

19. A. G. Perikhanian, "Agnatičeskie gruppy v drevnem Irane [Agnatic Groups in Ancient Iran]", *VDI* (1968/3), pp 28—52; "Notes sur le lexique iranien et arménien" *REArm*, n. s. V (1968), pp. 9—23; "Sur arm. *panduxt*", *REArm*, n. s. VI (1969), pp. 1—14; "On Some Pahlavi Legal Terms", *W. B. Henning Memorial Volume*, M. Boyce and I. Gershevitch edd. (London, 1970), pp. 349—357. A. Périkhanian, "Le contumace dans la procédure iranienne et les termes pehlevis *hačašmānd* et *srāδ*", *Mémorial Jean de Menasce* (Louvain, 1974), pp. 305—318; A. G. Perixanjan, Ordalija i kljatva v sudoproizvodstve do-islamskogo Irana, *Peredneaziatskij Sbornik* III (Moskva 1979), pp. 182—192; "Un terme pour la 'dot' en iranien et en arménien", *REArm*. XX (1986—1987), pp. 47—53; "'Protivnik (v sudebnom protsesse)' i 'vrag' v iranskom i v armjanskom" in A. G. Perixanjan, *Materialy k etimologičeskomu slovarju drevnearmjanskogo jazyka*, (Erevan, 1993), pp. 107—125 (hereafter *Materialy*).

20. A. G. Perixanjan. *Obščestvo i pravo Irana v parfjanskij i sasanidskij periody* (Moskva, 1983), 381 pp.; Iranian Society and Law, *CHI*, 3, 2 (Cambridge, 1983), pp. 627—680.

21. A. G. Perixanjan, *Sasanidskij sudebnik* "Kniga tysjači sudebnyx rešenij" (Mātakdān ī hazār dātastān), Erevan, 1973.

22. The one given by S. J. Bulsara (*The Laws of the Ancient Persians*, Bombay, 1937) is too far from the standards of modern European scholarship to serve scholarly purposes.

23. M. Macuch, Das sasanidische Rechtsbuch "Mātakdān ī hazār dātistān" (Teil II), Wiesbaden, 1981 [Abhandlungen für die Kunde des Morgenlandes, Bd. 45, 1], 268 pp.; *Rechtskasuistik und Gerichtspraxis zu Beginn des siebenten Jahrhunderts in Iran*, (Wiesbaden, 1993), 807 pp.

LIST OF CHAPTERS

The list of chapter headings is given in according with the order of their appearance in the manuscript. The roman numerals preceeding the heading of the chapter indicates the sequential order attributed to it in the manuscript. The first series of Arabic numbers following the heading refers to the pagination and line of the Facsimile editions, the second series refers to the pagination of the present edition.

Hataria Ms.

Anklesaria Ms.

TEXT AND TRANSLATION

Farraxvmart ī Vahrāmān

MĀTAKDĀN Ī HAZĀR DĀTASTĀN

[*Hataria Ms.*]

[XVI]

[Dar ī bandakīh]*

1, 1—2:

... īh ut bandakīh dahēt ōγōn bavēt čiγōn mart-ē(v) ī dehkān ī šāhān šāh pat bandakīh ō mart-ē(v) (2) dahēt.

1, 2—4:

Gōβēnd kū tā xvatāyīh (ī)Vahrām martōxmān anšahrīk ān xvēš būt^{+} ī (3) hač pitar zāt^{+} nē ān ī hač māt ē(t)$^{+}$ rāδ čē Sōšyans guft kū vaččak pit xvēš (4) ut nūn gōβēnd kū māt.

1, 4—6:

Zan ut anšahrīk hamē(v) pat dīt ut vēnišn ī xvatāy ut sardār (5) žahm ayāp staxm kunēnd tāvān dō ēvak xvatāy ayāp sardār ēvak ōy kē vinās (6) kart.

1, 6—7:

Mart-ē(v) ka-š anšahrīk-ē(v) pat 10 bahr ē(v) bahr xvēš āzāt bē kart frazand-ič (7) hač ān anšahrīk zāyēt harv ēvak pat 10 bahr ē(v) bahr āzāt.

1, 7—10:

Ka ātaxš-ē bandak mart (8) 2 ut anšahrīk mart 2 hast ut mart xvāstak-ē(v) rāδ kart kū-m ō bandakān ī ān ātaxš (9) dāt hač ān čiγōn anšahrīk bandakīh ī ātaxš nē bavēt ō anšahrīk (ī) ātaxš čiš-ič (10) nē dahēt.

---

* The beginning of the chapter has not survived. The heading is reconstructed from the content of the chapter.

Farraxvmart Son of Vahrām

THE BOOK OF A THOUSAND JUDGEMENTS

[*Hataria Ms.*]

[XVI]

[Chapter on slavery]*

1, 1—2:

... and hands over into slavery, (then) this is equivalent to a person's handing over a subject of the King of Kings into slavery to someone.

1, 2—4:

It is said that up to (the reign) of Vahrām, persons became the owners of a slave born of a father (belonging to them — *A. P.*), but not of (such a) mother. For Sōšyans stated that the child belongs to the father, but now, it is said (that he belongs) to the mother.

1, 4—6:

If a woman or ("and") a slave commits an act of physical violence before the eyes of (his / her) master or ("and") guardian, (then) the master or guardian (shall pay) half the fine, and the other half (shall be paid) by whoever committed the offence.

1, 6—7:

If a man frees one-tenth of a slave / slave-woman, the children born (subsequently — *A. P.*) from this slave / slave-woman shall likewise be, each of them, one-tenth free.

1, 7—10:

If a fire-temple has two sacred-slaves (= *hierodulo*i) and two *anšahrīk*-slaves and a man makes (the following) disposition regarding a thing: "I conveyed (this thing) to the sacred-slaves of this temple", (then) insofar as an *anšahrīk*-slave is not a sacred-slave, he (= the bestower) has not conveyed anything (through this action) to the *anšahrīk*-slaves of the Fire-temple [1].

1, 10—13:

Gyākē nipišt kū anšahrīk ī tarsāk xvēš ka ō hudēnīh (11) ut nazdīkīh ī hudēnān āyēt vahāk ī anšahrīk bē dāt apāyēt ut anšahrīk āzāt (12) u-š ōy apēziyān kunišn ka ō nazdīkīh ī kas nē bē ō hudēnīh āyēt (13) xvat vahāk (ī) xvēš bē dāt apāyēt.

1, 13—15:

Anšahrīk ō aγdēnān frōxt+ ne pātixšāy (14) ka frōšēnd pat anšahrīk harv 2 andar rat ī hudēn duz bavēnd ⟨i⟩ u-šan drōš bē kunišn (15) drahm pas hakar pat rāh ī  (?) ī zamān pat ōy kē dārēt bē mānēt.

1, 16—17:

Anšahrīk (ī) aγdēn ka apāk xvatāy ayāp pas hač xvatāy ō aγdēnīh āyēt hamē(v) (17) anšahrīk.

XVII

1, 17—**2**, 1:

En dar* ī čiš pat hambāγān ut hamxvāstakān (I) ut hampāyandānān hilišn.

2, 1—4:

Mart ⟨ī⟩ 3 xvāstak apām stānēnd (ut) vičīr ăvartēnd ān kē (2) [a]pām bē dāt pas hač ān ān xvāstak pat xvēšīh ō avēšān mart ō mart 1 dahēt (3) ān mart ān xvāstak ān ī frēh hač ān ī-š xvat niyāpēt hač hambāγān xvāst nē pātixšāy.

2, 4—6:

Ka tōžišn ī pitarān apāč ō pus (ī) pātixšāyīhā pat aparmānd (5) [xv]āstakdār(ān) dahēnd čiγōn hač Xvatāybūt ī Dipīr bē gōβēnd tōžišn hišt bavēt (6) ut ān kē aviš dahēnd hač hambāγān xvāst nē tuvān.

2, 6—8:

Ka 2 mart pat ākanēn apām (7) stanēnd ut ān apām ast-ē(v) bē hilēnd avēšān mart ēvak bahr ī xvēš vičārēt ān ī (8) bē hilēnd ētōn bavēt čiγōn ān ī pat pāyandān hilēnd.

* In the manuscript, the ordinal number 17 is placed above the word *dar* "chapter".

1, 10—13:

It is written in one place that if a slave belonging to a Christian converts to Zoroastrianism ("the Good Religion") and (enters the service) of a Zoroastrian, (the latter) must return the value ("price") of the slave to (his former master) and free the slave, and the latter (= the slave) must compensate him for this loss. But if a slave does not enter (the service) of a Zoroastrian and yet converts to Zoroastrianism, (then) he himself must repay his own price (to his master).

1, 13—15:

A slave may not be sold to a non-Zoroastrian. If, however he is sold, (then) both of them (the buyer and the seller) shall be considered thieves by the Zoroastrian *rat* on account of the slave (*i. e.* the action shall be equated with theft — *A. P.*) and they shall be branded. As for the money, if subsequently (it was to have been paid?) on the basis ... (?) of a term ("time"), it shall remain with the one who has it.

1, 16—17:

Whether an unbeliever-slave has converted to another (non-Zoroastrian) faith at the same time as ("together with") his master or subsequently, in either case ("always") he (remains) a slave.

XVII

1, 17—**2**, 1:

This is the chapter* concerning the discharge from a debt (= *solutio*) of partners, joint-debtors (*correi*) and co-warrantors.

2, 1—4:

Three persons borrow money ("a thing") on credit and make a contract. (And) he who gave the loan subsequently conveys this money ("thing") to one of them to become that man's personal property. (Then), this person (= the beneficiary of the transfer) shall not be entitled to claim this money ("thing") from his partners (in an amount) superior to the one to which he was entitled (under the terms of the contract).

2, 4—6:

If the heirs [2] lay on the legitimate son and successor the settlement of (his) father's debts, then it is said, on the authority of (the work of) Xvatāybūt the Scribe, that the obligation for the settlement is (thereby) removed (from the heirs and rests wholly upon the successor). And he who has been charged (with the obligation to settle the debt, *i. e.* the successor) shall have no right to demand reimbursement ("to make a claim") from his co-heirs [3].

2, 6—8:

If two persons jointly receive a loan and repay it in part, (*i. e.*) one of them repays his share, then, the régime of discharge from the debt shall be the same as in warranty contracts.

2, 8—10:

Ka tōžišn bē (9) hilēnd pēš hač brīn zamān pat pasēmār ut pas hač brīn zamān pat pāyandān hišt+ (10) bavēt.

2, 10—11 = **2**, 8—10

2, 11—13:

Ka pat 3 gōβišn ō pāyandān gōβēt kū-m hač (12) pāyandānīh hišt hēh aδak-iš hač pāyandānīh hišt bavēt ut tōžišn hakar pēš (13) [hač] brīn zamān gōβēt nē hišt bavēt ut hakar pas hač brīn zamān uskārtan apāyēt.

2, 14—16:

Ka mart 3 xvāstak 100 hač mart-ē(v) Farraxv nām apām stanēnd ut pas Farraxv pat ān (15) xvāstak hač mart 1 apāyišn bavēt Farraxv-Zurvān ut Veh-Ōhrmizd guft kū bahr ī ōy ⟨ī⟩ (16) hač-iš apāyišn bavēt ut ān ī apārīk hač apārīk xvāst tuvān bavēt yuttar.

XVIII

2, 17:

Dar* ī vičīr ī pēšak sardārān ut xonsandīh ut axonsandīh ī pat vičīr.

2, 17—**3**, 1:

Vičīr ī pēšak (1) sardārān kart bē pat framān ī dehpatān ⟨ī⟩ nē šāyēt.

3, 1—3:

Ka pat vičīr xonsand būt (2) pas bē ka yuttar kartan apāyistan paytāk bavēt enyā axonsandīh ī pat vičīr nē (3) patigīrišn.

3, 3—5:

Ka pēšēmār pat vičīr ī dātaβar hač apāmdān-ē(v) ēvar brīn vičārtan (4) apāyistan ī pasēmār (ut) xvāstak rāδ kart xonsand būt ut pas vičārt āβarēt xonsandīh ī (5) pat vičīr rāδ+ ērangīh.

* In the manuscript the ordinal-number 18 is placed bove this word.

2, 8—10:

When a debt is discharged, then, until the expiration of the time-limit the discharge of the debt shall be from the respondent, and, after the expiration of the time-limit — from the warrantor.

2, 10—11 = **2**, 8—10.

2, 11—13:

If after repeating the formula three times, he (= the creditor) declares to the warrantor: "you are released by me from the warranty", then, he shall be released from the warranty. As for the debt, if he (= the creditor) made the declaration before the expiration of the stipulated time-limit, (the debtor) shall not be considered released (as a result of the creditor's release of the warrantor — *A. P.*). If, however (the declaration regarding the release of the warrantor was made) after the expiration of the stipulated time-limit, an inquiry must be made into the matter [4].

2, 14—16:

If three men borrow 100 (*drahms*) of money from someone named Farraxv, and subsequently Farraxv claims this money from one (of these men), then, as has been stated by Farraxv-Zurvān and Veh-Ōhrmizd, (only) his share can be required of him, the remainder may be claimed separately from the others.

XVIII

2, 17:

Chapter* concerning decisions taken by the heads of the estates (in civil or criminal actions) and agreement or non-agreement with a decision.

2, 17—**3**, 1:

A decision given by the heads of the estates shall not have the force of law (lit. "is not allowable, is not lawful") without the confirmation of the "rulers" [5].

3, 1—3:

If (he) was satisfied with the decision (*i. e.* publicly declared himself satisfied — *A. P.*), then — exept in cases where one must clearly act otherwise — his subsequent (declaration of) dissatisfaction with the (same) decision shall not be taken (into account by the court).

3, 3—5:

If the plaintiff has declared himself satisfied with the decision of the judge regarding the debtor's obligation to settle (pay) a definite share of a debt (and) with the thing (*i. e* with the determination of the amount and form of the payment — *A. P.*), and subsequently he (= the plaintiff) brings forth the payment (?) [6], he is liable to some measure of punishment owing to (his previous) declaration of satisfaction with the decision (of the judge).

3, 5—6:

Ut xvāhišn ī drōš rāδ pat tōžišn ut xonsandīh ī pat vičīr rāδ (6) pat vičārtan ut pat atōžišnīh nakīrā(k)īh kam nē patigīrišn.

3, 6—8:

Bē pat vičīr kart ī (7) pat hačašmānd apārīk vičir ī dātaβar ⟨ut⟩ (ī) kas kunēt axonsandīh ī pasēmār kunēt ōh (8) ⟨ōh⟩ patigīrišn ut zamān ī ō dātaβar ī mas ōh dahišn.

XIX

3, 9:

Dar* ī hištan ī hač zanīh.

3, 10—11:

Ka ō zan gōβēt kū-m pat xvēš tan sardār pātixšāy kart hēh nē hišt bē-š (11) pātixšāyīh pat šoy ī čakar kartan dāt bavēt.

3, 11—14:

Ka gōβēt kū duxtak (ī) pātixšāyīh (12) ō zanīh ī man mat ut man pat xonsandīh ī duxtak duxtak hač zanīh ī (man) hišt bē čiγōn (13) pat ān aδvēnak gōβēt enyā apar ēstāt ī duxtak čiš nē paytāk aδak hišt (14) nē bavēt duxtak (ut) ōy mart zan ut mērak.

3, 14—15:

Hakar ka pat baxt šavēt zan ut frazand nēst (15) stūr ⟨nē⟩ gumārišn.

3, 15—**4**, 1:

Gyākē nipišt kū ka mart zan hač zanīh hilēt bē (16) čiγōn ān zan pat xvēš tan sardār pātixšāy kunēt enyā-š pat sardārīh ō kas (17) nē dahēt ut ān zan pas hač ān žīvandakān ān mart šoy kunēt ut frazand zāyēt frazand (ī) (l) ⟨ōy frazand⟩ ān zan ōy ⟨ī⟩ xvēš+ kē ān zan pat ān aδvēnak hač zanīh hišt.

4, 1—4:

Ka (2) mart pat xonsandīh (ī) zan zan hač zanīh hīlēt (ut) pat zanīh ō apurnāyak ī xvēš (3) dahēt ut apurnāyak andar apurnāyīh pat baxt šavēt aδak-ič ān zan ōy čim rāδ stūrīh ī (4) ān mart kem avi-š nē rasēt .

---

* The (*abǰad*) ordinal-number 19 is placed above this word.

3, 5—6:

And, as for the demand (by the plaintiff) for branding (as punishment of the defendant — *A. P.*) in cases of settlement (of a debt), or for a declaration of agreement with a decision requiring the settlement (of a debt), or for (a statement of) protest (against a judicial decision) discharging from payment ("about non-payement"), minor matters [7] shall not be admitted.

3, 6—8:

Except in cases of judgement given by default, the defendant's declaration of dissatisfaction with any decision given by a junior judge must be admitted and a court session with the participation of a senior judge must be arranged ("given").

XIX

3, 9:

Chapter * concerning divorce ("dissolution of a marriage").

3, 10—11:

If he declares to his wife: "I have granted you the right of 'self-guardianship'", the marriage is not dissolved (thereby), but she is given the right to enter into a *čakar* marriage.

3, 11—14:

When he declares: "A daughter (of mine) from a *pātixšāyīh* marriage entered into a marriage with me and I, with the daughter's consent, dissolve my marriage with her", then — unless the declaration was made in this (precise) form — nothing is clear about the status of the daughter and her marriage is not dissolved at that time, and the daughter and the man are still wife and husband.

3, 14—15:

If at the time of his death he had neither a wife nor children, a *stūr* must be appointed.

3, 15—**4**, 1:

In one place it is written that if a man divorces his wife and — except for the case where this (woman) receives from him the right of "self-guardianship" — does not transfer the guardianship to anyone, and (if) this woman subsequently enters into a marriage during the lifetime of this man and bears children, then, the children of this woman belong to him who divorced her in this manner.

4, 1—4:

If a man, with the consent of his wife, dissolves his marriage with (this) wife and gives her in marriage to his minor son, and the minor (son) dies without reaching his majority, then because of this (*i. e.* because the young man's death occurred while he was still a minor — *A. P.*) the woman still receives the *stūr*ship of that man (*i. e.* her first husband — *A. P.*).

4, 4—9:

Ka mart (ut) zan ⟨ut⟩ hambāγ ut ēn-ič patmān kunēt kū (5) ēn xvāstak ōy kē tō xvēš+ būt gōβēh xvēš hēβ bavēt ka zyānak hač zanīh (6) bē hilēt aδak-ič ka zyānak ān xvāstak kas xvēš būt xvap gōβēt apāč (7) nē āβarišn. Bē hambāγīh apāč āβarišn+ ut Pusānūč (ut) Martak hamdātastān (8) būt hend Pusānūč ēn-ič guft kū-m saxvan-nāmak dīt ī apar hambāγīh rāδēnīt (9) ēstāt (ut) vičīr kart ēstāt hač-šān hambāγīh apāč āβurtan.

4, 9—10:

Hišt (10) būt kē guft kū yut hač sardār nē bavēt u-š kartak ōγōn ⟨ī⟩ apāk kū ō (vahmān kas)? ōh bavēt.

4, 11—13:

Hišt būt kē guft kū ān ī zanīh rāδ andar burt čiγōn pašadātakān ut vāspuhrakān (12) bē barēt ut vindišn ī andar zanīh ⟨ī⟩ bē mānēt u-š kartak ōγōn apāk kū: "saxtak bē (13) šavēt".

4, 13—14:

Zan xvāstak ī-š šōy andar zanīh dāt ka-š šōy pat xonsandīh hač (14) zanīh bē hilēt bē nē barēt (ut) pat šoy bē mānēt.

4, 14—**5**, 3:

Ka gōβēt kū-m (15) zyānak hač zanīh hišt ut pat zanīh ut sardārīh ō Farraxv dāt ut Farraxv zyānak (16) pat zanīh patigīrēt pat sardārīh andar nē apāyēt gōβēt. Būt kē guft kū (17) hišt kār nēst. Vahrām guft kū ē(t) rāδ čē pat sardārīh andar nē apāyēt (1) guft zanīh rāδ guft bavēt. Čē zanīh yut yut hač sardārīh nē šāyēt (2) būt. Pas ōγōn bavēt čiγōn kē pat xvāštak ī aviš dahēnd andar nē apāyēt gōβēt (3) dāt nē bavēt.

XX

5, 3:

Dar* ī dastaβar.

* In the manuscript the ordinal-numeral 20 is placed above this word.

4, 4—9:

If a husband and wife are partners and (the husband) makes this agreement: "this thing shall belong to him about whom you declare that it is his", (then) — if he divorces (this) wife and the wife then declares: "this thing belongs to such a person, it is well!" — it (= the thing) shall not be liable to return (to the relinquisher — *A. P.*) but the partnership shall be subject to cancellation ("return, removal"). Pusānūč and Martak are unanimous on this point. And Pusānūč has also said the following: "I saw a record of (judicial) proceedings drawn up in a case of partnership, and the decision was to cancel ('remove, take away') their partnership".

4, 9—10:

This opinion has been given regarding the dissolution of a marriage, namely that there is no (valid) divorce without the appointment of a guardian, and according to the procedure in such a case (the following declaration must be made): "let (her) be given (in guardianship to such a one?)".

4, 11—13:

Divorce: some have said that everything brought (by her) in connexion with the marriage — such as, for instance, (her) *paraphernalia* and (her) dowry (lit. "her 'daughter's share' in her father's estate") shall be taken away by her, but that which was acquired during the marriage shall remain. And the (proper) procedure (or formula) in such a case is this: "let (her) go provided for (equipped, endowed, established)".

4, 13—14:

The wife is not entitled to take ("does not take away") the property conveyed to her by her husband during the marriage if he dissolves the marriage with her consent, and it (= the property) remains with the husband.

4, 15—**5**, 3:

If he declares: "I have dissolved my marriage with (this) woman and have given her in marriage and guardianship to Farraxv", and (if) Farraxv takes the woman as a wife but declares regarding the guardianship: "there is no need ('not needed')"; some (authorities) have stated that (in such a case) the divorce is not valid. Vahrām has stated that the reason for this is that to declare: "not needed" with regard to the guardianship is to declare (the same) with regard to the marriage. For a marriage cannot ("may not") exist without guardianship. Then the procedure is the same as in the case where a person to whom a thing is conveyed declares: "not needed". The transfer (of the thing) does not take place (*cf.* **87**, 7—10).

XX

5, 3:

Chapter* concerning a fully empowered (= entitled) person (= a representative, mandatary, disposer — *A. P.*)

5, 4—5:

Vāyayār nipišt kū pasēmār ka-š xvāstak ī pat xvēšīh ī xvēš guft zamān ī (5) ō dastaβar nē bavēt.

5, 5—8:

U-š ēn-ič nipišt kū ka Farraxv ī hač Gōr xvāstak-ē(v) bē ō (6) Mihrēn ī hač Kāzarōn frōšēt (ut) pas Mihrēn pat ān xvāstak pēš Kāzarōn dātaβar hamēmār (7) bavēt+ Farraxv nē pātixšāy bē ka ō ⟨bē ō⟩ Kāzarōn āyēt pat dastaβarīh andar ēstēt (8) bē-š patkārišn andar būt kē guft kū pātixšāy ka nē āyēt.

5, 9—6, 2:

Ka pēšēmar pat ēn kū xvāstak man xvēš ut apātixšāyīhā pasōmār dārēt (10) pasēmār hamēmār (ut) pasēmār nē xvēšīh (ī) pēšēmār pat tāšt gōβēt pas (11) ⟨ō⟩ zamān ō dastaβar xvāhēt Pusānveh ī Āzātmartān guft kū ka ōtōn gōβēt (12) aδak-iš zamān ōh dahišn. Bē ka gōβēt kū tō nē xvēš čē man xvēš zamān ī (13) ō dastaβar nē dahišn. Čē dātastān bē rāδēnītan čiγōn ēhrpatān gōβēnd. Mēt̲ō⟨k⟩ (14) māh guft kū-š zamān ō dastaβar nē dahisn. Ut Aparak guft kū zamān ī ō (15) dastaβarān zamān ī ō ēvarīh bavēt ka-č-iš xvēšīh ī pasēmār+ (Ms.: dstwbl) xvēš guft ēstēt (16) aδak-ič-iš zamān ī ō dastaβar ōh dahišn. Gyākē nipišt kū ka-š pat xvēšīh (17) būt ī dastaβarān guft ka-č ēn nē gōβēt kū-m ⟨ka⟩ pat ān dastaβarīh xvēš (1) aδak-ič-iš dastaβarīh ī ōy guft bavēt kū-m xvēš čē anī aδvēnak būt nē šāyēt.

6, 2—6:

Vahrām guft kū ka pēšēmār gōβēt kū ēn xvāstāk Āturfarnbaγ (3) xvēš būt Āturfarnbaγ ō Mihrēn (ut) hač Mihrēn ō man mat ut man xvēš ut apātixšāyīhā (4) Farraxv dārēt Farraxv pat nakīrā(y/k) pat nē ētōnīh ī ān hamāk čiš ētōnīh ī xvēš (5) apāč apāyēt guft. Ka dātastān pat var (ut) pasēmār vehdātastāntar var ēvāč pat nē (6) xvēšīh ī Āturfarnbaγ varzišn.

5, 4—5:

Vāyayār has written that if the respondent has made a declaration (during the trial) concerning his ownership of a thing, the disposer (or "mandator") need not be summoned before the court.

5, 5—8:

And he (= Vāyayār, *cf.* 5, 4—5) has also written that if Farraxv, from the town of Gōr, sells a thing to Mihrēn from Kāzarōn (and if) Mihrēn subsequently brings suit concerning this thing before the judge of Kāzarōn, then Farraxv is not entitled to act in this case as the fully empowered disposer (of the disputed thing in order to confirm Mihrēn's title — *A. P.*) unless he presents himself in Kāzarōn. However, as regards his participation in the case (as respondent or as representative of one of the litigating parties — *A. P.*), some (authorities) have said that he is entitled not to appear (in Kāzarōn — *A. P.*) [8].

5, 9—6, 2:

If a plaintiff is in litigation with the respondent concerning the following: "(this) thing belongs to me whereas the respondent possesses it unlawfully", but the respondent declares specifically that the thing does not belong to the plaintiff and subsequently demands a court session with the participation of the disposer; then, according to the opinion of Pusānveh ī Āzātmartān, if (the respondent) makes such a declaration, the session (with the participation of the disposer for the purpose of establishing the respondent's title — *A. P.*) must be arranged. But if he (= the respondent) declares (to the plaintiff): "the thing does not belong to you because (it) belongs to me", then a session with summons to the disposer need not be arranged. For such a trial must take place according to the precepts of the *ēhrpat*s. (And) Mēδōmāh has said that a session with the participation of the disposer need not be arranged (in response to the demand of the respondent). But Aparak has said that a court session with the participation of the disposer is a session (purporting to demonstrate) trustworthiness and (therefore) that a session with the participation of the disposer must be arranged in such a case even if a declaration has been made regarding the ownership of the thing by the plaintiff (Ms.: 'disposer') [9]. It is written in one place (by Aparak? — *A. P.*) that if he (= the respondent) made a declaration about the ownership of a thing by the disposer without adding thereupon: "(and) on the basis of ('this') empowering (='title, mandate' — *A. P.*) received from him it belongs to me", then he has (thereby) said regarding his (= the respondent's) right (= title): "(the thing) belongs to me", for otherwise it is not allowable.

6, 2—6:

Vahrām has said that if a plaintiff declares: "this thing belonged to Āturfarnbaγ and Āturfarnbaγ (conveyed it) to Mihrēn and from Mihrēn it came ("passed") to me and (it) belongs to me whereas Farraxv possesses it unlawfully", then Farraxv — in order to object that everything did not occur (as asserted by the plaintiff) — must make a statement of the way in which this occurred in his opinion. If the trial is under oath (= by ordeal) and the right to take an oath is given to the respondent ("the respondent has the legal advantage"), then, it is sufficient to take an oath only that the thing did not belong to Āturfarnbaγ.

6, 6—9:

Hač dastaβarān pat^{+} (Ms.: BR') gyākē nipišt kū ka dastaβar (7) kē xvāstak ō kas ut kas kē ān xvāstak avi-š frōxt pat ān xvāstak pat anī (8) šahr hamēmār hend ō ānōδ kū-š xrītarīh hamēmār kart ēstēt nē pātixšāy (9) bē ka šavēt u-š uzēnak hač xvēš.

6, 9—11:

Ka pasēmār pat ē(v)$^{+}$ čiš 2 dastaβar (10) (ut) mart 2 zamān ō dastaβar kart ut dastaβar ēvak āyēt (ut) pat dātastān andar ēstēt ut ēvak (11) nē āyēt (ān ī āyēt) dastaβarīh ut rāδēnišn ī (dātastān) pat hamāk ān dātastān kart nē tuvān.

6, 11—12:

Ka dastaβar (12) hač dastaβarīh nakīrāk bavēt (ut) pas (pat dātastān) andar ēstēt apāk pēšēmār dātastān rāδēnītan kār nēst.

6, 13—14:

Ka mart 2 ākanēn xvāstak-ē(v) ō mart-ē(v) frōšēnd ut pašt kunēnd kū drust (14) dārēm^{+} Vahrām guft kū drust dārišnīh hač harv kē kāmēt xvāst pātixšāy.

6, 15—17:

Apāk anī nipišt kū mart 2 apāk mart 2 patmān kunēnd kū ēn čiš (16) kunēm hakar yuttar kunēm^{+} tāvān dahēm ka hač avēšān kē ān patmān kart mart-ē(v) (17) ān patmān ast čē yuttar kart ān tāvān ō tōžišn ī harv dō mart rasēt.

6, 17—7, 2:

Apāk-ič anī (1) nipišt kū ka gōβēt kū xvāstak ī ō xvēšīh ī amāh ākanēn ēt-ič čē ō xvēšīh (2) ī amāh yut-yut mat ān ī ākanēn mat ut yut-yut mat rāδ guft bavēt nikerītan.

7, 3—4:

Dastaβar ka mātak nē mat ēstēt (ut) nē dānēt pātixšāy ka tā mātak āstavēt pat (4) dastaβar(īh) andar nē ēstēt.

6, 6—9:

It is written in one place with a citation of the commentary on the *Avesta* that if a disposer (or "mandatary") having (sold) a thing to someone and the person to whom he sold the thing litigate in another *šahr* (= town, province), then, it is inadmissible for him (= the "disposer/agent") not to go where the litigation regarding the thing bought (or "the purchase") is taking place, and he shall bear the expenses himself.

6, 9—11:

If a respondent has two disposers (or "mandataries") for one thing and an appearance at a court session with the participation of the disposer is set, and if one of the disposers (or 'agents') appears (and) is present in court but the other one does not appear; (the one present) cannot act as the disposer (confirming the title of the respondent) nor conduct his affairs in this entire case.

6, 11—12:

If an agent (representing the respondent — *A. P.*) resigns and subsequently continues to attend (the court session), then (his title) to conduct the case with the plaintiff is null and void.

6, 13—14:

If two men jointly sell a thing to one person and make the (following) agreement: "we shall preserve (it) intact (evidently until the new owner should take possession of it — *A. P.*)", then, Vahrām has said that he (= the buyer) has the right to demand the preservation of the thing from whichever (of them) he pleases.

6, 15—17:

At the same time it is written that if two men make the (following) agreement with two persons: "we shall do this (in this way) and if we do it otherwise we shall pay a fine"; then, if one of those who made this agreement does anything (of what has been stipulated in the agreement) in another way (*i. e.* violates any point of it — *A. P.*), the obligation to pay the fine shall fall on each of the two men.

6, 17—7, 2:

At the same time it is written that if he makes the declaration: "the estate which belongs to us jointly as well as that which passed to us severally", then attention must be paid that a statement be made about the joint (property/possession) and about the one obtained severally.

7, 3—4:

If the principal (= the principal respondent in a suit or the giver of the mandate — *A. P.*) is absent ("does not appear") and has not been informed ("does not know"), then, the person having disposed of a thing (or "the agent") is entitled not to act (in court) as one empowered (as a representative at the trial or as a disposer confirming the title of the respondent — *A. P.*) until the former approves.

7, 4—6:

Pasēmār pat xvāstak-ē(v) patkārēt kū vindišn ī (5) anšahrīk ī-m hač Mihrēn xrīt (Mihrēn? ... ...) Mihrēn-ič pat anšahrīk ⟨i⟩ patkārēt kū ⟨anšahrīk ī-m hač (6) Mihrēn xrīt⟩ * (... ... ...) zāt zamān ō dastaβar ōh dahišn**.

7, 6—8:

Ka pasēmār pat xvāstak (7) dastaβar (ut) vikāy būt kē guft kū pat 2 vikāy būt kē guft kū pat 2 dastaβar (8) dārišn. 2 dastaβarīh dārišnīh rāδ vičīr kunišn.

7, 8—11:

Dastaβar ka āyēt⁺ ut pat dastaβarīh (9) andar ēstēt ut bē ēraxtēt pasēmār pātixšāy ka ān ērangīh nē patīgīrēt bē (10) xvat pas(s)axv gōβēt (ut) dātastān rāδēnēt bē-š nipišt-ē(v) hač-iš ō xvāhišn pat (11) dāt zamān ō dātaβar⁺ (Ms.:dstwbl) ōh bavēt.

7, 11—15:

Vahrām guft kū ka pasēmār gōβēt kū harv (12) čē dastaβar (ī) man pat ēn (h)ēr gōβēt, kunēt ut rāδēnēt pat guft kart ut rāδēnīt ⟨tā⟩ (ī) xvēš (13) dārom ka dastaβar hačašmānd bavēt mā hakar vināskārīh pat hačašmānd ēvak (14) dastaβar bavēt ēvak pasēmār bē ētōn dānom kū ētōn čiγōn ka hač pasēmār (15) hačašmānd būt hē vičīr apāyēt kartan.

7, 15—**8**, 2:

Ka dastaβar gōβēt kū-m xvāstak frōxt⁺ (16) bē hač xvēš nē būt pēšēmār vināskārīh hakar-iš kāmēt vas-ič guharīk hač dastaβar (17) bē kart⁺ pātixšāy ka guharīk vas pat graβīh kart mātak hač pasēmār xvāhēt (1) ka mātak guharīkān (hač ān ī) dastaβar pat xvēšīh bē kunēt aδak-iš apak pasēmār rāδēnišn nē (2) bavēt.

* The passage in pointed brackets is a repetition of the preceding line.
** The text of this article is seriously corrupted by the omissions of the copyist.

7, 4—6:

The respondent litigates ("objects") concerning a thing: "the revenue from the slave bought by me from Mihrēn, (to Mihrēn? ... ...)". But at the trial Mihrēn asserts regarding the slave: "⟨the slave bought by me from Mihrēn⟩* (... ... ...) born", then a court session with the participation of the disposer must be arranged ("given")**.

7, 6—8:

If the respondent as regards a thing brings forth both a disposer (confirming his title — *A. P.*) (and) a witness, some (authorities) have said that they should be considered as two witnesses, while others (have said) — as two disposers. In order for them to be considered as two disposers, a special decision must be rendered.

7, 8—11:

If the disposer (or "agent" — *A. P.*) appears (in court), acts (there) as the empowered representative (of the respondent), and loses the case ("is found guilty"); then, the respondent is entitled to reject this sentence and to respond himself and to conduct the case. However, a written obligation that he shall appear in court at the time designated must be demanded from him.

7, 11—15:

Vahrām has said that if the respondent declares: "I will consider ('hold, accept') everything said, done and directed concerning this property ('thing') by my empowered representative (or 'agent' — *A. P.*) at the trial as said, done and directed by myself", and if the empowered representative defaults at the trial; then — even though either the representative or the respondent (himself) may be at fault — this is my understanding (of such a case): the decision must be rendered as though the respondent were guilty of default.

7, 15—**8**, 2:

If the empowered representative (of the respondent, who disposed of a thing, or his mandatary — *A. P.*) declares: "I sold the thing but not in my own right (or, 'not from property belonging to me personally' — *A. P.*)", then — should he so desire — the plaintiff is entitled to claim ("extract") a compensation equivalent to the loss, from the property belonging to the representative. If, however, a value equal to the loss has been given as security, then he (= the plaintiff) claims the principal (*i. e.* the compensation for his loss — *A. P.*) from the respondent. If, however, he exacts (a sum of money) equal to the principal from the property belonging to the representative (of the respondent), then no suit (= claim by the plaintiff — *A. P.*) can be brought against the respondent.

8, 2—10:

Ka pasēmār andar pēšēmār ī fratom pat dastaβar nakīrā(k) bavēt ut andar (3) pēšēmār ī ditīkar dastaβar (nē) ān kunēt ī-š andar pēšēmār ī fratom kart (4) pasēmār ka apar xvēš būt (ī) dastaβar [ī pas] guft bē ēstēt (ut) pat mat ī (5) hač ān dastaβar patkārēt ēt rāδ ka-š andar pēšēmār ī fratom dastaβar nē ān (6) kart ī-š andar pēšēmār ī ditīkar guft būt kē guft kū pat vaštakīh⁺(7) ēraxt. Vahrām guft kū pat ān vaštakīh nē ēranǰēnišn čē andar pēšēmar (8) ī ditīkar čiš-ič vaštakīh nē kart ut vaštakīh ān bavēt ka andar pēšēmār ⟨ī⟩ nakīrā(k) (9) bavēt dastaβar nē ān ī (andar) pēšēmār ī (fratom) kart (ut) nazdist Farraxv ē(v) ut pas Mihrēn ē(v) pat dastaβar kart.

8, 10—11:

Dastaβar ka pat xvāstak kē pat-iš dastaβar ō dātaβarān⁺ (Ms.: dstwbl'n) zamān (11) xvāhēt zamān ōh dahišn.

8, 11—13:

Zamān ī ō dastaβar nē mātak bē (dastaβar) anāsān-tan āmār ka-č mātak (12) hač nērōk ut mizd kam aδak-ič sāl drahnāδ zamān dahišn pat kartak ka has šāyēt pat (13) āmat⁺ zamān vēš nē dahišn kū ān ī tā hangām ka pat mat tuvānīk.

XXI*

8, 15:

Dar ī vaštakīh ut apārīk-ič ērangīh.

8, 15—16:

Pat xvārastān pat vičārt pat-ič man bē hišt (16) harv 2 ēvarīh xvāst.

8, 16—**9**, 1:

Gyākē nipišt kū pat man bē hišt ka andar rāδēnišn ī (17) dātastān gōβēt varōmand kart bavēt hač-ič dipīrīh 1 ī-m dīt pat xvārastān kart (1) ēstāt ētōn paytāk būt.

---

* The (*abǰad*) ordinal-number 21 is placed in line 14 above the heading of the chapter.

8, 2—10:

If a respondent (argues) with a first plaintiff about the disposer (of the disputed thing or title — *A. P.*) while in a dispute with a second plaintiff he does not specify as disposer the same (man) whom he declared as disposer (defending his title to a thing) in the case of ("as regards") the first plaintiff, (and if) the respondent conducts the case, insisting that (the thing) belonged to that disposer whom he designated later and that (he) obtained it from that disposer; then — inasmuch as he did not specify as disposer (defending his title) in the case of the first plaintiff the same (man) as he designated in the case of the second plaintiff — some (authorities) have said that he should be condemned for (or "found guilty of") a change in declaration. But Vahrām has said that such a divergence ("change") in declaration is not liable to condemnation (= cannot be imputed as guilt) because he made no deviation (from the declaration made in the case of the first plaintiff — *A. P.*) in the case of ("as regards") the second plaintiff; whereas there would be a divergence ("change") if — in the case of the plaintiff with whom he is in dispute — he were not (to designate) as disposer the (same) person whom he had designated in the case of (the first) plaintiff: (if he were to designate as a disposer in the first case ("at first") a certain Farraxv, but in the second case ("later") — a certain Mihrēn.

8, 10—11:

If a mandatary demands from the judges a court session regarding the thing over which he (was given) full powers, then a session must be arranged ("given") [10].

8, 11—13:

As regards the setting of a time limit for the appearance in court of a disposer (or "agent / representative" — *A. P.*), the sickness of the disposer and not of the principal (= the litigant himself, or the giver of the mandate — *A. P.*) is taken into consideration. Even if the principal has little physical strength or earnings (the court session) must be set within one year. According to the existing judicial (norms), if (this) can be arranged earlier, then, no more time should be granted for the appearance (in court) than that in which he (= the disposer / representative) is able to appear.

XXI *

8, 15:

Chapter concerning the making of contradictory statements (= concerning "change" in declaration) and other offences.

8, 15—16:

In an ordeal court, (an oath — *A. P.*) is required concerning the trustworthiness of each of these two (statements): "it is paid", or "I am released (from the debt)".

8, 16—**9**, 1:

It is written in one place that if he declares at a court trial: "I am released (from the debt)", then (the trustworthiness of this particular statement — *A. P.*) is verified through the ordeal procedure (= by oath). This was also evident from an ordeal court record / document seen by me.

9, 1—3:

Vaštak-saxvanīh ka ō ēvarīh vartēt (2) nē ēranǰēnišn ut ka nē ō ēvarīh vartēt ēraxtan (nē) ētōn čiγōn Ātur-Ōhrmizd (3) guft (kū) ka-č nē ō ēvarīh vartēt aδak-ič nē ēraxtan.

9, 3—6:

Ka pasēmār pat (4) vaštak saxvanīh ēranǰēnīt ut pas paytāk bavēt kū pēšēmar dātastān drōγ (5) xvāst pēšēmār xvāstak ī-š hač pasēmār bē grift hač bar ī-š burt (6) hammis pat tāvānīh-ič ō pasēmār dahišn.

9, 6—8:

Ka pasēmār vaštak bavēt (7) pēšēmār pat ān vaštakīh pat ēvak+ čiš nē vimāyēt ut saxvan-nāmak bē āvartēt (8) pas pat ān vaštakīh nē ēranǰēnišn.

9, 8—11:

Ka saxvan-nāmak hač rāδēnišm mānēt (9) pasēmār ka patkārēt kū-m pas hač ān vičārt nē ērangīh hakar gōβēt kū-m (10) pēš vičārt ērangīh. Ut apāk ān pat man bē hišt ī andar rāδēnišn ī dātastān rāδ (11) hačapar nipišt nikerītan.

9, 11—14:

Ka pēšēmār pat xvāstak 2 ī-š ēvak xvēš ut ēvak (12) nē xvēš ⟨ut⟩ pasēmār anbassān (ut) andar rāδēnišn ī dātastān pēšēmār ān xvāstak hač pasēmār (13) bē ap(p)urēt aδak-ič ān xvāstak ī pēšēmār xvēš ō pasēmār nē rasēt (14) ōy ap(p)ur rāδ hač pasēmār kem bē nē stanišn.

9, 1—3:

If — altering his declaration (= testimony) — he turns to the trustworthy one (*i. e.* if his last testimony is trustworthy — *A. P.*), then, (he) should not be sentenced (to the punishment provided for contradictory testimonies — *A. P.*); but if he turns to (the one) unworthy of trust, he should be convicted (for this), and (one should) not (follow) what was said by Ātur-Ōhrmizd: that even if he turns to the false (testimony), (he) should still not be sentenced (to a punishment for this).

9, 3—6:

If a defendant has been found guilty of making contradictory statements (= of altering his declaration in court) and it is subsequently discovered that the plaintiff sought a false judicial decision (*i. e.* deliberately led the court into error), then the plaintiff must give to the defendant — along with the fine — the thing taken by him from the defendant and all the fruits (= revenue) brought by it.

9, 6—8:

If the respondent alters his statement (but) the plaintiff suffers no damage through this alteration of testimony, and he (= the respondent) seals the minutes of the testimony (with his own seal); then, he should not be sentenced thereafter (to a fine) for this alteration in his testimony.

9, 8—11:

If the minutes of the testimony at a judicial session are preserved but the respondent objects at the trial: "I paid subsequently to this", then (such a divergence from his testimony as recorded in the minutes — *A. P.*) is not deemed to be an offence. But if he declares: "I paid before this", then that is assessed as an offence. And (this case) must be considered together with what has been written above on the one regarding the declaration: "I am released (from the debt)".

9, 11—14:

If a plaintiff litigates with a respondent as regards two things — one of which belongs to him and the other does not — (and if) the plaintiff seizes this thing (= the one which is not his) from the respondent, then even in this case, the thing which belongs to the plaintiff does not pass to the respondent. But he (= the plaintiff) — despite his having commited a robbery — shall receive (his thing) in full from the respondent (as well as the reimbursement for the loss born by him because of the interruption in his possession thereof; *cf.* 9, 3—6 — *A. P.*).

9, 14—**10**, 7:

Ka hangām ayāp dastaβar ayāp (15) čē aδvēnak ⟨ut⟩ xvēšīh vartēnēt ēraxtan ut hangām vartēnītan ān bavēt ka naxvist (16) gōβēt kū sāl ēvak hač Mihrēn ō man mat ut pat ān dastaβarīh dārom ut pas gōβēt (17) kū sāl 2 mat ut pat ān dastaβarīh dārom ut ka apar ān ī pat ⟨ī⟩ sāl ēvak patkārēt (1) ēt nē gōβēt kū pat ān dastaβarīh dārom ka-č pas hangām vartēnēt ut pat dārišn (2) sāl ditīkar kunēt aδak-ič nē ēraxtan ut dastaβar vartēnītan ān bavēt ka naxvist+ (3) gōβēt kū Farraxv xvēš būt u-š bē ō man dāt ut pat ān dastaβarīh dārom (4) (ut) pas gōβēt kū Mihrēn xvēš būt u-š bē ō man dāt ut pat (ān) dastaβatīh (5) dārom. Ut ka pat ān ī pat mat ī hač Farraxv patkārēt ēt nē gōβet kū pat ān (6) dastaβarīh dārom ka-č pas dastaβar vartēnēt ut pat dārišn dastaβar ān ī aptom gōβēt (7) aδak-ič nē ēraxt(an) ut čē aδvēnak xvēšīh-ič dātastān ān ham.

10, 7—9:

Ka pasēmār andar (8) rāδēnišn naxvist gōβēt kū-m zan ī tō nē gāt ut pas gōβēt kū-m gāt (9) bē-m nē andar zanīh ī tō gāt vaštak-saxvanīh rāδ ēraxt(an).

10, 9—11:

Ut pat-ič (10) žahm ka gōβēt kū-m nē zat hēh ut pas gōβēt kū-m andar abōδīh ⟨ī⟩ zat (11) hēh aδak-ič ēraxt.

XXII

10, 12:

Dar* ī hačašmānd.

* The ordinal-number of this chapter is 22.

9, 14—**10**, 7:

If he changes (gives a contradictory testimony at the trial — *A. P.*) the time, or the disposer, or the origin and nature (lit. "the manner = the way in which") of the holding (= possession of a thing), he should be sentenced (to some measure of punishment, to a fine — *A. P.*). An alteration of the time occurs when at first he declares: "it is one year (since) (this thing) came ('passed') from Mihrēn to me and I possess it on the basis of this title (= disposition of the thing by him)", and subsequently he says: "it is two years (since) (it) passed to me and I possess (it) on the basis of this disposition". (Then), if in his declaration in court regarding one year he does not say: "(and) I possess (it) on the basis of this title", (then) — even though he subsequently alters the time and indicates ("declares") another year for the (length of) possession (of the thing) — he should still not be sentenced to (a punishment, a fine). A change (= substitution) of disposer occurs when at first he declares: "(the thing) belonged to Farraxv, and he conveyed (it) to me, and I possess (it) on the basis of this empowering (= disposition of the title)", and subsequently he says: "(the thing) belonged to Mihrēn, and he conveyed (it) to me, and I possess (it) on the basis of this empowering (= his disposition)". If in his assertion at the trial that (the thing) passed to him from Farraxv he does not say: "(and) I possess (it) on the basis of this title (= of this disposition of the thing)", then — even though he subsequently substitutes the disposer and designates the one whom he named last (*i. e.* Mihrēn — *A. P.*) as the disposer of the possession — even in such a case, he should not be sentenced. And similarly, (in cases of statements) regarding the origin and nature of (one's real right), the decision is the same.

10, 7—9:

If the respondent at first declares at the trial: "I did not commit adultery with your wife", and subsequently declares: "I did commit adultery but not during the period when she was married to you"; then, he should be found guilty of making contradictory statements ("a change in declaration").

10, 9—11:

And similarly as regards acts of physical violence (= "blows"), when he declares: "I did not strike you", and subsequently says: "I struck you while in a state of unconsciousness"; then in this case as well, he should be found guilty (= sentenced to a punishment).

XXII

10, 12:

Chapter * concerning contumacy (default).

10, 12—**11**, 7:

Ka gōβēt kū man xvēš dārom u-m pasēmār (13) hač dārišn vizāyēt ut hačašmānd bavēt pat ēvak hačašmānd pat dārišn (tā) dātastān (14) sar (vičīr kunišn) ka-š nōktar vizāyēt paštak hend ut ka gōβēt kū man xvēš dārom (15) u-m ⟨u-m⟩ pasēmār hač-iš vizāyēt ut hačašmānd bavēt ast kē ētōn gōβēt (16) kū ēn-ič ētōn bavēt ka gōβēt kū man xvēš dārom u-m pasēmār hač (17) pat xvēšīh dāštan vizāyēt ut pat ēvak hačašmānd vičīr kunišn kū tā dātastān (1) sar bavēt ma vizāy ut pat hačašmānd ī ditīkar graβ hāvand-ē(v) bē apispārišn ut pat sitīkar (2) ēraxt. Ut apar Dātastān-nāmak ōγōn nipišt kū ka gōβēt kū man xvēš dārom u-m (3) pasēmār hač-iš vizāyēt ut hačašmānd bavēt vičīr kunišn kū tā dātastān sar bavēt ma (4) vizāy ut tā 2 yāvar hačašmand bavēt vičīr hamgōnak kunišn. Ut yāvar ī sitīkar ēraxt ut pat xvēšīh (5) bē apaspārišn. Zurvāndāt anī-č būt^{+} kē guft kū pat hačašmānd ī ditīkar (6) graβ hāvand-ē(v) bē apispārišn ka hač pēšēmār bavēt tā 3 yāvar harv yāvar-ē(v) graβ (7) hāvand-ē(v) bē apispārišn. Ka pat 3 ēraxt xvāstak ō pasēmār apispārišn.

11, 8—13:

Ka gōβēt kū mart 3 bē ap(p)urt ut mart 1 hamēmār hom ut hač pasēmār hačašmānd (9) bavēt srāδ-ē(v) [Ms.: 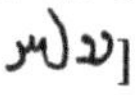] ut tāvān 12 graβ bē apispārišn ut pat ditīkar hamgōnak ut pat sitīkar ēraxt (10) ut pat xvēšīh bē apispārišn ut pas hač-ič avēšān ī apārīk harv ēvak tāvān 12 (11) xvāst pātixšāy ut ka-č hač pēšēmār bavēt hamgōnak ut ka harv 3 mart pat dātastān (12) hend ⟨ut⟩ hač harv 3 mart pat bahrak čiγōn šōn niyāpēt bē kunišn ut pēšēmār-ič hamgōnak (13) apispārišn.

11, 13—16:

Būt kē guft kū ka gōβēt kū apātixšāyīhā tō dārēh (ut) hač (14) pasēmār hačašmānd bavēt apar (tāvān) ut pat-ič srāδ vičīr kunišn kū tā dātastān sar bavēt (15) apāč apispār ut pat ditīkar graβ hāvand-ē(v) bē apispārišn ut pat sitīkar ēraxt ut pat xvēšīh (16) bē apispārišn. Ut ka-č hač pēšēmārān bavēt hamgōnak vičārišn.

10, 12—**11**, 7:

If he declares: "(this thing) belongs to me but the respondent is depriving me of (its) possession", and there is default (= contumacy, or suspension of judgement because of the non-appearance of the respondent — *A. P.*); then, at the first default, a decision must be rendered as to the status of the possession until the end of the case. But if he (= the respondent) again deprives him (of this possession), they bind themselves with an obligation (*i. e.* they make a judicial wager). And if he declares: "(this thing) belongs to me but the respondent is depriving me of it", and there is default, some (authorities) say that this case is analogous to the one where he declares: "(this thing) belongs to me but the respondent is depriving me of the rightful possession". (Then), at the very first default (the first non-appearance of the respondent — *A. P.*), the following decision is rendered: "do not deprive him (of it) until the end of the case!". And at the second default (both parties) must deposit a stake of equal value, and at the third — the sentence is pronounced. And it is written in the *Dātastān-nāmak* that if he declares: "(this thing) belongs to me but the respondent deprives me of it", and there is default, then (the following) decision must be rendered as to the detention of the disputed thing: "do not deprive him (of it) until the end of the case!". And in the case of a second default the same decision must be rendered. And in the case of the third default — the sentence is pronounced and (all the stakes along with the disputed thing) must be delivered (awarded to the plaintiff — *A. P.*) as his personal possession. Another (authority), Zurvāndāt, has also stated likewise that at the second default (each of the parties) must furnish a stake of equal value. But if the defaulter is the plaintiff, then — at every default — stakes of equal value must be deposited (by the litigants). And the third time — the sentence is pronounced, and (the thing and all the stakes) are awarded to the respondent.

11, 8—13:

If he declares: "(I) have been robbed by three men and I am litigating with one (of them)", and the respondent defaults, then a trial stake as well as 12 (*drahms*?) of fine must be deposited as security, and the same (is done) the second time; and the third time — the sentence is pronounced and (the securities furnished — *A. P.*) are delivered (to the plaintiff) as his personal property; and he is subsequently entitled to demand (the payment of) a fine of 12 (*drahms*?) from each of the others (= the two other men who took part in the robbery but were not summoned to court — *A. P.*). And the same is done if the defaulter is the plaintiff. But if all three (= those accused of the robbery) participate in the case, then — as custom requires — a share (= an amount equivalent to his part in the obligation to deposit a stake — *A. P.*) shall be demanded of each of then. And the plaintiff's party (if it consists of several persons — *A. P.*) must furnish (a trial stake) in the same manner.

11, 13—16:

Some (authorities) have said that if he declares: "you possess (this thing) unlawfully", and the respondent defaults, then (the following) decision must be rendered as regards the fine as well as the pledge of the judicial wager: "deposit them (in court) until the end of the trial!". And at the second (non-appearance), a stake (or stakes) of equal value must be furnished (to the court — *A. P.*), and at the third — the sentence (must be) pronounced (= in favour of the plaintiff — *A. P.*) and (the disputed thing as well as all the stakes) are awarded as personal possessions/"his own property" (to the plaintiff — *A. P.*). And when the defaulter is the plaintiff's party, (the case) shall be resolved in similar fashion.

11, 16—**12**, 4:

Ka gōβēt kū man (17) anšahrīk hēh u-t anšahrīkih ī man kunišn ut hačašmānd bavēt vičīr kunišn kū tā dātastān (1) sar bavēt kār ī pēšēmār kunēt ut pat-ič zan hamgōnak anī gyākē nipišt kū ka hač pasēmār hačašmānd bavēt vičīr kunišn kū tā (3) dātastān sar bavēt zanīh ōγōn čiγōn zan ī xvēš (4) hēβ kunēt.

12, 4—9:

Martak anšahrīk rāδ ōγōn nipišt kū pat nazdist hačašmānd rōčkār and čand (5) dātastān rāδēnītan rāδ andar apāyēt ut apārīk bē apispārišn ut pat ān ī ditīkar hakar-iš (6) attānīh hast graβ apispārīšn ut pat sitīkar sar graβ hakar pēšēmār guft ēstēt (7) kū anšahrīk čē aržēt pat ān arž ut ka yuttar pat 500 drahm bē apispārišn ut zan rāδ ōγōn nipišt ku pat nazdist hačašmānd vičīr kunišn kū zanīh ī yut hač gātan (9) kunēt ut pat ditīkar graβ 500 drahm bē apispārišn ut pat sitīkar sar.

12, 9—13:

Ka gōspand (10) 2 ī Farraxv ut Mihrēn ākanēn ayāp yut-yut xvēš Mihrēn dārēt ut Farraxv gōspand 1 (ō) Pusak (11) dahēt+ ut Pusak ān gōspand ān ī Farraxv xvēš nē šnāsēt ut Mihrēn-ič ān gōspend ān ī ōy (12) xvēš paytāk nē kunēt u-š hačašmānd hač-iš bavēt Pusak pātixšāy ka ān gōspand (13) harv 2 pat graβ bē gīrēt ut bar hač-iš barēt.

12, 13—16:

Ka gōβēt kū ēn zan man (14) xvēš+ tō apātixšāyīhā dārēh ut hačašmānd bavēt tā 3 yāvar hačašmānd (15) bavēt zan bē nē apispārišn čē dārišn ēvar ut bunxvēšīh varōmand ut ka (16) pat xvāstak saxvan pēšēmār hamgōnak gōβēt aδak-iš dātastān hangōnak bavēt.

12, 17:

Ka mart apar mart-ē(v) hamēmār kū-t ⟨pat⟩ xvāstak ō man dahišn ut hač pasēmār hačašmānd...*

* The text of this article breaks off here and the next folio of the manuscript is missing.

11, 16—**12**, 4:

If he declares: "you are my slave and you must be in servitude to me" and there is default (on the part of the respondent — *A. P.*), then the decision to be rendered is that he (the slave-respondent — *A. P.*) must work for the plaintiff untill the end of the case. Equally, in the case of a wife, (the decision to be rendered is) the same. And the same (is done) if the defaulter is the plaintiff. In another place it is written that if judgement is suspended through the fault of the respondent, then, the decision must be rendered that until the end of the case (the disputed wife appearing in this case as respondent's party — *A. P.*) must perform her wifely duties (for the plaintiff) as though she were his wife, while the slave (must perform his duties as a slave) as though he were his (= the plaintiff's) slave.

12, 4—9:

Martak has written this as regards a slave: at the first ("nearest") default, (he must work for the plaintiff) as many days as are required for the conduct of the case, and the other (litigant) must furnish a stake, and at the second default — if he (= the slave-respondent) is capable of payment — he must furnish a stake, but at the third default — it is the end (of the case). (As regards the value of) the stake — if the plaintiff states the value of (this) slave — the amount of the stake is set by this price, otherwise a pledge valued at 500 *drahms* must be furnished. And as regards a wife he (= Martak) has written as follows: at the first ("nearest") default the decision shall be rendered that she should perform the duties of a wife (of the plaintiff — *A. P.*) except for sexual intercourse, and at the second default a stake valued at 500 *drahms* must be furnished, but at the third — it is the end (of the case).

12, 9—13:

If two sheep belonging jointly or separately to Farraxv and Mihrēn are in the possession of Mihrēn, and Fahraxv conveys one sheep to Pusak but Pusak is not able to identify the sheep belonging to Farraxv, and Mihrēn does not make a declaration as to which of the sheep belongs to him, and judgement is suspended through his fault; then Pusak is entitled to take both sheep as security and to benefit from them (until the sentence is pronounced — *A. P.*).

12, 13—16:

If he declares: "this is my wife and you hold her illegally", and the respondent defaults, then, — until the third default — the wife shall not be given (to the plaintiff) because possession is certain while the fundamental title is uncertain. And if the plaintiff makes an analogous declaration in a case regarding a thing, the decision of the court is the same.

12, 17:

If a person litigates with another (and makes the following declaration): "you must deliver the thing to me" and the respondent defaults...*

13, 1—4*:

... tōžišn ī pitarān hamēmār hend ⟨ut⟩ pasēmār pat tōžišn pat nē dānist ka var ī dēnīk (?) (2) pēšēmār+ (Ms.: pasēmār) var pat nē ētōnīh varzišn ut apārīk Mēnō⟨k⟩martān (? Ms.: mynwkGBR"n) ētōn guft kū ka var ān ī pāδ nišān var pat nē dānom varzišn pas pēšēmār pat ēvarīh paytākēnišn.

13, 4—5:

Čiγōn pat Nipištak dīt Mahraspand ī rat būt (guft kū) pat tōžišn ī katak-xvatāy (5) kē sardār ut katak-bānūk ka-šān pat nē dānist var varzīt būt bē (nē) hilišn.

13, 6—13:

Gyākē nipišt kū ka pat dātastān pēšēmār sardār ut katak-bānūk hamēmār ut pat var (7) pasēmār hač pēšēmār vehdātastāntar ⟨pēšēmār⟩ sardar ut katak-bānūk har(v) 2 var dāt (8) apāyēt ut sardār ut katak-bānūk sardār nē bē katak-bānūk var varzišnīh rāδ patkārēnd (9) ut dātastān pat var ī pat sōkand sardār ut katak-bānūk ka dātastān hač ān xvēš būt ī (10) katak-xvatāy vičārtan apāyēt ī (katak-xvatāy dastaβarān) tōžišn saxvan ka pat var xvēš būt ī (11) katak-xvatāy ut dastaβarān xvāstak vičārtan apāyēt ī katak-xvatāy tōžišn pat nē (12) dānist gōβēnd pat ān ī pat ān aδvēnak gōβēnd var dāt apāyēt ut harv 2 var varzišn (13) u-šān āhang kart kū ma hakar ēvak varzēt ut ēvak nē varzēt.

13, 13—15:

Ka pēšēmār ⟨pēšēmār⟩ (14) pat ēt kart ēstēt kū šumā dūtak rāδ apām stāt (ut) nakīrā(k) hend pat ān ī nakīrā(k) (15) hend harv 2 pat tāšt var varzišn ut hakar var nē varzēnd pat hačašmānd dārišn.

---

* The beginning of this article is missing.

13, 1—4 *:

... litigate as regards estate debts ("the debts of fathers"), then, the respondent must take the oath, stating: "I did not know", if it is a case of *dēnīk* (?) ordeal, while the plaintiff [11] (must take the oath, stating): "it is not so". And Mēṯō⟨k⟩martān has said moreover ("another") that in a case of *pāδ nišān* ordeal ("tied feet" — the name of a variety of ordeal — *A. P.*), he (= the respondent) must take the oath, stating: "I did not know" and subsequently make a declaration regarding the truthfulness (of the claim, of the declaration — *A. P.*) of the plaintiff.

13, 4—5:

As I have seen in the *Nipištak* ("*Memorial*" or "*Rescript*"), Mahraspand, who was a *rat*, has said that as regards the obligation to settle the debts of a (deceased) head of household/*pater familias* — the guardian and the mistress of the house are (not) released, even though they have taken the oath (stating): "(we) did not know".

13, 6—13:

It is written in one place that if a plaintiff litigates in court with the guardian and the mistress of the house, and the taking of the oath is adjudicated to the respondent and not to the plaintiff; then both (= each of them) the guardian and the mistress of the house must take the oath. And if a contestation arises between the guardian and the mistress of the house as to the taking of the oath by the mistress of the house but not by the guardian, the trial is to be conducted by oath ordeal (or "by sulphur ordeal" = a variety of ordeal imposing the drinking of a liquid containing sulphur — *A. P.*). (And if) — in a case where the decision of the court (was) that the debts of the (deceased) head of household/*pater familias* must be settled from his estate (by the persons empowered as regards the estate) — the guardian and the mistress of the house declare at the taking of the oath that they "did not know" about the existence ("belonging") of (the debts) of the head of household and about the obligation of the empowered persons (in this case themselves — *A. P.*) to settle the debts of the head of household; then, an oath must be taken about this (specific) circumstance (*i. e.* about their ignorance of their duty to settle the debt — *A. P.*) and the oath must be taken by both of them. And as it is prescribed by regulations for their (case), it should not happen that one of them does take the oath and the other does not.

13, 13—15:

If the plaintiff declares the following: "you (*i. e.* the widowed mistress of the house and the guardian appearing jointly as the respondent — *A. P.*) have received (a loan) for the family" and they deny it, then they must both undergo the ordeal (= take an oath) concerning (the very thing that) they are denying (*i. e.* swear that they did not receive a loan — *A. P.*) as a demonstration of the trustworthiness (of their statement). But if they refuse the ordeal (= refuse to take the oath), then this is to be treated as a case of contumacy.

13, 16—**14**, 2:

Hač dastaβarān pat⁺ (Ms.: BR' = bē) gyākē nipišt kū ka pēšēmār gōβēt kū xvāstak Āturfarnbaγ (17) xvēš būt ⟨hač xvēš⟩ (ut) apātixšāyīhā Farraxv dārēt Farraxv pat nē ētōnīh ī (1) ān hamāk čiš ētōnīh ī xvēš apāč apāyēt guft ut hakar dātastān pat var ut pasēmār vehdāta(2)stāntar var (pat xvēšīh ī xvēš) ayāp pat nē xvēšīh ī Āturfarnbaγ varzišn.

14, 2—5:

Pēšēmār goβēt kū (3) xvāstak man xvēš ut apātixšāyīhā pasēmār dārēt (ut) dātastān pat⁺ (Ms.: BR' = bē) var ī pāδ nišān mat (4) pasēmār ka var ētōn varzēt kū nē tō xvēš Pusānveh ī Āzātmartān guft kū (5) var bavandak Farraxv-Zurvān-ič hamgōnak guft.

14, 5—7:

Ka gōβēt kū Āturfarnbaγ xvēš būt ut hač (6) Āturfarnbaγ ō man mat Pusānveh guft kū ka var ētōn varzēt kū Āturfarnbaγ xvēš (7) nē būt var bavandak.

14, 7—12:

Ka dūtak sardār (ut) katak-bānūk pat tōžišn hač dūtak ō mart ī šahr (8) kart apāyist xvastūk bavēnd ut xvāstak pat tōžišn apispārēnd ut pas andar dūtak (9) pus ō purnāyīh rasēt (ut) apāk ōy kē xvāstak dārēt (pat) tōžišn kartan nē apāyēt patkārēt (10) ut dātastān rāδēnēt pat var pus vehdātastāntar bē ka pēš dātaβarān xvastūk bavēnd ut pēšēmār (11) xvāstak pat vičīr ī dātaβarān bē kunēt/gīrēt pat ēn kū tōžišn būt pat var ōy kē xvāstak (12) dārēt vehdātastāntar kū pus.

14, 12—17:

Anī gyākē nipišt kū pat hačašmānd ī pasēmār (13) kart ka graβ hač pasēmār bē kart/grift būt vināskārīh ī pasēmār ut ēt-ič rāδ (...)* (14) ka ēn guft ēstēt kū dārišn ī pat vičīr ī dātaβarān bē pat ēvarīh enyā apāč (15) nē āβarišn⁺ (? Ms.: YḤSNWšn = dārišn) ka čak (?/ka-č ō?) tā ān hangām pat var pasēmār vehdātastāntar būt (...)** aδak-ič hač-iš (16) xvāstak pat vičīr ī dātaβarān bē kart/grift dārišn bōžišn ut pat var pēšēmār vehdātastān(17)tar.

---

* A line has been omitted in the manuscript.

** Line 15 cannot be translated coherently; omissions and corruption are clearly present.

13, 16—**14**, 2:

It is written in one place with a citation from the authorities (= the commentators on the *Avesta* — *A. P.*), that when the plaintiff declares that a thing belonged to Āturfarnbaγ but Farrxv possessed it illegally, then, Farraxv must make an answering declaration that everything is not so and that the thing belongs to him. And if there is a trial by ordeal and the ordeal — oath — is adjudicated to the respondent, then, he must take an oath (stating that the thing belonged to him), or that it did not belong to Āturfarnbaγ.

14, 2—5:

The plaintiff declares: "the thing belongs to me and the respondent possesses it illegally", and the trial has reached (the stage of — *A. P.*) the *pāδ nišān* ("bound feet" — a variety of ordeal — *A. P.*) ordeal, then, if the respondent swears as follows: "(this thing) does not belong to you", the oath is sufficient according to Pusānveh ī Āzātmartān; Farraxv-Zurvān has said the same.

14, 5—7:

If (the plaintiff) declares:"(this thing) belonged to Āturfarnbaγ and from Āturfarnbaγ (it) came to me", (then), as has been said by Pusānveh, if he (= the respondent) takes an oath in this fashion: "(it) did not belong to Āturfarnbaγ", (such) an oath is sufficient.

14, 7—12:

If the guardian and the mistress of the house agree that a settlement from the family estate is due to a fellow-citizen and deliver a thing in payment, and subsequently, a son from (this) family reaches his majority and brings suit against the one (= the citizen) who received ("has") the thing — maintaining that the payment was unnecessary; then, the son has the legal advantage in the taking of the oath. But if they (= the family guardian and the mistress of the house) declare their agreement before the judges, and the plaintiff takes the thing according to a judicial decision, then the one who received ("holds") the thing — and not the son — shall be the right person to take the oath (stating that) "the payment was due".

14, 12—17:

In another place it is written that if — as the result of contumacy on the part of the respondent — a pledge (or judicial wager) was taken from the respondent because of the respondent's guilt as well as because (...) * if it is declared that his title of possession is based on a judicial decision, then (it) should not be returned (? withheld?) except upon the presentation of trustworthy proof. If the document (? containing the judicial decision) until that time the respondent has the legal advantage in the oath taking (= the ordeal) (...) ** , in that case too, the thing should be taken away by judicial decision, the possession liquidated ("freed, dissolved") and the plaintiff should be given the legal advantage in the taking of the oath.

14, 17—**15**, 1:

Apāk ān guft kū pat markaržān pat-ič ēvak hačašmānd sar brīt apāyēt (1) hač Apastāk (Ms.: 'pystk') paytāk nikerītan.

XXIII

15, 2—3:

Dar * ī tōžišn ī (3) hač dūtak kunišn ut ēt-ič ī ō dūtak xvāhišn.

15, 3—7:

Gyākē nipišt kū (4) ka tōžišn hač dūtak xvāst ut zan ut sardār harv 2 hamēmārīh kart ut ēvak nē šūt+ (5) ut hačašmānd bavēt hakar hač sardār bavēt graβ hač dūtak nē bē (apispārišn) hakar hač zan ut sardār (6) yut-yut hačašmānd bavēt ōγōn čiγōn ka pat ēv+ yāvar būt hē graβ hač dūtak (7) bē apispārišn. Ut Zurvāndāt guft kū ka yut-yut graβ čiš-ič nē apispārišn.

15, 8—9:

Ka hač dūtak tōžišn bē kunišn ut zan 3 pat dūtak bē ka harv 3 hamēmārīh bē (9) kunēnd enyā nē šāyēt.

15, 9—10:

Zan ī pat dūtak stūr ka tōžišn ō dūtak xvāhēt (10) ut ka-č hač dūtak tōžišn-ē(v) xvāhēnd yut hač sardār nē šāyēt.

15, 10—11:

Ka dūtak sardār ut pus (11) katak-bānūk pat pēšēmārīh ī ut pasēmārīh ī (h)ēr ī dūtak ō dātastān nē xvāhišn.

15, 12—14:

Ka sardār ut katak-bānūk pat tōžišn ī katak-xvatāy xvastūk bavēnd (ut) pat tōžišn xvāstak (ī) (13) dūtak bē apispārēnd (ut) pus-ē(v) ī andar dūtak ō purnāyīh rasēt (pat) ōy kē xvāstak (14) bē kart / grift hamēmār bavēt pat pēšēmārīh dātastān xvap.

---

* The (*abǰad*) ordinal-number is placed in line 1 above the title of the chapter.

14, 17—**15**, 1:

In addition it is said that the head of the one accused of a capital offence shall be cut off at his very first failure to appear in court; (this) is evident from the *Avesta*. Take note!

XXIII

15, 2—3:

Chapter* concerning payments (= in settlement of the debts of a deceased person / *de cuius* — *A. P.*) from the family estate ("from the family") as well as payments liable to claim by the family.

15, 3—7:

It is written in one place that if a claim was made for the settlement of a debt (of the *de cuius*) by the family, and if both the wife (= the widow) and the guardian acted (jointly) at the trial, and one of them did not appear (in court), and the case was suspended; then — if (the case) is suspended through the fault of the guardian — no pledge (= trial stake — *A. P.*) need be (furnished) from the family (estate), but if the case is suspended through the fault of the widow ("wife") and the guardian — because of each of them separately — then, the pledge must be furnished from the family estate ("by the family") as if it were a case of a single (default). But Zurvāndat has said that even when (the trial is suspended) through the fault of each of them separately, (in this case also) no pledge need be furnished.

15, 8—9:

If a payment (for the debts of the deceased *paterfamilias* — *A. P.*) is due from his family estate and there are three wives in the family, then, unless all three take part in the case — it is not allowed ("it is not fitting").

15, 9—10:

A woman who is a *stūr* in a family is not empowered (to conduct the case) without the guardian when claiming the settlement (of a debt due) to the family, and similarly, when (others) claim a settlement from the family.

15, 10—11:

If the guardian and a son (of the deceased head of household are in litigation), then, the mistress of the house need not be summoned to court (to act) with the suing or respondent party (in a case concerned with) the family estate.

15, 12—14:

If the guardian (and) the mistress of the house declare (in court) their agreement to settle a debt of the (deceased) head of household and deliver as payment a thing belonging to the family, but — upon reaching his majority — a son from this family brings a claim against the one (the person) who exacted/took the thing; (then), the decision (of the judge) to entertain this claim is good (*i. e.* it is legal — *A. P.*).

15, 14—**16**, 1:

Gyākē nipišt kū ka (15) dārišn bē kart pasēmār pat ēn kū ān apām būt paytāk kunišn ut hakar-aš (16) paytāk kartan nē tuvān xvāstak pat ān dastaβarīh bē apispārišn. Ut ka dārišn asūn (? Ms. 'swn/'dyn') (17) pat dūtak bē ka ēvar paytāk kunēt kū ān tōžišn ō apāyēt kartan enyā (1) xvāstak dārišn hač dūtak bē nē kunišn.

16, 1—2:

Ka tōžišn ī pitar xvāhēnd zan ī pat dūtak ī (2) pit ut ān-ič ī pat dūtak ī pus hač sardār hammis hamēmār kunišn.

16, 2—5:

Gyākē nipišt kū hač (3) pit ō dūtak ī pus ī patigriftak ī žīvandakān pit pat baxt šavēt čiγōn Pusānveh ī Burzātur (4) Farnbaγān guft xvāstak pat aparmānd ōh rasēt ut hač dūtak ī pus tōžišn ī pit and kunišn (5) čand xvāstak ⟨ī⟩ pit xvēš būt.

16, 5—10:

Ka čiš ō dūtak kē katak-bānūk andar xvāhēnd (6) hakar+(Ms.: BYN = andar) dūtak sardār xvāstan nē kāmēt katak-bānūk xvāst nē tuvān. Ka katak-bānūk (7) xvāstan kāmēt dūtak sardār andar rāδēnēt ēn bē gōβēt kū katak-bānūk nē kāmēt (8) pat dātastān guft dūtak sardār yut hač katak-bānūk dātastān dāt pat xvap dāštan ēn (9) tā zamān ka rāδēnišn ī dātastān nē sar enyā ka rāδēnišn ī dātastān sar tā (10) čiš ō dūtak apāyēt apispārtan pat čiš patigriftan+ katak-bānūk-ič andar apāyēt.

16, 11:

Yātakgōβ ī xvastūk ⟨ī⟩ būt ī sardār rāδ pat dūtak gumart xvastūkīh rāδ patigīrišn.

16, 12—14:

Zan ī dūtak stūr ka žahm kunēt ka-č stahm ut apārīk vinās kunēt ut ka(13)-č apātixšāyīhā apar xvāstak patkārēt pat dātastān apar xvāst sardār andar nē apāyēt.

16, 14—17:

Vāyayār nipišt kū ka hač dūtak tōžišn bē kunišn ut katak-bānūk (15) nakīrā(k) ut sardār xvastūk bavēt xvastūkīh ī sardār bē āvartišn ut dātastān rāδēnītan (16) rāδ katak-bānūk sardār gumārišn ut ka andar rāδēnišn katak-bānūk xvastūk bavēt sardār (17) ī ōh gumārēnd nakīrā(k) bavēt nakīrākīh ī sardār ī pas kār nēst.

15, 14—**16**, 1:

It is written in one place that when property is removed (through a court decision), then the respondent must make a (public) declaration that this was a debt (*i. e.* a loan — *A. P.*). And if he is unable to declare this, the thing must be delivered according to this disposition (the decision of the court is evidently intended here — *A. P.*). But if the family property is of meager income (?), then, unless he (= the plaintiff — *A. P.*) declares explicitly (or, "trustworthily") that this payment must be made, the possession of the thing cannot be taken from the family.

16, 1—2:

If the settlement of a debt of the (deceased) father is demanded, the wife from the father's family as well as the wife from the son's family must take part in the case together with the guardian.

16, 2—5:

It is written in one place that — as has been said by Pusānveh ī Burzātur Farnbaγān — the estate of a father passes by transmission (with successory rights) [12] to the family of an adopted son who died in the father's lifetime [13], and the father's debts must be settled by the son's family within the limits of the estate belonging to the father.

16, 5—10:

If a thing is claimed for ("into") a family having a mistress of the house, and if the guardian does not wish to claim (the thing), the mistress of the house cannot make a claim. If the mistress of the house wishes to make a claim and the case is conducted by the guardian of the family (who) declares the following: "the mistress of the house does not wish to appear ('speak') at the trial", the arrangements ("giving") of the case in which the guardian appears without the mistress of the house are to be considered valid (= lawfull) and this (is so) as long as the case has not ended. It is otherwise after the case is closed and up to the moment when the thing is to be delivered to the family: (then), for the receipt of the thing, (a declaration of her willingness to accept) is required from the mistress of the house as well.

16, 11:

An advocate (= a legal representative; a defender) appointed for a family with the agreement of the guardian shall be admitted (to take part in the case) inasmuch as (such an) agreement existed ("because of the agreement").

16, 12—14:

If a woman who is the *stūr* of a family commits an act of violence or another offence and likewise if she shall illegally dispute a thing, then, there is no need of a guardian for her being summoned to court (as the respondent — *A. P.*).

16, 14—17:

Vāyayār has written that if a debt (of the late head of household) is to be settled from the family estate ("out of/from the family") and the mistress of the house denies (this) while the guardian admits (it), then, the admission of the guardian must be (set down in writing and) sealed and the mistress of the household shall designate (another) guardian to conduct the case in court. And if during the trial the mistress of the house admits (the debt and the necessity for its settlement) but the guardian appointed denies (this), then the denial of the second guardian is valueless.

17, 1 *:

... Āturfarnbaγ mat pas hač ān pat ān dāt ō Āturfarnbaγ rasēt ⟨rasēt⟩.

17, 1—4:

Ka gōβēt (2) kū xvāštak ī ō man rasēt ō tō dāt ān ī-š andar ān ē xvēš būt⁺ ka apāč rasēt (3) nē dāt bavēt ut ka-š andar ān ē nē bē-š pēš hač ān pašt xvēš būt ut pas hač ān (4) pašt rasēt dāt bavēt.

17, 4—5:

Ka gōβēt kū pas hač 1 sāl xvāstak ī man xvēš (5) tō xvēš ān dāt bavēt ī pas ⟨hač⟩ ān 1 sāl xvēš.

17, 5—9:

Ka Farraxv ō Mihrēn gōβēt kū (6) ⟨kū⟩ xvāstak ī ō ⟨Farraxv⟩ xvēšīh ī man rasēt tō xvēš pas kas ō Farraxv xvāstak (7) dahēt ut Mihrēn andar nē apāyēt gōβēt ān xvāstak pat Farraxv bē nē ēstēt čē Mihrēn (8) pat dāt ī bun patigīrišn paytākēnīt nē ōγōn bavēt čiγōn ka ō apurnāyak xvāstak (9) dahēnd ut pit gōβēt kū-m andar nē apāyēt.

17, 9—16:

Ut ka šōy xvāstak ī rasēt bē (10) dahēt pas zan ī xvēš pat vindišn pātixšāy kunēt ut ka-č-iš xvāstak dahēnd gōβēt (11) kū-m nē apāyēt. Būt kē ētōn guft kū zan pat vindišn pātixšāy nē pātixšāy (12) kartan bē xvāstak ī-š dahēnd pātixšāy ka patigīrēt ut ka nē patigīrēt hač bun bē (13) nē āyēt. Vahrām guft kū zan pat vindišn pātixšāy kartan ⟨ut⟩ čē vindišn pat zan (14) bē ēstēt ō šōy nē rasēt Mēṯō⟨k⟩māh-ič ēn vāčak pat uskārišn guft (15) ut būt kē guft kū ka-š zan pat vindišn pātixšay kart ā-š patigīrišn paytākēnīt (16) bavēt.

17, 16—18, 1:

Ka gōβēt kū asīm ī ō xvēšīh ī man mat ut zarr ī ō xvēšīh ī (17) man rasēt čand arž 200 vahāk aržēt tō xvēš hēβ bavēt ut zarr nē rasēt (1) asīm 70 bē dahišn.

* This is the end of an article whose first part was to be found on one of the missing folios.

17, 1*:

"... passed to Āturfarnbaγ", then, according to this transfer (the thing) shall pass thereafter to Āturfarnbaγ.

17, 1—4:

If he declares: "the thing which will come to me is given to you", (then) if a thing which belonged to him at that time (at the moment when the agreement was made) is returned to him it is not considered to be transferred (by this declaration of transfer — *A. P.*). But if it did not (belong to him) at that time, but belonged to him before (the time of the agreement) and returned to him once more after (the conclusion of the agreement), (then it) is to be considered as transferred.

17, 4—5:

If he declares: "the property ('thing') belonging to me shall belong to you in a year's time", (then according to this declaration): (all) these (things) which make up the property belonging (to the giver) after the passage of one year (following the declaration) are considered as having been conveyed.

17, 5—9:

If Farraxv declares to Mihrēn: "a thing which will come into my personal possession belongs to you", and subsequently someone conveys a thing to Farraxv but Mihrēn declares: "(it is) not needed", then, this thing will not belong to Farraxv (either), inasmuch as Mihrēn declared his acceptance of the original transfer; this is not the same case as (the one) where a thing is conveyed to a minor but the father declares: "I do not need (it)".

17, 9—16:

If a husband conveys a thing to be received by him and subsequently makes/declares his wife empowered with regard to income (=endows her with an income — *A. P.*), and likewise if (the wife) declares: "I do not need it", at the time when the thing is conveyed; some have said as follows: a wife cannot be empowered with regard to income (= cannot be entitled to dispose of an income; cannot be endowed with an income — *A. P.*), but she is entitled to receive a thing conveyed to her; if, however, (she) does not accept (it), then (this thing) does not leave the conveyor (the "original" possessor/disposer). Vahrām has said that a wife can be made/declared empowered with regard to income, and — inasmuch as the income will (then) belong to the wife — it does not go to the husband. But Mēδō⟨k⟩māh has said that this question should be investigated. And the opinion has likewise been emitted that when he endows his wife with an income her acceptance (of the transfer) must be declared.

17, 16—**18**, 1:

If he declares: "from the silver which will come to me and from the gold which will pass into my property let a definite amount valued at 200 (*drahms*) be yours!", but he received no gold, then, he must convey 70 (*drahms*) of silver.

18, 1—6:

Ut ka gōβēt kū asīm ī ō xvēšīh ī man mat ut asīm ī ō (2) xvēšīh ī man rasēt čand arž 200 vahāk aržēt tō xvēš ut pas hač ān asīm nē rasēt (3) aδak-ič 200 hač asīm ī avi-š mat pat nāmčišt paytāk kunišn ut bē apispārišn ut ka ēvak (4) zarr ut ēvak asīm gōβēt yuttar nē bavēt čiγōn ka gōβēt ku zarr ut asīm ī ō (5) xvēšīh ī man mat čand arž 200 vahāk aržēt tō xvēš ut nēm zarr ut nēm asīm (6) dahišn.

18, 6—7:

Ka gōβēt kū-m ēn dastkart ō tō dāt ān dastkart ut harv čē (7) pat ān dastkart dāšt ēstēt dāt bavēt.

18, 7—8 = **18**, 6—7

18, 9—10:

Ut ka gōβēt kū-m ēn dastkart ut harv čē pat ēn destkart dāšt ēstēt ō tō (10) dāt stōr-ič anšahrīk-ē(v) kē kār ān gyāk kunēt dāt bavēt.

18, 10—13:

Ka gōβēt (11) kū-m ēn dastkart hač[+] harv čē-š andar hammis ō tō (dāt) vičīr-ič ēv ī andar ān dastkart (12) ēstēt ut xvāstak-ič ēv ī pat anī gyāk pat vičīr šāyēt dāštan ut kahas-ē(v) ī hač ēn gyāk (13) rāδēnīt ēstēt ut kār pat apārīk gyāk kunēt dāt bavēt.

18, 13—17:

Ka gōβēt kū-m (14) ēn dastkart hač harv čē-š andar hammis ō tō ut ān dastkart ō tō dāt ēn dast(15)kart ō ōy ut ān dastkart ō ōy dāt bavēt vičīr ī andar ēn dastkart kart ēstēt u-š (16) xvāstak ī pat ān dastkart pat-iš šāyēt dāštan ut kahas ī hač gyāk rāδēnīt ēstēt (17) ut kār pat ān gyāk kunēt nēm ō ōy ut nēm ō ōy dāt bavēt.

18, 17—**19**, 2:

Ka gōβēt (1) kū-m ēn katak ō tō dāt aδak-iš sarāy ut stūn ut rōčpānak ut dar ⟨ī⟩ ut kardar ut hamāpēr ut (2) čāh ī pat hamāpēr dāt bavēt.

18, 1—6:

And if he declares: "(from) the silver which passed into my property and (from) the silver which will pass into my property, a definite amount valued at 200 (*drahms*) belongs to you", and subsequently, the silver (which was to pass to him) does not come to him; then in such as case, (a sum equal to) 200 (*drahms*) from the silver which came to him must be accurately declared and conveyed. But if in one case he mentions gold and in the other silver (*i. e.* if he speaks of the gold as already belonging to him but of the silver as still expected), then, this is equivalent to his declaring: "(from) the gold and silver which have come into my property a sum valued at 200 (*drahms*) belongs to you" — (in that case), he must convey half in gold and half in silver.

18, 6—7:

If he declares: "I have conveyed this *dastkart* to you", then (as a result of this declaration — *A. P.*), this *dastkart* and all the possessions in that *dastkart* are transferred.

18, 7—8 = **18**, 6—7

18, 9—10:

If he declares: "I conveyed to you this *dastkart* and everything in this *dastkart*", then the draught animals and the slaves [14] working on it are likewise transferred (thereby).

18, 10—13:

If he declares: "I conveyed to you this *dastkart* together with everything it contains", then, the document(= title) concerning this *dastkart* as well as property (located) in another place — (but of which) according to that document — he is the rightfull possessor, and the canal dug from this place but irrigating other plots ("serving in another place"), are also transferred (as a result of this declaration of transfer — *A. P.*).

18, 13—17:

If he declares: "I conveyed this *dastkart* together with everything in it to you, and that *dastkart* — to you", then, this *dastkart* is conveyed to one person ("to him") while that *dastkart* (is condeyed) to another ("to him"). (However the title) documents regarding this *dastkart* — but according to which he possess property located in another *dastkart* — and the canal dug from this place — but irrigating a plot in the other ("serving in that place") — are transferred half to one and half to the other.

18, 17—**19**, 2:

If he declares: "I have conveyed this house to you", then: the hall, and the porch ("the columns"), and the window, and the gates, and the platform (?) and the utilitarian building, and the well in the building are (thereby) conveyed by him.

19, 2—3:

Ka gōβēt kū-m ēn xānak pat mānišin (3) dāštan ō tō dāt yāvētānīk pat xvēšīh dāt bavēt.

19, 3—7:

Ka gōβēt (4) kū-m xānak-ē(v) ō tō dāt hač Pusānveh ī Āzātmartān bē guft kū ⟨ka⟩-š ast ī (5) bun dāt bavēt ka gōβēt kū-m zamīk ō tō dāt aδak-iš ēvkartakīhā dāt (6) bavēt. Ēvkartakīhā ōγōn bavēt ka-š zamīk ī hambarakān zamīk ī kasān ut yōy kē (7) āp ō xān ut xvāstak barēt ut katak ut kardar⁺ (*cf.* **19**, 1; Ms.: srd'l = sardār) ut rāh ⟨ut⟩ andarg nēst.

19, 7—10:

Ka (8) xvāstak ō apurnāyak kē sardār ut zan kē šōy hast dahēnd ut šōy ut sardār gōβēnd (9) kū-mān andar nē apāyēt aδak-ič ān ī ō apurnāyak dahēnd apurnāyak ka ō purnāyīh (10) mat ut ān ī ō zan dahēnd zan xvēš.

19, 10—12:

Gyākē nipišt kū ka ō apurnāyak (11) xvāstak dahēnd ut pit andar nē apāyēt gōβēt pas (apurnāyak andar) apurnāyīh ut pit-ič pat baxt šavēnd (12) ān xvāstak ō dūtak ī pit rasēt.

19, 12—16:

Ut apāk anī gyākē nipišt kū ka mart apāk (13) zan kē hač šoy stūrīh ut sardārīh nēst kart kū ēn xvāstak frazand ī nazdist (14) hač tō zāyēt xvēš ut pas hač ān zan frazand zāyēt ut andar apurnāyīh pat baxt šavēt (15) ⟨ut⟩ ān xvāstak apāč ō ōy rasēt kē⁺ bē dāt ut apāk-ič anī Martak nipišt kū bē⁺ (16) ān ī pat nīrmat ēstēt pat ēn dārišn kū apurnāyak andar apāyēt.

19, 16—**20**, 1:

An-ič guft ēstēt kū (17) Vehak xvāstak ō Farraxv dahēt ut Farraxv patigīrišn nē paytākēnēt ut mīrēt patigīrišn (1) pat paytākēnīt dārišn ut Farraxv pat ān xvāstak stūr gumārišn nikerītan.

19, 2—3:

If he declares: "I conveyed this house to you for you to live (in it)", then, (this house) is conveyed (to him) forever as personal property (= as his personal share with the right of transmission to his successors — *A. P.*).

19, 3—7:

If he declares: "I conveyed a house to you", then (according to such a transfer formula — *A. P.*), only a part of the plot (= property, possession; lit. "capital; basis; principal") has been conveyed — as was confirmed on the basis of a citation from Pusānveh ī Āzātmartān. If he declares: "I conveyed the land (= the plot) to you", then (it) is conveyed to him as a whole ("united", "as one"). And (a transfer) as a whole unit ("as one") takes place when he has a plot ("land") joined to the plots of other persons, and there is in it neither a canal bringing water to the house and the plot, nor a house, nor a platform (?. *cf.* **19**, 1), nor a road.

19, 7—10:

If a thing is conveyed to a minor having a guardian and to a woman having a husband, and (if) the husband and the guardian declare: "we do not need (it)", then, that (which is conveyed to the minor (will belong to him) when he comes of age, and that which is conveyed to the wife will become her property.

19, 10—12:

It is written in one place that if a thing is given (as a gift) to a minor, but his father declares that it is: "not needed", and (the minor) then dies without reaching his majority and (his) father (also) dies, then this thing shall go to the father's family.

19, 12—16:

And in addition it is written in one place that if a man concludes (the following agreement) with a woman who is not under her husband's guardianship and is not his *stūr*: "this thing shall belong to the first child born to you" and (if) the woman subsequently bears a child and (this child) dies without reaching his majority, then, this thing returns to the man who conveyed it. And in addition, Martak has also written the following: "except for what is needed ("usefull") for the maintenance expenses required for a minor".

19, 16—**20**, 1:

The following is also said: Vehak conveys a thing to Farraxv, but Farraxv does not declare (his) acceptance (of the transfer), (and Vehak — *A. P.*) dies. The acceptance (of the transfer) is to be considered as having occurred ("been declared") and Farraxv is to be appointed (Vehak's — *A. P.*) *stūr* on the basis of this thing (conveyed to him). To be examined carefully.

20, 2—6:

Ka mart xvāstak ī-š rasēt apurnāyak^{+} mart-ē(v) xvēš būt rāδ gōβēt (3) xvāstak ī andar apurnāyīh^{+} ī ān apurnāyak rasēt pit xvēš ut apāk ān ī nipišt kū (4) pat dāt ī bun patigīrišn paytākēnīt ut ēn-ič nikerītan kū-š rāh pat xvēšīh pat gyāk (5) dāt bavēt nē ōγōn bavēt kū-š xvāstak pas hač 10 sāl ō apurnāyak dāt būt^{+} (6) ēstēt^{+}.

20, 6—7:

Ka gōβēt kū-m xvāstak ī vitart man ō ḍūtak ī man rasēt ō tō dāt (7) ān ī hač katak xvatāy apar zan ut frazand mānd nē dāt bavēt.

20, 7—10:

Vahrām guft kū (8) ka pit (xvāstak ī-š) mat ut rasēt bē ō zan ut frazand (ī) xvēš dahēt ut pas anšahrīk āzāt kunēt (9) Syāvaxš guft kū anšahrīk hač šāhān šāh bandakīh apāč aβurt (10) nē šāyēt man-ič hamgōnak gōβom bē Rāt-Ōhrmizd yut-dātastānīh-ē(v) andar ōh kart.

20, 11—13:

Syāvaxš guft kū ka mart-ē(v) apāk Farraxv patmān kunēt kū-m ēn xvāstak (12) (pas) hač 10 sāl ō tō dāt Farraxv andar 10 sāl bē mīrēt ān xvāstak ō zan ut frazand (13) ut dūtak ī Farraxv nē rasēt.

20, 13—16:

Ka pit pat^{+} apurnāyak ayāp šōy pat zan vičīr ăvišt (14) kū xvāstak ī ō xvēšīh ī man rasēt tō xvēš (ut) pas hač ān anī kas ō ān zan (15) (ut) apurnāyak xvāstak dāt ān ī ō zan dahēt pat zan ut ān ī ō apurnāyak dahēt (16) pat apurnāyak bē ēstēt.

20, 16—**21**, 3:

Ka Farraxv sāl ēvak apar Mihrēn kart kū xvāstak ī (17) man xvēš ut ēt-ič ō xvēšīh ī man rasēt tō xvēš ut sāl 5 andar Kērēn (?) kart kū (1) xvāstak ī man xvēš ut ēt čē ō xvēšīh ī man rasēt tō xvēš xvāstak ī Farraxv (Ms.: Mihrēn) pas (2) hač pašt ī andar Mihrēn ō Mihrēn (Ms.: Farraxv) ān ī andar 5 sāl frāč bavēt pat rāh ī rasīt (3) Kērēn(?) xvēš.

20, 2—6:

If a person declares that a thing which is to come to him (= *bona adventicia — A. P.*) belongs (through this declaration) to a minor, then — if the thing comes to him (= the giver) before the minor reaches his majority — it shall belong to the (his) father. And it is also written that the acceptance of the transfer must be declared and care must also be taken that the real rights be opened ("granted, given") to him at once, so that (the following should not occur): that the thing be conveyed to the minor (only) after a lapse of 10 years.

20, 6—7:

If he declares: "I have conveyed to you the estate ("thing") which will pass to my family after my death" [15], then (the estate) left by the head of household to his wife and children is not included in the transfer ("is not conveyed").

20, 7—10:

Vahrām has said that if a father transmits to his wife and children (the estate which) he will receive and he subsequently frees a slave (from servitude), then, according to the opinion of Syāvaxš, the (former) slave cannot ("may not") be brought back from his (acquired status of) a "subject of the King of Kings", and I express the same opinion, but Rāt-Ōhrmizd has rendered a different judgement on this question [16].

20, 11—13:

Syāvaxš has said that if a man concludes (the following) agreement with Farraxv: "I convey this thing to you after the passage of ten years", but Farraxv dies during these ten years, (then), the thing does not pass to Farraxv's wife, children and family.

20, 13—16:

If a father has drawn up ("sealed") the following contract as regards his minor (son) or a man — as regards his wife: "a thing which will pass into my personal possession ("property") shall belong to you" and subsequently the thing is conveyed by another person to the woman and the minor, then, that which he conveys to the woman shall belong to the woman, and that which he conveys to the minor — to the minor [17].

20, 16—**21**, 3:

If in year one Farraxv makes as regards Mihrēn (the following declaration): "the estate which belongs to me and that which will pass into my personal possession/property belongs to you", and in year five he concludes (this agreement) with Kērēn (?): "the estate which belongs to me and that which will pass into my personal possession/property belongs to you", then the estate of Farraxv (Mihrēn in the ms.) (will belong) to Mihrēn (Farraxv in the ms.) after the conclusion of the agreement with Mihrēn, and that which after five years will be found to have passed (to Farraxv) — since it consists of *bona adventicia* — shall belong to Kērēn (?).

[*Numberless*] *

21, 4—5:

Dar ī *ayōγēn / ayuγēn. Yō hē pasčaēta* (5) 'ywk' ps'čyt' *.

21, 5—8:

Nipišt kū mart zan ut frazand bē duxt 1 anī kas nēst (6) ut ān ī duxt šōy ān duxt hač zanīh bē hilēt (ut) pat sardārīh apāč ō pit nē (7) dahēt aδak-iš stūrīh ī pit pat xvāhišn ut ka-š pat sardārīh apāč patigīrēt (8) aδak-iš apar ōh mānēt (ut) xvāhišn pat kār (nē) apāyēt.

21, 8—10:

Sōšyans guft kū (9) duxt ī baγaspān+ ka-š bē hilēt ka-č-iš vitart pit bē hilēt aδak-ič-iš (10) *ayōγēn* apar ōh bavēt.

21, 10—15:

Nipišt kū ka frazand ī pas zāt+ (Ms.: zāyēt) duxt [žīvandakān pit šōy] (11) kunēt hač zanīh hišt+ apāč šavēt vitart stūr ī kart(ak) ān stūrīh apar ān duxt (12) ōh mānēt ut ka-š dātastān ōγōn ⟨ī⟩ pitar ⟨i⟩ stūr andar apāyēt pat ān ī pit ōh gumārišn ut hast (13) kē ētōn gōβēt kū ka-č-iš andar ān ē ka stūr ī kartak pat baxt šut+ (Ms.: 'ZLWNyt) šōy kart ut (14) nē hišt ēstēt aδak-ič *yō hē pasčaēta* (Ms.: ywk hy psčyt'). Vahrām guft ku ka-š andar ān ē (15) šōy kart ētōn apāyēt dāštan čiγōn ka nē žīvandak hē.

21, 15—**22**, 1:

Duxt ī pas (16) zāt kē stūrīh apar mānēt hač čiγōn xvēš ka stūr aparmānd ī (17) [pita]r nē bavēt andar-ič aparmānd ī pat stūrīh aparmānd ī pat xvēšīh būt nē (1) šāyēt.

22, 1—2:

Pat guft ī dastaβarān ēt nipišt kū *yō hē pasčaēta* ka živandak pit šōy (2) kunēt xvap.

---

* This chapter carries no ordinal-number.

[*Numberless*] *

21, 4—5:

Chapter concerning auxiliary succession — the *epiklerate* [18].

21, 5—8:

(The following) has been written: if a man has no one — no wife, no children — except for one daughter, and the man who is the husband of that daughter divorces her (but) does not return her to (her) father's guardianship; then, she can become her father' *stūr* (= be charged with her father's succession, become *epikleros*) (only) upon request. But if (her father) takes her back under his guardianship, then she will inherit (the status of her father's *epikleros*) and the request is not necessary.

21, 8—10:

Sōšans has said that: if a daughter (having entered into a *bayaspān* (marriage) is divorced, she shall become her father's *epikleros* even if she is divorced after her father's death.

21, 10—15:

It is written that (if) the child born afterwards (= after the father has instituted a *stūr* for himself — *A. P.*) is a daughter, and she [marries during her father's lifetime], and returns (to her father's house) upon the dissolution of her marriage; then — after the death of the *stūr* instituted (by her father) — this daughter will inherit the *stūr*ship (= she will have to take up her father's *epiklerate* through natural calling without the formal procedure of request and appointment — *A. P.*). But if a judicial decision (has been rendered) that: "(the late) father requires a *stūr*", then, she shall be appointed her father's *stūr* [19]. Some say that: even if she has married and does not divorce at the death of the instituted *stūr*, in that case also, she shall become her father's *stūr* (= *epikleros*). Vahrām has said that if she entered into a marriage at that time (*i. e.* after the death of the instituted *stūr* — *A. P.*), then this (case) is to be equated with (the standard case of an *epikleros*-daughter's marriage) after the death (of her father) [20].

21, 15—**22**, 1:

A daughter born after (her father instituted a *stūr* for himself) (*cf. supra*, **21**, 10—15) (and) who will inherit his *stūr*ship — inasmuch as, being his *stūr*, she is not her father's personal successor (= an heir receiving her father's estate as a personal share — *A. P.*) — then, within the limits of her father's succession on the basis of the *stūr*ship, she is not entitled (at the same time) to be her father's personal heir.

22, 1—2:

The following is written from the words of the commentators on the *Avesta*: if an *epikleros*-daughter enters into a (*pātixšāyīh*) marriage during her father's lifetime, then this is lawful ("good").

22, 2:

(...) šut u-š ān stūrīh pat ān dastaβarīh avi-š nē rasēt *.

22, 2—3:

Ut ēn-ič ōγōn nipišt kū (3) *yō hē pasčaēta* ka duxt aparmānd ī pit nē bavēt ut ka pus ā-š ōh bavēt.

22, 3—6:

Ka-š (4) brāt 2 ut xvah 1 ān gyāk ut ān xvah apāk brāt 1 hambāγ u-š brāt ī dit apar sardār ⟨ī⟩ (5) ut brāt 2 harv pat ēv yāvar pat baxt bē šavēnd pat čāštak ī Aparak sardār pat ān ī Mēṯō(k)māh (6) hambāγīh gōβēnd kū ka-š hast ā-š apar ōh mānēt.

22, 6—8:

Ka māt andar dūtak xvah stūrīh (7) ī brāt apar nē mānēt u-š čim ēn kū ⟨kū⟩ xvah pat zanīh māt bē pātixšāy (8) dāt pat ān čim sardārīh ī andar brāt nē bavandak.

22, 9—12:

Duxt ī pit pat sardārīh ō mart ī šahr dāt (10) ēstēt ayōγēn ī pit ut brāt kem apar nē mānēt ka-š ayōγēn ī pit apar mānēt sardār (11) ān (ī) māt ut ka-š ān ī brāt apar mānēt sardār hač nabānazdištān+ ī brāt bavēt. Ka pat sardārīh (12) (ī) brāt bē dāt ēstet aδak-ič-iš ayōγēn apar ōh mānēt ut sardār hač xvēšāvandān ī brāt ⟨ī⟩ bavēt.

22, 13—14:

Ka brāt 2 ut xvah 1 ān gyāk baxtīkīh kunēnd ut brāt ī kas ut xvah ākanēn bahr gīrēnd (14) xvah-sardārīh-ič bē ō brāt ī kas rasēt.

22, 14—**23**, 1:

Apāk-ič ān pas-ič ka brāt ī mas pēš (15) mīrēt ēt rāδ čē xvah sardārīh hač brāt nē pat dāt ī brāt bē nē patkār[tan ⟨ī⟩] (16) ka bažišn+ (? Ms. w/nbčšn) kart brāt apar sardārīh ī xvah rāδ u-š ap(p)ār būt ēstēt [xvah ayōγēn ī] (17) brāt ī mas ut ka naxvist brāt ī kas mīrēt ka-č harv 2 pat ēv+ [tāk mīrēnd aδak-ič] (1) xvah ayōγēn ī brāt ī kas.

* The beginning of this article has been omitted by the copyist.

22, 2:

(...) died (?) then this *stūr*ship will not pass to her through this empowering (= title)*.

22, 2—3:

And it is also written in this manner: if the *stūr*ship (for the deceased passes) to a daughter, then she does not become her father's personal heir, but if — to a son, then he becomes (a successor and an heir).

22, 3—6:

If in one family ("place") there are two brothers and a sister, and the sister is in co-partnership with one of the brothers (= they hold undivided shares in their father's estate — *A. P.*), while the other is her guardian, and (if) both brothers die simultaneously, then, according to the *Čāštak* (= "*Commentary*") of Aparak, she must become (the *epikleros* of the brother who was her) guardian, but according to (the *Čāštak*) of Mēδō⟨k⟩māh, in a case (because of the existence) of partnership (= the joint share in the estate), she inherits (the *epiklerate* of the brother who is her co-heir).

22, 6—8:

If in a family there is a mother, then the *stūr*ship for a brother does not go to the sister. The reason for this is that the mother is entitled to give the daughter in marriage, and as the result of this circumstance, the guardianship of the brother over the sister is insufficient (for her calling to assume his *stūr*ship — *A. P.*).

22, 9—12:

A daughter given by her father into the guardianship of a fellow-citizen nevertheless inherits the *epiklerate* for her father or her brother. If she receives the *epiklerate* for her father, her guardian must become the same as the guardian of (her) mother, but if she inherits the *epiklerate* for her brother, then one of (her) brother's nearest agnates becomes her guardian. But if she was put under the guardianship of (her) brother, then, in this case, also, she will receive the status of *epikleros* and one of the relatives (= agnates) of the brother will become her guardian.

22, 13—14:

If in a family ("in that place") there are two brothers and a sister, and they divide (the inheritance) and the younger brother and the sister jointly receive ("take") a (common) share; then the guardianship over the sister goes to the younger brother.

22, 14—**23**, 1:

And in addition — the following: if subsequently the older brother dies before (the younger), a suit regarding the transmission (to the sister of the *stūr*ship) for her brother should not be initiated inasmuch as (that) brother did not exercise the functions of a guardian over the sister. If a division (?) took place because of (or, "for the sake of") the brother's guardianship over the sister, and he was removed (from the guardianship), then [the sister becomes the *epikleros*] of the older brother. But if the younger brother dies first, and even when both (brothers) die simultaneously, the sister must become the *epikleros* of the younger brother. (*Vide supra*, **22**, 13—14).

23, 1—4:

Vāyayār nipišt kū ka duxt [pat] dastaβarīh ī pit (2) andar kas kunēt kū tā 10 sāl zan ī tō hom ut pit pēš hač 10 sāl mīrēt pit tā (3) 10 sāl stūr gumārišn ut ka 10 sāl uzīt duxt zanīh ī kas nēst ut ayōγēn ī (4) pit.

23, 4—10:

U-š ēn-ič ōγōn nipišt kū xvah ayōγēn ī brāt andar hambāγīh ⟨ī aδak⟩ apar mānēt. (5) Ka brāt pat baxt šavēt u-š zan ut frazand ⟨ut⟩ bē xvah aδak-iš ayōγēn ī brāt apar nē (6) mānēt ut ka baxtīkīh kart ān ī ōy brat apar mānēt kē-š bahr pat hambāγīh (7) apāk stat^{+} ayāp-iš pat aparmānd ⟨ī⟩ dastaβarīh apar sardār būt ka baxtīkīh (8) kart ut brat-ē(v) kē bahr pat hambāγīh apāk stat^{+} brāt-ē(v) kē-š pat aparmānd dastaβarīh (9) apar sardār būt frāč raft ayōγēn ī ōy brāt apar mānēt kē-š apar sardār (10) būt ut ka-š apāk brāt 2 pat hambāγīh bahr stat ēstēt hač pēš paytāk.

23, 10—11:

Ka brāt (11) 2 ut xvah 1 ān gyāk xvah sardārīh pat brāt ī mas.

23, 11—13:

Ut būt kē guft kū ka xvāstak (12) nēst aδak-ič hambāγ ōh bavēt ut ka hast aδak-ič pat rāh ī hamvindišnīh apāč gumaštēt. (13) Apāk-ič ēt kū ayōγēn xvāstak xvāst nē āmār.

23, 13—17:

Pas-ič ōγōn čiγōn pit kē pus hast (14) ayōγēn apar duxt nē mānēt brāt-ič ka brāt ī hambāγ hast ayōγēn apar xvah nē mānēt. (15) Bē-šān ōγōn dāšt kū hambāγ ī dēnīk^{+} (?) ō kartak nē kart ēstēt hamē(v) sardārīh (16) kār ut ka brāt ī mas mīrēt aδak-iš ayōγēn apar ōh mānēt ut ka ān ī kas mīrēt ā-š (17) nē mānēt.

23, 17—**24**, 2:

Ka pit duxt 1 ut dūtak ī pus 1 ut pat ān dūtak xvāstak 80 hast ut duxt (1) sardārīh pat pit ka pit frāč ravēt ayōγēn ī brāt čē vitart pit apāk dūtak (2) ī pus hambāγ.

23, 1—4:

Vāyayār has wrtitten that if a daughter — empowered by her father — concludes (the following agreement) with someone: "I shall be your wife for ten years", and (if) the father dies before the ten years are up, (then) a *stūr* must be appointed for the father untill the (end of the) ten years limit. At the end of the ten years, however, she ceases to be that man's wife and becomes her father's *epikleros*.

23, 4—10:

And he has also written this: the sister becomes the *epikleros* of the brother who is her co-partner (= co-heir). If the brother dies and he (also) has a wife and a child in addition to the sister, then she (= the sister) does not become her brother's *epikleros*. And if a division (of the estate) took place, then she will become the *epikleros* of the brother with whom she received a joint share, or of (that brother) who has become her guardian according to the (testamentary) disposition ("empowering"). If a division took place and (both) — the brother with whom she received a joint share as co-partner and the brother who was her guardian according to the (testamentary) disposition of the inheritance — have died, then she becomes the *epikleros* of the brother who was her guardian; and if she received a joint share as co-partner with both brothers, then (the decision) is obvious from (what has been stated) above.

23, 10—11:

If in a family ("in that place") there are two brothers and a sister, then the guardianship goes to the older brother.

23, 11—13:

Some (authorities) have said that even when there is no estate, (an *epikleros*-sister) is a co-partner (with her late brother). And if there is (an estate), then, in that case also, (a certain share of its revenue) — on the basis of the joint share in the revenue — is deducted. And the following has been said in addition: a claim on the estate made by the *epikleros* is not to be taken into consideration.

23, 13—17:

And furthermore (the following): just as when the father has a son, a daughter does not become (her father's) *epikleros*, so when a brother has a co-partner brother, a sister does not become (her brother's) *epikleros*. But such cases (lit., "they") must be considered (as follows): (if) the co-heir — so instituted by religious law (? "the living heir" is not a likely reading. *cf.* also **24**, 2—3 — *A. P.*) — does not go through the formal procedure (for the confirmation of the guardianship — *A. P.*), his assumption of the functions of guardian is valid. And if the older brother dies, she (= the sister) becomes his *epikleros*, but she does not become (*epikleros*) if the younger one dies.

23, 17—**24**, 2:

If (a family consists of) the father, a daughter, and the family of a (deceased) son, and this family has an estate of 80 (drahms/*satērs*?), and the daughter is under her father's guardianship, then in the case of the father's death, the daughter will become her brother's *epikleros* since, after the death of the father, she becomes a co-heir with the son's (= her late brother's) family.

24, 2—3:

Manuščihr guft kū hambāγ ī dēnīk (?) ō kartak nē kart ēvāč pat (3) rāδēnišn ī stūr.

24, 3—4:

Būt kē guft kū duxt ī andar xānak ī pitarān zāt ēstāt (4) ka-š māt andar žīvandakānīh ī pit ī māt šōy kart ayōγēn ī pit ī māt apar nē mānēt.

24, 4—7:

Māhvindāt⁺ (5) guft kū duxt ī pat ān ayōγēn ka-š māt andar žīvandakānīh ī pit ī māt šōy ayāp markaržān ayāp (6) *paratāčaēta* kart ā-š nēm bahrak ī māt apar nē mānēt enyā (7) ka pat ayōγēn andar apāyēt ā-š ayōγēn apar ōh mānēt.

24, 7—10:

Ka duxt apēdastaβār ī (8) pit ⟨ī⟩ gātār kunēt hakar gātār nē hač ān ī⁺ hamēyīk kunēt aδak-iš sardārīh ut aparmānd (9) ī pitar yuttar bē nē bavēt ut ka gātār hač ān ī hamēyīk kunēt ā-š aparmānd ī pitar (10) avi-š nē rasēt ut pit-ič kār vindišn ī duxt hač-iš ap(p)ār bē bavēt.

XXVI

24, 11:

Dar ī sardārīh *.

24, 12—13:

Ka xvāstak ruvān rāδ paytāk kunēt ut pat dāštan ō kas nē dahēt hač frazand ī ōy (13) ēvak ī sažāktar dārišn čē ētōn bavēt čiγōn sardārīh ī ātaxš.

24, 13—16:

Ka xvāstak (14) ruvān rāδ paytāk kunēt ut pat dāštan ō mart-ē(v) dahēt ⟨kū⟩ uzīt [ān mart] kē-š ān (15) xvāstak avi-š dāt⁺ ān xvāstak pat patvand ī ōy mart bē ravēt kē-š avi-š dāt (16) ēstēt hamēv ēvak ī sažāktar dārišn.

* The (*abǰad*) ordinal-number 26 is plased above the heading of this chapter.

24, 2—3:

Manuščihr has said that one who is co-partner/co-heir by religious law (?) need not go through the formal procedure, (he must undergo it) only to assume the functions of a *stūr*.

24, 3—4:

Some (authorities) have said that a daughter born to her father's house does not inherit the *epiklerate* of her mother's father if the mother marries during her (= the mother's) father's lifetime.

24, 4—7:

Māhvindāt has said that a daughter (= granddaughter — *A. P.*) (is called) to the *epiklerate* (for her maternal — grandfather — *A. P.*) (in such cases): if (her) mother entered into a marriage (with full rights) during her (the mother's) father's lifetime, or if she (= the mother) committed a capital crime, or (an offence punishable) by exile (from the community). Then she does not inherit her mother's "half-share" (*i. e.* her daughter's share of the inheritance — *A. P.*) except for the benefit of the *epiklerate* ("when it is indispensable for the *epiklerate*"), and in such a case she receives (it) through transmission, as the *epikleros* (*i. e.* as a *stūr* possession and as the *epikleros* for her maternal grandfather — *A. P.*).

24, 7—10:

If a daughter enters into a sexual relationship without her father's sanction, then — if it is not a case of adultery as a habitual offence — this will not result in an alteration of her status as ward and as successor to (her) father. But if (it is a case) of adultery continually committed by her, then she will not receive the inheritance and the succession of her father, and her father shall likewise lose his right over the daughter's income (= revenue).

XXVI

24, 11:

Chapter * concerning guardianship.

24, 12—13:

If he declares (the transfer) of a thing "for the soul" and yet does not convey it to the possession (= the trusteeship — *A. P.*) of anyone, then one of his children must possess ("hold") this thing, and specifically the one most suited (to do so); for this case is analogous to the (case) regarding the trusteeship over a Fire-temple.

24, 13—16:

If he declares (the transfer) of a thing "for the soul") and conveys it to the possession ("holding" = trust) of someone, then — after the death of the man to whom he gave the thing — this thing shall pass to the kinsmen of the man who gave it, and let one of them (*i. e.* of the kinsmen of the man who endowed the foundation "for the soul" — *A. P.*) possess it, (namely the one who is) most suited (to assume the charge).

24, 16—17:

Gyākē nipišt kū ka gōβēt kū-m ēn xvāstak (17) ruvān rāδ paytāk kart zan ut frazand ī ōy mart pat ākanēn dārišn.

24, 17—**25**, 1:

Ka xvāstak ruvān ī xvēš (1) anī-č kas rāδ paytāk kunēt aδak-ič ān xvāstak pat patvand ī ōy mart ravēt (2) kē pat ān aδvēnak dāštan rāδ paytāk kunēt.

25, 2—5:

Gyākē ōγōn nipišt kū ka Farraxv (3) xvāstak ⟨anī⟩ pat ruvān ī xvēš ut (ān) ī Mihrēn dāštan rāδ paytāk kunēt ut kas daštan (4) rāδ framān nē bavēt ān xvāstak pat ān aδvēnak ī paytāk kart xvāstakdārān ī (5) Farraxv (ut) xvāstakdārān (ī) Mihrēn pat ākanēn dārišn.

25, 5—8:

Gyākē nipišt kū ka xvāstak (6) ruvān rāδ paytāk kunēt ut pat dāštan ō zan ēv dahēt ut ān zan šōy kunēt ān xvāstak (7) pat ān aδvēnak ī ō ān zan mat bē ō ān mart rasēt ut pat patvand ī ān mart bē (8) ravēt.

25, 8—11:

Ut apāk anī gyākē nipišt kū ka ātaxš pat sardārīh ō duxt ī xvēš (9) dahēt ut duxt šōy kunēt ō šōy barēt ut ka-š šōy hač zanīh bē hilēt (10) ayāp bē mīrēt ēn kū sardārīh ānōδ bē mānēt ayāp apāč ō bun šavēt saxvan (11) ut patkār pat-iš nikerītan.

25, 11—13:

Ka gōβēt kū ēn dūtak pat sardārīh tō dār ut dūtak sardārīh (12) bē ō pēš dahēt ut dūtak sardār ī ditīkar bē mīrēt sardārīh ī dūtak apāč ō bun (13) šavēt.

25, 13—15:

Ka gōβēt kū-m ēn dūtak pat sardārīh ⟨ī⟩ ō tō dāt ayāp gōβēt kū-m (14) ēn dūtak sardār kart hēh ut dūtak sardār dūtak sardārīh bē ō pēš dahēt dūtak sardār ī (15) ditīkar bē mīrēt sardārīh ī dūtak apāč ō ōy ī fratōm rasēt.

24, 16—17:

It is written in one place that if he declares: "I have declared this thing (conveyed) 'for the soul'", then the wife and children of this man must possess ("hold, keep") it jointly.

24, 17—**25**, 1:

If he declares (the transfer) of a thing (as the endowment of a foundation) for his soul, as well as for the soul of another person, then this thing must pass to the kinsmen of the one who made the declaration concerning the nature of (the) possession of this thing.

25, 2—5:

It is written in one place as follows: if Farraxv declares the transfer of the possession of a thing (as an endowment) for his soul and the soul of Mihrēn without making (any) disposition as to the person who is to possess (this thing), then the heirs of Farraxv and the heirs of Mihrēn must possess it jointly in the manner for which it was declared (*i. e.* as an endowment "for the soul" of Farraxv and Mihrēn — *A. P.*).

25, 5—8:

It is written in one place that if he declares (the transfer) of a thing as (an endowment) "for the soul", and conveys it to the possession (= trusteeship) of a woman, and this woman marries; then this thing will pass to that man (= her husband) and to his kinsmen on the same basis as it passed to the woman.

25, 8—11:

In addition it is written in one place that if he conveys a Fire-altar to the possession ("the trusteeship") of his daughter and the daughter marries, then she will bring (the trusteeship over the Fire-altar) to her husband. And if the husband divorces her or (if he) dies, then the testimonies given in court and the responses to them must be investigated in order to (decide) whether the trusteeship (over the endowed Fire-altar) shall remain in that family ("there") or return to the family of the endower.

25, 11—13:

If he declares (the following): "Keep this family under (your) guardianship", and (that one subsequently) transfers (the guardianship to another person), and if the second guardian dies, then the guardianship shall return to the family of the disposer (*i. e.* the *status quo ante* shall be re-established; *cf.* **25**, 13—15 — *A. P.*).

25, 13—15:

If he declares: "I have conveyed this family to your guardianship", or if he declares: "you are made/proclaimed by me the guardian of this family", and (if) the guardian of the family (= the one who became guardian through the above declaration — *A. P.*) transfers the guardianship over the family further (*i. e.* appoints another guardian), and (this) guardian dies; then the guardianship over the family shall return to the first guardian (= to the family of the first guardian; *cf. supra* **25**, 11—13).

25, 15—16:

Ka gōβēt (16) kū ēn ātaxš sardārīh ō tō kart sardārīh pat patvand bē barišn.

25, 16—**26**, 1:

Ka gōβēt (17) kū ēn ātaxš pat sardārīh tō dār sardārīh pat patvand bē barišn sardārīh ī pat (1) patvand bē ravēt ān ī ātaxš ut ān ī xvāstak ī ō ruvān dahēnd.

26, 1—3:

Ka pat dūtak (2) sardār gumārtan pus-ē(v) ō purnāyīh rasēt (ut) ān pus frāč ravēt būt kē guft (3) kū dūtak sardār ī pus gumārišn.

26, 3—5:

Dūtak sardār ī gumārtak ka katak-bānūk zan (4) kunēt ut pas pus ō purnāyīh rasēt aδak-iš pat zanīh hamdātastānīh ī pus (5) apāyēt.

26, 5—7:

Sardār ī katak-xvatāy gumārt pātixšāy ka zan ut frazand pat sardārīh (6) bē dahēt pat čāštak gōβēnd kū sardār ī būtak ī sardārīh ō pēš pātixšāy dāt (7) u-š and dāt bavēt čand dahēnd⁺.

26, 7—8:

Pus ka xvāstak ī pitar gīrēt ut dārēt (8) nē pātixšāy kū sardārīh ī apurnāyakān nē kunēt.

26, 8—10:

Gyākē nipišt kū sardārīh ī dūtak (9) kē sardār⁺ ō pēš pātixšāy dāt ut ēvāč ān ēvak ī katak-xvatāy gumārt⁺ ut stūr ī kartak (10) andar žīvandakānīh ī xvēš ō harv kē kāmēt pātixšāy dāt.

25, 15—16:

If he declares: "the trusteeship over this Fire-alter is declared (to be transferred) to you", then the trusteeship must be transmitted (by way of inheritance) to the kinsmen (of that man).

25, 16—**26**, 1:

If he declares (the following): "hold this Fire-altar in (your) trust", then (the trusteeship) is transferred to the family (= "kinsmen" of that man). The trusteeship which passes to the kinsmen (of that man) (consists of): (the guardianship) over the Fire-altar and (the guardianship) over the estate conveyed (as a foundation) "for the soul".

26, 1—3:

If at the time of (the official) appointment of a family guardian one of the sons (of that family) has reached his majority and died, (then), as has been said by some (authorities) a family guardian must be appointed, proceeding from the assumption that son was the head of the household [21].

26, 3—5:

If the "*appointed*" guardian marries the mistress of the house and the son (of the mistress of the house) subsequently comes of age, then the agreement of the son is required for (the continuation/legality of) the marriage (of the mistress of the house and the guardian).

26, 5—7:

A guardian appointed by the head of household is (in turn) entitled to convey the wife and children (of the family under his guardianship) to the guardianship of another person. In the *Commentary* on the *Avesta* it is said (by the authorities) that the "*natural*" (*i. e.* the one who has assumed the guardianship *via* natural calling — *A. P.*) guardian is fully empowered to convey the guardianship further (lit. "forward", *i. e.* to another person — *A. P.*), and it may be transferred as many times as it is transferred.

26, 7—8:

If a son receives ("takes") and possesses his father's estate, he is not entitled to refuse (= "not to carry out") the responsibilities of the guardianship for the minors (in his father's family).

26, 8—10:

It is written in one place that he who is the guardian of a family is entitled to transfer the guardianship (to another person) and the only guardian (having this right) is the one appointed by the head of household (himself). And likewise, an "*instituted*" *stūr* (*i. e.* one who was designated as *stūr* through the disposition of the late head of household — *A. P.*) is entitled to transfer (the *stūr*ship) during his (own) lifetime to whomsoever he desires.

26, 10—12:

Čāšt ēstēt kū (11) dūtak sardār ī būtak ēn 4 bavēt pus (ī) pātixšāyīhā ut patigriftak ut stūr ī kartak ut brāt ī hambāγ.

26, 12 (= **69**, 9—10):

Gyākē nipišt kū sardārīh ī dūtak ī pit ō pus ī patigriftak nē rasēt.

26, 13—14:

Ka ātaxš pat sardārīh ō 2 mart dahēt ut ēvak gōβēt kū-m andar nē apāyēt (14) ō ōy ī dit nē rasēt čē-š ōstaβarīh ⟨ī⟩ ō 2 mart dāt bavēt.

26, 14—17:

Ka ātaxš (15) nišāyēt ut sardārīh rāδ framān nē dahēt sardārīh pat pus ī mas ut ka ān ī mas ut pat (16) dāt hāvand 2 hast ō ān ī pat dēn kartārtar ut veh ut ka-č pat dēn kartārīh ut vehīh (17) hāvand hēnd pat ākanēn dārišn.

26, 17—**27**, 1:

Āturōk ī ⟨kas nišāyēt⟩ kas pat Varahrānīh ō (1) dātgāh nišāst pat dūtak ī ōy kē pat Varahrānīh ō dātgāh nišāst ravēt.

27, 2—4:

Sardār ī gumārtak sēnak masā ut bāzūk+ masā ōh bavēt ut ān kē sardārīh apar frāč (3) mānēt nē bavēt. Ān-ič kē sardārīh apar frāč mānēt bē ka aparmānd gīrēt ut (4) dārēt+ enyā-š ōh bavēt ut ka gīrēt ā-š nē bavēt.

27, 4—5:

Ka gōβēt kū-m dūtak pat (5) sardārīh ō tō dāt ātaxš-ič dāt bavēt.

27, 5—9:

Gyākē nipišt kū ka Āturfarnbaγ+ (6) aturōk nišāst ut xvāstak avi-š dāt ut sardār pat-iš gumārt u-š pas zūr-xvart (7) bē kart ⟨ut pat Varahrānīh ō dātgāh nišāst⟩ Vāyayār guft kū būt kē patkārišn (8) ēn būt kū čiš ī sardārīh yuttar bē būt čē ān zamān āturōk būt bē-šān (9) yuttar bē nē kart.

26, 10—12:

It is indicated (in the *Commentary* on the *Avesta*) that the following (categories of persons) may become "*natural*" guardians: a son from a *pātixšāyīh* marriage (of the late head of household), an adopted son, an "*instituted*" *stūr*, and a co-heir (co-partner) brother.

26, 12 (= **69**, 9—10):

It is written in one place that (the prerogatives) of a guardian of his father's family do not pass to an adopted son.

26, 13—14:

If he conveys the trusteeship over a Fire-altar to two persons and one (of them) declares: "I do not need it", then (this Fire-altar) shall not pass to the trusteeship of the other (= the second individual), since the title was given to the two individuals (jointly).

26, 14—17:

If he sets up a Fire-altar but makes no disposition regarding (its) trust, then the trusteeship (passes) to (his) eldest son. If there are two of them having the same age, then the trusteeship for the Fire-altar shall pass) to the one (of them) who is more devout and virtuous, and if they are equal in religious and other virtues, then they shall possess (it) (= carry out the trust) jointly.

26, 17—**27**, 1:

An altar set up by someone at an appropriate place in (the temple) of the Varahrān-fire is transmitted (to the trust) of the family of the person who instituted (that altar) at the given place in (the temple) of the Varahrān-Fire.

27, 2—4:

Payment-rations commensurate with his maintenance are allotted to the "*appointed*" guardian (from the revenues of the family). But one who inherits the guardianship (= one to whom it is transmitted, *i. e.*, the "*natural*" guardian — *A. P.*) is not entitled to it (= the payment). Likewise, if the one who has inherited the guardianship has not accepted the estate (of the late head of household) and does not possess it, he is entitled (to a payment), but if he has received (a share from) the estate (of the deceased), then he is not entitled to a payment.

27, 4—5:

If he declares: "I have placed (my) family under your guardianship", then the (trusteeship over the) Fire-altar is thereby conveyed (to him).

27, 5—9:

It is written in one place that if Āturfarnbaγ has set up a Fire-altar, and conveyed an estate ("a thing") to it, and appointed a trustee over all this, and subsequently has (himself) committed (the offence) of giving a false oath; (then), as has been said by Vāyayār, some (authorities) have considered (Āturfarnbaγ's disposition) doubtfull in (the sense) that the situation regarding the trusteeship has been altered thereby, since the Fire-altar was already in existence at that time [22]. However, they have not acted otherwise.

27, 9—12:

Ātaxš ī Varahrān ī čand mart pat ākanēn nišānēnd (ō) avēšān kē (10) pat ākanēn nišānēnd bahr ut dāštārīh nē dahēnd nē bahr bē dāštārīh. Ut ān ī mart (11) tanīhā nišānēt ka-š bahr sūtōmandtar bahr ut ka-š dāštārīh sūtōmandtar dāštārīh (12) apāyēt dāt.

27, 12—14:

Ka mart xvāštak ruvān rāδ paytāk kart ut nipišt kū-m zan ī (13) xvēš dāštan rāδ framān dāt zan hač framān ī šōy bē ēstāt nē pātixšāy (14) u-š sardārīh kunišn.

27, 14—15:

Pat sardārīh ī dūtak kē apurnāyak andar pus ī čakar nē gumārišn (15) čē-š apāk apurnāyak ī pat ān dūtak patvand nēst.

27, 15—16:

Ātaxš ī zan kē šōy ut frazand (16) hast ut anandarz murt nišāst ō frazand nē bē ō šōy rasēt.

27, 16—**28**, 5:

Ka mart (17) dūtak pat sardārīh ō mart-ē(v) dahēt (ut) andar dūtak ⟨ī⟩ apurnāyak (ut) purnāy (hast) ut ka purnāy (ō šōy) dahēt (ut) pit ī (1) ōy (ut) pit ī sardārīh nabānazdišt hend ut dūtak sardār ān māt (ut) katak-xvatāy kart kū-mān+ duxtak+ (Ms.: dūtak) pat (2) sardārīh ō Mihrēn dāt būt kē guft kū hač+ ān čiγōn sardārīh pat dāt ī pit būt (3) ēstēt māt ⟨pat⟩ duxt pat šōy bē dāt kār nēst. Pusānveh ī Burzātur Farnbaγān (4) guft kū ka pat ān aδvēnak pat ān čiš dātastān yuttar nē bavēt čiγōn ka sardār būtak (5) hē.

28, 5—7:

Gyākē nipišt kū ka ātaxš rāδ gōβēt kū-m pat sardārīh ō avēšān ī (6) man pus dāt (ut) ō avēšān ī man brāt dāt ⟨hēnd⟩ ēvak ī pat dāt ī mas dāt (ut) ō avēšān (7) ī hač dātastān pus (ut) dātastān brāt ī čakar zāt ēstēt nē rasēt.

27, 9—12:

If several persons jointly set up a Varahrān-Fire, then the share [23] and maintenance (= the payment assigned to the trustee — *A. P.*) are not given to the persons who jointly set up (the Varahrān-Fire), nor is a share without maintenance. (If, however, it is a case of) a Fire-altar set up by a single individual, then (he) shall be given a share — if a share is more beneficial, and maintenance — if maintenance is more beneficial.

27, 12—14:

If a person has declared (the transfer) of an estate / property (as a foundation intended) "for the soul" and has written (the following): "I have given a disposition so that my wife should exercise the trusteeship ('should hold it')", then the wife is not entitled to withdraw from (the fulfillment of) her husband's disposition and she must exercise the trusteeship (over the foundation instituted).

27, 14—15:

A son from a *čakar* marriage cannot be appointed guardian over a family with a minor, since he is not a kinsman of the minor in that family.

27, 15—16:

A Fire-altar set up by a woman — having a husband and children — who died without leaving a will, passes (under the trusteeship of) the husband and not (under that of) the children.

27, 16—**28**, 5:

If a man conveys his family to the guardianship of another and the family comprises a minor (son) and a major (daughter), and the major daughter is given (in marriage), and her father and her guardian ("her father according to guardianship"?) are agnates, and (if) the family guardian, the mother (of the girl) and the head of household make (the following) declaration: "We⁺ have conveyed the daughter⁺ ('family' in the ms.) to the guardianship of Mihrēn", (then), as has been expressed by some (authorities), inasmuch as the transfer of the guardianship was effected by the father (himself), the right of the mother to give the daughter in marriage is invalid. Pusānveh ī Burzātur Farnbayān has said that if the matter took place in this way, then the decision in such a case must be the same as the one rendered when the guardian is (a) "*natural*" (one).

28, 5—7:

It is written in one place that if he makes (the following) declaration regarding a Fire-altar (set up by himself): "I have conveyed (this Fire-altar) to the trust of (the successors) of my son and of (the successors) of my brother", then (the trust is thereby) transmitted to the successors of one (son and one brother), specifically of the eldest (son and the eldest brother — *A. P.*), but it does not pass (to the children) of a "*legal*" son and a "*legal*" brother born from a *čakar* marriage.

28, 7—9:

Apāk anī guft kū ka (8) gōβēt kū-m yuma ī zan ut frazand hambāγ kart hēh ka pātixšāyīhā (ayāp) patigriftak hast (9) ⟨2⟩ čakar nē kunišn ka nē ān-ič ī čakar ōh kunišn nikerītan.

28, 9—11:

Hač dastaβarān ōγōn nipišt (10) kū pit sardārīh ī apurnāyak ī-š pat sardārīh bē dāt hamē(v) ka-š kāmak kāmēt (11) apāč stat pātixšāy.

28, 11—12:

Pit sardārīh ī duxt yavētānak ut brāt ān ī xvah tā žīvandakīh ī (12) xvēš+ (Ms.: BNPŠH = xvat) bē pātixšāy dāt.

28, 12—13:

Ka dūtak pat sardārīh ō 2 mart dahēt ut ēvak nē (13) patigīrēt ayāp harv 2 patigīrēnd ēvak pat baxt šavēt sardārīh aframān.

28, 13—15:

Ka kunēt (14) kū-m ēn ātaxš hač xvāstak hammis nēm pat sardārīh ō tō dāt sardārīh xvap (15) u-š ān nēm pat patvand bē ravēt.

28, 15—17:

Dūtak sardārīh (ī) pus+ (Ms.: BRTH = duxt) ōγōn vēš gōβēnd kū (16) ka ziyān kunēt ā-š sardārīh appār nē bavēt mart pat guft ī Zurvāndāt nipišt (17) kū ka nē hanbārēt (ziyān) kartan ut nē vičārtan rāδ apurnāyak sardār gumārišn.

28, 17—**29**, 3:

Sardār ī (1) gumārtak ka ziyān kunēt ā-š sardārīh appar. Ut ka apāč nē hanbārēt dūtak (2) sardārīh ōh dārēt ka sāl drahnāδ Aparak+ guft (kū) dūtak asardār kartan rāδ mark[aržān] (3) ut ka andar sāl drahnāδ ān ziyān bē vičārēt apāč gumārišn.

28, 7—9:

In addition it is said that if he declares: "I have made you a co-partner with (my) wife and children", then — if there are (a wife and son) from a *pātixšāyīh* marriage, (or) an adopted son — (the wife and children) of a *čakar* marriage cannot be made co-partners (= co-heirs), but if there are not, then the wife and children of a *čakar* marriage may be made co-partners. Take note.

28, 9—11:

The following has been written with a reference to the commentators of the *Avesta*: a father who has transferred the guardianship over his minor son (to another person) is entitled to receive (the guardianship) back whenever he expresses the desire (= demands it).

28, 11—12:

A father is entitled to transfer the guardianship over a daughter (to another person) forever, but a brother (is entitled to transfer) the guardianship over his sister to the end of his (own) life.

28, 12—13:

If he transfers the guardianship over his family to two persons, and one (of them) does not accept (it), or if both accept it but one (of them) dies, then the guardianship is not valid.

28, 13—15:

If he declares: "I have conveyed one half of this Fire-altar with (its) estate (= endowment) to your trust", then such a trust is legal ("good"). And the other ("that") half passes to the trust of the kinsmen (of the endower).

28, 15—17:

The following is said for the most part (regarding) the guardianship of a son over the family (of his father): he is not to be removed from the guardianship even if he causes damage. Someone has written from the words of Zurvāndāt, that if he does not reimburse the loss, then a (new) guardian must be appointed over the minors (in the family) because of the damage caused and the failure to make up for it.

28, 17—**29**, 3:

But if an "*appointed*" guardian causes damage, then he is removed from the guardianship. And if he does not compensate (the damage caused by him), (then in this case also) he shall (continue) to exercise the guardianship over the family for the duration of one year. Aparak has said (that): the abandonment of a family without a guardian deserves a punishment (of the category intended) for capital offences. And if he reimburses this loss within the period of one year, then he shall again be appointed as guardian.

29, 3—6:

Ka xvāstak ruvān (4) rāδ paytāk kunēt ut pat dāštan ō Farraxv dahēt ut Farraxv gīrēt ut dārēt vitart Farraxv (5) ⟨ut⟩ pat patvand ī Farraxv bē ravēt hakar⁺ ōy ī sardār vināš pat-iš kunēt ⟨ut⟩ ap(p)ār bavēt (6) ut čiγōn Dāt-Farraxv guft sardārīh apāč ō bun šavēt nē ō Farraxv.

29, 6—9:

Gyākē nipišt (7) kū ka ātaxš nišānēt u-š ⟨ut⟩ pus ī pātixšāyīhā ut patigriftak hast ut sardārīh (8) rāδ (ō) Farraxv nē dahēt vitart katak-xvatāy ka pus ī patigriftak pat dāt mas sardār (9) pus ī patigriftak ut hakar-iš nīrmat-ē(v) andar apāk hamdūtakān.

29, 9—11:

Ka xvāstak ruvān rāδ paytāk (10) kart u-š yazišn ⟨ut⟩ nihātak apar nihāt ut pat dāštan framān nē dāt vitart pit (11) pus ī mas pat sardārīh dārišn ut hakar-iš nīrmat-ē(v) andar apāk hamdūtakān.

XXVII *

29, 12:

Dar ī āgraβīh.

29, 12—17:

Paštōžišnīh⁺ (13) dāt pātixšāy bavēt ut pātixšāy nē bavēt. Mart apām ⟨ut⟩ tōžišn ī-š pat kasān ut xvāstak (14) ī-š tā anī aδvēnak sahēt ut ēt čē-š handarz ut xvāstak-ič ī-š dastvarz⁺ (Ms.: YDH-w-wrč) tā anī (15) aδvēnak dāt patmān apar kart ēstēt pat apām tōžišn ī ō kas ka-š anī-č (16) xvāstak hast xvat u-š xvāstakdār-ič pātixšāy hend ka bē nē apaspārēnd (17) ut ka-š anī-č xvāstak nēst aδak-ič tā žīvandakānīh pātixšāy ka bē nē apaspārēt.

30, 1—3:

Ka mart kē ō kas tōžišn ut dehišn hamaδvēn xvāstak ī xvēš rāδ kunēt kū (2) nēm tā 10 sāl ō Farraxv ut nēm pas hač 10 sāl ō Mihrēn dāt ut andar 10 sāl apām xvāhend (3) xvāstak žīvandakān⁺ (Ms.: PL-BḤY⁺) tōžišn nēm tā 10 sāl ut nēm pas hač 10 sāl bē apaspārišn.

* The (*abǰad*) ordinal-number 27 is plased in line 11 above the heading of the chapter.

29, 3—6:

If he declares (the transfer) of a thing (as an endowment) "for the soul" and conveys it to the possession (= guardianship) of Farraxv, and Farraxv receives and holds it, then — after Farraxv's death — the guardianship will pass to his family. And if the person exercising the guardianship causes damage, then he shall be removed from the guardianship; and, as has been said by Dāt-Farraxv, (in such a case) the guardianship returns to the family of the endower and (does) not (remain in the family of) Farraxv.

29, 6—9:

It is written in one place that if he sets up a Fire-altar and he has a son from a *pātixšāyīh* marriage and an adopted son, and (if) he does not transfer (the Fire-altar instituted) to the trusteeship of Farraxv, then after the death of the head of household, the trustee is the adopted son, if the adopted son is older, and (he shall exercise the trust) together with the members of the family, should this prove beneficial.

29, 9—11:

If he declared (the transfer of) a thing (as a foundation) "for the soul" and allotted ("laid down") an endowment for the performance of the religious ritual but gave no orders regarding possession (= trust), then, after the father's death, the eldest son shall be trustee — together with the members of the family — should this prove beneficial.

XXVII *

29, 12:

Chapter concerning seizures (of property in settlement of debts — *A. P.*).

29, 12—17:

The settlement after death of a debt (of the deceased by his heirs or by persons having benefitted from his estate — *A. P.*) may or may not take place. A man (may hold back) the settlement of (his) debt to (other) persons and (the transfer of) a thing (according to an earlier contract) as long as a different form (or "situation") is satisfactory (presumably to the creditors or to the other party — *A. P.*). Insofar as equipment (or "clothing") and (technical) implements / tools are concerned — even if he has property — he, himself, and his heirs are entitled not to convey (them) for the settlement of a debt as long as an agreement (exists) concerning a different form of transfer (*i. e.* a different manner of settling the debt — *A. P.*). And if he has no other property, then he is entitled not to transfer (them) untill the end of his life.

30, 1—3:

If a man who must make a settlement with someone and convey (a thing) makes the following declaration regarding his entire estate: "half (of my entire estate) is conveyed to Farraxv for a period of ten years, and the second half — to Mihrēn after ten years", and (if) the settlement of the debt is demanded of him in (these first) ten years; then he must settle (the debt) in his own lifetime and he must give half of the debt before ten years elapse and the second half in ten years' time.

30, 4—8:

Ka mart kē ō kas xvāstak ut čiš tōžišn ut dahišn kunēt kū-m xvāstak ī man (5) xvēš frāč hač man ō Āturfarnbaγ dāt hač ān frāč bē kunēt[+] ān xvāstak bavēt (6) anī xvāstak avi-š nē rasēt ut hakar and bavēt čand pat tōžišn bavandak ut hamaδvēn (7) pat (h)ēr ī xvēš uzēnak kunēt aδak-ič xvāstak pat arž ī tōžišn hač Āturfarnbaγ (8) apāč āβarišn.

30, 8—9:

Ka vaxš ut 'nw'n ī pat patmān ī sāl ēvak kart sāl 3 (9) ō tōžišn mat apām ī sāl 2 hast pat kartak pat apām ī sāl 2 bē apaspārtan.

30, 10—11:

Ka xvāstak pat dāt bē dahēt ka-č-iš ō zan ētar aδak-ič xvarišn ut dārišn (1) ī zan (ut) apurnāyak apāč āβarišn. Ka pat (h)andarz bē dahēt aδak-ič apāč āβarišn.

30, 12—13:

Ka xvāstak pat dāt bē dahēt ut žahm kunēt apāč nē [āβa]rišn ut ka pat (13) handarz bē dahēt apāč āβarišn.

30, 13—15:

Duxt ut zan ut apurnāyak xvāstak ī pēš hač (14) ān ka-šān šōy kart ⟨ut⟩ pit apām stat ut hač pit ut šōy ut šāhān šāh ō xvēšīh (15) mat pat tōžišn ī šōy ut pit bē nē[+] vičārišn.

30, 15—17:

Gyākē nipišt kū vičīr ī mart andar (16) zan ut frazand ăvašt rāδ apām ut tōžīšn ī pas hač ān hač xvāstak ī (ān mart dăšt) hakar ēvbār (17) ān vičīr ăvartēt ⟨ān mart dăšt⟩ kem nē tōžišn.

30, 17—**31**, 2:

Gyākē nipišt kū paš-tōžišn(1)īh rāδ pat vaxš ut 'nw'n apārīk-ič ān ī hač ān šōn xvāstak kē dārišn bē kart apāč nē (2) āβarišn.

30, 4—8:

If a man who must make a settlement (of a debt) to someone and convey a thing declares (the following): "I have conveyed my entire estate after my death to Āturfarnbaγ", and since (the time) that he has made the declaration (concerning this transfer) the estate (remains) the same and (no) other estate passes to him; then — if this estate is sufficient for the settlement (of the debt), but he (= Āturfarnbaγ — *A. P.*) has spent it for his own needs — a thing equivalent to the amount of the debt must be seized ("taken back") from Āturfarnbaγ in this case as well.

30, 8—9:

If interest and smart-money (?) are stipulated in the case ("on the condition") of (his non-fulfillment of his obligation — *A. P.*) within one year, he is faced with the obligation to settle (lit. "it has come to the payment") in the third year; then his indebtedness (to pay the interest and smart-money (?) — *A. P.*) is a two-year one and, according to judicial regulations ("according to procedure"), (a sum) equivalent to a two year indebtedness must be conveyed (in settlement of this debt; *cf.* **A12**, 17—**13**, 2).

30, 10—11:

When he conveys a thing for transfer — even if he (conveys it) to a wife (who is) there — the means required for the maintenance of the wife and minor (child) must be retained ("returned"). And if he conveys (it) by testament, then (it) must be retained ("returned"; removed from the transfer), in this case as well.

30, 12—13:

If he alienates an estate ("thing") in accordance with a (transfer) agreement and (subsequently) commits a crime of physical violence, then (nothing) is retained (from the estate) conveyed by him. But if he alienates (it) by testament, then it must be retained [24].

30, 13—15:

A daughter, wife or minor (child) need not transfer — in payment of a debt (contracted) by the husband or father — a thing lent to the father before the marriage and (which) was given into their personal possession by the father, the husband, or "the King of Kings".

30, 15—17:

It is written in one place that even when there is a contract (regarding the transmission of the estate) sealed by the husband with (his) wife and son, the debts and payment obligations subsequently undertaken by him must be paid in full from the estate in that man's possession (at that time) — (this is the case), even if he sealed the contract immediately.

30, 17—**31**, 2:

It is written in one place that a thing formally transferred (to another person) may not be seized ("returned") for the settlement after death (of the *de cuius's* liability) for percentages (interest on the debt), smart-money, and all other (payments) of this type.

31, 2—3:

Būt⁺ kē guft kū pat apām ut ahravdāt ut markaržān enyā pat (3) apārīk⁺ harv čiš paš-tōžišnīh aδak kār ka xvāstak-dārišn bē nē kart.

31, 4—6:

Vāyayār guft kū ka kunēt kū-m xvāstak ī man xvēš frāč hac man ō vāhmān ⟨ī⟩ (5) mart dāt pat kartak ōγōn kunēnd kū parvārišn ī zan (ut) apurnāyak apāč āβarišn ut apārīk (6) hamgōnak čiγōn dāt ⟨ī⟩ frēh rāst.

31, 6—8:

U-š ēn-ič guft kū ka kunēt kū frāč hač man (7) ēn xvastak tō xvēš hēβ bavēt Martak ut Pusānveh guft kū pat kartak ka mat (8) aδak-šān ōγōn kart čiγōn dāt nē ōγōn čiγōn andarz.

31, 8—15:

Vahrām guft kū ka Farraxv (9) xvāstak hamāk ō zan ut frazand ī pātixšāyīhā dāt u-š pas āturōk dāt (10) nišāšt ut xvāstak hamāk avi-š dāt rāδ⁺ vičīr ăvašt kū āturōk dāštārīh pat (11) miyān xvāstak hač zan ut frazand apāč stat ut ō āturōk dāt man vičīr pat-iš (12) kart ut ⟨nē⟩ ăvašt⁺ u-š xvat-dātastān nēst če ēn yuttar bavēt kū ka xvāstak bē (13) ō zan ut frazand-ē(v) dāt ut pas bē frōšēt ayāp graβ kunēt ayāp apām stānēt čē (14) zan ut frazand kē xvāstak avi-š dat pat-ič rāh ī xvāstak sardārīh ān apām (15) bē apāyēt tōxtan ut ān xvāstak drust apāyēt dāštan.

31, 15—**32**, 17 = **20**, 7—10:

U-š ēn-ič guft kū ka (16) katak xvatāy xvāstak (ī-š) mat ut rasēt ō zan ut frazand dahēt ut pas anšahrīk āzāt (17) kunēt Siyāva(x)š guft (kū) anšahrīk hač šāhān šāh bandakīh apāč aβurtan nē šāyēt (1) ut man-ič ētōn dānom bē-š Rāt-Ōhrmizd yut-dātastānīh-ē(v) andar ōh kart.

31, 2—3:

Some (authorities) have said that except in cases of settlement of (the principal — *A. P.*)debt, of fulfillment of obligations of religious devotion, or of (payments adjudicated for the commission of) capital crimes, in all other cases, (a demand) for the after death settlement of (the *de cuius*'s) debt is valid only if there was no alienation of the possession of the thing (at the entry of the new possessor into his rights).

31, 4—6:

Vāyayār has said that if he declares the following: "I have transferred the estate belonging to me to so-and-so, after my death", then this decision is rendered according to the judicial regulations: (the means required) for the maintenance of the wife and minor (child) must be retained ("returned") and the remaining estate (must be treated) in accordance with his disposition as to the transfer — (this will be) more equitable.

31, 6—8:

He (= Vāyayār) has also said that if anyone makes the following declaration: "let this thing be yours after my death!", (then) — as has been said by Martak and Pusānveh — when (the case) is brought before the judges (lit. "comes to the judicial procedure"), they judge (the case) as one of bestowal by deed, not by testament.

31, 8—15:

Vahrām has said that if Farraxv (bequeathed) his entire estate to (his) wife and son (= children) from a *pātixšāyīh* marriage, and subsequently he has set up a Fire-altar and has sealed a document (with the following content) regarding the transfer to it (= the Fire-altar) of the entire estate: "I have made a disposition and sealed (a document) regarding the maintenance of a Fire-altar at the expense of the estate taken ("received") back from (my) wife and son and transferred to the Fire-altar"; then (this question) is not (resolved) *ipso iure* (*i. e.* this question requires special investigation — *A. P.*) because this case is different from the one where (someone) having conveyed an estate by testament to (his) wife and children, subsequently sells it, or gives it as security, or contracts a debt ("receives it as a loan"). For — insofar as they are the guardians of (this) estate (= the endowed foundation — *A. P.*) — the wife and son to whom he has bequeathed the estate are obligated to settle this debt and to preserve the estate intact.

31, 15—**32**, 1:

And he (= Vahrām) has also said that if a head of household conveys to his wife and children the estate belonging to him and that which he will receive, and he subsequently frees a slave; then, according to the opinion of Siyāva(x)š, the (freed) slave may not be brought back from his (acquired status of) a subject of the King of Kings (to his former servile status). And I express the same opinion, but Rāt-Ōhrmizd has expressed a different judgement on this question [25].

32, 1—4:

Zāmasp (2) guft kū čiγōn-am āšnūt xvāstak ī mart ō zan ut frazand dāt ēstēt ut pas (3) bē frōšēt hač mart ī rāt apāč nē āβarišn ān-ič ī čakar rāδ framān būt (4) ēstāt.

32, 4—10:

Ka mart 2 ēvak pat muhr ī ēvar ēvak pat muhr ī vičurt ī pēš hač (5) ān vičīr dārēt ut zan-ē(v) rāδ yut yut patkārēt kū man zan ut dātastān apāk ziyānak (6) kunēnd ut ziyānak dārišn andar ēvak-ič nē paytāk gōβēt kū ōy zan hom kē vičīr ī (7) varōmand dārēt dārišn. Hast kē ētōn gōβēt kū bē ō ōy kunišn kē vičīr ī (8) pēš dārēt ut ⟨hast kē ētōn gōβēt kū bē ō ōy kunišn kē vičīr ī pēš dārēt⟩ (9) hast kē ō ōy guft kē vičīr ī ēvar dārēt bē ka dātastān mart ēvak apāk dit (10) kunēnd harv aδvēnak dārišn ō vičīr ī ēvar kunišn.

XXVIII

32, 11:

Dar * ī xvarišn ut dārišn ī kas hač kas.

32, 12—14:

Pus tā purnāy bavēt duxt tā šōy kunēt zan tā žīvandak ān ī pātixšāyīhā xvarišn (13) ut dārišn. Ka hač ⟨ān⟩ (h)ēr+ (Ms.: PWN < ṢB/PWN) ī pit pat miyān kartan šāyēt hač ān ī pit ut ka hač ān ī pit (14) pat miyān kartan šāyēt ōγōn kū-š guharīk hač ān ī pit apāč rasēt hač ān ī pus.

32, 15:

Apurnāyak ī čakarīhā ka hač (hēr ī) dūtak nēst hač ān ī pit ī čakarīhā ān-ič ī purnāy hamgōnak.

32, 16—**33**, 1:

Pit ka-š hač (h)ēr ⟨ī⟩ ut xvāstak ī xvēš nēst hač (h)ēr ī pus duxt (ut) zan (ī) (17) pātixšāyīhā. Pit ī čakarīhā hač vāspuhrakān ī zan ut frazand (ī) čakarīhā (1) u-š guharīk apāč dahišn.

* The (*abǰad*) ordinal-number 28 is placed above the heading of this chapter.

32, 1—4:

Zāmasp has said: "As I have learned, a thing transferred by the husband to (his) wife and child and subsequently sold by him shall not be taken back ("returned") from whoever received the gift (lit. 'from the man of the gift')". (The situation is) the same in the case of a disposition (for a transfer) made in favour of a *čakar*-wife.

32, 4—10:

If two man — one having a document with a valid (or: "trustworthy") seal, the other with a seal set earlier and then valid — each separately conduct a judicial case concerning one (= the same) woman (declaring): "(this woman) is my wife", and a court session with the participation of the woman is arranged, but the woman does not make a declaration regarding her belonging to one of them (as a wife), namely: "I am his (that man's) wife"; then she shall belong to the one having the document sealed earlier. Some hold to the opinion that she should be adjudicated to the one (of them) having the earlier document, but there were also those who said that (she) should be adjudicated to the one having the document with the trustworthy seal. However, when one person litigates with another, a possession of whatsoever nature should be adjudicated to the one (of them having) a document with the seal actually valid.

XXVIII

32, 11:

Chapter* concerning the support of one person by another.

32, 12—14:

(The following) must be supported: a son — until he comes of age, a daughter — until she marries, a wife from a *pātixšāyīh*-marriage — for life. If the maintenance can be provided from the funds of the father (= the head of household), this should be done from the funds of the father; but if the funds of the father provided for this maintenance (are such) that the amount (provided) from the funds of the father are insufficient to cover (the expenses) of the members of the family — then the funds of the son (should likewise be used).

32, 15:

In the absence (of funds) in his family, a minor (son) from a *čakar*-marriage (must be supported) at the expense of (his) *čakar*-father. The same for a major (daughter) (from a *čakar*-marriage).

32, 16—**33**, 1:

If a father does not have his own means (he must be supported) at the expense of his son, daughter or wife from a *pātixšāyīh*-marriage. But a *čakar*-father (must be supported in the absence of his own means — *A. P.*) from the inherited share of (his) wife or daughter from the *čakar*-marriage. And he is obligated to return the equivalent (to them) (= reimburse their expenses).

33, 1—3:

Duxt ka pat vināskārīh ī pit ⟨i⟩ gātār, kunēt (2) xvarišn ut dārišn ut ka-š ⟨hač⟩ kār-vindišn ī xvēš hast hač kar-vindišn ī xvēš ut ka-š kār(3)-vindišn ī xvēš nēšt hač ān ī pit ⟨ī⟩ bavēt.

33, 3—6:

Apurnāyak kē-š pit pat vināskārīh xvarišn (4) ut dārišn nē dahēt kas bē parvarēt parvartār pātixšāy ka kār-vindišn čand (5) parvarišn guharīk ī parvarišn rāδ apāč kunēt ka kār-vindišn pat parvarišn nē bavandak ān ī (6) nē bavandak guharīk pit bē dahišn.

33, 6—9:

Zan apurnāyak pusakānīh duxtakānīh stūrīh (7) zanīh ⟨ut tarsakāyīh⟩ sardārīh bē pat atvadāt pit pat (8) ān ī xvat+ (Ms.: NPŠH = xvēš) pat-ič ān ī apārīk avēšān ut māt andar apāyēt pat ān ī xvēš pat ⟨ān ī⟩ ōy kē (9) apar ēstēt frōxt pātixšāy.

33, 9—11:

Zan ī pātixšāyīhā ī tarsākāy sāl-sāl hač xvāstak ī (10) šōy xvēš ut šōy nē guft ēstēt ma dahēt yut hač zamīk āp ut urvarān (ut) xānak (11) ut anšahrīk tā 2 bandak bavēt bē dāt pātixšāy.

33, 11—13:

Duxt ut zan (ut) anšahrīk ⟨ī⟩ mart-(12) mart ⟨ut⟩ pat vinās varōmand kart ēstēt uzēnak ī-š pat xvarišn ut dārišn ut ēt čē-š pat (13) passāxtan andar apāyēt xvatāy ut sardār dahišn.

33, 13—17:

Frazand pat anšahrīkīh ēvāč pit (14) pātixšāy frōxt ut pat markīh ut rištakīh pātixšāy frōxt ēvāč pat ān ī ōy ī (15) pātixšāy frōxt pat atvadāt pit pat ān ī xvēš pat-ič ān ī ōy ut māt pat ān (ī) xvat (andar apāyēt) (16) ut pat ān ī ⟨xvat⟩ ōy kē apar mat ēstēt ut apārīk sardār pat ān ī xvat ut ōy kē apar mat (17) ēstēt frōxt pātixšāy.

33, 1—3:

A daughter having committed adultery through her father's fault must be supported. If she has a personal income — then (the means for her maintenance are to be drawn) from that income, but if she has no personal income — she is to be supported at her father's expense.

33, 3—6:

(Concerning) a minor whom his father does not support through his own (= the father's) fault and who is reared by someone else: the maintainer is entitled to retain from the personal income (of his nurseling) a sum equivalent to the one indispensable for his maintenance expenses. If the personal income (of the minor) is insufficient for his maintenance, then the lacking portion of the amount (= of the means), its "equivalent", is paid by the father.

33, 6—9:

A wife, minor (child), adopted son and daughter, *stūr*ship (or) guardianship over a woman may not (be sold) except in cases of utmost destitution. And even in cases of utmost destitution the father (may do this only) (insofar as) it corresponds to what is indispensable for him and also for the others (= the members of the family — *A. P.*) and for the mother (*i. e.* on the basis of the calculation of the minimal requirement for the survival of the family — *A. P.*); and he is entitled to sell (them only) to one of his kinsmen, to the one who comes forward (or "is present").

33, 9—11:

A well-behaved and pious wife from a *pātixšāyīh*-marriage (must be supported) year after year at her husband's expense, and the husband may not say: "do not give (funds for her) support!" He is entitled to convey (to his wife) (anything) except land, water, plants, and the house; as for slaves — no more than that she have two slaves.

33, 11—13:

A daughter, a wife (and) a slave must each be subjected separately to the ordeal procedure in connexion with an offence; the expenses for her / his maintenance and those required for the arrangement (of the ordeal procedure) shall be born by the master (of the slave)25 or the guardian (of the daughter or wife).

33, 13—17:

Only the father is entitled to sell children into slavery. And on his deathbed or in a state of physical helplessness he is entitled to sell (them) only to someone to whom it is permissible to sell in the state of "*atvadāt*" (= in a state of utmost destitution; *cf.* **33**, 6—9 — *A. P.*), namely: the father — to his (kinsman), likewise — to (the kinsman of) that (= the child's) mother; and (only) insofar as this corresponds to what (is indispensable) for his (life) and for those whom he has (= the members of his family). As for the rest (*i. e.* property of any type), a guardian is entitled to sell it — insofar as this is indispensible for his (survival) and for those (in his family).

XXIX

34, 1:

Dar ī yazišn⁺ ut nihātak ī apar (h)ēr ī āta(x)š ut xvāstak ī ruvān (rāδ) nihāt ut paytāk kart *.

34, 2—3:

Xvāstak ī ō ruvān dahēnd hakar barōmand bar hakar abar bun (ut) ān ī hač hark (ut) bār ut uzēnak ī pat (3) bun ut mizd ut rōčīk ī sardārān bē par(r)ēčēt / pardačēt.

34, 3—6:

(Ka) ōγōn nipišt kū-m⁺ ruvan ⟨ut⟩ yazišn rāδ paytāk (4) kart ēvāč pat āyazišn ut hakar ōγōn nipišt ēstēt kū-m⁺ ruvān (rāδ) nē paytāk kart pat ān ē (5) ōy ī kē pat dāštan avi-š dat pat ruvān rāδ paytāk kart sūtōmandtar sahēt dahišn (6) ut uzēnak kunišn.

34, 6—9:

Ka xvāstak ruvān ut yazišn rāδ paytāk kunēt ut yazišn pat nāmčišt (7) nihātak nihēt bar ān ī hač nihātak pardačēt / par(r)ēčēt sardārān xvēš ut ka ōγōn nipēsēt⁺ kū-m (8) ruvān rāδ paytāk kart ut yazišn pat nāmčišt nihātak nihāt bar ān ī (hač) nihātak pardačēt / par(r)ēčēt (rāδ)? (9) yazišn kem hač-iš nē kunišn.

34, 9—12:

Ut ka xvāstak ruvān rāδ paytāk kart ut pat dāštan ō (10) kas ut bar ast-ē(v) ōy kē avi-š dāt ō xvēš barēt / burt rāδ⁺ (Ms.: L'-nē) framān dāt ka-č nē (guft / kart) (11) ēstēt kū kartan ī sardārīh rāδ aδak-ič ōy kē avi-š dāt bar frēh hač ān ī-š barēt / burt (12) rāδ framān dāt nē xvēš.

* The (*abǰad*) ordinal-number 29 is placed above the heading of this chapter.

XXIX

34, 1:

Chapter concerning religious services, and special appropriations to the treasuries of Fire (temples) and endowments instituted and declared (as foundations) "for the soul"*.

34, 2—3:

If a thing conveyed (as an endowment) "for the soul" bears fruit (= brings revenue), the fruit is (also) dedicated; but if it does not bear fruit, then the "principal" (shall be dedicated as well as) that which remains after the payment of the taxes and dues (with which the thing is encumbered — *A. P.*), and of the expenses for the maintenance of the "principal", and of the payments ("payments and rations") to the trustees.

34, 3—6:

If he has written the following: "I have declared (the transfer of an estate as an endowment) for the performance of rituals "for the soul"", then (the revenue from the estate) may be used only for the performance of religious rites. But if it is written in this manner: "I have declared (the transfer of an estate as an endowment) 'for the soul'", then the man having received possession (= the trusteeship) of the estate) may transfer it and make expenditures (in whatever way) he considers more suitable/beneficial for the soul (of the endower).

34, 6—9:

If he makes a declaration regarding (the transfer) of a thing (as a foundation) "for the soul" and for the performance of religious rites, and sets a definite (=fixed) appropriation for the performance of the rites, then the surplus fruits (=surplus revenue) from this endowment shall belong to the trustees. And if he writes (as follows): "I have made a declaration (concerning the transfer of a thing) 'for the soul' and I have made ('set down') a definite (=fixed) appropriation (lit. 'outlay, deposit') for the performance of religious rites", then, a lesser number of religious rites than (was set down by the endower — *A. P.*) may not be performed (for the sake) of preserving a surplus revenue from the endowment.

34, 9—12:

If he has declared (the transfer of) a thing (as a foundation) "for the soul" and conveyed it to the trust ("holding") of someone, and made a disposition that the one to whom he transferred the trusteeship (of the endowment) should take for himself a (certain) share of the fruits (=revenue); then in that case also, fruits (=a revenue) superior to that indicated in the disposition of the endower do not belong to the person to whom he (=the endower) conveyed (the trusteeship of the foundation), even if he did not (specify): "for the performance of the trusteeship" (*i. e.* the right to take a fixed part of the revenue as a payment for the trusteeship — *A. P.*).

34, 12—15:

Ka kart kū-m xvāstak ruvān rāδ paytāk kart (13) (ut) xvāstak ī-m ruvān rāδ paytāk kart Mihrēn hēβ dārēt aδak-iš hač ruvān apāč nē (14) stat bavēt čē ahravdāt-ič andar ruvān ut Mihrēn tuvān guft kū pat ahravdāt (15) dāt.

34, 15—**35**, 6:

Ka gōβēt kū ēn xvāstak pat graβīh ayāp gōβēt kū pat ruvān (ut) yazišn (16) dāštan ō man mat ut man xvāstak ī-m ō man mat guft ō Mihrēn dāt ka-č nē (1) nipēsēt+ kū pat ān aδvēnak ī-m ō man mat guft xvap ut pat āhang dahēt ut ka gōβēt (2) kū ēn xvāstak ruvān rāδ yazišn nē paytāk ut xvāstak ī-m paytāk kart Mihrēn hēβ (3) dārēt ēn-ič nē nipēsēt kū-⟨m⟩ pat ān aδvēnak ī-m paytāk kart nē xvap ut ka gōβēt (4) kū-m xvāstak ruvān raδ paytāk kart ut pat dāštan ō Mihrēn dāt Mihrēn ut anī-č (5) kas ān xvāstak frōxt ut bē dāt nē pātixšāy ēvāč+ (Ms.: 'DYNč) bar pātixšāy frōxt ut bun (6) pat ān aδvēnak ī-š avi-š mat bē dāt nē pātixšāy u-š pat patvand ōh ravēt.

35, 7—9:

Ka mart xvāstak ī-š pat ruvān (ut) yazišn avi-š mat vinās ut ziyān bē (8) vičārēt+ (Ms.: vičārišn) sardārīh ap(p)ār nē bavēt čē-š pat patvand ōh ravēt apāk ān ī (9) hačapar pat guft ī Dāt-Farraxv nipišt nikerītan.

34, 12—15:

If he declares the following: "I have declared (the transfer) of a thing (as a foundation) 'for the soul', and let Mihrēn possess (=be trustee of) the thing which I declared transferred 'for the soul'!", then it (=the thing) cannot be taken back from "the soul" (=from the endowment "for the soul") because piety (lies) in (the transfer) "for the soul" (lit. "in the soul"). And Mihrēn can say that it was transferred for a pious purpose.

34, 15—**35**, 6:

If he declares (the following): "this thing came (=passed by transmission — *A. P.*) in my trust ('into my possession') as a security", or if he declares: "as an endowment set up 'for the soul' and for religious rites, and I have transferred to Mihrēn (this) thing of which I said that (it) had come to me"; then — even if he does not write (the following): "in the same manner (*i. e.* on the same basis — *A. P.*) as I said that it had passed to me" — it is well and the transfer is regular. If, however, he declares: "this thing is declared (as having been transferred to me as an endowment) 'for the soul', not for religious rites, and let the thing, regarding which I made this declaration, be in the trusteeship of Mihrēn ('let Mihrēn hold/possess' it)", but he does not write: "in the same manner (*i. e.* on the same basis — *A. P.*) as I declared (it)" — then it is not well (=is irregular). And if he declares: "I declared this thing (as an endowment set up) 'for the soul' and transferred it to the trusteeship of Mihrēn", then neither Mihrēn nor any other person is entitled to sell or transfer the thing, and he (=Mihrēn) is entitled to sell only the fruits (=revenue), but he is not entitled to transfer the principal on the same basis ("in the same manner") as he received it (to anyone else), and it must pass to (the trusteeship of) his kinsmen.

35, 7—9:

If a man makes good the damage wrought by him on an estate (endowed) "for the soul" and for the performance of religious rites which came (by transmission — *A. P.*) into his trust, then he shall not be removed from the trusteeship, because (a trust) passes through kinship ("to the kinsmen"). (This case) should be examined together with what has been written above on the basis of the statement of Dāt-Farraxv [*cf. supra* **29**, 3—6 — *A. P.*].

35, 9—17:

Ka kart kū hač bar ut vaxt ī hač xvāstak (10) māh Fravartīn pat ruvān (ī) Farraxv ⟨ī⟩ ut māh Tīr pat ruvān ī Mihrēn ēn yazišn (ut) harv sāl pat ān (11) rōč ka man fražām bavēt yazišn čand šāyēt hēβ kunēt ka vaxt and nē bavēt čand (12) ān yazišn hamaδvēn hač-iš kartan šāyēt ān (ī) kunišn ⟨i⟩ ka kunēt kirpak vēš bavēt yuttar (13) nē bavēt čiγōn ka kunēt kū māh Ātur pat ruvān ī man Visprat-ē(v) rōč Ōhrmizd ut Yašt-ē(v) (14)rōč Vahman ut Drōn-ē(v) rōč Artvahišt hēβ yazēt. Ut hakar ka Visprat yazīhīt Yašt (15) ut Drōn kartan nē šāyēt pat ēn čim kū apāč ō saxvan ut framān ī pas ēstāt Visprat (16) kem nē yazišn ut yazišn ī pat ruvān ī mart mart nihēt ut kunēt pat-ič ruvān ī xvēš nihāt (17) ut kart bavēt.

35, 17—**36**, 1:

Ka kunēt kū rōč Ōhrmizd Aštāt-ē(v) kē šnōm (ī) Ōhrmizd xvatāy (1) ut rōč Srōš Yašt-ē(v) šnōm (ī) Srōš heβ yazēt ka ēvak šāyēt kartan Aštāt kartan.

XXX *

36, 2:

Dar ī zanīh ⟨zan⟩ (ī) pātixšāyīhā.

36, 2—5:

Apar Dātastān-nāmak (3) ōγōn nipišt ēstēt kū xvah ut duxt ka yut hač xonsandīh ī sardār tan pat zanīh bē (4) dahēt zanīh nē⁺ xvap. Ut ka-š yut hač xonsandīh ī sardārān frēpēnd⁺ (5) ut nayēnd būt kē guft kū-š dātastān dahišn bē pat kartak nē dahēnd⁺ (Ms.: YḤSNWnd = dārēnd).

36, 6—9:

Ka mart zan kē sardār ī pat nāmčišt ut stūrīh ī kas nēst gāyēt (7) ut pat ān gāt frazand zāyēt ut ān zan xvāstak ōγōn nēst kū-š xvēš tan (8) ut frazand dāštan tuvān ōy mart ān frazand tā purnāy bavēt ut ān zan tā ān frazand (9) purnāy bavēt pat parvārišn ut xvarišn ut vistarg dārišn.

* The (*abǰad*) ordinal-number 30 is placed between lines 1 and 2 above the heading or this chapter.

35, 9—17:

If he has made (the following) disposition: "these religious services shall be performed in the month Fravartīn for the soul of Farraxv and in the month Tīr — for the soul of Mihrēn, on the fruits (=revenue) and accretion (or 'profit' — *A. P.*) from this thing, let them also perform the service every year on the anniversary of my death insofar as this is possible". If the profit is insufficient to perform the liturgy for him in full, then, if the one entrusted with this performance fulfills it (evidently drawing additional funds from his own means — *A. P.*), it shall (be reckoned to him) as an act of great (religious) virtue. This case is identical with the one in which he sets out this disposition: "in the month Ātur, let him perform for my soul the *Visprat* ritual on the day Ōhrmizd, the *Yasna* ritual on the day Vahman, and the *Drōn* ritual on the day Artvahišt". And if it is impossible (for lack of funds — *A. P.*) to perform the *Yasna* and *Drōn* rituals after the *Visprat*, then — under the pretext that he will (thereby) default from the subsequent statement and injunction (*i. e.* from the disposition regarding the performance of the *Yasna* and *Drōn* rituals — *A. P.*) — (he) must not omit the *Visprat* ritual. And the performance by a man at (his own) expense of the service for the soul of (another) person is equivalent to his expenditure of funds and performance (of the service) for (the benefit of) his own soul.

35, 17—**36**, 1:

If he declares (the following) disposition: "on the day Ōhrmizd, let him perform the *Aštāt* (ritual) of gratification (with invocations) of the Lord Ōhrmizd, and on the day Srōš — the ritual of gratification (with invocations) of Srōš", then, in case (only) one (ritual) can be performed, the *Aštāt* (ritual) must be performed.

XXX *

36, 2:

Chapter concerning a wife with full-rights (*pātixšāyīhā*).

36, 2—5:

It is written thus in the *Dātastān-nāmak*: if a sister or ("and") a daughter enters into a marriage (lit. "gives herself/her body in marriage") without the permission of her guardian, then (this) marriage is invalid ("not good"). And if she (=the sister or daughter) is seduced and taken away against the will of her guardian, then, as has been said by some (authorities), (she) should be granted a legal trial; this is not granted, however, according to the norms of procedure.

36, 6—9:

If a man enters into sexual intercourse (or "commits adultery") with a woman who has no definite guardian and who is no one's *stūr*, and if a child is born from this intercourse but the woman does not have sufficient property to support herself and the child; then this man must support the child untill his majority and the woman — until the child reaches his majority.

36, 9—12:

Zurvāndāt ī Yuvān-Yam (10) guft kū ka mart ō duxt ī xvēš gōβēt kū šav ut stūrīh ī vahmān kas (11) kun duxt pātixšāy ka nē kunēt čē ēn-ič ōγōn bavēt čiγōn ka-š gōβēt (12) kū šav ut zanīh ī vahmān mart kun ut ka nē kunēt pātixšāy.

36, 12—16:

Ut apāk anī guft (13) kū mart duxt ī xvēš pat akāmakōmandīh ī ān duxt pat stūrīh bē dāt pātixšāy (14) ut pat zanīh bē dāt nē pātixšāy. Ut pat stūrīh ēt rāδ bē pātixšāy dāt čē-š (15) vindišn pat pit ēstēt ut pat zanīh ēt rāδ nē pātixšāy čē duxt gāt pat (16) xvat ēstēt nikerītan.

36, 16—17:

Ut xvēšīh ī duxt (pat) gāt (rāδ) apāk anī nipišt kū (ka) zan (17) ut duxt ī pātixšāyīhā ī pat vindišn pātixšāy gāt ut tāvān pit ut šōy ut žahm tāvān *

37, 1—2 ** :

... (1) aržīh and ka handarz ō vidranǰ / nidranǰ (? Ms.: [illegible]) dahēt ān ī frēh ahravdāt ut ka yuttar hamē(v) (2) frēh arž bē dahišn.

37, 2—10:

Ka šōy ō zan gōβēt kū guharēn kun zan (3) guharēn (ī) rāst pātixšāy kart ut ka šōy nē guft ēstēt pat 4 bahr ēv bahr pat (4) šōy nīrmattar pātixšāy kartan ut ka frēh kū pat 4 bahr ēv bahr hač vēš pat ān ī hač vēš (5) duž čē guhārēn ētōn pātixšāy kartan ka frēh kū 4 ēvak hač vēš nēst ut ziyānak (6) apāč nē pātixšāy ēstāt. Ut ān kē guharēn apāk hamē(v) kunēt (andar) 3 šapak apāč pātixšāy (7) ēstāt ⟨ī⟩ paytāk kū ka mart 1 ō kas 1 gōβēt kū guharēn kun ān kē avi-š gōβēt (8) guharēn (ī) rāst pātixšāy kartan ut andar-ič 3 šapak apāč nē pātixšāy ēstāt. Ut ēn-ič kū (9) ān kē ōy kas pat guharēn kartan pātixšāy kunēt andar 3 šapak pātixšāy (apāč) ēstāt (10) ōh apāyēt uskārtan.

XXXIII ***

37, 11:

Dar ī graβakānīh.

---

* The text of the article breaks off at this point.

** This is the end of an article whose first part was to be found on one of the missing folios.

*** The (*abǰad*) ordinal-number 33 is placed above the heading of this chapter.

36, 9—12:

Zurvāndāt i Yuvān-Yam has said that if a man declares to his daughter: "go and become the *stūr* of such-and-such a man!", the daughter is entitled not to become (the *stūr* of the designated person) bacause this is identical with his saying: "go and become the wife of such-and-such a man!". And she is entitled not to carry out (this order).

36, 12—16:

In addition it is said that a man is entitled to give his daughter as a *stūr* against her will, but he is not entitled (to give her) as a wife. He is entitled to give her as a *stūr* on the basis that her income belongs to her father, but he is not entitled to give her as a wife because (the decision regarding) sexual intercourse belongs to the daughter. (This is) to be noted.

36, 16—17:

And in addition to other (opinions), this is (also) written (regarding the right) of a daughter (to decide) independently (the question) of sexual intercourse: (if) a wife or ("and") daughter of a *pātixšāyīh* marriage (and who is) endowed with (a personal) income has entered into (unlawful) sexual intercourse (= has committed adultery), (then) the father or husband (must be paid?) a fine, but the fine for violence...*.

37, 1—2 **

37, 2—10:

If a husband says to his wife: "exchange (this thing)!", then the wife is entitled to make an equivalent exchange. But if the husband does not say this (*i. e.* did not empower her to make the exchange — *A. P.*), then she is entitled to make an exchange with one-quarter (*ad valorem*) profit to her hasband. But if the profit exceeds one-quarter (*ad valorem*) of the thing, then such an excess (above the norm) of one-quarter is theft, because exchanges are permitted in such a manner that the profit shall not exceed one quarter (*ad valorem* of the thing exchanged). And the wife may not back out of the exchange (already made). But the one with whom she made the exchange may reject it (within a period of) three days. It is known (?) that if one person declares to another: "exchange!", then the one to whom this declaration is made is entitled to make an equivalent exchange, and in such a case, this exchange cannot be rejected even within the three day limit. And an investigation must also be made whether the person empowering the exchange is entitled to withdraw from the exchange during the three day period (following) the exchange.

XXXIII ***

37, 11:

Chapter concerning securities/pledges.

37, 11—13:

Ka graβakāndār xvāstak ī pat 100+ pat (12) graβ dārēt nēm pat 50 pat Farraxv pat graβ bē nihēt ut Farraxv 50 bē patigīret (13) ut xvāstak hač graβīh bē hilēt graβīh nē višuft bavēt.

37, 13—15:

Ka graβakāndār zamīč māh (14) Ātur graβ gīrēt ut bun-xvēš māh Tīr apāč vēčēt dastkarīh ōγōn kunišn čiγōn bar(15)-xvēš.

37, 15—**38**, 1:

Ka kart kū-m drahm vičārtan ut ēn xvāstak hač graβ ⟨ut⟩ apāč vēxtan rāδ (16) Mihrēn pātixšāy kart ut Mihrēn ān xvāstak hač graβīh vēčēt drahm pat dastaβarīh (17) vičārt bavēt ān ī apāč āβarēt ān ī bē vičārt rāδ pat graβīh dāštan pātixšāy (1) gyākē nipišt kū pātixšāy kartan pat čiš ī xvēškār.

38, 1—3:

Mart kē xvāstak ī (2) kasān hač anērān apāč xrīnēt tā ān ī bē vičārt apāč dahēnd pat graβīh dāštan (3) pātixšāy.

38, 3—6:

Xvāstak ī graβakān ka hač ān ī harv sāl bar 2 gīrēt pat 6 māh (4) ut ka harv sāl bar ēvak gīret pat 12 māh čē bar pat I sāl ēvak gīrišn. Ka (5) tangīh ī zamīk rāδ kam kunēt hač ān čiγōn zamīk ka-č apēr tanūk aδak-ič hamāk bar čē-š [Ms.: čiš-ē(v)] (6) bavēt pat ēv sāl ut ka nē bavēt tā āp rāδ kam gīrēt pat 2 sāl baxšišn.

38, 7—9:

Ka Farraxv pat apām statan ī xvāstak ut graβakānīh ī xvāstak andar Mihrēn vičīr ăvartēt (8) (ut) pas Mihrēn xvāstak xvāhēt hač Syāva(x)š bē guft kū tā ān vičīr apāč dahēt (9) pātixšāy ka drahm nē vičārēt.

37, 11—13:

If the pledgee who holds a thing pledged against 100 (*drahms*) (lent by him), gives one half (of the thing) against 50 (*drahms*) as a security to Farraxv, and Farraxv (subsequently) receives 50 (*drahms*) (from him) and releases the thing (= the half he holds) from pledge, the security-contract [26] is not dissolved (thereby).

37, 13—15:

If a creditor (= "holder of a pledge") accepts a plot of land as a pledge in the month Ātur and the original possessor (of this plot = the debtor — *A. P.*) is to redeem it (= must buy it back according to the contract) in the month Tīr, then the (agricultural) work must be done (by the creditor) as it is incumbent upon an usufructuary.

37, 15—**38**, 1:

If he makes the following declaration: "I have empowered Mihrēn to pay money and redeem the thing from pledge", and Mihren redeems the thing from pledge by paying the money in accordance with the mandate (of that person); (then) he (= Mihrēn) may keep the thing as security against the money he has paid (to redeem it). It is written in one place that (the agent — *A. P.*) may deal ("act") with it as with a pledge object (= as with a thing confirming and guarenteeing a debt obligation on the part of the giver of the mandate or the agent's right of regression — *A. P.*).

38, 1—3:

If a man redeems a thing belonging to other persons from a non-Zoroastrian, he is entitled to hold (this thing) as a pledge until (the sum) paid (by him) is returned to him.

38, 3—6:

Regarding a plot of land ("thing") given as a pledge if (the possessor) collects from it two crops per year, then (the term of pledge for such a plot is of) six months, but if he collects one crop per year, then — of twelve months. Because (the pledgee) is entitled to receive one crop per year. If (the crop) he collects is small because of lack of land or because the soil ("land") in it is very poor, then the entire crop raised on that plot in the course of an entire year (shall belong to the pledgee; *i. e.* in such a case the pledgee is entitled to receive both the yearly crops — *A. P.*). And if there is no (crop that year) including (the case) when the crop collected is small because of (lack of) water, (the pledgee) shall be given (the crops of) two years.

38, 7—9:

If Farraxv (concludes a written) and sealed contract with Mihrēn concerning a loan and the giving of a pledge, and Mihrēn subsequently demands the return of the loan ("thing"); then, as has been said with a citation from Syāva(x)š, until the latter (= Mihrēn) returns the document of the contract, he (= Farraxv) need not pay him the money [27].

38, 9—11:

Ka ān kē xvāstak xvēš graβ hač graβakānīh (10) bē duzēt ut xvāstak ō ratān appār ⟨ut⟩ rat hamēmārīh ī ōy kē xvāstak ⟨ō ratān⟩ xvēš (11) pātixšāy kartan kū drahm bē vičār ut xvāstak apāč stān čē man xvēš.

38, 11—13:

Kart xvāstak (12) ī-š pat graβ frōxt nē pātixšāy (ut) ān bavēt ka-š anī-č xvāstak nēst čē (13) xvāstak ī agraβ frōxt nē ⟨ut⟩ ān ī graβakān frōxt pātixšāy.

38, 13—17:

Ka dastkart ut anšahrīk (14) graβ ut xvāstak pat zamān ī nāmčišt dāt rāδ ut ēn-ič apāk ān mart patmān kart kū (15) uzīt ān zamān ka ān xvāstak nē vičārt ēstēt ān dastkart ut anšahrīk ōy xvāstak (16) rāδ tō xvēš ut pēš hač zamān anšahrīk mīrēt čiγōn Syāva⟨x⟩š guft graβakāndār (17) pātixšāy ka xvāstak pat xvēšīh pātixšāy ka pat graβīh gīrēt.

38, 17—**39**, 2:

Ka dastkart (1) graβ kunēt u-š sarv ut činār (Ms.: čnd'l = čandāl?) aβzāyišn nē be hanbāhišn ⟨ut⟩ graβakāndār xvēš (2) dastkart ēvkartakīhā dātastān ētōn čiγōn draxt ī barōmand.

39, 2—5:

Ka anšahrīk (ī pat) graβ (3) āzāt kunēt bē hakar xvatāy anattān enyā anšahrīk pat gyāk āzāt ut xvāstak (4) ī graβakānīh^{+} xvatāy pat graβakāndār ut hakar anšahrīk vičārt guharīk pat anšahrīk vičārišn (5) ut tā drahm vičārēnd graβakāndār anšahrīk pat graβīh dāštan pātixšāy.

39, 5—9:

Ka anšahrīk (6) pat graβakān pat kār ō anī šahr frēstēt ut drahm vičārēt tā apāč apispārtan ī (7) anšahrīk guharīk (ī) anšahrīk ō ōy ⟨i⟩ apispārišn kē anšahrīk xvēš ka graβakāndār (8) nē anšahrīk mat ēstēt zan ut frazand ī graβakāndār pātixšāy ka tā graβakāndār (9) apāč āyēt drahm nē patigīrēnd (ut) anšahrīk hač dārišn nē hilēnd.

38, 9—11:

If the posssessor of a thing (deposited as a pledge = the debtor — *A. P.*) steals it from deposit, and the thing is removed (from him and passes) to the *rats*, then the *rat* is entitled to try the case against the possessor of (this) thing (in the following manner/according to the following formula): "pay the money and receive the thing, for (at present) it is mine!".

38, 11—13:

A man is not entitled to sell a thing which he has hypothecated. This is the case even when he has no other property, because it is permissible to sell only an unpledged thing but not a pledged (one).

38, 13—17:

If he makes the following agreement with this man regarding the pledging (= hypothec) of a *dastkart* and a slave, and regarding the transfer (= return) of the money within a time-limit set (by the contract): "if the money is not paid at the expiration of this time-limit, this *dastkart* and slave shall belong to you because of this money"; then — if the slave dies before (the expiration of) the stipulated time-limit — according to the statement of Syāvaxš, the creditor is entitled either to take the thing (= the *dastkart*) into his personal possession or to take it as pledge (presumably as an *antichresis* security — *A. P.*).

38, 17—**39**, 2:

If he (= debtor) pledges a *dastkart* which contains cypresses and plane-trees (probably not "sandalwood trees"), (then) what belongs to the creditor ("the holder of the pledge") is not the growth (or "the shoots"), but that which has fallen (= been cut off); for the decision regarding a *dastakart* taken as a whole is the same as (the one regarding a single) fruit-bearing tree (*cf. infra* **40**, 13—17).

39, 2—5:

If he (= the master) manumits a slave who has been pledged as a security, (then) except (in the case when) the master (= the owner of the slave, *i. e.*, the debtor — *A. P.*) is insolvent, the slave is immediately free, but the master (leaves) the thing [28] pledged with the creditor (= pledgee). And if the slave is released, then an equivalent (sum) must be paid (to the creditor) in place of the slave. And untill (this) money is paid, the creditor ("the pledgee") is entitled to hold/keep the slave in pledge.

39, 5—9:

If (a creditor — *A. P.*) sends a slave whom he holds as a pledge (= an *antichresis* — *A. P.*) to work in another town, and (the debtor) pays the money (= settles the debt), then a sum equal to the value of the slave must be conveyed to the owner of the slave [29] until his return. If the creditor-holder of the pledge has not (returned) but the slave has returned, the wife and son (or "children") of the creditor are entitled not to accept the money (= the debt returned by the debtor — *A. P.*) and not to release the slave from their possession until the return of the creditor.

39, 9—12:

Ka xvāstak 1 (10) graβakān kart hamē(v) andar ān sāl ka bar hambun-ič nē āβarēt 3 sāl apāč ō pas (11) kunišn ut andar ēt sāl ka-š bar miyānak āβarēt ziyān ī ōy ī graβakāndār bē (12) vičārišn.

39, 12—**40**, 1:

Ka bun-xvēš drahm kē xvāstak pat-iš graβ pat zamān ī nāmčišt bē (13) dāt rāδ apāk ān mart patmān kunēt ayāp ka graβakāndār drahm xvāhēt apāč nē (14) dahēt ut pas graβakāndār andar ākāsīh[+] ut dānišn ī bun-xvēš xvāstak grāβ kunēt ut hakar (15) ēvbār[+] graβakāndār xvāstak graβ kunēt bun-xvēš dārišn ī xvāstak ⟨i⟩ xvāhēt (16) graβakāndār pātixšāy ka gōβēt kū drahm xvat vičār xvāstak xvat vēč (17) graβakāndār kē graβ apaytāk bavēt ān ī katak-xvatāy kart guharīk nē ut ān ī dātaβar kart (ī) guharīk pātixšāy xvāst.

40, 1—4:

Ka mart xvāstak-ē(v) ī-š pat-iš graβ hač graβīh bē (2) hilēt xvāstak rāδ čiš-ič nē gōβēt. Būt kē guft kū-š xvāstak nē hišt (3) bavēt u-š bōžišn ēn guft kū ka graβakān kunēt bar graβakān kart bavēt ut ka (4) agraβ kunēt bun agraβ kart bavēt. Ut ka hač graβīh hilēt bar hišt bavēt.

40, 5—13:

Ka Āturfarnbaγ hač Mihrēn apām stānēt ut xvāstak (ī) graβakān (rāδ) patmān kunēt kū hark-ič (6) bār ī ēn xvāstak rāδ hač tō xvāhēnd rāδ xvāstak pat graβakānīh dāštan pātixšāy (7) hēh būt kē guft kū ka xvāstak bē vičārēt hark ut bār rāδ pat graβakānīh (8) nē pātixšāy dāštan čē ka-š guft kū hark-ič (bār) rāδ xvāstak ī apāmdān hark ut bār (9) rāδ guft bavēt kū pat tō graβakān xvāstak ī āpāmdān nē pātixšāy bē ka stānēt (10) čē nazdist apām būt ut pas hark ut bār u-š pat hark ut bār pat graβakān dāštan (11) tā ān tāyak guft ka apām bē vičārēt. Ut būt kē guft kū ka-č apām apāč (12) stānēt aδak-ič hark ut bār rāδ pat graβakān dāštan pātixšāy. Ut ēn-ič pātixšāy ka apām (13) ut hark ut bār pat ēv yāvar apāč stānēt.

39, 9—12:

If a plot of land ("a thing") given as a pledge does not bear the slightest crop, then after three years it must be returned to the pledger. And in the year that it bears an average crop, the loss born by the creditor must be made good ("paid").

39, 12—**40**, 1:

If the owner (*i. e.* the original possessor of a pledged thing, the debtor — *A. P.*) has made an agreement — regarding the return of money (received as a loan) within a stipulated time-limit to the man who holds the thing as a pledge — with that man, or if the creditor (= "the pledgee") demands (the return of the loaned) money and the former does not return it, and the creditor subsequently [30] pledges the thing (to another person) [31] with the knowledge of the owner (= the debtor), and if after the creditor has pledged the thing the owner demands the return (lit. "the possession") of this thing; then the creditor is entitled to declare: "pay the money yourself and redeem the thing yourself!" A creditor to whom (the value of) the pledge was not (formally) declared is entitled to claim an (amount) equivalent not to that declared by the head of household but to (the amount) declared by the judge.

40, 1—4:

If a man (= the creditor — *A. P.*) releases a thing which is (pledged to) him and says nothing about (this) thing, the following opinion has been given: that (in such a case), the thing has not been released (from pledge) by him. And this was the decision presented ("stated") for this problem: when he (= the debtor — *A. P.*) pledges a thing, then the fruits of the thing (= the revenue brought by the thing) are (also) pledged; but when (he) redeems the pledge, then the principal is released; and when he (= the creditor — *A. P.*) releases the thing from pledge he (thereby) releases the fruits (= the revenue) (as well).

40, 5—13:

If Aturfarnbaγ receives a loan (= "debt") from Mihrēn and makes the following agreement regarding the thing (= the plot of land; *vide infra*) (conveyed) as a pledge: "you are likewise entitled to hold the plot as a pledge for (= against) the taxes and dues which will be demanded from you for this plot ('thing')"; this opinion has been given: that when he pays the money (= settles the debt), the latter is not entitled to hold the plot ("thing") for the taxes and dues, because when he declared: "likewise for the taxes and dues", then: "(the thing is conveyed) to you as a pledge" was said at the same time as (that which) regarded the taxes and dues on the thing pledged. And he (= the debtor who has settled his debt — *A. P.*) cannot fail to receive the plot ("thing") he pledged, because the debt came first and the taxes and dues — later. And he (= the authority on whom the author of the *Law-Book* bases himself — *A. P.*) has said that a plot ("thing") is to be kept as a pledge against taxes and dues until the time that he (= the debtor) settles ("pays") the debt. But (some) have spoken as follows: that (the creditor — holder of the pledge) is entitled to hold the plot as a pledge for (= against) the taxes and dues (which he has paid — *A. P.*) even after he has received back his loan (debt). It is also permissible for (the creditor) to receive back immediately the debt as well as the taxes and dues (*i. e.* a sum equivalent to the loan plus the reimbursement to the creditor of the payments for taxes and dues — *A. P.*).

40, 13—17:

Ka draxt-ē(v) graβ kunēt kē bar hast graβakān+(14)dār ēvāč bar xvēš ka-š bar nēšt hakar ka zanēnd apāč nē rōδēt čiγōn sarv (15) graβakāndār ēvāč hanbāhišn ut hakar ka zanēnd apāč rōδēt čiγōn čanār+/čandāl (Ms.: čnd'l) ut amrāv hanbāhišn-ič (16) ut aβzōn xvēš ut tā ān ē ka andar aβzōn ēstēt bē xonsandīh ī ōy kē graβ kart enyā (17) zatan nē pātixšāy u-š aβzōn-ič ī andar graβīh vahāk ayāp guharīk stānišn.

40, 17 — **85**, 2:

Ka (1) anšahrīk ī āpustan bē frōšēt ka āpustanīh āšnāk āpustanīh-ič frōxt+ (2) bavēt.

85, 2—4:

Būt kē guft kū ka 50 apām stanēt ut xvāstak-ē(v) graβ kunēt (3) harv 1 drahm ī bē vičārēt xvāstak drahm marīhā čand ān ī apāč stanēt niyāpēt hač graβīh (4) bē hilišn.

85, 4—5:

Ka zamīk-ē(v) graβ kunēt u-š pas xānīk andar āxēzēt xānīk-ič (5) graβakān dār[išn].

85, 5—6:

Xvāstak pat 2 mart graβakān ka drahm vičārēt dārišn ī xvāstak (6) hač harv kē kāmēt pātixšāy xvāst.

41, 1—2:*

[...............] nipēsēt aδak-iš nē šāyēt ut ka katak-xvatāy kart kū ō (2) ān ī sažāktar nē (?) [........] dātastān kartakīhā.

41, 2—5:

Ka Farraxv stūr gumārišn (ut) Mihrēn andar (3) dūtak ī Pusak ī hač pus ī Farraxv mat ēstēt ut Vasak hač patvand ī ō Farraxv pat duxtdātīh (4) ut Zahak frāč mat ēstēt dūr patvandtar mat ēstēnd+ (ut) ān ⟨ī⟩ stūrīh xvāhēnd pat (15) ān stūrīh Mihrēn sažāktar.

* Lines 1 and 2 contain the (corrupted) ending of a chapter whose beginning is altogether missing together with the preceding folios of the manuscript.

40, 13—17:

If he (= the debtor) has pledged a fruit-bearing tree, then only the fruit belongs to the pledgee (= the creditor). And if the tree bears no fruit, or if it does not grow back again after being cut — as for instance the cypress — then only what has been cut off (belongs) to the creditor. And if it does grow back again after being cut — as for instance the plane tree (or "sandalwood") and the palm — then both what has been cut off and the offshoots belong to him (= the creditor). And during the time that it is growing, he (=the creditor) is not entitled to cut it unless he has the agreement of the pledger. And he (= the creditor to whom the pledger-debtor has not given the permission to cut — *A. P.*) shall receive (from the debtor) the amount (in money) or the equivalent for the offshoots pledged as well.

40, 17 — **85**, 2:

When he sells a pregnant female-slave — if the pregnancy is visible — then the pregnancy is also sold (*i. e.* the fruit is included in the transaction — *A. P.*).

85, 2—4:

The following has been said: if he receives a loan of 50 (*drahms*) and pledges a thing, then — with each *drahm* paid — this thing shall be released from pledge (to the degree) corresponding with the number of *drahms* that he (= the creditor) has received back.

85, 4—5:

If (anyone) pledges a plot of land and subsequently a spring gushes forth on it, then this spring is to be considered as a pledge (= the spring is included in the pledge — *A. P.*).

85, 5—6:

A thing is held as a pledge by two persons: when (the debtor) pays the money (= settles the debt), he can demand the thing ("possession of the thing") from whichever of them he desires.

41, 1—2 *

41, 2—5:

If a *stūr* must be appointed for Farraxv, and Mihrēn — from the family of Pusak who is from (= *via* the line of — *A. P.*) Farraxv's son — presents himself, (and) Vasak — a kinsman of Farraxv on his daughter's side [32], and Zahak — who is a still more distant relative — (likewise) present themselves and request the *stūr*ship; then Mihrēn is the most suitable person for the *stūr*ship under consideration [33].

41, 5—8:

Ut Pusānveh ut Veh-Ōhrmizd ut Siyāvaxš hamdātastān būt (6) ka+ (Ms.: MNW = kē) pat hangōšītak frazand ī čakar ī pus ī ōy mart duxtdāt guft kū+ pat stūrīh (7) purnāy ut yut hač purnāy apurnāy sažāktar ka-č purnāy stūrīh andar nē apāyēt rāδ gōβēt (8) aδak-ič apurnāyak ut ān ī hač apurnāyak kam sažāktar nē gumārišn.

41, 8—9:

Martak guft kū stūrīh-(9)ič nīrmat ēv ut ān ī nīrmat ōγōn dārišn čiγōn ka apurnāyak ōh apāyēh bē gumārišn.

41, 9—13:

Duxt ī (10 baγaspāndāt kē duxt ī pat xvă̄s̱rāyōnīh zāt ēstēt sažāktar ka-š brāt pat baxt (11) šavēt u-š xvah 3 hast ut anī kas nēst ān ī mas stūr ut ka pit pat baxt šavēt u-š duxt (12) 3 hast ut anī kas nēst ka ān ī mas apāyēt ān ī mas ut ka nē ān kē apatom šōy kunēt (13) stūr.

41, 13—14:

Ka duxtdāt-ē(v) andar xānak+ ī pit ī māt andar apāyēt bahr ī māt pat xvēšīh hamaδvēn duxt (14) apar ō mānēt ut ēn kū ka ān ī mas šōy kunēt ō ān ī ditīkar rasēt ayāp nē uskārtan.

41, 15:

Ka stūr(īh) ī kartak apāč ō bun šavēt duxt 2 ān gyāk ān ī mas ōh apāyēt xvāst.

41, 16—**42**, 1:

Ka kunēt kū-m ēn xvāstak pat stūrīh paytāk kart u-š duxt 2 hast ān kē framān (17) apar nē dāt ēstēt pat xvēšīh pat duxt harv 2 ut ān ī paytāk kart pat stūrīh duxt ī (1) mas dārišn.

41, 5—8:

Pusānveh, Veh-Ōhrmizd and Syāva(x)š were unanimous when they said concerning the collaterally-related children of a *čakar*-marriage of the son of an *epikleros*-daughter of this man (= the deceased for whom a *stūr* must be appointed — *A. P.*) that the one most suitable for the position of *stūr* (is the one of them who is) of age, and if none is of age — a minor. And if (the one existing) who is of age declares: "(I) do not need (it)", in such a case also, a minor shall be named, and the one who is less suitable (according to degree of kinship — *A. P.*) than the minor shall not be appointed (as *stūr*).

41, 8—9:

Martak has said that the *stūr*ship also (presents / gives) an advantage, and that which (presents / gives) an advantage is to be received as though it were needed for the minor (= as though the declaration: "I need it" had been made regarding the *stūr*ship — *A. P.*), (and he) should be appointed (*cf. supra*, **41**, 5—8 and **19**, 15—16).

41, 9—13:

(As regards) a daughter born from a *baγaspān*-marriage — *i. e.* a daughter (lit. "one who is a daughter") born from the *xvǎs̱rāyōnīh*-marriage (of her parents — *A. P.*) — if her brother who has three sisters and no one else dies, the one most suited (to assume his *stūr*ship) is the eldest sister. And if the father who has three daughters and no one else dies, then (it shall be) the eldest if she consents ("needs it"); and if not, (then) the one (of these daughters) who marries last shall become his *stūr*.

41, 13—14:

If a successor-heir by way of an *epikleros* is required in the family ("in the house") of the mother's father, then the inheritance-share of the mother comes entirely to her daughter [34]. It is also necessary to note (or "investigate") whether it (= the inheritance) goes to a second daughter if the elder (daughter) marries [35].

41, 15:

If an instituted *stūr*ship returns to the family of the one who instituted it (*i. e.* if the *stūr* whom he designated dies or is unable to give him a successor — *A. P.*), and there are two daughters in that family; then the elder shall be called (to the *stūr*ship).

41, 16—**42**, 1:

If he declares the following: "I have declared this thing conveyed for *stūr*ship", and he has two daughters, (then) that (part of the estate) regarding which he made no disposition passes as personal inheritance-shares (= "daughter's" shares) to both daughters, but that (estate) regarding (whose transfer for *stūr*ship) he made the declaration, shall go to the elder daughter on the basis of a *stūr*'s possession. [Repeated in **44**, 16—**45**, 1; *cf.* also **45**, 1—6 — *A. P.*].

42, 1—5:

Ka mart [pus ī patigriftak hast ut xvāstak pat stūrīh dahēt ō pus ī patigri](2)ftak nē rasēt nē-č gumārišn. Vāyayār [nipišt kū ka pus ī patigrif]tak pat (3) dāt mas kū ān ī pātixšāyīhā pat stūrīh pus ī patigriftak gumārišn ut ka pit ī (4) pātixšāyīhā xvāstak pat stūrīh paytāk kunēt pus ī-š pat pusakānīh bē dāt (5) ēstēt pat ān xvāstak pat stūrīh ōh gumārišn.

42, 5—9:

Andar dūtak-zāt pat kart(ak) guft (6) ēstēt kū pat stūrīh (ī) pit nē gumārišn. Vāyayār guft kū ōh apāyēt gumārtan ut pat (7) Artaxšahr-xvarreh ōh gumārēnd ut pat-ič Dārāβkart ōh gumārēnd ut Martak Pusānveh-ič hamdātastān (8) būt hend kū-šān ōh gumārtan ut dātastān brāt-ič ōh apāyēt gumārtan ut dātastān (9) xvah-ič ōh apāyēt gumārtan.

42, 9—14:

Rāt-Ōhrmizd guft kū dātastān duxt yuttar nēst kū (10) pus ī patigriftak čē ān-ič pat zanīh patigrift ī māt rāδ ut ka-š dātastān duxt-iš hast pus-ič ī (11) patigriftak pat pašt bavēt. U-š ēn-ič guft kū dātastān duxt ka-š ōh apāyēt (12) xvāst nē ēn kū-š apar mānēt (ut) pas pus ī čakar sažāktar ut Vāyayār hamdātastān nē būt (13) u-š ēn-ič pat bōžišn guft kū hakar datastān duxt kas-ič+ (Ms.: MND'Mč = čiš-ič) nēst pas stūr čim apāyēt gumārtan (14) kē+ (Ms.: 'MT = ka) ān ōh zāyēt+ hamē(v) dātastān pus ut hamē(v) dātastān duxt hend.

42, 14—15:

Ka dūtak-zāt katak-xvatāy(15)īhā valāδ patvand ut tōxmak apar nē mānet.

42, 15—17:

Gyākē nipišt kū pat stūrīh ut sardārīh (16) dātastān brāt hač brāt ut pus ut duxt ī andar dūtak ī brāt zāt ēstēnd hač ān ī apārīk brātarān sažāk(17)tar+ ut dātastān yuttar nēst.

42, 1—5:

If a man has [an adopted son, and (that man) conveys a thing for *stūr*ship (= institutes a *stūr*ship for himself — *A. P.*), then it (= the *stūr*ship)] does not pass (by transmission — *A. P.*) [to the adopted son] and he should likewise not be appointed. (However), Vāyayār [has written that if the adopted son] is older than the son from a pātixšāyīh-marriage, then the adopted son should be appointed. And if the father by blood declares the transfer of a thing for *stūr*ship, then the son given by him for adoption to (another person) must be appointed *stūr* (for his own blood-father — *A. P.*) with (the transfer) of this thing (to him) as a *stūr* (possession).

42, 5—9:

In procedural regulations it is said regarding one "born in / into a family": that he shall not be appointed as stūr for the (late) father (of the family). (But) Vāyayār has said that he shall be appointed, and he is (so) appointed in (the province of) Artaxšahr-Xvarreh, and he is appointed in (the city of) Dārāβkart. Martak and Pusānveh were in agreement that they (= those "born in / into a family") should be appointed. And likewise the "legal" brother (= "the brother according to law"; of the deceased — *A. P.*) shall be appointed (as *stūr*), and the "*legal*" sister (= "the sister according to law") shall be appointed.

42, 9—14:

Rāt-Ōhrmizd has said that (the case of) a "*legal*" daughter (= "a daughter according to law") does not differ from that of an adopted son, for she too (is suitable for the *stūr*ship? — *A. P.*) as the result of her mother's having been taken into (a *pātixšāyīh*) marriage. And if he has a "*legal*" daughter, then the adopted son is also included in the agreement (?). And he has also said the following: if it is indispensable to call the "*legal*" daughter (to assume the *stūr*ship for her father — *A. P.*), (then) this is not (the case) where they inherit from him. And after (her), the most suitable are a son / daughter from a *čakar* marriage. Vāyayār, however, did not agree with this. And he also said this regarding the solution (of this problem): if there is neither a "*legal*" daughter (in the family) nor another person, then a stūr must be appointed, and all those born from her / him (= the appointed *stūr*) shall be "*legal*" sons and "*legal*" daughters (of the late head of household — *A. P.*).

42, 14—15:

The one "born into / in a family" does not inherit the dignities (lit. "the height; the high position") of the head of household, (or his) kinships and succession through kinship ("clan, family").

42, 15—17:

It is written in one place that a "*legal*" brother (= a "brother according to law" — *A. P.*) is more suitable for the position of *stūr* or guardian than a brother (by blood), and the son and daughter born into the family (of a "*legal*") brother (are more suitable) than the children of other brothers. And there is no other decision.

42, 17—**43**, 1:

(Hač) Pēšaksēr gōβēnd kū dātastān brāt ka-šān zahakīh/zāyākīh hač ēt gyāk (1) pat uskārišn kū ēvak andar dit šāyēnd.

43, 1—4:

Zan ī pat stūrīh sažāktar ka-š (2) ō xvāhišn kart bahr ut pašadātakān bē dāt pātixšāy ut ka ān (ī) kam sažāktar xvāhēt (3) bē hišt pātixšāy ut ka pat axonsandīh+ ī ōy ān ī kem sažāktar ō xvāhišn kart (4) aδak nē gumārišn ut ān ī sažāktar xvāhēt aδak-ič ān (ī) sažāktar gumārišn.

43, 4—6:

Ka brāt (5) stūrīh has ō xvāhišn kart kū xvah pat ān stūrīh xvah nē bē brāt gumārišn (6) Pusānveh-ič ī Āzātmartān hamgōnak guft.

43, 6—8:

Ka brāt stūrīh andar xvāhišn dāšt xvah (7) rāδ ēn nipišt ēstēt kū pātixšāy kas zan gumārēt pat xvap dāštan (ut) pursišn ī (8) hač xvah kār nēst.

43, 8—11:

Ka mart pat baxt šavēt u-š xvastak 60 nēst ut māt+ xvah (9) ut brāt hast ut māt pat dūtak ī kas stūr ut xvah kas zan ān xvāstak ō brāt ut apāk-ič ān (10) kū zan kē šōy hast pat stūrīh pat sažāk ut ān ī stūr pat asažāk dārēnd pas-ič (11) ō xvah nē bē pat xvēšīh ō brāt rasēt.

43, 11—13:

Xvāstak ī pat dūtak kē stūr (12) gumārišn arž ī šahr rāδ hač 60 apāč arž ka pēš hač ān ē ka stūr gumārēnd (13) apāč arž stūr nē gumārišn. Ut hakar pas (apāč) arž stūrīh yuttar bē nē bavēt.

42, 17—43, 1:

It is said, on the basis of Pēšaksēr's (authority), that an investigation must be made regarding a "*legal*" brother (="a brother according to law") (to find out) whether they are born in the same family ("place") and whether they are suitable for each other.

43, 1—4:

If a (married) woman who is the one most suitable (for the assumption of the *stūr*ship for her kinsman —*A. P.*) has made a request (=has requested the *stūr*ship), he (=her husband —*A. P.*) is entitled to transfer her share (=her daughter's share in her father's estate which she brought as a dowry —*A. P.*) to her, as well as the paraphernalia. And if that (married woman) who is least suitable requests (the *stūr*ship), he (=her husband) is entitled to divorce (her). And if she requests (this) in the face of his opposition, she should not be appointed. (But) if the one who is most suitable makes the request (in the face of her husband's opposition —*A. P.*), then even in such a case, the one most suitable shall be appointed.

43, 4—6:

If a brother requested (="declared a request for") the *stūr*ship earlier than his sister, then the brother and not the sister shall be appointed to this *stūr*ship. And Pusānveh ī Āzātmartān has said the same.

43, 6—8:

If a brother has been attributed ("has had") the requested *stūr*ship, the following has been written regarding the sister: a man may appoint his wife (as *stūr*), this is to be considered lawful (and) a demand coming from a sister is devoid of force.

43, 8—11:

If a man dies and he does not have a thing (valued at) 60 (*satērs*) and he has a mother, a sister and a brother, (and moreover) his mother is a *stūr* in the family of another person and his sister is married to someone; (then) the thing (=his estate —*A. P.*) (goes) to his brother. And it is also (written) that a woman who has a husband is to be considered suitable to become a *stūr*, whereas one who is the *stūr* (of another person) — is unsuitable. And furthermore: the inheritance does not pass as a personal share to the sister but to the brother.

43, 11—13:

(The value) of the estate belonging to a family for which a *stūr* must be appointed becomes (less than 60 *satērs*) as the result of a conjunction of prices in the *šahr*: if the price fell before the time of appointment of the *stūr*, then the *stūr* should not be appointed. But if the fall in value occurred subsequently, it has no effect on the *stūr*ship.

43, 13—16:

Ka katak-bānūk (pat) (14) bē vitīrišnīh stūrīh bē dahēt hakar ōγōn nipišt kū-m frāč hač man dāt būt kē guft (15) kū pat ēn čim čē pat ān zamān hamē(v) dahēt ka dātaβarān stūr gumārišn nē xvap ut ka kart (16) kū-m pat bē vitīrišnīh dāt pat xvap dāštan.

43, 16—**44**, 2:

Ka stūr ī kartak stūrīh bē ō (17) apurnāyak ī xvēš dahēt ut apurnāyak andar apurnāyakīh pat baxt šavēt yuttar nē bavēt čiγōn ka-š (1) zan apar kart hē ka-š zan apar kunēt ētōn uskārišn kū ētōn bavēt (2) čiγōn ān-ič ī gumārtak.

44, 2—3:

Stūrīh ka xvēšāvandān hend ut nē xvāhēnd ādehīk čiγōn (3) hač Dātastān-namak ī pat Gurgān kartak sahist kū paytāk ōh gumārišn.

44, 3—6:

Ka mart (4) xvāstak pat stūrīh ī xvēš zan ī pātixšāyīhā ī xvēš dāšt rāδ ut ēn-ič framān (5) dahēt kū kas pat ziyānak ut ān xvāstak sardārīh pātixšāyīhā mā hēβ⁺ bavēt ziyānak (6) pat pēšēmārīh ut pasēmārīh ī (h)ēr ī ān stūrīh sardār andar nē apāyēt.

44, 6—8:

Mart ka-š (7) bē zan ayāp ān ī anērīh dārēt ayāp-iš bē apurnāyak ī ō aγdēnīh šavēt anī frazand (8) nēst stūr ōh gumārišn.

44, 8—12:

Ka mart bē duxt 2 anī kas nēst xvāstak ut xān pat bahr (9) ut xvēšīh ō duxt ī mas dahēt (ut) anandarz mīrēt būt kē guft kū duxt ī mas (10) bahr ī duxtīh rāδ bahr pat stūrīh kem apar nē mānēt ut yuttar nē bavēt čiγōn (11) ka-š naxvist bahr ī duxtīh dāt ut pas pat zanīh kart bahr ī zanīh kem (12) nē rasēt. Ut būt kē guft kū ⟨ka⟩ bahr-ič ī stūrīh duxtīh rāδ hamē(v) rasēt.

43, 13—16:

If the mistress of the house transfers the *stūr*ship (to another person) (in case of) her death, then — if she has written this: "I have transferred (the *stūr*ship) after my death ('after myself')" — the opinion has been given that: inasmuch as she is transferring (the *stūr*ship) at the time that a *stūr* must be appointed by the judges, this is unlawful (= invalid). If, however, she uses the following formula: "in case of my death, I have transferred", then (a transfer formulated in this manner) is to be considered lawful [36].

43, 16—**44**, 2:

If an *instituted stūr* (= one instituted by the deceased himself during his lifetime — *A. P.*) transfers the *stūr*ship to his minor (son/daughter) and the minor dies before coming of age, then (the decision in such a case) does not differ from the one when he proclaims/designates his wife as *stūr*; and if he transfers the *stūr*ship to his wife, attention must be paid that (this matter) take place as in the case of an *appointed stūr* (= a *stūr* "by appointment").

44, 2—3:

If — (although) they are kinsmen — they do not wish (to accept) the *stūr*ship (or: "they do not claim the *stūr*ship"), (then), as follows from the *Dātastān-nāmak*, a fellow-citizen ("one belonging to the same community"; *cf. infra* "Glossary" *s. v. ādehīk* — *A. P.*) must be appointed (as *stūr*) in accordance with the procedural norms operative in Gurgan (= Hyrcania).

44, 3—6:

If a man makes a disposition of a thing intended as a foundation for his *stūr*ship to his wife from a *pātixšāyīh*-marriage and he likewise orders the following: "let no one be entitled to be the guardian (of) this woman (= wife) and to hold the guardianship over this thing!", then the woman does not need a guardian to participate — as plaintiff or respondent — in a suit relating to the estate of this *stūr*ship.

44, 6—8:

If a man has no wife, or if his wife does not belong to the Zoroastrian faith, or if he has no children other than a minor son who has converted to a non-Zoroastrian faith, a *stūr* must be appointed for him.

44, 8—12:

If a man has no one besides two daughters, (and) he transfers ("gives" by transfer — *A. P.*) a house and homestead to his elder daughter as her personal share of the inheritance, and dies without leaving a will; then, as has been stated by some (authorities), the elder daughter shall receive the share for (her father's) *stūr*ship as well, despite the daughter's-share (she has already received). And this case is identical with the one where (the father) first transfers a daughter's share (to his daughter) and then marries her: a wife's share (= the share received by a wife after her husband's death — *A. P.*) shall still go to her. And some have said that the share (alloted) for the *stūr*ship (of her father) shall also go to her inasmuch as she is his daughter.

44, 13—14:

Duxt ha-š zan kunēt bahr ī zanīh nē duxtīh rāδ hamē(v) rasēt u-š apārīk (14) xvāstak apar nē mānēt.

44, 14—16:

Ut apar Dātastān-nāmak ōγōn nipišt kū (ka) duxt ī mas stūr (15) ⟨ut⟩ xvāstak ī ka katak-xvatāy pat baxt šavēt pat katak-xvatāy ēstāt ō duxt ī kas (16) rasēt.

44, 16—**45**, 1:

Ka gōβēt kū-m ēn xvāstak pat stūrīh paytāk kart u-š duxt ⟨ī⟩ (17) 2 hast ān kē framān apar nē dāt ēstēt pat xvēšīh pat duxt harv 2 ut ān ī paytāk (1) kart pat stūrīh ⟨ō⟩ duxt ī mas dahišn.

45, 1—6:

Ut Vāyayār-ič hamgōnak gyākē (2) nipišt kū ka pit xvāstak 60 pat stūrīh paytāk kunēt ut pat dāštan ō (3) kas nē dahēt u-š duxt 2+ ut anī-č xvāstak hast ān 60 pat stūrīh ō duxt ī (4) mas ut apārīk pat xvēšīh nēm ō ān duxt ut nēm ō ān duxt rasēt čē pit xvāstak (5) pat stūrīh ān and paytākēnīt duxt xvāstak andar ō xvēšīh+ (Ms.: stūrīh) nē barēt čē pat (6) ān and xvāstak stūr(īh).

45, 6—8:

Ka gōβēt kū-m ēn xvāstak pat stūrīh ō ziyānak (7) ayāp ō mērak dāt ka ētōn dāt ī pat nāmčišt paytāk nē kart katak-xvatāy (8) mīrēt xvāstak ō ziyānak rasēt čē pat dūtak ētōn nīrmattar.

44, 13—14:

If he marries (his) daughter, then (in the case of his death *ab intestato* — *A. P.*), she shall receive (as inheritance) a wife's share (and) not (the share alloted) to a daughter. And she does not inherit the rest of the estate.

44, 14—16:

And it is written thus in the *Dātastān-nāmak*: "(if) the elder daughter is a *stūr* (for another person — *A. P.*), the estate belonging to the head of household at the time of his death shall go to the younger daughter".

44, 16—**45**, 1:

If he declares: "I have declared this thing (conveyed) for *stūr*ship", and he has two daughters; (then) that (part of his estate) regarding which he made no disposition (shall pass) as personal inheritance-shares to both daughters, but that (estate) regarding (whose transfer for *stūr*ship) he made the declaration shall go to the elder daughter on the basis of a *stūr*'s possesion. [A repetition of **41**, 16—**42**, 1; *cf.* **45**, 1—6. — *A. P.*].

45, 1—6:

And Vāyayār has also written in one place in the same manner that if a father declares the transfer for *stūr*ship of a thing (valued at) 60 (*satēr*s) without transferring it to the guardianship of anyone (= without designating a *stūr* — *A. P.*), and he has two daughters and also other properties; (then) this (thing valued at) 60 (*satēr*s) shall go to the elder daughter as a *stūr*'s (possession) and the remainder (of his estate) (shall go) as personal inheritance-shares: half to this one (= the elder daughter), half to that one (= the younger), because a daughter does not acquire ("take away") as her personal inheritance-share that portion ("that much") of her father's estate which the father declared (transferred for *stūr*ship) because that portion of the estate is a *stūr*'s possession.

45, 6—8:

If he declares: "I have transferred this thing as a *stūr*'s possesion ('for *stūr*ship') to a woman/wife or to a man", then upon the declaration of the transfer (for *stūr*ship) without precise indication (specifically to whom), after the death of the head of household the thing shall pass (as a *stūr*'s possession) to the woman/wife, since this is more advantageous for the family.

45, 8—17:

Ka mart (9) xvāstak pat stūrīh paytāk kart u-š duxt nē pus ī pātixšāyīhā hast ut ān xvāstak (10) kas dāštan rāδ framān nē dāt ⟨ut⟩ pus ut apārīk nabānazdišt pat ēn kū ka ōy mart (11) xvāstak pat stūrīh ō man dāt hē man nē kart tā ān stūrīh pātixšāy būt hē (12) mart ān stūrīh yut hač framān ī katak-xvatāy pat rāh ī nabānazdištīh kunišn enyā nē (13) kart pātixšāy hend ān stūrīh nē kunēnd. Būt kē guft kū frazand ut nabānazdišt ī (14) ān mart ī andar ān ē ka-š ān xvāstak paytāk kart ut ēt čē pas hač ān būt hend (15) nē pātixšāy hend bē ka (sardārīh) kunēnd ut yuttar nē bavēt čiγōn ka ātaxš nišānēt ayāp (16) xvāstak ruvān rāδ paytāk kunēt ut pus ut apārīk nabānazdišt nē pātixšāy hend bē ka-š (17) sardārīh kunēnd.

45, 17—46, 2:

Ut ka mart-ē(v) xvāstak pat stūrīh ō katak-xvatāy dahēt katak-xvatāy (1) bē patigīrēt (ōy ut pus) ī pātixšāyīhā ī katak-xvatāy pas hač ān naxvist zāyēt ka dātastān ōγōn ⟨ī⟩ (2) pat ān stūrīh andar apāyēt ān stūrīh nē pātixšāy bē ka (sardārīh) kunēnd.

46, 2—4:

Ka ātaxš pat (3) stūrīh nišānēt ut (ō) ātaxš vizand ī pat sazišn rasēt ōγōn sahēt kū pēš-ič (4) hač apāč nišāst ī ātaxš stūr nē gumārišn.

46, 4—9:

Vāyayār nipišt kū ka mart xvāstak (5) 60^+ rāδ kart kū-m harv 2 sāl sāl ī nazdist stūrīh ut sāl ī ditīkar ruvān rāδ paytāk (6) kart ut ān xvāstak kas dāštan rāδ framān nē dāt murt u-š pus 1 ut duxt 1 (7) hast ut anī kas nēst pat ān xvāstak fratom duxt pat stūrīh bē gumārišn ut harv (8) 2 sāl ī nazdist pat stūrīh duxt ut sāl ī ditīkar pat ruvān pus dārišn ut duxt hamē(v) (9) stūrīh ut dūtak ut ān xvāstak sardār pus.

45, 8—17:

If a man has declared the transfer of a thing for *stūr*ship, and (if) he has no daughter but he has a son from a *pātixšāyīh*-marriage, and if no disposition was made by him regarding the transfer of this thing to the (*stūr*'s) possession of a specific person; then — unless there is a disposition from the head of household (to the effect that) it shall be exercised in agnatic line — neither the son nor any other agnate, no one of them — is entitled to exercise this *stūrship* on the strength of the following declaration made by him: "even (if) this man had transferred this thing to me for *stūr*ship, I would not have become (his) *stūr* until (the acceptance of — *A. P.*) the *stūr*ship had become lawful", and they shall not exercise this *stūr*ship. And (the authorities) have stated (this opinion): that the son and nearest agnates of this man — both those whom he had at the time of the declaration (= the institution of the *stūr*ship — *A. P.*) and those who appeared subsequently — are not entitled (to receive this *stūr*ship — *A. P.*) unless they fulfill (the obligations of guardian over the disposer's family — *A. P.*). And this is equivalent to (the case where) someone sets up a Fire-altar or declares the transfer of a thing (as a foundation) "for the soul", and neither the son nor any of the nearest agnates of this person is entitled (to become its trustee — *A. P.*) unless they act as ("are") guardians (of the endower's family — *A. P.*).

45, 17—**46**, 2:

If a man transfers a thing for *stūr*ship to a head of household (and) the head of household accepts, (then he and) the first (son) born thereafter to the head of household from a *pātixšāyīh*-marriage are not entitled (to exercise) this *stūr*ship — (even) if the decision regarding the acceptance of this *stūr*ship was "it es needed" — unless they fulfill the obligations (of guardian over the family of the person who instituted the *stūr*ship — *A. P.*).

46, 2—4:

If (anyone) sets up a Fire on a *stūr*ship (= on the endowment set up for a *stūr*ship — *A. P.*) and destructive damage is wrought to (this) Fire, then (the matter) stands thus: no *stūr* shall be appointed until the Fire (altar of temple) is rebuilt (= reinstated).

46, 4—9:

Vāyayār has written that if a man declares the following regarding a thing (valued at) 60 (*satērs*): "I have declared (this thing transferred) every two years: in year one — for *stūr*ship, in year two — as a foundation 'for the soul'", and he dies without having given instructions regarding the transfer of the rights of possession/the trust of this thing to anyone, and he has a son and a daughter and no one else; then the daughter must first be appointed *stūr* as regards this thing. And (in the course of) every two subsequent) years: (in) the first ("nearest") year — the daughter shall hold it as a stūr's possession, and (in) the following year — (this thing) shall be in the possession (= under the trust) of the son as a foundation "for the soul". And the daughter always (acts as) *stūr* and the son as guardian of the family and trustee over this thing.

46, 9—12:

U-š ēn-ič guft kū ka kart kū-m ēn xvāstak (10) harv 2 sāl ēv sāl pat stūrīh dāštan ⟨dāštan⟩ ō Mihrēn dāt u-š zan ut frazand (11) ut anī xvāstak nēst stūr-ē(v) pat ham xvāstak bē gumārišn ut harv 2 sāl ēv+ sal stūr⟨īh⟩ (ī) (12) gumārtak ut ēv+ sāl stūr ī kartak dārišn.

46, 12—14:

Apāk ān ī-š gyākē nipišt kū ka kunēt (13) kū-m hač 10 sāl frāč ēn xvāstak pat stūrīh ō tō dāt ā-š tā 10 sāl stūrīh pat(14)īrānēnēt nikerītan.

46, 14—15:

Gyākē nipišt kū pat zan hamdātastān būt hend kū tan (15) stūr ut zēnīk stūr harv ⟨ōh⟩ 2 ōh bavēt.

46, 15—17:

Ka kunēt kū-m ēn xvāstak pat stūrīh (16) dāštan ō 3 mart dāt hast kē ōγōn gōβēnd+ kū šāyēt čē avēšān harv 3 (17) mart hamdātastān bavišn.

46, 17:

⟨Ut⟩ mart-ē(v) ut zan-ē(v) ō dūtak-nāyišn ka hamdātastān nē bavēnd...*

47, 1—2:

...] (l) ut mīrend hast kē pus hast kē [duxt ī mas hast kē] duxt ī pas zāt čē pat būtakīh (2) ō duxt ī pas zāt rasēt **.

47, 2—4:

Ka Mihrēn xvāstak 60 harv 2 sāl ēv+ (3) sāl pat xvēšīh ō Farraxv dahēt Farraxv ut Mihrēn harv dō anandarz pat baxt šavēnd (4) u-šān zan ut frazand ut anī xvāstak nēst harv 2 stūr gumārišn.

47, 4—7:

Ut ka pat ān aδvēnak (5) kart ēstēt ut Farraxv ut Mihrēn harv 2 žīvandak hend Mihrēn apāk Farraxv ēn rāδēnišn (6) nē bavēh kū baxtīk ut bahr ī man nāmčištīktar paytāk kun būt kē guft kū (7) ōγōn bavēt čiγōn xvāstak 60 ī pat 2 mart xvēš.

---

* The article breaks off here.

** This is the end of an article whose beginning has not been preserved.

46, 9—12:

And he (= Vāyayār) has also said this: if he has made the following declaration: "I have conveyed this thing as a *stūr*'s possession to Mihrēn for one year out of every two", and he has neither a wife, nor any other property; then one (additional) stūr shall be appointed for this thing. And in every two year (span), (this thing) shall be: one year — in the possession of the *appointed stūr* (= the one appointed by a judge or by the agnatic group of the deceased — *A. P.*), and (the other) year — in (that) of the *instituted stūr* (= the one instituted by the deceased himself, *i. e.* Mihrēn — *A. P.*).

46, 12—14:

In addition he (= Vāyayār) has written in one place that if (someone) makes (the following) declaration: "after the passage of ten years this hing is conveyed by me to you as a *stūr*'s possession ('for *stūr*ship')", then care must be taken that (or: "it must be looked into whether" — *A. P.*) until the ten years have elapsed, the *stūr*'s possession is kept by him (= is preserved by the institutor of the *stūr*ship — *A. P.*).

46, 14—15:

It is written in one place that all were in agreement as regards a wife: she can become both a *tan stūr* and a *zēnīk/dēnīk stūr* (*cf. infra* **48**, 10—12; see Glossary, *s. v. stūr*).

46, 15—17:

If he declares the following: "I have given this thing as a *stūr*'s possession to three persons", (then) some say that (this) is possible inasmuch as all three persons are in agreement (with it).

46, 17:

If a husband and wife disagree over (questions regarding) the management of the family...*

47, 1—2 **.

47, 2—4:

If Mihrēn conveys a thing (valued at) 60 (*satērs*) to Farraxv as his personal inheritance-share for one year out of every two, (and if) both Farraxv and Mihrēn die without leaving a will and without having a wife or children or any other estate, a *stūr* shall be appointed for both (= for each one of them).

47, 4—7:

If the disposition is formulated in this manner (*cf. supra* **47**, 2—4), and if both Farraxv and Mihrēn are alive, and if the transaction between Farraxv and Mihrēn was not such (= as is presupposed by the following declaration — *A. P.*): "make a division and declare my share more precisely!"; then, as some have asserted, this is identical with the case of a thing belonging (jointly) to two persons.

47, 7—11:

Vāyayār nipišt kū (8) ka mart-ē(v) xvāstak pat stūrīh ī xvēš paytāk kart ut pat dāštan harv 2 sāl ēv sāl (9) ō Farraxv ēv+ sāl ō Mihrēn dāt Farraxv ut Mihrēn yut-yut pat ān xvāstak *yō hē* (10) *pasčaēta* ōh bavēt čē ēt-ič patixšāy (ut) ka frāč hač xvēš bē dahēt yut-yut xvēš+ (Ms.: NYŠH < NPŠH) (11) pat-iš kart xvap čē ēt-ič pātixšāy.

47, 11—12:

Ka bē ō zan ō dahēt *yō hē pasčaēta* ān (12) bavēt ī pat ān sāl zāyēt ka-š stūrīh pat ō zan pat ān sāl kunišn.

47, 12—14:

Ka-š (13) stūrīh pat-iš ēstēt ka hač kust ī būtak bē bavēt andar būtakīh pat xvēšīh bē (14) ō mart-ē(v) rasēt hač ēn kust pat xvēšīh ut hač kust ī dit pat stūrīh ravēt.

47, 15—**48**, 2

Ka Āturfarnbaγ xvāstak 200 pat ⟨pat⟩ stūrīh ō Mihrēn dahēt ut Mihrēn ān xvāstak (16) nēm pat stūrīh ī Āturfarnbaγ ō Farraxv dahēt ut pas hač ān Farraxv ut Mihrēn frazand (17) zāyēt ān xvāstak rāδ framān nē dahēnd ut pat baxt šavēnd ān xvāstak vitart avēšān (1) ō frazand ī Mihrēn ut nē bē o frazand ī [Farraxv] rasēt. Ut (ō frazand ī) Farraxv+ (Ms.: Mihrēn) bē čiγōn tā žīvandak (2) ut ān xvāstak nēm bar barēt dastaβarīh būt enyā-š pas hač ān stūrīh nēst.

48, 3—7:

Pit xvāstak pat stūrīh ō duxt ī čakar ī apurnāy kē apar sardār frāč hač xvēš dahēt (4) ut ka duxt purnāy bavēt sardār anī-č mart bavēt. Būt kē guft kū ka dātastān (5) ōγōn ī pit ī čakar stūr andar apāyēt ut ān sažāktar hamdātastānīh ī sardar ī pas andar nē apāyēt (6) ut ka yuttar ōγōn bavēt ka yut hač dastaβar ō zanīh ut stūrīh ī kasān kartan šut (7) hē.

47, 7—11:

Vāyayār has written that if someone has made a declaration regarding the transfer of a thing for his *stūr*ship and has conveyed it alternately, for one year out of the two — to Farraxv and for the next ("one") year — to Mihrēn, then Farraxv and Mihrēn, each of them separately, become *stūr*- (possessors) as regards this thing; for this is permissible. And if — in a case of transfer at his death — he conveyed the title to the personal possession of this thing (*i. e.* in a case of ordinary transfer unconnected with the institution of a *stūr*ship — *A. P.*) to each of them singly, then (it) is lawful, for this too is permissible.

47, 11—12:

If he transfers (a thing) to his wife (for *stūr*ship; a transfer with an alternating regime of real right; *cf. supra* **46**, 4—8; **46**, 9—12; **47**, 2—4; **47**, 9—12), then the legitimate succession to the *stūr*ship shall pass to him/her whom (the wife) bore in the year in which she exercised the function of *stūr*.

47, 12—14:

If he obtains a *stūr*'s title (to a thing) then, if it came to him in the line of ("on the side of") "natural" calling (to the *stūr*ship; *i. e.* if he is a "*natural*" *stūr* — *A. P.*), (this thing) is held by the man on the basis of a personal inheritance-share. It shall come according to the regime of inheritance-share — if it is in this line ("on this side") of calling, and according to the regime of ("as") a *stūr*'s possession — (if it is) by way of another calling [37].

47, 15—**48**, 2:

If Āturfarnbaγ conveys a thing (valued at) 200 (*drahms*?/*satērs*?) to Mihēn for *stūr*ship (= as a *stūr*'s possession) and Mihrēn conveys half of this to Farraxv for the *stūr*ship of Āturfarnbaγ, and children are subsequently born to Farraxv and Mihrēn, and both of them die without leaving dispositions regarding the thing; then this thing must pass after their death to the descendant (= daughter) of Mihrēn and not to the descendant (= daughter) [of Farraxv]. (And) after this (*i. e.* after the death of Farraxv — *A. P.*) (the descendants) of Farraxv have no title to the given *stūr*ship (= the stūrship of Āturfarnbaγ), except if his title to the *stūr*ship was for life, and the thing brings only half of the revenue.

48, 3—7:

A father conveys a thing for *stūr*ship on the occurrence of his death to (his) minor daughter from a *čakar*-marriage whose guardian he is, but when the daughter comes of age another man is her guardian; the opinion has been given that if the decision (rendered in this case) is that a *stūr* for the *čakar*-father is indispensable, and (if) this (*čakar*-daughter) is the most suitable person, then the consent of the subsequent guardian is not necessary (for her assumption of the *stūr*ship). In another case, however, this (= the absence of the guardian's consent — *A. P.*) is equivalent to her entering into a marriage or becoming someone's *stūr* without the participation of the entitled person (= her guardian).

48, 7—10:

Mart andar ān šahr kū pat uzdehīkīh pat baxt šavet stūr ut dūtak sardār ōh gumārišn (8) ut andar ān šahr kū-š xvāstak ka-č xvat nē mat ēstēt kār-framān nēst pat kār-framān (9) gumārtan apāyēt. Yutdātastānīh pat-iš uzdehīkīh kē stūr ut dūtak sardār gumārišn (10) mānišn nē āmār.

48, 10—12:

Mart žīvandakān dūtak (stūr) ōh bavēt čē pat zan hamdātastān būt hend (11) kū tan stūr ut žēnīk stūr harv 2 ōh bavēt ut apurnāyak murt-ič pit dūtak⟨īh⟩ (stūrīh) ōγōn čiγōn nūn-ič čē-š (12) čiš-ič čiš yuttar bē nē bavēt.

48, 12—13:

Ka šōy pat zan stūrīh ō xvāhišn kart (13) pēš tā gumārēnd šōy bē mīrēt zan pat ān stūrīh bē gumārišn.

48, 13—16:

Ka (14) anšahrīk 1 ō Farraxv mat Farraxv nēm āzāt kart ut apārīk pat xvēšīh ō Mihrēn dāt (15) stūr ōh gumārišn. Būt kē guft hač vahmān apastāk ētōn paytāk kū Farraxv (16) sažāktar ut pat-ič xvēšīh hamgōnak.

48, 16—17:

Ka stūr ut dūtak sardār gumart ut ān ī sažāktar (pas) hač ān (17) mīrēt (ān) ī pas hač ān zāt stūrīh nē sardārīh bē kanišn ut pat sardārīh ān ī sažāktar...*

49, 1—2:

[... ... ...] pus rasēt [... ... ...] kē andar [... ... ...]īk (?) pat 7 bahr (2) ō pusarān ēv+ bahr ō ān duxt rasēt **.

49, 2—3:

Zan ī čakar ka barvar ā-š ayōγēn apar (3) ōh bavēt (ut) tā dāt ī 70 sālak pat barvar dārišn.

* The article breaks off here.
** Only the very damaged ending of this article has survived.

48, 7—10:

A *stūr* and a guardian (for his) family must be appointed for a man in that *šahr* (or "town") in which he died while in a foreign land. And a manager must be appointed in the *šahr*/town in which his estate is located in the case that there is no manager (of this estate) — even if he does not appear there personally (for that purpose). In a conflict of opinions as to who is to be appointed as his *stūr* and as guardian of the family in the foreign land (in such a case), the fact of (the candidate's) residing (elsewhere — *A. P.*) does not matter.

48, 10—12:

And (a wife) can (likewise) be the family *stūr* during the man's life, for all (authorities) were in agreement as regards a wife that she can be both a *tan stūr* and a *zēnīk/dēnīk stūr*. (As regards) a minor (daughter), even after her father's death the matter of (her father's) family *stūr*ship shall remain the same as it is now, since in such a case nothing is altered. (*cf. supra* **46**, 14—15; see *Glossary*, *s. v. stūr*).

48, 12—13:

If a husband has (formally) claimed a *stūr*ship for his wife, and he has died before she was appointed, then the wife shall be appointed to this *stūr*ship (= the one claimed for her by her husband).

48, 13—16:

If Farraxv received one slave and Farraxv freed one-half of him (from servitude) and transferred the other (= the non-manumitted half of the slave — *A. P.*) to Mihrēn as an inherited possession ("in personal ownership"), then (should the slave die without a successor — *A. P.*) a *stūr* shall be appointed for him. Some have said that it is evident from such a regulation (or "from the *Avesta*") that Farraxv is the person most suitable (for the *stūr*ship of the half of the slave manumitted by him) as well as for (that half) which is the personal ownership (of Mihrēn — *A. P.*).

48, 16—17:

If someone is appointed *stūr* and also guardian of the family, and (this man) who is most suitable (= the nearest agnate of the deceased — *A. P.*) dies after this, then the *stūr*ship is not (taken away) from (the daughter/son) born (from this man) after this, but the title to the guardianship must be taken away ("destroyed") and the one most suitable (shall be appointed) guardian...*

49, 1—2 **

49, 2—3:

If she is able to bear children ("is fertile"), a *čakar*-wife may become the *stūr-epikleros* (of her *čakar*-husband) [38]. And she is to be considered as able to bear children until the age of seventy [39].

49, 3—6:

Ka mart zan ī-š pātixšāy(4)īhā ⟨zan⟩ rāδ stūrīh xvāhēt ō ān stūrīh hilišn. Būt kē guft (5) kū-š sardārīh ī ān zan būtakīhā čē-š hač sardārīh bē nē hilišn. (6) Ut būt kē guft kū-š gumārtakīhā ut pat kartak ōγōn dārēnd kū-š būtākīhā.

49, 7—8:

Ka duxt ī apurnāyak rāδ stūrīh xvāhēt sardārīh hač patvand ī ōy bavēt kē-š (8) pat stūrīh gumārēnd pus rāδ ētōn vēš gōβēnd kū sardār pit bavēt.

49, 8—10:

Gyākē (9) nipišt kū ka mart xvāstak pat stūrīh ō mart-ē(v) ayāp ō zan dahēt apāč (10) statan pātixšāy.

49, 10—12:

U-š bōžišn ēn guft kū ka xvāstak pat stūrīh bē dahēt (11) ut pas-ič apām stanēt ut mīrēt xvāstak pat ān apām apāč āβarišn. Ut būt (12) kē guft apāč statan nē pātixšāy.

49, 12—15:

U-š bōžišn ēn guft kū ka ⟨pat⟩ xvāstak (13) pat stūrīh bē dahēt ut pas apām stanēt ān kē ān xvāstak avi-š dahēt pas-(14)ič hač ān xvāstak bar barēt dastaβarīhā ut ka xvāstak pat ān apām nē bavandak aδak-ič (15) bar apāč nē āβarišn.

49, 15—17:

Hač Rāt-Ōhrmizd bē ōγōn guft kū ka zan (ī) Āturfarnbaγ (16) pat xonsandīh ī Āturfarnbaγ stūrīh (ī) Mihrēn pat xvāhišn dārēt ka dātaβarān aparmat (17) kart hač ān ē ka dātaβarān aparmat kart frāč stūr ī Mihrēn ut xvāstak avi-š ōh apaspārišn.

50, 1—3:

U-š ēn-ič guft kū [ka gōβēt kū ēn xvāstak tā 10 sāl pat stūrīh Zanbūt hēβ] (2) dārēt ut Zanbūt andar 10 sāl frazand zāyēt ān xvāstak pat xvēšīh bē ō ān frazand (3) rasēt.

49, 3—6:

If a man claims a *stūr*ship for his wife from a *pātixšāyīh*-marriage, then (the *pātixšāyīh*-marriage) must be dissolved because of this *stūr*ship. Some (authorities) have said that he (continues to be) the *natural* guardian of this woman, since he is not obliged to free her from his guardianship. (This opinion) has also been given that he is the *appointed* guardian (*i. e.* that he may remain the guardian of his wife from a *pātixšāyīh*-marriage when she assumes a *stūr*ship only if he is appointed to that position — *A. P.*), but according to procedural regulations (or "norms") he is held to be the *natural* guardian.

49, 7—8:

If he claims a *stūr*ship for his minor daughter, then one of the kinsmen (of the deceased) to whose *stūr*ship she is being appointed shall become her guardian. (As for the case where the father claims the *stūr*ship) for (his minor) son, most (authorities) say this: the father continues to be (his) guardian.

49, 8—10:

If is written in one place that if a man conveys a thing as a foundation for *stūr*ship to a man or a woman, then he may obtain the thing back.

49, 10—12:

And he has formulated this decision: if he conveys a thing for *stūr*ship and subsequently receives (money) as a loan ("debt") and dies, then the thing must be returned for (the settlement of) the debt. Some (authorities) have said that (it) cannot be received back.

49, 12—15:

And he has formulated this decision: if (a man) conveys a thing for *stūr*ship and subsequently receives (money) as a loan ("debt"), even after that the person to whom he conveyed this thing is entitled to take the fruit (= revenue) and is not bound to return it, even in the case where (this) thing is insufficient for (the settlement of) the debt.

49, 15—17:

The following has been said with a reference to (the authority of) Rāt-Ōhrmizd: if Āturfarnbaɣ's wife says claim to Mihrēn's *stūr*ship with Āturfarnbaɣ's consent, she becomes Mihrēn's *stūr* (only) after the judge has announced (his) decision and from the moment that the judge has announced (his) decision, and the thing (= the foundation for Mihrēn's *stūr*ship) shall be conveyed ("entrusted") to her.

50, 1—3:

He (= the commentator) has also said this: [if he makes the following declaration: "let Zanbūt"] possess [this thing as (a foundation) for *stūr*ship during the course of (the next) ten years"], and during (these) ten years Zanbut has a son; then this thing shall pass to this son as his personal inherited possession (= as a son's share in his father's estate — *A. P.*).

50, 3—4:

Ka apām hač āturān ut ātaxšān stūr nē gumārišn ⟨ut⟩ čē pat apām ī (4) āturān ut ātaxšān hilišn dāt būt nē šāyēt ut xvāstak (pat ān) apām bē apaspārišn.

50, 5—6:

Gyākē nipist kū mart ka hambun-ič ast-ē(v) nē bavandak pat stūrīh šāyēt u-š (6) xvat-ič stūr ōh gumārišn.

50, 6—7:

Ut apāk anī nipišt kū mart-ē(v) pat vas stūrīh šāyēt (7) nikerītan.

50, 7—12:

Ka xvāstak pat stūrīh ō zan-ē(v) (ut) mart-ē(v) dahēt hast kē ōγōn guft kū (8) ka xvāstak 2 stūrīh hast stūr 2 ōh bavēt ēvak ziyānak ut apārīk mērak dārišn (9) ut ka ēv stūrīh hast ziyānak apāk mērak dārišn. Ut hast kē ōγōn gōβēt kū ka 2 (10) stūrīh hast aδak-ič stūr ēvak bavēt ut ziyānak ut mērak dārišn ut hast kē ōγōn gōβēt (11) kū ka ēv stūrīh hast ziyānak dārišn bē ēvar kū ān zan pātixšāy ka zanīh (ī) (12) ān mart nē kunēt.

50, 12—13:

Gyākē nipišt kū ka xvāstak pat stūrīh ō zan-ē(v) ut mart-ē(v) (13) dahēt ka zan mīrēt xvāstak apāč ō ān mart rasēt.

50, 13—17:

Aparakīk(ān) gōβēnd kū⁺ ka-š (14) pit pat apurnāyīh pat stūrīh bē dahēt ka ō purnāyīh rasēt nē pātixšāy bē ka-š (15) apar ēstēt. Mēṯō⟨k⟩māhīk(ān) gōβēnd kū⁺ Mēṯō⟨k⟩māh guft kū ka ō purnāyīh mat ham pus (16) ut ham duxt pātixšāy ka-š apar nē ēstēt ut Veh-Ōhrmizd guft kū⁺ tā ō purnāyīh rasēt (17) stūrīh pat apurnāyak hamē(v) rasēt.

50, 17:

(Hač)? Pēšakser gōβēnd kū⁺ pus pat pusakānīh ut duxt * (pat duxtakānīh ēvāč pit pātixšāy dāt)... .

* The article breaks off here. The phrase in parentheses is reconstructed from the presumed sense of the context.

50, 3—4:

If (the deceased received) a loan ("debt") from Fire temples or altars, then a *stūr* shall not be appointed [40]; since in cases of indebtedness to Fire temples and altars, the remission of the debt cannot be granted/take place, and the estate (of the deceased) must be conveyed (to the temple-creditor — *A. P.*) in settlement of the debt.

50, 5—6:

It is written in one place that if (a man's estate) fails by (only) a small amount to reach (the minimal value for a *stūr*ship foundation — *A. P.*), the man is entitled to convey it for *stūr*ship, and (in such a case) he shall appoint the *stūr* himself.

50, 6—7:

In addition to this it is written that a man may accept several *stūr*ships (= in contrast with a woman, he is entitled to serve simultaneously as *stūr* for several persons — *A. P.*). This should be noted.

50, 7—12:

If (he) conveys a thing for *stūr*ship to a certain wife and husband, then, according to the opinion of certain (authorities): if a thing is encumbered with a dual *stūr*ship, there must be two *stūrs* — the wife shall hold one *stūr*ship and the husband, the other. But if there is one *stūr*ship(= if the *stūr*ship is single), then the wife shall hold it together with her husband. And there is also the opinion that a single individual becomes *stūr* even in a dual *stūr*ship, and (either) the wife (or) the husband may hold it. And some say that if this is a case of single *stūr*ship, then the wife must hold it; however, it is (absolutely) clear that (in such a case) this woman is entitled to cease being that husband's wife.

50, 12—13:

It is written in one place that if (he) conveys a thing for *stūr*ship to a (certain) wife and husband (jointly), then, should the wife die, the thing (conveyed for the *stūr*ship foundation) returns to that man (= to the person who conveyed the thing for *stūr*ship or to his family — *A. P.*).

50, 13—17:

The followers of Aparak say that: if a father hands over a son ("him"/daughter ("her") as *stūr* (for some person) when (they are) not of age, then upon coming of age, he/she is not entitled (to act) otherwise than to become *stūr*. (But) the followers of Mēt̠ō⟨k⟩māh (= Meδōmāh) assert that, as was said by Mēt̠ō⟨k⟩māh, that son and that daughter are entitled not to become *stūr* when they come of age. Veh-Ōhrmizd has (likewise) said that a *stūr*ship goes to a minor (only) for the period until he comes of age [41].

50, 17:

It is said, with a reference to the *Čāštak* of Pēšaksēr, that (only a father is entitled to give) a son and a daughter (for adoption)...*

51, 1—2:

(....................)*īh bahr (2) ēstēt vēš uskārtan ut nikerītan apāyēt.

51, 2—6:

Katak-xvatāy pus ut duxt hamvaxš [pat] (3) [Varahrān]īh(?)/[baxtīk]īh(?) kunēnd ut pas xvāstak ō dūtak dahēnd. Pusānveh guft kū-[šān] (4) [āṭ]axš/[ham]ṿaxš pat ākanēn xvēš čē ātaxš ka-š bahr sūtōmandtar bahr ōyōn čiyōn [.....] (5) [ut ka-š dāš]tārīh sūtōmandtar dāštārīh apāyēt dāt ⟨ī⟩ ut hakar-iš bahr ōyōn [čiyōn] (6) [pus?] 2. Ān čē ō dūtak rasēt čiyōn pus xvēš xvēš apāyēt būt.

51, 6—12:

Ka [pat] (7-8) [dūtak bē] pus 1 ut katak-bānūk kas nēst ut dastkart-ē(v) pat hamdātastānīh bē ō mart ī šahr dahend [ut pas] (9) [katak-bānūk pus]-ē(v) zāyēt pat Čāštak ī Mēṭō⟨k⟩māh guft ēstēt kū ka bē [pat] (10) [hamdātastānīh ī pus nē] ka pat hamdatastānīh ī [pus dāt xvap] u-š čiš-ē(v) andar nēst (11) [... katak]-bānūk frazand zāyēt ayāp pus ī (mas?) pēš hač katak-bānūk pat baxt šavēt ut pas [hač] (12) [ān stūr] apāyēt gumārtan a-mān nē kart ēstēt.

51, 12—16:

Ut gyākē nipišt kū [apar] (13) [bahr ī] katak-bānūk ān čē-š bē dāt (ut nē) apar bahr ī pus ān ī-š bē ⟨nē⟩ būt ōh zāyēt (14) [ut ka ka]tak-bānūk ut duxt ēv⁺ pat dūtak ut naxvist duxt šōy kunēt ut pas hač katak-bānūk [frazand] (15) [zāyēt] Vahrām guft kū apar bahr ī duxt nē zāyēt čē duxt ka-š šōy kart (16) [bahr] ō xvēšīh ī dūtak ī ka-sān mat.

* There is a lacuna of some fifty characters. This is the end of an article whose beginning was to be found on one of the missing folios of the manuscript.

51, 1—2 *

51, 2—6:

A head of household, (his) son and daughter declare the entire profit ("increment") [42] conveyed to a Varahrān-fire (or: "carry out a division of the common increment/profit"), after which, property ("a thing") is conveyed to (this) family (from the side): as has been said by Pusānveh (in such a case), the Fire (or "the increment/profit") belongs to them jointly; for if it is more advantageous for the Fire that they (= the members of the family) be paid ("be given") a share (= the institutor's share; *cf. supra* **27**, 9—12 — *A. P.*) then such a share corresponds to (= acts on the same basis as)... [... ... ...] [but if what is more advantageous is main]tenance (= the pay-rations assigned to a trustee — *A. P.*), then maintenance shall be provided ("given"). And if a share is paid, then (it is apportioned) as (though there were) two [sons] (in the family) [43]. Whereas the property which came (subsequently) to the family (from the side), shall be (acquired) as the personal (inheritance)-share of the son.

51, 6—12:

If there is no one [in a family] except for one son and the mistress of the house and (they) convey a *dastkart* by joint agreement to a certain fellow-citizen (= a member of the same community), [and subsequently] [another (son)] is born [to the mistress of the house], it is said in the *Čāštak* of Meδōmāh that (if the transaction concerning the *dastkart* was concluded) without [the consent of the son (= the elder, *i. e.*, of the son whom the mistress of the house already had at the time — *A. P.*), then it is invalid]; but if [(the *dastkart*) was conveyed] with the consent [of the son — then this is lawful] and there is nothing in this (= the birth of the second son, that casts doubt on the legality of the transaction — *A. P.*). [... ... mistress] of the house bears a son, or (if the elder?) son predeceases the mistress of the house and after [that a *stūr*] must be appointed, (then), the one not having reached maturity (?) shall not be appointed ("made").

51, 12—16:

And it is written in one place that he (= the second son; *cf. supra* **51**, 6—12 — *A. P.*) shall inherit [the share] of the mistress of the house, the one conveyed to her (from the estate of the head of household — *A. P.*), (and not) the share of the son whom she had (at the time that the inheritance of the head of household fell open — *A. P.*). [But if] the family consists (only) of the mistress of the house and one daughter, and first the daughter marries, and later the mistress of the house [bears a son], Vahrām has said (of such a case) that (the son) does not inherit the daughter's share [44], because after the daugher's marriage [her share (of the inheritance)] passed into the ownership of another family.

51, 16—**52**, 15:

Ka katak-bānūk ut pus ut duxt ī purnāy ut apurnāy [ān] (17) [gyāk] hambāγ hend ut pus ī purnāy ayāp duxt 1 pat baxt šavēt xvāstak bahr ī ōy apāč [ō] (1) ēn hakar pat(?) [(... ... ...) * pat baxt] (2) šavēt pat stūrīh ayāp pat xvēšīh ō ān ī sažāktar rasēt (ut hakar) apurnāyāk [andar apurnāyākīh pat] (3) baxt ⟨pat⟩ šavēt pat Čāštak ī Mēṯō⟨k⟩māh (bahr ī ōy) pat katak-bānūk ēstēt ut pat ān ī Aparak [... ...] (4) hamaδvēn u-š kartak ān ī Mēṯō⟨k⟩māh. Ka hambāγ baxtīkīh kunēnd ut pur[nāy ut] (5) apurnāy ākanēn bahr stanēnd ō ān ī purnāy ut apurnāy xvāstak dahēnd ān ī ō [apurnāy] (6) ēt rāδ ka apurnāyak vindišn dūtak xvēš bē ō dūtak rasēt ut ān ī ō p[urnāy] (7) ēt rāδ čē-š hambāγīh ī apāk apurnāyak yuttar nē būt ēstēt nēm-ē(v) bē ō [ōy ut nēm-ē(v) ī] (8) hač apurnāyak bē ō dūtak rasēt ētōn čiγōn Aparak [guft] (9) harv čē+ (Ms.: MNW = kē) pat dūtak ētōn čiγōn Mēṯō⟨k⟩māh guft katak-bānūk dārišn [N. guft kū ka] (10) pus ut duxt pat dūtak hend u-šān katak-xvatāy xvāstak bahr ī [pusīh ut duxtīh] (11) ut zanīh bē dahēt ut vitart mērak hač katak-bānūk+ frazand zāyēt [ut pas xvāstak ō dūtak] (12) dahēnd frazand apar bahr ī katak-bānūk zāyēt ut ān xvāstak ō dūtak dah[ēnd Pusānveh ī] (13) Āzātmartān guft kū pat katak-bānūk ut frazand ī pas hač katak-bānūk zāyēt ē[stēt man-ič] (14) pat ēt dārom kū ēt rāδ ētōn čē-š pus andar katak-bānūk pat kas dār [... ... ...] (15) Mēṯō⟨k⟩māhīkān-ič hamgōnak gōβēnd.

52, 15—17:

Ka katak-bānūk ut pus ī purnāy ut apurnāy pat dūtak baxtīkīh (kunēnd ut) ēvak pat baxt šavēt [Pusānveh] (16) guft kū bahr ī ōy pat katak-bānūk ut frazand ī pas hač katak-bānūk ⟨zāt⟩ zāyēt. (17) (Hač)? Pēšaksēr-ič hamgōnak gōβēnd. Ka-č pit ō zan ut frazand xvāstak pat bahr (bē dahēt...) **.

53, 1—3:

(...) *** rāδ pat baxtīkīh kartan nē apāyēt patkārēnd bē ka avēšān kē baxtīkīh xvāhēnd (2) avēšān apurnāyakān ut armēštan hač xvāstak hammis sardārīh kunēnd enyā baxtīkīh kartan (3) nē pātixšāy.

* There is a lacuna of over fifty characters.
** The article breaks off here.
*** The beginning of this article is missing.

51, 16—**52**, 15:

If in a family the mistress of the house, the sons and the daughters — (both) those of age and the minors — are partners, and (if) a son who is of age or one of the daughters dies, then his (or "her") share of the estate returns ... ...* dies, then as a *stūr*'s possession or as a personal inheritance-share (it) shall go to the one (of them) who is most suitable. (But if) a minor [before having reached his majority] dies, (his share in the family estate) shall pass to the mistress of the house according to the *Čāštak* of Mētō⟨k⟩māh, and, according to the *Čāštak* of Aparak [... ... ...] similarly; and judicial practice (in this case follows the *Čāštak*) of Mētō⟨k⟩māh (= Meδōmāh). If the partners/co-heirs divide (the estate) and one [of age together with] a minor receive a common share, and (if) a thing is conveyed (from the side — *A. P.*) to the one who is of age and the minor, then that which (is conveyed) [to the minor] shall go to the family inasmuch as his income belongs to the family as long as he is a minor, whereas that which (has passed through the transfer — *A. P.*) [to the one who is of age] falls under the following *régime* inasmuch as he is the partner of a minor: one half [shall go to him, whereas the other half (of the conveyed thing) — the one (to be acquired by his minor partner — *A. P.*)] — shall pass from the minor to the family, as this [has been said] by Aparak. And the mistress of the house shall possess all that passes to the family, as was said by Meδōmāh. [(Commentator N — *A. P.*) has said that: if] in a family there is a son and a daughter, and the head of household conveys to them [a son's, a daughter's] and a wife's share, and (if) the mistress of the house bears a son after the death of her husband, [after which a thing] is conveyed [to the family] (from the side — *A. P.*), then (this) son shall inherit the share of the mistress of the house. (As regards) the thing which was (subsequently) conveyed to the family, [Pusānveh ī] Āzātmartān has said that it [shall] belong to the mistress of the house and to the son born to the mistress of the house after (the apportionment of the estate by the head of household — *A. P.*), [and I] also consider that this (should be) so, because the son as regards the mistress of the house [... ... ...]. And the followers of Meδōmāh say the same.

52, 15—17:

If a family consists of the mistress of the house, a son who is of age and a minor son, (and) they divide (the estate), (after which) one (of the sons) dies: [Pusānveh] has said that his (= the deceased son's) share shall pass to the mistress of the house and to the son (= child) born to the mistress of the house after (the division). The same is said (on the authority)? of Pēšaksēr. But if the father (transfers) the estate as shares to his wife and children...**

53, 1—3:

... ...*** are in litigation over (... ... ...), a division shall not be carried out; then — unless those demanding the division exercise guardianship over the minors and invalids (in that family) and guardianship over their estate — the division is not lawful.

XXXVIII *

53, 4:

Ēn dar ī hambāγān ut hamxvāstakān čiš vičārtan.

53, 4—6:

Hambāγ kē apām⁺ (Ms.: NKSY' = xvāstak) ut vaxš ī pitarān (5) vičārišn hamaδvēn yut hač xvāstārīh bē vičārt guharīkān hač hambāγān apāč xvāst (6) pātixšāy.

53, 6—10:

Ka mart apām ī pitarān kē⁺ vaxš nēst bahr ī xvēš pat patigriftan⁺ frāč (7) dārēt ut ān kē-š avi-š dahišn gōβēt kū tā apārīkān vičārēnd nē patigīrom ka apārīk-ič (8) bē vičārēt guharīkān hač hambāγān apāč xvāst nē patixšāy. Ka gōβēt kū apārīk-ič bē (9) vičārēnd patigīrom ut apārīk-ič bē vičārēt hač hambāγān apāč xvāst pātixšāy čē ka-š (10) guft kū bē vičār aδak-iš xvāstārīh kart bavēt.

XXXIX

53, 11** :

Dar ī nēm bahr ut arž ī andar xvāstak kē pašt apar kunēnd.

53, 12—13:

Ka gōβēt kū-m ēn xvāstak nēm ō tō dāt arž ōγōn bavēt čiγōn andar ān ē ka (13) xvāhēt.

53, 13—15:

Ka gōβēt kū-m ēn xvāstak nēm ō tō dāt tā dahēt⁺ pātixšāy ka (14) nē paytākēnēt ut ka paytākēnēt bar pātixšāy burt ut tā-č bar hamē(v) barēt vizand ī pat avināsīh ī (15) rāt ō bun rasēt ō harv 2 nēm mat bavēt.

* This article carries the (*abǰad*) ordinal-number 38.

** The (*abǰad*) ordinal-number of this chapter — 39 — is placed in line 10.

XXXVIII *

53, 4:

This is the chapter concerning the settlement of a debt with partners (= co-heirs) and joint-debtors (= *correi*; persons jointly responsible).

53, 4—6:

A partner/co-heir who without awaiting legal action ("before a claim takes place") has fully settled all the financial obligations of the (late) *paterfamilias* ("of the fathers") — both the debt itself and the interest — is entitled to demand the equivalent (of the expenses born by him; *cf. supra* **2**, 4—6) from the (other) partners/co-heirs.

53, 6—10:

If a man delays (= puts off) the assumption of his share (in the payment) of a non-interest-bearing debt of the late *paterfamilias*, and to the one to whom he should pay ("give") he declares the following: "until (all) the others (the co-heirs — *A. P.*) pay, I shall not accept"; then — (even) if (another co-heir) pays all the rest — he is not entitled to claim a compensation from the co-heirs. But if he declares: "(if) the rest is also paid, I shall accept", and (another) pays the rest, then he (= the one who paid) is entitled to claim a compensation (for his expenses within the limits of each one's share in the common debt — *A. P.*) from his partners/co-heirs; for if he said "pay!", he has thereby presented a claim.

XXXIX

53, 11 **:

Chapter concerning a half-share and the value of a thing regarding which there is a transaction (=agreement).

53, 12—13:

If he declares: "I have conveyed one-half of this thing to you", (then) the value (of the thing) is determined in accordance with the value (of the thing) at the time that (the latter) claims his share.

53, 13—15:

If he declares: "I have conveyed one-half of this thing to you", then (the latter) is allowed not to make a declaration (regarding his acceptance of the transfer) until (there is) an act of transfer. But if that one (= the acquirer) makes a declaration, he is entitled to take the income ("fruits"). And as long as he takes the income (*i. e.* as long as he receives an income from one-half of the thing after having declared his acceptance of it, whereas the thing remains in the hands of the transferer — *A. P.*), any (damage) wrought to the thing itself ("the principal") through no fault of the conveyer (shall be taken as damage) to each of the two halves of the thing.

53, 15—54, 2:

Čiγōn ka gōβēt kū-m 3 bahr ēv bahr (16) ō tō dāt čē ka bahr gōβēt aδak-iš ēn patkārišn andar hast kū-š abaxt dāt (17) bavēt pēšēmār+ (ka) mat ⟨ī⟩ (ut) kart ēstēt kū pit xvāstak pat 3 bahr ēv bahr ō man dāt (1) u-š xvāstārīh pat-iš kart ēstēt dātaβarān ōγōn čiγōn ka abaxt dāt ēstāt (2) hē vičīr kartan bē apāyēt+ (Ms.: apaspārēt) ut bē dātaβar vičīr nē kartan.

54, 2—5:

Pat guft ī Vāyayār (3) nipišt kū ka gōβēt kū ēn xvāstak 3 bahr ēv bahr Mihrēn xvēš hēβ bavēt u-š (4) abaxt apāk nē guft ētōn bavēt čiγōn ka-š nēm-ē(v) dahēh ut kāmak pat rāt. Ut anī (5) gyākē nipišt kū ka-š pat bahr dahēt abaxt dāt bavēt.

54, 5—11:

Ka Farraxv apāk (6) Mihrēn patmān kart kū uzīt+ rōč vāhmān ka ān xvāstak nē vičārt ēstēt xvāstak (7) ī tō gōβēh čand ān xvāstak vahāk aržēt ān xvāstak rāδ tō xvēš Mihrēn pat xvāstak ka+ (8) bar ⟨ī⟩ 13 aržēt ut pat bavandak nē pa(z)zāft pat-iš mih ēstēt gōβišn gōβēt. Ut ān xvāstak andar ān ē (9) ka patmān kart bar pat-iš nē būt ut ān drahm frēh nē aržist (N. guft) kū nūn guharēn ōγōn bavēt (10) čiγōn andar ān ē būt. Syavāxš guft kū bar bē nē šavēt čē ka ōγōn xvāstak pat (11) arž ī 13 frēh hamē(v) gīrēt.

54, 11—15:

Ka Farraxv apāk Mihrēn patmān kart kū xvāstak ī man xvēš (12) ut tō gōβēh (čand) arž 200 vahāk aržēt to xvēš Mihrēn pat čand anšahrīk ī andar ān ē apurnāyak pat ākanēn (13) 200 aržist ut nūn yut-yut 200 aržēt sahišn gōβēt hač ān čiγōn nē arž ī šahr (14) bē tan ī xvēš veh bē kartan rāδ arž aβzūt nē pat arž ī andar ān ē bē pat arž ī nūn (15) apaspārišn ut gōβišn kār nēst.

53, 15—**54**, 2:

As when he declares: "I have conveyed to you one-third share", (and) inasmuch as he has said "share" the following disputable (factor) is present, namely that the share is conveyed to him without a division (having been made); if the plaintiff comes (to court) and declares: "(my) father has given to me one-third share of a thing/estate" and he presents a claim for it, then the judge shall render a decision (in accordance) as though (the share of the thing/estate) had been given without a division, and no decision may be taken without a judge.

54, 2—5:

It is written from the words of (= with a reference to — *A. P.*) Vāyayār, that if he declares: "let a third share of this thing/estate belong to Mihrēn", and on this occasion he has not said (the word) "undivided", then this is equivalent to the case where he (= the conveyer) were to transfer one-half and there was willingness (on the part of the receiver — *A. P.*) (to accept) the gift. But in another place it is written that if he conveys (the estate) as a share/by share, then (the thing) is conveyed undivided (= without division, as an ideal share).

54, 5—11:

If Farraxv concludes the following agreement with Mihrēn: "if no payment is made (for) this thing (= the debt is not settled) by such-and-such a day, then (any) thing of equivalent value (belonging to me) that you name shall belong to you on account of it ('this thing' = 'the debt')". And Mihrēn makes the declaration (in court — *A. P.*) with regard to the thing (loaned): that the income from it is equivalent to 13 (*drahms*) and (the thing) has not been fully redeemed and he objects (to this compensation — *A. P.*). But at the time of the agreement this thing brought no income (= fruits) and was not worth this addition to its price. (N has said) that the compensation now (shall be) equivalent to its (= the thing's) value at that time (= at the time that the agreement was concluded). Siyāva(x)š has said that the income (= the fruits) is not to be taken into account, since, in the opposite case, he (= the creditor) shall take a thing valued at 13 (*drahms*) more (than that stipulated in the agreement — *A. P.*).

54, 11—15:

If Farraxv makes the following contract with Mihrēn: "whatever you choose ("name") that has a value of 200 (*drahms*) (from) the estate belonging to me, shall belong to you". And if Mihrēn declares his agreement to the receipt (= the transfer to him) of several slaves who were minors at that time and valued at 200 (*drahms*) altogether and who now are valued each separately at 200 *drahms*, then — since their value has grown because of their (= the slave's) bodily improvement (*i. e.* the minors are now fully grown — *A. P.*) and not because of a conjunction of prices in the town/*šahr* — the transfer shall be made in accordance with their present value and not with what they were worth at the time of the drawing up of the contract. And the declaration (made by Mihrēn regarding his agreement to receive several slaves — *A. P.*) is not in force.

54, 15—17:

Ka gōβēt kū-m xvāstak nēm ō tō dāt pat ān arž ī (16) andar ān ē ka xvāhēnd dahišn+ čē pātixšāy ka-š ān nēm abaxt dahēt ut ka-š abaxt (17) dahēt arž ōγōn bavēt čiγōn andar ān ē ka xvāhēnd.

54, 17—55, 1:

Ka gōβēt kū-m xvāstak pat arž [ī] (1) 250 ō (tō) dāt pat ān arž dahišn ī (andar) ān ē ka gōβēt.

55, 1—3:

Pat guft ī dastaβarān nipišt (2) kū ka gōβēt kū ēn xvāstak ēt bahr ⟨ī⟩ to xvēš hēβ+ bavēt kartak ōγōn apāk kū-š tan (3) xvēš hač miyān bē āβurt bavēt xvāstak hamaδvēn avi-š+ bē rasēt.

55, 3—7:

Ka gōβēt (4) kū xvāstak ī man xvēš ut xvāstak ō xvēšīh ī man rasēt čans arž+ 200 vahāk aržēt (5) tō xvēš ut ān xvāstak kē kāmak apar dōšīt ast-ē(v) andar ān ē ka-š gōβišn guft xvēš (6) būt ut ast-ē(v) pas hač ān mat ān ī andar ān ē xvēš pat arž ī andar ān ē ka gōβišn guft (ut) ān ī (7) pas hač ān mat pat arž ī andar ān ē ka mat paytāk kunišn.

55, 7—8:

Ka zamīk ēv kartak rāδ gōβēt (18) kū pat+ 3 ēvak ⟨ī⟩ tō xvēš pat kartak ōγōn kart kū arž ⟨ī⟩ marīhā dāt bavēt.

XL*

55, 10:

Dar ī hampāyandānīh ut pāyandānīh ut hambāγīh.

* The (*abǰad*) ordinal-number of this chapter — 40 — is placed in line 9.

54, 15—17:

If he says: "I have conveyed ("given") one-half of a thing to you", then the transfer shall be made in accordance with the value (of the thing) at the time that (this half) is claimed. Because he can (also) give this half without a division ("undivided"), and if he gives it undivided, then the calculation must be made in accordance with the value of the thing at the time that it is claimed.

54, 17—**55**, 1:

If he declares: "I have conveyed (to you) (any — *A. P.*) thing having a value of 250 (*drahms*)", then the transfer (= the receipt of the thing by the receiver) shall be made in accordance with the calculation of its value at the time that he (= the conveyer) made (his) declaration.

55, 1—3:

It is written with a citation of the commentators ("from the words of; in accordance with the statement of the commentators") of the *Avesta*, that if he declares: "let this part of a given thing belong to you!", then this is the precedure in such a case: should that (= the part of the thing) which (continues) to belong to (= remains with) him (= the conveyer) be destroyed, the thing shall pass totally to that man ("him" — the receiver) [45].

55, 3—7:

If he declares the following: "a (share) valued at 200 (*drahms*) shall belong ("belongs") to you from the estate that belongs to me (now) and from the estate that will belong to me (in the future)", and if one part of the estate which he (= the receiver) declares his willingness to receive (consists of) what (already) belonged (to the conveyer) at the time of the declaration of transfer, and the other half (consists of) what passed to him later, then the value of the share which (already) belonged (to the conveyer) is determined in accordance with (its) value at the time of the declaration of transfer, whereas (the value of) the share which passed to him (= the conveyer) later is determined ("shall be declared") in accordance with the value (of this share of the estate) at the time that (these things) passed into the ownership (of the conveyer — *A. P.*).

55, 7—8:

If he makes (the following) declaration regarding a plot ("piece") of land: "one-third (of it) belongs to you", then according to the procedure (or "in the procedural regulations") it is laid down (or "formulated") thus: (the share of the plot) is conveyed in accordance with its value (*i. e.* the value of the share of the plot to which the title of the acquirer is being established must be equivalent to one-third of the value of the entire plot — *A. P.*).

XL*

55, 10:

Chapter concerning joint warranty, warranty, and partnership.

55, 10—11:

Ka gōβēt kū mart 2 pat ākanēn 200 ō man dahišn (11) ākanēn kār ētōn framūt ēstēt kū rāst.

55, 11—13:

Ka gōβēt kū mart 2 200 hač man apām stat (12) gyākē nipišt kū magupatān magupat guft kū hamaδvēn hač mart 1 bē xvāstan pātixšāy čē (13) dārišn ākanēn barēnd ⟨Vahuman⟩ hamxvāstak hend [46].

55, 13—17:

Ka gōβēt kū mart 2 hač man apām stat (14) pat ēn šōn frāč guft čiγōn ka-šān ākanēn stat hānd⁺ u-š pat andāčak ēn gōβēt (15) kū ka gōβēt kū ēn xvāstak mart 2 xvēš ut nē gōβēt kū-šān pat ākanēn xvēš būt (16) kē guft kū ka⁺ nē paytāk kū čand ōy ut čand ōy pat⁺ yāvar-ē(v) kār ētōn framūt ēstēt (17) kū rāst xvēš.

55, 17—56, 5:

Ka gōβēt kū mart 3 hač man apām stat (ut) patmān kart kū (1) hampāyandānān hēm hač harv kē kāmēt pātixšāy xvāst gōβēnd kū [Dāt]-Farraxv ⟨ī⟩ guft (2) kū ka ⟨ō⟩ harv 3 attān hend aδak-ič hač harv kē kāmēt pātixšāy xvāst (ut) ōy kē bē vičārēt (3) bahr ī ōy ī dit pātixšāy hač ōy ī dit xvāst ut ka hampāyandān nē bē gōβēnd⁺ kū hač harv kē (4) kāmēt pātixšāy (xvāst ut) ka ⟨ō⟩ hamāk ēvak bē vičārēt aδak-ič hač ōy ī dit nē pātixšāy (5) xvāst.

56, 5—8:

Ka gōβēt kū-m pat ēn xvāstak vāhmān mart pāyandān kart rāh (6) ō pāyandān pat ān zamān bavēt ka mērak anattān ayāp nē mat ēstēt ut ka pāyandānīh (7) yut hač hamdātastānīh ī ōy kē vičārišn kunišn ka xvāstak vičārēt ētōn bavēt čiγōn ka (8) apēdastaβar vičārēt u-š apāč nē rasēt.

55, 10—11:

If he declares: "two persons must jointly transfer 200 (*drahms*) to me", then (the expression) "jointly" has the force of the injunction "equally".

55, 11—13:

If he declares: "two persons received 200 (*drahms*) from me as a loan ('debt')", it is written in one place that he is entitled to claim the entire sum ("in full") from one of these persons, as was said by the *magupatān magupat*, because — inasmuch as the possession (received as a loan — *A. P.*) is theirs jointly ("they hold the possession jointly") — they are jointly-responsible (individuals; that is *correi* — *A. P.*).

55, 13—17:

If he declares: "two persons have received money from me as a loan ('debt')", then what is said thereby is as though they had received (this money) jointly. And, as proof, he (= the commentator) says the following: if (anyone) declares that: "the given thing belongs to two persons" but does not by the same occasion say: "it belongs to them jointly", the opinion has been given that — if no declaration has been made that so-much (belongs) to one and so-much to the other — (the expression) "jointly" (lit. "at the same time", "simultaneously") acts as a disposition to the effect that (the thing) belongs to them equally.

55, 17—56, 5:

If he declares: "three (persons) have received (money) from me as a loan ('debt') (and) have concluded the agreement (that): 'we are co-warrantors'", then he is entitled to claim (the settlement of this debt) from whichever (of them) he pleases. It is said that [Dāt]-Farraxv said that if all three are solvent, he is entitled to claim (the settlement of the debt) from whichever of them he pleases in this case too, and he who settles (=in full — *A. P.*) the share of the other one (in the common debt) is entitled to claim it from that person ("the other one"). But if (they) did not (say): "we are co-warrantors", but it was said (that): "he is entitled (to claim the settlement of the debt) from whichever he pleases", then if one pays everything (= for everyone), he is not entitled to make a claim from another (within the limits of his share of the debt).

56, 5—8:

If he declares: "I have made/declared such-and-such a man guarantor as regards a given thing (= money, debt)", then the reversion (from the creditor) to the guarantor shall take place in the occurrence that the principal debtor ("man") proves insolvent or does not appear (to settle the debt). And if the guarantor pays the money (= settles the debt) without the consent of the debtor, then this is equivalent to his paying without being empowered, and (in such a case) he shall not receive a compensation (from the debtor for his expenses).

56, 8—12:

Gyākē nipišt kū ka gōβēt kū-mān (9) xvāstak apām stat (ut) hampāyandān hēm ayāp gōβēt kū pat ān xvāstak ēvak ut ōy ī dit (10) hampāyandān hēm attānīh ut nē attānīh ī ōy ī dit pat tōžišn vičārtan ut mat ēstēt (11) nē mat ēstēt ī ōy ī dit nē hamār čē hač harv kē kāmēt xvāst pātixšāy ut ōy kē hač-iš (12) xvāst hač ōy ī dit bahr apāč rasēt.

56, 12—15:

Ka gōβēt kū ēn xvāstak duxtak čiγōn (13) purnāy bavēt ut Farraxv pat ākanēn xvēš hēβ bavēt ētōn dānom kū ēt rāδ ka pat ākanēn (14) xvēš nipišt ēstēt ō-č Farraxv pat ān zamān rasēt ka duxtak purnāy bavēt (15) čē pat ān zamān xvēš šāyēt būt.

56, 15—17:

Ka mart-ē(v) apāk mart-ē(v) patmān kunēt kū man (16) pāyandānīh ī văhmān rāδ xvāstak and ō tō dahom ka ān patmān hamē(v) kartan (17) xonsand aδak-iš rāh ō pāyandān u-š apāč ō bun nē bavēt.

56, 17—57, 2

Pusānveh ī Āzātmartān (1) ōγōn guft kū ēt ka gōβēnd^{+} kū hampāyandān hēm tā ka gōβēnd^{+} kū pat ēn xvāstak (2) văhmān mart pāyandān hēm ka mātakvar attān rāh ō pāyandān nēst.

57, 2—12:

Vahrīč guft (3) kū-m āšnūt kū Āturparzkar guft kū ka-m bē ō xvārastān (4) kāmist šutan zan mart^{+} (?) 3 pat rāh nišast (būt) hend. Ut ēvak guft kū (5) ōstāt ēn dātastān hēβ bē vičār ka mart 2 xvāstak apām stānēnd ut gōβēnd kū (6) hampāyandānān čiγōn. Ut man guft kū mātakvar attān rāh ō pāyandān nē bavēt. U-š (7) pas guft kū ka ēvak apām stanēt ut ān ī ditīkar gōβēt kū-š pat ēn xvāstak (8) pāyandān hom čiγōn bavēt. Ut man guft kū ēn-ič hamgōnak bavēt. U-š pas guft (9) kū nūn mātakvar anattān bavēt ut hač pāyandān tōžišn xvāhēt (ut) pas mātakvar ō tuvānīkīh (10) rasēt. Ut man bē ēstāt hom u-m pa(s)saxv guftan nē dānist. Ut pas ēvak (11) guft kū ōstāt ma handēš u-š vistāxvīhā pa(s)saxv kun kū nē dānom. (12) Hač ān ī moγān (h)andarzpat vičīr kart ut ō pēš nipišt paytāk.

56, 8—12:

It is written in one place that if he declares: "we have received a thing (= money) as a loan ('debt') (and we are co-guarantors", or if he declares: "(both) of us, one (as well as) the other are co-guarantors as regards this thing", then the solvency or insolvency of the other, as regards the settlement of the financial obligation, just as the appearance or non-appearance of the other (on the date stipulated for the payment — *A. P.*) are not taken into consideration, for he (= the creditor) is entitled to claim (the settlement of the entire debt — *A. P.*) from whichever of them he pleases. And the one against whom he (= the creditor) laid the claim shall receive from the other (co-guarantor) (the latter's) share (in their common indebtedness).

56, 12—15:

If he declares (the following): "let this thing belong jointly to (my) daughter when she comes of age and to Farraxv", then I understand this in the following manner: inasmuch as it is written: "(let it) belong jointly", (then) Farraxv, too, shall obtain it (only) when the daughter attains her majority, for (only) then may (this thing) belong to her.

56, 15—17:

If one person concludes the following agreement with another: "I shall convey to you such-and-such a sum ("so much") under the guarantee of such-and-such a person", and if (both sides express — *A. P.*) their acceptance of the conclusion of this agreement, then (the creditor) shall be entitled to address his claim (directly) to the guarantor, and he does not have the right to address his claim to the principal contractor (= the debtor).

56, 17—**57**, 2:

Pusānveh ī Āzātmartān has spoken in this fashion: if he makes use of the formula: "we are joint-guarantors", or even if he declares: "we are guarantors for such-and-such a person as regards a given sum of money (= a thing, a debt)"; then if the principal contractor (= the debtor) is solvent, (the creditor) is not entitled to address (his claim) to the guarantor.

57, 2—12:

Vahrīč has said: "I have learned that Āturparzkar has said the following: (Once upon a time) when I was going to the ordeal court, three women were sitting by the road. And one of them said: "Master, decide this legal case. If two persons receive money (= 'a thing') (separately — *A. P.*) as a loan and declare that they are joint-guarantors, then how shall it be?" And I said: that if the principal contractor (= debtor) is solvent, then no claim may be addressed to the guarantor. And then she said: "and if one receives (the money) as a loan and the other declares: 'I am the guarantor as regards this money ('thing'), what then?'" And I said that this case too is resolved likewise. Ans she then said: "well, now what if the principal contractor is insolvent and (the creditor) claims the payment from the guarantor, but subsequently the principal contractor becomes solvent?" And I stood and did not know what answer to give. And then one (of the women) said: "Master, do not hesitate but say truthfully ("confidently") — 'I do not know'!" (But the answer to this question) is evident from the decision rendered by the *(h)andarzpat* of the Magi, and (regarding which) it is written below (*cf. infra* **59**, 1—10 — *A. P.*).

57, 12—14:

Ka gōβēt kū-m (13) Farraxv pat tan hač tō grift ut ēn nē gōβēt kū-š apāč apaspārom tuvān guftan kū-t (14) dārišn ō man (apāč) nē apaspārt.

57, 14—16:

Ka Ōhrmizd rōč Farraxv ut Vahuman rōč (15) Pusak andar Āturfarnbaγ kart kū-m Mihrēn pat tan hač tō patigrift pāyandānīh harv 2 (16) xvap.

57, 16—**58**, 3:

Ka Ōhrmizd rōč Farraxv ut Vahuman rōč ka Mihrēn kart kū-m tā ēv sāl Farraxv (17) pat tan hač Āturfarnbaγ patigrift tā ēv sāl. Ut ka gōβēt kū-m Farraxv pat tan hač (1) Āturfarnbaγ ⟨i⟩ patigrift hač ān čiγōn dārišn+ (Ms.: xvāhišn) ī tan sāl drahnāδ hač ān ē ka [xvāhēt] frāč tā (2) ēv sāl bavandak bavēt ka tan nē mih ēstēt pātixšāy ka apāč nē apaspārēt (3) ut ka tan mih ēstēt apāč apaspārišn (ut) Āturfarndaγ nē pātixšāy bē ka apāč patigīrēt.

58, 4—9:

Ka Farraxv apāk Āturfarnbaγ patmān kunēt kū hakar ka tō Mihrēn xvāhēh Mihrēn (5) ō tō apaspārom enyā 200 bē dahom ut pas Āturfarnbaγ Mihrēn hač Farraxv xvāhēt ut Farraxv (6) Mihrēn nē apaspārēt hakar Farraxv pat apaspārtan ī Mihrēn atuvānīk ut pat ān atuvānīkīh (7) avinās ka-č pas ō tuvānīkīh rasēt tan nē apaspārišn ut 200-ič nē (dahišn) hakar-iš guft (8) kū-m patigrift ka-č pat ān aδvēnak atuvānīk bē bavēt aδak-ič čiγōn ō tuvānīk(īh) rasēt (9) tan apāč apaspārišn.

58, 9—14:

Ka Farraxv Mihrēn pat tan hač Āturfarnbaγ apāč patigīrēt (10) Āturfarnbaγ hakar ka xvāhēt Farraxv Mihrēn apaspārēt enyā pātixšāy ka pat guharīkānīh (11) ī Mihrēn Farraxv griftār kunēt. Ut ka Farraxv yut hač xvāhišn ī Mihrēn pat tan (12) hač Āturfarnbaγ apāč patigīrēt Farraxv Mihrēn bē hišt pātixšāy ut tā dārēt pat dāštan (13) ut tā+ (Ms.: 'MT-ka) xvāhend pat-ič kart dāštan pātixšāy ōγōn čiγōn Āturfarnbaγ-ič būt ut ka bē (14) hilēt tā xvāhēnd yut hač xonsandīh ī Mihrēn apāč apaspārtan nē pātixšāy.

57, 12—14:

If he declares: "I have received Farraxv from you, as a slave (*i. e. servi loco — A. P.*)", without saying in addition: "I shall return him", (then in this case too, the person conveying Farraxv to him) may (address a claim to him and) declare: "you have not returned my possession to me".

57, 14—16:

If Farraxv concludes the following agreement with Ātufrarnbaγ — on the day Ōhrmizd, and with Pusak — on the day Vahuman (*i. e.* on the following day — *A. P.*): "I have received Mihrēn from you, as a slave", (then) the warranty of both of them is valid.

57, 16—**58**, 3:

If Farraxv made the following declaration on the day Ōhrmizd, and Mihrēn — on the day Vahuman: "I have received Farraxv as a slave (= *servi loco — A. P.*) from Āturfarnbaγ for the term of one year", then the term (of validity of the title of possession of the given slave, for the one as for the other) is one year (from the day of each one's declaration of acceptance — *A. P.*). And if he declares: "I have received Farraxv from Āturfarnbaγ, as a slave", then — inasmuch as the term for the possession of the slave is of one year — he is entitled not to return him (to Āturfarnbaγ) from the time [that the demand] (of Āturfarnbaγ for the return of the slave) took place and up to the expiration of the one year (term), if the slave does not object. But if the slave objects, he shall be returned, and Āturfarnbaγ must take him (= the slave) back (lit. "Āturfarnbaγ cannot but receive him back").

58, 4—9:

If Farraxv concludes (this) agreement with Āturfarnbaγ: "as soon as you claim Mihrēn (= the name of the person pledged to the creditor as a slave — *A. P.*), I shall hand over ("reintrust") Mihrēn to you, or I shall pay 200 (*drahms*)", and Āturfarnbaγ then demands Mihrēn from Farraxv, but Farraxv does not hand Mihrēn over; (then) if Farraxv is unable to hand Mihrēn over and this inability is not his fault, he need not hand over the slave nor the 200 (*drahms*) even if he subsequently becomes able (to do so). But if he (= Farraxv?) declared: "I have accepted", then even if his inability is the same (*i. e.* though no fault of his own — *A. P.*), he must return the slave as soon as he is able (to do so).

58, 9—14:

If Farraxv receives Mihrēn from Āturfarnbaγ, as a slave (= *loco servi*) once again, then — if Āturfarnbaγ makes a claim — Farraxv must hand Mihrēn over, otherwise (Āturfarnbaγ) shall be entitled to seize Farraxv (himself) in compensation ("exchange") for Mihrēn. But if Farraxv receives Mihrēn from Āturfarnbaγ, once again as a slave, against Mihrēn's will, then Farraxv is entitled to let Mihrēn go [or: "release Mihrēn (from pledge)" — *A. P.*]. And as long as he (= Faraxv) possesses him, he is as entitled as Āturfarnbaγ himself to possess him and to dispose of him, until such a time as he (= Mihrēn) is claimed from him (= Farraxv). And if he lets him go (= releases him from pledge) before he is claimed, he is not entitled to return him without Mihrēn's consent.

58, 14—16:

Ka (15) Farraxv ⟨ut⟩ Āturfarnbaγ pat tan hač mart-ē(v) apāč patigīrēt vitart-ič Farraxv xvāstakdārān ī (16) Farraxv Āturfarnbaγ apāč apaspārišn.

58, 16—**59**, 1:

Yut hač zan ut anšahrīk ut apurnāyak ⟨ut⟩ apārīk-ič (17) ān ī hač ān šōn čiγōn bē ka paytāk attān hend enyā pat anattān dārišn. (1) Bē ka paytāk kū anattān hend enyā pat attān dārišn.

59, 1—10:

Māhvindāt guft (2) kū ka Farraxv man ut Mihrēn tō hač Āturfarnbaγ apām stānēm ut patmān kunēm⁺ kū ēvak ōy ī (3) dit pāyandān hēm ā-š kār ēn kū Āturfarnbaγ ka Farraxv anattān ā-š pat man rāh (4) ō Mihrēn ut ka Mihrēn anattān ā-š pat tō rāh ō Farraxv. Ka gōβēnd kū hampāyandānān (5) hēm ā-š ēn guft bavēt kū hamtōžišn hēm u-š attānīh ut anattānīh nē (6) āmār. U-š ēn-ič guft kū ka ōγōn gōβēnd kū ēvak ōy ī dit pāyandān hēm (7) ut Farraxv anattān bē bavēt ut Āturfarnbaγ pat tōžišn apāk Mihrēn rāδēnišn kunēt (8) ut pas Farraxv ō tuvānīkīh⁺ rasēt Āturfarnbaγ pātixšāy ka rāδēnišn bē hilēt (9) ut apāč ō rāδēnišn ī Farraxv ēstēt apar ēn vāčak čiγōn-am pat nipištak dīt (10) Vehpanāh čē moγān (h)andarzpat būt vičīr hamgōnak kart.

XLI*

59, 11:

Dar ī xvāstakdārīh

59, 12—16:

Pus ka-š xvāstak ī pitar drahm 1 pat aparmānd grift (ut) dāšt hamāk tōžišn ī (13) pitar bavēt ut pēšēmār tōžišn hač harv kē kāmēt xvāst pātixšāy ut ōy kē hač-iš (14) xvāst bē bahr ī xvēš apārīkān hač hambāγān apač rasēt bē ān ī pat nīrmat ī (15) katak-xvatāy ēstēt ayāp ān kē ka-š tōžišn hač-iš xvāhēnd hač hambāγān apāč (16) rasēt enyā hač ēvak nē pātixšāy xvāst.

59, 16—**60**, 1:

Ut ka pus ēvāč ēvak anōδ u-š (17) pit xvāstak dahēt gyākē nipišt kū harv čiγōn-iš dahēt pat ⟨pat⟩ xvāstakdārīh (1) dāt bavēt.

---

* The (*abǰad*) ordinal-number of this chapter — 41 — is placed in line 10.

58, 14—16:

If Farraxv receives Āturfarnbaγ from a certain person, as a slave (= *loco servi*), then on the occurrence of Farraxv's death, Farraxv's heirs shall give Āturfarnbaγ back.

58, 16—**59**, 1:

In addition to a woman, a slave, and a minor, others from the same category are also to be considered insolvent unless it is evident that they are solvent. Except for the cases where they are unquestionably insolvent, they should be considered solvent.

59, 1—10:

Māhvindāt has said the following: if Farraxv and I (on one side) and Mihrēn and you (on the other) take money as a loan ('debt') from Āturfarnbaγ and conclude the agreement that we are co-guarantors one for the other (= one pair for the other — *A. P.*), then this is the effect of (such an agreement): if Farraxv proves insolvent, Āturfarnbaγ shall address himself to Mihrēn for a claim against me, and if Mihrēn proves insolvent, then (Āturfarnbaγ shall address himself) to Farraxv for a claim against you. If the declaration: "we are each other's warrantors (warrantors 'one for the other')" has been made, then what has been said is: "we are reciprocally obliged to pay", and solvency or insolvency are not taken into account. And he (= Māhvindāt) has also said this: if this declaration has been made: "we are each other's warrantors (warrantors for each other)" and Farraxv proves insolvent, and Āturfarnbaγ brings a legal action against Mihrēn for the settlement of the debt, then — should Farraxv subsequently become solvent — Āturfarnbaγ is entitled to break off this legal action and bring a claim against Farraxv. This problem was resolved in this fashion by Vehpanāh the (h)andarzpat of the Magi, as I have read ("seen") in the *Nipištak*. (*Cf. supra* **57**, 2—12).

XLI*

59, 11:

Chapter concerning inherited possessions (or "concerning heirs")

59, 12—16:

If a son inherits (merely) one *drahm* of his father's estate and possesses it, then he is liable for his father's entire indebtedness and the plaintiff is entitled to claim the settlement of (the deceased man's) debts from whichever (of his successors) he pleases. And the one from whom he makes the claim shall receive everything back from his co-heirs minus his own share (in the settlement of the debt). Except in the case of the man who has an advantageous (position as against the other heirs) of the head of household [47], or if the one from whom the settlement of the (father's entire) debt is claimed receives back from his co-heirs (the sum laid out for their share of the indebtedness), (the settlement of the entire indebtedness) may not be sought from one of the heirs.

59, 16—**60**, 1:

If there is only one son in a family ("there") and the father has transferred the estate to him, then everything that he has transferred (= everything that the son acquires by transfer from the father — *A. P.*) is given as an inheritance (= as to an heir).

60, 1—2:

[Ut ka pus čand hast u-šān pat ēv yāvar pat ahravdāt xvāstak dahē]t (2) tōžišn bahr marīhā bavēt ut mart-mart ān ī xvēš tōžišn.

60, 2—3:

Ut xvāstak-tōžišn bavēnd ut ka (3) pēš ut pas dāt paytāk hač ān ī pas dāt.

60, 3—5:

Ut ka xvāstak ō čand mart ī šahr pat (4) ēv yāvar pat xvēšīh dahēt hamgōnak čiγōn ān-ič ī pus. Ut ka pat yut bahr dahēt hamgōnak (5) čiγōn ān-ič ī pus.

60, 5—7:

Ut ka ō čand pus pat xvāstakdārīh dahēt ēt+ ka pēš ut pas dahēt (6) ut ēt+ ka pat ēvbār dahēt hamēv hamāk tōžišn hend. Ut ka ō mart ī šahr pat xvāstak(7)dārīh dahēt hamēv xvāstak-tōžišn hend.

60, 7—10:

Ēt ka pus ēt ka mart ī šahr pat (8) 3 gōβišnīh gōβēt kū xvāstakdār hom hamēv xvāstakdār bavēt. Ut ka anattān (9) ut gōβēt kū xvāstakdār hom čiš-ič nē bavēt.

60, 9—10:

Pat apām rāh ō xvāstak bavēt (10) pat aptom bē šut+.

60, 10—16:

Ka pus xvāstak pat xvāstakdārīh grift ut ka (ān ī) bē (11) grift hač ān ī xvēš hammis pat tōžišn nē bavandak bavēt+ hakar andar ān ē tōžišn xvāhēnd (12) ka xvāstak pat xvāstakdārīh bē grift pat ān ī nē bavandak rāh ō xvāstak bavēt ī (13) hač pit aptom bē šut hakar andar ān ē tōžišn xvāhēnd ka-š xvat hač xvāstak pat (14) xvāstakdārīh grift and xvāstak ī andar ān ē ka tōžišn xvāhēnd ōγōn šut ēstēt (15) kū ān ī par(r)ēxt pat tōžišn nē bavandak handōxt pat ān ī pat ān aδvēnak nē bavandak rāh ō (16) xvāstak bavēt ī hač pus aptom bē šut.

60, 1—2:

[And if there are several sons and (the father) transfers a thing for a pious purpose to them at one time (= to all of them together — *A. P.*)], then payment shall be made in accordance with the shares and each of them shall pay his share (of the common debt — *A. P.*).

60, 2—3:

And they are obliged to pay (their late father's debts). And where it is known what was transferred earlier (out of the father's estate) and what later, (then the settlement of the debt should be made starting) from what was transferred later.

60, 3—5:

And when he transfers a thing to several fellow-citizens (= members of the same community) at one time (= together — *A. P.*) as personal possession/(their) own property, then (the decision in this case is) the same as in the case of sons (*cf. supra* **60**, 1—2). And where he transfers a separate share to each, (the decision) is the same as in the case of sons.

60, 5—7:

If he transfers an estate to several (of his) sons as an inheritance, then each of them is obliged to pay (his father-legator's) entire indebtedness — whether he has transferred/bequeathed (the estate) to them separately or has transferred/bequeathed (it) at one time (= to all together). And when he bequeathes a thing as an inheritance to fellow-citizens (= members of the same community), then each of them becomes obliged to pay (the legator's debts, but only within the limits of the legacy acquired by him — *A. P.*).

60, 7—10:

Everyone — be he a son or a fellow-citizen — who has spoken three times the (formula of) declaration: "I am an heir", becomes an heir. And if an insolvent person declares: "I am an heir", then this has no effect.

60, 9—10:

At (the settlement) of a debt, payment should be made (starting) from that thing (lit. "regression takes place to that thing") which was last alienated by (lit. "last left") the debtor.

60, 10—16:

If a son has received an estate (from his father), and if the estate he has received together with the one which is his own (= the one accumulated by him — *A. P.*) are insufficient (for the settlement of the father's debts: a) if settlement (of the debts) is demanded of him at the moment when he receives (his father's) estate as an inheritance, then the claim for the coverage of the deficit (= for the sum lacking to settle the debt) shall bear on the thing of which the father disposed (not in the son's favour — *A. P.*) last (lit. "which went last from the father"); b) but if settlement is demanded of him when he has already disposed in such a fashion of part of the estate received by him as an inheritance (lit. "part of the estate has gone from him in such a fashion") that what remains in his hands ("to him") proves ("adds up" as) insufficient to settle the debts, then the deficit so created shall be covered through a claim bearing on the thing of which the son disposed last ("which went last from the son").

60, 16—**61**, 1:

Aγdēn(ān) nē hamāk tōžišn bē xvāstak[dār] (17) bavēnd. Aγdēnān bē čiγōn-šāh stūr nē gumārišn ut ān čiš ī pat rāh ī zahakīh ut patvand (1) apāyēt [.......... dā]rēnd(?) enyā-šān apārīk dātastān ōγōn čiγōn ān ī vehdēnān.

61, 1—3:

[Pus žīvandakān pit] (2) xvāstakdārīh ī pit ōh bavēt u-š apām tōžišnīh pat and mātak bavēt čand xvāstak (3) dārēt.

61, 3—5:

Katak-xvatāy ka frāč (šavēt) u-š xvāstak ō zan ut frazand ētōn dahēt ⟨ī ka⟩ (kū)-(4)šān pat aparmānd rasēh aδak-šān ētōn bavēh ayāp-šān pat bahr dahēt xvāstakdār (5) bavēnd.

61, 5—7:

Ka andar žīvandakīh xvāstak pat bahr ayāp hamgōnak čiγōn pat aparmānd bavēt dahēt (6) pat ān xvāstak xvāstakdār hend u-šān apām ī pēš hač ān ē ka-š xvāstak bē dāt (7) stat vičārišn u-šān ham and vičārišn čand xvāstak dārēt.

61, 7—9:

Apāk anī nipišt kū (8) pus žīvandakān pit xvāstakdārīh ī pit ōh bavēt u-š apām tōžišnīh pat and xvāstak bavēt (9) čand xvāstak dārēt nikerītan.

61, 9—12:

(Hač)? Pēšaksēr gōβēnd kū mart ī šahr ka-š xvāstak (10) dahēnd bē ka gōβēt kū xvāstakdārīh kunom enyā nē xvāstakdār pus bē ka gōβēt (11) kū nē kunom enyā xvāstakdār mart ī šahr kē$^+$-š (Ms.: MNŠ < MNWŠ) xvāstak pat xvāstakdārīh aviš (12) dahēnd apām ī pēš$^+$ (Ms. 'ḤR = pas) hač dāt ōh apāyēt vičārtan.

61, 12—14:

Duxt ka-š pit xvāstak dahēt (13) bē ka-š pat arž ut xvēšīh dahēt enyā harv aδvēnak čiγōn-iš dahēt bahr dāt bavēt (14) u-š rāh ō ān ī dit nē bavēt.

60, 16—**61**, 1:

Non-believers (= non-Zoroastrians) are not obliged to settle all (the debts of a deceased Zoroastrian-head of household as this must be done by his successors — *A. P.*), (just as) they (also) do not become his heirs. As regards non-believers — except for the fact that they shall not be appointed *stūrs*, as well as for everything which comes/is due in line of direct family succession or (agnatic) kinship [... ... ... they ha]ve (?) — decisions concerning everything else are the same as those for Zoroastrians.

61, 1—3:

[During (his) father's lifetime, a son] may become his father's heir (= a simple heir but not a successor — *A. P.*); and (in such a case) his settlement of his father's debts must be carried out in accordance with the value of the estate that he possesses. (*cf.* the correspondence of **61**, 7—9 with this article — *A. P.*).

61, 3—5:

If a head of household dies having bequeathed his estate to his wife and children as follows: "let it pass to them as my successors ('in succession')!", then they become heirs — whether it was bequeathed to them in this fashion or whether he gave (it) to them as (inheritance)-shares.

61, 5—7:

If (a head of household) transfers (= bequeaths) his estate as (inheritance)-shares in his own lifetime, or as (this) happens, on the basis of succession (*i. e.* as an endowment for his succession — *A. P.*), then they are heirs as regards this estate and are liable for the debts he contracted before the time that he transferred the estate. And they are obliged to pay within the limits of the value of (the) estate which (each of them) possesses.

61, 7—9:

In addition to other (things) it is written that (if) a son becomes (his) father's heir during the father's lifetime, he is liable for (his father's) debt to the extent that the estate in his possession (makes it possible). Take note! (*cf supra* **61**, 1—3 — *A. P.*).

61, 9—12:

It is said, (with a reference to) Pēšaksēr, that if a fellow-citizen (= a member of the same community) does not declare (formally): "I shall be an heir", at the time that a thing is transferred to him, then he does not become an heir. But a son becomes an heir unless he declares (formally): "I shall not be an heir". A fellow-citizen to whom an estate is transferred/bequeathed as an inheritance is obliged to settle the debts (contracted by the previous owner/possessor) before the transfer.

61, 12—14:

If a father (conveys) a thing to his daughter, then — except in the case where he gives it for money ("by value") and in ownership when he transfers it in any other manner, (the thing) is conveyed to her as an (inheritance)-share, and she is not entitled to lay claim to another thing.

61, 14—16:

Pus bē ka-š pat ahravdāt ut xvēšīh dāt⁺ (15) enyā-š pat xvāstakdārīh dāt bavēt bē ka gōβēt kū-m bahr rāδ pat bahr hangārišn (16) hač bahr hangārišn ō tō dāt enyā-š ne bahr rāδ dāt bavēt.

61, 16—**62**, 2:

Vahrām guft kū-m (17) ētōn āšnūt kū-šān pat kartak ōγōn kart kū duxt-ič ētōn čiγōn pus-ē(v) bē ka gōβēt (1) kū-m bahr rāδ pat bahr hangārišn hač [bahr] hangārišn ō tō dāt enyā-[š ... ...] hač ān (2) ōh bavēt.

62, 2—4:

Ut Vāyayār gyākē ōγōn nipišt kū pus ut duxt ka-šān pit xvāstak pat stūrīh (3) avi-š dāt patigīrend aδak-šān aparmānd ōh bavēt ut ka mart xvāstak pat xvāstakdārīh (4) ō mart ī šahr dahēt ut patigīrēt hamāk tōžišn [48].

62, 4—6:

Ka gōβēt kū-m tā 10 sāl ayāp gōβēt (5) kū-m pas hač 10 sāl bahr ī pusīh rāδ ēn xvāstak ō tō dāt bahr ī pusīh fraškartīk (6) dāt bavēt.

62, 6—7:

Ka gōβēt kū-m ēn xvāstak ō pus dāt pat xvāstakdārīh (7) dāt bavēt. Ka gōβēt kū-m pat xvēšīh dāt nē pat xvāstakdārīh dāt bavēt.

62, 8—10:

Dūtak katak-bānūk ka-š pat bahr ut xvēšīh ut ēt⁺ ka-š pat bahr ut stūrīh dahet⁺ aparmānd (9) hamdātastān būt hend kū bē pat rāh ī 2 kasīh enyā-š nē bavēt. Gyākē nipišt (10) kū zan kē šōy xvāstak pat bahr avi-š dahēt bahr vindāt bavēt.

62, 10—12:

Apar Dāta(11)stān-nāmak ōγōn nipišt kū ka xvāstak pat stūrīh ō duxt ī xvēš dahēt ān (12) duxt aparmānd ī hač pitar bē pat rāh ī 2 kasīh nē bavēt.

61, 14—16:

(An estate conveyed by a father) to (his) son is transferred to him as an inherited possession (= as an inheritance) unless he conveyed (this estate) to him as a foundation for fixed purposes of pious character or as (his) own personal possession. Except in the case where the declaration has been made: "I conveyed (it) to you, considering it a share, as an (inheritance)-share, so that it be considered an (inheritance)-share", the estate is not transferred as ("for", "for the sake of") an (inheritance)-share.

61, 16—**62**, 2:

Vahrām has said: I know that they decided in accordance with procedural regulations (or "according to the procedure") that the position of a daughter (in this connexion) is analogous to the (position of) a son. Except where (the father declares: "I have conveyed a thing to you, considering it an inheritance-[share], as an (inheritance)-share, so that it be considered as an (inheritance)-share", [the thing ... ...] (after) this (?) becomes/passes(?).

62, 2—4:

And Vāyayār has written thus in one place: if a son and a daughter accept the estate transferred by (their) father for *stūr*ship, they become his successors [48]. And if a man transfers a thing to a fellow-citizen as an inherited possession, and (the latter) accepts (it), then he is obliged to settle the entire debt of the conveyer.

62, 4—6:

If he declares (the following): "I shall give this thing to you as a son's share (of the inheritance) after a lapse of ten years", or he declares: "I (shall give this thing to you) before ten years have alapsed", then the son's share is conveyed forever.

62, 6—7:

If he declares: "I have given this thing to (my) son", then (this thing) is transferred as an inherited possession. (But) if he declares: "I have given (it) as (your) own possession/as personal property", then (the thing) is not transferred as an inherited possession.

62, 8—10:

(All the authorities) have been unanimous that if (on the occurrence of his death — *A. P.*) (he) transfers an estate to the mistress of the house — either as an (inheritance)-share and as (her) own/personal possession, or as an (inheritance)-share for *stūr*ship — then she may become his heiress only jointly with another person (lit. "*via* two people" = jointly with one of his kinsmen — *A. P.*). It is written in one place that a wife to whom (her) husband transferred a thing as (her) share (in the estate) has acquired the share.

62, 10—12:

It is written thus in the *Dātastān-nāmak*: if a father transfers a thing to (his) daughter for *stūr*ship, then she may become his heiress/acquire his inheritance only jointly with another person (lit. "*via* two people"; *i. e.* when there is another successor in her father's family — *A. P.*).

62, 12—15:

Duxt ka pat dūtak ī (13) pitarān u-š xvāstak ī pitarān pat xvāstakdārīh grift ut dāšt būt kē guft (14) kū tā šōy kunēt ētōn čiγōn pus. Ut ka-š šōy kart ā-š **va-sasə.yānā̆*- pat kār-(15)vindišn nē bavēt bē-š pat rāh ī āgraβīh tōžišn and čand xvāstak dārēt ōh kunišn.

62, 16—**63**, 1:

Pus duxt ut katak-bānūk ānōδ hač katak-bānūk nē bē hač pus ayāp duxt ān kē kamēt xvāst⁺ (17) pātixšāy ut ka hač pus ayāp hač duxt bē xvāhēt ōy kē hač-iš xvāhēt hač hambāγān bahr (1) apāč [stā̆n]ēt.

63, 1—3:

[Katak-bānūk ut duxt] ān xvāstak ī pēš hač ān ka-šān šōy kart pit [ut šōy] (2) apām stat hač pit šōy šāhān šāh ō xvēšīh mat tōžišn ī pit ut šōy bē nē (3) vičārišn.

63, 3—4:

Gyākē nipišt kū ka hač dūtak tōžišn xvāhēnd ut ēvāč duxt 1 pat dūtak hamāk (4) tōžišn ka-š šōy kart ka-č-iš nē kart.

63, 4—5:

Gyākē nipišt kū ka-č pus ut duxt ut katak-bānūk (5) hamahl bavēt xvap ut ka-č yut-yut bavēt xvap ut duxt bahr marīhā tōžišn ut vičārišn.

XLII *

63, 6:

Dar ī xvēš būt guft.

* This chapter carries the (*abǰad*) ordinal-number 42.

62, 12—15:

If there is one daughter in the father's ("fathers'") family, and (if) she has received (a share from) her father's estate as inheritance, and she possesses it, the opinion which has been given (is that) (her position as heiress — *A. P.*) until she marries is equal to (the position of) a son. But if she is married, then she does not have unlimited rights on the use of the income (from the inheritance she has received — *A. P.*; lit. "as regards the income, she is not a taker and disposer as she pleases"); but as regards claims (against her father's debts), she is obliged to pay them within the limits of the estate she possesses (= of the portion she inherited from her father — *A. P.*).

62, 16—**63**, 1:

If there are in a family ("there") a son, a daughter and the mistress of the house, then he is entitled to claim whatever he pleases (out of the father's house) from the son or from the daughter, but not from the mistress of the house. And if he demands (= the settlement of the late father's debt) from the son or from the daughter, then the one from whom he makes the claim shall receive back from (his/her) co-heirs (their) share (in the common indebtedness).

63, 1—3:

[A mistress of the house or ("and") a daughter] is not obliged to convey ("pay") as settlement of her father's or husband's debt that which the father [("and") or husband] received as a loan ("debt") before the marriage (and which then) passed to her as (her) own property (or "as a personal possession") from her father, (or) from her husband, (or) from the King of Kings.

63, 3—4:

It is written in one place that if the settlement (of the financial obligations of the late head of household) is demanded from the family, and (this) family consists of only one daughter, then — whether she be married or not — she is liable for settling the entire debt.

63, 4—5:

It is written in one place that if the son, the daughter and the mistress of the household are partners (in the settlement of the indebtedness of the late head of the family — *A. P.*), then — this is good (= lawful); and if (the settlement) is made separately — this is good. The financial obligations of a daughter (= as regards the indebtedness of the father-*de cuius* — *A. P.*) and their settlement shall correspond to her share (in the common inheritance).

XLII *

63, 6:

Chapter concerning declarations regarding the ownership (of a thing by a certain person).

63, 7—8:

Gyākē nipišt kū ka kart kū ōy kē Mihrēn xvēš būt gōβēt xvēš (8) ut Mihrēn ⟨i⟩ (man) xvēš būt gōβēt gōβišn kār nēst ut nōk gōβišn guftan xvap.

63, 8—12:

Ka⁺ (19) xvāstak 1 nēm Āturfarnbaγ ut apārīk Mihrēn xvēš ut Āturfarnbaγ nēm ēv rāδ kart kū ōy kē Mihrēn (10) xvēš būt gōβēt xvēš gōβišn ka nē ογōn nipēsēt kū-m ān (nēm ī) Āturfarnbaγ ōy kē man (11) xvēš būt rāδ gōβom xvēš būt rāδ guft bē ōγōn nipēsēt kū-m nēm (12) mērak⁺ xvēš būt rāδ guft ān nēm ī-š xvat xvēš dāt bavēt.

63, 12—15:

Ka gōβēt kū ēn xvāstak Farraxv ut ēt kē Farraxv xvēš būt rāδ gōβēt xvēš hēβ bavēt (14) xvāstak ī Farraxv gōβišn apar gōβēt nēm pat Farraxv ēstēt čiγōn gōβišn hakar mart 1 rāδ (15) gōβēt nēm ut hakar 2 mart rāδ gōβēt pat 3 bahr ēv bahr xvēš.

63, 15—17:

(Ka) gōβišn ōγōn gōβēt kū (16) xvāstak ī mērak ōy kē man xvēš būt rāδ gōβom xvēš būt rāδ guft mērak (17) xvēš hēβ bavēt (mērak xvēš).

63, 17—**64**, 2:

Apāk anī gyākē nipišt kū ka gōβēt kū kas kē tō xvēš (1) būt (rāδ) gōβēh xvēš hēβ bavēt [... ... ... xvēš] būt (2) rāδ gōβēt aδak-ič xvap nikerītan.

64, 2—9:

Ka katak-xvatāy andar zan ī pātixšāyīhā vičīr (3) ăvašt kū ēn xvāstak ōy kē tō xvēš būt rāδ gōβēh xvēš hēβ⁺ bavēt (4) ut pas hač ān (h)andarz kunēt ut pat (h)andarz xvāstak ō kas dahēt ziyānak apar (h)andarz bē (5) ēstēt ayāp hač xvāstak apēsaxvan būt ēstēt pas-ič ka ziyānak ān xvāstak (6) kas xvēš būt rāδ bē gōβēt pat ān gōβišn ān xvāstak bē rasēt (ut) apē(7)saxvanīh rāδ yuttar bē nē bavēt tā ka-š ōy kē xvāstak xvēš būt guft (8) ēstēt ān xvāstak apāč avi-š dāt ēt rāδ čē-š pat (h)andarz apar ēstāt (9) ēstēt apar patkārtan nē tuvān.

63, 7—8:

It is written in one place that if (the following) declaration was made: "(the given thing shall) belong ('belongs') to the person whom Mihrēn designates as the possessor (lit.: 'of whom Mihrēn says that it is his')," and (if) Mihrēn declares that he is himself the owner (of that thing); then (this) declaration (made by him) is null and void, and (the possibility granted to him) of making a new declaration is lawful.

63, 8—12:

If one half of a thing belongs to Āturfarnbaγ but the other to Mihrēn, and (if) Āturfarnbaγ made the following declaration regarding one of the halves: "(let it) belong to the one of whom Mihrēn says: it is his", and if he (= the scribe drawing up Mihrēn's subsequent declaration — *A. P.*) writes down not: "I (convey) the (half) regarding which Āturfarnbaγ said that it belongs to the one whom I name as possessor/owner", but "I have declared that half of the thing belongs to (this) man"; then (as a consequence of the second formulation of the declaration), the half (of the thing) conveyed shall be the one which belongs to him (= to Mihrēn — *A. P.*) personally.

63, 12—15:

If he makes the following declaration: "let this thing belong to Farraxv and to the one whom Farraxv names as (its) possessor/owner!", then, as regards the thing concerning which (Farraxv makes a subsequent declaration), half of it shall belong to Farraxv, if he states in (his) declaration that (this thing belongs) to one (other) person, but if he declares that (the thing belongs) to two (other) persons, then his ownership thereof shall be one third.

63, 15—17:

If he makes the (following) declaration: "let the thing — regarding which (this) man declared that it belongs to the person whom I shall name its owner — belong to that man", (then it must belong to the man so designated).

63, 17—**64**, 2:

At the same time it is written in one place that if he makes the (following) declaration: "let it belong to the man whom you name as (its) possessor!", [... ... ...] he declares, that (the thing) belongs (......), then this is valid. Take note.

64, 2—9:

If a head of household has made ("sealed") the following contract with his wife from a *pātixšāyīh*-marriage: "let this thing belong to the one whom you name as its owner", and afterwards he (= the head of household) makes a will and conveys (this) thing through (his) will to some man, whereas the wife is passed over ("remains outside") in the will or is dispossessed ("is recalled, dismissed") of the thing; then, if the wife subsequently makes a declaration concerning the ownership of that thing by (a given) person (other than the one indicated in her husband's will — *A. P.*), this thing shall go (to him) as a consequence of (her) declaration, and the ousting of the wife does not alter the transaction, unless the one whom the wife named as the owner returns the thing on the grounds that he cannot contest (or "challenge") what is laid down ("included, stands") in the will.

64, 9—15:

Rāt-Ōhrmizd guft kū ka Mihrēn gōβēt kū (10) ēn xvāstak ōy kē Farraxv xvēš būt rāδ gōβēt xvēš hēβ bavēt ut pas hač (ān) Farraxv (11) xvāstak-ē(v) bē ō Dāt-Farraxv frōšēt ut patmān kunēt kū hamē(v) ka druvist nē (12) dārom anšahrīk kē Mihrēn ān gōβišn apar guft tō xvēš hēβ bavēt ut ka-č gōβēt (13) kū hamē(v) ka ān xvāstak druvist nē dārom aδak-im ān anšahrīk tō xvēš būt rāδ (14) guft ka xvāstak druvist nē dārēt ān anšahrīk pat ān gōβišn bē šavēt. Vahrām (15) guft kū vēš uskārtan apāyēt.

64, 15—17:

U-š ēn-ič guft kū ka gōβēt kū⟨m⟩ ēn tā tō (16) kas xvēš gōβēh tō xvēš hēβ bavēt ka kas xvēš būt bē (17) gōβēt apāč ō bun šavēt. Ut ka nē gōβēt aδak-iš tā žīvandakīh pat-iš ēstēt ut pas (apāč ō bun šavēt).

65, 1:

...) āβurt ētōn guft kū pat 3 bahr 2 bahr dāt *.

65, 1—2:

Ka gōβēt kū xvāstak ī man xvēš (2) 3 bahr yumāy Mihrēn tō xvēš pat 4 bahr 3 bahr dāt apar kart.

65, 2—6:

Vehdāt ōγōn nipišt (3) kū ka gōβēt kū-m xvāstak ēv bahr ō tō dāt bē čiγōn Dipīr guft kū-š (4) nēm 1 bē rasēt enyā-šān pat xvārastān vičīr pat-iš nē ut bahr rāδ čiš-ič (5) paytāk nē kart ka-č gōβēt kū-m ēv bahr ō tō ut ēv bahr ō tō dāt aδak-ič hamgōnak (6) bavēt.

65, 6—7:

Gyākē nipišt kū (ka) gōβēt kū ēn xvāstak yumāy Farraxv ut Mihrēn tō xvēš (7) aδak-iš hamāk dāt bavēt.

65, 7—9:

Ka gōβēt kū tō yumāy Farraxv ut Mihrēn ēn xvāstak (8) xvēš aδak-iš pat 3 bahr ēv bahr dāt bavēt bē ka mih enyā⁺-šān hamāk kār bahrak (9) ōšmurt framūt.

* Only the end of the line has survived.

64, 9—15:

Rāt-Ōhrmizd has said that if Mihrēn makes the (following) declaration: "let this thing (= a slave, *vide infra* — *A. P.*) belong to the one whom Farraxv shall designate as its owner", and if Farraxv subsequently sells some thing to Dāt-Farraxv and concludes (the following) agreement with him: "if I do not safely preserve (this thing), then the slave concerning whom Mihrēn made (his) declaration shall belong to you", or if he says (= if the agreement with Dāt-Farraxv is formulated as follows — *A. P.*): "if I do not safely preserve this thing, then the ownership of this slave by you (may be considered as) having been declared by me", (and) if he does not safely preserve the thing uninjured, then, as a consequence of this declaration, the slave must be transferred ("must go"). Vahrām has said that this must be carefully ("well") investigated.

64, 15—17:

And he (= Vahrām) has also said that if he declares: "let this thing belong to you until you declare that it belongs to another man!", then, if the latter makes a declaration of (its) ownership by (another) person, the thing shall return to its original owner [49]. But if the latter makes no (such) declaration, then the thing shall belong to him until the end of his life, after which (it shall return to the original owner or to his successor — *A. P.*).

65, 1:

...) brought, then it is said (thereby) that two-thirds have been transferred *.

65, 1—2:

If he declares: "three shares from my estate (shall) belong to you jointly with Mihrēn", then (he) has thereby declared the transfer of three-quarters (of the estate).

65, 2—6:

Vehdāt has written as follows: if he declares: "I have conveyed one share of a thing to you", then — except for the fact that half (of the thing) shall go to him, as was said by (the) Dipīr — no decision concerning this (matter) is (taken) in ordeal-courts, and (the conveyer) has given no indication concerning the share in his declaration (*i. e.* regarding which half is intended and what is included therein — *A. P.*). Similarly, if he declares the following: "I have conveyed one share to you, and one share to you (*i. e.* to a third person — *A. P.*)", the (transaction is treated) in the same fashion in this case as well.

65, 6—7:

It is written in one place that if he declares: "this thing shall belong ("belongs") to you jointly with Farraxv and Mihrēn", then this thing is transferred in (its) entirety ("all, wholly").

65, 7—9:

If he declares: "this thing belongs to you jointly with Farraxv and Mihrēn", then one third of the thing is conveyed to him (= the person to whom the declaration is addressed). And he has conveyed to them the entire thing apportioned into (ideal) shares, unless (one of the persons designated) refuses (it).

65, 9—11:

Vahrām guft kū čiγōn-am ašnūt pat dīvān ī ōstāndārīh+ (Ms.: 'wst'nd'ršn') (10) ka nipišt kū ēn xvāstak yumāy ān xvāstak apāč ō šāhīkān kart harv 2 (11) pat apāč kart ō mar kart.

65, 11—12:

Ka gōβēt kū zan ut frazand ī man hend ut zan (12) ut frazand ī man bavēnd bahrak 8 ōh kunišn.

65, 12—14:

Vahrām guft kū ⟨kū⟩ ka gōβēt kū (13) frazand ī ziyānak pat zanīh ī man u-š zāt ut bavēt+ ēt rāδ ka bavend čē yut hač zāt+ (14) ō bavēt bahrak 4 ōh kunišn. Māhvindāt ī Vazurgbūtān guft kū bahrak 2 kunišn.

65, 15:

Duxt+ (Ms.: BRH = pus) harv ēvak 1 bahr ēvāč ī ēvakīh pus (harv) ēvak ēv bahr ēvāč ī dō(v)īh.

65, 15—17:

Ka gōβēt (16) kū ēn xvāstak frazandān ī to xvēš ut frazand ēvak gyākē nipišt kū hamāk bē rasēt (17) čē ēvak-ič veh vehān paytāk ut Vahrām guft kū pat kartak nē kunēnd.

XLIII *

66, 2:

Dar ī sahišn ut kāmak dōšīt.

66, 3—5:

Ka gōβēt kū ān ī tō sahēt ayāp ān ī tō kāmēh+, ayāp ān ī tō pas(s)andēh ayāp ān ī (4) tō apāyēt harv 4 ēv aδvēnak ut ka aδak kāmak nē dōšēt ut mīrēt xvāstakdārān kāmak dōšišn+.

66, 5—6:

Ka gōβēt kū ān ī tō gōβēh tō xvēš bē ka ōy gōβēt enyā (6) nē šāyēt.

---

* The (*abǰad*) ordinal-number of this chapter — 43 — is placed in line 1.

65, 9—11:

Vahrām has said. "as I heard/learned in the department for the management of royal lands (= the royal domain), if it is recorded that this thing has been confiscated ('taken away') into the royal treasury, together with that one, then both these things (each of them) were entered into the register of accounts ('were registered, were taken into account') at their confiscation".

65, 11—12:

If he declares: "(let this thing belong jointly — *A. P.*) to my present wife and son and to the wife and son whom I shall have", then a division into eight (ideal) shares must be made.

65, 12—14:

Vahrām has said that if he declares: "(this thing shall belong) to the children of the woman married to me, both (to the son whom) she has (already) born (and to the one who) will be", then, since (the thing) shall go ("be apportioned"), as a result of this declatarion, to the one "who will be" separately from the one "already born", a division into four (ideal) shares must be made. Māhvindāt ī Vazurgbūtān has said that the apportionment should be made (on the basis) of two (ideal) shares.

65, 15:

Each daughter receives one share, but only a single (one), each son (likewise receives) one share, but only a double (one).

65, 15—17:

If he declares: "(let) this thing belong to your children", but there is only one child, it is written in one place that (the thing will go to him entirely (= as a whole, altogether), because even one ... ... (?) is evident (?). But Vahrām has said that — according to judicial norms — (this) is not done.

XLIII

66, 2:

Chapter concerning the selection (of a thing) and the approval (= acceptance) of a will *.

66, 3—5:

Whether he declares: "whatever you choose", or "whatever you wish", or "whatever pleases you", or "whatever you need", then all these four methods (formulae) are equivalent. And if he (= the acquirer) does not declare his acceptance of the will at that time and dies, then (his) heirs should make a declaration of acceptance.

66, 5—6:

If he declares: "whatever you name (= designate) shall belong to you", then this (*i. e.* the transfer of the real right — *A. P.*) is possible only in the case where he (= the acquirer) declares (his selection of a thing — *A. P.*).

66, 6—8:

Ka gōβēt kū xvāstak ī ⟨tō⟩ pat xvēšīh ī man ⟨ut⟩ (čand) arž 200 vahāk aržēt (7) (tō) gōβēh tō xvēš pat ēv yāvar ut pat xvāstak and čand arž 200 vahāk aržistan rāδ (8) gōβēt pātixšāy dōšīt.

66, 8—10:

Ka gōβēt kū xvāstak man xvēš ut arž 200 vahāk aržēt (9) tō xvēš hēβ+ bavēt pat ēv yāvar ut pat xvāstak čand arž 200 vahāk aržēt pātixšāy (10) dōšīt.

66, 10—13:

Ka gōβēt kū xvāstak ī man xvēš ān ī Mihrēn sahēt čand arž 200 (11) vahāk aržēt Mihrēn hēβ bavēt ka Mihrēn ān sahišn pat 70 bē gōβēt (12) ut ān ī dit rāδ xvat sahišn nē gōβēt bē ō Farraxv dahēt Farraxv sahišn (13) bē gōβēt xvap.

66, 13—14:

Ān ō xvāstakdārān rasēt ī pat nīrmat enyā ān ī nē pat (14) nīrmat ō xvāstakdārān nē rasēt.

66, 14—17:

Ka gōβēt kū xvāstak ī man xvēš hakar (15) Mihrēn sahēt Mihrēn xvēš hēβ bavēt ā-šān/kasān+ (Ms.: 'š'n/'(Y)Š'n) ētōn guft kū ka Mihrēn sahišn (16) nē guft ut pat baxt šut sahišn pat guft ut xvāstak pat xvēšīh (ī) xvāstakdārān ⟨ut⟩ (ī) Mihrēn (17) dāšt(an).

66, 17—67, 2:

Sahišn ī ō xvāstakdārān rasēt ān bavēt ka gōβēt kū hakar tō (1) sahēt ēn xvāstak tō xvēš ayāp anī ka gōβēt kū xvāstak ī man xvēš ān ī tō sahēt (2) tō xvēš kas kē ān ⟨ī⟩ sahišn avi-š dāt ān sahišn bē pātixšāy dāt.

66, 6—8:

If he declares: "(anything) valued at 200 (*drahms*) that you name (= declare to have selected from the estate belonging to me, shall belong to you", then — having designated a single time and only as regards a thing valued at 200 (*drahms*) — he (= the acquirer) is entitled to state his acceptance (of this declaration of transfer — *A. P.*).

66, 8—10:

If he declares: "let a thing belonging to me and valued at 200 (*drahms*) belong to you!", then — a single time and only as regards the thing worth 200 (*drahms*) — he (= the acquirer) is entitled to declare his acceptance (of the given transfer — *A. P.*). (*cf supra* **66**, 6—8).

66, 10—13:

If he declares: "let anything valued at 200 (*drahms*) selected by Mihrēn (from) the estate belonging to me belong to Mihrēn!", and if Mihrēn declares his selection (and acceptance of a thing) valued at 70 (*drahms*) and makes no declaration himself concerning his selection (and acceptance) of the rest, but transfers (this right — *A. P.*) to Farraxv; then, if Farraxv makes a declaration concerning his selection (and acceptance), this is lawful (= valid).

66, 13—14:

Only that (declaration concerning the selection of a thing and its acceptance — *A. P.*) which is to the advantage of the heirs (of the acquirer — *A. P.*) passes on (extends) to them, whereas that which is not to the advantage of the heirs does not pass on to them.

66, 14—17:

If he declares: "If Mihrēn declares his agreement to (= acceptance of the transfer of) a thing belonging to me, let it belong to Mihrēn!" certain (authorities, commentators) have expressed themselves in this fashion: if Mihrēn did not declare his agreement/acceptance and died, the agreement should be considered as having been declared and the thing as belonging to Mihrēn's heirs.

66, 17—**67**, 2:

The right of an heir to declare his selection of a thing and his acceptance of the transfer consists in this (the following), that if he declares (thus): "if you declare your agreement (= 'if (it) pleases you') this thing shall belong to you", or if he makes a different formulation: "the thing belonging to me that pleases you shall belong to you", (then) the person to whom he gave the right of declaring his selection and (his) acceptance of the transfer may transfer (his) right (to another person).

67, 3—10:

Ka Āturfarnbaγ xvāstak 200 hač Farraxv ut Mihrēn apām stānēt ut patmān ētōn kunēt (4) kū ka ān xvāstak nē vičārt ēstēt šumā xvāstak ī man xvēš ān ī šumā sahēt (5) and čand 200 vahāk aržēt pat xvēšīh ayāp pat graβakānīh ōγōn čiγōn šumā sahēt apāč (6) kart pātixšāy hēt ut pas hač ān Mihrēn pat baxt šavēt u-š apurnāyak pat dūtak avēšān (7) apurnāyakān (ī) ān dūtak sardār Farraxv (ut) Farraxv patkārēt kū man sahišn ut sardārīh-ič ī apar dūtak (ī) (8) apurnāyak rāδ bē gōβom hač Siyāvaxš ut Rāt-Ōhrmizd bē ētōn guft kū ān sahišn (9) (tā) apurnāyak purnāy bavēnd guft nē šāyēt uskārtan apāyēt kū ka apurnāyak ēvak ō (10) purnāyīh mat pātixšāy guft ayāp tā hamē(v) ō purnāyīh rasēnd.

67, 10—13:

Ēn dātastān apāk (11) anī nipišt kū sahišn ān ō xvāstakdārān rasēt ī pat nīrmat ut ka pus (12) ut duxt purnāy ut dūtak katak-bānūk ān gyāk ā-šān ākanēn kāmak dōšišn čē ka yut-kāmak (13) bavēnd xvāstak bē nē rasēt nikerītan.

67, 13—**68**, 1:

Ka apāk mart 1 patmān kunēt kū (14) vǎhmān čiš pat ēn mātak ō tō dahom ut ka ān mart ān čiš xvāhēt gōβēt kū-m (15) xvāstak hač sarṯak dāt nē tuvān bē-t anī xvāstak pat ān mātak avi-š apispārom (16) (ut pas)? andar apārīk kāmak pat [illegible] (?) (ī)? hamsarṯak dahēt hač Rāt bē ⟨ān xvāstak ī⟩ guft ēstēt (17) kū ka ān ī apārīk hast hač ān pātixšāy ka nē apispārēt (ut ka) apārīk hač ān [illegible] (?) (1) sahēt pat ān mātak bē apispārišn.

68, 1—4:

Ka apām stānēt ut patmān kunēt (2) kū xvāstak ī tō pat xvēšīh (ī) man sahēt čand ān xvāstak vahāk aržēt ān xvāstak (3) rāδ^{+} apāč pātixšāy hēh kart ut pat 2 yāvar sahišn guft ut xvāstak grift (4) ⟨nē⟩ pātixšāy.

68, 4—6:

Ut ka gōβēt kū xvāstak man xvēš čand ān xvāstak vahāk aržēt (5) apāč pātixšāy hēh kart pat-ič 2 yāvar pātixšāy. Ut ka nēm-ē(v) xvāstak gīrēt nēm-ē(v) drahm xvāhēt nē pātixšāy.

67, 3—10:

If Āturfarnbaγ receives a thing (valued) at 200 (*drahms*) as a loan from Farraxv and Mihrēn and makes this (the following) agreement (with/them): "if this debt is not settled (by the expiration of the stipulated time-limit — *A. P.*), then you are entitled to seize (as a forfeit; lit. 'to take away') whatever satisfies you (= you choose) amounting to 200 (*drahms*) from the estate belonging to me, (and take it) as (your) property (= personal possession) or as security (= *antichresis* — *A. P.*), whichever is more satisfactory to you"; and if Mihrēn dies thereafter and there are minors (left) in his family and Farraxv is the guardian of the family's minors, and (if) Farraxv appears in court (with the following declaration: "I (declare) my selection and acceptance of this (thing), and I make this declaration as ('for, because') the guardian of the minors in this family"; (then) it is said (in the *Dātastan-nāmak* with reference to the authority of the commentators — *A. P.*) Syavaxš and Rāt-Ōhrmizd, that such a declaration concerning selection and acceptance should not be made (until) the minors come of age. (And) it is necessary to clarify whether (this) declaration may be made when one of the minors comes of age, or whether one ought (to wait) until all of them come of age.

67, 10—13:

In addition to others, this decision is also written (= in the *Dātastān-nāmak* — *A. P.*) that only a decision concerning the selection and agreement (to accept the thing conveyed) made (by the guardian of the deceased man's family — *A. P.*) which is to (their) advantage passes on to (his) heirs. And if in this family there are a son and a daughter of full age as well as a mistress of the house, then they must make a joint declaration concerning their approval of the will (of the conveyer), since if there are disagreements among them, the thing does not go (to them). Note (this).

67, 13—**68**, 1:

If he makes the following agreement with a man: "I shall convey such-and-such a thing to you against this sum of money", and (if) when the latter claims the thing, he declares: "I cannot convey to you a thing of this type, but I shall transfer to you another thing against that sum of money", (and if the latter subsequently?) expresses his agreement (or: "his wish") to (accept) another but a similar thing (?); it is said with a reference to (the opinion) of the *rat*, that even if (he) has another (thing of the same kind. — *A. P.*), he is entitled not to convey it, (but if the latter) declares his agreement to receive another object (?), then it should be conveyed against that sum of money [50].

68, 1—4:

If he receives as a loan a thing/money and makes this agreement: "you are entitled to take anything belonging to me (and) having a value equivalent to this thing/money that pleases you for (against) this thing/money", then he (= the creditor) is ⟨not⟩ (*cf. infra* **68**, 4—6; **68**, 6—8; **68**, 9—12) entitled to effectuate in two instances both (his) selection of the thing, and (his) taking it (from the debtor).

68, 4—6:

If he declares: "You are entitled to take a thing with equivalent value to that thing (= *i. e.* the one loaned — *A. P.*)", then the latter is entitled (to do this) in two instances also. But if he takes a thing for half (the amount) and demands money for the other half, that is not allowed.

68, 6—8:

Ut anī gyākē nipišt kū ka gōβēt kū xvāstak ī (7) tō pat xvēšīh ī man sahēt čand 70 vahāk aržēt tō xvēš ka+ xvāstak ēv 10 rāδ (8) nazdist+ sahišn ut pas ān ī apārīk pat čand yāvar sahišn gōβēt aδak-ič pātixšāy.

68, 9—12:

Gyākē nipišt kū ka gōβēt kū xvāstak ī tō pat xvēšīh (ī) man sahēt čand (10) arž+ 70 vahāk aržēt tō xvēš ka pat xvāstak ēv arž+ 10 vahāk aržēt ut frēh (11) nē aržēt sahišn gōβēt xvap čē ka 70 pat 10 bār gōβēt aδak-ič šāyēt (12) apāk ān ī hačapar nipišt nikerītan.

68, 12—14:

Gyakē nipišt kū ka gōβēt kū xvāstak (13) ī man xvēš čand arž+ 200 vahāk aržēt ī tō kāmēh+ tō xvēš ut ān kē avi-š gōβēt (14) ⟨ut⟩ kāmak dōšēt guft kāmak pas xvāstak pat ōy ī ⟨xvāstak⟩ (kāmak dōšīt) xvēš.

68, 14—17:

Ka gōβēt (15) (kū) xvāstak man xvēš čand arž 200 vahāk aržēt ī mērak sahēt tō xvēš ut mērak (16) kāmak nē dōšēt aδak-ič 200 paytāk kartan (ut) bē apispārtan apāyēt čē pat ān (17) mātak tōžišnōmand.

68, 17:

Ka gōβēt kū+ ān ī mērak sahēt tō xvēš....*

69, 1—3:

[... ... ...] pat duxtakānīh ētōn bē dāt ēstēt kū tō-č duxt ut man-ič duxt (2) [... ... ...] mart bē pat hamdātastānīh ī ōy ī dit enyā pat duxtakānīh bē dāt nē (3) [pātixšāy ?] hend.

69, 3—6:

Ut apāk anī nipišt kū ka kunēt kū-m ēn anšahrīk harv 2 sāl (4) [ēv] sāl ō Mihrēn dāt ān anšahrīk bē pat hamdātastānīh ī ākanēn enyā āzāt (5) kartan nē pātixšāy ut ka ēvak bahr (ī) xvēš pat xonsandīh ī ōy dit āzāt kunēt hamaδvēn (6) ⟨hamaδvēn⟩ āzāt nikerītan.

---

* The article breaks off at this point.

68, 6—8:

It is also written in another place that if he declares: "a thing valued at 70 (*drahms*) which belongs to me and pleases you shall belong to you", then if the latter first declares his acceptance of a thing (valued at) 10 (*drahms*) and subsequently declares his selection and acceptance of the remainder in several instances, that too may be done.

68, 9—12:

It is written in one place that if he declares: "any thing belonging to me (and) valued at 70 (*drahms*) which pleases you shall belong to you", if he declares his selection of a thing valued at 10 (*drahms*) and worth no more; then that is lawful, for even if he makes a declaration ten times (= in ten instances about his selection and acceptance out of a sum of) 70 (*drahms*), that too is permitted. To be examined together with what has been written above.

68, 12—14:

It is written in one place that if he declares: "(whatever) thing belonging to me valued at 200 (*drahms*) which you desire shall belong to you", and if the one to whom he made this declaration declares his selection of a thing and his approval of the disposition (concerning the transfer); then, after the declaration concerning the approval has been made, the thing belongs to the person who (made the declaration concerning his approval of the disposition).

68, 14—17:

If he declares: "a thing from my estate valued at 200 (*drahms*) of which a certain man has declared that '(it) pleases (me)', shall belong to you", and the man (referred to) does not express (his) approval of (the given) disposition (*i. e.* does not declare specifically his selection of a thing — *A. P.*), then in this case also, it is necessary to make known and declare (a thing valued at) 200 (*drahms*) and give (it), since within the limits of that amount, he (= the conveyer) is obliged to pay.

68, 17:

If he declares: "whatever a certain man shall approve (= select) shall belong to you" *....

69, 1—3:

[... ... ...] is conveyed for adoption (as a daughter) in this manner (= according to this formula —*A. P.*): "both a daughter to you and a daughter to me", [(then).......] a man, they are not [entitled] to convey for adoption (as a daughter) without the consent of the one and of the other.

69, 3—6:

Alongside it is written that if he makes the following declaration: "I have conveyed this slave to Mihrēn for one year out of every two", then this slave cannot be manumitted without mutual consent. And if one of them frees his share (= his share of the real right on the slave — *A. P.*) with the consent of the other, then note should be taken (that the slave) is entirely free (one year out of every two).

69, 6—9:

(Ut ka kunēt kū-m xvāstak harv 2) sāl ēv sāl pat stūrīh (ō Farraxv) ut ēv+ sāl ō Mihrēn dāt Farraxv (7) (ut) Mihrēn yut yut pat ān xvāstak *yō hē pasčaēta* ōh bavēt. Ut ka hač kust ī būtak (8) bē būt andar būtakīh pat xvēšīh ō mart-ē(v) rasēt hač ēn kust pat xvēšīh ut hač (9) kust ī dit pat stūrīh rasēt nikerītan.

69, 9—10 (*Cf.* **26**, 12):

Gyākē nipišt kū sardārīh ī dūtak ī (10) pit ī (pātixšāyīhā) ō pus ī patigriftak nē rasēt.

69, 10—12:

Hač pit ō dūtak ī pus ī patigriftak ī žīvandakān (11) pit pat baxt šut+ čiγōn hač Pusānveh ī Burzātur Farnbaγān bē guft xvāst(ak) pat (12) aparmānd ōh rasēt.

69, 12:

Duxt ī patigriftak ayōγēn ī brāt apar nē mānēt.

69, 12—14:

Apurnāyak ī (13) patigriftak vitart pit čiγōn Vahrāmšāt ut Rāt-Ōhrmizd guft hač kust ī pit kē (14) patigrift.

69, 14—17:

Pus ī patigriftak kē xvāstak ī pit ī patigriftak pat xvāstakdārīh (15) gīrēt hamāk tōžišn. Ka pēš hač pit (ī) patigriftak mīrēt aparmānd (ō) pit ī (16) patigriftak čiγōn hač Siyāvaxš bē nipišt ka-š zan ut apurnāyak hast ā-š ōh (17) rasēt ut ka ēvāč pus ī purnāy ānōδ ā-š nē rasēt.

69, 17—**70**, 2:

Ka mart pus ī apurnāy (1) pat pusakānīh+ bē dahēt ayāp pat vahāk bē frōšēt u-š anī kas nēst [stūr ōh] (2) gumārišn.

70, 2—3:

Duxt bē ka-š pit bē dahēt enyā ka-š kas pat dux[takānīh patigīrēt] (3) čiš-ič nēst (u-š) aparmānd ī pit ī patigriftak nē barēt.

69, 6—9:

(If he declares the following: "out of every two years) I have conveyed (a thing) for *stūr*ship one year to Farraxv and the other year to Mihrēn", then Farraxv and Mihrēn, each separately, become the possessor of this thing on the basis of *stūr*ship. And if (the *stūr*ship passed) through "natural" calling the thing goes to the man as a personal possession (*i. e.* as a share of inheritance — *A. P.*); when it is through this line, (it is) as a personal possession; but when it is through another line (of calling), then it is as a possession for *stūr*ship. Take note.

69, 9—10 (*Cf.* **26**, 12):

It is written in one place that the guardianship over the family of the (natural) father does not go to the adopted son.

69, 10—12:

According to the opinion of Pusānveh ī Burzātur Farnbaγān, the estate of an (adoptive — *A. P.*) father shall pass to the family of the adopted son who died in his father's lifetime as (his, *i. e.* of the adopter — and not of the adopted son who died earlier — *A. P.*) succession (= patrimony).

69, 12:

An adopted daughter does not inherit the *epikler*ate of her (own — *A. P.*) brother.

69, 12—14:

As has been stated by Vahrāmšāt and Rāt-Ōhrmizd, after the death of his (adoptive) father, an adopted (son) (comes under the guardianship of an agnate) on the side of the father who adopted him.

69, 14—17:

An adopted son who has inherited the estate of his adoptive father is obliged to settle all the debts (of his adoptive father). If he dies before his adopter, then the inheritance of his estate passes to (his adoptive) father if, as has been written with a citation of (the opinion of) Siyāvaxš, he has a wife and minor children; but if there is only a son of full age in the family, then (it) shall not pass to him.

69, 17—**70**, 2:

If a man gives (his) minor son for adoption to another person, or if he sells (him) for money ("for a price", "at a price"), and he has no one else, then [a *stūr*] must be appointed.

70, 2—3:

Unless (her) father has given her up for adoption, even if some person [has accepted to receive her as] a daughter, this has no (legal) force, (and she) is not called to ("does not bear") the (charge of) the succession (*i. e.* the *epikler*ate) of (such) an adoptive father.

70, 3—12:

Mart ī šahr [ka-š kas] (4) pat pusīh bē patigīrēt čiγōn Vahrām guft ā-š aparmānd pat ān zamān bavēt [ka] (5) ān-ič pat pusīh ī ōy kartan andar ēstēt. Čē pat pusīh ī ōy tuvānīk nē ōγōn bavēt čiγōn (6) ka zan ī dūtak stūr pat pātixšāyīhā zanīh patigīrēt ut ka-č gōβēt kū-m pat (7) pusīh patigrift hēh ut hač xvāstak ī man yumāy zan+ ut frazand ī man ēv bahr tō xvēš (8) hač ān čiγōn ōy mart ān xvāstak pusīh rāδ ō ōy kas dāt ka kas pat pusīh ī (9) ōy mart andar nē ēstēt aδak-iš ān xvāstak nē rasēt čiγōn Māhdāt-Gušnasp ī (10) Gyānaβzōt guft ka šōy andar zan (ī) čakar kunēt kū-m pat pātixšāyīhā zanīh (11) patigrift hēh pat ēn kū-š xvāstak pat aparmānd avi-š ōh rasēt pat Dārāβ(12)kart vičīr apar ōh kunēnd.

70, 13—14:

Xvāstak ī apurnāyak ī patigriftak ka pat baxt šavēt (13) čiγōn hač Rāt-Ōhrmizd bē nipišt ō pit ī pātixšāyīhā rasēt ut apāk anī guft (14) kū pus ī patigriftak a-patvand(?) hēβ bavēt.

70, 14—16:

Apāk-ič ān nipišt+ kū pat stūrīh ī pus ī (15) patigriftak ka ōγōn bē dāt kū tō-č pus pit ī pātixšāyīhā ut ka nē ōγōn bē (16) dāt ēstēt ī pit ī patigriftak sažāktar nikerītan.

70, 16—71, 2:

Rāt-Ōhrmizd guft kū (17) ka Mihrēn mart ī šahr pat pusīh bē patigīrēt u-š xvāstak dahēt u-š xvāstak (1) [ruvān rāδ bē kunēt?] bē hakar ōy mart pat pusīh ī Mihrēn andar ēstēt enyā+ (2) [tōžišn ī pat apā]m ī Mihrēn hač xvāstak ī ruvān apāyēt dāt.

71, 2—4:

Ka gōβēt kū (3) [xvāsta]k frazandan (ī) tō xvēš gyākē ōγōn nipišt kū pus-ič ī patigriftak xvēš (4) [bavēt].

71, 4—7:

Martak nipišt kū pus ī patigriftak sardārīh (ī) dūtak ī pit ī patigriftak (5) bē pat rāh (ī) ēv-+kasīh ut stūrīh čē hač kust ī pit ī patigriftak ō-š nē rasēt (6) čē-š sažakīh ⟨ī⟩ pat stūrīh (ut) ⟨ī⟩ sardārīh ⟨ī⟩ hač dātastān pusīh ut dātastān brātarīh bē (7) šāyēt būt nē hač kust ī anītarān(?).

70, 3—12:

[If anyone] adopts (his) fellow-citizen, then — as has been said by Vahrām — he (= the adopted fellow-citizen) shall become the successor of his adopter only [if] he agrees to perform the functions of his son. Because the matter of his legal competence as the son and successor of that person is treated differently from (the case where) someone contracts a *pātixšāyīh*-marriage with the wife-*stūr* of a family. If he declares (the following): "I have adopted you and one portion of my estate shall belong to you jointly with my wife and children", then — inasmuch as that man transferred this estate to that person (= the fellow-citizen) as to a son ("for sonship") — if that person does not remain a son of that man, this estate does not pass to him.

As has been said by Māhdāt-Gušnasp ī Gyānaβzōt: if a man makes (this) declaration concerning his *čakar*-wife: "you are accepted by me into a *pātixšāyīh*-marriage", then a decision is taken in *Dārāβkart* so that his estate should pass to her as an inheritance.

70, 13—14:

As it is written with a citation from Rāt-Ōhrmizd, the estate of a minor adopted son passes to (his) legitimate (= own) father. And in addition to other (things), it is said that an adopted son (formally) has no relations of kinship (with the family of his adopter? — *A. P.*).

70, 14—16:

Moreover it is also written that (the most suitable *stūr* for an adopted son is his legitimate (= natural) father if he (the former) was given up (for adoption) with the pronouncement of this (formula) by his own father: "he is also a son to you". But if he was not given up (for adoption) in this manner [51], then the adoptive father is the one most suitable (to receive the *stūr*ship). Take note (of this).

70, 16—**71**, 2:

Rāt-Ōhrmizd has said that if Mihrēn adopts his fellow-citizen and conveys a thing to him, and the latter [declares] (this) thing [set-up as a foundation for the soul?], then — except in the case where that man remains Mihrēn's adopted son — [the settlement] of Mihrēn's [debts] is to be made from the thing set up as a foundation "for the soul".

71, 2—4:

If he declares: "(let) this [thing] belong to your sons", it is written in one place that (this thing) should belong to the adopted son as well.

71, 4—7:

Martak has written that the adopted son shall not obtain the guardianship over the family of (his) adoptive father, except where he is the only one or if he has been invested with the *stūr*ship on the part of his adoptive father. For *stūr*s and guardians should be (called) from among the sons "according to law" and the brothers "according to law" and not from outsiders (?) ("from the side of aliens"?).

XLV

71, 8:

Dar ī ۱۳۱۳ ut tāvān dahišnīh ut ahravdāt ut atuvānīkīh čē andar pašt ut patmān*.

71, 9—12:

Ka gōβēt kū rōč Anaγrān ēn čiš pēš ī dātaβar ō tō dahom hakar nē dahom (10) tāvān dahom ka pašt pat ān aδvēnak kunēt sē+ (Ms: 'yw — ēv) rōčak pat gōβ pāyišn+ ut ka gōβēt (11) kū dahom hakar yuttar+ kunom tāvān dahom hamēv ka yuttar kart nām kunēt sē rōčak pat gōβ (12) bē+ pāyišn+

71, 12—16:

Ka gōβēt 200 hač xvēš māh vǎhmān ut rōč vǎhmān ō tō dahom (13) ut hakar nē dahom tāvān dahom hamēv ka ۳۱۳ ayāp tāvān nām kunēt mātak ut tāvān (14) anōδ ut ka-č mātak ahravdāt gōβēt bē ۳۱۳ nām kunēt aδak-ič harv 2 bē dahišn (15) ut ka gōβēt kū-m 200 ō tō dahišn ut rōč vǎhmān bē dahom ut hakar nē dahom 300 bē (16) dahom aδak-ic harv 2 bē dahišn.

71, 16—72, 3:

Ka gōβēt kū 200 pēš (ī) dātaβar ō tō dahom ut hakar nē dahom 300 bē dahom ka pat ān hangām nē dahēt ēvāč (17) 300 anōδ čē-š mātak ahravdāt guft ut ۳۱۳ nām nē kart. Būt kē guft kū ka (1) gōβēt (kū) 100 rōč vāhmān bē dahom ut hakar nē dahom ētōn kunom [200 dahom ۳۱۳] (2) guft bavēt ut ahravdāt ān bavēt ka gōβēt kū hakar rōč vāhmān 200 bē [dahom] (3) enyā ētōn kunom.

72, 3—5:

Martak ōγōn nipišt kū ka gōβēt kū hakar rōč Ōhr[mizd] (4) asp ō tō apispārom enyā tāvān dahom ⟨ī⟩ būt kē ōγōn guft kū ka (5) pēš hač Ōhrmizd rōč asp bē mīrēt aδak-ič tāvān ō+ tōžišn ōh rasēt.

---

* The (*abǰad*) ordinal-number of this chapter — 45 — is placed in line 7.

XLV

71, 8:

Chapter concerning the payment of smart money and fines, concerning transfers for charitable (or "pious") purposes, and concerning the incapacity to fulfil the conditions of (verbal) agreements and (written) contracts *.

71, 9—12:

If he declares: "I shall convey this thing to you in the presence of a judge on the day Anaγrān (and) if I do not convey it I shall pay a fine", then, if he formulates the agreement in this fashion, he (= the other party) must wait three days (counting from the expiration date stipulated). And if he declares: "I shall convey and if I act otherwise I shall pay a fine", in both cases if he acts in a manner other than the one declared (in the agreement) he (= the other party) must wait three days (counting from the one designated in the declaration of agreement before he demands the payment of the fine — *A. P.*).

71, 12—16:

If he declares: "I shall convey to you 200 (*drahms*) from (the means) belonging to me in such-and-such a month on such-and-such a day, and if I do not give (them) I shall pay a fine", then whether he stipulates smart-money or a fine (in both cases the obligation to pay) both the principal sum and the fine (is presumed) here. And similarly if he declares the transfer of the money (= the principal) for a pious pupose, but (at the same time) stipulates smart money; then in this case too he must convey (= pay) the one and the other (if he does not fulfil the obligation to transfer which he assumed — *A. P.*). And if he declares: "I assume the obligation of conveying to you 200 (*drahms*) and I shall convey them to you on such-and-such a day, and if I do not convey (them) I shall pay ('give') 300 (*drahms*)"; then in this case too he must convey the one and the other (*i. e.* the original debt plus the stipulated smart-money — *A. P.*).

71, 16—**72**, 3:

If he declares (as follows): "I shall convey 200 (*drahms*) to you in the presence of a judge, and if I do not convey (them), then (I shall be obliged) to convey ('I shall convey') 300 (*drahms*)"; then if he does convey (them) within the designated time-limit (or "under these circumstances"), (he will) then (be obliged to pay) only 300 (*drahms*), since he declared the transfer of the principal for pious purposes and stipulated no smart-money. Certain (authorities) have said that when he declares: "I shall convey 100 (*drahms*) on such-and-such a day, and if I do not convey (them), I shall act in this manner [I shall convey 200 (*drahms*)]", (then) [smart-money] was (thereby) stipulated by him. And (a transfer) for pious purposes takes place when he declares: "either [I shall convey] 200 (*drahms*) on such-and-such a day, or I shall act in this manner".

72, 3—5:

Martak has written thus, if he declares: "either I shall convey a horse to you on the day Ōhrmizd, or I shall pay a fine", then according to the opinion expressed by certain (authorities), (even) if the horse dies before the day Ōhrmizd, the fine must be paid in this case as well.

72, 5—10:

Apāk-ič (6) ān ī Pusānveh ī Burzātur Farnbaγān guft kū ka gōβēt kū tā hač Sūristān apāč (7) āyom ēn xvāstak ⟨ī⟩ tō xvēš ut andar Asūristān bē mīrēt ā-š xvāstak apāč (8) nē rasēt ut Dāt-Farraxv ī Marbūtān guft kū-š apāč rasēt čē ōγōn bavēt čiγōn (9) ka ān gōβēt kū tā apāč ō bun āyom tō dār ka mīrēt pat mat ī ō (10) bun dārišn.

72, 10—13:

Apāk-ič ān ī hačapar nipišt kū ka gōβēt kū hakar rōč vǎhmān Farraxv ō tō (11) apispārom enyā 200 bē dahom (ut) rōč vǎhmān pat apispārtan ī Farraxv atuvānīkīh (12) avinās ka-č pas (ō) tuvānīkīh rasēt aδak-ič tan nē apispārišn ut 200-ič nē dahišn (13) nikerītan.

XLVI

72, 13:

Dar ī task+ (Ms.: t'/hk) *.

72, 14—15:

Ka gōβēt kū ēn xvāstak rāδ task 400 ō tō dahom ka vaxt hambun-ič nē bavēt (15) task pat bavandak bē vičārisn.

72, 15—16:

Ka gōβēt kū čiš xvāstak (rāδ) task 50 ō tō dahom (16) ka hač xvāstak (ī) task 50 nē vaxt and dahišn čand vaxt.

72, 16—17:

Ka mart 1 xvāstak pat task (17) patigīrēt gyākē nipišt kū pat ān sāl ka vizand ī ō bun rasīt rāδ vaxt (...) ** .

73, 1—2:

Ka 4 bār drōš kart ut pas-ič anī vinās ī pat ān aδvēnak kunēt (2) [hakurč] hač zēndān bē nē hilišn. ⟨Ut drōš hamēmārān xvēš⟩*** .

73, 2—7:

Ka pēš dātaβarān (3) gōβēt kū man hač anī mart ī nāmčištīk ham(m)is duž kart ān zamān duzīt man dārom (4) apar-ič avēšān ī apārīk pat vikāyīh šāyēt čē-š ān gōβišn nē pat nīrmat ī xvēš (5) guft. Ka gōβēt kū mān duž kart ut ān zamān dužīt avēšān ī apārīk dārēnd (6) apar avēšān ī apārīk pat vikāyīh nē šāyēt čē-š ān gōβišn pat nīrmat ī xvēš (7) guft.

---

* The (*abǰad*) ordinal-number of this chapter of which only the beginning has survived, is 46.

** The article breaks off at this point.

*** The phrase in pointed brackets is devoid of sense and is presumably the result of a corruption in copying.

72, 5—10:

In addition here is what has been said by Pusānveh ī Burzātur Farnbaɣan. If he declares: "this thing shall belong ('belongs') to you until my return from Babylonia", and if he dies in Babylonia, then the thing is not subject to return to him (*i. e.* to the disposer' heirs — *A. P.*). But Dāt-Farraxv ī Marbūtān has said that (it) is subject to return because this is the same as though he declared thus: "you possess it (= the thing) until I return!", (and) if he dies, this should be taken as a return (= be equated with a return — *A. P.*).

72, 10—13:

In addition to what was set out above it is written that if he declared thus: "I shall convey to you (the slave) Farraxv on such-and-such a day, or convey 200 (*drahms*)", (and if) he is guiltless of the incapacity of conveying (the slave) Farraxv on the day stipulated, then, even if he subsequently acquires the capacity (to convey Farraxv), he is not obliged to convey the slave, nor the 200 (*drahms*). Take note.

XLVI

72, 13:

Chapter concerning the payment of rent *.

72, 14—15:

If he declares (the following): "I shall pay ('give') you 400 (*drahms*) for the lease of this thing", then, even if (the lessee — *A. P.*) has no profit, (lit. 'increment, increase'), the rent must be paid in full.

72, 15—16:

If he declares (the following): "I shall pay you 50 (*drahms*) as rent for (this) thing", and if 50 (*drahms*) of income/profit is not received from the thing leased, the lessee shall pay as much as he received as income ("as much as there was income/profit").

72, 16—17:

If a person accepts a thing as a lease, it is written in one place that in the year in which, because of damage to the principal (= to the thing leased — *A. P.*), the benefit (...) **.

73, 1—2:

If he was punished four times with branding and subsequently commits one more offence of the same type, he must [never again] be released from prison ***.

73, 2—7:

If he declares before judges: "I have committed a theft, together with a certain ('a definite', 'a named') person (and) I hold stolen (things) at that time", (then this) may be taken as the statement of a witness as regards the other persons (involved in this affair — *A. P.*) as well, because he has not made this declaration in his own favour. But if he declares: "we have committed a theft and the others (= the participants in the theft) hold the stolen (thing)", then this may not be taken as the statement of a witness as regards the others, because he has made this declaration in his own favour.

73, 7:

Zan ī kasān apātixšāyīhā gāt tāvān 300 satēr.

73, 8—9:

Ka zan ī mart 1 dužēt ut apātixšāyīhā gāyēt 700 (Ms.: 300 + 400) gāt tāvān ut (9) 500 drahm duž rāδ bē dahišn.

73, 9—10:

Ka apurnāyak⟨ān⟩ rūnēt 600 (Ms.: 100 + 500) drahm bē dahišn (10) ut apurnāyak apāč apispārišn.

73, 10—12:

Āturfarnbaγ yāmak-ē(v) hač Mihr-Āturfarnbaγ bē dužēt (11) Āturfarnbaγ pasēmār nē šavēt ⟨ut apurnāyakān⟩ pēšēmār pātixšāy ka tā (12) hač pasēmār nē šut hačašmānd bavēt saxvan-nāmak hač kart muhr nē brīnēt.

73, 13—**74**, 5:

Ut gyākē nipišt kū ka pāt dātastān pēšēmār ēvak pasēmār dō saxvan-(14)nāmak rāδ ō pēš dātaβarān dēmān kunēnd (ut) pat ān dēmān pasēmār ēvak nē ēvak (15) pēšēmār šavēt pasēmār (ī) ō gōβ šut^{+} apar pēšēmār saxvan pat kār (16) rāδēnīt ut pēšēmār apar pasēmār ī ō gōβ nē šut ⟨saxvan⟩ pat nē āmat/dāt^{+}/rāδēnīt^{+} (17) čak dahišn. Pat ān hačašmānd harv 2 andar ān pasēmārīh ī ō gōβ ⟨ī⟩ nē šut (1) [vič]īr kunišn. Ut hakar ān saxvan-nāmak brīnīhēt aδak ān saxvan-nāmak andar p[asēmār ī] (2) ō gōβ ⟨ī⟩ nē šut^{+} pat a-vāvarīkānīh dārišn ut pat ān pasēmār ī ō gōβ ⟨ī⟩ šut apar (3) pēšēmār ⟨ pēšēmār⟩ saxvan pat kār nē rāδēnīt čak dahišn ēn-ič bōžišn (4) čē pasēmār gōβēt kū ka pēšēmār saxvan-nāmak yutāk bē kart hē (5) man ēn ziyān nē būt hē.

74, 5—9:

Gyāke nipišt kū ka pēšēmār 2 pasēmār (6) ēvak pēšēmār (ēvak) nē ēvak ut pasēmār-ič šavēt pasēmār apar pēšēmār ī (7) šut (saxvan) pat kār nē rāδēnīt ut apar ān ī nē šut saxvan pat nē āmat čak dahišn ut (8) pēšēmār kē nē šavēt ziyān ī pat nē šut ⟨nē⟩ vičārišn čē-š xvat vināš (9) būt ka-š saxvan-nāmak yutāk nē kart.

73, 7:

For adultery with another man's wife the fine is 300 *saters*.

73, 8—9:

If anyone abducts ("steals") a married woman and enters into an illicit sexual relation with her, then 700 (*drahms*) must be paid as a fine for adultery and 500 *drahms* (as a) fine for abduction ("theft").

73, 9—10:

A fine of 600 *drahms* shall be paid for the deflowering of a minor and the minor shall be returned (to her family).

73, 10—12:

Āturfarnbaγ steals clothes from Mihr-Āturfarnbaγ. Āturfarnbaγ does not appear in court as the respondent. (Then) as long as the trial is suspended ("in default") because of the non-appearance of the respondent, the plaintiff is entitled not to affix (...)? his seal to the record of the deposition.

73, 13—**74**, 5:

And it is written in one place that if one plaintiff and two respondents are summoned to court for a session before the judges intended for the drawing up of the record (of the deposition), and if one respondent and one plaintiff appear ("betake themselves" to) at this session; then the respondent who is present at the judicial session must give a testimony set down in a written document, stating that the plaintiff participated in the (given) trial ("conducted the case"), whereas the plaintiff must present a (written) deposition regarding the respondent who did not appear in court, (specifically a testimony) that he did not appear. The decision on this "delayed" trial (or trial "by default") must be rendered as though both respondents had not appeared. But if a record of the deposition is made up, then this record is to be considered unreliable as concerns [the respondent] who did not appear in court, and a document regarding the fact that the plaintiff did not testify in this matter must be given to the respondent who appeared in court. And the decision rendered is such, since the respondent will say that if the plaintiff had drawn up the record in another manner, I should not have sustained this loss.

74, 5—9:

It is written in one place that if there are two plaintiffs and one respondent, and (if) one of the plaintiffs and one respondent appear (in court), then the respondent must make a statement set down in a document: as regards the plaintiff (who appeared in court) — that he made no statement in (this) matter, and as regards the one who did not appear — that he did not appear. And the plaintiff who did not appear at the court session shall pay for the loss sustained through his non-appearance, since he is the one at fault that the record of the depositions was not drawn up otherwise.

74, 9—12:

Ka pēšēmār pat ān ī pasēmār (10) anbassān saxvan-nāmak rāδēnīt apāk pasēmār kart kū-t pat ēn saxvan-nāmak hamēmār(11)īh hēβ nē kunēh pat-ič anī saxvan-nāmak rāδēnišn apāk pasēmār pat ān dātastān guftan (12) nē tuvān.

[*Numberless*]

74, 12:

Dar ī yātakgōβānak*.

74, 13—15:

Pātixšāy kartan (ēt) ka gōβēt kū-m ēn xvāstak frōxtan ayāp ēn dāta(14)stān rāδēnītan ut sar kartan rāδ Gušnasp pātixšāy kart ut Gušnasp nē (15) pātixšāy pat ān ī Mihrēn Gušnasp pātixšāy kart anī mart pātixšāy kartan.

74, 16—17:

Ka gōβēt kū-m yātakgōβ kart būt kē guft kū-š tā var kart būt kē guft kū-š (17) tā graβ kart bavēt.

74, 17—75, 1:

Ut ka gōβēt kū-m ākanēn yātakgōβ kart hēt avēšān (1) [... ... mar]t 1 yātakgōβ kunēt/kunēnd xvap ka ēvak ōy ī dit yātakgōβ kunēt nē xvap.

75, 2—5:

Ka yātakgōβ gumārt ēstēt pas anī-č yātakgōβ ut yātakgōβ ī pas gumārt ō (3)  ī hamēmārān gumārt ⟨lyt⟩ hangām tā yātakgōβ ī pas gumart ō dātastān šavēt (4) guft ut kart ī yātakgōβ ī fratom pat ān dātastān kār ōγōn hač-iš kart čiγōn ka pas (5) hač ān yātakōβ ⟨i⟩ nē gumārt hē.

75, 5—8:

Ka pēšēmār pat xunsandīh ī yātakgōβ ī pasēmār (6) dātastān ast ī g/yānvar-ē(v)? (Ms.: 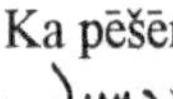) hač rāδēnišn hilēt ayāp dātaβar pat xunsandīh ī yātakgōβ ī (7) pēšēmār ut yātakgōβ ī pasēmār ⟨ yātakgōβ yātakgōβ ī pasēmār⟩ g/yānvar-ē(v)? hač gōβ visēh (8) kunēt xvap.

* The ordinal-number of this chapter is not given.

74, 9—12:

If the plaintiff concludes with the respondent (such an agreement) as regards the opposition of the respondent (to the giving of a deposition) for the drawing up of the judicial record: "you will not participate in the trial to (draw up) this record of deposition", then he (= the plaintiff) may not give a deposition for the drawing up of another record jointly with the respondent in this case.

[*Numberless*]

74, 12:

Chapter concerning legal representation *.

74, 13—15:

To provide someone with legal power — (this occurs) when he declares (as follows): "I have empowered Gušnasp for the sale of this thing", or "for the conduct of this legal case to its very end". But Gušnasp is not entitled to transfer to another person the empowering given to him by Mihrēn ("is not entitled to empower another person").

74, 16—17:

If he declares (thus): "I have designated (such-and-such a person) as (my) representative", some (authorities) have said that his title as a representative is valid right up to the taking of an oath, but others have said up to (the presentation) of a security (= pledge / stake).

74, 17—**75**, 1:

If he declares: "you are both ("jointly") appointed by me as (legal) representatives", (then if) they [.....] act as (joint) representatives of one man, that is valid, but if they proclaim each other ("one another") (legal) representatives, then that is not valid.

75, 2—5:

If (one) legal representative is appointed and later another one, and the representative subsequently appointed, to ...... of the litigants is appointed, then until the subsequently appointed representative appears in court everything said and done by the first representative has the same force in this case as though a second representative had not been appointed.

75, 5—8:

If the plaintiff with the consent of the respondent's legal representative excludes ("omits, leaves out") from the conduct of the case a ......? part of the judicial procedure, or if the judge with the consent of the legal representative of the plaintiff and the legal representative of the respondent eliminates ("sends off / away, dismisses; cancels") a ......? from the evidence given at the trial; then that is lawful (= valid).

75, 8:

Yātakgōβ (ī) gumārt ēvarīh apāyēt ut ka dātaβarān frāč patigīrēnd ēvar.

75, 9—11:

Ka pēšēmār ut pasēmār 2 mart ākanēn ut yut-ič yut yātakgōβ kunēnd harv 2 yātakgōβ ō (10) dātastān šavēnd pat kartak yātakgōβ ēvak patigīrēnd. Ut ka 2 mart ākanēn yātakgōβ kunēnd harv (11) 2 pat dātastān apāyēt būt.

75, 11—12:

Ka yātakgōβ ēvak hač dit yuttar gōβēnd saxvan nē patigīrišn (12) ut pat hačašmānd dārišn.

75, 12—13:

Ka katak-bānūk ut dūtak sardār pat čiš vičīr xvāst ka katak-bānūk (13) dūtak sardār ⟨ut⟩ yātakgōβ kunēt xvap.

75, 13—14:

Ka dūtak sardār katak-bānūk-ē(v) yātakgōβ kunēt nē (14) xvap u-š čim ēn kū katak-bānūk tanīhā pat čiš ī dūtak nē ōstaβār.

75, 14—17:

Harv ān ī (15) mātakvarān ēt aδvēnak guft ēstēt yātakgōβān anī aδvēnak guftan nē pātixšāy hend. (16) Ut ka gōβēnd nē patigīrišn ka patigīrēnd hač yātakgōβīh ānāft bavēt (ut) hač ān ī (17) patigrift⁺ kār nē kunišn.

75, 16—76, 1:

Ut ka ēvāč ēt⁺ gōβēt kū-m yātakgōβ kart yātakgōβ pat rāδēnišn (1) ut yātakgōβ ī xvēš pātixšāy gumārtan ut pat ān ī (apārīk) mātakvarān nē pātixšāy.

76, 1—3:

Ka [pēšēmār] (2) yātakgōβīh pat muhr (ī) pasēmār ka-č ō pasēmār muhr āšnāk aδak-ič nē šāyēt (ut) vikāy (ī) (3) dātastān apar ham dātastān pat yātakgōβīh šāyēt.

75, 8:

A confirmation of the authenticity (of his mandate) is indispensable for a person appointed as representative of (one) of the parties in a case, and if the judge accepts him (as a representative), (then his right to appear in the case) has been authenticated.

75, 9—11:

If the plaintiff and the respondent appoint two persons jointly and each of them separately as (their) legal representatives, and both representatives betake themselves to court, then, according to the rules of judicial practice, (the judges) will accept one representative (for each of the litigating parties — *A. P.*). And if two persons have jointly been appointed as representatives (of a single party — *A. P.*), then both of them are obliged to appear in court.

75, 11—12:

If one of the representatives states (at the trial) something different from what is asserted by the other representative (of the same party), then their testimonies may not be accepted, and the trial is to be considered as defaulted.

75, 12—13:

If a mistress of the house and the guardian of the family request a court decision (= bring action in court) concerning a certain thing or matter, and if the mistress of the house appoints the guardian of the family as representative, this is good (= valid, lawful).

75, 13—14:

If the guardian of a family appoints the mistress of the house as legal representative, then this is not good (= not valid). The reason for this is that the mistress of the house is not entitled to (represent / conduct) the affairs of the family, alone.

75, 14—17:

Everything stated ("said") in a given way by the principal litigants, (their) representatives are not entitled to present otherwise, and should they state (otherwise), (their testimonies) may not be accepted. Should they be accepted, then (such a person) is removed from the representation, and one may not rely on (the testimonies) which were accepted (lit.: "one may not act from what was accepted").

75, 16—76, 1:

If all that he has declared is: "I have appointed (such-and-such a person) as representative", then he is entitled to appoint (only) a legal representative to conduct the case and (as) his own personal representative, but he is not entitled (to appoint) one to act as such of other litigants.

76, 1—3:

If the representative of [the plaintiff] (?) has (a document confirming his mandate, sealed) with the seal of the respondent, (this) is illicit even if the respondent acknowledges his seal. But a witness participating in a case may appear as the representative (of one of the parties) in the same case.

XLVII

76, 3:

Dar ī pēšēmār *.

76, 4—13:

Pēšēmār gōβēt kū tō ō kasān čiš tōžišn dahišn kas hač čiš avi-š (5) tōžišn dahišn xvāstan ut statan rāδ+ az pātixšāy kart hom ka pātixšāy-kart (6) nē apāk dārēt čiγōn hač dastaβarān bē nipišt ēstēt tā ō var rāδēnišn ī pat dātastān (7) dāt ka pēš hač var rāδēnišn ī pat dātastān (dātastān) sar nē bavēt var apar apāyēt varzītan (8) ka ō var mih var nē dāt(an). U-š bōžišn ēn kū ī-m fratom pēšēmar rāδ (9) nē paytāk kū pat dātastān mātakvar ayāp yātakgōβ ut ētōn dānom kū ka ētōn (10) gōβēt kū čiš dahišn ut ⟨ka⟩ (hač kas) čiš avi-š dahišn būt xvāst ut stat rāδ az pātixšāy (11) kart hom xvēšīh ī xvēš rāδ guft ēstēt čē mart-ē(v) ka čiš ī xvēš rāδ (12) gōβēt kū-m xvāst ut stat rāδ tō pātixšāy ⟨īh⟩ kart hēh pātixšāyīh ī (13) pat xvēšīh ⟨i⟩ xvāstan dāt bavēt.

76, 13—17:

Ka gōβēt kū tō hač Mihrēn apām (14) stat ut Mihrēn ān apām pat xvēšīh ō man dāt ut pasēmār gōβēt kū man apām (15) nē stat ut Mihrēn ō tō nē dāt ka apām stat paytāk apar pasēmār pat (16) apām framān dahišn. U-š čim ēn čē ka-š guft kū-m apām nē stat guft (17) bavēt kū andar kas-ič nē tōžišnōmand hom ut ka tōžišnōmandīh paytāk (...) **.

77, 1—3:

... ... Āturak dāt pat pusakānīh (ut) sardārīh ō Zurvāndāt ...... (2) ...... Āturak dāt rāδ kart kū (hakar) Āturak andar apurnāyīh pat baxt šavēt Zurvāndāt (3) ....n]ē (?) bavēt gāt tāvān nē andar dastīk ***.

[*Numberless*]

77, 4—5:

Dar ī pat ēn kū čand dātastān kē paytākīh hač nipišt (ut) (5) ǎvašt (ī) pēšēnīk ****.

---

* The (*abǰad*) ordinal-number of this chapter is 47.

** The end of this article is missing.

*** The beginning of this article is missing. The remaining part has survived in a corrupt state. The translation given is highly hypothetical. The logical connexion between the textual content of line 3 and what precedes it is likewise unclear.

**** The ordinal-number of this chapter is not given.

XLVII

76, 3:

Chapter concerning the plaintiff*.

76, 4—13:

A plaintiff declares: "you are obliged to pay and convey a thing to people, (and) through the person to whom you are obliged to pay and convey (this) thing, I am entitled to lay claim to and receive (the thing)". If he does not have with him the document confirming his title (= mandate), then — as it is written in the *Dātastān-nāmak* with a citation of the commentators on the *Avesta* — he should be allowed ("given") to participate in the case ("conduct the case") right up to the taking of an oath. If the conduct of the case is not concluded before (an oath is required), he should take an oath concerning (this, *i. e.* the existence of his mandate as representative — *A. P.*). If he is opposed to (the taking of) such an oath, then he should not be granted the right to take an oath (concerning the case; *i. e.* he should be kept from participating in the ordeal portion of the trial on the given case — *A. P.*). (Commentary by the compiler of the *Law-Book* — *A. P.*): the resolution of this case is such that first of all it is unclear to me as regards the plaintiff: is he (present) in court as the principal litigant or as his representative? And I understand (it) thus: if he makes the declaration in this fashion: "(such-and-such) a thing is to be returned, and through the person to whom it was to have been conveyed, I am entitled to lay claim to it and receive (it)", then his ownership of this thing is stated thereby, since when a man declares the following concerning a thing belonging to him: "you are empowered by me to lay claim and to receive", then the power to claim the thing in his own (= the representative's) real right has been conferred to him thereby.

76, 13—17:

If he (= the plaintiff) declares: "you have received a loan from Mihrēn, and Mihrēn has conveyed this loan to me as a personal possession/property", but the respondent declares (regarding this matter): "I did not receive a loan and (consequently) Mihrēn did not convey it to you"; then, when the fact of the receipt of the loan is established, a court order should be rendered against the respondent regarding (his return) of the loan (= debt). The basis for this is that, when he declared: "I did not receive a loan" he has (thereby) said: "and I am not obliged to pay anyone". And when his obligation to pay is established and declared, (...) **.

77, 1—3:

... ... conveyed Āturak, and concerning the transfer of Āturak to Zurvāndāt for adoption and guardianship .... he made arrangements that "if Āturak dies before coming of age, then Zurvāndāt ..... will not (?) be/become", the payment of the fine for adultery (thus! — *A. P.*) does not (enter) into the (given) agreement (?) ***.

[*Numberless*]

77, 4—5:

Chapter **** containing a number of legal decisions evident from (that which) was written (and) sealed in the past.

77, 6—9:

Ēvak ēn kū ka xvāstak pat ēmōčan hangārišn ō asaβār (ut) asaβăr (7) kē avi-š dāt pat baxt šavēt tā ān xvāstak apāč ō šāhīkān kart sāl (8) sāl pat arž ī ēmōčan kē rāδ xvāstak bē dāt hač xvāstakdār ī asaβār (9) ⟨ut⟩ kē xvāstak dāšt xvāst(an).

77, 9—10:

Ēvak ēn kū pasēmār ān ī-š pat xvastūkīh (10) guft ēstēt ka nakīrā(k) bavēt nakīrā(k)īh frāč patigīrišn bē ēranǰēnīt(an).

77, 11—12:

Ēvak ēn kart ī dātaβar pat-ič ēn kū pasēmār xvastūk+ būt kū pēšēmār (12) mart-ē(v) yātakgōβ ⟨i⟩ kart andar pasēmār ēvar.

77, 12—14:

Ka pat hačašmānd ⟨i⟩ yātakgōβ ī (13) pēšēmār graβ ī pat nāmčišt rāδ patkārēt kū nē pēšēmār xvēš (14) ut mātakvar ānīt rāδ zamān xvāhēt patkārišn patigīrišn ut ān zamān dahišn.

77, 15—**78**, 2:

Ka naxvist hač gōβišn ī yātakgōβ ī pēšēmār čiγōn-iš guft kū dātastān (16) apāk pasēmār rāδēnom ut mātakvar ānayom mātakvar ānīt rāδ zamān (17) dāt pas ka pasēmār patkārēt kū tā vičārtan ī ān ī pātīrān (1) saxtan ī dātastān rāδ ō tōžišn mat apāk yātakgōβ ⟨i⟩ dātastān [nē rāδēnom (?)] (2) pat xvap dāštan.

77, 6—9:

One (decision) is this: if a thing intended "for outfitting" (is conveyed) to a horseman, (and) the horseman to whom it is conveyed, dies, then up to the time when this thing is returned to the treasury, (an amount equal) to the coast of the outfitting for which the thing was issued shall be claimed for each year (overdue) from the horseman's heir who holds this thing.

77, 9—10:

One (decision) is this: if a respondent repudiates what he confessed (or "what he agreed with"), then the acceptance (by the judges — *A. P.*) of the objection (or of the "denial" following the confession) is subject to condemnation.

77, 11—12:

One (decision) is this: the declaration of a judge, that the respondent declared his consent to the appointment by the plaintiff of a certain man as his (= the plaintiff's) legal representative has absolute force ("is valid, unchallengeable, unquestionable") as concerns the respondent.

77, 12—14:

If in the case of a *defaulted* trial the representative of the plaintiff argues — as regards a specific object put up as surety (= as a stake — *A. P.*) — that this thing does not belong to the plaintiff and demands time to bring in the principal litigant (= the plaintiff himself; *cf infra* 77, 15—**78**, 2 — *A. P.*), then his objection should be sustained and the time (indispensable for the summoning of the plaintiff) given.

77, 15—**78**, 2:

If — on the basis of the declaration of the plaintiff's legal representative in which he stated: "I shall conduct the case with the respondent and I shall bring in the principal (litigant)" [52] — time was granted to him at the beginning for the summoning (to court) of the principal litigant (or: for the presentation of the document — *A. P.*); then, if the respondent subsequently declares (in court): "I shall not conduct (?) the case with the representative (of the plaintiff) until whatever has to be paid (lit.: 'came to be paid') because of the delay in the case is paid", this should be sustained.

78, 2—11:

Apar ōy ī baγ Xusrav ī Kavātān pat vičīr ī ratān ut [anī? kār](3)-framānān apar Artaxšahr-xvarreh nahang mānākān (?) ⟨i⟩ (Ms.: ) rōtastāk rōtas[tāk ...pat](4) vēšist andar apāyēt ut dipīr 4 frēh pat kār nē dāštan ut pargā[r ut pursišn](5)-nāmak ī nōk apāyēt kartan pat (h)anǰaman ut pat hampursakīh ī čašmak(āy)ān ut [šahrīkān rāh](6) ut pat nikerišn kartan ut pat muhr ī čašmak(āy)ān ut šahrīkān ī mat ēstēnd ǎvaštan ut ān ī (7) nōk nikerišn kunēnd ut apārīk-ič pursišn-nāmak ut pargār pat vināskārīh ut saxvan (8) ān kē vināskār pat āstūt fratom ut kē vināskār nē pat āstūt bē ka (9) vināskār apāč ō miyān āβarēt ut ān čē varōmand kart ēstēt bē pat (10) nāmak-pas(s)āč hangām ut apārīk-ič bē ān kē yātūk ut vinās ut dusravīh ī pat nāmčišt (11) gōβēnd enyā nē brīt rāδ nipišt ēstēt.

78, 11—14:

Ēvak ēn kū (12) ātaxš ī Varahrān hamβarakān xvēš nāmak kē ēn and dātastān hač-iš paytāk pat nāmak(13)-nidān ī ātaxš ī Xurram-Artaxšahr ī Artaxšahr-Xvarreh nahang Xabr Xurram-Ar[taxšahr] (14) deh nišāst dārēnd.

78, 14—15:

Ēvak ēn kū pursišn-nāmak (ut) uzdāt-nāmak pat-ič (15) ǎvišt ī ōy kē pursišn-nāmak pat-iš ǎvišt(an) apāyēt.

78, 15—17:

Ēvak ān ī pat (16) yātakgōβ gumārtan nipišt kū-m pat var ī pat sōkand+ ut var ī pat nāmāk-passāč (17) yātakgōβ kart.

78, 17 + **93**, 1—3 *.

* *Vide infra* after article **96**, 16—17 + **97**, 1—3.

78, 2—11:

In the decree issued by the *rat*s and [other? official] persons during the reign of Xusrav son of Kavāt it was set down that in the province of Artaxšahr-Xvarreh there should be a maximum of [.....] judicial offices (?) in each *rōtastāk*, and that no more than four scribes should be kept at work and that (documents concerning) sentences? and records of interrogations should be drawn up new (anew) at a judicial session ("assembly") by means of the interrogation of eye-witnesses and [citizens], and (these) should be re-examined and sealed with the seals of the eye-witnesses and of the citizens who appeared (in court); and that: (the documents / court decisions) to be re-examined, as well as other records of interrogation and sentences (?) regarding crimes, and the statement that the offender acknowledged at first (during the first investigation of the affair — *A. P.*), and the one that he did not acknowledge (or "did not approve") — except for the one that the offender furnishes afresh, and also someone's subjection to the ordeal (or "oath-taking") — except for the ordeal / oath taken in conformity with an "ordeal-letter" (*i. e.* in conformity with the court-issued document containing the designation of an ordeal — *A. P.*), as well as everything else — except for the cases where he (= the accused) is spoken of with absolute certainty as a sorcerer, a criminal, (or: "a sinner"), and a person of ill repute; that all these (documents) should not be regarded as valid (lit. "drawn up, laid down").

78, 11—14:

And the following: the document concerning the Varahrān Fire-temple, which belongs jointly to the persons who drew it up and in which each one's share ("how much to whom") is set out, is preserved in the archives ("the depository of documents") of the Xurram-Artaxšahr Fire-temple which was founded in the province of Artaxšahr-Xvarreh in the village of Xurram-[Artaxšahr] near the city of Xabr.

78, 14—15:

And the following: the record of interrogation, as well as the document concerning the designation of an ordeal related to it must be sealed with the seal of the person concerning whom the record of interrogation (was drawn up).

78, 15—17:

This (too) is written concerning the appointment of a legal representative: "I have appointed (so-and-so as my) representative for the taking of a verbal oath (or "for the sulphur-water ordeal") designated in the ordeal-letter" [53].

78, 17—**93**, 1—3 *.

79, 3—13 *:

Pat nām ī Ōhrmizd ī xvatāy ī mēnōkān ut gē[tīkān ... ... apātīh ī vehdēn ī] (4) Mazdēsnān. (5) Ēn (mātakdān) mātakdān (ī) 1000 dātastān xvānēnd kē masīh ut vehīh ut aržōmandīh (ī) martōhmān (6) yut hač čiγōnīh ī-šān hač tuxšīšn [ut dahišn ī yazdān pat] xvat gōhrīh mātakdān ān (7) aβzār^{+} (ī) nērōk^{+} ī dātār pat harvispākāsīh apasīhēnītan ī druž ut apāč ō xvēš kartan (8) ut dām vinnārtan a-hambatīkīh ut anōšak ⟨ut⟩ šētāk ut hamāk-rōšnīh ut purr-pātixšāyīh pat fražām (9) rāδ ōγōn vazurg mātīk dāt andar gōhr ī martōhmīh^{+} dāšt ēstāt rāδ būtan (ī) ān sūtōmand (10) rāδ yazdān martōhm āfrīt ut stāyēnītan šāyist⟨an⟩ pat fražām drang ēn bun-dārīh hač dānākīh (11) ut dahišn ut vičītārīh ut (h)ōšyārīh^{+} ākāsīh ut martōhmān pat čiš hač čiš ... [... ...] (12) ṢLYBH (*sic*!) harv ušt(ān)ōmandān gavākīh ut  [= āšna-vākānīh?] gannākīh (h)ōš-ākāsīh vičītārīh ī (13) ō martōhmān dāt ēstēt gartakīh (<vartakīh — *A. P.*) ī-š hast pāyakīhā ut bōδīhā$^{+}$ [... ... ...] **.

[*Numberless*]

79, 15:

[Dar ī] *** arž [ī dēn ut] sahmān ī šnāsakīh.

79, 16—**80**, 17:

Frahaxtišnīh pat martōhmān ān sūtōmandtar pat ān čiš andar gētīk (17) tan pat-iš darīhēt pat mēnōk (ut) ruvān ut ān čiš kē harv bahr andar vaxt^{+}? pat dāt [.. ...] **** (4) yazdān apartom pānakīh ī dāmān ī huyōδ hač dēn paytāk ēstāt ut pat ākāsīh (5) hač dēn ō sarakīh (?) pat harv šnāsakīh paytākīh pat harv dānišn ut vičītārīh (6) ut pat harv xvēškārīh matan šāyēt aδak ān arg ī andar dēn apar xvāhišn ut pursišn ī (7) pat ākāsīh būt (ut)? andar māṣr šnāxt / šnāyīt [... ... ...] (8) ut (h)amōxtan čiš ī čiš ī [... ...] hač harv 2 šnāsakīh ī dānišn ut ākāsīh burzišnīh-ič (9) ut bahr ī patīrak ēt (h)ēr ī pat mat hač yazdān rāh ut mānyakān hač harv āpātīh (10) [ut nām]-burzišn pat mas ut veh ⟨ī ut⟩ (pat) mātakvartom sūtōmandtom ut ⟨ō-š⟩ frahaxtišnīk(11)tom ut vičīrišnīktom dārišn. Bē ōy kē-šān bahr ī yazdān hač-iš andar? (12) ap(p)urt ēstāt ut ān bahr hač-iš ap(p)urtārīh rāδ hač kām-framān ī vehān / yazdān vēxt (? Ms.: [Pahlavi]) u-š (13) mēnišn gōβišn ut kunišn rāh vanī būt^{+} ēstēt apārīk kas apēgumān nikēžīt (14) bavēt kū ōy pat farraxvtar dārišn kē pat tuxšišn ut kunišn ī xvēš bahr ī anōšak (15) ut āpātīh ī yāvētānīk vindāt ēstēt čiγōn hač dēn yazdān ākās būt pat xvāhišn ut (16)

* This is the beginning of the *Law-Book*. The upper part of this folio has been torn away.

** The phrase breaks off at this point. There is no text on line 14 of the manuscript.

*** This chapter carries no ordinal-number.

**** A lacuna of three lines — **80**, 1—3 — intervenes at this point.

79, 3—13 *:

In the name of Ōhrmizd, Lord of all (things) spiritual and [material ... ... for the prosperity of the Good] Mazdā-worshipping [religion]!

This (book) is called *The Book of One Thousand Judgements*, which (examines) only in their very essence the greatness, piety and merits of people, whosoever they be, as a result of (their own) zeal [and also as a consequence of the mercy of the gods]. This book is a weapon of the creator's power (serving for) the rout of evil ("the lie") through omniscience, for the re-establishment of his (= Ōhrmizd's) rule (in the world), for the regulation of creation, for the removal of enmity, and for the final establishment of the immortal truth (or "righteousness") and all-powerfulness of light. So great a text has been given into the keeping of the human race (or "the essence, nature of mankind") that gods and men should be blessed to the end of time [53a], for its beneficial existence. This is a repository of the bases of the wisdom of creation, of discernment (in the understanding of things and in deeds), and of prudent consciousness and people ... ... [... ...] the cross (? Ms. ṢLYBH). Every increase of the animate and (every) understanding/perception of what is corrupt/evil, the consciousness and discernment (in deeds — *A. P.*) given to the human race (...) gradually and consciously the state of captivity (to the evil principle — *A. P.*) in which (mankind) finds itself... ...**.

[*Numberless*]

79, 15:

[Chapter concerning] *** the value [of religion and] the limits of knowledge.

79, 16—**80**, 17:

The most useful education for men concerns the things in this material world containing their (= men's) body that serve the spiritual principle (and) the soul, as well as those things in which the increase (?) of each part (takes place) in accordance with the law [...] ****... (that) the gods are the highest bastion for creatures struggling for righteousness was clarified by religion. And with the help of knowledge (drawn) from religion, it is possible to reach perfection (? "completeness"?) through every manifestation of understanding, through every (piece of) knowledge and capacity to discern ("discernment, discrimination, selectiveness"), and through (any) type of activity ("function, obligation"). Then, the respect found in religion as regards claims (= lawsuits) and judicial investigation ("trial, interrogation") carried out with awareness, (and that which) is accepted/praised by the divine word [... ... ...] and to teach (?) ... ... [.... ....] to each of the two [varieties] of knowledge, namely wisdom and information, and to the exaltation [of one's name]. And that portion (in a man) which comes from the gods and (from) the *manes* (= *fravahrs* — *A. P.*) as against the estate obtained (through inheritance or acquisition), is to be considered the most important, the most beneficial, the most deserving of being learned and the most determinant in all the aspects of the prosperity and exaltation of one's name in the Great and the Good. But (the man) from whom the portion (received) from the gods ("the divine share") was stolen, and who as the result of the theft of this portion abandoned the spiritual teachings of the righteous/the design and the command of the gods, he pursišn xvēštan avinās kart ut rāh ī xvēškārih šnāxtan mēnišn ut gōβišn ut kunišn (17) pat rāstīh apēč dāštan ut man Farraxvmart ī Vahrāmān ēn āpātīh āpātīhāta[r] (...)*.

81, 1—11**:

(2) ayāp ān ī māt ut brāt ka bē mīrēt xvāstak apāč gumā[r∾... ... ...] (3) nē šāyēt aδak-iš xvāstak apāč gumārēt ut xvah [... ... ...] (4) ut ka pit pus ēv ut duxt 1 ān gyāk ut pit pus pat ēv-t[āk ... ...] (5) drahm ēt būt stūr ān ī pus gumārišn ut pat stūrī[h ... ...] (6) ut pit hamāk 90 hast ān pus 1 drahm xvāstak ī pit [... ... ...] (7) v/bar? ō duxt stūr ān ī pus gumārišn. Pus-ič ēt n[ē/rāδ ... ...] (8) u-š stūr gumārtan nē šāyēt ut ka-m ēt guft kū [... ... ...] (9) ēt guft kū ān ī pit nē gumārišn. Ut ka stūr ī pit nē gu[mār∾ ... ...] (10) ī pit nē bavēt ut pas xvāstak 61 drahm pus pat rāh ī nabānazdištīh bē ō duxt (11) stūrīh ī kas nēst.

81, 11—17:

Ut ka pus 2 duxt 1 ut pit ān gyāk pus harv 2 ut pit pat ēv-tāk (12) mīrēnd pusarān yut-yut handōxt ī xvēš 1 drahm hast ut pit xvāstak 95 bavēt (13) ā-m ēt guft kū stūr ān ī pus gumārišn ut nūn pusarān yut-yut xvāstak 31 drahm (14) hast pat ān čim stūr ī avēšān gumārtan nē šāyēt ut pas 31 drahm ī ān pus (ut) 31 drahm ī (15) anī pus duxt pat rāh (ī) ⟨rāh⟩ nabānazdištīh bē barēt hač ān čiγōn pusarān ka-šān (16) yut-yut xvāstak 60+ hē aδak-šān stūr apayēh gumārtan ut ān duxt stūrīh-ič (17) ī pit apar nē mānēh+.

81, 17—**82**, 7***:

Gyāk-ē nipišt kū pus andar dūtak (ut) katak-bānūk pat 2 kas (1) ... ... [pus ut katak-bānūk] (2) [... ... ...] dūtak ī katak-xvatāy xvāstak dahēnd ō katak-bānūk rasēt (3) [... ... ...] ... ō dūtak xvāstak dahēnd+ aδak-ič pat katak-bānūk ēstēt (4) [... ... ... st]ūr ī kartak xvāstak dahēnd andar ō katak-xvatāy barīhēt+ (5) [... ... ... ka ō zan ī] xvēš gōβēt kū frazand ī hač tō zāyēt stūrīh (ī) man (6) [... ... ...] yut-yut xvāstak 80 frāč kunišn ut xvāstak (7) [... ... ...] pat xvēšīh ut duxt pat stūrīh dārišn.

82, 7—9:

Ut ka ō zan (8) [ī xvēš gōβēt kū frazand ī hač tō zāy]ēnd stūrīh ī man hēβ kunēnd (9) [aδak-šān xvāstak ī pat stūrīh] nē frāč kunišn. Ut duxt hamaδvēn zan ī pātixšāyīhā (10) ī ōy hend.

82, 10—12:

Ut ka gōβēt kū-m frazand ī hač tō zāyēnd pat xvāstak ī man stūr kart hend ēv (11) ka ō zan ī xvēš ēv ka ō ān ī hač šahr gōβēt hamē(v) pus ut duxt bahr rāst ut hamē(v) (12) pat stūrīh pātixšāyōmand dāštan.

---

* The text of the "Prologue" by the compiler of the *Law-Book* breaks off at this point.

** The corner of this folio has been torn away; almost nothing has survived from the first line of the folio and only the right hand half of the text in lines 2-9 has been preserved.

*** From the first line on the page 82 only traces of the last letters have survived; in the lines 2—9 only the left hand half of the text has been preserved.

perishes through his thoughts, words, and deeds. It has been shown beyond question by others that the (man) who through his own striving and zeal has obtained a share of immortality and eternal prosperity, (who) being versed in matters of religion and of the gods has made himself invulnerable ("guiltless") to claims and judicial investigations through a knowledge of (his) obligations, and who has kept the form of (his) thoughts, speech, and actions pure in accordance with righteousness is to be considered more fortunate (than any other). And I Farraxvmart son of Vahrām this prosperity more prosperous...*

81, 1—11**:

81, 11—17:

(And) if in a family there are two sons, a father and a daughter, and (if) both sons and the father die at the same time, and if the sons — each of them separately — have accumulated one *drahm* apiece, whereas the father's estate amounts to 95 (*drahms*), then (here) is what I have said in this case: a *stūr* must be appointed for the son [54]. And now (this case): the sons — each of them separately — have an estate ("a thing") amounting to 31 *drahms* apiece, then, because of this, no *stūr* should be appointed (for either of them — *A. P.*), but subsequently the 31 *drahms* of the one son (and) the 31 *drahms* belonging to the other son shall be received by the daughter (as her father's *stūr* — *A. P.*) on the basis of the right of succession *via* kinship. Since, if the sons — each of them separately — had a thing (with a value of) 60 (*drahms*), a *stūr* would have to be appointed for them and this daughter would not have inherited her father's *stūr*ship.

81, 17—**82**, 7***:

82, 7—9:

If he makes [the following declaration to his] wife: "let [the children whom you will bear] be my *stūrs*", and if children are born (to her) and assume the *stūr*ship, [then the estate conveyed for the *stūr*ship] shall not be taken [from them]. (When it is addressed to) a daughter, (this declaration shall have an effect that is) entirely similar (to the one which it has when it is addressed) to his *pātišxāy*-wife.

82, 10—12:

And if he declares: "I have instituted as *stūr*-possessors of my estate the children whom you will bear", then irrespective of whether he has made the declaration to his wife or merely to a female fellow-citizen, all (the children), son or daughter, receive equal shares, and all of them should be considered as entitled to the *stūr*ship.

82, 12—14:

Ut ka ō mart 1 gōβēt kū stūrīh (ī) man kun aδak-iš (13) xvāstak 60+ (Ms.: 80) pat stūrīh avi-š dāt bavēt. Ut ka ān-īč patigīrēt+ (apāč) ēstāt nē pātixšāyōmand. (14) Ut ān ī kē apāč ēstēt pat sāl drahnāδ markarž(ān).

82, 14—16:

Ka ō zan (ī) šahr gōβēt kū frazand ī hač tō zāyēnd (15) stūrīh ī man hēβ kunēnd ka zāyēnd ut stūrīh nē kunēnd ut mērak zan ut frazand ī pātixšāyīhā hast ō zan (16) ut frazand rasēt.

82, 16—17:

Ut ka (ō) zan ī xvēš gōβēt kū frazand ī hač tō zāyēnd stūrīh ī man hēβ kunēnd (17) nipišt kū ka pus 2 duxt 2 zāyēnd pus 1 ut duxt 1 stūrīh kunēnd apārīk nē kunēnd.

83, 1—3:

[... ...]šn p[...] bōžišn [... ...] ut gumā[rišn ... ...] ēstēt kū xvāstak ī pat dūtak (2) mērak dārišn ut dāštan rāδ+ framān dāt ut xvāstak pat dūtak dāštan apāyist (3) andar pēšēmār ut pasēmār pat ēvār dārišn *.

83, 3—6:

Pasēmār kē xvāstak rāδ patkār[ēt] (4) kū ka hač kas bērōn pat graβakānīh ayāp pat passandārīh ayāp pat yāmdārīh (5) ayāp pat anī aδvēnak man dāšt ut ō xvēšīh ī man mat ut (pēšēmār) kē-č patkārēt kū-šān (6) āzāt kart hom ayāp-am pat ⟨pat⟩ xvāstak apāk hambaγān nē tōžišnōmand hom (...) **.

83, 7—8:

Ut ka gōβēt kas-ič zan nē būt ut gāt bē dāt pātixšāy bavēt+ (8) pat zanīh ut gāt(ā)r (nē) kunišn.

83, 8—11:

Xvāstak 1 Farraxv hač Mihrēn stat ut pēšēmār (9) gōβēt kū Mihrēn ō man dāt ut pasēmār pat dāt ⟨ō pasēmār pat dāt⟩ ī (10) ō pēšēmār nakīrā(k) ut patkārēt kū ō anī kas ut pat ōy kē avi-š dāt vičārt (11) [... ha]kar pasēmar pat ān ī nakīrā(k) bōxt pēšēmār vatxvāh.

* End of an article whose beginning has not survived.
** The second half of this article has been left out by the copyist.

82, 12—14:

If he has declared to a man: "be my *stūr*!", then a thing valued at 60 /80 (*drahms*?) is conveyed to him as a *stūr*-possession (from the declarer's estate on the strength of this declaration — *A. P.*). And if he accepts this (= thing), he is not entitled to deviate (from the performance of a *stūr*'s obligations). And one who deviates within a year (following his acceptance of the *stūr*ship) should be considered to be a person who has committed a capital offence.

82, 14—16:

If he declares to (one of his female) fellow-citizens: "let the children whom you will bear be my *stūrs*", (and) if children are born from her, but do not perform (the functions of) a *stūr*, and (this) man has a wife and children from a *pātixšāyīh*-marriage, then (the *stūr*ship instituted by him) shall go to (his) wife and children.

82, 16—17:

If he declares (the following) to his wife: "let the children whom you will bear assume my *stūr*ship!"; it is written that, if two sons and two daughters are born, then one son and one daughter shall assume (their father's) *stūr*ship, whereas the others need not assume it.

83, 1—3 *.

83, 3—6:

The respondent gives the following testimony regarding a thing at a trial: "I possess it from a certain person as a pledge (= *antichresis*- security of immoveable property — *A. P.*)" or "as an emphyteutic (tenure)?" or "as a pledge-deposit (moveable property — *A. P.*)" or on some other basis, "and it has become my personal possession (= "became my personal property")". Whereas (the plaintiff) gives the following testimony: "they (= the partners and co-heirs) have freed me (from the obligation to pay this debt)", or (he formulates it in this manner): "I am not obliged to pay this debt jointly with (my) partners/co-heirs". (...) **.

83, 7—8:

And if he declares: "she was no one's wife and she has committed fornication", then she is entitled to be given in marriage and she shall not commit adultery (thereafter).

83, 8—11:

Farraxv received a thing from Mihrēn, and the plaintiff declares: "Mihrēn conveyed (it) to me", whereas the respondent denies the fact of the transfer (of the thing by Mihrēn) to the plaintiff, and he asserts the following at the trial: "(Mihrēn conveyed it) to another person and (I) have paid the one to whom he conveyed (the thing)", [then if] the respondent is justified in that which he denied (in the testimony of the plaintiff), the plaintiff must be proclaimed malicious (*i. e.* he should be charged with legal chicanery — *A. P.*).

83, 11—17:

Ut ka ēraxt hač ān (12) [...] y'/īh nē guft kū ō pēšēmār nē dahišn (ut) vičīr kunišn kū bē dah! U-š (13) (h)andāčak ēn hamē(v) gōβēt kū ka pēšēmār gōβēt kū sāl 3 ō zanīh ī (14) man mat ut pasēmār gāt pasēmār gōβēt kū sāl 3 ō zanīh ī Kd/yl/ryn mat ut pat (15) ān aδvēnak ī pēšēmar guft andar zanīh ī K... pat K... vičārt ka pasēmār (16) [pat vičārt ī andar K... bōxt?] pēšēmār vatxvāh ut ka ēraxt vičīr kunišn kū bē (17) [... ... ...] nē tāvānōmand hom.

83, 17—**84**, 5:

Ka pēšēmār (1) [ut zan-ē(v)] pat ēn kū-t aδvēnak [... ... ...] ī man kart hamēmār ān zan-ič [... ...] (2) rāδ nikīrā(k) ut gōβēt kū mart-ē(v) Mihrēn nām zan hom ut pas pēšēmār dip (3) ō dātastān āβarēt ⟨i⟩ ōy zan guft ēstēt kū nē Mihrēn zan hom (4) vičīr kunišn kū zanīh ī pēšēmār kun čē ōy zan nē tuvān guft kū-m (5) šōy nēst.

84, 5—10:

Ka pēšēmār gōβēt kū ēn xvāstak sāl ēvak ō Mihrēn (6) mat u-š sāl 2 ō man dāt ⟨pēšēmār⟩ pasēmār gōβēt kū pēš mat (7) u-š pas (ō) man dāt pēšēmār (ut) pasēmār harv dō zamān ī ō xvāhišn dahišn. Ut ka (8) pēšēmār gōβēt kū sāl ēvak (ō) Mihrēn mat u-š sāl 10 ō man dāt pasēmār (9) gōβēt kū pat ān hangām mat u-š sāl 8 ō man dāt pasēmār zamān dahišn (10) ut pēšēmār nē dahišn.

84, 10—17:

Ka pēšēmār gōβēt kū ēn xvāstak Farraxv (ō man dāt ut apātixšāyīhā pasēmār) (12) dārēt ut pasēmār gōβēt kū sāl ēvak Farraxv xvēš būt u-š bē ō man (13) dāt u-š sāl 3 dārišn bē ō man kart pat ān dastaβarīh man dārom pasēmār (14) pat dārišn ēraxt, čē hamdātastān būt kū sāl 2 nē man dāšt čē pat (15) dārišn (ī) Farraxv būt u-š pat ān dātastān pat pēšēmār gōβišn. Pēšēmār (16) gōβēt kū ēn xvāstak sāl ēvak Farraxv xvēš būt u-š bē ō man dāt (17) pat ān dastaβarīh man xvēš [hamdātastān? ... ...].

85, 1—6: (See **40**, 17).

83, 11—17:

If he is sentenced (for malice; *cf. supra* **83**, 8—11 — *A. P.*) it does not [...] derive (? lit.: "did not say") (from it) that the thing should not be conveyed to the plaintiff (?), (and) the decision: "hand (the thing) over!" must be rendered. And he gives this example: if the plaintiff declares: "three years (ago) she entered into a marriage with me, and the respondent committed adultery (with her)", whereas the respondent declares: "three years (ago) she entered into a marriage with K..., and as regards the occurrence which ('the manner in which') the plaintiff recalled, (when she was) married to K..., I paid (a fine — *A. P.*) to K...". If the respondent [is justified in the part of his testimony relating to his payment of a fine to K... (*i. e.* if it is confirmed — *A. P.*)], then the plaintiff is proclaimed malicious. And if he is sentenced (to a fine for malice — *A. P.*), then a decision must be rendered that ... [... ... ...] "I am not obliged to pay the fine".

83, 17—**84**, 5:

If a plaintiff brings suit [against a woman] concerning this: "you ... [... ... ...]", and this woman [... ...] denies (it) and declares (the following): "I am the wife of a man named Mihrēn", but upon the presentation in court of a document (= of the marriage contract — *A. P.*) by the plaintiff, this woman declares that: "I am not Mihrēn's wife"; then the following decision must be rendered: "perform (your) obligations as the wife of the plaintiff", since this woman may (no longer) say: "he is not my husband".

84, 5—10:

If the plaintiff declares: "this thing went (= passed) to Mihrēn a year (ago), but he gave it to me (= conveyed it through a will or a bill of transfer — *A. P.*) two years (ago)", whereas the respondent declares: "it went first (to Mihrēn) and (he) subsequently conveyed it to me"; then in such a case, the plaintiff as well as the respondent — both of them — must arrange for a judicial session to investigate the claim (to the thing under dispute — *A. P.*). But if the plaintiff declares: "(the thing) went to Mihrēn a year (ago), but he gave it to me ten years ago", but the respondent declares: "at that time (or "under these circumstances") it went (to Mihrēn), and he gave it to me eight years (ago)", then a judicial session (with the attendance) of the respondent must be arranged (for the investigation of the respondent's claim, but a judicial session) with the plaintiff in attendance need not be arranged.

84, 10—17:

If the plaintiff declares: "Farraxv (conveyed) this thing (to me and the respondent possesses it unlawfully", whereas the respondent declares: "(this thing) belonged to Farraxv a year (ago) and he conveyed it to me and already three years (ago) he transferred to me the right of possession of this thing and I possess it on the basis of this title (= of this disposition by Farraxv — *A. P.*)"; then the respondent (should be condemned) for the possession of this thing since he agreed to this (= the following) that: "two years (out of three — *A. P.*) I did not possess the thing since it was in Farraxv's possession". And according to this decision (= according to the decision in this legal case — *A. P.*), it must be declared (as belonging to the plaintiff. (Whereas if) the plaintiff declares: "this thing belonged to Farraxv one year (ago) and he conveyed it to me, and on the basis of this title (= of this disposition of the thing), I possess it", [... ... ...].

85, 1—6: (See **40**, 17).

XXXIV*

85, 7—8:

Dar ī hambāγīh ī dō ut kahas ut xvāstak ī (8) pat 2 mart.

85, 8—11:

Kahas ī mart pat zamīk ī xvēš ayāp pat zamīk ī hamβarakān kunēt ka-š gōš-bālāδ (9) kand ka-š pērāmōn hamāk zamīk ī kasān aδak-ič avēšān kē ān zamīk xvēš nendar dašt (10) mizd ī ān kahas bē pat xunsandīh ut bērōn dašt mizd ī ān kahas⁺ (Ms.: ks < kts) bē pat apēziyānīh ī (11) ōy kē kahas xvēš enyā kahas⁺ kand(an) nē pātixšāy.

85, 11—13:

Kanas⁺ (Ms.: ks < kts) pat 2 mart kand (12) tā spurr bavēt hamēv ka ēvak kanēt ān ī did nē pātixšāy bē ka kanēt (13) ayāp aβzōn bahr ī xvēš apar ōy ī dit bē hilēt / hilišn.

85, 13—16:

Kahas-ē(v) 2 mart pat ākanēn (14) kanēnd ut bē rāδēnēnd ut ēvak patkārēt kū āp aβzāyēm. Būt kē guft kū ān ī (15) dit nē pātixšāy bē ka pat aβzūtan andar ēstēt ayāp aβzōn pat xvēšīh apar ōy ī dit (16) bē hilēt.

85, 16—**86**, 2:

Gyākē nipišt kū kahas-ē(v) 2 mart pat ākanēn rāδēnīt ēstēt ut ēvak nē (17) mat ēstēt ut ān ī dit yut hač ākāsīh ī ōy ī nē mat ēstēt āp aβzāyēt (1) [pātixšāy ka?] aβzāyēt ut tā uzēnak apāč dāt aβzōn bahr ī ōy ī nē mat ēstēt pat (2) graβ dāštan pātixšāy.

86, 2—15:

Mart uzēnak ī pat xānak ut kahas ut xvāstak ī-š hač anī (3) mart ham(m)is xvēš ān ī andar ān ē ka xānak ut kahas ut xvāstak āpātān pat ēvak(?) virāδišn ī (4) ān xānak ut kahas ut varz ī pat ān xvāstak kart⁺ andar apāyēt hakar andar kart pat patkārišn (5) ō hamxvāstakān pat garzišn ō dātaβarān rōčkār andar apāyēt ka-č ⟨ō⟩ hambāγ mih ēstēt (6) aδak-ič⁺ yut hač dastaβarīh ī hambāγān kartan ut uzēnak ī kunēt ān ī pat kartan apārīk hambāγān (7) niyāpēt guharīk xvāst pātixšāy. Ka-š apar gōβišnīh dāt ēstēt aδak-ič hamgōnak [.] (8) Ut ān ī andar ān ē ka ān kahas ut xānak

* The (*abǰad*) ordinal-number of this chapter is 34.

XXXIV*

85, 7—8:

Chapter concerning the co-partnership of two (persons) and concerning canals and plots of land ("a thing") belonging to two persons.

85, 8—11:

(Concerning) the canal which a man lays on his own land or on common (= public) land: if he has dug it to a depth ("height") "up to the ears", and if he (has laid it) all around the entire land of other persons; then, under these circumstances, the persons owning this land are not entitled to dig (lateral, out-flow? — *A. P.*) canals: inside (their own) field — except (against) the payment for such a canal set through an agreement (with the possessor of the canal — *A. P.*), and/or outside the field — except (against) the payment for such a canal corresponding to the compensation (due) for the damage caused to the possessor of the canal.

85, 11—13:

Two men (jointly) dig a canal: up to the completion (of the work on the canal), whenever one is digging the other is not entitled to (refrain from) digging, otherwise he must cede his share in (the common) profits to the other (= the one who dug).

85, 13—16:

Two men jointly dig a canal and operate it (or "exploit" it), and one of them starts a quarrel: "let us increase the water!". Certain (authorities) have said that the other one must either consent to the increase (in the level, or in the number of times the water is turned on — *A. P.*), or cede his share in the common profits to his partner ("the other").

85, 16—**86**, 2:

It is written in one place: a canal is put into operation and it is managed jointly by two persons, and one of them does not appear, and the other increases the water (level, or the number of times it is turned on — *A. P.*) without the knowledge of the one who did not appear; (then he is entitled) to increase (the water), and until his expenditures (*i. e.* the part of the expenditures born by him which falls to his partner's share — *A. P.*) are repaid, he is entitled to keep as security the share of the benefits (from the common revenue) of the one who did not appear.

86, 2—15:

As regards the expenditures connected with a house, a canal, and a plot of land ("a thing") — which a man possesses jointly with another person — (specifically) those (= expenditures) which are indispensable exclusively for putting the house and canal in order and for the cultivation of the plot of land ("thing") after the house, canal and plot are ready ("set up") — and also should a (daily) allowance be required to lay a complaint before the judges over a suit with his partners regarding (the necessity) of hanbast ēstēt pat apāč kartan ī ān kahas ut xānak andar (9) apāyēt ka hamxvāstakān mih ēstēnd⁺ yut hač patkārišn ō hamxvāstakān kunēt uzēnak (10) apāč nē rasēt ut ka-(šān) ō hamxvāstak patkārišn nē kunēnd pātixšāy kartan ut hakar (11) kunēt ān ī apārīk hamxvāstakān dahišn guharīk xvāst ut tā guharīk dahēnd xvāstak (12) bahr ī apārīk hambāγān ka uzēnak andak mātak ut xvāstak apēr staβr mātak aδak-ič uzēnak (13) rāδ pat graβīh dāšt pātixšāy u-š pat patkārišn ī ō dātaβarān ⟨ut⟩ čandīh ī uzēnak (14) ēvarīh xvāhišn ut pat vēšist ēvar šāyēt kartan ut dātaβar pat vēš[istīh] pat hamēmār (15) ēvar.

86, 15—17:

En dātastān apāk anī guft ēxtēt kū ka hambāγ tōžišn [... ... ...] (16) kart ēstēt andar ān ē ka hambāγ(ān) mih [ēs]tēnd⁺ yut hač patkārišn ī hambāγān bē (17) vičārēt pat vičārtan a[pārīk ham]bāγān niyāpēt apāč xvāst [pātixšāy].

87, 1—2*:

[... ... ...] (2) pat stūrīh ō ān ī ditīkar sažāk dāt pātixšāy.

87, 2—3:

Ka gōβēt kū-[m pat 10 sāl] (3) tan pat zanīh ō tō dāt aδak-iš andar 10 sāl *ayuγēn* apar ōh mānēt.

87, 3—7:

[Mart-ē(v) ka-š pat] (4) xunsandīh ī zan zan hač zanīh hilēt ut pat zanīh ō apurnāyak ī xvēš dahēt ut apurnāyak (5) andar apurnāyakīh pat baxt šavēt aδak-ič ān zan ōy čim rāδ stūrīh ī ān mart kem avi-š (6) nē rasēt ēn dātastān apāk ān ī guft ēstēt kū ka-š sardārīh apāk bē nē (7) hilēt hišt nē bavēt.

* This is the end of an article whose beginning has not survived since line 1 of the folio is missing.

making these expenditures; thus, even if his partner ("co-possessor") denies (the necessity of such expenditures, refuses to bear the expenses — *A. P.*); even in such a case, he ("the man") is entitled to make them (= the expenditures) without his partners' commission, and he is entitled to demand that (the portion) of the expenditures made by him which should (have been born) by the other co-possessors should be repaid (by them) to him. And if a court decision is rendered concerning this, it is the same. And as regards those (expenditures) related to the destruction of the canal and house which are indispensable for the reconstruction of the canal and house: if (his) partners deny (the necessity of such expenditures; refuse to participate in them — *A. P.*) and he bears these expenses without litigating with his co-possessors, then he is not reimbursed for the costs. But if they do not bring suit against their partner, then he is entitled to make the expenditures and if he has made them, he is entitled to demand that they reimburse him the part (of the expenditures) which should have been born by the other partners. And until he has been reimbursed, he is entitled to hold as security — against the expenses born by him — the part of the estate (= the house and the plot of land; lit. "thing") belonging to the other co-possessors — no matter how small the amount of the expenses or how much greater the value ("amount") of the estate ("thing"). And during the trial before the judges he must demand the exact sum of (his) expenditures, and this must be fixed with maximum precision, and the setting (of the amount of the expenditures) with maximum precision enters into the competence of the judge at the trial.

86, 15—17:

Together with the other, this decision is rendered: if a co-partner/co-possessor made (?) a payment/debt [... ... ...] and (he) makes the payment or ("settles the debt") at the time that (his) co-possessors deny (the necessity of paying, refuse to pay — *A. P.*); then he (is entitled) to claim the portion of the sum paid which ought to have been paid by the other co-possessors.

87, 1—2 *:

(...) (he) is entitled to convey as a *stūr*-possession to another suitable person.

87, 2—3:

If she declared (the following): "(I) gave myself in marriage to you [for a ten year term]", then during the course of (these) ten years she will remain in the status of an *epikleros*.

87, 3—7:

[If a man, with] his wife's consent, divorces her and gives her in marriage to his minor son, and (this) minor dies before coming of age; then even in this case, the woman, as a result of this [55], still receives the *stūr*ship of that man (= of the husband who divorced her — *A. P.*). This decision (was formulated) side by side with the one stating that: "if he does not dissolve (the marriage) together with the guardianship (*i. e.* he does not give the woman into the guardianship of another person when he divorces her — *A. P.*), then the marriage is not to be considered as dissolved". (*Cf. supra* **4**, 1—4).

87, 7—10:

Apāk-ič ān ī hačapar nipišt kū ka gōβēt kū-m hač zanīh (8) hišt ut pat zanīh ut sardārīh ō Mihrēn dāt ut Mihrēn ziyānak pat zanīh patigīrēt (9) ut p(at) sardārīh andar nē apāyēt ⟨rāδ⟩ gōβēt būt kē guft kū hišt+/hilišn+ kār nēst ut ān čē (10) pat hišt+/hilišn-nāmak naxvist sardārīh hanǰāmēnd ut pas hišt+/hilišn nikerītan.

87, 10—12:

Ka xvāstak (11) pat stūrīh ō apurnāyak dahēt ut apurnāyak andar apurnāyākīh pat baxt šavēt (stūr) apāč gumārišn (12) ut ēn kū rētak hač kanīžak yuttar bavēt uskārtan.

87, 12—15:

Ka xvēšāvand nabānazdišt nē paytāk (13) dūtak katak-bānūk pat bē vitīrišnīh stūrīh ō harv kē kāmēt dāt pātixšāy ka xvēšāvand (14) stūrīh nē xvāhēnd ō stūrīh+ (Ms.: sardārīh) anī mart ī ōstaβar gumārtan pātixšāy hend stūr ī (15) kartak pat ān xvāstak apar mānēt ayāp ō ān stūrīh dahēnd pat bar āmār ōh bavēt.

87, 16:

Pat stūrīh ka ān ī ham-pit pat dāt mas kū ān ī ham-māt ut ham-pit ān ī ham-pit gumārišn.

87, 17—**88**, 2:

Ka zan 1 tā 10 sāl tan ō zanīh ō mart 1 dāhēt andar 10 sāl naxvist mart ut pas zan (1)* [... ... ...] (2) [... ... ...] andar ān ī bē dāt dastaβarīhā būt.

88, 2—4:

Ka stūr (3) [... ... ...] xvēšāvandīh ēvaktom stūrīh xvāhēnd ān ī mas gumārišn ut ka 2 (4) tan st[ūr] gumārišn u-š pat harv 2 sažākīh ēvaktom pat ān ī ōy [ī]? mas gumārišn.

88, 5—6:

Ka xvāstak ī 90 aržēt rāδ kart kū-m ēv bahr frāč hač man pat stūrīh (6) ō tō dāt pat 3 bahr 2 bahr dāt bavēt čē pat stūrīh ōγōn šāyēt būt.

* Line 1 of this folio has not survived.

87, 7—10:

In addition to the above it is written, that if he declares: "I have divorced (you) and given (you) as a wife and into the guardianship of Mihrēn", and Mihrēn accepts her as a wife, but as to the guardianship (over her he declares: "(there is) no need"; certain (authorities) have maintained that the divorce is not valid (in such a case), and attention should be paid that the question of the guardianship (over the woman) be resolved (that "they resolve, settle" this question) first in the divorce-document, and only then (the question of the divorce). (*Cf. supra* **4**, 14—**5**, 3 — *A. P.*).

87, 10—12:

If he conveys his estate as a *stūr*-possession to (his) minor child, and this minor dies before coming of age, then (a *stūr*) should be appointed again and the difference between a boy and a girl (should) be taken into consideration at that time.

87, 12—15:

If it is not clear which of the agnates is the closest (*i. e.* who has the most rights among the possible agnate-candidates — *A. P.*), then the mistress of the house has the right to transfer the *stūr*ship at her death to whom(ever of them) she prefers. If the agnate-kinsmen do not claim/desire the *stūr*ship (*i. e.* evade the acceptance of the *stūr*ship), then they are entitled to appoint another person (*i. e.* a non-agnate — *A. P.*), specifically a man whom they trust, as *stūr*. An *instituted stūr* has the right to a revenue (lit.: "is taken into account as regards revenue") from the estate remaining (= escheated) from the family or from the one conveyed (especially) for the *stūr*ship (= as a foundation for *stūr*ship).

87, 16:

If a consanguinous (brother or sister of the dead man) is older than (the brother or sister) from the same father and mother (as the dead man), then the half-brother ("from the same father") should be appointed as *stūr*.

87, 17—**88**, 2:

If a woman gives herself (lit.: "her body") in marriage to a man for a term of ten years, then during the course of these ten years first the husband then the wife [... ... ...] * he/she is entitled to give (?).

88, 2—4:

If a *stūr* [is appointed *via*] kinship, then at the first demand for a *stūr*ship the eldest (of the agnates) should be appointed. And if a *stūr* must be appointed for two (persons from the same family) and he (= the eldest of the agnates) is equally suitable to assume the *stūr*ship for each one of them, he should be appointed first as *stūr* for the elder (of the dead men) [56].

88, 5—6:

If he declares (the following) regarding a thing which costs 90 (*drahms/saters*?): "I have conveyed to you after me (= in case of death) a part (of this thing) as a foundation for *stūr*ship", (then) two thirds (of this thing, *i. e.* property amounting to 60 *drahms/saters* — *A. P.*) are (thereby) conveyed, since this is the case (in transfers) for *stūr*ship.

88, 7—14:

Hač dastaβarān bē ōγōn gōβēnd kū ka katak-xvatāy ut katak-bānūk ut pus 1 ān gyāk ut katak-(8)xvatāy bē mīrēt pus apāk katak-bānūk hambāγ bē hakar-iš zan-ē(v) ayāp apurnāyak-ē(v) (9) ayāp xvāstak ī-š andar žīvandakīh (ī) pitar handōxt 60 (Ms.: 80) hast enyā$^{+}$ ka-š andar (10) hambāγīh ī katak-bānūk xvāstak ēv^{+} drahm nē handōxt ka-č-iš yut hač aparmānd (11) ī pit xvāstak ī-š andar zīvandakīh ī pit handōxt 59 (Ms.: 79) hast ēt rāδ čē apāk katak- (12) bānūk hambāγ u-š andar hambāγīh ⟨i⟩ čiš nē aβzūt ka pat baxt šavēt xvāstak-ič (13) 59 (Ms.: 79) pat rāh (ī) hambāγīh frāč ⟨2⟩ (ō) katak-bānūk mānēt u-š stūr gumārtan nē (14) šāyēt ut ka katak-bānūk frāč ravēt stūr ān ī katak-xvatāy gumārišn.

88, 14—17:

Ka (15) katak-bānūk ut pus (ut duxt 1) ān gyak ut harv 3 hambāγ hend ka-č-iš handōxt ī andar žīvandakīh ī pitar (16) 59^{+} (Ms.: 79) hast bē-š andar hambāγīh ⟨andar hambāγīh⟩ čiš-ič nē aβzūt pas-ič ka (17) bē mīrēt apāk-ič ēt^{+} kū-š apāk xvah hambāγīh ut sardārīh harv 2 hast pat-ič (...) *.

89, 1:

(...) (1) dārom uzīt^{+} ān zamān dārišn ō xvēšāvandān apispārisn **.

89, 1—3:

Apāk anī [nipišt/guft] (2) kū ka gōβēt kū-m tā ēv sāl pat tan hač tō patigrift uzīt ēv sāl pāyandānīh (3) nēst bē tan apāč apispārišn.

89, 3—5:

Ut ān guft kū ka graβakāndār pat xvāstak ī (4) graβakān vinās kunēt aδak-iš graβ pat graβīh dāštan ō ratān ap(p)ār u-š drahm ap(p)ār (5) nē bavēt čē pat ān vinās nē kart.

89, 5—6:

Apāk anī guft kū ka hač xvāstak ī (6) graβ apēsaxvan bavēt aδak-iš drahm nē hišt bavēt.

89, 6—7:

Ut apāk anī Syāvaxš guft (7) kū ka drahm kē xvāstak pat-iš graβakān bē dahēt aδak-iš xvāstak-ič dāt bavēt.

---

* The chapter breaks off here.

** This is the end of an article whose beginning has not survived.

88, 7—14:

The following is said with a reference to the commentators of the *Avesta*. If a family consists of a head of household, a mistress of the house and one son, and the head of household dies, and the son and the mistress of the house are co-partners (= co-heirs), then — except when he (= the son) has a wife or a minor (child) or an estate valued at 60^+ (the ms. has 80) (*satērs*?) accumulated in his father's lifetime — if he did not accumulate a single *drahm* in his co-partnership with the mistress of the house and he has at the same time an estate valued at 59^+ (the ms. has 79) (*satērs*?/*drahms*?) accumulated in his father's lifetime in addition to the share he inherited from his father; inasmuch as he is in co-partnership with the mistress of the house, and while in co-partnership he has added nothing (to their common estate), upon his death the estate valued at 59^+ (*drahms*/*satērs*?) shall go to the mistress of the house in accordance with the law of co-partnership and no *stūr* need be appointed for him (= the son). But when the mistress of the house dies, a *stūr* must be appointed for the late head of household.

88, 14—17:

If a family contains a mistress of the house, a son and a daughter, and all three are co-partners (= co-heirs), then — even if what has been accumulated (by the son) in his father's lifetime amounts to 59^+ (the ms. has 79) (*drahms*/*satērs*?), and nothing was acquired in co-partnership — when he (= the son) dies, in addition to what he held jointly with his sister *via* co-partnership and guardianship, and after (...) **.

89, 1:

(...) I possess", then after the expiration of this time limit, the possession should be transferred to the agnates *.

89, 1—3:

(This) is also written at the same time as that, (namely) that if he declares: "I have received from you (such-and-such a man) as a slave for a term of one year", then upon the expiration of one year (the obligation of) the warranty ends ("does not exist") and the slave must be returned.

89, 3—5:

And this has been said, that if the creditor ("the holder of a security") causes damage to the thing held by him as security, then this thing is taken from him and transferred to the *rats* to be kept as security, but his money (= loan, credit — *A. P.*) is not taken away, since he caused no damage to it (= the money).

89, 5—6:

At the same time as the other it has been said, that if he declines the thing held as security, then he has not thereby discharged from the debt (lit.: "the money").

89, 6—7:

And in addition to that, this is what was said by Syāvaxš: when he gives back (= returns) the money to the person who holds the thing as security, then the thing (= the security) is also given back. (*Cf. supra*, **89**, 5—6 — *A. P.*).

89, 8—9:

Ut apāk anī gōβēnd kū Yuvān-Yam guft kū mart xvāstak ī apāmdān hakar hač xvāstak ī (9) ōy kē ān xvāstak tōžišn apēsaxvan bavēt hilišn čē xvāstak pat apām āgraβ.

89, 10—11:

Apāk anī guft kū ka drahm kē vaxš kart ēstēt bē dahēt vaxš čē pas-ič (11) hač ān ōy xvēš kē mātak avi-š dāt.

89, 11—15:

Ut apāk anī guft kū ka xvāstak-ē(v) Farraxv (12) hač Mihrēn apām stat ut pat zamān ī nāmčišt dāt rāδ ⟨ut⟩ ēn-ič patmān kart kū (13) hakar pat zamān dahom enyā xvāstak tō xvēš Mihrēn pēš hač zamān pat xvēšīh (14) bē dāt hakar ān xvāstak pat zamān vičārēnd enyā xvāstak ōy xvēš kē+ drahm avi-š (15) dāt.

89, 15—17:

Ut anī guft kū ka pit duxt ī apurnāy pat zanīh bē dahēt duxt hakar (16) [ka] purnāy bavēt pat ān dāt axunsand pas ka xunsand bavēt nōk (?) xvāst+/būt(?) ī hač (17) sardārān ōh apāyēt*.

89, 17—**90**, 1:

Apāk anī guft kū duxt ī pit kart kū zanīh ī Mihrēn kun (1) [zanīh] ī Mihrēn nē kunēt ayōγēn ī pit apar ōh mānēt (ut) aparmānd ōh bavēt.

90, 1—4:

Apāk anī (2) guft kū ka katak-bānūk kart kū-m pat bē vitīrišnīh xvāstak pat stūrīh ō kas dāt (3) ut pas frazand zāyēt frazand ī zāyēt andar apurnāyīh ut katak-bānūk-ič anandarz pat baxt šavēt ān (4) dāt kār nēst.

90, 4—6:

Ut anī guft kū ka pēšēmār+ (Ms.: pasēmār) saxvan-nāmak yut hač ākāsīh ut dānišn ī (5) pasēmār bē dahēt nē šāyēt čē pasēmār tuvān guft kū ēn (saxvan-nāmak apāk) pēšēmār bē (6) nē brīnom+ (Ms.: has ŠB̲QWNm for PSQWNm).

---

* One or two words followed by a guestion mark (at the end of line 16 of the manuscript) are doubtful. They are badly rubbed out in the Facsimile edition, and presumably in the manuscript as well.

89, 8—9:

In addition to that, it is said that Yuvān-Yam stated (the following): a man must consider a debt settled (lit.: "must remit, resolve") if he declines the estate of the person who was obliged to pay this money, since an estate is claimed ("seized") in settlement of a debt [57].

89, 10—11:

At the same time as the other it is said, that if he conveys (= alienates) money (= a loan) which has accumulated a percentage (of interest), then the interest (= the percents) which shall accumulate after this (= after the act of transfer) belong to the person to whom he transferred the principal [58].

89, 11—15:

In addition it is said, that, if Farraxv received a certain sum of money ("a thing") as a loan from Mihrēn and made the following agreement regarding the return (of the loan) within a definite term: "If I do not give back the loan within the term set, the thing (set up as security) will belong to you". But Mihrēn, before the end of the term (set for the settlement of the debt) conveyed (the capital loaned by him to Farraxv) to (another person) as property/personal possession. Then — unless the debt is settled within the given term — the thing (serving as security) shall belong to the person to whom he (Mihrēn) conveyed the money (*i. e.* to Farraxv's new creditor replacing the former one — *A. P.*).

89, 15—17:

And another (thing) has been said, that if a father gives (his) minor daughter in marriage, (and) if the daughter — when she comes of age — does not consent to this marriage ("transfer"), but subsequently declares her consent, then ... ... of the guardians is indispensable.

89, 17—**90**, 1:

Furthermore, another (thing) has been said, that (if) a daughter to whom (her) father said: "be Mihrēn's wife!", does not become Mihrēn's [wife], (then) she shall remain in the status of her father's *epikleros*, (and) she shall become his successor (of "*stūr*" type — *A. P.*).

90, 1—4:

Together with another (thing) it has been said, that if the mistress of the house declared the following: "I have given a thing to such-and-such a person upon my death for *stūr*ship (= as a *stūr*-possession or foundation)", and a son is subsequently born to her; then if the child she bore (dies) before coming of age, and the mistress of the house also dies without making a will, this conveyance (of the thing for *stūr*ship — *A. P.*) is null and void.

90, 4—6:

And another (thing) has been said, that if the plaintiff (the ms. gives "the respondent") conveys the record of the testimonies (of the parties at a trial) without the knowledge of the respondent; then (this) is not proper, since the respondent may declare: "(I) will not sign (this record with) the plaintiff".

90, 6—8:

Apāk anī (guft kū ka) pēšēmār kē čand dātastān pat rāδēnišn dāšt dātastān ēv rāδ (7) guft kū-š nūn vičīr apar nē bē ka-m kāmist+ (ut) xvāhom ōγōn patigīrišn ka pasēmār+-ič (8) xunsand būt.

90, 8—14:

Ut anī guft kū ka pus xvāstak ī xvēš pat stūrīh bē dahēt (9) frazand ī pas hač ān hač katak-bānūk zāyēt hač ān čiγōn stūr ī kartak bar-xvēš ⟨ut⟩ frazand ī pas (10) hač ān ē ka hambāγ xvāstak pat stūrīh+ (Ms.: xvēšīh) bē dahēt+ hač katak-bānūk zāyēt hač xvāstak ī (11) pat stūrīh+ (Ms.: xvēšīh) bē dāt bahr nē rasēt ut dātastān (ī) dūtak katak-bānūk ut frazand ī andar dutak (12) zāyēt apāk stūr ī kartak nē ōγōn čiγōn apāk stūr ī gumārtak ut būtak ut frazand ī pat ān (13) aδvēnak hač katak-bānūk zāyēt apar xvāstak ī pus pat stūrīh bē dāt nē zāyēt čē veh (14) būt nē šāyēt kū frazand ī ōy pus hač zan ī pātixšāyīhā zāyēt (nē apar xvāstak / bahr ī) xvēš+ (?) zāyēt.

90, 15—17:

Apāk anī Pusānveh ī Āzātmartān guft kū tā baxtīkīh kunēnd ayāp hač pus xvāstak (16) nē pat aparmānd bē pat xvēšīh ō kas rasēt frazand ī hač katak-bānūk (17) zāyēt apar-ič bahr ī pus zāt bavēt ut pus ī hač katak-bānūk zāyēt xvāstak (...) *.

91, 1—15 **:

(...) haštom paytāk ēvak ⟨ut⟩ ān ī ka xvāstak (rāδ andar) dātastān nē gōβēt kū čē; ditīkar ka nē [gōβēt] (2) kū kē; sitīkar ka drōγ gōβēt; čahārom ka pat gumēčak gumēčak gōβēt; panǰom (3) ka avikāy gōβēt; šašom ka dārišn ī xvāstak ān gōβēt ī nē dārēt; haftom (4) ka xvēšīh ī xvāstak nē ān gōβēt ī hast; haštom ka saẋvan nihānīk gōβēt; (5) nohom ka adastaβar+ (Ms.: adātaβar) gōβēt; dahom ka saxvan nazdist pat ēvarīh ut pas pat gumānīkīh (6) gōβēt hast (kē dātastān)? nē sar hilēt ut bē šavēt; yāzdahom ka gōβēt kū-m ētōn mēnīt; (7) dvāzdahom ka gōβēt kū-m ētōn ašnūt; sēzdahom ka ⟨gōβēt⟩ saxvan (8) nazdist pat ēvarīh ut pas pat gumānīkīh gōβēt; čahārdahom ka nē pēš ī hamēmārān (9) gōβēt; pānzdahom ka andar miyān ī saxvan ka hamēmār vēnēt xāmōš bavēt; (10) šāzdahom ka nē ētōn gōβēt kū dātaβar pat rāstīh vičīr tuvan kartan; haftdahom (11) ka vikāy-druž; haštdahom ka ō gyāk kū zamān ⟨zamān⟩ kunēt nē āyēt; (12) nōzdahom ka vikāy ī gōβēt fratom ayāp bavandak nē

* The text of this article breaks off at this point.

** The beginning of this article has not survived.

90, 6—8:

Together with another (thing) it has been said, that if a plaintiff who conducted several judicial cases (simultaneously — *A. P.*) declares (this) concerning one of them: "no decision (regarding the given case) need be (rendered) now, but (only when) I demand it", then this should be accepted in this manner, if the respondent also has stated his consent (to this).

90, 8—14:

And this has been said, that if a son conveys his estate for *stūr*ship and the mistress of the house subsequently bears a son, then — insofar as an "*instituted*" *stūr* is the usufructuary — the child born to the mistress of the house after her co-partner / co-heir has conveyed his estate for *stūr*ship (the ms. reads "in personal ownership") does not receive a share of the estate conveyed for *stūr*ship. And — (inasmuch as) the decision rendered in the case of the mistress of the household, the child born in the family, and an "*instituted*" *stūr* differs from (the decision rendered in the case) of an "*appointed*" *stūr* or a "*natural*" *stūr* — the child born under these circumstances ("in this way") to the mistress of the house shall not inherit the estate given by the son for *stūr*ship. For it is not right that a child born to the son from a *pātixšāyīh*-wife should (not) inherit (his own share in the family estate). (*Cf. supra* **51**, 16—**52**, 12; **52**, 15—17; *et infra* **90**, 15—17).

90, 15—17:

Together with that, Pusānveh ī Āzātmartān has said, that (if) (a son is born to the mistress of the house) before the division of the inheritance, or (if) the estate of the (dead) son should not go to another person neither on the basis of succession (= in *stūr*ship — *A. P.*) nor as a personal possession (= as a personal portion of the inheritance), (then) the child (= the son) born to the mistress of the house inherits also the share of a son, and the son born to the mistress of the house,...*

91, 1—15**:

... is evident from the eighth (point). One: when he does not say regarding the thing at the trial, what (type of thing it is); two: when he does not [say] specifically who (= does not name the person — *A. P.*); three: when he lies; four: when he speaks confusedly; five: when he testifies without having witnesses; six: if to an enquiry regarding the possession of a thing, he designates the one (=a thing) which he does not possess; seven: if he does not indicate his real right ("the ownership of a thing") which (he) has; eight: if (he) gives his testimony in a hidden (= veiled) manner; nine: if he comes forward in court without having the title (of a legal representative); ten: if in giving testimony he first presents them as reliable and subsequently as unreliable, and there are also (among litigants) those who give up and leave before the end of the trial; eleven: when he declares: "it seemed so to me"; twelve: when he declares: "I heard it thus"; thirteen: when he first presents (his) testimony as exact (= reliable) and subsequently as doubtful; fourteen: if he testifies when the opposing party is not present; fifteen: if on seeing his opponent he stops in the middle of a word (= of his testimony); sixteen: when he does not speak (at the trial) in such a fashion as to make it possible for the judge to render an equitable decision; seventeen: if he is a false ānayēt; vīstom ka pat gyāk ut (13) gāh ī kū gōβēt kū ēstom nē ēstēt; vīstēvakom ka pat gāh (ut) gyāk kū (14) ēstāt⁺ apāyēt nē xvap ēstēt; 22-om ka xvāstak ut (h)ēr kē patmān ut patkār apar (15) druvist ō peš ī dātaβarān nē āβarēt.

91, 15—**92**, 2 *:

[... ... ...] (16) 3 rōč ut 7 rōč dart  ut māh drahnāδ pat [... ... ...] nišast ut murt (17) ētōn bavēt čiγōn ka gōβēt kū [pat] gyāk murt ān mart hač ān zat bār (1) kē xāst?/murt⁺ pat xvārtar nē nišast ut ān mart murt. Būt kē guft (2) [var]ōmand ut pargār pat-iš kunišn.

92, 2—6:

Gyākē nipišt kū mart ka nē parēžvān (3) bē xvat frāč šavēt ō dātaβar (ut) gōβēt kū-m mart-ē(v) ⟨i⟩ ētōn ōzat (4) ka vikāy apāk nēst pat markaržān nipištak pat-iš nē ⟨kart⟩ kunēnd bē ka (5) pat parēžvān frāč šavēt ut vinās ī markaržān xvastūk⁺ bavēt ka-č vikāy apāk (6) nēst aδak-ič pat vinās ī markaržān nipištak pat-iš kunēnd.

92, 6—10:

Gyākē nipišt (7) kū ka gōβēt kū mart ī nāmčišt nē dānom (ut) Mihrēn Pusak zat (8) Pusak hač zat ī Mihrēn ayāp hač zat ī ān mart ī-m guft kū-š (9) nāmčišt nē dānom bār murt Mihrēn nē varōmand ut apāk anī gōβēnd kū (10) vēs/šak ut ramak varōmand nē kunišn.

92, 10—13:

Ka gōβēt kū Farraxv ut Mihrēn Pusak zat (11) ut Pusak hač ān zat ī Farraxv ayāp hač ān zat ī Mihrēn bār murt ut ēn (12) kū hač ān zat hač ān ī kē bār murt nē dānom ka-č pas gōβēt kū (13) hač zat ī (...) bār murt [... ... ...] kem nē bōxtišn.

92, 14—16:

Ka gōβēt kū sāl ēvak [ōy] zat ⟨i⟩ (ut sāl 2 anī zat ut) hač ān zat ī sāl ēvak (ayāp hač) ān (15) zat ī sāl 2 bār (murt) ⟨ut⟩ nē varōmand. Ut ka gōβēt kū-šān ākanēn zat (16) hač ān ī ōy ⟨i⟩ ayāp hač anī bār [murt] harv 2 varōmand hend.

92, 16—17 + **97**, 1—3:

Ut ka gōβēt (17) kū Farraxv ut Āturfarnbaγ yut-yut pat Mihrēn žahm kart ut ēn kū ān žahm kē (1) pēš kart nē bē ēn dānom kū žahm pat yut bār kart. Ut ka ān ī dit[īkar] (2) kart (hač) ān ī fratom kart nē xvārtar būt andar axvārtarīh ī žahm ī pas kart (3) Mihrēn murt Farraxv ut Āturfarnbāγ harv 2 varōmand hend.

* This article is too corrupt to be translatable.

witness; eighteen: if he does not appear in the place where the court is in session; nineteen: if he does not bring the witness whom he mentioned at first, or if he brings (no one); twenty: if he does not live in the locality and place of which he has stated: "I am staying (= live there)"; twenty-one: if he does not conduct himself well in the place in which it is incumbent for him to be; twenty-two: if he does not bring intact to the judges (= does not present in court — *A. P.*) the thing regarding which the contract and litigation (took place).

92, 2—6:

It is written in one place that, if a man presents himself before a judge on his own initiative ("himself") and not under constraint (and) declares: "I killed a man in such-and-such a manner", and if there is no witness with him then no decision is rendered ("no document is drawn-up") concerning the commission of a capital offence, as regards this man. But if he presents himself under constraint and confesses to a capital offence; then — even if he brings no witness — even in such a case, a judicial decision is rendered ("a document is drawn up") regarding (his commission) of a capital offence.

92, 6—10:

It is written in one place, that if he makes (the following) declaration: "a man whom I do not know, and Mihrēn struck Pusak, and Pusak died immediately from the blow (struck) by Mihrēn, or from the blow of the man of whom I said that I do not know precisely (who he is)"; (then) Mihrēn need not take an oath (or be subjected to ordeal — *A. P.*). And together with this it is said that slaves/servants and "plebeians" (= the *ramak*, "the common people") are not subject to an oath (or: "to an ordeal").

92, 10—13:

If he declares: "Farraxv and Mihrēn struck Pusak, and Pusak died at once from Farraxv's blow or from Mihrēn's blow, but I do not know (specifically) from whose blow he immediately died"; then even if he subsequently says: "he died at once from (...) blow [... ... ...], he should not be condemned ("he is nevertheless subject to acquittal") for it (= the change in his testimony — *A. P.*).

92, 14—16:

If he declares the following: "[this one] struck him one year (and another one on the next and) he (died) from the blow struck the first year (or from) the blow struck the second", then there is no need for subjection to an ordeal (oath-taking — *A. P.*). But if he declares: "they struck together and he [died] at once from the blow of this man or the blow of that [man]", then they are both to be subjected to the ordeal.

92, 16—17 + **97**, 1—3:

And if he declares: "Farraxv and Āturfarnbaγ, each of them separately struck a blow (= committed an act of physical violence) against Mihrēn, I do not know which one (of them) struck the earlier blow, I merely know that the act of violence (= 'the blow') was committed at different times". If the blow struck by the second was not heavier than the first blow, then, in the case of Mihrēn's death, both Farraxv and Āturfarnbaγ must take an oath (or "be subjected to an ordeal") regarding the fact that the second blow was not heavier than the first.

78, 17 + **93**, 1—3:

Ēvak ēn kū vičīr ī apāmdān ka-č ōγōn nipišt kū (1) vičārtan ut bē nē dahišnīh rāδ ka ēvar nē patkārom pat xvap dāštan (ut) k[artak?] (2) ōγōn hač-iš kart čiγōn ka nipišt kū vičārtan ut ō tō nē dahišnīh rāδ ka (3) nē ēvar nē patkārom.

93, 3—4:

Dātaβar hač fravartak hampačēn ō dāt rāδēnišn (hač ān) ī (4) Zartušt Bīšāhpuhr magupat pat (h)ēr ī ātaxš kart paytāk.

93, 4—9:

Ēvak (5) ēn kū muhr ī pat kār framān dāštan ān ī magupatān ut hamārkarān fratom (6) pat framān ī Kavāt ī Pērōžān ut ān ī dātaβarān fratom pat framān ī Xusrav [ī] (7) Kavātān ka muhr ī magupatān ī Pārs kand magupat nē pat nām ī magupatīh (8) bē pat nām ī driγōšān yātakgōβīh xvānd nipišt ut pat ān čim apar muhr ī (magupat ī Pārs) (9) hamgōnak kand ēstēt.

93, 9—11:

Ēvak ēn kū ka axunsandīh ī pāsēmār pat vičīr (10) rāδ hač dātaβarān ō magupatān visēh kart ut magupat ān vičīr pat vičār dāšt⟨an⟩ (11) apar ān (h)ēr ī pat uzēnak ut pātrōč apar pasēmār framān dāt.

93, 11—14:

Ēvak (ēn kū) mart (12) kē pašt kunēt kū būt ī ēn čiš raδ pat muhr ī vāvarīkān mart nāmak (13) āβarom ka pat muhr ī ōy kē+ pat vikāyīh muhr ī pat vāvarīkānīh patigrift (14) ēstēt nāmak āβarēt xvap.

93, 14—**94**, 2:

Ēvak ēn kū ka nipēsēt kū mērak pat (15) yātakgōβīh ī mērak pēš ī man mat aδak-iš pat yātakgōβīh ⟨i⟩ nē patigrift (16) bavēt pat čand nipišt ut ǎvašt ī pēš dastaβarān kart (kū) ka yātakgōβ-ič pat (17) yātakgōβīh nāmak ō dātastān āβurt pēš tā nāmak kē yātakgōβīh hač-iš (1) [paytāk] frāč patigīrēnd ōγōn nipištan kū mērak ī pat yātakgōβīh ī mērak mat čiγōn (2) yātakgōβ (ī) gumārt ō dātastān patigīrēnd ōγōn nipištan kū mērak ī mērak yātakgōβ.

78, 17 + **93**, 1—3:

One (decision) is this (the following). If (this) is written in a contractual document regarding credit (= "a debt"): "If it is exactly (known, established) that (the debt has already) been settled and that nothing is subject to transfer (in repayment), then I shall not bring suit"; then this formula is lawful (and) [the procedure?] is the same as though it were written in the following manner (in the document): "if it is not (established) precisely that (the debt) is to be settled and that (I) am obliged to pay you, I shall not litigate".

93, 3—4:

A judge must prepare a copy of a document (= the title of possession — *A. P.*) to be given out, as is evident from (the document) prepared by Zardušt, the *magupat* of Bīšāhpuhr, for the temple treasury (or perhaps "for the temple archives", *cf.* **78**, 11—14 — *A. P.*).

93, 4—9:

In addition, the following: The official seal(s) of the *magupat*s and finance officials was first introduced at the order of (king) Kavāt son of Pērōž, and the official seal(s) of judges under (king) Xusrav son of Kavāt. When the seal of the *magupat* of Pārs was cut, the *magupat* was inscribed (on its legend) as being ("called") not according to (his) *magupat*'(s office), but according to (his) defense of the interests ("representation; advocacy") of the poor / destitute (or "deprived") [59]. And for this reason this legend ("this") is engraved on the seal of (the *magupat* of Pārs).

93, 9—11:

This, as well: if an affair is sent from the judges to the *magupat* because of the dissatisfaction of the respondent with the judicial decision, and if the *magupat* takes up this decision (of the judges) for examination; (then) (a judicial) directive is given ("an order is given") as regards the respondent, concerning the sum (required) for expenses and daily allowance.

93, 11—14:

And this also. A certain person makes an agreement (with the court) in the following manner: "I shall present ("bring") a letter sealed with the seal of a trustworthy man, to the effect that everything was so". If he brings a letter sealed with the seal of the one bearing witness, (with the type of) seal that will be accepted (by the court) as trustworthy; then this (*i. e.* the acceptance by the court of the testimony of a person not present at the trial — *A. P.*) is lawful.

93, 14—**94**, 2:

And there is also this. If he (= the judge or the court official charged with the taking of the minutes — *A. P.*) writes as follows: "(such-and-such) a man appeared before me for the legal representation (= as the legal representative) (of this other man)", then (this indicates that) the former has not yet been (officialy) admitted (by the court) as a representative. In their formerly written and sealed instructions authoritative persons have said, (that) if the representative presents ("brought") to the court a document confirming his mandate, then what must be written — until the document ("letter") from which [it is evident] that (he is empowered as) a representative is accepted — is: "(such-and-such) a man has arrived (to assume the functions) of legal representative for (this other) man". (But) when he is admitted as the representative appointed to take part in the trial, what (must be) written is: "such-and-such a man is the (legal) representative (of this other) man".

94, 3—6:

Ēvak anī ham Pusānveh guft kū 1000 āturōk ī mart ka dātaβar pat gyāk (4) kū uzdēs-katak būt uzdēs hač-iš kand nišāst ka-š sardār (5) xvēšāvand ī pat nāmčišt nē paytāk būt mart ī pat Varahrānīh ō dātgāh (6) nišāst pat sardār dāštan.

94, 6—10:

Ka pit ⟨ut⟩ zan ī anšahrīk rāδ kart kū (7) pat čiš-ič aδvēnak ō Mihrēn ī man pus mā hēβ rasēt ut pēš hač ān ē ka pit (8) pat baxt šavēt ut ān ansahrīk pat aparmānd ō apārīk frazandān rasēt hač ān zan (9) frazand zāyēt vitart pit ō Mihrēn ⟨ut⟩ ān zan nē ut pat aparmānd frazand ī pat ān (10) aδvēnak hač ān zan zāyēt rasēt.

94, 10—14:

Zan ī anšahrīk ī ō zan ī pat (11) dūtak stūr ōγōn dat kū ō dūtak nē rasēt ut pas hač ān zan ī anšahrīk (12) frazand zāyēt frazand ī pat ān aδvēnak hač anšahrīk zāyēt hakar tā hač apārīk xvāstak ī pat (13) ān aδvēnak bē dāt bavēt hač ān čiγōn anšahrīk xvāstak pat xvēšīh bē ō katak-bānūk (14) mat andar xvēšīh ī katak-bānūk hamē(v) bavēt⁺ (ut) ō dūtak nē rasēt.

94, 14—**95**, 2:

Ka katak-xvatāy (15) sāl ēvak xvāstak ī-š xvēš čand 100 vahāk aržēt pat xvēšīh ō Mihr-(16)Āturfarnbaγ ī pus dāt ut sāl 2 ⟨(h)andarz⟩ pat (h)andarz kart kū-m xvāstak ī ō man mat (17) abaxt nēm ō Āturfarnbaγ ⟨i⟩ apārīk ō Mihr-Āturfarnbaγ ī pus dāt Mihr-Āturfarnbaγ (1) kart kū pat ān ī katak-xvatāy (h)andarz kart xunsand ut hamdātastān hom gumānīkīh kū Mihr-(2)Āturfarnbaγ dāt ī pēš hišt bavēt.

95, 2—4:

Apāk anī guft kū ka sāl ēvak (3) xvāstak ī mat abaxt nēm anī mart xvēš xvāstak ī pat 4 bahr ēv bahr pat katak-(4)xvatāy ēstēt čē-š hač ān ī andar ān ē pat xvēšīh ēstēt dāt bavēt nikerītan.

[*Numberless*]

95, 5—6:

Dar * ī apar ēn (6) kū čand dātastān ī dastaβar kē hač-iš ašnūt pat nāmčišt nipišt.

* This chapter carries no ordinal-number.

94, 3—6:

The same Pusānveh has also said the following: if a man sets up 1000 [60] altars in the (very) place where there was an idol shrine — the idols having been destroyed ("dug out") of there by a judge — without appointing a particular person from among his agnates as the guardian over these altars, then the man who has set up a Varahrān Fire should be considered the guardian of these altars.

94, 6—10:

If a father declares this, concerning a female-slave: "let her in no way pass to my son Mihrēn!", and if this (slave)-woman bears a son before the father dies and this woman passes to his other children as an inheritance; then this (slave)-woman does not pass to Mihrēn after the father's death, (but) the child born to this woman in such a fashion (*i. e.* before the opening of the inheritance — *A. P.*), shall go (to him).

94, 10—14:

A slave-woman is conveyed to a woman who is the family *stūr* in such a manner (under these conditions) that she (= the slave-woman) should not pass to the family, and after this, a child is born to the slave-woman; inasmuch as it (forms a part) of the remaining ("other") thing which was conveyed in this manner (under these conditions), (and) as a result of the fact that the thing — the slave-woman — went to the mistress of the house as a personal possession/property, (this child) shall belong to the mistress of the house and shall not pass to the family.

94, 14—**95**, 2:

If a head of household in one year conveyed a thing valued at 100 (*drahms*?) as a personal possesion/property to his son Mihr-Āturfarnbaγ, and in the next ("second") year he gave the following disposition in his will: "I have conveyed a thing received by me, in an undivided fashion: half to Āturfarnbaγ and the other (half) to my son Mihr-Āturfarnbaγ ". (And if) Mihr-Āturfarnbaγ declares: "I consent ("am satisfied and agree") to the disposition given by the head of household in his will", then the doubt created by the original transfer of the thing to Mihr-Āturfarnbaγ is thereby cleared up.

95, 2—4:

Besides other (things), it is said: if half of the thing which passed to him undivided one year (out of each two — *A. P.*) belongs to another person, then one-fourth of the thing must belong to the head of household since the transfer was made from what belonged to him at the time.

[*Numberless*]

95, 5—6:

Chapter* concerning the following: certain legal decisions (recommended) by the authorities (= the commentators on the legal *nasks* of the *Avesta* — *A. P.*), written down precisely by (those) who heard (these decisions) from them.

95, 7—10:

Ēvak anī zan ī hač zanīh hišt[+] ⟨ut⟩ patkārēt kū šōy apāk xvāstak (8) hišt hom ut šōy xvāstak hištan rāδ nakīrā(k) ut xvāstak dārišn pat ziyānak (9) ān zan rāδ Pusānveh ī Āzātmartān guft kū darišn ī ān xvāstak nē ut Pērōž (10) guft kū-š dārišn ī ān xvāstak bōžišn.

95, 10—12:

Ēvak ān ī ⟨Pusānveh⟩ ham Pusānveh (11) guft kū pēšēmār ut pasēmār ka[+] gōβēt kū-m xvāstak hač pitarān apar mānd (12) dastaβar ut čē aδvēnak xvēšīh harv 2 guft bavēt.

95, 12—15:

Ēvak ān ī Pusānveh guft (13) kū ka xvāstak ī-šān (rāδ) kart kū kas kē Mihrēn xvēš būt gōβēt xvēš (14) Mihrēn pat 3 yāvar ⟨yāvar yāvar⟩ pat 3 bahr ēv bahr Farraxv xvēš būt guft gōβišn (15) harv 3[+] (Ms.: 2) kār (ut) xvāstak hamāk Farraxv xvēš.

95, 15—**96**, 3:

Ēvak anī ham Pusānveh guft kū (16) vāhmān ī magupat būt ātaxš ī Rām-Šāhpuhr kē nē hamēšak-sōz būt (17) hamēšak-sōz kart ut vitart Māh-Ātur Frēh-Gušnasp ka ān ātaxš hač (h)ēr ī xvēš (1) hamēšak-sōz dāštan nē šāyēt hač (h)ēr ī dūtak ī Māh-Ātur Frēh-Gušnasp (2) hamēšak-sōz dāštan rāδ pātixšāy dastaβarān ī mat ēstāt hend framān (3) dāt.

96, 3—8:

Ēvak anī Siyāvaxš guft kū ka kunēt kū xvāstak ī pat aparmānd (4) ō frazand ī man rasēt frazand ī man pat stūrīh ī man hēβ dārēnd ut pus ān xvāstak pat (5) stūrīh andar nē apāyēt rāδ gōβēt ān xvāstak ō pus ut duxt rāst dāt (6) bavēt ut hač ān čiγōn duxt nē ut pus pātixšāy ka stūrīh nē kunēt ān ī ō duxt (7) dāt pat duxt bē ēstēt ut ān ī ō pus dāt aframān bavēt ut pat aparmānd (8) rāstīhā ō duxt pat stūrīh ō pus pat xvēšīh rasēt.

95, 7—10:

Here is another (case). A woman who has received a divorce brings suit: "in dissolving (my) marriage with my husband, I simultaneously (with it) settled (my) debt", (but) the husband denies the fact of the settlement (or "discharge / remission") of the debt, and the thing (is) in the possession of the woman: as regards this woman, Pusānveh ī Āzātmartān has said that the possession of this thing should not (be left to her), whereas Pērōž has said that she should enjoy the possession of the (that) thing.

95, 10—12:

The same Pusānveh has also said another (thing): that if the plaintiff or the respondent declares: "the thing came to me as an inheritance from my fathers", then both the *de cujus* (lit.: "the disposer, giver of the mandate; the former holder of the title to the thing conveyed or transmitted") and the variety of the (acquired) real right must be indicated.

95, 12—15:

One more decision from what was said by Pusānveh. If anyone disposes of his own thing in the following manner: "this thing shall belong to (the man) whom Mihrēn shall declare (to be its entitled) possessor / owner", and if Mihrēn shall make the declaration in three instances: "one-third (of this thing) belongs to Farraxv", then this declaration is valid all three (times) and the entire thing belongs to Farraxv.

95, 15—**96**, 3:

The same Pusānveh has also said this. So-and-so who was a *magupat* turned ("made") the Rām-Šāhpuhr Fire which did not burn continually, into a perpetually burning one. And after the death of Māh-Ātur Frēh-Gušnasp (= the *magupat* of Artaxšahr-Xvarreh, *cf. supra* **99**, 3—8 — *A. P.*), the entitled persons ("the disposers") who were gathered together established ("gave an order") that if it should turn out to be impossible to preserve the Fire perpetually burning on its own (= the temple's) means, it is lawful (to use) the means of Māh-Ātur Frēh-Gušnasp's family to keep the Fire burning perpetually.

96, 3—8:

Siyāvaxš has also said, that if (a man) has made a disposition in the following manner: "Let the estate which should pass to my children as inheritance be possessed by my children as my *stūrs*", and if the son declares that (he) does not need this estate on the basis of *stūr*ship, (then, on the strength of this testamentary disposition of the father), this estate is transmitted equally to the son and the daughter, but — inasmuch as the daughter is not entitled (to refuse the assumption of the *stūr*ship), whereas the son is entitled to refuse the assumption of the *stūr*ship — what is transmitted to the daughter shall go to the daughter (as he father's *epikleros* and on the basis of a *stūr*-possession — *A. P.*), whereas the injunction is removed (*i. e.* the disposition of the father concerning the transmission for *stūr*ship is rescinded — *A. P.*) from what is transmitted to the son, and (thus) it passes equally to the daughter — for *stūr*ship (= as a *stūr*-possession), and to the son — as a personal possession (= on the basis of his inheritance portion of his father's estate — *A. P.*).

96, 8—10:

Ēvak anī (9) ham Siyāvaxš guft kū zan ī mart kē-šān tā 10 sāl xvāstak pat stūrīh avi-š (10) dāt ō ān stūrīh nayēnd pas hač 10 sāl stūrīh nēst[+].

96, 10—13:

Ēvak anī ham Siyāvaxš (11) guft kū xvāstak ī mart abaxt nēm pat stūrīh (ī) xvēš ō Āturfarnbaγ ut apārīk (12) pat stūrīh ī xvēš ō Mihrēn dāt[+] Āturfarnbaγ ut Mihrēn baxtīkīh pat-iš kartan nē (13) pātixšāy.

96, 13—16:

Ēvak anī ham Siyāvaxš guft kū ka mart kart kū frazandān ī man pat (14) frōxtan ī ēn anšahrīk pātixšāyīhā mā hēβ bavēnd avēšān frazand ⟨frazand⟩ (15) ut aβγātak ī hač avēšān anšahrīk ān ī zan zāyēt frōxtan nē pātixšāy hend.

96, 16—17:

Ēvak anī ham Siyāvaxš guft kū ka gōβēt kū Mihrēn ī man pus harv sāl (17) xvāstak arž 50 ayāp hač vaxt ī ēn xvāstak⟨īhā⟩ 200 ō Farraxv hēβ dahēt vitart (...) *.

97, 1—3:

Vide supra **92**, 16—17 + **97**, 1—3.

97, 3—7:

Ka anšahrīk (4) guft kū šavom ut K... bē ōzanom ut xvatāy guft kū čim gōβēh ka-t kartan (5) nē tuvān ut anšahrīk šut u-š ⟨i⟩ ān mart ōzat gyākē nipišt kū pat magupatīh ī (6) Burzak mat u-š[+] (Ms.: u-šān) nipištak pat-iš kart ut pas Zurvāndāt guft kū nē varōmand (7) u-šān hač ān nipištak bē hilišn.

97, 7—9:

Gyākē nipišt kū zan ka šōy ī (8) xvēš rāδ gōβēt kū-š markaržān kart xvāstak ī šōy apar nē mānēt nē-č (9) stūr ī šōy bavēt.

97, 9—10:

Ka mart zan (ī) xvēš rāδ gōβēt kū-š markaržān (10) kart vitart ān mart ān zan šōy apar ōh mānēt ut stūr ī ān mart bavēt.

* This article breaks off at this point.

96, 8—10:

And the same Siyāvaxš has said another (thing): that a married woman to whom a thing has been conveyed for ten years as a *stūr* (possession; lit.: "into *stūr*ship"), (and who) is brought to (the assumption of this) *stūr*ship, ceases to be a *stūr* at the expiration of ten years.

96, 10—13:

And the same Siyāvaxš has said another (thing), that (if) a man conveyed half of a thing in an undivided state to Āturfarnbaγ for his (own) *stūr*ship, and the other (half of it) to Mihrēn (likewise) for his *stūr*ship, then Āturfarnbaγ and Mihrēn are not entitled to divide the thing.

96, 13—16:

The same Siyāvaxš has also said that, if a man has declared the following (disposition): "let my children not be entitled to sell this slave-woman!", (then) these children and their descendants are not entitled to sell a slave born from that (slave)-woman as well.

96, 16—17:

The same Siyāvaxš has also said that if (a man) declares this: "let my son Mihrēn yearly convey to Farraxv (any) thing valued at 50 (*saters* — *A. P.*) or 200 (*drahms* — *A. P.*) from the accretion (= revenue) furnished by this thing", (then) after the death (...) *.

97, 1—3:

Vide supra **92**, 16—17 + **97**, 1—3.

97, 3—7:

If a slave has said: "I shall go and kill K....", and his master has said: "you will give a reason if you prove unable to do this", and the slave set out and killed the man; it is written in one place that this occurred when Burzak was *magupat* and an edict ("letter, document") concerning this was drawn up by him. And subsequently Zurvāndāt said, that (the slave?, the given case?) is not subject to an ordeal-court, and (that) they (= the slave and his master) should be judged on the basis of this edict (= "the letter or document" drawn up by the *magupat* Burzak — *A. P.*) [61].

97, 7—9:

It is written in one place that if a woman declares of her husband that he has committed a capital offence, then she will not inherit her husband's property, nor does she also become his *stūr*.

97, 9—10:

If a husband makes an (unfounded) declaration concerning his wife: that she committed a capital offence, then after the death of this husband, the wife shall inherit from her husband and she may (also) become his *stūr*.

97, 11—12:

Ka kart [kū ... ...] būt kē guft (12) kū-š stūr ōh gumārišn bē xvat pat stūrīh ī kas nē šāyēt.

97, 13—15:

Ut ka pat stūrīh gumārt ut pas hač gumārt pat markaržān varōmand kart būt (14) kē guft kū ān stūrīh bē kanišn ut anī mart ī sažāktar bē gumārišn (15) ut būt kē guft kū nē kanišn.

97, 15—98, 1:

Ka pat markaržān ēraxt aδak-iš xvāstak ī (16) hast hač-iš ap(p)ār būt kē guft kū-š rōčīk ī zan ut frazand hač-iš bē kunišn (17) [ut] pat kartak nē kunēnd čē ka markaržān būt aδak-iš zan ut frazand (1) [ut] gēhān hač-iš ap(p)ār bavēt.

98, 1—5:

Vahrām hač Pusānveh (ī) Āzātmartān bē guft kū (2) nipištak-ē(v) hač vikāyīh ī zan 2 ⟨ut⟩ pat magupatīh ī (... ... ...) ī Staxr ⟨i⟩ magupat kart ēstāt (3) ut moγān (h)andarzpat frāč patigirift bē Zurvāndāt guft kū ān pat kartak nē kart. (4) Vahrām guft kū vikāy ēvak zan ut ēvak mart aδēnišn pursišn-nāmak ōh kart(an) (5) zan ut anšahrīk nē.

98, 5—6:

Pat ēn 2 čāštak guft ēstēt kū pat vinās ī šahr (6) šoy ut xvatāy nē pātixšāy [...].

98, 13*:

(...) nē magupatān bē ratān kart.

98, 13—14:

Gyāk-ē nipišt kū ka markaržān kunēt xvāstāk ī (11) andar ān ē hač ōy bērōn pat avināsīh kas dārēt ō ōy ī dārēt ap(p)ār.

---

* Only the beginning of this article has survived.

97, 11—12:

If he declares [(the following) ... ... (then)] the opinion has been expressed that a *stūr* should be appointed for him, but he, himself, may not become anyone's *stūr*.

97, 13—15:

If a man is appointed as *stūr* and (after his) appointment, he is sentenced to undergo the ordeal procedure for an accusation of a capital offence, then — in the opinion of certain authorities — this appointment to *stūr*ship should be rescinded ("destroyed") and the most suitable other person (in the agnatic line of calling — *A. P.*) should be appointed; but in the opinion of others, (this appointment to *stūr*ship) should not be rescinded.

97, 15—**98**, 1:

If (a man) is condemned for a capital offence, then (all) the property in his possession should be confiscated/seized. An opinion has been expressed according to which the means required for the support of (his) wife and children should be drawn (from the bulk of the property of the condemned man — *A. P.*), but this is not done in court practice (or "according to judicial practice" = *kartak*), because if a man has been condemned for a capital offence, he is deprived of (his) wife, children and property.

98, 1—5:

Vahrām, citing Pusānveh ī Āzātmartān, has said that a document was drawn upon the basis of the witnesses' deposition of two woman, in the *magupat*ate of (... ... ...), the *magupat* of Staxr, and the *(h)andarzapat* of the Magi accepted (this document). Zurvāndāt, however, has said that according to judicial norms (or "in judicial practice") this was not done. Vahrām has said that (in a case where) a woman and a man are brought in as witnesses, a court record is drawn up, (but) not (in a case involving) a woman and a slave.

98, 5—6:

It is said in these two "*Teachings*" (= commentaries on the legal *nasks* — *A. P.*) that — if (it is) to the prejudice of the state/city (= *šahr*) — a husband and a master (= slave owner) are not entitled [...] [62].

98, 13 *:

98, 13—14:

It is written in one place, that if he commits a capital offence, then the property belonging to him which is not in his (possession) at the time, (and) is in the (actual) possession of an innocent person, shall be removed (from the estate of the criminal — *A. P.*) for the benefit of the person who possesses it.

98, 14—17:

Anī (15) gyākē nipišt kū ka pasēmār nazdist hačašmānd ut pas markaržān kart (16) hakar pat hačašmānd xvāstak bē kart būt ōy ⟨ī⟩ xvēš kē bē kart (17) ō ōy kē markaržān andar kart nē rasēt.

98, 17:

Markaržān ka pat patīt bavēt (...) *.

99, 1—3:

... (1) nāmak ī mart pat muhr ī xvēš ka-š anī-č muhr vāvarīkān+ muhrān apar ēstēt (2) u-š anāstīh ⟨i⟩ nē paytāk būt andar ōy kē pat ăvišt (ut) nipišt pat ēvarīh (3) kār hač-iš kartan.

99, 3—8:

Apāk anī Pusānveh ī Āzātmartān guft kū nāmak-ē(v) ī pat muhr ī (4) pasēmār būt ut pasēmār ăvišt rāδ pat nakīrākīh ēn-ič guft kū muhr (5) kē pat-iš ăvišt andar ān ē vanī nē pat miyān būt (ut) apāč ō man nē mat ⟨raδ⟩ (6) hač ān ⟨i⟩ čiγōn paytāk būt kū pasēmār ān muhr pas-ič hač ān pat kār (7) dāšt Māh-Ātur Frēh-Gušnasp ī Artaxšahr-Xvarreh magupat būt ut Zurvāndāt (8) pat ēvarīh kār hač-iš kart.

99, 8—13:

Anī Pusānveh ī Āzātmartān guft kū kurt harv (9) ka rasēnd ka-č nē pat viδānmānīh rasēt bē ka hakurč ō (10) ān gyāk pat viδānmānīh nē mat hend u-š hamē(v) dātaβarān dātaβarīh pat-iš. (11) Apāk anī pat hamēmārīh kart ī martōhm ī kurt nipišt kū pat viδānmānīh (12) apar ān gyāk raft ēstēt ut ēn nē nipišt kū nūn pat ān gyāk viδānmānīh (13) mat ēstēt.

99, 13—15:

Ut anī guft kū Farraxv hač andar Mihrēn ēt+ hač-iš apēsaxvan (14) būt pat apām ī andar ān ē ka apēsaxvan būt Mihrēn ō Farraxv apāyist dāt (15) apāč kart nē pātixšāy.

99, 15—17:

Ut anī guft kū pat tōžišn ōy ⟨ī⟩ kē xvāstakdār (16) nē ut xvāstak hast ān ⟨i⟩ xvāstak hakar kas pat ān tōžišn vičārtan andar nē (17) ēstēt pat grāβ apāč kart rāδ dātaβarān vičīr kunišn.

---

* Only the beginning of this article has survived.

98, 14—17:

In another place it is written that if the defendant first defaulted at the trial and subsequently committed a capital offence, and if a thing was taken away from him in connexion with his non-appearance at the trial (= the security requisitioned from the property of the defendant after his first or second non-appearance at the trial — *A. P.*); then it (= the thing) belongs to the one who took it away (= the plaintiff in the defaulted trial — *A. P.*), and it does not go to the one (the man) with regards to whom the capital offence was committed.

98, 17:

If a man who committed a capital offence, expiates his crime (...) *.

99, 1—3:

...the document ("letter") which a man sealed with his seal, if (among) the trustworthy seals on (this document) there is also another seal whose forgery/destruction has not been declared, then, inasmuch as it concerns the man who wrote and sealed this document with his authentic seal, it (= the spoiled seal on this document) is to be considered as valid.

99, 3—8:

Besides another (statement), Pusānveh ī Āzātmartān has said (the following): The seal of the respondent was on a document, but the respondent declared — as a denial of (the fact) that he had affixed his seal to (this document): "(this) seal with which (this document) is sealed, was not in use having been lost at that time (*i. e.* the time when the document was composed — *A. P.*), and (it) has not returned to me (since that time)"; (then) — inasmuch as it was demonstrated that this seal was used by the defendant after that (time) as well — Māh-Ātur Frēh-Gušnasp, who was the *magupat* (of the district) of Artaxšahr-Xvarreh, and Zurvāndāt considered it valid.

99, 8—13:

Pusānveh ī Āzātmartān has also said that every Kurd sojourning in (a given district), even if not on his (periodic) migration — unless he never sojourned in this district on his migration — is subject to the jurisdiction of the judges (of that region). In addition, as regards the jurisdiction over the Kurdish population is written (= formulated) thus: "(A Kurd) who has set out to nomadize in that region", but it is not formulated ("written") thus: "at the present time he arrived to nomadize there".

99, 13—15:

And it is also said that Farraxv is not entitled to make a claim for ("to retain, seize") (anything) from the property which Mihrēn renounced against a debt which Mihrēn was obliged to repay to Farraxv at the time when he renounced (this property).

99, 15—17:

And another (thing) is said. The judges must render a decision as regards the repayment ("in payment, in settlement") of a debt by one who is not the heir (of the debtor — *A. P.*), but who holds ("has") the thing, (and specifically) as regards the necessity to seize the thing as security if the person obligated to repay the debt is not present.

99, 17—**100**, 5:

Apāk anī (1) Pusānveh ī Āzātmartān guft kū xvāstak ī mart kē zan ut frazand nē būt (2) pat stūrīh ō kas dāt ka pat ān stūrīh ⟨ō⟩ kas kē avi-š dat mih (3) ēstēt pat vičīr ī apāmdān ī ōy kē dāt kart andar ōy kē xvāstak avi-š dat (4) ăvašt dastaβarīh ī pat graβīh dāštan rāδ Burzak ī Artaxšahr-xvarreh magupat (5) būt vičir kart.

100, 5—7:

Ut anī guft kū magupat pat yut šahr ut dātaβarān pat yut ⟨ī⟩ (6) tasūk būt ⟨ī⟩ ka pat muhr ī pat kār-framān dāštan nipišt ut ăvašt (7) kart.

100, 7—11:

Apāk anī apar pursišn-nāmak ī sāl 26 Xusrav ī Ōhrmizdān (8) rāδēnīt ⟨ut⟩ andar Artaxšahr-xvarreh pat-ič ōstīkānīh ī Māh-Ātur Frēh-Zartušt ī (9) Ōhrmizd-Artaxšahr magupat nāmak pat-iš pas(s)āxt⁺ (Ms.:PWN s'xt') ut andar Gōr ī Artaxšahr-xvarreh (10) pat-ič muhr ī Ōhrmizd-Artaxšahr magupat pat kār-framān dāštan ăvišt ī (11) ham pursišn-nāmak rāδ nipišt ēstēt.

100, 11—15:

Ut apāk anī apar ōy bay Ōhrmizd šāhān šāh (12) pat dip ī Gōr dātaβar ō Artaxšahr-xvarreh magupat kart nipišt ēstēt kū (13) im dip ut dip-ič ī dit ka mērak muhr apar nihāt hač gōβišn ī pēšēmār ut (14) mērak ī pasēmār ēn dip ut dip-ič ī dit pat muhr ī Xūnāpakān mānāk (? Ms. 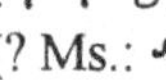) pat kār-framān (15) dāštan ⟨ut⟩ Anōšzāt kē tasūk ī Xūnāpakān pat mānākīh (? Ms.: ) dastaβar (= PQDWN) ăvišt.

100, 16—**101**, 1:

Ut anī Pusānveh ī Burzātur Farnbayān guft kū xvāstak ī pit pēš hač ān ī (17) ka duxt ī pātixšāyīhā stūr kart ō ān duxt dāt apāč ō dūtak (1) stūrīh rasēt.

101, 1—4:

Apāk anī guft kū duxt kē pit ī pātixšāyīhā xvāstak (2) pat stūrīh avi-š dahēt ān stūrīh nē pātixšāy bē ka kunēt ut hakar xvāstak ī (3) pēš hač ān dāt apāč (nē) āβārēt guft bavēt kū pit xvāstak ī pat (4) xvēšīh ō duxt dāt ka-š kāmēt vaštan pātixšāy.

99, 17—**100**, 5:

Besides this, Pusānveh ī Āzātmartān has said about a thing conveyed by a man having neither wife nor children to a certain man as a *stūr*(-possession), that if the man to whom (the thing) was conveyed renounces this *stūr*ship, Burzak, who was *magupat* of (the district of) Artaxšahr-Xvarreh, rendered a decision as to the right (of the man who renounced the *stūr*ship while being the former's creditor — *A. P.*) to hold this thing as a security guaranteeing ("against; of") the loan contract, that the one who declared the transfer (of the thing for *stūr*ship; the institutor of the *stūr*ship — *A. P.*) made ("sealed") with the one to whom he conveyed the thing (as a *stūr*-possession).

100, 5—7:

And it is also said, that a *magupat* (when sending letters, judicial documents) to another *šahr*, or a judge to another *tasūk* — sealed it in former times with his official seal (*Vide supra* **93**, 4—9, *et infra* **100**, 7—11).

100, 7—11:

In addition (the following) is written concerning the record of a judicial investigation drawn up in Artaxšahr-Xvarreh in the twenty-sixth year of (the reign of) Xusrav son of Ōhrmizd in the *ōstīkān*ate of Māh-Ātur: that Frēh-Zartušt, the *magupat* of (the city of) Ōhrmizd-Artaxšahr, composed a letter on this (subject), and that (he) sealed it with the official seal of the *magupat* (of the city) of Ōhrmizd-Artaxšahr (to send it — *A. P.*) to (the city of) Gōr which is in (the province of) Artaxšahr-Xvarreh.

100, 11—15:

And another. Under (our late) sovereign Ōhrmizd, King of Kings [63], this was written in a document drawn up by the judge of (the city of) Gōr and sent by him to the *magupat* (of the province) of Artaxšahr-Xvarreh: "this document — and another document to which the man affixed his (own) seal — is the record of the deposition ("declaration") of the respondent and the plaintiff. And Anōšzāt, head ("empowered manager") of the judicial department (?) of the district of Xūnāpakān sealed this document — as well as the other document — with the official seal of the judicial department"(?).

100, 16—**101**, 1:

Pusānveh ī Burzātur Farnbaγān has also said, that a thing conveyed by a father to his daughter from a *pātixšāyīh*-marriage before he designated this daughter as (his) *stūr*, must be returned to the foundation for *stūr*ship of (this) family.

101, 1—4:

Besides other (things) it is said, that a daughter to whom her father (married to her mother according to) a *pātišxāyīh*-marriage has conveyed a thing as a *stūr*-possession is not entitled to act otherwise than to assume the given *stūr*ship (= become her father's *epikleros* — *A. P.*). And if she does (not) return the thing which her father conveyed to her earlier (= before her institution as *epikleros* — *A. P.*); then it is said in this connexion that her father if he (so) wishes is entitled to take back ("turn") the thing that he gave to the daughter as a personal possession (= as her personal inheritance-share in her father's estate).

101, 4—8:

Ut apāk anī (5) Dāt-Farraxv ut Siyāvaxš guft kū mart zan ī pātixšāyīhā ō ōy ī pat zan ut (6) frazand niruzd ut pat ān niruzdīh avinās ut xvāhišn ī pat zan dātīhā kart (7) ēstēt yut-ič hač hamdātastānīh ī zan dāt pātixšāy ut ka dahēt xvāstak ī (8) zan ō ōy kē zan avi-š dahēt nē rasēt.

101, 8—11:

Ut anī guft kū ka (9) xvatāy bandak pat bandakīh ō āturān dahēt ā-t ōh-ič kū-š pat frazand ī bandak pātixšāyīh (10) nēst pas-ič frazand ut aβγātak ī bandak bavēnd āturān bandak bavēnd čē-šān frazandīh (11) ut aβγātakīh ī bandak āturān bandakīh ⟨raδ⟩ hamē(v) bavēt.

101, 11—15:

Apāk anī guft kū bandak 1 ī Farraxv ut (12) Mihrēn xvēš ā-t ⟨KN 'YK⟩ Farraxv pat vindišn ī ⟨ut⟩ bandak bahr ī Mihrēn čiš-ič pātixšāyīhā (13) nēst pas-ič ka Farraxv bandak bahr ī xvēš āzāt kunēt bandak zan ut frazand ōh (14) bavēt pašadātakān/pasādātakān ut vāspuhrakān ī zan andar ō bandak barēt hač-iš hamaδvēn pat-iš (15) bē ēstēt.

101, 15—17:

Xvāstak ī ka bun+ (Ms.: bandak) nēm mart anšahrīk ut vindišn nēm ān mart (16) xvēš būt hač anī kas ō bandak mat ut andar ō xvatāy nē šavēt ētōn (17) šāyēt būt.

101, 17—**102**, 3:

Anī guft kū ka pēšēmār (hač) pasēmār anbassān kū-m yām-ē(v) ī (1) pat 10 pat tō graβ kart ut 10 bē patigīr ut yām apāč dah ut pasēmār hač apamdān ut graβīh (2) anbassān ut pēšēmār bōxtēt pasēmār yām apāč dahišn apāk-ič anbassānīh pas-ič (3) 10 ap(p)ār nē bavēt.

102, 3—9:

Apāk anī guft kū ka pēšēmār pat xar 1 hač pasēmār (4) anbassān ut pasēmār ān xar pat guharīkānīh ī gāv 1 hač pasēmār stat ut ān gāv ō (5) pēšēmār apispārt ut pēšēmār ān gāv pat ziyānak ⟨i⟩ hač pasēmār dāštan rāδ+ (6) patkārt hakar pasēmār+ (Ms.: pēšēmār) bōxtēt (ut) pēšēmār xar ap(p)arakīhā bē kunēt ut gāv (7) apāk-ič ān ī pasēmār hač xvēšīh ī xvēš nakīrā(k) pas-ič ka pasēmār xvāhēt (8) ō pasēmār apispārišn ut hakar pasēmār ēraxtēt pasēmār tāvān ī pat xar (9) bē kunēt ut gāv pat pēšēmār bē mānēt.

101, 4—8:

And besides other (things) Dāt-Farraxv and Siyāvaxš also said, that a man is entitled to hand over his wife from a *pātixšāyīh*-marriage, without the wife's consent to a man bereft of wife and children and innocent of this bereavement, who has legally (officially) requested (= presented a demand for) a wife. And if he hands her over, then the wife's property does not go to the one to whom he conveyed (his) wife.

101, 8—11:

And another (thing) is said, that if a man gives his (slave) as a slave to a Fire-temple, then he has no authority (= title) over the offspring of (this) slave. And if the slave subsequently has children and grand-children, then they shall be slaves of the Fire-temple; because they are children and grand-children of a slave, they (= each of them) will always (= inevitably) be slaves of the Fire-temple.

101, 11—15:

Together with another (thing) it has been said, that (if) a slave belongs jointly to Farraxv and Mihrēn, then Farraxv has no rights/power as regards Mihrēn's share in the income of the slave. And if afterwards Farraxv frees his share of the slave (and) the slave has/acquires a wife and children, the dowry (= daugher's portion of her father's estate — *A. P.*) and the paraphernalia brought by the wife to the slave shall belong entirely to him and to her.

101, 15—17:

If a thing of which half of the principal belonged to a slave and half of the income — to this man has come to the slave from a third party ("another man") and does not go to the (slave's) master, (then) this is licit.

101, 17—**102**, 3:

And another (thing) is said, that if a plaintiff prefers a charge (and declares): "I conveyed a vessel to you as a pledge against the ten (*saters*) (loaned to me). (Now) take the ten (*saters*) and return the vessel!", but the respondent denies the fact of the loan and security, and the plaintiff wins the case ("is acquitted"), (then) the respondent is obliged to return the vessel and despite (his) denial (in court of the fact of the loan — *A. P.*), he shall not lose the ten (*satērs*).

102, 3—9:

Besides other (things) it is said, that if the plaintiff litigates with the respondent over a donkey, but the respondent received this donkey from the plaintiff in exchange for a bull, and he conveyed ("re-entrusted") this bull to the plaintiff, but the plaintiff contended that he received this bull from the respondent as a loss (to himself). (Then) if the respondent (the ms. has "plaintiff" — *A. P.*) is acquitted (= wins the case), but the plaintiff forcibly ("as a brigand") takes away the donkey, then the bull must be returned to the respondent at the respondents's first demand, even despite (the fact) that the respondent denied (at the trial) that (this bull) belonged to him. But if the respondent is convicted (= loses the case), then the respondent must pay a fine for the donkey, and the bull shall go to ("remain with") the plaintiff.

102, 9—11:

Ut apāk anī guft kū mart (10) xvāstak ī naxvist pat graβīh ut pas pat xrītakīh ī ēvar pat xvēšīh apar patkārēt (11) vaštakīh rāδ nē ēranǰēnišn.

102, 11—12:

Ut apāk anī guft kū ka ō ēvarīh vartēt nē (12) ēranǰēnišn.

102, 12—13:

Ut apāk anī guft kū ap(p)ārīh ī ⟨nē⟩ pat čiš ī kas ō kartak nē (13) kart ēstēt.

102, 13—14:

Hambāγ ut pāyandān ka tōžišn pat nakīrākīh vičārēnd guharīk apāč (14) nē rasēt.

102, 14—15:

Anī guft kū ka gōβēt kū ēn muγ bar brīn ⟨ut⟩ tō xvēš aδak-iš (15) bun dāt bavēt nē bar.

102, 15—16:

Apāk anī guft kū dip muhr-vēxt ut saxvan-nāmak (16) muhr-brīt ⟨ut⟩ višāt višāt dip ut saxvan-nāmak rāδ guft bavēt.

102, 16—17:

Ut anī guft (17) kū mart xvāstak ī dit sāl ī pat nāmčišt rāδ nipišt ut kart kū māndan...*

103, 1—2 **:

(...) pat dastaβarīh avi-š hamē(v) rasēt ⟨i⟩ ō-č pus kē xvāstak pat stūrīh bē dāt (2)  (?) nē ōγōn bavēt čiγōn frazand ī hač zan ī pātixšāyīhā ī ān ⟨ut⟩ pus zāyēt.

103, 2—4:

Ut anī (3) guft kū ka gōβēt kū ēn saxvan-nāmak (ī) muhr-⟨i⟩-brīt ēn dip (ī) muhr-⟨i⟩-vēxt (4) ⟨ut⟩ višāt aδak-iš[+] višāt nē muhr bē dip ut saxvan-nāmak rāδ guft bavēt.

103, 4—6:

Apāk (5) anī guft (kū) ka gōβēt kū-m Aβzūtxvatāy nēm āzāt kart ut pat 3 bahr ēv bahr pat bandakīh (6) ō ātaxš dāt aδak-iš pat 3 bahr ēv bahr nē hač ān nēm guft bavēt kū-m ⟨dāt⟩ (āzāt kart).

---

* The text of this article breaks off at this point.

** Only the end of this article has survived. No coherent translation of it is possible.

102, 9—11:

In addition to other (things), it is said that if a man litigates over his ownership of a thing — first as a pledge (*i. e.* citing his right as the creditor to possess the thing as security — *A. P.*), and subsequently on the strength of an authentic (= proven) purchase thereof, then (he) should not be sentenced to a fine for (this) shift from (the original statement) [64].

102, 11—12:

Together with this it is said, that if making a shift from (his original testimony) he turns to a trustworthy one, then a fine should not be adjudicated (for this) (as for a judicial offence — *A. P.*).

102, 12—13:

And together with this it is said that (actions concerned with) losses (or "seizures"; lit. "deprivation, taking away") of small amounts ("things") are not accepted for judgement through legal procedure (= trial).

102, 13—14:

If a co-partner or warrantor settles a *correal* (joint) debt ("obligation to pay") through a court decision ("through a trial") [65], then he loses his right to a regression [lit.: "no restitution (for his expenditures) reaches (him)"].

102, 14—15:

And another (thing) has been said, that if he declares: "this date palm belongs to you except for the fruit", then the base (= the tree itself) is conveyed ("given") but not the fruit (brought forth by it).

102, 15—16:

Together with this it is said, that a document with the seal removed and a record of depositions whose seal has been cut off are — open ("opened"). "Open" is said of the document and of the record. (*Cf. infra* **103**, 2—4).

102, 16—17 *:

103, 1—2 **:

103, 2—4:

And another (thing) is said, that if he declares: "this record of depositions with the seal cut off, (or) this document with the seal removed (are) open (= opened)", the (designation) "open" refers not to the seal, but to the record of depositions and to the document (*cf. supra* **102**, 15—16).

103, 4—6:

Besides other (things) it is said, (that) if he declares: "I manumitted one half of Aβzūtxvatay (= proper name of a slave — *A. P.*) and conveyed one-third (of him) in servitude to the Fire-temple", then the "one-third" is not (taken) from the one-half of which it was said: "I manumitted".

103, 7—8:

Ut apāk anī guft kū ka gōβēt kū sardarān ī rētak rētak hač (h)ēr ī xvēš (8) hač dušmanān pat vahāk xrīt hač (h)ēr ī rētak guft bavēt kū⟨-m⟩ xrīt.

103, 9—10:

Apāk anī pat aparmat ī ratān pat (h)ēr ī Ātur ī Farnbaγ kart ut nipišt kū bandakān ī (10) ātur (ī) Farnbaγ Ātur ī Farnbaγ hač (h)ēr ī xvēš hač dušmanān pat vahāk xrīt.

103, 10—12:

Ut apāk (11) anī (guft) kū ka gōβēt kū-m ziyānak pat handōčišn ut vindišn ī xvēš pātixšāy kart (12) handōčišn ut vindišn ī ziyānak rāδ guft bavēt.

103, 12—13:

Ut apāk anī guft kū ka gōβēt (13) kū bar ī muγ ī man xvēš (ō tō) hēβ bavēt aδakiš xvēšīh muγ rāδ guft bavēt.

103, 13—15:

Anī (14) guft kū ka gōβēt kū ēn xvāstak tā amā žīvandak hēm ākanēn darēm ka (15) ēvak mīrēt ⟨kū⟩ ēn (xvāstak) ōy-ič ī dit nē dārišn.

103, 15—**104**, 1:

Apāk anī guft kū ka gōβēt (16) kū tā amā žīvandak hēm ēn xvāstak amā darēm ayāp gōβēt kū amā tā žīvandak (17) hēm ēn xvāstak pat ākanēn dārēm ka ēvak mīrēt ōy ī dit [nēm] 1 ōh (1) dārišn.

104, 1—4:

Ut apāk anī guft kū ka gōβēt kū tā ān ē xvāstak vičārom vaxš dahom (2) ayāp xvāstak druvist dārom ut pas mātak ast-ē(v) vičārēt xvāstak xvāstak-(3)marīhā hač graβīh hišt bavēt ut apārīk nē hišt bavēt ut vaxš xvāstak-(4)marīhā apāč ut apārīk apāč nē ēstēt.

103, 7—8:

And together with another (thing) it is said, (that) if he declares: "the guardians of a youth have ransomed ('bought') the youth from the enemy with (his) own means", then it is thereby said that they ransomed (him) with the youth's (own) means.

103, 9—10:

Besides other (things) it is declared and written down concerning the decree of the *rat*s relating to the treasury of the Farnbaγ Fire-(temple), that the Farnbaγ Fire-temple ransomed the slaves of the Farnbaγ Fire-temple (the *hieroduloi* are evidently intended here — *A. P.*) from the enemy with money ("at a price") (taken from) its own means.

103, 10—12:

And together with another (thing) (it is said), that when he declares: "I have empowered my wife as regards her accumulation (= the estate personally acquired or accumulated — *A. P.*) and income", then (this is thereby) said concerning the acquisitions ("accumulation") and the income of the wife.

103, 12—13:

And besides other (things) it is said, that when he declares: "let the harvest of the date-palm which belongs to me be (yours)", then the indication concerning his ownership (of the thing) refers to the date-palm (lit.: "is said about the date-palm").

103, 13—15:

(And) another (thing) is said. If he declares: "we will possess this thing jointly as long as we live", (then) when one (of them) dies, the other must likewise not possess (the thing).

103, 15—**104**, 1:

Together with another (thing) it is said, that if he declares: "we will possess this thing as long as we live", or if (he) speaks in this manner: "we will possess this thing together as long as we live", then, when one of them dies, the other shall possess (merely) one [half] (of the thing).

104, 1—4:

Together with this another (thing) is said, that if he declares: "until such a time as I settle the debt I shall pay interest", or: "I shall preserve the thing intact (in other words the debtor is stipulating a hypothec-security — *A. P.*)", and he subsequently pays back part of the amount; then the (pledged — *A. P.*) thing is freed from the pledge (= is redeemed) in proportion with (the repaid portion) of the debt, whereas the remaining portion (of the hypothecated thing) is not freed. And the interest is retained in accordance with the amount of the debt (*i. e.* of the remaining portion of the debt — *A. P.*), but from the other part (= from the settled portion of the debt), it is not retained.

104, 4—5:

Ut anī guft kū graβakāndār ⟨kē⟩ graβakān (5) (graβ) kartan pātixšāyīhā nē bavēt (ut) ōy kē graβakān andar nihāt mātak-ič ap(p)ār bavēt.

104, 6—8:

Apāk anī guft kū ka ō mart-ē(v) kē gōspand nēst drahm dahēt kū-m gōspand (7) pat vahāk dah drahm ap(p)ār bavēt ut apāč nē rasēt ēn harv 2 dātastān apāk ān ī hačapar (8) nipišt ēstēt kū drahm ap(p)ār nē bavēt čē-š pat ān vinās-ē(v) nē kart nikerītan.

104, 9—11:

Ut anī guft kū ka gōβēt kū zarrēn ī man xvēš zan ut asīmēn ī man xvēš (10) duxt ī man xvēš hēβ bavēt ka-č naxvist dāt ī ō duxt ut pas dāt ī (11) ō zan gōβēt duxt ī-š zan asīmēn nē bē zarrēn xvēš.

104, 12—14:

Apāk anī guft kū ka gōβēt kū zarrēn ī man xvēš zan ī man ut asīmēn ī man (13) xvēš duxt ī man bavēt xvēš hēβ bavēt hakar duxt zāyēt ut ā-š zan bavēt (14), pēš-ič tā ō zanīh ī kas rasēt asīmēn ut pas zarrēn-ič xvēš.

104, 15—17:

Ut apāk anī guft kū ka gōβēt kū-t yumāy zan ī man hast ut zan ī man (16) bavēt pat hambāγ dārom zan ī-š andar ān ē zan būt ut pas hač zanīh (17) hišt ut apāč ō zanīh mat pat hast ut pat-ič bavēt harv 2 ō bahr mar(īhā)...*

105, 1**:

(...) kunišn ayāp nē.

105, 1—3:

Ut apāk-ič anī guft kū ka gōβēt kū xvāstak ī (2) ō man mat (ut) ān ī pit ī man xvēš būt duxt ī man xvēš ut ān ī ka pit ⟨i⟩ pat baxt (3) šut māt xvēš būt ō duxt dāt bavēt.

105, 3—5:

Ēn dar ī ō ān dar ī (4) nipišt kū ka xvāstak ī 2000 ō 3 mart rāst gōβēt ōγōn bavēt patmūt (5) apāyēt.

* The text of this article breaks off at this point.
** This is the end of an article whose beginning has not survived.

104, 4—5:

And another (thing) is said, that the holder of the pledge (= the creditor) is not entitled to pawn (to someone else — *A. P.*) the pledge that he holds, and the one (the creditor) who has re-pledged the security (to another), likewise loses the sum of money (which he loaned to the principal owner of the pledge).

104, 6—8:

Besides another (thing) it is said, that if he conveys a sum of money to a man who has no sheep (and says): "give me a sheep for this money ('at this price')!", he loses the money and does not receive it back. Both of these decisions should be investigated together with what has been written above (specifically), so that he should not be deprived of the money, since he has not committed any offence regarding it.

104, 9—11:

(Together with that) another (thing) is also said, that if he declares: "let the gold ('golden' things) belonging to me (belong) to my wife, and the silver ('silver' things) to my daughter", then even if he makes first the declaration of transfer to the daughter and subsequently (the declaration) of transfer to the wife, and the daughter is his wife, (in such a case) the gold ("golden" things) shall belong to her and not the silver.

104, 12—14:

Besides the other (thing) it is said, that if he declares: "let the gold ('golden' things) belonging to me belong to my wife, and the silver ('silver' things) belonging to me, to the daughter whom I shall have", (then) if a daughter is born to him and subsequently becomes his wife; then, until she marries — the silver — and subsequently (= after she marries her father — *A. P.*) — the gold ("golden things") shall belong to her.

104, 15—17:

Together with that it is said, that if he declares (the following): "I take as co-partners yourself together with the wife I (now) have and with the wife I shall (subsequently) have", then the woman — who was then his wife, and whom he subsequently divorced, and who afterwards became once more his wife — (is considered to be) both "the one I have" and "(the one) I shall have", (and) both (times) in accordance with the shares (...) *.

105, 1 **:

105, 1—3:

And together with this another (thing) is said, that if he declares (thus): "(let) the property that came to me (and) the one which belonged to my father belong to my daughter", then the thing which belonged to the mother after the father's death shall also pass to the daughter.

105, 3—5:

There also is an addition/supplement to what was written (above): if he declares (the transfer) of a thing (valued) at 2000 (*drahms*) equally to three persons, it is necessary to measure (it) (so that) it should be so.

105, 5—10:

Ut apāk anī guft kū mart dastkart 2 harv ēvak pat yut stūrīh (6) dāštan paytāk kart ut ān dastkart ēvak ī pat nāmčišt frazand ī naxvist pusak (7) bavēt čiγōn ō purnāyīh rasēt ēvak frazand ī naxvist hač duxt zāyēt (8) dāštan rāδ framān bavēt ut pas hač ān duxtak ō zanīh (ī) pusak rasēt (9) pat ān zanīh naxvist duxt-ē(v) pas pus-ē(v) zāyēt ut duxtak ut pusak anī frazand nē (10) bavēt framān ī pas kār ut ān ī pēš kār nēst.

105, 10—12:

Ut anī guft kū ka pat zamīk (11) ī-š ō Farraxv ut āp ī-š ō Mihrēn pat (h)andarz dāt āsyāp kart āsyāp pat (12) (h)andarz bē nē rasēt.

105, 12—14:

Apāk anī guft kū ka pat (h)andarz kart kū dastīk ī (13) man xvēš Farraxv xvēš apām ī-š andar ān ē pat kasān dāt bavēt (ut) ān ī pas (14) pat apām bē dahēt pat (h)andarz bē nē rasēt.

105, 14—16:

Ut anī guft kū ka gōβēt (15) kū xvāstak ō man rasēt tō xvēš bar ī bun ī hač xvāstak ī-š nūn xvēš bavēt (16) pat pas mat dārišn bē šavēt.

105, 16—**106**, 1:

Apāk anī guft kū anšahrīk ka bē (17) frōšēt ut zan ka bē hilēt u-š rēš pat-iš būt ēstēt šnāvīh? [ī] (1) pas ravēt xvatāy ut šōy ī pēš xvēš.

106, 1—4:

Ut apāk anī guft kū xvāstak ī (2) pēš hač ān ē ka xvatāy bandak xrīt anī kas ō bandak dāt ut xvatāy patigīrišn (3) apar nē paytākēnīt ēstāt hakar xvatāy ī pēš patigīrišn paytākēnēt xvatāy ī (4) pēš ut hakar yuttar bandak xvēš.

106, 4—5:

Ut anī guft kū ka gōβēt kū-t pas hač 10 (5) sāl pat hambāγ dārom pat ān xvāstak hambāγ kart bavēt ī-š nūn xvēš.

105, 5—10:

And together with this it is said: a man made a declaration concerning the transfer of each of two *dastkart*s to a separate *stūr*ship. And there is a disposition that: one of these *dastkart*s, which is fully specified, shall go to the first child born to his son when (that) child comes of age, and the other (*dastkart*) to the first child born to his daughter — as (*stūr*)-possessions. And subsequently this daughter marries the son (= her brother — *A. P.*), and first a daughter and then a son are born of this marriage, and there are no other children of the daughter and son (of the testator). The second ("subsequent") disposition is valid, but the first ("former") is not.

105, 10—12:

And another (thing) is said, that if he has built a mill on the land that he conveyed by testament to Farraxv and on the water willed to Mihrēn, then the mill does not pass on the strength of this testament (either to Farraxv or to Mihrēn (*i. e.* the transfer of the land and water does not carry with it the transfer of the mill — *A. P.*).

105, 12—14:

After that it is said, that if the following is declared in a testament "let those of my properties which are actually at my disposal belong to Farraxv"; then a loan he had made at that time to people, (and) that which he will subsequently convey as a loan, shall not pass (to Farraxv) according to (this) testament.

105, 14—16:

And it is also said, that if he declares: "let the property that I shall receive (= *bona adventicia* — *A. P.*) belong to you", then the income from the estate ("principal") belonging to him now (*i. e.* at the time of the declaration — *A. P.*) shall pass into (the category of) *bona adventicia* (lit.: "to the subsequent possession").

105, 16—**106**, 1:

Besides another (thing) it is said, that if he suffers a loss in connexion with the sale of a slave or the divorce of his wife, then the satisfaction (? compensation?) [which] shall follow belongs to the former master (of the slave) and to the former husband.

106, 1—4:

It is also said, that if a master does not declare (his) acceptance of a thing conveyed (presented) to a slave by a third party before the (present — *A. P.*) master bought (that) slave, then, should the former master (of that slave) make a declaration of acceptance (of the thing), it shall belong to the former master; in the opposite case (it shall belong) to the slave.

106, 4—5:

And another (thing) is said, that if he declares: "you shall be my partner in ten years", the/latter (thereby) becomes (his) partner as regards the property he owns now.

106, 6—7:

Ut anī guft kū ka gōβēt kū vitart man xvāstak ī man xvēš tō xvēš (7) aδak-iš ān dāt bavēt ī-š nūn xvēš.

106, 7—9:

Ut apāk anī guft kū ka gōβēt (8) kū-m pas hač 10 sāl tan pat zanīh ō Mihrēn dāt paš(a)dātakān ut vāspuhrakān ī (9) andar ān ē ka gōβišn gōβēt pas hač 10 sāl šōy xvēš.

106, 9—11:

Ut anī guft kū (10) bandak ka pat āzātīh patkārēt ut bōžišn ī varōmand apāk xvap ut vikāy ī pat (11) pāδ nē šāyēt.

106, 11—12:

Apāk anī guft kū yātakgōβ gumārt ka pat muhr ī xvēš (12) nē šāyēt.

106, 12—13:

Ut anī kū ka pat āp ī xvēš apar zamīk ī kasān āsyāp kunēt (13) ut 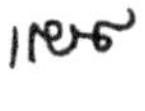 nišānēt āp ap(p)ār nē bavēt.

106, 13—17:

Apāk anī guft kū ka pat hamdātastānīh [ī] (14) ōy kē kahas xvēš pat āp ī hač ān kahas āsyāp kunēt ut dār ut draxt nišānēt (15) ayāp-iš pat āpvarīh(?) apar bē mānēt ān kē kahas xvēš ān āp ān ī pat āsyāp (16) andar apāyēt apāč kart nē ut ān ī pat dār ut draxt ut āpvarīh(?) andar apāyēt apāč kart (17) pātixšāy.

106, 17—**107**, 2:

Ut apāk anī čāšt ēstēt kū ka rāh ī (1) kasān pat āp ī xvēš kunēt aδak-iš āp ap(p)ār nē bavēt ut ka rāh ī (2) ⟨kasān⟩ xvēš pat āp ī kasān kunēt aδak-iš rāh ap(p)ār bavēt.

107, 3—4:

Ut anī guft kū⟨-m⟩ (ka) pus (hač) xvastūkīh+ (Ms.: NQSY' = xvāstak) (ī) katak-bānūk ut sardār pat apāmdān vičīr āvišt (4) ka-č stānēnd ut pat (h)ēr ī dūtak uzēnak kartan rāδ nakīrā(k) aδak-ič bē tōžišn.

106, 6—7:

It is also said, that if he declares: "the property belonging to me shall belong to you after my death", then the property transferred thereby to (the other person) is that which now (at the moment of the declaration) belongs to him (= the declarer).

106, 7—9:

In addition to the other it is said, that if she declares: "in ten years I shall enter into a marriage (= of a type *sine manu* — *A. P.*) with Mihrēn (lit.: 'I shall give myself as a wife to Mihrēn')"; then after the passage of ten years the paraphernalia and dowry (= her "daughter's share" of her father's estate brought to her husband's house as her dowry — *A. P.*), which (the woman) had at the time of the declaration, shall belong to (her) husband (from a *pātixšāyīh, i. e. cum manu* marriage — *A. P.*) after the passage of ten years.

106, 9—11:

It is also said, that if a slave argues for his freedom in court, and if the solution (of the given case) requires an ordeal procedure, then (the assignment of an ordeal for this slave) is lawful, (but if the slave appears) as a witness (testifying) after (a free person?), then it is not permissible (to assign an ordeal procedure to him — *A. P.*).

106, 11—12:

Besides another (thing) it is said, that the appointment as legal representative (or "the mandate of a legal representative" — *A. P.*) is not valid if (it is authenticated) by his own seal.

106, 12—13:

And also another: if he has built a mill and established a dam (?) on water belonging to him and land belonging to other people, (the possession)? of the water shall not be taken (= witheld) from him.

106, 13—17:

It is also said, that if he builds a mill on the water of a canal with the consent of the person owning the canal, and he also plants trees, or (if) he detains (water) for an aqueduct (?); the person who owns the canal is not entitled to withhold ("retain, take away") the water indispensable for the mill, but he is entitled to withhold (the water) needed for the trees and the aqueduct (?).

106, 17—**107**, 2:

Besides another (thing) it is said, that if he lays a people's road (= a public road — *A. P.*) over his own watercourse, then he does not lose (possession of) the water. But if he lays his own road over other people's watercourse (*i. e.* a public canal or stream — *A. P.*), then he loses (possession of) the road.

107, 3—4:

It is also said, that (if) a son makes ("seals") a loan-contract with the consent of the mistress of the house and the guardian, then, once the money has been borrowed, (the debt) must be repaid — even if they (the guardian and the mistress of the house — *A. P.*) protest against the expenditure from the family estate required to settle the debt.

107, 5—7:

Apāk anī guft kū xvāstak ī hač xvastūkīh (ī) pit pat vināskārīh ī apurnāyak (6) bērōn bē apispārēnd ayāp bē apispārtan rāδ vičīr kunēnd apurnāyak (7) purnāy ut nakīrā(k) bavēt aδak-ič vičīr kunišn ut bē apispārišn.

107, 7—9:

Apāk anī guft (8) kū xvastūkīh ī dūtak sardār (ut) katak-bānūk kart andar-ič katak-bānūk ut sardār ī hač ān (9) frāč bavēnd pat ēvarīh kār hač-iš kunišn.

107, 9—12:

Ut anī guft kū ka pēšēmār (10) pasēmār hamēmār kū-m anšahrīk hēh ut pasēmār anī mart pat nāmčišt (11) rāδ gōβēt kū-š anšahrīk hom u-š vikāy apāk pat anī (h)ēr apāk pasēmār (12) dātastān nē rāδēnišn.

107, 12—14:

Apāk anī guft kū ka pēšēmār pasēmār hamēmār (13) kū xvāstak man xvēš apātixšāyīhā pasēmār dārēt pasēmār gōβēt (14) baxškarīh ī anī mart dārom u-š vikāy apāk (ō) pēšēmār nē dahišn.

107, 15—17[*]:

circa 35 letters
Ut anī guft kū ka Farraxv [... ... ...] (16) xvēš hamaδvēn Mihrēn xvēš hēβ bavēt [... ... ...] (17) tōžišn ī andar ān ē Farraxv ō Mihrēn [... ... ...].
circa 30 letters

108, 1—5[**]:

108, 6—8:

... (6) Anaγrān rōč dāt u-m dārišn bē kart ut zanīh rāδ apāč ō man mat aδak-iš (7) pat dārišn bē kart ēvarīh apāyēt (ut) pat apāč matan aδak-iš vikāy-ič-ē(v) nē (8) apāyēt čē ētōn bavēt čiγōn raxt ut bizišk (= 'SY').

108, 8—11:

Ut anī guft kū ka zan (9) anšahrīk rāδ Farraxv apāk Mihrēn patmān kart kū frāč hač man tō [xvēš...] (10) Pērōž ī Veh-Ōhrmizdān ut Pusānveh ī Burzātur Farnbaγān [... ... ...] (11) [... ...] frazand ī žīvandakān Farraxv zāyēt nē dāt bavēt.

108, 12—17[***].

109, 1—3[****].

[*] So little of this article has survived that no coherent translation is possible.

[**] In lines 1—4, only the first word has survived. Not a single character has survived in line 5.

[***] Only disjointed words have survived in lines 12—17.

[****] The top of the page up to line 4 is filled with scribal exercises: the eight-fold repetition of the words, *nūn avi-š dahēt*: "... now conveys to him...".

107, 5—7:

Together with this it is said, that if a thing is given away (alienated) to the detriment (of the interests) of a minor with (his) father's consent, or a transfer-agreement is concluded, but the minor protests (against the transfer) when he comes of age, then even in this case, the agreement must be concluded and (the thing) handed over.

107, 7—9:

It is also said, that the agreement (with this or that legal action or with a court decision) expressed by the guardian of a family and the mistress of the house is also to be considered valid and binding as regards the mistress of the house and the guardian that (this family) shall subsequently have.

107, 9—12:

It is also said, that if a plaintiff litigates with a respondent (declaring): "you are my slave", whereas the respondent says of another particular person: "I am his slave", and he (= the slave-respondent) has a witness with him, then no suit about (any) other thing should be brought against (the given) respondent.

107, 12—14:

Furthermore it is said, that if a plaintiff litigates with a respondent (declaring the following): "the respondent unlawfully possesses a thing belonging to me". (But) the respondent declares "I possess it as a gift (received) from another man", and he has witnesses ("a witness") to this; (then) (this thing) should not be conveyed to the plaintiff.

107, 15—17*:

108, 1—5**:

108, 6—8:

"... conveyed on the day Anaγrān, and I transferred the possession (of this thing) (to another person), and (subsequently) it (=the right of possession over the thing) returned to me through marriage", then it is necessary to verify the transfer of the possession and the return of (the thing) to him, and no witness is required, since this (case) is analogous to the one of the patient and the physician(?).

108, 8—11:

It is also said, that if Farraxv concluded (the following) agreement concerning a slave-woman with Mihrēn: "[she shall belong (?)] to you after my death", Pērōž ī Veh-Ōhrmizdān and Pusānveh ī Burzātur Farnbaγān [... ... ...] (if) a child is born (to the slave-woman) in Farraxv's lifetime, then he should not be conveyed (to Mihrēn).

108, 12—17***.

109, 1—3****.

109, 4—6:

... (4) bavēt kū ān drahm apāč dāt nē šāyēt aδak-iš stūr gumārišn ut ka (5) ān kē xrīt+ mīrēt tā apāč dāt ī ān drahm aδak-iš ān zan stūr ut frazand (6) ī zan andar ān ē zāyēt ōy (ī) xrīt frazand bavēt.

109, 6—8:

Apāk anī guft (7) kū ka mart xvāstak 80 (ayāp) apām 80 aδak-iš stūr gumārišn čē šāyēt (8) būt kū xvāstak ō dūtak rasēt ayāp apām pat dūtak bē hilēnd.

109, 9—11:

Ut apāk anī guft kū ka gōβēt kū-m xvāstak ō Farraxv dāt ut Farraxv (10) nē mat ēstēt tā Farraxv rasēt andar nē apāyēt gōβēt stūrīh ī ōy (11) kē pat ān aδvēnak guft pātīrān nē gumārišn.

109, 11—13:

Ut apāk anī guft kū ka (12) gōβēt kū-m pas hač 10 sāl ēn xvāstak pat stūrīh ō tō dāt andar 10 sāl (13) stūr ī ōy kē bē dāt pat-iš gumārišn.

109, 13—15:

Ut anī guft kū (ka gōβēt kū) pat ān rōč (14) ka Mihrēn pat baxt šavēt hamākdēn yazom enyā 1000 bē dahom ka (15) pat ān rōč kē nām ān rōč yazēt aδak-ič 1000 ō tōžišn nē rasēt.

109, 16—**110**, 1:

Apāk anī guft kū ka gōβēt kū hakar pat ēn vēmārīh mīrom aδak-im (17) ēn xvāstak ō tō dāt ka-š ān vēmārīh druvist bavēt ka pat ham ān (1) vēmārīh mīrēt aδak-ič (h)andarz vašt bavēt.

110, 1—2:

Ut anī guft kū duxt andar dūtak ī (2) katak-xvatāy⟨ān⟩ zāt (.......) nē bavēt čē pat katak-xvatāyīh nē šāyēt.

109, 4—6:

... it is not possible to return that money, then a *stūr* must be appointed for him. And if the buyer dies before the return of that money, then this woman must become his *stūr*, and the child born to the woman at that time shall be the child of the buyer.

109, 6—8:

After the other it is said that if a man (conveyed through transfer — *A. P.*) a thing (valued at) 80 (*drahms*/*satērs*?) (or) lent 80 (*drahms*/*satērs*?), then a *stūr* must be appointed for him, since it is possible that the thing (which he relinquished through the transfer — *A. P.*) will pass to (his) family (= will return to the family), or the debt will be repaid to the family [66].

109, 9—11:

Besides the other it is said that if he declares (the following): "I have conveyed a thing to Farraxv", but Farraxv is not present; then, until Farraxv appears ("arrives") and "declares: 'not needed'" (*i. e.* refuses to acquire it through transfer — *A. P.*), the *stūr*ship of the one who made the declaration in this fashion (= the *stūr*ship of the conveyer — *A. P.*) is held up, (a *stūr*) should not be appointed.

109, 11—13:

It is also said, that if he declares (the following): "upon the passage of ten years this thing is conveyed to you for *stūr*ship (= as a *stūr*-possession)", then in the case of the declarer's death — *A. P.*) during the ten years (*i. e.* before the expiration of the time-limit indicated in the declaration for the entry into effect of the transfer — *A. P.*), he should be appointed as the *stūr* of the man who conveyed (the thing) to him.

109, 13—15:

It is also said, that (if he declares): "I shall perform a liturgy in accordance with the full ritual on the day of Mihrēn's death, in the opposite case I shall pay 1000 (*drahms*)", then even if he performs (this) liturgy (not on that day, but) on a homonymous day (of the death of Mihrēn), in that case too, (he) will not be obliged to pay 1000 (*drahms*).

109, 16—**110**, 1:

Besides that it is said, that if he declares (the following): "if I die from this (the present) sickness, this thing is conveyed by me to you", if he recovers from this sickness — even if he dies from the same sickness — the testamentary disposition (regarding the transfer) shall be overruled ("reversed").

110, 1—2:

It is also said, that a daughter born into the family of a head of household (= a daughter born to the *epikleros*-daughter or to the *stūr* of the late head of household — *A. P.*) shall not become his (heir, successor?), since she is not fit for the position of head of household.

110, 2—3:

Apāk (3) anī guft (kū) duxt pat ātaxš sardārīh nē šāyēt ut duxtdāt ōh gumārišn.

110, 4:

Ut anī guft kū ātaxš veh kartan ī āturgāh rāδ vidāštan pātixšāy.

110, 5—11:

Apāk anī guft kū apar GT'k ī Farraxvyān ī Zartuštān ⟨būt⟩ (ī) šahr dātaβarān (6) dātaβar būt dō-vartān ăvašt ēstēt ōγōn nipišt kū-m ō xvēš kartan ī (7) kār ut kirpak ī hač has nišāst ī ān ātaxš rāδ ān ātaxš pat Varahrānīh ō (8) dātgāh nišāst hač ān čiγōn-⟨am⟩ tā kartan (ī) katak^{+} ut mān ī ān ātaxš andar dāšt (9) dāštan gyākē ān dip ōstaβartar sahist ōγōn ⟨i⟩ (kū) ka ān katak ut mān kart (10) bavēt ō ān katak ut mān nayīhēt andar ān xānak ut mān darīhēt andar ān dip (11) čiγōn apāyēt dārom.

110, 11—13:

Ut anī guft kū ka gōβēt kū xvāstak ī Ātur(12)farnbaγ arž 100 aržēt ut frēh nē aržistan rāδ nipēsēt ut ăvartēt tō xvēš (13) bē ka nāmak pat nipēk ī Āturfarnbaγ enyā nē šāyēt.

110, 13—15:

Apāk anī pat apāč (14) dāt ī magupatān ō dātaβar nipēsēnd kū čē aδvēnak ēn čiš hāt ō (15) man hēβ nipēsēt.

110, 15—17:

Ut anī guft kū pus ī patigriftak ī apurnāy sardārīh pat (16) pit ī pātixšāyīhā ut ka andar apurnāyīh frāč ravēt xvāstak ī-š pit ī (17) pātixšāyīhā dāt apāč ō pit ī pātixšāyīhā rasēt.

110, 2—3:

Together with that it is said, (that) a daughter may not become the trustee of a Fire-(temple/altar), but the successor born by an *epikleros*-daughter shall be appointed (trustee).

110, 4:

It is also said that a Fire may be shifted (to another place) for the improvement of the fire-bed.

110, 5—11:

Besides the other it is said, that the following is written in the testament of Farraxvyān ī Zartuštān who was the chief judge ("the judge of judges") of the *šahr* (= empire) — (it) was twice sealed with a seal: "In fulfilment of religious duty and piety, (and) for the sake of this formerly instituted Fire, I have placed this Fire in a special place in (the temple of) the Varahrān-Fire, so that it should be kept (there) until the building ('house and dwelling') in which this Fire was kept is ready ('made')". And in one place this document expresses the following in the most specific (or "most positive") manner: "I have properly indicated ('I duly have') in this document that when that building shall be ready, the Fire shall be transported into that building and shall be kept in that building".

110, 11—13:

It is also said, that if he declares the following (in a written disposition): "(Let) the thing, about which Āturfarnbaγ writes and seals that it is worth 100 (*drahm*s) and is worth no more, belong to you", then (it) is not valid ("permissible"), unless Āturfarnbaγ's document is affixed to the letter containing (the given disposition).

110, 13—15:

It is also said, (that) in connexion with the *magupats*' return (to a judicial institution of the affairs which were forwarded for their examination — *A. P.*), (the interested parties) write to the judges ('judge'): "(please)! write to me how this affair (stands/was resolved)".

110, 15—17:

It is also said, that the guardian of a minor adopted son is his own (= natural) father, (and not the adoptive one). And if the minor dies without coming of age, the thing conveyed to him by his own father shall return to his own father.

[Anklesaria Ms.]

[XLVII]

A1, 1*:

A1, 1—2:

... (1) hend kū-t f[raška]rtīk pat ahravdāt dā[t] bav[ēt ...] duxt ka-š šōy (2) kart tan pat zanīh yut⁺ (Ms.: xvat) hač vindišn bē [... ... ...] pit xvēš.

A1, 2—6:

Ka mart 1 (3) apāk zan 2 ī pātixšāyīhā ī xvēš patmān kart kū-m tō ut tō hamvindišn kart hēt (4) zan yut yut apāk šōy hamvindišn ut zanān ēvak hač dit yut vindišnōmand (5) ut ān hamvindišnīh zan vartēnītan nē ut šōy pātixšāy ut ka vartēnēt vindišn dātastān ōγōn (6) čiγōn p[... ...] būt.

A1, 6—12:

Ka zan (ut/apāk) šōy ī pātixšāyīhā ī xvēš yut⁺-vindišn (7) anī mart-ē(v) [... ... ...] kē ān vindišn xvēš ān zan pat vindišn pātixšāy kunēt (8) aδak ān [zan ān vindišn ō] šōy nē b[arišn] ut Dāt-Farraxv ī Farraxv-Zurvān (9) guft kū hakar-iš tan pat [zanīh bē d]āt yut hač vindišn bē dāt ka-š pas (10) apāč avi-š rasēt andar ō šōy nē barišn bē hakar ka-š tan pat zanīh bē dāt (11) vindišn ō anī kas dāt ēstāt u-š andar zanīh ⟨i⟩ apāč avi-š rasēt (vindišn) andar ō (12) šoy barišn.

A1, 12—13:

Ka ma[rt 2 hamvindi]šn bavēnd hamē(v) ka ēvak kāmēt yut-vindišn (13) bavēnd.

---

* The beginning of the chapter has not survived. The heading is reconstructed from the content of the chapter.

[*Anklesaria Ms.*]

[XLVII]

A1, 1:

(Chapter concerning revenue) *.

A1, 1—2:

..: "is conveyed to you forever for pious purposes", [...] if the daughter marries [she is given] into a (temporary or *sine manu* type *A. P.*) marriage without (her own personal) income, [and (the daughter's) income] shall belong to (her) father.

A1, 2—6:

If a man makes (the following) agreement with his two wives from *pātixšāyīh*-marriages: "I have made you and you co-possessors of (my) income", then each of (these) women separately is co-possessor of the income with (her) husband, and each of the wives is endowed with an income separately from the other, and a wife is not (entitled) to alter ("overturn") this joint possession of the income, but the husband is (so entitled). And if (the husband) revokes/alters this agreement, the question of the income is resolved in the same way as in the case with [...].

A1, 6—12:

If a wife (and) her husband from a *pātixšāyīh*-marriage have a divided income, (and if) another man [... ... ...], to whom the income belongs, empowers the woman as regards (this) income; then this [woman] must not [bring this income] to (her) husband. And Dāt-Farraxv ī Farraxv-Zurvān has said, that if, having been given [in marriage (= term-marriage — *A. P.*)], she was given (by her husband) without an income; then when she subsequently returns to him, she is not obliged to bring to her husband the income (acquired during the term-marriage). But if an income was (also) conveyed to the other person when he (= the husband) gave her in (a term) marriage, and she returns to her *pātixšāy*-husband, then she must bring (the income) to (her) husband.

A1, 12—13:

If two [men] are [co-possessors of an income], then they shall become separate possessors of the income as soon as one of them so desires.

A1, 13—**2**, 1:

Ka Farraxv vindišn [ō Mih]rēn dahēt vitart Mihrēn ka Mihrēn zan ut frazand (14) ut xvāstak-ē(v) nēst xvāstak 60⁺ (?) ō Mihrēn (Ms.: Farraxv) dahēnd hač ān čiγōn ka zan ut frazand ut xvāstak (15) nēst ayāp pat vindišn xvāstakdār būt nē šāyēt pēš hač ān ē ka xvāstak (16) rasēt vindišn pat hastakīh apāč ō Farraxv rasēt. Ka-č Mihrēn xvāstak ut čiš (17) anī ō kas tōžišn ut dahišn būt hē aδak-ič pat apām vindišn bē apispārtan (1) nē ⟨pat šōy sahēt⟩ (pātixšāy).

A2, 1—2:

Ka bandak ī pat 2 mart xvēš ēvak pat vindišn pātixšāy (2) kunēt vindišn ī-š pat-iš pā[tixšāy kart] nēm apāč ō xvatāy ī ditikar barišn.

A2, 3:

Ka gōβēt kū xvāstak ī man handōžom tō xvēš aparmānd nē dāt bavēt.

A2, 4—5:

Ka gōβēt kū-m handōžišn vindišn ō tō dāt apāk ān ī guft kū ka gōβēt kū (5) bar ī ēn muγ tō xvēš nikerītan.

A2, 5—6:

Ka gōβēt kū-m handōžišn (ō) tō dāt ān ī tā ān (6) rōč handōxt nē dāt bavēt.

A2, 6—7:

Vindišn kār ī stōrān andar nē ut ān ī vindišn [ī an]šahrīk (7) ahravdāt čiγōn bavēt harv mizd ut bar ut sūt ut vahāk xrīt-ič andar [ahravdāt].

A2, 7—11:

Ka gōβēt (8) kū-m tā 10 sāl tan pat zanīh [ō Mih]rēn dāt [andar 10 sāl ka zan mīrēt] pašadātakān/pasadātakān ut (9) vāspuhrakān pat Mihrēn bē mānēt. Ka nē [apāč ō bun] āβarēt. Ut vindišn ī (10) andar 10 sāl Mihrēn xvēš. Būt kē guft kū ān ī pat zanīh andar šavēt pašadātakān/pasadātakān (11) ut vāspuhrakān nē andar vindišn.

A1, 13—**2**, 1:

If Farraxv conveys an income to [Mih]rēn, then in the case where after Mihrēn's death, Mihrēn leaves ("has") no wife of children or estate, (but) a thing (valued at) 60^{+} (*drahm*'s/*satērs*?) is relinquished [67] to Mihrēn [68] — inasmuch as (Mihrēn) has no wife nor children, or (if there is someone but) incapable of being the heir of (his) income — then until the time when the thing well be received [69], the income (conveyed to Mihrēn by Farraxv — *A. P.*) shall be acquired by Farraxv (lit.: "shall return to the acquisition of Farraxv"). And even if Mihrēn were obliged to pay or convey money or any thing to someone, it is not right to transfer (this) income to cover (Mihrēn's) debt.

A2, 1—2:

If a slave belonging to two persons is endowed by one of them with an income ("is empowered as regards an income"), then the slave must give ("bear") to his second master one half of the income with which he (= the slave) is endowed.

A2, 3:

If he declares (the following): "the possessions which I shall accumulate belongs to you", the inherited possessions are not included in the transfer ("are not transferred").

A2, 4—5:

If he declares: "I have conveyed to you the income from (the possessions which I shall accumulate", then (this case) should be examined together with the one given (above; specifically) where he declares: "the fruit of this date-palm belong to you". (*cf. supra* **103**, 12—13).

A2, 5—6:

If he declares: "I have conveyed to you the possessions which (I) shall accumulate", the possessions accumulated up to that day are not conveyed (according to the given formula of the declaration of transfer).

A2, 6—7:

There is no piety (?) in the income (derived) from cattle; but in the income (provided by) a slave — if it (= the income) is conveyed for pious purposes — (then) piety (?) (is included) in (the transfer of) any (form of this income): in the salary (received from the renting out of a slave and handed over for pious purposes — *A. P.*), in income and profit, or likewise, in the value (= "the sale price") (obtained from the sale of the slave and handed over for pious purposes — *A. P.*).

A2, 7—11:

If she declares (the following): "I have handed myself over for ten years to [Mih]rēn as a wife", then [if (this) woman dies during the ten year term], (her) dowry and *paraphernalia* shall remain with Mihrēn. But if she does not (die), [she] will bring (them) back [to the house of her husband/father]. And the income provided (by the wife's possessions) shall belong to Mihrēn during the ten years. Certain (authorities) have (however) said, that the *paraphernalia* and the dowry of the one who entered into (a temporary) marriage are not included in the income.

A2, 11—14:

Ka gōβēt kū-m vindišn ī ēn anšahrīk tā 3 sāl ō (12) tō dāt ān ī andar 3 sāl pat vindišn andar dahēt tā [3 sāl] dāt bavēt ka gōβēt (13) kū-m vindišn ī ēn anšahrīk⟨īh⟩ ī tā 3 sāl ō tō [dā]t vindišn ī andar 3 sāl tā (14) fraškart dāt bavēt.

A2, 14—15:

Ut ka zan andar zanīh kār vindišn (ī) xvēš (Ms.: BNPŠH = xvat) xvat (Ms.: NPŠH = xvēš) (15) bē ō šōy dahēt ut pas (šōy) zan hač zanīh hilēt kār vindišn bē nē barišn.

A2, 16—17:

Ka mart vindišn ī anšahrīk bē dahēt ut pas anšahrīk āzāt kunēt vindišn ī (17) anšahrīk apāč nē āβarišn.

A2, 17—**3**, 1:

Ka mart vindišn ī zan bē dahēt ut pas zan (1) hač zanīh hilēt vindišn ī zan apāč āβarišn.

A3, 1—6:

Ka mart 2 ākanēn (2) hamvindišn hend ut ō avēšān mart ō mart 1 xvāstak dahēnd ut gōβēt kū-m andar nē (3) apāyēt ⟨ut⟩ būt kē (guft) kū bahr-ič ī ōy ī dit bē nē rasēt. Ut gyākē ōγōn nipišt kū (4) bahr ī ōy ī dit bē rasēt u-m ōγōn sahēt kū harv 2 patigīrišn ōh paytākēnišn. (5) Ut ka ēvak andar nē apāyist gōβēt ōy ī dit patigīrišn ōh paytākēnišn u-š (6) nēm 1 bē rasēt.

A3, 6—13:

Pat čāstak guft ēstēt (kū) anšahrīk ī nēm Farraxv ut apārīk Mihrēn (7) xvēš ka[-š Fa]rraxv pat vindišn pātixšāy kunēt u-š kas xvāstak dāt+ rāδ+ (8) kart ēst[ēt ut nāmak] andar ō Farraxv (ut) Mihrēn barēt nēm hač Farraxv apāč ō anšahrīk (9) rasēt ayāp nāmak ⟨i⟩ pat [anšahr]īk bē ēstēt ut andar ō Farraxv nē barēt ut hakar pat (10) anšahrīk bē ēstēt ut andar ō Farraxv nē barēt nēm anšahrīk nēm Mihrēn xvēš (11) ut hakar nāmak andar ō Farraxv barēt apāč ō anšahrīk rasēt ut pas vindišn+ ī nōk hač (12) ān-ič nāmak bē ō Mihrēn rasēt. Ut būt kē guft kū ka-š pat vindišn pātixšāy (13) kunēt xvāstak pat anšahrīk bē ēstēt ut andar ō xvatāy nē barišn.

A2, 11—14:

If he declares (thus): "I have conveyed to you for three years the revenue (brought) by this slave, (or "the income of this slave")", then what is conveyed by him during three years as the income (from/of the slave) is conveyed with a term of three years. But if he declares (thus): "I have conveyed to you a three-year income from this slave (or 'income of this slave')", then the three-year income is conveyed forever.

A2, 14—15:

If a married woman herself transfers to her husband the income belonging to her, and (the husband) subsequently divorces this woman, then she does not take the income away (with her).

A2, 16—17:

If a man conveys the income of a slave (to another person), and subsequently manumits this slave, then the slave's income is not subject to return.

A2, 17—**3**, 1:

If a man conveys his wife's income (to another person) and subsequently dissolves this marriage with his wife, then the wife's income is subject to return.

A3, 1—6:

If two men are co-possessors of an income and a thing is conveyed to one of them but he declares: "I do not need (it)", certain (authorities) have said that a share will not go to the other one, as well (in such a case). But it seems to me that both of them must make a declaration regarding the acceptance (of the thing). And if one declares that (he) does not need (it), then the other one must declare his acceptance (of the thing) and he will (then) receive one half (of it).

A3, 6—13:

It is said in the "Commentary" to the *Avesta* that if Farraxv endows a slave of which one half belongs to Farraxv and the other (half) to Mihrēn with the right to an income ("gives him a title as regards income"), and (if) there is a disposition regarding the transfer of a thing to him (= the slave) by a certain person and [the title-document] is addressed to (both) Farraxv and Mihrēn; then one-half (of Farraxv's share) shall pass from Farraxv to the slave. Or there is (another case where) the entitling document ("letter") is drawn up for the slave and does not reach Farraxv. If it has been drawn up for the slave and does not reach Farraxv, then one-half shall belong to the slave and one-half to Mihrēn. And if the document is addressed to Farraxv, then (the income) shall go to the slave, and subsequently the new income shall go to Mihrēn on the basis of the same document. Whereas some have said, that if he (= the master) endows him (= the slave) with the right to an income, then the thing shall belong to the slave and (the right of possession) shall not extend to the master.

A3, 13—**4**, 4:

Ut apāk-ič ān ī-š (14) ētōn guft pas-ič guft kū ka zan pat vindišn pātixšāy kunēt u-š (15) pas atarsakāy gōβēt ētōn xvaptar dārom ka xvāstak apāč ō šōy (16) rasēt ut Vahrām guft kū man-ič hamgōnak dānom čē ka-š atarsakāy apar (17) stanēt harv nīrmat ī-š hač šōy apāč ō šōy rasēt ut nūn atarsakāy (rāδ)? (1) guft (ēstēt) kū⁺ (Ms.: MNW = kē) nē pat vindišn nē patixšāy ut ka-š pat vindišn pātixšāyīhā nēst aδak xvāstak ī (2) varγ (?ڒلا ı) nūn pat zan ēstēt⁺ Pusānveh-ič ī Āzatmartān ētōn guft kū ka šōy (3) zan pat vindišn pātixšāy kart u-š pas atarsakāyīhā guft ān ī⁺-šān vindišn apāč (4) ō šōy apispārtan.

A4, 4—5:

Rāt-Ōhrmizd guft kū mart 2 ākanēn xvēš ut ēvak xvāst[ak] (5) vindēt ut ēvak zan xvāstak ākanēn ut zan ōy ī veh xvēš.

A4, 5—10:

Gyākē nipišt (6) kū ka mart-ē(v) gōβēt kū-m ēn xvāstak ō zan ī Mihrēn dāt ut Mihrēn gōβēt (7) kū pat ān ī ōy ⟨i⟩ mart dāt kart xunsand hom (ayāp) ka Mihrēn [andar apāy]ēt gōβēt (8) ō Mihrēn rasēt. Ut ka gōβēt kū-m pat xvēšīh ō [zan ī] Mihrēn dāt (9) ut Mihrēn gōβēt kū pat ān ī ōy mart pat xvēšīh bē dāt xunsand hom pat zam (10) bē ēstēt ut ō šōy nē rasēt.

A4, 10—11:

Frazand ka-š gātār ī mātar parvartār (11) u-š vindišn nē mātar čē parvartār xvēš ⟨ut pit parvartār nām⟩.

XLVIII

A4, 12:

Dar ī atarsakāyīh*.

A4, 13—14:

Gyākē nipišt patvand⁺ (? Ms.: ptw/nd) pēšēnīkān ōγōn nipišt kū atarsakāy ān ō kār šut ī (14) zan ī pātixšāyīhā rāδ gōβēnd enyā ān ī čakarīhā rāδ gōβēnd ō kār nē šavēt.

A4, 15—**5**, 2:

⟨Pursišn⟩ Dāt-Farraxv ī Āturzandān pat pursišn ī Dāt-Farraxv ōγōn nipišt kū (16) atarsakāyīh ī frazandān ōγōn čiγōn ān ī zan ayāp yuttar ān ī čakarīhā ōγōn čiγōn (17) ān ī pātixšāyīhā ayāp yuttar ut ka-š xvāstak andar purnāyīh dahēt ōγōn bavēt (1) čiγōn ka pat apurnāyīh ayāp yuttar ut atarsakāyīh čē ān ī zan ut čē ān ī frazandān (2) pus ut duxt ēvkānak ⟨ayāp yuttar⟩ ān ī anšahrīkān čiγōn bavēt.

---

* The (*abǰad*) ordinal-number of this chapter is 48.

A3, 13—**4**, 4:

And together with what he had said in this manner, he (= the commentator — *A. P.*) said a little farther: "if a husband endows (his) wife with the right to have her own income, and subsequently he declares her guilty of misconduct, then I consider the best (decision to be the one according to which) the thing is returned to the husband". And Vahrām has said: "I too think the same, because if she receives (a judicial document regarding her) misconduct, then any material benefit ('advantage') that she has (received) from her husband shall return to the husband". Now, however, it is said concerning a disobedient wife: that she cannot be left without income. And if she is not endowed with the right to an income, then the possessions that ..., now go to the wife. But Pusānveh ī Āzātmartān has spoken thus: "if a man endowed ('entitled') the wife with (to) an income, and subsequently declared her guilty of misconduct, then her income (should) be conveyed back to the husband".

A4, 4—5:

Rāt-Ōhrmizd has said: "two men hold a common estate, and one of them acquires/receives a thing and the other — a wife, the thing shall belong to them jointly and the woman to the (more) pious and dutiful of them".

A4, 5—10:

It is written in one place, that if a man declares: "I convey this thing to Mihrēn's wife", and Mihrēn declares: "I approve of what this man has conveyed", (or) if Mihrēn declares: "needed"; then (the thing) goes to Mihrēn. But if he declares (thus): "I conveyed into the personal possession of Mihrēn's [wife]", and Mihrēn declares: "I approve of what this man has conveyed into personal possession", then the thing shall belong to the wife and shall not go to the husband.

A4, 10—11:

If a child is reared by the husband (= from a marriage *sine manu mariti*; lit.: "the cohabiter") of (his) mother, then the income of the child shall not go to the mother, since (by right) it belongs to the rearer (of the child) ⟨and to the father, named rearer⟩.

XLVIII

A4, 12:

Chapter concerning misconduct (or "disobedience") *.

A4, 13—14:

It is written in one place, (that) ... (?) of the earlier (commentators) wrote (thus): "a wife who goes to the others [70] is called disobedient, however a *čakar*-wife is said to be of bad conduct if she does not go to the others" [71].

A4, 15—**5**, 2:

Dāt-Farraxv ī Āturzandān answered ("wrote") thus to the question of Dāt-Farraxv: "the disobedience/misconduct of children is (evaluated/examined) in the same way as the misconduct of a wife, and vice-versa; (the disobedience) of a *čakar*-wife like (that of) a *pātixšāy*-wife, and vice-versa. And when he conveys a thing to one who is of age, then this is the same as when he (conveys it) to a minor, and vice-versa. And the disobedience of both wife and children — a son or daughter equally — (is evaluated in the legal sense) like (the disobedience) of slaves".

A5, 2—6:

Dāt-Farraxv ōγōn guft (3) ēstāt kū ka zan guft ⟨ut⟩ andar frazandān rāstīh ī ān ī guft āmār. Ān ī čakarīhā (4) mart ī pat nāmčišt rāδ framān būt nē hamāk gēhān rāδ ut purnāyīh ut apurnāyīh harv (5) 2 ēvak (ut) pusarān pat rāh (ī) atarsakāyīh ī andar pitarān ān čē pahlom axvān xvēš nē (6) būt rāδ guft ēstēt.

A5, 6—8:

Atarsakāyīh ī zanān ēn bavēt kār ī frārōn ī-š (7) šōy framāyēt nē kartan ut ān ī apārōn ī nē kartan gōβēt ut harv 2 pat 3 bār (8) bavēt.

A5, 8—15:

An ī [pus] nē pusīh druvist ăšnūt ān ka+ (Ms.: MNW-kē) gōβēt kū nē pus ī tō hom (9) ut pusīh ī tō nē kunom [dātastān] ōγōn čiγōn zan patkār pat-iš ut pus ut duxt rāst (10) ut anšahrīk ōγōn čiγōn zan bē ō vistar nē šut ān ī zan ī pātixšāyīhā raδ (11) čiγōn pat Mustaβar-nāmak nipišt ēstēt ut ān ī zan ī čakarīhā (ī) mart-ē(v) Burzōy nām (12) būt rāδ ōh parmāt nipišt kū hač ān čiγōn šāyēt dānist kū Burzōy ān vičīr (13) nē sut ut nēvakīh ī dūtak (rāδ) kē ziyānak pat-iš stūr bē tarsakāyīhātar būt ī (14) ziyānak andar zanīh (ī) mērak andar zan (Ms.: mērak) ē(t) rāδ ăvašt ān mān parmāt ut anī kas pat (15) ān vičīr dastaβarīh ān xvāstak hač Burzōy apāč nē kart.

A5, 15—**6**,1:

Ut zan ī pātixšayīhā (16) ka-š pat hambāγīh patigīrēnd ayāp-iš šōy xvāstak pat xvēšīh avi-š dāt (17) ēstēt ka-š atarsakāy gōβēt xvāstak ī-š pat-iš ēstēt apāč ō šōy (1) rasēt ut zan ēn dātastān nē bavēt ka+ paytāk kunēt kū tarsakāy būt hom.

A6, 2—5:

Ut ka-š zan ut frazand-ič ī hač ān zan zāt pat hambāγīh patigrift ēstēt ut atarsa(3)kāyīh ī zan gōβēt xvāstak pat ziyānak ēstēt apāč nē rasēt ut ān ī frazandān (4) tā paytāk bavēt kū ziyānak atarsakāy būt apāč nē rasēt. Ut ān-ič ī ōy frazand (5) apāč rasēt ī pas hač atarsakāyīh ī ziyānak zāt.

A5, 2—6:

Dāt-Farraxv has spoken thus: it is said (that) if a wife has said something, then the children must pay attention to the justice of what she has said; and that (a woman) in a *čakar*-marriage must obey a particular man and not the whole world; and that one of age and a minor hold an equal position (vis-à-vis the head of household — *A. P.*); and that the sons are deprived of a better world (= paradise) for disobedience to (their) fathers.

A5, 6—8:

The disobedience / misconduct of a wife consists in the following: not to fulfil a just task ordered by her husband, but to perform an injust (one) of which he has said that (it) should not be done. And any (of these infringements of the husband's orders) must be committed three times (for the wife's conduct to be legally considered as an offence of misconduct / disobedience — *A. P.*).

A5, 8—15:

The decision (concerning) a son who does not acknowledge his filiation and declares: "I am not your son and I shall not assume filial obligations for you" is the same as in the case of a similar suit by a wife; moreover, it makes no difference whether the matter concerns a son or a daughter. (And the decision concerning) a slave (who deviates from the performance of his master's orders — *A. P.*) is the same as in the case of a wife who scorns her husband's bed. In the case of a *pātixšāy*-wife (the matter is settled as) it is written in the *Mustaβar-nāmak* ("*The Book of Appeals*"). But as regards (the decision) concerning a former *čakar*-wife, of a man named Burzōy this was specifically written: "(judging) from what (?) may be seen ('known'), Burzōy (sealed the document containing) this decision as regards the (his) wife (the ms. has 'husband') not because of the advantage and profit of the family of which (this) woman (was) the *stūr*, but (so that) (this) woman should be more obedient / well-behaved in the (*stūr*) marriage with (her) husband: (it was) for this reason, that he sealed the document (and) specified (or 'ordered') this measure. And — owning to the title conferred by this document — no one ('other persons') seized (or 'took away') this possession from Burzōy".

A5, 15—**6**, 1:

If a *pātišxāy*-wife is taken into co-partnership, or if (her) husband conveyed her a thing as a personal possession, and if he (subsequently) declares her disobedient: then the property belonging to her shall go (= return) to her husband. But this right does not extend to the wife if she declares publicly: "I was of good-conduct / obedient".

A6, 2—5:

If he took (his) wife and the children born by her into co-partnership, and (after that) he declares the wife disobedient, then the possessions belonging to the wife as well as the possessions of the children shall not go to him until it is publicly / officially declared stated that the wife (truly) was disobedient. And the property of that particular child who was born to the wife after her misconduct (is the one that) shall pass to him (= the woman's husband).

A6, 5—14:

Ka Farraxv apar⁺ (Ms.: MH = čē) Zanbūt (6) ī-š (zan ī) pātixšāyīhā atarsakāyīh stānēt ut ēn nē nipēsēt kū-š xvāstak ī man avi-š (7) mā hēβ ōh rasēt aδak-iš xvāstak bahr ī katak-bānūkīh avi-š ōh rasēt ka nipēsēt (8) kū-š xvāstak ī man avi-š mā hēβ rasēt ka ev⁺ kas ān gyāk [aδak-iš] nē rasēt (9) ut ka nē aδak-ič-iš pat rāh ī 2-kasīh avi-š ōh rasēt [ut ka] gōβēt kū-š xvāstāk ī (10) man pat čiš-ič aδvēnak mā hēβ rasēt aδak-iš pat-ič [rāh] ī 2-kasīh avi-š nē rasēt. (11) Ut xvāstak pat dūtak ī Farraxv ēstēt u-š pat-iš patkārtan nē tuvān Ut hakar pas hač ān (12) andar dūtak frazand zāyēt bē ō ān frazand rasēt. Būt ke patkārišn kart kū bē (13) ō xvēšīh ī xvēšāvandān rasēt ut apāč ō ān frazand nē rasēt u-m ān nē xvap (14) sahist.

A6, 14—7, 2:

Gyākē nipišt kū ka andar zan ī pātixšāyīhā vičīr ăvartēt kū-t pat (15) hambāγ dārom ān zan xvāstak ī ān mart xvēš būt ut pat ān dastaβarīh ō ān zan (16) rasīt bē dāt pātixšāy ut ka zan xvāstak bē dahēt šōy atarsakāyīh ī (17) zan gōβēt ān xvāstak apāč ō šōy rasēt. Ut gyākē nipišt kū zan (1) xvāstak ī [šōy] avi-š dahēt ka-č-iš ō pat čē kāmēt kartan pātixšāy kunēt aδak-ič (2) yut hač dastaβarīh ī šōy bē dāt nē pātixšāy.

A7, 2—7:

Ka mart pat atarsakāyīh (3) raft ī zan ī xvēš dip stānēt frazand ī pēš⁺ (Ms.: pas) hač ān zan zāyēt (4) xvāstak ī oy mart xvēš bavēt ut ān ī ka frazand ī pas hač atarsakāyīh guftan zāyēt (5) xvāstak xvēš nē bavēt. Pat ān zamān bavēt ka atarsakāyīh (nē) ēvar ut ka-č tarsa(6)kāyīh ēvar aδak-ič-iš xvāstak ān xvēš nē bavēt ī-š pat pašt ī apāk māt kart (7) dastaβarīh (ī) xvēš šāyēt būt enyā-š⁺ aparmānd (ī) pitar bē nē bavēt.

A7, 8—11:

Vāyayār guft kū xvāstak ī šōy pat bar-xvart ō zan dahēt zan (9) ētōn kū šōy avi-š dahēt harv čiγōn-iš kāmēt kart pātixšāy u-š xvarišn ut (10) vastrak hač dūtak ut apāk ān ī hačapar xvāstak ī šōy ō zan dahēt rāδ (11) nipišt nikerītan.

A7, 11—13:

U-š ēn-ič guft kū Pusānveh guft kū ka šōy zan (12) pat vindišn pātixšāy kart u-š pas atarsakāyīh apar stānēt ā-š ān vindišn apāč ō (13) šōy apispārtan.

A6, 5—14:

If Farraxv obtains (a document) regarding the misbehavior of his *pātixšāy*-wife Zanbūt, and does not write: "let my estate not go to her!", then the share of the mistress of the house shall go to her from his estate (= from the bulk of the inheritance left by him — *A. P.*). But if he writes: "let my estate not go to her!". Then if there is (even) one person in that family [she] shall not receive it; but if (he) does not (write so) then, in that case too, she will receive her share (only) in co-partnersip with another person ("by way of association of two persons"). [But if] he declares: "let my estate in no way go to her!", then she will not receive it even in co-partnership with another person. The estate shall remain in (= shall belong to) Farraxv's family and she is not entitled to claim it through the court. And if a child is subsequently born into the family, it shall go to that child. Some have disputed (this position — *A. P.*), asserting that it shall belong to the agnates and shall not go to the child, but this does not seem right to me.

A6, 14—7, 2:

It is written in one place that if he makes ("seals") a contract concerning his *pātixšāy*-wife: "I take you as a co-partner", then this woman is entitled to convey ("alienate") to another person a thing which belonged to that man and which came to her in accordance with the given title. And if the wife conveys the thing, but the husband makes a declaration regarding the disobedience of the wife, then that thing shall return to the husband. And in one place it is written that even if he (= the husband) endows her with the right to deal with a thing as she pleases, even then, the wife is not entitled to alienate the thing conveyed to her (by her husband) without her husband's permission (= the title to do this).

A7, 2—7:

If a man receives a document regarding (the fact) that his wife is guilty of the offence of misconduct/disobedience, then the child born previously (the ms. has "subsequently") to that wife shall inherit the estate of that man. But the child born after (his father's) declaration of (his mother's) misconduct shall not inherit (his father's) estate. He becomes (heir to the estate) only when (his mother's) misconduct is (not) proven. And even if her good behaviour is positively proven, even then, he does not inherit that property which was conveyed by the father in accordance with the contract made with the mother. He does not become (his) father's heir otherwise than through his (= father's — *A. P.*) personal disposition.

A7, 8—11:

Vāyayār has said that a wife may dispose at her discretion of the thing that (her) husband conveyed to the wife with (the right) of usufruct — within the framework of the rights stipulated by the husband at (the time of) the transfer — but her subsistance and clothing (come) from the family (= from the family's means — *A. P.*). (This) should be examined together with what has been written above concerning the transfer of a thing by the husband to the wife.

A7, 11—13:

And he (= Vāyayār) has also said that Pusānveh said, that if a husband endowed his wife with the right to acquire an income ("he empowered her as regards income"), and he subsequently receives (a document, a judicial confirmation — *A. P.*) regarding (his wife's) misconduct, then this income must be returned to the husband.

A7, 13—17:

U-š ēn-ič guft kū ka mart apāk ān ī-š pātixšāyīhā zan (14) patmān kart kū ēn xvāstak ōy kē tō xvēš būt rāδ gōβēh xvēš hēβ bavēt (15) pas hač ān atarsakāyīh ī ān zan guft ka ān zan pas hač ān atarsakāyīh (16) guft ān xvāstak kas xvēš būt rāδ guft ā-šān hamgōnak (17) pat⁺ (Ms.: BR' = bē) ōy bē hilišn kē hač ān zan xvēš būt rāδ guft.

A7, 17—**8**, 2:

Gyākē nipišt kū (1) xvāstak ī šōy ō zan (ī) čakar dahēt⁺ ka atarsakāyīh ī ān zan gōβēt framān-ē(v) (2) būt rāδ apāč ō šōy apispārtan.

XLIX

A8, 3:

Dar ī xvāstak ī man xvēš*.

A8, 4—7:

Ka gōβēt kū xvāstak ī man xvēš ō tō dāt (Ms.: YHWWNt = būt) ān čē-š andar ān ē kart ēstēt⁺ (5) kū-m tā 10 sāl ō anī-č kas dāt pas-ič hač 10 sāl bar ī xvāstak ī-š pat (6) dāt dastaβarīh pat stūrīh xvāstak ī-š pat graβīh ut vaxš ī xvāstak ī-š pat (7) xvēšīh avi-š mat dāt bavēt.

A8, 7—12:

Ka gōβēt kū xvāstak ī tō gōβēh⁺ tō xvēš (8) tā gōβēt ka xvāstak ī nāmčišt rāδ gōβēt kū frazand ī tō bavēt xvēš hēβ (9) bavēt⁺ tā frazand bavēt bar pātīrān nē kunišn. Ut ka xvāstak 1 ī nāmčišt rāδ gōβēt (10) kū Mihrēn xvēš tā-ič Mihrēn patigīrišn⁺ (Ms.: pātīrān) paytākēnēt ut ka xvāstak 1 ī nāmčišt rāδ (11) gōβēt kū ōy kē tō xvēš būt gōβēh xvēš tā-ič gōβīšn gōβēt bar pātīrān (12) kunišn.

A8, 12—13:

Gyākē nipišt kū ka xvastak-ē(v) ⟨nē⟩ pat vahāk frōxšēnd⁺ ayāp bē dahēnd (13) u-š pas bē ō xvēšīh rasēt pat ān frōxt⁺/frōxšišn⁺ (ut) dāt bē šavēt.

---

* The (*abǰad*) ordinal number of this chapter is 49.

A7, 13—17:

And he (= Vāyayār) also said the following, that if a husband makes an agreement with his *pātixšāyīh*-wife: "let this thing belong to the person whom you designate as its owner", and (he) subsequently declares the wife disobedient; then if this wife has declared that this thing belongs to a certain person — even after his declaration of her misconduct — this thing should be left (by the judges) to the person whose ownership of the thing was declared by her.

A7, 17—**8**, 2:

It is written in one place that a thing which a husband conveyed to (his) *čakar*-wife must be returned to the husband should be declare her disobedient, because an offence of "*framān*" degree has occurred.

XLIX

A8, 3:

Chapter * concerning (declarations beginning with the words:) "a thing which belongs to me".

A8, 4—7:

If he declares: "I convey to you the possessions belonging to me", then (a thing) of which he disposed at that time in the following manner: "I have also conveyed it to another person for a term of ten years" is likewise (considered as transferred to the man to whom this transfer is addressed — *A. P.*), after the passage of ten years. (And the following) are transferred: the fruit (= income) from the thing conveyed, which (= the thing) — according to the title of transfer (given to the receiver) — will pass as a *stūr*-possession, and the thing pledged (held by a creditor) at the time of the declaration, and the benefit/increase from the property that had entered his personal possession.

A8, 7—12:

If he declares: "the thing which you name shall belong ('belongs') to you", the fruit (= the income from the thing conveyed — *A. P.*) should not be retained (= belongs to the conveyer — *A. P.*) until the other names (it), or — if he declares regarding a concrete thing: "let it belong to the child you will have" — until the child appears. But if he declares regarding a concrete thing: "(let it) belong to Mihrēn!)", then — until Mihrēn declares his acceptance of the thing, or if he declares regarding some specific thing: "(let) it belong to the (man) whom you declare (to be) its owner!", then — until the time when the other (one) makes a declaration — the fruit from (the thing conveyed) is subject to retainment (= is retained, is claimed from the conveyer — *A. P.*).

A8, 12—13:

It is written in one place, that if a thing is sold (to someone of the family — *A. P.*) or conveyed, and subsequently (this thing) passes (to this person) as a personal possession (= as an inheritance-portion — *A. P.*), then the sale or conveyance is thereby annulled ("goes away, leaves").

A8, 13—17:

Anī gyākē (14) nipišt kū Farraxv dastkart 1 ī-š nĕ xvēš rāδ kunēt kū-m pas hač 10 sāl (15) ō Mihrēn dāt ut ōy kē ān dastkart xvēš pas hač ān ōy dastkart rāδ (16) kunēt kū-m pas hač 10 sāl ō Farraxv dāt ān xvāstak pat dāt ī Farraxv (17) ō Mihrēn rasēt.

A8, 17—**9**, 5:

Ut ka gōβēt kū-t dahom u-š nē xvēš bē xrīnišn⁺ (1) ut bē dahišn. Ut ka gōβēt kū-t dahom u-š xvēš gyākē nipišt kū yut hač zan (2) tā žīvandakīh pātixšāy pātīrānēnītan ut ka zan gōβēt kū-š pat zanīh ō tō (3) dahom aδak-iš andar zamān⁺ (Ms.: dm'n) bē dahišn ut gyākē nipišt kū ka gōβēt kū ēn ō (4) tō dahom bē xvāhišn ut hakar bē dahēt tā hamāk pat hačašmānd graβ apispārišn (5) tā bē apispārēt.

A9, 5—7:

Vahrām hač Vahrāmšāt ut Rāt-Ōhrmizd bē ōγōn guft kū (6) ka dastkart ī nē xvēš rāδ kunēt kū ō tō dahom u-š pat vahāk xrīt ut (7) bē dāt nē tuvān arž ī ān dastkart bē dahišn.

A9, 7—9:

Pat 3 gōβišnīh ut 2 gōβišnīh (8) būt kē guft kū dāt pat sar bavēt ut būt kē guft kū ka and bē (9) uzīt čand šāyēt guftan kū-m nē dāt adāt bē bavēt.

A9, 9—**10**, 1:

Ut ka mart-ē(v) xvāstak (10) 3000⁺ (Ms.: 2000) hast nē pat (h)andarz ut ăvišt bē gōβēt kū-m 2000 ō Farraxv dāt ut 2000 ō (11) Mihrēn dāt ut 2000 ō Āturfarnbaγ dāt ān kē hēβ gōβēt kū dāt pat sar bē (12) bavēt ētōn gōβēt kū 3000⁺ (Ms.: 2000) 2000 ōy (ī) aptom 500 ōy 500 ōy xvēš čē (13) ka ahanūn dāt nē būt ēstāt u-š 2000 hač 3000 apāč stānēt (Ms.: stānēnd) u-š ō (14) ōy ī aptom dāt ān kē hēβ gōβēt ⟨kū⟩ ka and

A8, 13—17:

In another place it is written, that (if) Farraxv declares (the following) regarding a *dastkart* which does not belong to him: "I have conveyed (this *dastkart*) to Mihrēn after the passage of ten years", whereas the man to whom this *dastkart* belongs subsequently declares regarding the same *dastkart*: "after the passage of ten years it is conveyed to Farraxv", then this thing shall go to Mihrēn in accordance with Farraxv's transfer.

A8, 17—**9**, 5:

And if he declares (thus): "I convey to you", but (the thing) does not belong to him; then he must buy (it) and convey (it). But if he declares: "I convey to you", and (the subject of the fransfer) belongs to him; then it is written in one place, that he (= the conveyer) is entitled to retain (the thing in his possession — *A. P.*) to the end of his life — except for the case where a woman is involved (= where the subject of the transfer is a woman — *A. P.*). But if he declares concerning a woman (= his wife): "I convey (her) to you as a wife", then he must convey her at once [lit.: 'at (that) time']. And it is written in once place that if he declares: "I convey this to you", then a claim should (be made). And if he conveys the thing to another person, then until everything (= until he transfers it in full), he is obliged to give a security for what is retained until such time as he delivers (everything stipulated in the transfer).

A9, 5—7:

Vahrām — citing (the words, authority) of Vahrāmšāt and Rāt-Ōhrmizd — has spoken in this manner, that if he declares regarding a *dastkart* which does not belong to him: "I convey (it) to you", and he is unable (or "not entitled") to buy it for money and transfer it, then he must convey (an amount equal) to the value of the *dastkart*.

A9, 7—9:

As has been said by certain authorities, in the case of three or two declarations (concerning the transfer of the same thing — *A. P.*), the transfer takes place in accordance with the last (declaration of will; or "the transfer is joint" — *A. P.*). But others have said, that if the amount of time allowed for the declaration: "I have not conveyed" has elapsed (between the first and the subsequent declarations), then the thing is not transferred (according to the first declaration) (= the first declaration is annulled; *cf. infra* **A9**, 9—**10**, 1).

A9, 9—**10**, 1:

If a man having an estate worth 3000 (*drahms*) (the ms. has 2000) declares — neither in a will (nor in any other) sealed document: "I have conveyed 2000 (*drahms*) to Farraxv", and "I have conveyed 2000 (*drahms*) to Mihrēn", and "I have conveyed 2000 (*drahms*) to Āturfarnbaγ". If he said the following (at the same time): "the transfer takes place in accordance with the last (declaration of will? lit.: 'the end, the summit'; or 'the transfer is joint' — *A. P.*)"; then he has thereby declared that 2000 (*drahms*) out of the 3000 (the ms. has 2000) belong to the last named, 500 (*drahms*) belong to the first ("him") and 500 (to) the second ("him"); because — inasmuch as the transfer of the right (= the transfer in accordance with the first declaration of zamān uzīt čand nē ⟨hač⟩ dāt hēβ (15) bē šāyēt guft adāt bē bavēt ēt^{+} gōβēt kū ka-š ō ōy kē-š pas (16) nām kart dāt ān ī fratom dāt bē būt ēstāt u-š apāč stātan (Ms.: stānēnd) (17) nē tuvān būt. Ut ān ī ditīkar ahanūn dāt nē būt ēstāt u-š/hač-iš apāč stānēnd (1) u-š bē ō ōy ī sitīkar dāt 2000 ōy ī fratom ut 1000 ōy ī [sitīkar] xvēš.

A10, 2—8:

Bē ka xvāstak 1000 hast ut gōβēt kū-m 1000 ō Farraxv ut 1000 ō Mihrēn (3) ut 1000 ō Āturfarnbaγ dāt būt kē guft kū ōy ⟨i⟩ xvēš kē ō [ān mart] (4) nazdisttar ut būt kē guft kū-šān ākanēn xvēš ut Veh-Ōhrmizd ēn-ič guf[t] (5) kū man pat-ič hamčašmānīh ī Zurvāndāt hač Yuvān-Yam ī Vahištbahr apāč pursīt (6) u-š guft kū man ētōn čāšt (kū) ka gōβēt kū-m 1000 ō tō dāt ut 1000 ō (7) tō dāt ut 1000 ō tō dāt enyā ka dāt ēvāč ēvak gōβēt ā-šān (8) rāst xvēš.

A10, 8—13:

Ut pat (h)andarz pat-ič ǎvišt ka ēvak-ēvak dāt apar bē (9) gōβēt ā-š hamāk ō ēv (Ms.: 2) ī aptom dāt (h)andarz ēt^{+} rāδ čē pātixšāy vartēnītan ǎvišt (10) ēt^{+} rāδ čē tā bē ǎvišt hamāk apāč statan ut ō ān ī dit dāt pātixšāy. Ut čim ī (11) ǎvišt hač guft ī nē pat ǎvišt yuttar būt ēn kū ⟨i⟩ pat ǎvišt dit (12) bē ǎvišt kār nēst ut ān ī pat guft ka bē guft vas u-š ēvarīh hač 3 (13) vikāy ut guft ī magupatān magupat nē (Ms.: NWR' = ātaxš!).

will — *A. P.*) has not yet taken place and he receives back 2000 (*drahms*) out of 3000 — he has conveyed (them) to the last named. But had he made the declaration (concerning the transfer to the second person — *A. P.*) upon the expiration of the time limit within which it would be possible to declare "not transferred" [72] — then (the immediately preceding) transfer would (thereby) be annulled and he (is assumed to have — *A. P.*) declared this: the transfer to the first person had already taken place at the time of the transfer of the right ("the conveyance") to the person designated last, and it was impossible to obtain the return (of the sum conveyed to him); but since the transfer of the right ("the conveyance") to the second person has not yet taken place, (the amount conveyed to him through the declaration) is (= can be) taken back (= retained), and (it should be) conveyed to the third person. (Thus): 2000 (*drahms*) shall be conveyed to the first person, and 1000 (*drahms*) to the third. (*cf. supra* **A9**, 7—9, *et infra* **A10**, 2—8, 8—13).

A10, 2—8:

But if he has a thing (worth) 1000 (*drahms*) and he declares: "I have conveyed 1000 (*drahms*) to Farraxv and 1000 (*drahms*) to Mihrēn, and 1000 (*drahms*) to Āturfarnbaγ", (then) — as has been said by some (authorities) — (the thing) should belong to the one (of the persons named) who is the closest agnate [of that man (= the declarer)]. But others have said that (the thing) should belong to them together (= as common property). And Veh-Ōhrmizd said the same as well as the following: "in the presence of Zurvāndāt, I asked Yuvān-Yam, (son of) Vahištbahr (or else: 'having received a better portion of paradise' = an epithet used of the dead — *A. P.*)", and he said: "I maintain this, that if (this) declaration took place: 'I conveyed 1000 (*drahms*) to you, and I conveyed 1000 (*drahms*) to you (= the second person), and I conveyed 1000 (*drahms*) to you (= the third person)', then (here) — as in any other (formula) — if he utters the word 'conveyed' only once, the thing must belong to them equally".

A10, 8—13:

But if he makes a declaration in a will/or in a sealed (document) regarding a transfer to each one singly ("one by one"), then he has conveyed the entire thing to him alone (the ms. has 2) who was mentioned last. (The matters stands thus) in (the case of) a will — because it may be altered (= he is entitled to alter it), and in the case (of a transfer set down) in a sealed (document) — because until it has been sealed, he is entitled to take everything back and convey it to another (person). The reason that a declaration in a sealed (document) differs from an unsealed (= oral) declaration is the following: that a second sealing (or "second seal") is not required (for the authentication of a declaration made in) a sealed (document); whereas (in the case of) an oral declaration, whenever an oral declaration of will is made, its trustworthiness (must be confirmed) by three witnesses ⟨but (this) is not required for the declaration of the *magupatān magupat*⟩ [73].

A10, 13—**11**, 10:

Vahrām guft kū ka Mihrēn patmān (14) kunēt kū-m ēn xvāstak pas hač 10 sāl ō Zanbūt ī Āturfarnbaγ duxt dāt (15) andar 10 sāl Zanbūt ⟨i⟩ bē mīrēt ōy kē ēt⁺ guft kū dāt pašt xvaš⁺ (Ms.: NPŠH-xvēš) (16) guft bavēt kū xvāstak bē ō pit rasēt čē-š pašt ān zamān kart (17) ka Zanbūt ⟨i⟩ vindišn pat pit ēstāt ōy kē ēt guft kū pašt dāt xvaš⁺ (1) guft bavēt kū hakar Zanbūt andar 10 sāl bē mīrēt ēt rāδ ka xvāstak pat zan (2) andar šāyēt šut ut zan mīrēt xvāstak hač rāt bē nē āyēt. Ka Zanbūt (3) andar 10 sāl šōy kunēt ut andar ham 10 sāl bē mīrēt aδak-ič hamgōnak bavēt čē hakar (4) pašt dāt xvaš⁺ Zanbūt mīrēt xvāstak ō kas matan nē šāyēt ut hakar (5) dāt pašt xvaš⁺ ka-č pit mīrēt aδak-ič xvāstak bē ō dūtak ī pit (6) rasēt yuttar nēst kū ka gōβēt kū-m ēn xvāstak pas hač 10 sāl ō (7) pit dāt ut ka pit andar 10 sāl bē mīrēt aδak-ič xvāstak bē ō dūtak ī pit (8) rasēt u-š ēn-ič guft kū ēn dātastān kartak ōγōn apāk kū pašt dāt (9) xvaš⁺ ēn kū ka pit andar 10 sāl bē mīrēt aδak-ič xvāstak pat⁺ dūtak ī pit (10) rasēt apāk ān ī hačapar pat guft ī Siyāvaxš nipišt anbassānīk.

A11, 10—12:

(Hač) Pēšaksēr (11) gōβēnd kū ka gōβēt kū-m ēn xvāstak ō duxt ēv ī tō dāt ō ān ī mas dāt (12) bavēt.

A11, 12—17:

Vahrām guft kū ka Farraxv apāk Mihrēn patmān kunēt kū anšahrīk ī (13) man xvēš ēvak ī tō andar apāyēt (gōβēh) tō xvēš ut Mihrēn andar apāyēt pas hač 10 sāl gōβēt (14) andar 10 sāl hač anšahrīk kē-š andar apāyēt pat-iš gōβēt anšahrīk-ē(v) bē zāyēt (15) ān-ič ī pat ān aδvēnak zāyēt bē šavēt. U-š ēn-ič guft kū pat ēn vāčak vas (16) kas hamdātastān bē-š Yuvān-Yam hač-ič Vahrāmšāt bē pat-ič yutdātastān (17) būt.

A11, 17—**12**, 3:

(...)* tō ō Mihrēn frōxt ut Mihrēn pas hač 3 šapak andar apāyēt gōβēt (1) ēt kū Farraxv andar 3 šapak ī hač ān ka Mihrēn andar apāyēt gōβēt apāč ēstāt nē (2) pātixšāy čē-š 3 šapak ī xvēš šut ut ka-š 3 šapak ī xvēš šut 3 šapak ī (3) Mihrēn andar Farraxv ēv(?) kār nēst.

* The beginning of this article has been omitted by the copyist.

A10, 13—**11**, 10:

Vahrām has said that if Mihrēn makes (the following) contract: "upon the passage of ten years this thing is conveyed by me to Zanbūt, daughter of Āturfarnbaγ", and (if) Zanbūt dies in the course of these ten years; this is (the opinion) expressed by one (of the commentators): that (what) is said (= presumed) (by pronouncing the formula?): "a covenant is made ('given')" — "(it is) good" [74], is that the thing should go to the father, since the contract was made at a time when Zanbūt's income belonged (= went) to (her) father. But there was one who said, that what is stated (= presumed) by (the formula): "a covenant is made" — '(it is) good' is that if Zanbūt dies during the course of (these) ten years, then — inasmuch as the thing must go to the woman and the woman is dead — the thing does not go from the conveyer. And if Zanbūt marries in the course of these ten years and dies in the course of the same ten years, then (the decision is) the same, because if Zanbūt dies (after the formula): "a covenant is made" — "(it is) good" (has been pronounced), the thing must not go to anyone. And if the father also dies (after the formula): "a covenant is made" — "(it is) good" (has been pronounced), then in this case too, the thing goes to the family of the father. And this case is not different (from the one) in which, he (= Mihrēn) declares: "upon the passage of ten years, this thing is conveyed by me to the father (of Zanbūt — *A. P.*)", and the father dies in the course of these ten years, then also the thing shall go to the father's family.

He (= Vahrām — *A. P.*) has also said that this decision corresponds to/accompanies the established judicial rule (?) (in accordance with which the formula): "a covenant is made" — "(it is) good" (indicates) the following: if the father dies in the course of the ten years, then also, the thing shall go to the father's family — which contradicts what was said above from the words of Siyāvaxš.

A11, 10—12:

It is said (with a reference to the *Čaštak*) of Pēšaksēr, that if he declares: "I have conveyed this thing to one of your daughters", then (the thing) is conveyed to the eldest.

A11, 12—17:

Vahrām has said, that if Farraxv concludes (the following) agreement with Mihrēn: "from (among) the slaves that belong to me, one (male or female) of whom you say 'needed', shall belong to you", and Mihrēn declares "needed" after ten years, but in the course of these ten years the slave-woman about whom he declared ("declares") "needed" has born a slave; then the one born under these circumstances ("in this manner") also passes (to Mihrēn). He has also said that many are in agreement on this question, but Yuvān-Yam together with Vahrāmšāt held to another opinion in this (matter).

A11, 17—**12**, 3:

(...)* you/your (?) is sold to Mihrēn, and Mihrēn declared "(it is) needed" after three days; then Farraxv's revocation (of the agreement/transaction) is not possible during the course of the three days following Mihrēn's declaration "it is needed" since his own three days (*i. e.* those following the time of the declaration of the agreement and during which his right of revocation of the agreement or the transaction is operative — *A. P.*) have already elapsed, and Mihrēn's three days (= those over which Mihrēn's right of refusal extends — *A. P.*) are not valid as regards Farraxv.

A12, 3—7:

Dāt-Farraxv ī Farraxv-Zurvān bōžišn ēvak ēn guft (4) kū ka zan guharēn kunēt ut šōy andar 3 šapak ī zan rasēt u-š apar (5) ēstēt ka 3 šapak ī zan šut (guhart) bē bavēt. U-š ēvak (ēn) guft kū ka (6) zan gōspand pat *pasuš.haurva*-īh bē patigīrēt ut šōy andar 3 šapak ī (zan) āyēt (7) u-š apar ēstēt ka 3 šapak ī zan šavēt *pasuš.haurva*-īh bē bavēt.

A12, 8—9:

Nāmčištīk dāt ⟨hēβ⟩ ā-š xvāst nē apāyēt nāmčištīk dahom nāmčištīk (9) hēβ dāt (?) dahom ā-š hamēv bē xvāst apāyēt.

L

A12, 10—11:

Dar ī vāčak čand ī pat kartak dāštan gōβēnd ut apar-ič (11) Dātastān-nāmak⟨īhā⟩ nipišt ēstēt*.

A12, 11—13:

Hač dātaβarān ō var tā rat aparmat hač dātaβarān (12) ut hač-ič magupatān ō xvārastān zamān nē dāt. Zamān ī ō dātaβar ī mas tā ō magupatān (13) pat hamēmār ut hač ān frāč pat tan-ē(v) kart.

A12, 13—17:

Magupat ut dātaβar kē hač kār guharīk (14) kart muhr tā muhr-dāt ăvartēt pātixšāy ka bē nē dahēt čiγōn hač Yuvān-Yam (15) bē gōβēnd ăvaštak kartan rāδ muhr apāč ō dātaβar ī pēš dāt nē pātixšāy (16) u-š ān-ič bōžišn ī tā muhr-dāt ăvartēt bē nē dāt pātixšāy ī muhr (17) rāδ nipišt.

* The (*abǰad*) ordinal-number of this chapter is 50.

A12, 3—7:

Dāt-Farraxv ī Farraxv-Zurvān has stated such a decision: if a wife makes an exchange and the husband comes (to the place where the transaction is taking place) within the wife's three days (= the three days following the wife's declaration during which her right to revoke the agreement remained in effect — *A. P.*), and he supports her; then (the exchange) takes place (= is concluded) at the end of the wife's three days. And he (= Dāt-Farraxv) also said this: if a wife takes a sheep for safekeeping and the husband appears during the wife's three days and supports the agreement, then (the agreement regarding) the keeping of the small cattle takes place (= is concluded) at the end of the wife's three days.

A12, 8—9:

(If the transfer is formulated in the following fashion — *A. P.*): "(I) have conveyed a definite (thing) to you", then he need not bring a claim (to receive the thing in such a transfer — *A. P.*). (But if the transfer or the relinquishment are formulated in one of the manners given below: "I shall convey a specific (thing)", "I would give a specific thing (if)" (should the receiver observe some condition stipulated by the conveyer — *A. P.*)"; then it is indispensable to bring suit (to obtain the thing).

L

A12, 10—11:

Chapter concerning certain regulations ("formulae") which, it is said, must be adhered to ("had; held") in judicial proceedings and which are also set down in the *Dātastān-nāmak* ("*The Book of Judgements*") *.

A12, 11—13:

A session (= the investigation of an affair) in (an ordeal) court is not appointed by the judges — the judges and likewise the *magupat*s — until a decision (regarding this matter is rendered by the *rat*s. The session (= the investigation of the affair) — before a senior judge and all the way up to a judicial session before the *magupat*s — takes the form of a trial ("is through trial, a litigation between parties") but in higher instances ("after this") — (it takes place) singly (= independently, *i. e.* by way of an individual investigation of the affair and (the individual) rendering of a decision — *A. P.*).

A12, 13—17:

A *magupat* and (or) a judge who is being removed from office is entitled not to return (his) seal (of office) until (the document regarding) their transfer (= surrender, return) of (this) seal has been sealed. As it has been said, with a citation of Yuvān-Yam, it is not permitted to convey an (official) seal for the sealing (of documents) to a former judge. He has also written down this decision: that (an ex-*magupat* or an ex-judge — *A. P.*) is entitled not to return (his) seal until he has sealed with it (the document) regarding the surrender of (this) seal.

A12, 17—**13**, 2:

Ka xvāstak 100 vaxš ut 'nw'n (?) ī pat patmān ī sāl ēvak kart (1) ut sāl 3 [ō tō]žišn mat ut apām ī sāl 2 hast pat kartak pat apām ī sāl 2 bē (2) apispārtan.

A13, 2—3:

Yō hvā.daēna- pat kas ō kartak kart ēstēt ut pat apārīk hišt (3) ēstēt.

A13, 3—4:

Pat bōžišn ī andar hambāγān ka andar hambāγīh ēvak yāvar staβrtar xvarēt (4) vastrak veh dārēt pat bahr bē nē hangārišn u-šān pat vaštīh bē hangārtan.

A13, 5—7:

Ka katak-bānūk gātār kart ut pat dūtak anī zan ayāp apurnāyak būt (6) pat katak-bānūk ut xvāstak bahr ī katak-bānūk sardār nē ut pat apurnāyak ut apārīk harv kē pat dūtak (7) sardār gumārtan.

A13, 7—8:

Yazišn-nāmak pat Čāštak Artvahišt rōč ăvartišn ut pat kartak (8) Xordat rōč ăvartēnd.

A13, 8—9:

۳۱۳ ka pat rāδēnišn xvāhēt ō kartak kart ēstēt (9) ka pat ēvarīh xvahēt hač kartak hišt ēstēt.

A13, 9—11:

Zēndānīk ravāk būt zēndānpān (10) pat vināskārīh bē ēraxt ut pas zēndānīk apāč ō miyān āmat ut pat kartak (11) mat ēstēt u-šān zēndānpān nē ōzat.

A13, 11—13:

Mart-ē(v) tan-ē(v) andar ō Diglīt apakanēt (12) ān tan apāč kart hač ān bār nē mīrēt ut pat kartak mat ēstēt u-šān pat (13) andar apakandān pursišn-nāmak pat-iš kart.

A12, 17—**13**, 2:

If a thing/sum (amounting to) 100 (*drahms*) was stipulated as interest or ("and") smart-money in case (of his non-fulfilment of an obligation) by the end of one year (from the day that he assumed it), and if he appears in the third year intending to pay, but (his) indebtedness is a two-year (one); then according to judicial rules ("*kartak*") he must pay (the interest or smart money — *A. P.*) calculated (on the basis of) a two-year indebtedness.

A13, 2—3:

One who is a Zoroastrian must be subjected to judicial procedure even for a minor (offence; in minor matters — *A. P.*), whereas (the necessity to investigate the matter within the framework of judicial procedure) is set aside in the case of others (*i. e.*. unbelievers).

A13, 3—4:

In the settlement (of affairs) between co-partners, if one of the partners eats more and has better clothing (than the other), this should not be added on (= taken into account for) his share, but (if one of) them is sick (? "in sickness"), (this) should be taken into account.

A13, 5—7:

If the mistress of the house has entered into a sexual relationship (*i. e.*. "has entered into a marriage of the type without full rights" — *A. P.*), and there is another woman or minor in the family, then a guardian (should) not (be appointed) for the mistress of the house and (for) the estate representing the portion of the mistress of the house, whereas a guardian should be appointed for the minor and (for) all the other members of the family.

A13, 7—8:

According to the *Teaching* (*Čāštak* = the commentary on the legal *nasks* of the *Avesta* — *A. P.*), a document regarding an ordeal should be sealed on the day Artvahišt, whereas according to the procedure (*kartak* = the norms of judicial practice — *A. P.*) it is sealed on the day Xordat.

A13, 8—9:

If he demands the payment of smart-money, then (the investigation of this matter) takes place by way of judicial procedure. If he demands (it) on the basis (of his having) an unquestionable ("authentic") right (to it), then the affair is removed from judicial procedure (= is freed from the obligation of going through a trial — *A. P.*).

A13, 9—11:

A prisoner fled (from prison), and the gaoler was condemned (= sentenced to a punishment) for (his) offence (= for allowing the flight of the prisoner — *A. P.*), after which, the prisoner appeared again and presented himself before the court, and they (= the judges) did not condemn [75] (or: "kill") the gaoler.

A13, 11—13:

A man throws a slave into the Tigris. This slave having been pulled out (of the river) does not die on this occasion and appears at the court trial, and they (= the judges) have drawn up a record regarding his being thrown into the river (= the attempt to drown him — *A. P.*).

A13, 13—15:

Tan kē dārišn ī pat zēndān paytāk (14) dātaβar pat vičōδišn mat ēstēt bē vičust vināskārīh-ē(v) nē paytāk pat kartak (15) hač zēndān bē nē hilēnd.

A13, 15—16:

Ka pēšēmār apāyēt ēranǰēnītan dātaβar ī (16) pasēmār bē ēranǰēnēt u-šān zamān bē ō dātaβar ī pēšēmārān kart.

A13, 17:

Pat kartak žīvandak anattān nē kunēnd.

A13, 17—**14**, 1:

Čak ut hačašmānd pat harv 2 var andar (1) frayar (= Avest. *frayara-*) pat dastaβarān (Ms.: dātāβarān) pat dēp *hū frāšmō.dāt*(*i*-) dahēnd.

A14, 1—4:

Hakar [ātaxš] 1 (2) zan ⟨dō⟩ nišāst sardārīh pat zan kē nišāst (ut) zan ī stūr kē (3) gātār ut andar ān ē ka-š gātār kart sardār nē būt sardārīh pat gātār bē hilišn.

A14, 4—5:

Pat gāt tāvān ka šōy ayāp zan ayāp (5) gātār murt ō xvāhišn nē kart ēstāt vičīr nē kartan.

A14, 5—6:

Pat vičīr ī (6) nē ōγōn kart čiγōn sažist ham dātaβar dip hač pas kartan nē pat xvap dāštan.

A14, 7—9:

Pat xvāstak ī varōmandīh stūr ōγōn gumārtan kū hač ān čiγōn ⟨hakar⟩ mērak stūr aδvēn (8) gumārt ⟨an⟩ pat stūrīh ī mērak mērak sažāktar. Hakar mērak stūr aδvēn gumārt⟨an⟩ (9) ā-mān mērak pat stūrīh ī mērak gumārt.

A14, 9—10:

Pat stūrīh ut dūtak-sardārīh (10) pus ut duxt ī čakardāt ī ōy kē stūr ut dūtak-sardār ⟨i⟩ apāyēt gumārtan nē gumārt(an).

A13, 13—15:

A man (not likely "a slave") known to be in prison, and whom a judge — having come (there) for an investigation (probably relating to another matter that he was examining in court — *A. P.*) — finds entirely innocent upon inquiry, is not released from prison according to the norms of judicial practice.

A13, 15—16:

If it is incumbent to condemn the plaintiff, (then) the verdict is rendered by the respondent's judges and they (= the respondent's judges) must set a (court) session before the plaintiff's ("plaintiffs'") judge.

A13, 17:

According to judicial norms, the insolvency of a living man (or "for life") is not proclaimed.

A13, 17—**14**, 1:

A document (regarding the court decision) or (a document regarding) contumacy is conveyed to both litigating parties in the morning ("before noon"), but to the representatives at sunset (lit.: "at the meeting of the sunset, evening").

A14, 1—4:

If a woman has instituted (a Fire), then the trusteeship (over it) belongs to the woman who instituted it. And (if) this woman as a *stūr* enters into a marriage (*sine manu* — *A. P.*); then even if she has not been the trustee over the Fire when entering into (the marriage), the trusteeship (over the Fire) is transferred to her (*čakar* — *A. P.*)-husband.

A14, 4—5:

As regards a fine for adultery: if by the death of the husband, of the wife, or of (her) lover the claim has not been presented, a (judicial) decision should not be rendered.

A14, 5—6:

As regards a judicial decision which was improperly rendered: the drawing up of a subsequent document by the same judge is to be considered invalid [76].

A14, 7—9:

In the case of a "doubtful" estate (evidently an estate to which the dead man's title is not clear — *A. P.*) a *stūr* is to be appointed in this manner: inasmuch as (such-and-such) a (dead — *A. P.*) man designated a "conditional" *stūr* (lit.: "sort of" a *stūr*, a "kind of" *stūr*), this man is the most suitable to be that (dead) man's *stūr*. If (such-and-such) a (dead) man has designated a "conditional" *stūr*, we have appointed this man to be that (dead) man's *stūr*.

A14, 9—10:

Neither the son nor the daughter born from a *čakar*-marriage of the person for whom a *stūr* or a family guardian should be appointed shall be appointed (that man's — *A. P.*) *stūr* or family guardian.

A14, 11—12:

(...) apāyēt hač ē(v)kart ōrōn magupatān gumārt u-šān pat framānīh (ī) šāhān šāh (12) gumārt *.

A14, 12—13:

Zan būt ī-šān sažākān rāδ pātīrānēnīt u-šān pat šōy bē nē (13) dāt u-šān Xvatāyduxt⁺-ič Veh-Šāhpuhr rāδ ōh pātīrānēnīt.

A14, 13—15:

Vikāyīh ī pat žahm (14) ēn and vas ka gōβēt kū-š and žahm kart tōžišn bē kunišn. Spurrīkīh ī (15) sneh ut čandīh (ī) rēš (ut) nāmčištīkīh ī gyāk ⟨i⟩ guftan nē apāyēt.

A14, 15—**15**, 1:

Pat žahm hamāk (16) pat rēš ut masrūk⁺ ut vars rūnišnīh ut karp apakanišnīh ut dart (ut) xūn tōžišnīh ut pat-ič žahm (17) sardak čiγōn žahm sardak āhanǰišn ut āspōžišn ut kašišn ut *miϑō.sāst*(*a*)- tā (1) nē drōγ [r]āh nimūt hangart/handart ut *a̱tvadāt* bavēt.

A15, 1—2:

Pat hačašmānd harv ān kē (2) mātak hast mātak ut ān kē nēst *pāk*(*a*) *pasu.čāša-*/ *čaxša-*(?).

A15, 2—5:

Pat duž drōš ī šahr mātak 10 bāγ (3) pat ap(p)ur mātak tasubāγ pat bōδō.ǰat ut kātō.ǰat guharīk ī mātak ō bun-xvēšān (ut) rēš (= *raēšā*) (4) ō vināskārān dāt rāδ vičīr kartan pat gāt tāvān pat ēv vičīrkart ī (5) dātaβarān frēh kū 300 vičārtan rāδ vičīr nē kartan.

A15, 5—7:

Ka vikāy 2 nē būt (6) pursišn-nāmak (rāδ) ⟨ut⟩ ka guft kū vizūt ut asar ⟨nē⟩ nipišt pat ap(p)ur rāδēnišn nē (7) ut ka yut-dātastānīh rāδ nām bē nē guft attānīh pat dastaβar ōh (bavēt).

* The beginning of this paragraph has been left out by the copyist.

A14, 11—12:

(...) it is necessary that *magupats* henceforth (?) be appointed, and they are appointed (?) by order (or "according to the order") of the King of Kings *.

A14, 12—13:

There have been women who refrained (from marriage with the man offered to them as a husband — *A. P.*) for the sake of (a bridegroom more) suited to them. Thus Xvatāyduxt refrained for the sake of Veh-Šāhpuhr (= for the sake of becoming Veh-Šāhpuhr's wife — *A. P.*).

A14, 13—15:

If he gives a witness' testimony regarding the degree ("size") of an act of physical violence ("a blow") in this fashion: "he struck so many blows", then the fine should be set (in accordance with this). It is not necessary to make a declaration regarding the weapon, nor (regarding) the number of wounds, nor (regarding) their exact position.

A14, 15—**15**, 1:

A fine must be paid for every act of physical violence ("blow") corresponding to the *raēša-* (= an offence of deliberate damage against a body — *A. P.*): for the pulling out of the beard and hair, and (for) disfigurement, and (for the causing) of pain, and (for the spilling) of blood. As regards the variety (= the degree of seriousness? — *A. P.*) of an act of physical violence, namely when (there is an intentional) increase in the variety (= seriousness) of this offence: (a deliberate) intensification and stretching (of the wound — *A. P.*), and a false testimony (or "dissembling" — *A. P.*), (such acts) should be considered as (equated with an) "*at̠vadāt*" (offence) (*cf. DkM*, **698**, 2—17) in order to avoid any attempt to lead (the legal process) astray.

A15, 1—2:

For non-appearance in court, the one who has money (shall pay the fine and the stake — *A. P.*) in money, and the one who has none, in "*pāk*(*a*) *pasu.čāša-*/ *čaxša-*" (?).

A15, 2—5:

(The punishment provided) for theft is the brand of the *šahr*, for looting — a sum equivalent to ten *bāγ*s, for *bōdō.ǰat* and *kātō.ǰat* (= varieties of offenses of physical violence) — a sum equivalent to four *bāγ*s. A decision must be rendered concerning the transfer of the sum equivalent (to the fine — *A. P.*) to the owners, and the imposition of *raēša* (the obligation to reimburse the loss — *A. P.*) on the criminals. For adultery the judges should not render in a single sentence a decision requiring the payment of a fine in an amount superior to 300 (*satēr*s? *drahm*s?).

A15, 5—7:

If two witnesses were not present, if it is said of the record of investigations / interrogation: "(it is) shortened and is not written in full ('is written without the beginning / ending')"; then a trial regarding a case of robbery cannot be conducted. And if it named no name because of a divergence in opinion, (then) the solvency (is determined?) according to that of the representative / disposer(?).

A15, 7—8:

Zamān ī (8) ō dastaβarān sāl drahnāδ.

A15, 8—9:

Stūrīh ī katak-bānūk bē dāt dātastān gumārtak(9)īhā būt rāδ nipišt ut ǎvašt ēstēt.

A15, 9—11:

Duž kē hamēmār pat hamēmārīh (10) andar ēstēt ut vat-āhangīh ut zūr-vikāy ut drōγ-čāš ut *virāδkar (? Ms.: الاسرو) bastār ut anayār (11) ut stūr-škand ut nasā⟨k⟩-nikān ut nasā⟨k⟩-pāk ōh bast(an).

A15, 11—12:

Pat yātūk ka daxšak nē (12) gōβēt nipištak nē kunišn ut ka kart nē āhōkēnišn.

A15, 12—15:

Katak-bānūk stūrīh ō (13) ōy ī kem sažāktar nē pātixšāy dāt ut pat-ič kartak ōγōn kartan čiγōn ōstaβarān (14) guft būt kē ō ōy ī kem sažāktar dāt (rāδ) pēš Dāt-Farraxv ī moγān (h)andarz(15)pat mat ēstāt u-š bē nē vartēnīt.

A15, 15—17:

Yātūk ī pātram dusrav čambar ō (16) gartan ut gōšvār ō duškartan tā varōmand kart ayāp bōxt bē hilišn ka-š (17) čambar ayāp gōšvār ēvak šikast pat varōmand dāštan.

A15, 17—**16**, 5:

Uzēnak ī pat nāmak (1) pas(s)āč pat kartak pat xvāstak gyākē guft kū 9 drahm 2. Ut gyākē guft (2) kū harv 10 drahm 3 ut pat markaržān 95 ut ka dātastān hač ān ī apēr vas ⟨ī⟩ aδak-ič pat (3) markaržān vēš nēst kū 95 ut pat xvāstak ōγōn paytāk čiγōn ka vēš nē hē (4) kū 18 drahm 2 pat kartak uzēnak ī pat nāmak pas(s)āč andar apāyēt hač ātaxšān (5) bē dahēnd ut hač pēšēmārān (ut) pasēmārān apāč xvāhēnd.

A15, 7—8:

(The time limit for the appointment) of a court session with the participation of a legal representative (is) one year.

A15, 8—9:

It has been written and sealed, that the transfer of the *stūr*ship (to another person) by the mistress of the house is carried out by means of a judicial appointment (= at the designation of the court — *A. P.*).

A15, 9—11:

A thief who participates in a trial ("is present in court") as one of the litigating parties, as well as a malicious man, and a false-witness, and a preacher of false doctrine (heresy), and a man who binds (= impedes) the officer of order (?), and he who does not give help; and a *stūr* who scorns his obligations (lit.: "a breaker of *stūr*ship"), and he who buries corpses, and he who cremates corpses must be arrested ("bound").

A15, 11—12:

As regards a sorcerer, if he does not declare about distinctive signs, a document should not be drawn up, but if it has been drawn up (it should) not be flawed [or: "it should not wrong (the man)" — *A. P.*].

A15, 12—15:

A mistress of the house is not entitled to convey the *stūr*ship (laid upon her — *A. P.*) to the one less suited (*i. e.*. to a more distant agnate — *A. P.*), and (in this matter) action should be taken in the judicial procedure in the same way as was stated by the commentators of the *Avesta*. Some presented themselves before Dāt-Farraxv, the *(h)andarzpat* of the Magi (concerning) the possibility) of transferring (the *stūr*ship) to a less suitable person, but he did not alter (the regulation given — *A. P.*).

A15, 15—17:

The neck hoop and earrings of a sorcerer who has a bad reputation among the neighbouring persons should be left until he has been subjected to an ordeal as regards his committing of evil deeds, or (until) he (has been) acquitted (during a normal judicial investigation — *A. P.*). If he has broken the hoop or one of the earrings, then he must be held subject to trial by ordeal.

A15, 17—**16**, 5:

As it is written in one place, according to the norms adopted by the courts that the costs for the drawing up of a document correspond to (the value of the disputed) thing (in the proportion of) 2 *drahms* (for each) 9 (*drahms*). (But) in (another) place it is said, that 3 (*drahms* of costs) (are calculated) on every 10 *drahms* (of the value of the thing), and at (a trial on) a capital charge (the costs are) 95 (*drahms*). And if the trial (is being conducted) regarding (a thing) which (costs) much more, even then, (the costs of drawing up the documents) in a capital charge do not exceed 95 (*drahms*). As regards the (disputed) thing, it is known, that if (its value) does not exceed 18 (*drahms*), (then) 2 (*drahms* out of those which are) indispensable, according to judicial regulations, to cover the drawing up of the documents, are paid by the Fire-(temples) and (subsequently) claimed from the plaintiffs or ("and") the respondents.

A16, 5—6:

Ka vičīrkart ēvar (6) ut vizūtan/nizūtan varōmand pursišn-nāmak ōh kunēnd.

LI

A16, 7—8:

Dar ī dātastān ē(v)-čand ī ēvāč rāδ pat (8) nāmčišt apāyēt nikerītan *.

A16, 8—11:

Ka gōβēt kū ēn ātaxš hamāk hač frazandān ī (9) man mart-ē(v) ī pahlom hēβ dārēt hamāk ān ī hast ān ī pahlom dārišn. Ut ka gōβēt (10) kū hač frazandān ī man hamāk mart-ē(v) ī pahlom hēβ dārēt hač frazandān andar ān ē hast ān ī (11) pahlom guft bavēt.

A16, 11—14:

Ka gōβēt kū frazand ut aβγātak ī Farraxv pat asāβar-nipēk (12) ma hēβ ăvartēnd ān ī frazand ut aβγātak rāδ guft bavēt ī andar ān ē ka gōβēt hast+ (13) ut ka gōβēt kū Farraxv frazand ut aβγātak pat asaβār-nipēk mā hēβ ăvartēnd (14) ān ī andar ān ē hast ut ān-ič ī pas hač ān rāδ guft bavēt.

A16, 14—**17**, 1:

Vahrām hač Pusānveh ī (15) Āzātmartān bē guft kū Dāt-Farraxv ī Kĕrakān rāδ framān būt kū-š (frazandān? — *A. P.*) pat asaβār-(16)nipēk ma hēβ ăvartēnd u-šān dipīrīh ōγōn virāst kū frazand ut aβγātak ī Dāt-Farraxv (17) ut Dāt-Farraxv xvāhišn kart kū ōγōn nipēsēt kū Dāt-Farraxv frazand ut aβγātak pat (1) asaβār-nipēk [m]a hēβ ăvartēnd.

A17, 1—4:

Ka gōβēt kū-m ēn xvāstak pat stūrīh ī (2) man dāštan tā 10 sāl ō Farraxv dāt pas-ič hač 10 sāl pat stūrīh ēstēt. (3) Ka gōβēt kū-m tā 10 sāl pat stūrīh ī man dāštan ō Farraxv dāt pas hač (4) 10 sāl nē pat stūrīh ēstēt.

* The (*abǰad*) ordinal-number of this chapter is 51.

A16, 5—6:

If the document (presented? — *A. P.*) is trustworthy whereas the fact of causing an injury (?) is dubious, a record of the interrogation (or: "of the judicial enquiry") is drawn up.

LI

A16, 7—8:

Chapter concerning certain judicial cases in which attention should be paid to the particular ways in which statements ("declarations") are formulated *.

A16, 8—11:

If he declares (thus): "out of all my sons, let the best (= the best behaved, the most pious — *A. P.*) possess (= carry out the trusteeship over) this Fire", then (the one who) possesses (exercises the trusteeship over) it must be the best of all the sons whom he had. But if he makes the declaration (in this manner): "let the best of my sons (= those whom I have — *A. P.*) possess (become trustee)", then the best among the sons whom he had at that time is intended.

A16, 11—14:

If he makes a declaration (thus): "let them not enter (lit.: 'not seal', 'not affix a seal') the sons and descendants of Farraxv in the *List of Horsemen*", then what is intended (are) those sons and descendants whom (Farraxv) had at the time that he made (this) declaration. But if he declares (thus): "let them not enter Farraxv's sons and descendants in the *List of Horsemen*", what is intended ("said") are both (the sons and grandsons of Farraxv) whom (he) had at that time (= at the time of the given declaration — *A. P.*) and those who (will be / were) subsequently (born to Farraxv).

A16, 14—**17**, 1:

Vahrām has said from the words of Pusānveh ī Āzātmartān, that there was a disposition regarding (the sons) of Dāt-Farraxv ī Kĕrakān: that his (sons) should not be entered (lit. "sealed") in the *List of Horsemen* but the scribe formulated ("arranged") it (in the document) in this manner: "the sons and descendants of Dāt-Farraxv". But Dāt-Farraxv demanded that (the scribe) write down this: "let Dāt-Farraxv's sons and descendants not be entered into the *List of Horsemen*".

A17, 1—4:

If he makes a declaration (in this fashion): "until ten years (are over — *A. P.*) I conveyed this thing — as a possession instituted for my *stūr*ship — to Farraxv", then (this thing) shall remain a *stūr*-foundation even after the passage of ten years. But if he makes the declaration (in this fashion): "I have conveyed (this thing) to Farraxv so that it be possessed for ten years as a foundation instituted for my *stūr*ship", then at the end of ten years (this thing) ceases to be a *stūr*-possession (= foundation).

A17, 4—7:

Ka gōβēt kū man nē patkārom ut ōγōn kunom (5) kū pat-ič dastaβarīh ī man kas nē patkārēt ut hakar yuttar kunom tāvān dahom (6) bē ka ōγōn čiγōn patkārēt ut paytāk kū-š ān kē patmān kart pat-iš dastaβar (7) hamdātastān būt enyā tāvān tōžišn nē rasēt.

A17, 7—11:

Ka gōβēt (8) kū man nē patkārom ut ōγōn kunom kū kas pat-ič dastaβarīh ī man nē patkārēt ut hakar (9) yuttar kunom tāvān dahom bē ka ōγōn čiγōn patkārēt ut paytāk kū-š ān kē (10) patmān kart pat-iš dastaβar hamdātastān būt enyā tāvān tōžišn nē (11) rasēt.

A17, 11—13:

Ut ka gōβēt kū man nē patkārom ut ōγōn kunom kū kas pat-ič (12) dastaβarīh ī man nē patkārēt ut hakar yuttar kunom tāvān dahom ka-č nē pat (13) dastaβarīh ī ōy ⟨i⟩ patkārēnd aδak-ič tāvān ō tōžišn rasēt.

A17, 13—16:

Ka gōβēt (14) kū ēn xvāstak tā+ man (ut) tō žīvandak hēm ākanēn darēm ka ēvak mīrēt ōy ī dit (15) nē dārišn. Ut ka gōβēt kū man ut tō tā žīvandak hēm ākanēn dārēm ut ka ēvak (16) mīrēt aδak-ič ōy ī dit žīvandak dāštan dastaβarīhā.

A17, 16—**18**, 2:

Ka ō Mihrēn gōβēt (17) kū ēn xvāstak pat stūrīh ayāp pat xvēšīh tō dār Mihrēn pat stūrīh (1) ut xvēšīh ēvak ī-š kāmēt dāštan dastaβarīhā ut ka gōβēt kū[-m pat] stūrīh (2) ayāp pat xvēšīh ō tō dāt pat stūrīh dāt bavēt.

A18, 2—7:

Ka dastkart (3) ō pusak dāt ut kart kū hakar pusak pat ēn anšahrīk patkārēt ān dastkart (4) pusak xvēš mā hēβ+ bavēt čiγōn Vāyayār nipišt andar žīvandakīh ī pusak (5) hamāk xvāstak aframān ut ka ōγōn kart kū hakar patkārēt dastkart ī-m ō (6) pusak dāt pusak xvēš mā hēβ bavēt hač ān čiγōn-iš dāt pat dahišn apāč (7) kart tā patkārēt xvāstak xvap ēstēt.

A17, 4—7:

If he makes (this) declaration: "I shall not bring suit, and I shall arrange that no one brings suit on my instruction and empowering either, and if I act otherwise I shall pay the fine", then — except (for the case) where he brings suit and it is known that the person who made (this) contract gave him (his) sanction and consent for it — he should not be obliged to pay the fine (*cf. infra*, **A17**, 7—11; 11—13 —*A. P.*).

A17, 7—11:

If he makes a declaration (in this fashion): "I shall not bring suit and I shall arrange that no one brings suit on my instruction and empowering either, and if I act otherwise. I shall pay the fine"; then — except (for the case) where he brings suit and it is known that the person who made (this) contract gave him (his) sanction and consent for it — he should not be obliged to pay the fine.

A17, 11—13:

If he declares (this): "I shall not bring suit and I shall arrange that no one shall bring suit, not even on my instruction and empowering, and if I act otherwise I shall pay the fine", then — even if they bring suit without the instruction and empowering of the declarer ("him") — they should be obliged to pay the fime (*cf. supra* **A17**, 4—7; 7—11 —*A. P.*).

A17, 13—16:

If he makes a declaration (in this fashion): "while we are both ("you and I") alive we shall possess this thing jointly", then in the case of the death of one (of them), the other shall not possess (it). But if he declares this: "while we are alive, you and I shall possess jointly", and if one (of them) dies, then the other is entitled to possess (it) as long as he lives.

A17, 16—**18**, 2:

If he declared (this) to Mihrēn: "possess this thing on the basis of a *stūr*-possession or as your personal inheritance-share!", then Mihrēn is entitled to possess (this thing) on the basis of a *stūr*-foundation or as his share of the estate according (to one of these two titles), whichever one he selects ("wishes"). But if he formulates thus: "I have given (it) to you for the *stūr*ship or as a personal share of the estate", then (the thing) is conveyed on the basis of a *stūr*-possession.

A18, 2—7:

If he conveyed a *dastkart* to his son and declared (thus): "If (my) son should bring suit concerning this slave, let this *dastkart* not belong to (my) son"; then, as has been written by Vāyayār, during the son's life his title to the whole (thing, *i. e.*., the *dastkart* and the slave — *A. P.*) is not valid (= the transfer cannot legally go into effect — *A. P.*). But if he formulates it (thus): "if he (= the son) brings suit, then let the *dastkart* which I conveyed to (my son) not belong to my son", then — inasmuch as he conveyed on the condition ("through, by means") of the withdrawal of the gift, (if the son does not fulfil the condition set — *A. P.*) — until the time when the son brings suit, his title to (this) thing is valid.

A18, 7—12:

Ka kart kū-m ēn xvāstak (8) pas hač 10 sāl ō pus dāt ut xvāstak ⟨i⟩ ī-m ō pus dāt hakar pus duxt ī man pat (9) zanīh gīrēt pus xvēš hēβ bavēt pas hač 10 sāl ut hakar duxt pat zanīh gīrēt (10) pēš-ič hač 10 sāl dāt bavēt ut ka ōγōn gōβēt kū pas hač 10 sāl ō pus (11) dāt ut hakar pus duxt pat zanīh gīrēt pus xvēš hēβ bavēt apāč ō pašt ī (12) pas ēstāt ut hakar duxt pat zanīh nē gīrēt pas-ič hač 10 sāl nē xvēš.

A18, 12—15:

Ka (13) māh Ātur ut rōč Ōhrmizd kunēt kū-t andar ēt māhak ī nazdist+ harv rōč 1 drahm dahom (14) 30 drahm dahišn. Ut hakar gōβēt kū-t tā ēv māh ī nazdist bavandak bavēt harv rōč ēv (15) drahm dahom 31 drahm dahišn.

A18, 15—**19**, 2:

Ka gōβēt kū hakar pat muhr ī ratān ayāp pat muhr ī (16) magupatān nāmak nē dārom xvāstak tō xvēš bē+ ka pat harv 2 nāmak dārēt enyā (17) xvāstak bē rasēt. Ut ka gōβēt kū hakar pat muhr ī ratān ayāp magupatān nāmak (1) nē āβ[arom] xvāstak ⟨hač⟩ tō xvēš ka pat muhr ī ēvak nāmak āβarēt Vahrām (2) guft kū xvāstak nē rasēt.

A19, 2—6:

Ka gōβēt kū hakar pus ī man pat asaβār ayāp (3) pat nipēk nē ăvartēnd xvāstak tō xvēš bē ka harv 2 ăvartēnd enyā xvāstak (4) bē rasēt. Ut hakar gōβēt kū hakar pus ī man pat asaβār ayāp nipēk nē ăvartēnd (5) xvāstak tō xvēš ka pus ēvak asaβār (ayāp) ēvak pat nipēk ăvišt Vahrām guft kū (6) xvāstak nē rasēt.

A19, 6—9:

Ka gōβēt kū varzītan ī ān var rāδ pat muhr (ī Farraxv ayāp pat muhr) ī Gušnasp ī (6) Āturfarnbaγ pus nāmak stānom Farraxv pat pusakīh ī Āturfarnbaγ nē guft bavēt. (7) Ka gōβēt kū pat muhr ī Farraxv ayāp Gušnasp ī Āturfarnbaγ pus nāmak stānom (9) harv 2 pat pusīh ī Āturfarnbaγ guft bavēt.

A18, 7—12:

If he declares (this): "I have conveyed this thing to my son after the passage of ten years, and let the thing I conveyed to my son belong to my son in the case that (my) son marries my daughter", then, after the passage of ten years, (the thing) must be transferred (to the son); but if he marries the daughter (= his sister) (before that time — *A. P.*), then (it should be transferred even) before the passage of ten years. And if he declares (thus): "after the passage of ten years (this thing) is conveyed to (my) son, and if (my) son marries (my) daugher, let (it) belong to my son", then one (should) keep the last condition of the agreement ("the last stipulation"), and if the son does not marry the daughter (= his sister), then even after the passing of ten years (the thing) shall not belong (to him).

A18, 12—15:

If in the month Ātur on the day Ōhrmizd he declares in this manner: "in the course of this next month, I shall daily give you one *drahm*", then he must give 30 *drahms*. But if he declares (this, in this manner): "until one, the nearest, month elapses, I shall daily give one *drahm*", then he must give 31 *drahms*.

A18, 15—**19** ,2:

If he makes a declaration (in this fashion): "If I do not have a document with the seal of a *rat* ("*rat*s"), or with the seal of a *magupat* ("*magupat*s"), the (this) thing belongs to you"; then the thing shall go to (that man) only if he (= declarer) does not have a document (sealed) with the one and the other (= both) seal. But if he declares (this): "if I do not bring a letter with the seal of a *rat* or *magupat*, the thing belongs to you", then Vahrām has said that if he brings a letter with one seal, the thing shall not go to (that other man).

A19, 2—6:

If he declares: "In case they do not enter ("seal") my son among the '*Horsemen*', or into the '*List*', (this) thing shall belong to you", then the thing shall go (to that man) — except for the case when (his son) is included in the one and the other ("in both"). And if he declares (thus): "if they do not enter my son (either) among the '*Horsemen*' or into the '*List*' (this) thing shall belong to you", then, Vahrām has said that the thing shall not go (to that man) if the son is entered only among the '*Horsemen*', or only into the '*List*' [77].

A19, 6—9:

If he formulates his declaration (in this manner): "I shall receive a letter (= a document) concerning the performance of this ordeal / the taking of this oath sealed with Farraxv's seal, or sealed with the seal of Gušnasp son of Āturfarnbaγ", then it does not follow from this ("it is not said") that Farraxv is the son of Āturfarnbaγ. But if he declares (this): "I shall receive a letter (= document) sealed with the seal of Farraxv or Gušnasp the son(s) of Āturfarnbaγ", then it follows from this that both of them are sons of ("in sonship to") Āturfarnbaγ.

A19, 9—13:

Ka gōβēt kū xvāstak ī ō man (10) mat ān ī Farraxv ayāp Mihrēn gōβēt tō xvēš. Ut Mihrēn gāv 1 ut Farraxv xar 1 gōβēt harv (11) 2 bē rasēt ut ka pat ēv hangām ut ka-č pēš ut pas gōβēnd yuttar nēst. (12) Ut ka gōβēt kū ān ī Farraxv ayāp ān (ī) Mihrēn gōβēt tō xvēš ka harv 2 gōβēnd ēvak (13) rasēt ī rāt kāmak.

A19, 13—16:

Gyāk-ē nipišt kū ka gōβēt (kū) hakar rōč Ōhrmizd ō Kuvār (14) ut Xabr nē šavom drahm 30 bē dahom ka ō Kuvār ayāp Xabr šut 30 nē dahišn. (15) Ut ka gōβēt kū hakar ō Kuvār ayāp ō Xabr nē šavom drahm 30 bē dahom bē hakar (16) ō harv 2 gyāk šavēt enyā-š 30 (Ms.: 12) bē dahišn.

A19, 16—**20**, 1:

Ka Farraxv apāk Mihrēn patmān (17) kunēt kū hakar ō Kuvār šavom enyā drahm 12 bē dahom pat šut Farraxv paytākēnišn. (1) Ut ka gōβēt kū [hakar] nē šavom drahm 12 bē dahom pat nē šut Mihrēn paytākēnišn.

A20, 2—5:

Ka Farraxv apāk Mihrēn patmān kunēt kū hakar ō Kuvār šavom enyā drahm 12 bē (3) dahom ka Mihrēn gōβēt kū bē šav ayāp drahm bē dah nē pātixšāy bē ka (4) šavēt ayāp drahm dahēt. Ut ka gōβēt kū hakar nē šavom drahm 12 bē dahom (5) pātixšāy pātīrānēnītan.

A20, 5—8:

Ut ka gōβēt kū Aβzūtxvatāy čiγōn *vohu.(t)baēš(ah)*- (6) istēt (? Ms.: 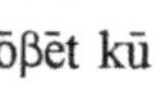 = ḤWYTNyt) kartan tō xvēš pat gyāk dāt bavēt. Čē-š daxšak guft. Ut ka (7) gōβēt kū čiγōn purnāy bavēt tō xvēš tā purnāy bavēt nē rasēt čē-š (8) hangām guft.

A19, 9—13:

If he declares (this): "whatever Farraxv or Mihrēn name among the things received by me shall belong to you". And if Mihrēn names a cow, whereas Farraxv names a donkey; then the one and the other ("both") shall go (to that person) — and it does not matter whether they designate (them) simultaneously or one earlier and the other later. But if he declares (this): "whatever Farraxv names, or else whatever Mihrēn names shall belong to you", then even if both designate (their choice), one (of the things named by them) shall go (to that person), (specifically) the one which the donor wishes (prefers).

A19, 13—16:

In one place it is written, that if he declares (this): "if I do not depart to Kuvār and (= or) Xabr on the day Ōhrmizd, I shall give thirty *drahms*", then if he departed to Kuvār or to Xabr, he is not obliged to pay thirty *drahms*. But if he formulates (his declaration thus): "if I do not depart either to Kuvār or to Xabr, I shall give thirty *drahms*", then unless he goes to both places, he shall, in either case, be obliged to pay ("give") thirty (*drahms*).

A19, 16—**20**, 1:

If Farraxv concludes (such an) agreement with Mihrēn: "either I shall go to Kuvār, or (= in the opposite case — *A. P.*) I shall give you twelve *drahms*", then Farraxv must make a public declaration regarding (his) departure. But if he formulates (his agreement with Mihrēn in the following manner): "if I do not depart, I shall give twelve *drahms*", then Mihrēn must make a public declaration that (his contractor = Farraxv) did not depart.

A20, 2—5:

If Farraxv and Mihrēn conclude (the following) agreement: "either I shall go to Kuvār or I shall pay ('give') twelve *drahms*", and if Mihrēn declares: "depart or else pay the money!", then Farraxv is not entitled (to act) otherwise than to depart (to Kuvār) or to pay the money. But if he (= Farraxv declares (this): "if I do not depart, I shall pay twelve *drahms*", then he is entitled to delay (his departure or the payment of the money ? — *A. P.*).

A20, 5—8:

If he declares: "inasmuch as (the slave — *A. P.*) Aβzūtxvatāy has committed a hostile act against Zoroastrianism, (the slave) shall belong to you", then (the slave) is handed over at once, because he (= the declarer) designated ("spoke") the sign (= the particular circumstance). But if he makes (this) declaration: "when (the slave) comes of age, (he) shall belong to you", then until the slave comes of age (the slave) shall not go (to that person), since he (= the declarer) mentioned the time (when the transfer would become effective — *A. P.*).

A20, 8—11:

Ka gōβēt kū xvāstak ī man xvēš frāč hač man frazand ī tō pat (9) zanīh ī man hač-iš zāyēt xvēš ān-ič frazand ī žīvandak katak-xvatāy pas hač ān zāyēt (10) xvēš ut ka gōβēt kū frāč hač man frazand ī tō pat zanīh ī man hač-iš zāyēt xvēš (11) frazand ān guft bavēt ī andar ān dūtak zāyēt.

A20, 11—15:

Ka gōβēt kū ēn dastkart (12) raz žīvandakān Mihrēn nēm ut vitart Mihrēn apārīk ō Farraxv dāt aδak-iš zamīk (13) fratom nē dāt bavēt ut ka gōβēt kū ēn dastkart žīvandakān Mihrēn raz (14) abaxt nēm ō Pusak ut vitart Mihrēn apārīk ō Farraxv dāt aδak-iš raz nēm ut zamīk (15) hamaδvēn ō Farraxv dāt bavēt.

A20, 15—**22**, 1:

Ka gōβēt kū-m ēn xvāstak ōγōn čiγōn-im (16) ō pus xvāstak dāt ō duxt dāt yuttar bavēt čiγōn ka gōβēt kū-m ēn (17) xvāstak čiγōn-im ō pus xvāstak dāt ō duxt dāt (ut) yuttar bavēt čiγōn ka (1) gōβēt kū-m ēn xvāstak čiγōn-im ō pusarān xvāstak dāt ō duxt dāt pa[t] (2) ēn čim ētōn čē ka dāt ōγōn čiγōn apar bē gōβēt u-š xvāstak ast-ē(v) pat (3) xvēšīh ut ast-ē(v) pat stūrīh ut ast-ē(v) pat ruvān dāštan ayāp ast-ē(v) tā xvat ast-ē(v) (4) tā pus žīvandak ast-ē(v) frāč hač xvēš ō pus dāt ēstēt aδak-iš 3 aδvēnak ut harv aδvēnak (5) ēt⁺ rāst guft bavēt kū dāt ut ka dāt ōγōn apar bē gōβēt aδak-iš hamaδvēn (6) pat xvēšīh dāt rāδ ēn-ič saxvan pat-iš kū ēt ⟨ēt⟩ guft bavēt kū-m ō duxt (7) [xv]āstak aδak dāt ka-m ō pus dāt ut ka dāt ōγōn apar nē ut pusarān apar (6) bē gōβēt u-š pus ēvak būt saxvan pat-iš kū dāt nē bavēt čē ān hangām nē būt. (9) Ut ka pus 2 būt u-š ēvak xvāstak sāl ēvak dāt ēvak sāl 2 (10) dāt aδak-iš saxvan pat-iš kū-š aδak guft bavēt ōγōn apar nē ut pus apar (11) gōβēt nē pusarān⁺ u-š pus 2 būt ēvak xvāstak sāl ēvak ut ēvak sāl 2 dat (12) aδak-iš saxvan pat-iš aδak guft bavēt kū-m dāt ka-š fratom xvāstak (13) dāt ut ka dāt ōγōn pusarān harv 2 apar bē gōβēt u-š pus frēh kū ēvak (14) nē būt nēm dāt ut nēm adahišnīh guft bavēt yuttar nēst čiγōn ka gōβēt (15)

A20, 8—11:

If he makes a declaration (in this fashion): "the thing belonging to me shall belong after my death to the child who will be born to you in (your) marriage to me", then (this thing) shall likewise belong to a child born after this (= after this declaration — *A. P.*) within the lifetime of the head of household. But if he declares (this): "(it) shall belong to the child born to you after my death from your marriage to me", then the child who will be born into this family is intended (= the *stūrīh* son and successor of the dead man born to his wife in a *čakar*-marriage with his agnate — *A. P.*).

A20, 11—15:

If he declares this: "the vineyard of this *dastkart* is half conveyed to Farraxv in Mihrēn's lifetime, and (all) the rest (is conveyed to him) after Mihrēn's death", then the land is not conveyed in the first case. But if he declares (this): "the vineyard of this *dastkart* is half conveyed to Pusak, without division, in Mihrēn's lifetime, and all the rest is conveyed to Farraxv after Mihrēn's death", then in this case, half the vineyard and all the land are conveyed to Farraxv [78].

A20, 15—**22**, 1:

If he declares: "I gave this thing to (my) daughter in the same way as I gave (my) estate to (my) son", then (this declaration) differs from (the one) in which he would have declared: "I gave this thing to (my) daughter at the same time as I gave (my) estate to (my) son", (and it(differs from (the one) in which he would have declared: "I gave this thing to (my) daughter at the same time as I gave (my) estate to (my) sons". And the reason for this is that when he declares regarding the transfer (that it is) "in the same way as", and the estate is conveyed to (his) son: partly as an inheritance-share, and partly as a *stūr*-possession (= as a *stūr*-foundation), or partly "for the soul" (= as a pious-foundation "for the soul" — *A. P.*), or else partly while he (himself) is alive, partly while the son is alive and partly after his (own) death (= in case of his death — *A. P.*); then in the (these) three varieties and methods it is equally said that he "transferred". And if he says; "in the same way" as regards the transfer of the thing (without specifying the character of the real right transferred — *A. P.*), then (what is intended is) his transfer (of the thing) in the same way/altogether as a personal inheritance-share. And likewise (in the case of) the declaration ("word") regarding this (also), specifically, when the following declaration takes place: "I transferred the thing to (my) daughter at the same time as I transferred (an estate) to my son". But if he speaks (= declares) not about the variety ("in what way") of the transfer but about "the sons", and he has only one son; then his declaration ("word") (is reduced) to the fact that the transfer is invalid ("does not take place"), because he has no other sons at the time. But if there were two sons, and if he transferred the estate ("the thing") (in alternate possession) for one year to one and for the second year to the other; then here too what was said regarded the fact that (the thing was transferred to the daughter — *A. P.*): "at the (same) time as" (= simultaneously with the conveyance to the sons — *A. P.*), and not: in what way. And if he speaks of "a son" and not of "sons", but he has two sons, and he transferred (the estate) "for one year to the one and for the second year to the other"; then the declaration ("word") he makes regards (the fact that) (the thing is to be transferred to the daughter — *A. P.*) "at the same time" (specifically): "I transferred (the thing to my daughter — *A. P.*) at the time that kū ōγōn čiγōn-im ō pit ut māt xvāstak dāt ō tō dāt u-š xvāstak ō māt⁺ nē (16) bē⁺ ō pit dāt ēstēt. Ut ka gōβēt kū-m ⟨čiγōn-im⟩ ēn xvāstak ōγōn čiγōn-im (17) ō Mihrēn xvāstak dāt ō duxt dāt u-š ō Mihrēn xvāstak nē dāt (1) ēstēt dāt nē bavēt.

A22, 1—17:

Ka xvāstak 1 ī nāmčišt rāδ gōβēt kū tā nūn ō (2) man dāt apāyītan ī Mihrēn rāδ Mihrēn nē patkārom pat dāt ī Mihrēn tā-ič (3) ān hangām apar patkārtan patixšāy. Ut ka xvāstak ayāp anī čiš ī Mihrēn patmān (4) kart kū bē ⟨kū⟩ dahom rāδ kart kū tā nūn ō man dāt apāyītan ī Mihrēn rāδ (5) nē patkārom aδak-iš ān xvāstak ut čiš pat dāt ī Mihrēn apar nē patkārišn (6) ut pat ēn čim ōγōn apar xvāstak ī-š Mihrēn pat nāmčišt avi-š dāt hakurč (7) (aδvēn) nē būt kū⁺-š Mihrēn avi-š dāt apāyist hē ut ān ī-š patmān kart kū (8) bē dahom tā dahēt hamēv dāt apāyēt ut ka xvāstak ī nāmčišt rāδ gōβēt (9) kū tā nūn ō man frōxt ut dāt aδvēn būt (ī) Mihrēn rāδ nē patkārom yuttar bav[ēt] (10) ⟨ut⟩ čiγōn ka gōβēt kū tā nūn ō man frōxt ut dāt pātixšāy būt ī Mihrēn rāδ nē (11) patkārom ut pat ēn čim ōγōn čē ēn būt nē šāyēt kū ka gōβēt kū-m (12) ēn xvāstak aδvēn ō tō frōxt ayāp tō dāt aδak-iš ēt guft bavēt kū (13) pātixšāy hom ō tō frōxt ut dāt u-š pat ān aδvēnak ī gōβēt frōxt ut dāt (14) nē apāyēh ut xvāstak ī frōšēnd ut dahēnd andar ōy kē avi-š frōšēnd ut dahēnd pēš (15) hač ān ut andar-ič ān ē ka frōšēnd ut dahēnd čiš-ič ī avi-š frōšēnd ut dahēnd ut aδvēn (16) būt nēst ut ka frōxt ut dāt nē frōxt ut dāt aδvēn būt bē xvat (17) frōxt (ut) dāt bavet.

A22, 17—**23**, 6:

Ka gōβēt kū-m tā rētak purnāy bavēt ayāp gōβēt (1) kū-m tā rētak apurnāy ēn čiš ō tō dāt harv 2 ēv aδvēnak. Ut ka gōβēt kū tā rētak (2) apurnāy ēn čiš ō tō dahom yuttar bavēt čiγōn ka gōβēt kū tā rētak purnāy (3) bavēt ēn čiš ō tō dāt čē ka gōβēt kū tā rētak apurnāy ēn čiš (4) ō tō dahom aδak-iš pat gyāk bē dahišn u-š hangām tā rētak purnāy bavēt (5) xvēš u-š pas nē xvēš ut ka gōβēt kū tā rētak purnāy bavēt ō tō dahom (6) aδak-iš pēš hač purnāyīh ī rētak bē dahišn u-š hamaδvēn xvēš.

I transferred the estate to (my) first (son)". But if he makes a declaration regarding the conveyance (of the thing to the daughter) in the same fashion (= on the same basis, with the same title — *A. P.*) as to both sons, but he has only one son; then this is to be understood as the conveyance of one half (to the daughter) and the non-conveyance of the other half (of the thing) in exactly the same way as though he had declared: "I have conveyed (this thing) to you in the same way as I conveyed (my) estate to (my) father and mother", but he conveyed the estate only to the father and not to the mother. And if he declares: "I have conveyed this thing to (my) daughter in the same way as I conveyed a thing to Mihrēn", and he has conveyed nothing to Mihrēn, then the transfer (of the thing to the daughter) is null and void.

A22, 1—17:

If he declares (the following) regarding a certain thing: "I shall not bring suit that Mihrēn was obliged to convey (it) to me before the present time (*i. e.*. regarding Mihrēn's obligation to convey the thing before the present time — *A. P.*)", then he is entitled to bring suit over (the thing) which Mihrēn had (already) conveyed (to him) before that time (*i. e.*. before the declaration was made — *A. P.*). And if he declares — regarding money or another thing, about which Mihrēn had contracted with him: "I shall convey (it to you)" — "I shall not bring suit over Mihrēn's obligation to convey (it) to me before the present day"; then he must not bring suit over the transfer of this money or thing by Mihrēn. And the reason for this is that regarding the thing which Mihrēn conveyed (= declared the conveyance — *A. P.*) to him in a certain way no agreement was made (with the stipulation) that Mihrēn was to have conveyed it already and since he (= Mihrēn) made this (the following) contract: "I shall convey"; then as long as he has not made the transfer he remains obliged to make (it). And if he has declared (the following) regarding a certain thing: "I shall not bring suit regarding (the fact that) Mihrēn has obliged himself to sell and convey (it) to me before the present time", then this declaration differs from another, (specifically from the one) in which he declares: "I shall not bring suit regarding (the fact) that until the present time Mihrēn was entitled to sell and convey (it) to me". And the reason for it is that this (= the sale, transfer) did not obligatorily have to take place, (since) if he declares: "it befits me to sell and convey this thing to you", he has thereby said: "I am entitled to sell and convey (it) to you", and the form of his declaration would not oblige him to sell and convey it. And as to the thing which people sell and convey, those who sell and convey it are not obliged to sell (or convey) anything of what they are selling and conveying to that person — either before or at the time of the sale and transfer. And if they have sold and transferred (it), this does not mean that it befitted them to sell and transfer, but (merely) that they themselves (*i. e.*. at their own initiative — *A. P.*) sold and conveyed (it).

A22, 17—**23**, 6:

And if he makes the declaration: "until the boy comes of age, I — ", or if he formulates it (this): "while the boy is a minor, I have conveyed this thing to you"; then in both these cases (the declaration formulae) are equivalent. But if he declares (this): "while the boy is a minor, I shall convey this thing to you", then (this declaration) differs (from the other, specifically) (it is as though) he had declared (this): "I shall convey this thing to you before the boy comes of age". Since if he says: "whilst the boy is a minor, I shall convey this thing to you", he must convey it at once, and it shall belong (to that person) until the boy comes of age, but after (that), (it) will not. And if he declares: "before the boy comes of age, I shall convey (it) to you", then in this case, he must convey (the thing) before the boy comes of age and it shall belong altogether to that man.

A23, 6—10:

Ka gōβēt (7) kū tā sāl ī nazdist bavandak bavēt var varzom yuttar bavēt čiyōn ka gōβēt kū hangām (8) tā ēv+ sāl (ī) nazdist bavandak bavēt var varzom čē ka gōβēt kū tā ēv+ sāl var varzom ka (9) pēš hač sāl var varzēt+ šāyēt ut ka gōβēt kū hangām tā sāl ī nazdist bavandak bavēt (10) var varzom hangām kār hamsālakīh bavēt u-š pas (hač) ham sālak var varzītan patigrift (nē) bavēt.

A23, 11—15:

Ka gōβēt kū tā ēt sāl ēn čiš ōyōn kunom hakar čiš hač ān ī ka-š ēt (12) apar nē gōβēt aδak-iš hamāk apāyēt kart ut andar ēv sāl hamāk ōh kunišn. Ut hakar čiš (13) hač ān ī ka-š ēt sāl apar nē gōβēt aδak-iš ēv yāvar kunisn andar-ič ēv sāl ēv yāvar (14) kunišn čiyōn ka gōβēt kū var varzom u-š ēv yāvar varzišn ayāp gōβēt kū kār ī (15) tō kunom u-š hamāk ōh kunišn.

A23, 15—17:

Ka gōβēt kū ēn xvāstak nēm hakar Zanbūt (16) frazand zāyēt apārīk hakar Zanbūt frazand nē zāyēt tō xvēš tā frazand zāyēt (17) ayāp paytāk bavēt kū frazand nē zāyēt xvāstak aframān ēstēt.

A23, 17—**24**, 9:

Ka (1) gōβēt kū ēn xvāstak ka man ut pus ī pātixšāyīhā ut ēt čē čakarīhā hast pus ī (2) man pat ān aδvēnak hast ut ka man pus ī pātixšāyīhā ut ēt čē čakarīhā nēst Farraxv (3) xvēš hēβ bavēt pus ī patixšāyīhā ut ēt čē čakarīhā hast ētōn bavēt čiyōn (4) ka gōβēt kū ka man pus ī pātixšāyīhā enyā čakarīhā (hast) pas (hač man)? pus ī man pat ān aδvēnak (5) xvēš hēβ bavēt. Ut ka pātixšāyīhā hast ut čakar nēst pat ān patmān ō pus nē rasēt. (6) Ka gōβēt kū (ka) man pus ī pātixšāyīhā ut ēt čē čakarīhā nēst ayāp gōβēt kū ka (7) pus ī pātixšāyīhā ayāp čakarīhā nēst ut ka-č kunēt kū ka man pus ī pātixšāyīhā (8) ut čakarīhā nēst Farraxv xvēš hēβ bavēt harv 3+ (Md.: 2) aδvēnak (ēv) bavēt. Ut ka pātixšāyīhā (hast) hakar čakar (9) nēst xvāstak ō Farraxv nē rasēt.

A23, 6—10:

If he declares: "I shall take an oath (or 'undergo the ordeal'), before the nearest (= first) year elapses", then (this declaration) differs (from the one in which) he declares (this): "I shall take an oath when one, the nearest, year elapses" (from the time of this declaration — *A. P.*). Because if he declares: "I shall take an oath before one year has elapsed", then he may take the oath before one year (*i. e.*. after the end of the given calendar year — *A. P.*). But if he declares: "I shall take an oath when the nearest year elapses", then the time question is reduced to the same year (= the calendar year in which the declaration was made — *A. P.*) and in such a case, his taking of the oath after that year may (not) be admitted.

A23, 11—15:

If he declares: "in the course of this/year, I shall carry out this matter ('thing') in this way", and if he is speaking of a matter regarding which he does not say "this" (*i. e.*. if he is speaking of a matter whose definite limits are not set down in the declaration — *A. P.*), then he must do everything (in full) and he must carry (it) out within one year. But if he is speaking of the type of matter regarding which he does not say: "(within) this year", then he must do it all at once (= at one go). And (it) should be done within one year and all at once, when (for instance) he declares: "I shall take an oath": he shall take it once. Or if he declares: "I shall do your work"; then he must do all of it.

A23, 15—17:

If he declares (this): "half of this thing shall belong to you — if Zanbūt bears a child, and the rest of it — if Zanbūt does not bear a child", then until the time that a child is born, the thing remains without assignment (*i. e.*. the disposition regarding this thing cannot go into effect — *A. P.*).

A23, 17—**24**, 9:

If he declares: "if I have a son from a *pātixšāyīh*-marriage and a son ("the one who") from a *čakar*-marriage, (let) this thing (belong) to the sons whom I have in this way, but if I have no son from a *pātixšāyīh*-marriage and no son from a *čakar*-marriage, let (it) belong to Farraxv", and if he has a son from a *pātixšāyīh*-marriage and a son from a *čakar*-marriage, then this is equivalent to his saying: "if I (shall have) a son from a *pātixšāyīh*-marriage (and) morover, from a *čakar*-marriage — then let (it) belong after (my death) to the son whom I (shall have) in this way". But if he has a son from a *pātixšāyīh*-marriage, but he has none from a *čakar*-marriage, then according to this condition/agreement, (the thing) shall not go to the son. If he declares: "if I have no son from a *pātixšāyīh*-marriage and no son from a *čakar*-marriage", or if he says: "if I have no son from a *pātixšāyīh*-marriage as well as (from) a *čakar*(-marriage)", and likewise if he declares (this): "if I have no son from a *pātixšāyīh*-marriage (and equally) from a *čakar*-marriage, let (the thing) belong to Farraxv", then these three modes (formulae) are equivalent. But if he has a son from a *pātixšāyīh*-marriage but no son from a *čakar*-marriage, then the thing does not go to Farraxv.

A24, 9—14:

Ka gōβēt kū xvāstak ō xvēšīh ī (10) man mat ut ēt čē ō xvēšīh ī man rasēt ut ka-č gōβēt kū xvāstak ī čē ō (11) xvēšīh ī man mat enyā ō xvēšīh ī man rasēt harv 2 ēv aδvēnak bavēt čiγōn (12) ka gōβēt kū xvāstak ī ō xvēšīh ī man mat ayāp ō xvēšīh ī man rasēt čē (13) ka ayāp gōβēt hast kē patkārišn ēn kū-š mat ayāp rasēt ēvak nē (14) dahēt.

A24, 14—**25**, 1:

Ka Farraxv andar Zanbūt kart kū ēn xvāstak hakar tō pat zanīh ī man frazand (15) hač-iš zāyēt hamāk ut hakar tō pat zanīh ī man frazand hač-iš (nē) zāyēt nēm tā tō žīvandak hēh (16) tō xvēš hēβ bavēt xvāstak ī-m pat ān aδvēnak patmān kart kū tā tō žīvandak hēh (17) tō xvēš hēβ bavēt frāč hač tō Mihrēn xvēš Zanbūt frazand nē zāyēt ān ⟨i⟩ (1) xvāstak ō Mihrēn nē rasēt.

A25, 1—6:

Ka Farraxv apāk Mihrēn patmān kart kū bē (2) ka nē vičārtan ī ēn xvāstak ēvar enyā xvāstak Mihrēn xvēš ka vičārtan ut ka-č (3) nē vičārt (nē) ēvar xvāstak Mihrēn xvēš ut ka gōβēt kū bē ka nē vičārtan nē (4) ēvar enyā xvāstak Mihrēn xvēš hamēv ka nē vičārtan ēvar Mihrēn xvēš ut ka (5) vičārtan ēvar aδak-ič ēn šāyēt guftan kū nē vičārtan nē ēvar xvāstak ō Mihrēn (6) nē rasēt.

A25, 6—8:

Ka kart kū xvāstak ī ō man mat bē ān ī bē nē dahom apārīk (7) Mihrēn xvēš Mihrēn ān ī xvēš ⟨ī⟩ bē dahēt enyā ān ī bē nē dahēt hač rāt (8) bē nē rasēt.

A25, 8—11:

Ka mart xvāstak ī-šān čand sāl pat task hač-iš (9) patigrift ut sāl-sāl task vičārtan patmān kart ⟨ut⟩ apāč kart pātixšāy būt rāδ (10) ōγōn framāt nipištan kū bē ka ān task nē vičārt enyā ān xvāstak ma (11) stān. Ka sāl-sāl hač task hambun-ič vičārt bē stat nē šāyēt.

A24, 9—14:

If he declares: "a thing which has come into my personal lawful possession (= personal inheritance-share — *A. P.*) and that which will come into my personal lawful possession", and likewise if he declares: "the thing which has come into my personal lawful possession or will come into my personal lawful possession"; then both these (formulae) are equivalent, (and) as though he declared: "the thing which has come into my personal possession or will come into my personal possession". And meanwhile [79], if he uses ("speaks") (the word) "or", there are people who argue that he must not convey ("does not convey") one of these: (either) the one that he received or the one that he will receive.

A24, 14—**25**, 1:

If Farraxv declares (the following) regarding Zanbūt: "if you bear a child from your marriage with me, let this thing belong to you wholly (= *in toto*) during your lifetime, but if you do not bear a child from your marriage with me, let one half (of it belong to you). And let the thing — regarding which I have contracted that it shall go to you during your lifetime — belong to Mihrēn after your death", (and) Zanbūt does not bear a child. (Then) this thing shall not go to Mihrēn.

A25, 1—6:

If Farraxv made the following agreement with Mihrēn: "except in the case where it is authentically established that the debt (or "this money" — *A. P.*) has not been paid, the thing (= the pledge — *A. P.*) shall belong to Mihrēn", then if it is authentically established that (the debt) was repaid, as well as if it is (not) established authentically that (it) was not repaid, the thing (= the pledge) shall belong to Mihrēn. But if he makes the declaration (in this manner): "with the exception of the case where it is not authentically established that the debt was not repaid, the thing shall belong to Mihrēn", then (the thing) shall belong to Mihrēn only if it is authentically established that (the debt) was not repaid. But if it is authentically established that (it) has been repaid, even then it might be said that it was not authentically established that (the debt) was not repaid, and the thing does not go to Mihrēn.

A25, 6—8:

If he declared (this): "except for that which I shall not convey (= except for what is not mentioned in the subsequent declaration of transfer — *A. P.*), (let) everything else from the estate that passed to me belong to Mihrēn", then only that which he conveys shall belong ("belongs") to Mihrēn, whereas (the portion of the estate) which he does not convey shall not go to him (= Mihrēn) from the giver (= relinquisher).

A25, 8—11:

If it was ordered to write this down — regarding the right of a man to take away (= exact, take back) a thing which they received from him on lease for several years and made an agreement regarding the yearly payment of the lease: "do not take away this thing except for the case where the lease is not paid!", then if even a very small portion of the lease is paid yearly, he should not take (this thing) away.

A25, 12—14:

Ka Farraxv kart kū xvāstak ī kas ō man tōžišn (ut) dahišn bē ān ī hač 500 (13) ut ēt[+] čē hač 100 frēh apārīk tō xvēš ⟨u-š ān⟩ aδak-iš ān kē hač 100 nē frēh (14) dāt apārīk čiš-ič nē dāt bavēt.

LII

A25, 15:

Dar ī ēvarīh ī kārdārān *.

A25, 16—**26**, 11:

Dātaβar pat čē ut čand ut čiγōn ut čē aδvēnak xvēšīh ut vikāy patigrift ut hamēmārīh (17) kart ut zamān kart ⟨ut zamān kart⟩ ut āβurt ut dāšt ut pāt ut nē pāt ut kār rāδēnīt (1) ut kār nē rāδēnīt ut hačašmānd ut čak patisāy dātastān ānayīhīt ut nihān būt ut *miϑō.paitīm* (2) ut vaštakīh ut apārīk vinās ī apar dātastān (ut) syāh ut spētīh[+] ut narīh ut mātakīh ut hamtanīh ⟨i⟩ (3) ut hamnāmīh ut hammuhrīh ut xvastūkīh ut dārišn ī pat vidāšt (? Ms.: [Pahlavi script]) ut andar ⟨andar⟩ 3 gām ut saxvan (4) ut pas(s)axv ut garzītan ī must ut hač pās virōpišn ī gizīrān (ut) dužītan ut burtan ī yāmak ut čiš (5) ut xonsandīh ut axonsandīh i pat vičīr ut dip (ī) pat[+] vičīr kū kē kart ut tan ut muhr kū kē pat āšnāk (6) guft ut nāmak ut vičīr kū ō dīvānpān ut tan kū ō zēndānpān ut gizīrān apispārtan pat-ič (7) apārīk harv čē ka dātaβar pat-iš nē ēvar rāδēnišn ī saxvan pātīrān pat kartak pat-ič (8) čē ut čand dužītan ut burtan ī yāmak ut čiš (ut) hač pās virōpišn ī gizīrān pat ēvar dārēnd (9) ut hač druž ⟨ī⟩ škastan ut nīšān kartan apāyēt rāδ ētōn paytāk čiγōn ka pat škastan (10) ut nīšān kartan ēvar ut būt kē guft kū dātaβar pat-ič vidāšt (? Ms.: [Pahlavi script]) ī nē pat dārišn (11) ēvar.

* The (*abǰad*) ordinal-number of this chapter is 52.

A25, 12—14:

If Farraxv declares (this): "let (everything) else from the estate/debt that a certain person is obligated to pay and convey to me belong to you — except for the (thing) (costing) more than five-hundred and the one (costing) more than one hundred (*drahms*)", then he has conveyed (only) what (costs) no more than one hundred (*drahms*), and nothing else is conveyed.

LII

A25, 15:

Chapter concerning the competence of officials *.

A25, 16—**26**, 11:

(The competence of) a judge (*dātaβar*) (lies) in: what (in particular) is owned — (specifically) how much, since when, and in what way (= the type of ownership, the variety of real rights — *A. P.*); and in the admittance/reception of witnesses; and in the opening of a case; and in the matter of appointing a court session; and in the presentation (of the disputed object or of the judicial security — *A. P.*), and in (its) safekeeping; and in what regards the grant of a postponement and the non-granting of a postponement; and in the conduct or non-conduct of the trial by one (of the) parties (what is intended here is the appearance or non-appearance of one of the litigating parties in court to participate in the trial — *A. P.*); and in what regards a case in which (the respondent) defaults, as well as the presentation (in court — the deposition in court — *A. P.*) of the documents (required) for the trial, or their (= the documents') concealment; and likewise ("and") in (the ascertainment of an offence of) barratry (= vexatious litigation) (?), the giving of contradictory evidence ("change of testimony" — *A. P.*), and other judicial offences. (A judge is likewise competent) in ascertaining blackness or whiteness (of hair, *i. e.*. the determination of the age of the participants in a case — *A. P.*), maleness or femaleness, the identity of a physical person (lit.: "identity of body"); and in the identification of a name or seal; and in (what regards) the confession (of guilt) and in the possession/keeping ... (?); and in (the placing of litigants at a distance of) three "paces" (from each other and from the judge — *A. P.*); and in what regards statements (in court), responses and appeals ("complaints"), and the removal of guards from their police posts (= the removal or dismissal of the watch — *A. P.*); (and in the) theft or abduction of the judicial security or of the disputed object (lit.: "vessel") deposited in court (*cf.* "Glossary" *s. v. yāmak* — *A. P.*), or (other) things; and in what regards (the declaration of the litigants, concerning their) satisfaction or dissatisfaction with the decision (of the court), as well as who drew up the document regarding the judicial decision, and (in particular) who made the declaration concerning the identification of the person or seal. (He is competent) to convey the (court) documents and the verdicts to the archivist ("the head of the chancellery") and the convicted man (lit.: "the body itself" — *A. P.*) to the prison warden and the guards; and likewise for everything else. For if a judge has not ascertained (or "is not competent" in) any of this, the conduct of the trial is delayed. Likewise, according to judicial norms ("*kartak*") he (= the judge) must determine precisely (= "in a trustworthy manner", exactly) what and how much of the juducial security, or deposit, or other thing has been stolen or carried off (= through open seizure as against theft — *A. P.*), (and also regarding) the removal of the guard from its post. And as regards the indispensability of crushing the demon and setting a mark (= brand, sign on a sorcerer — *A. P.*) it is known that he (= the judge) is competent in this (*i. e.*. this enters into his area of competence — *A. P.*). And some say that a judge is also competent in what regards ... (?) that which is not for possession.

A26, 11—16:

(Hač) Pēšaksēr gōβend kū⁺ dātaβar pat dārišn ī ōzītak (? Ms.: ’w/nčytk)/uzītak ēvar ut druvistak ān ī ka (12) ō stūrīh xvāhēt magupat pat gumārtan ī stūrīh ut pat apāč kart (13) ut sāk⁺/nisāk⁺ (? Ms.: 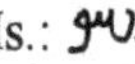) apar nihāt ī xvāstak ī apāč ō ātaxš ⟨i⟩ pat magupatān saxvan apāyēt (14) kart ut pat nižāδ/vižāδ (Ms.: n/wyz’d) hištan ut pargār brītan ut pat-ič ān kē dātaβar pat-iš ēvar būt (15) rāδ nipišt ut ēt čē ōγōn čiγōn apar xvēškārīh-nāmak ī magupatān nipišt (kū) ka (16) magupat pat-iš nē ēvar kār xvēškārīh ī magupatān pātīmār pātīrān ēvar.

A26, 17—**27**, 4:

Rat pat apāč kart ut sāk⁺/nisāk⁺ (? Ms.: 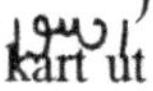) apar nihāt ut xrīt ut guharīk ut arž ut vahāk ī pat (1) (h)ēr ī ātaxšān apāyēt kart ut čand mat ut pat-ič nē mat ī čiš atēn ō ātaxš kē bun (2) ut handraxt pat dīvān ī kartak hangārēnd ut pat-ič nižāδ/vižāδ hištan ut pargār brītan ut apārīk (3) harv ān ī pat ān aδvēnak ut pat harv (h)ēr ī ātaxšān ka pat šāhīkān⁺ hē hamārkarān pat-iš (4) ēvar hē pat ēvar dārēnd.

A27, 4—5:

Magupatān magupat pat harv ān ī ka apārīk (5) kas gōβēt varōmand ka magupatān magupat gōβēt ēvar.

A27, 5—7:

Ut hačapar framān ī dehpatān (6) būt nē šāyistan ī čiš-ič ēvarīh rāδ pat ān čiš ī nē andar pēšak ī (7) ā̱sravanān ut pat framān ī dehpatān ut yāt-gēhān⁺ kār-framān pat-iš.

A27, 7—9:

Var-sardār pat (8) pātīrān ī var tā varzītan ī var ut pat yazišn pat var tā ǎvašt ī yazišn-nāmak ut pat-ič (9) ān čiš kē dātaβar pat-iš ēvar.

A26, 11—16:

It is said with reference to the authority of (with citation of) Pēšaksēr, that a judge is competent in matters regarding the possession of the escheated property(?), (specifically) when someone demands it for *stūr*ship (= as a *stūr*-possession). A *magupat* (is competent) in the appointment of a *stūr* and in the withdrawing (of a *stūr*-possession) from a person who has been removed from the exercise of the *stūr*ship — *A. P.*). And the assessment of taxes (or: "imposition of taxes/charges"? — *A. P.*) on the properties ("things") returned to Fire-temples (or "retained for the profit of Fire-temples" — *A. P.*) must be carried out in accordance with the word (= decision) of a *magupat*. (A *magupat* is competent) as regards the resolution of a claim (? "appeal"? — *A. P.*) and the issue of a verdict, and also in all that was written above concerning the competence of a judge. And it is in accordance with what is written in *The Book Regarding the Duties of Magupats*: that if a *magupat* is uncertain about something ("in this"), then the unquestionable right and duty of the *magupat* ("*magupats*") is to halt the verdict (= delay the entrance into effect of the sentence — *A. P.*).

A26, 17—**27**, 4:

A *rat* (is competent) in the matter of taking away/retaining (a possession), and of the charge/tax assessment (? on an estate — *A. P.*) and in what regards a purchase or exchange (and) the value and price of what should go to the temple-treasury; and (in what regards) how much has been paid and how much (remains) unpaid ("has not been entered") out of that which composes the revenue ("income") of the temple-treasury (lit. "of the Fire-temples" — *A. P.*) — the basic payments as well as those adjudicated — (and those) which are assessed ("they estimate, they reckon") in the department of pious institutions; and also in the resolution of claims/appeals and the issue of a verdict; and (in) everything else of this type. And (judges) accept as competent (a judgement, decision or information issuing from a *rat* — *A. P.*) in all matters (concerning) a temple-treasury — (the matters) concerning which financial officials (*hamārkars*) would have been competent, had these been matters regarding the royal treasury.

A27, 4—5:

Concerning the *magupatān magupat*: all that is subject to doubt (= verification — *A. P.*), when it is said by another person, is not subject to doubt ("is trustworthy") when the *magupatān magupat* states (it).

A27, 5—7:

And nothing may be above the edict of the rulers ("*dehpats*"), because of (their) competence in matters which lie beyond the (prerogatives and competence) of the priestly (*āsravanān*) class. And according to the order of the rulers ... ... [80].

A27, 7—9:

The head of the ordeal (*var sardār*) is competent in everything — from the delay ("impediment") of the oath/ordeal to its taking/undergoing, and from the performance of the ordeal procedure to the sealing of the document regarding the ordeal/oath; and likewise in everything in which a judge is competent.

A27, 9—11:

Parēžvān pat ān čiš kē dātaβar pat-iš (10) ēvar ut pat hamēmārīh kartan andar apāyēt ēvar. Ut ka-č šut ī parēžvān ō ganǰ būt (hē)? (11) (ān ī)? pasēmārān ēvar.

A27, 11—12:

Yāmak ī gōβēt ka duž⁺ kart pat ān ganǰ būt pat mat ī (12) ō ān ganǰ ēvar.

A27, 12—13:

Ōstāndār pat apāč kart ut sāk⁺/nisāk (?Ms.: 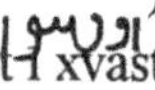) apar nihāt ut xrīt (13) ut vahāk patigrift ut dāt paytāk kart (ut) ō šāhīkān mat-ī xvāstak ēvar.

A27, 13—**28**, 3:

Hamārkar (14) pat arž ut vahāk ut ō šāhīkān matan ut hač šāhīkān bē matan ī xvāstak ut ka-č xvāstak 1 ī (15) dārišn pat apasēkōmandān būt apāč ō šāhīkān kart ut kas pat xvēšīh (16) apar patkārēt⁺ pat nē xvēšīh ī apasēkōmand ān xvāstak ut ka-č ōstāndār (17) nāmak apar ⟨nē⟩ xvāst čiγōn mizd ī stūr kē ǎvašt pat-iš ōh barišn/barēnd ut apārīk-ič (1) ān ī pat ān aδvēnak ut pat dāt ut ōzīt/uzīt (Ms.: 'w/nčyt) nāmak dāt pat-ič nē dāt ut nē ōzīt/uzīt (?) ī (2) xvāstak ut ka-č kas pat (h)ēr ī šāhīkān ziyān kart rāδ dip ut pat ān ⟨ī⟩ ziyān tāvān (3) kart pat-ič ān ī pat ān aδvēnak dip ut tāvān kart ēvar.

A28, 3—5:

Rat ut hamārkar pat-ič ān ī pat (h)ēr ī (4) šāhīkān čand ut hač kū ⟨nē⟩ vizīt ut apar kē (ut) čiγōn baxtan ut vidāštan rāδ pat pātimār (5) kartan⁺/kunēnd ēvar hamārkarān pat hangārtan ut ul statan⁺ ī sāk⁺ ēvar.

A27, 9—11:

A *parēžvān* (= a court official accepting a claim and taking part in the investigation and the preparation of a case for trial — *A. P.*) is competent in those things indispensable for a case in which a judge is competent. And even if (this implies) a visit by the *parēžvān* to the treasury of the respondent, he is competent (*cf. infra* **A27**, 11—12).

A27, 11—12:

(If the plaintiff or the respondent) declares that the vessel was in the treasury at the time of the theft, then (the *parēžvān*?) is competent to visit this treasury (= his right of visiting the treasury in the interests of the investigation is not open to question, since it enters into his prerogatives; *cf. supra* **A27**, 9—11 — *A. P.*).

A27, 12—13:

The *ōstāndār* is competent in matters of the removal of possession (what is evidently intended here is the right of the *ōstāndār* to take away the conditional title granted to a possessor on royal lands — *A. P.*); and (in) the assessment of rent? tax?/the adjudication of a fine; and in the acceptance of payments ("the price"); and in the declaration of conveyances (of plots on royal lands — *A. P.*); and in what regards the entry of property/money into the royal treasury.

A27, 13—**28**, 3:

A *hamārkar* is competent in everything regarding value and price and the entry of property into the royal treasury as well as disbursements from it; and also in the case where an estate of which the possession was burdened with liabilities/debts is taken away and returned to the royal treasury, but someone brings suit regarding (the variety of right) of his holding of this estate, asserting that it is not a tenure burdened with liabilities (*'psyk'wmnd*); and also if (in a case where) the *ōstāndār* has inquired about a document — for instance (if he has asked regarding a document dealing with) a payment for *stūr*ship: who sealed it with his own seal — (to have) it (= the document) brought to him (= the *hamārkar*); and also in matters of the same type. And he is competent to grant a document relating to the transfer of an estate (= a holding on the royal lands — *A. P.*) and to (its) removal (? "deprivation" or: "abandonment, relinquishment" — *A. P.*) or relating to (its) non-transfer and to (the fact) that (the estate) did not escheat (?) (or: "was not abandoned" — *A. P.*), and likewise to grant a document regarding the loss caused to the royal treasury by this or that person, and the setting of a fine related to this loss; and in other similar grants of documents and setting of fines.

A28, 3—5:

A *rat* and a *hamārkar* are also competent as regards what ("how much") and whence a loss to the royal treasury was caused, and (as regards) the disposition taken by them concerning among whom and through what means, it (= the shortage?) should be divided and distributed? (for it to be covered? — *A. P.*). The *hamārkar*s are also competent to assess and collect ("receive") taxes/duties.

A28, 5—7:

Xvastūkīh (6) guft ī magupatān magupat⟨ān⟩ ut var ⟨ut⟩ čiɣōn hač Dipīr bē gōβēnd guft ī magupatān (7) magupat⟨ān⟩ hač-ič var pat ēvartar dārišn.

A28, 7—10:

Hampačēn ī pat hamēmār ut vičīr ī pat gōβišn ī (8) mart ī bēšahrīk ut saxvan-nāmak harv čē andar pēšēmārīh ut hāmēmārīh kart ka čak⁺ (9) pat ăvašt ī pēšēmārān nē kart ēstēt aδak-ič hač ān ⟨i⟩ čiɣōn dātaβar pat hāmēmārīh (10) kart ēvar būt kē guft kū-š andar pēšēmār pat ēvarīh kār u-š ōh kunišn.

A28, 11—**29**, 5:

Zēndānpān būt kē guft kū ēvāč pat dārišn ī pat zēndān ēvar ut būt kē guft (12) kū pat-ič hamtanīh ut hamnāmīh ut hamvināsīh ēvar. Dastaβarān guft kū ān ēvarīh ī zēndānpān (13) pat hamtanīh ān bavēt ka ēvak Ōhrmizd rōč pat duž ēvak Vahuman rōč pat markaržān ō⁺ (14) zēndān kart ēstēt ut nē paytāk kū katām Ōhrmizd rōč katām Vahuman rōč ō⁺ zēndān kart (15) ēstēt ut zēndānpān gōβēt kū ēn Ōhrmizd rōč pat duž ut ēn Vahuman rōč pat markaržān (16) ō zēndān kart ēstēt ut pat hamnāmīh ōɣōn bavēt kū ēvak Mihr-Āturfarnbaɣ nām pat (17) duž ut ēvak Kay-Āturfarnbaɣ nām pat markaržān ō zēndān kart ēstēt ut nē paytāk (1) kū ka[tām Mi]hr-Āturfarnbaɣ ī pat duž ut katām Kay-Āturfarnbaɣ ī pat markaržān ō zēndān (2) kart ēstēt zēndānpān gōβēt kū ēn Mihr-Āturfarnbaɣ ī pat duž ut ēn Kay-Āturfarnbaɣ (ī) (3) pat markaržān ō zēndān kart ēstēt. Pat hamvināsīh ōɣōn bavēt ka ēvak pat duž (4) ut ēvak pat markaržān (ut) nē paytāk kū katām pat duž ut katām pat markaržān ō zēndān kart (5) ēstēt ut zēndānpān gōβēt kū ēn pat duž ut ēn pat markaržān ō zēndān kart ēstēt.

A29, 6—7:

Kōypān/kōδpān(?) pat ēn kū-m ō tō guft u-t ăšnūt ut pat-ič ēn kū gōhrak (guharīk⁺? — *A. P.*) ō tō mat (7) ēstēt ēvar.

A28, 5—7:

As regards the agreement (with a judicial decision — *A. P.*) expressed by the *magupatān magupat* and as regards the ordeal — as it has been said, with a reference to Dipīr: (the decision) rendered by the *magupatān magupat* is to be taken as more competent ("trustworthy, unchallengeable") than even the ordeal.

A28, 7—10:

A copy (of a document) regarding a judicial case, and a document containing the evidence of a person from another city (one who evidently cannot be present at the trial — *A. P.*), and a record of testimonies at the trial, and (in general) any (document) drawn up in connexion with a claim and trial is authentic — (even) in the case where (such a) document is not sealed with the plaintiff's seal — as a result of its drawing up by the judges in connexion with the case. Certain (authorities) have said that it (= the document) should be taken as authentic and valid as regards the plaintiff and (that) it should be drawn up (despite the absence of the plaintiff's seal — *A. P.*).

A28, 11—**29**, 5:

As regards the warden of a prison (*zēndānpān*), some have said that he is competent only as regards the keeping (of the criminal) in prison, but the opinion has also been emitted that he is likewise competent in matters relating to the identification of the person (of the prisoner — *A. P.*), of his name and crime. It has been said by the learned commentators (of the *Avesta*) that, (this is) the competence of the warden of a prison as regards the identification of a person: when one (man) is imprisoned on the day Ōhrmizd — for theft, and another on the day Vahrām — on a capital charge, and it is not clear which one was imprisoned on the day Ōhrmizd and which one on the day Vahrām, and the warden of the prison declares that this one was imprisoned on the day Ōhrmizd for theft, and that one on the day Vahrām — on a capital charge. And as to (the prerogatives of the warden of a prison as regards) the identification of a name, then it (takes place) in this manner: one person named Mihr-Āturfarnbaγ is imprisoned — for theft, and another person named Kay-Āturfarnbaγ is imprisoned — on a capital charge, and it is not clear which of them is Mihr-Āturfarnbaγ (imprisoned) for theft, and which (is) Kay-Āturfarnbaγ imprisoned on a capital charge, and the warden of the prison declares: this is Mihr-Āturfarnbaγ who is imprisoned for theft, and that is Kay-Āturfarnbaγ, who is imprisoned on a capital charge. And the identification of the crime takes place in this manner: if one man (is imprisoned) for theft, and another one on a capital charge, and it is not clear which of them is imprisoned for theft and which one on a capital charge, and the warden declares that this one is imprisoned for theft and that one — on a capital charge.

A29, 6—7:

A supervisor of a town quarter/of a major highway (? *Cf.* "Glossary" *s. v.* *kōδpān* — *A. P.*) is competent to (give evidence such as): "I said to you and you heard/learned", and also to (give evidence such as): "the capital?/equivalent? shall go to you" [81].

A29, 7—9:

(Pat) nē xvēšīh ī vikāy yātakgōβ ut xvāstak kē pat xvēšīh ī pēšēmār (8) ān vikāy (ut) yātakgōβ. Ut dātaβar muhr/muhrak-iš [82] ō dātastān patigīrēnd andar ān ē ka patigīrēnd+ hač ān (9) vikāyīh ut yātakgōβīh pat ēvar dārišn.

A29, 9—**30**, 2:

Veh-Ōhmizd guft kū hamnāmīh ān bavēt (10) ka gōβēt kū ēn mērak Farraxv nām enyā pat ēn kū Farraxv nām Mihrēn pus nē (11) ēvar. Ut hamtanīh ⟨ut hamtanīh⟩ ān bavēt ka dātaβar gōβēt kū ēn tan ān ⟨ān⟩ Šahrevar (12) rōč markaržān vikāyīh apar dāt. Ut Farraxv-Zurvān nazdist+ guft kū pat-ič pit (13) ut deh pat ēvar. U-š pas guft kū nē ēvar čē pit ut deh pat āšnākīh ī (14) tan ēvar enyā tan pat kē pusīh nē ēvar. Pusānveh ī Āzātmartān guft kū pat pit ēvar. (15) Ut ka-č gōβēt kū mērak ī apar ēn dip nipišt ān ham ī apar (16) ēn dip nipišt ēvar. Vahrām guft kū man ōγōn sahist+ kū ōγōn bavēt (17) čiγōn Veh-Ōhrmizd guft u-m ān ī Pusānveh guft nē varravīt čē ka gōβēt (1) kū-š+ (Ms.: 'YKm) mērak tā apar ēn dip nipišt ān ham ī apar ēn dip nip[išt] narīh-ē(v) (?) ut mātakīh-ē(v) bavēt.

A30, 2—3:

Veh-Ōhrmizd ēn-ič guft kū Rōšn-Ōhrmizd guft dātaβar tan āšnāk (3) xvat kunišn ut harv čiš xvat dānišnīk kunišn.

A30, 3—5:

Ut Aparak guft kū parēžvān (4) pātixšāyōmand tan āšnāk kartan ut muhr patigriftan ut ka anī aδvēnak paytāk bavēt (5) parēžvān griftārōmand.

[LIII?] *

A30, 5—6:

Dar ī ⟨1 ī⟩ pat čiš ī nipišt ut ǎvašt (6) anī-č vāč ī uskārtak.

* This chapter carries no ordinal-number.

A29, 7—9:

(As regards the fact that) a witness (is) "not his"(?), (the competence to judge and to testify — *A. P.*) belongs to the legal representative; as regards (the fact that) a thing belongs to the plantiff, (the competence belongs to) that witness and the legal representative. And the judges ("the judge") accept his (= the witness' and the legal representative's — *A. P.*) seal/entitling document [82] in court; after (the documents and the titles confirmed by them — *A. P.*) have been accepted (by the judges), the evidence presented (by these persons) and their representation must be taken as competent (= not open to challenge).

A29, 9—**30**, 2:

Veh-Ōhrmizd has said, that identity/identification of name (takes place) when he declares: "the name of that man is Farraxv"; however, (the fact) that he is the son of Mihrēn does not reliably follow from (the fact) that his name is Farraxv. And identification of a person (lit.: "body" — *A. P.*) (takes place) when a judge declares: "this man here gave evidence regarding a capital offence on that day Šahrevar". And Farraxv-Zurvān (one of the commentators — *A. P.*) first said that one should also ascertain the father and the village (= the residence). Subsequently, he himself said that it is not (necessary) to ascertain (this), since (who is his) father and (from what) village can be established with certainty by means of the identification of the person, whereas (the identity) of the person cannot be established with certainty by means of the discovery of whose son he is. Pusānveh ī Āzātmartān has said, that (the identity of a person) is established with certainty by means of (the clarification of who) is the father. And likewise, when he declares: "a man is the one who wrote on this scroll ('letter, document')", (the person) who wrote on that scroll (= document) is also established with certainty thereby (according to the opinion of Pusānveh — *A. P.*). But Vahrām has said: "in my opinion the matter stands as stated by Veh-Ōhrmizd". And I too (= the compiler of the *Law-Book* — *A. P.*) do not trust the statement of Pusānveh, because, when he declares: "he is a man inasmuch as he wrote on that scroll (='document')" [lit.: "he should have been a man to write on this scroll" — *A. P.*], that person, the very one who wrote on the scroll, might have been either a man or a woman.

A30, 2—3:

Veh-Ōhrmizd said the same: that, as it was said by Rōšn-Ōhrmizd, the judge must perform the identification of the person himself, and he must investigate everything himself.

A30, 3—5:

And Aparak has said, that a *parēžvan* (*cf. supra* **A27**, 9—11 — *A. P.*) is entitled to establish the identity of a person and to accept a seal (= establish the authenticity of a document presented in court — *A. P.*). But if it becomes evident that (the things) stand otherwise (*i. e.*. if a mistake of the *parēžvān* is revealed — *A. P.*), then the *parēžvān* is subject to arrest ("must be seized").

[LIII?] *

A30, 5—6:

Chapter concerning that which is written and sealed, and other questions (deserving) investigation.

A30, 7—9:

Nipišt ut ăvašt kē hampačēn hač-iš dāt nē šāyēt ⟨ut⟩ ? stahmakīhā ut dušpātixšāy (8) ap(p)urēnd hampačēn dahišn. Ut pat xānak čiš bē paytākēnišn ut pat dātastān⁺ bē (9) nihišn ut ka šāyēt pat bōžišn dāštan rāδ ō xvēšāvandān apispārišn.

A30, 10—12:

Ka šōy ut zan pat ēv⁺ yāvar hač mart 1 apām stānēnd ān mart ān apām (11) hamaδvēn hač zan xvāst tuvān ut pat rāδēnišn ī dātastān dastaβarīh ī šōy andar (12) nē apāyēt.

A30, 12—16

Ka gōβēt kū Farraxv ēn yāmak apātixšāyīhā hač man stat (13) ut burt ut ān yāmak man xvēš ut dārišn ut pat ān čiγōn Farraxv stat ut burt Farraxv (14) dārēt ut hač Farraxv hačašmānd bavēt pat ān hačašmānd pat graβ vičīr kunišn čē (15) xvāstak nē nāmčištīk ut ka xvāstak nāmčištīk hē vičīr kunišn kū dārišn (16) apāč kunišn⁺.

A30, 16—17:

Ka hač zamīk bun-xvēšān xvēš u-š pat bar graβakāndār ziyān (16) vičārišn *.

A30, 17—**31**, 3:

Ka pēšēmār pat apām ut vaxš pasēmār hamēmār ut pēšēmār (1) pasēm[ār harv] 2 xvastūk hend kū vaxš ī tā Farraxv ō Asūristān šut vičārt (2) ut pēšēmār⁺ (Ms.: pasēmār) patkārēt kū Farraxv sāl ēvak ō Asūristān šut (Ms.: šavēt) pasēmār (3) paytākēnišn.

A31, 3—5:

Pat rāδēnišn ī stūr ka (Ms.: MNW = kē) ān ī sažāktar nē mat ēstēt hast (kē) ōγōn (4) nipišt kū mērak pat ān kustak ī Xvarāsān u-š āmatan nē kāmēt mērak nē (5) pat bun ut pat katām gyāk būt nē āšnāk.

A31, 5—8:

Pat rāδēnišn ī apar gumārtan (6) apāyistan ī katak-bānūk dūtak sardār (ut) kart ī katak-bānūk gātār čiš ⟨ut⟩ apar (7) gumārtan ētōn nipišt kū katak-bānūk bē čiγōn-iš apēdastaβarīhā tan pat gāt (8) ō kas dāt guft enyā-š sardār nēst ut apar-ič katak-bānūk sardār gumārtan.

* This article has reached us in a damaged form. Part of the text has apparently been left out by the copyist.

A30, 7—9:

(If) a written and sealed (document) of which it is not proper to give a copy, is forcibly and impermissibly carried off, a copy should be given. And the property found in a house should be declared and deposited in court, and transferred to the kinsmen for usufruct whenever this can / may (be done).

A30, 10—12:

If a man and wife jointly ("as one, in one instance") receive a loan ("debt") from a person, then that person is entitled to claim (the settlement) in full of this debt from the wife, and (the wife) does not need to obtain from her husband the title to conduct (the case regarding this).

A30, 12—16:

If he declares: "Farraxv obtained this vessel from me unlawfully and carried (it) away, whereas this vessel belongs to me and I should possess it, but since Farraxv received and carried (it) away, Farraxv possesses (it)", and the case is suspended / defaulted (because of Farraxv's non-appearance in court); then a decision as to (the furnishing of) a security must be rendered in connexion with the contumacy, since the thing has not been determined with precision. Had the thing been precisely determined, a decision as to the return of the possession (of the thing, to the plaintiff — *A. P.*) should be rendered.

A30, 16—17:

If from the land which belongs to the original (= principal) owners but (whose) revenue (belongs to) a creditor, (... ... ...), then the loss should be reimbursed *.

A30, 17—**31**, 3:

If a plaintiff is carrying on a suit with the respondent over a matter of debt and interest, and [both of] them — the plaintiff and the respondent — admit that the interest which (accrued) before Farraxv's departure to Babylon has been paid; but the plaintiff (the ms. has "respondent" presumably through the copyist's mistake — *A. P.*) protests: "it is (already) a year (= a year has passed) (since) Farraxv left for Babylon!"; (then) the respondent must make a declaration concerning this.

A31, 3—5:

In connexion with a case regarding the appointment of a *stūr* (and) when the one most suitable (to assume the *stūr*ship) has not appeared, some have written: "(this) man is in the province of Xvarāsān (= Khorasan) and he does not wish to appear", (and): "(this) man is not in his principal residence, and it is not known in what place (he is to be found)".

A31, 5—8:

In connexion with a case regarding the necessity to appoint the mistress of the house (= the widow — *A. P.*) as the guardian of a family (and) regarding the cohabitation of the mistress of the house — the following has been written concerning the appointment: "except where she has declared that she entered into illicit cohabitation with a certain man, the mistress of a house is not the guardian of the family, and a guardian should be appointed also over the mistress of the house herself".

A31, 9—10:

Yuvān-Yam nāmak kart kū ōγōn čiγōn Nēv / Vēv-Gušnasp guft ka mart ut zan patvand (10) rāst mart gumārt stūrīh nē kanišn.

A31, 10—15:

Māhveh nāmak kart kū pat kartan (11) ut daštan ōγōn apar āβurt kū ka mart pat stūrīh gumārt u-š ziyān ī (12) pat dūtak kartan nē paytāk ka-č pas hač ān xvah ī ān mart pat gumārt apāyistan ī (13) xvah pat ān stūrīh andar patkārēt patkārišn ī xvah pat ān stūrīh nē (14) patigīrišn ut stūrīh pat mart pat raft dārišn ut xvāstak pat stūrīh ō (15) xvah nē apispārišn ut ān stūrīh pat ham mart bē hilišn.

A31, 15—**32**, 2:

Ka mart kē (16) dārišn ī pat anšahrīkīh pat mart 1 patkārēt kū(-m hač) xvatāy āzāt hišt hom (17) ut āzāt-hišt Pūsak dārēt apāk Pūsak pat saxvan-nāmak dātastān bun kartan rāδēnēt (11) aδak šāyēt ka nē pat xvatāy āšnāk kunēnd ut dātastān pat yātakgōβ xvāhēt (2) ka hačašmānd bavēt uskārtan apāyēt.

[LIV?] *

A32, 2:

Dar ī guft apāk guft.

A32, 3:

(Apāk) anī guft kū pat kartak žīvandak (drahnāδ)? anattān nē kunēnd.

A32, 4:

Apāk anī guft kū bavandak anattān [or: bandak (ka / ī) anattān — *A. P.*] pat kār ōh apispārišn.

A32, 4—5:

Ut apāk anī guft (5) kū ka mātakvar anattān apāk pāyandān.

A32, 5—7:

Apāk anī guft kū ka pus 1 (6) pat tōžišn ī pitarān hamēmārōmand anattān bē bavēt apāk apārīk xvāstak(7)dārān rāδēnišn ī var⁺ ō / ōh bavēt.

* This chapter carries no ordinal-number.

A31, 9—10:

Yuvān-Yam has written (the following): "in accordance with the opinion given by Nēv / Vēv-Gušnasp, if the kinsmen of the husband and wife have appointed a just man as *stūr*, then the *stūr*ship should not be dissolved / cancelled (lit.: "is not subject to destruction")".

A31, 10—15:

Māhveh has written that (the following) took place (as regards) the problem of an appointment (to *stūr*ship — *A. P.*) and the preservation (of a *stūr*ship — *A. P.*): if a man has been appointed *stūr* and it has not been discovered that he caused any damage to the family (= to the estate of the dead man's succession — *A. P.*); then, if the sister of that man (whose *stūr* he is — *A. P.*) subsequently brings action regarding the nessessity of appointing the sister (*i. e.*. herself — *A. P.*) as *stūr*, then the claim to the *stūr*ship made by the sister should not be accepted (for investigation), and the *stūr*ship is to be considered as having gone to (that) man, and the estate should not be given to the sister as a *stūr*-possession, and this *stūr*ship should be left to that man.

A31, 15—**32**, 2:

If a man who contests his ownership by another man as (his) slave (declares): "(my) master manumitted me (from slavery), but the manumission document is in the hands of Pūsak", then if (he) together with Pūsak will testify for the record (in order to) open the case; then the trial may (or "should, must" — *A. P.*) be declared in default in the case where the master cannot be brought to admit (the manumission) (in court), and he (= the master? the freedman?) demands legal proceedings with ("by means of, through") a legal representative. This is to be examined (carefully).

[LIV?] *

A32, 2:

Chapter in which one statement follows another.

A32, 3:

Besides that it is said, that according to judicial rules (or "in judicial procedure" — *A. P.*), (a man) is not declared insolvent for life (?).

A32, 4:

Besides other things it is said, that one who is completely insolvent [or "a slave if he is insolvent" — *A. P.*] should be handed over for labout (to pay off his debt).

A32, 4—5:

Besides other (things) it is said, that if the principal contractor is insolvent, (then it is) together with the warrantor [83].

A32, 5—7:

Together with that it is said, that if a son participating in a case regarding the settlement of inheritance-debts is (found to be) insolvent, then (he) together with the other heirs will have ("it falls to his lot / takes place; occurs, happens") to undergo the ordeal procedure ("oath-taking" — *A. P.*).

A32, 7—8:

Ut anī guft kū pasēmār tā dātastān hač (8) rāδēnišn mānēt pat yut dātastān pēšēmār hamēmārīh kartan nē pātixšāy.

A32, 9—13:

Apāk anī guft kū ka andar rāδēnišn ī dātastān pus purnāy bavēt dūtak (10) sardār dātastān rāδēnītan nē tuvān ut pasēmār (nē)? pātixšāy ka dūtak sardār hač (11) rāδēnišn bē nē hilēt ut hampačēn stānēt ut pat vatxvāh andar dūtak sardār (12) vičīr xvāhēt ēt rāδ⁺ čē dūtak sardār nūn nē pēšēmār ut andar dūtak sardār ēt (13) dātastān hač rāδēnišn mānd.

A32, 13—15:

Ut anī guft kū ka gōβēt kū tā man sahēt ēn (14) xvāstak tō xvēš pat vēšistīh tā žīvandakīh ut pat kamistīh tā sahēt dāt (15) bavēt.

A32, 15—17:

Apāk anī guft kū ka gōβēt kū tā rētak purnāy bavēt tō xvēš (16) pat vēšistīh tā 15 sāl guft bavēt. Ut Pērōž ⟨i⟩ guft kū ka rētak andar (17) purnāyīh mīrēt xvāstak hakarč apāč nē āyēt.

A32, 17—**33**, 2:

Ut apāk ān guft kū (1) ka gōβēt kū tā tō sahēt pat task az dārom tā ān tan ayāp xvāstakdār ī ān (2) tan kē pat task bē dāt nē sahēt kunēnd apāč kartan nē pātixšay.

A33, 3—7:

Ut apāk anī guft kū ka Farraxv andar Mihrēn kart kū ēn xvāstak tā apāk (4) tō pat pēšēmārīh gōβom tō hač-iš (nē) vizāyom pat vēšistīh tā žīvandakīh ī (5) Mihrēn ayāp Farraxv. Ut ka apāk tō nē nipēsēt pat vēšistīh tā žīvandakīh ī (6) Farraxv guft bavēt čē gōβišn pat patvand nē ravēt bē ān ē⁺ ka yātakgōβ (7) gumārēt.

A33, 7—9:

Ka mart 1 apāk pus⁺ (Ms.: 'B = pit) patmān kart kū xvāstak ī tō sahēt tō (8) xvēš ut čand pus hast ēvak sahišn paytākēnēt ut apārīk dušnīrmat ī (9) apārīk rāδ sahišn nē kunēnd.

A32, 7—8:

And this is said, that until the end of a legal case, the respondent is not entitled to bring another suit against the plaintiff [84].

A32, 9—13:

Beside other (things) it is said, that if a son comes of age during the course of a case, then the guardian of the family is not entitled (to continue) to conduct the case, but the respondent may (not) dismiss/release the guardian from the conduct of the case, nor obtain a copy of the document, nor ("and") demand a judgement (of the court) as regards(= against — *A. P.*) the guardian of the family (condemning him) for malice (= for malicious litigation — *A. P.*), because the guardian of the family now is no (longer the) plaintiff, and for the guardian of the family the case is finished.

A32, 13—15:

It is said that if he declares (this): "(this thing) belongs to you as long as I please", then in the best case ("at maximum") it is conveyed to the end of his life, and in the worst ("at minimum") — for the time that it will please him (= the conveyer).

A32, 15—17:

Besides other (things) it has been said, that if he declares (this): "(a thing) belongs to you until the boy comes of age", then in the best case ("at maximum") the statement regards ("it is said, it is declared") a transfer with a term of fifteen years. And Pērōz has said, that if the boy dies before coming of age, then the thing shall never return (to the declarer, the conveyer—*A. P.*).

A32, 17—**33**, 2:

And moreover it is said, that if he declares (this): "I shall lease (this) as long as it pleases you", then until that man, or the heir of the man who gave it out on lease declares: "(I am) not pleased!", he is not entitled to return the possession rented [or: "he is not entitled to revoke the lease agreement" — *A. P.*].

A33, 3—7:

Besides other (things) it is said, that if Farraxv and Mihrēn make the following agreement: "I shall not deprive you of this thing until I bring suit against you", then in the best case ("at maximum") (the thing is conveyed) until the end of Mihrēn's or Farraxv's life. But if he does not write: "against you"; then in the best case, this is declared (regarding the transfer of the thing) until the end of Farraxv's (= the conveyer's) life, since (this) declaration does not extend to the descendants/kinsmen except in the case where he appoints a legal representative.

A33, 7—9:

If a man has made (the following) agreement with (his) son: "(whatever) thing pleases you belongs to you", but there are several sons (in the family), then (only) one (of them) declares his choice of a thing, whereas the others do not make a declaration of choice since they ("the others") are deprived of this advantage (lit.: "because of the disadvantage of the others" — *A. P.*).

A33, 9—11:

Ut anī guft kū ka Farraxv ō Mihrēn (10) gōβēt kū tā ēn vičīr ō bōžišn dārēt tō hač ēn+ xvāstak nē vizāyom aδak-iš (11) andar Mihrēn ut dastaβarān ut xvāstakdārān ēt ō bōžišn āβarišn.

A33, 11—14:

Apāk anī (12) guft kū ka gōβēt kū tā pat pēšēmārīh gōβom tō hač ēn+ xvāstak nē (13) vizāyom aδak-iš andar ōy (ut) frazand xvāstakdār ī ōy ī hamēmār pat pēšēmārīh (14) gōβišn.

A33, 14—15:

Ut apāk anī guft kū ka nipēsēt kū xvāstak ka tō xvāhēh ō tō (15) dahom xvāhišn hač ōy ut xvāstakdār kunišn.

A33, 15—17:

Ut anī guft kū vičīr-ēv ī pat 3 bahr (16) ēv bahr ō Mihrēn ut apārīk+ ō Farraxv dahēnd mātakvar Farraxv dārīsn ut (ō) Mihrēn hampačēn dahišn.

A33, 17—**34**, 1:

Apāk anī guft kū ka stūr pat bahr mar bē dahēt kāmak ī (1) pat bahr kart hakar nēm ayāp kem dahēt pat rāt ut hakar vēš+ bavēt pat kas.

A34, 2—3:

Ut anī guft kū ka gōβēt kū-m ēn vičīr ō tō dāt aδak-iš gil (3) ut nāmak dāt bavēt.

A34, 3—6:

Ut apāk anī guft kū ka gōβēt kū-m ēn (4) dastkart hač harv čē-š andar hammis ō tō dāt vičīr-ēv ī pat ēn dastkart (5) ēstēt ut xvāstak-ič ⟨l⟩ ī pat anī gyāk pat ān vičīr šāyēt xvāst dāt (6) bavēt.

A33, 9—11:

And another one said (or: "and something else has been said") that if Farraxv declares to Mihrēn: "as long as you (pl.) are entitled to enjoy use of this contract (lit.: 'as long as you have this contract for use' — *A. P.*), I shall not deprive you (sg.) of this thing", then he must convey this (thing) for the use of Mihrēn and of his (Mihrēn's) empowered agents ("mandataries, representatives") as well as of his heirs.

A33, 11—14:

Besides this it is said that if he declares (the following): "I shall not deprive you of this thing until I bring a legal claim", then the claim (*i. e.*. the one stipulated by this declaration of the conveyer and which gives him the right to take back the thing — *A. P.*) must be brought against the contractor himself ("against him"), or against the son and heir of this contractor.

A33, 14—15:

Besides other (things) it is said, that if he writes: "I shall convey (this) thing to you when you demand it", then the demand must be made eiher to him (= to the author of the given written declaration — *A. P.*) or to his heir.

A33, 15—17:

It is also said, that the original copy of a document concerning a contract (by which) one third (of a thing) is conveyed to Mihrēn and the rest to Farraxv must be held by Farraxv, whereas a copy should be given to Mihrēn.

A33, 17—**34**, 1:

Together with this it is said, that if he conveys (a thing, an estate) to a (foundation) for *stūr*ship "as a share" (= he conveys — as a *stūr*-possession — a certain portion only of a thing or estate as the whole — *A. P.*), and if he conveys half or less (of the thing) in accordance with his declaration of will regarding the portion; then (the original copy of the document relating to the transfer with intention of instituting a *stūr*-foundation must be handed over) to the establisher of the foundation ("the donor"), but if it is more (than half), (the original copy of the document should be handed over) to that man (= the *stūr* — *A. P.*).

A34, 2—3:

It is also said, that if he declares: "I have handed this document over to you", then (according to this declaration) (both) the seal ("the clay") and the document ("the written text") are handed over to him [85].

A34, 3—6:

Besides this it is said, that if he makes a declaration (in this manner): "I convey this *dastkart* to you together with everything that it contains", then (any) document of contract relating to this *dastkart*, and anything (located) in another place but liable to claim according to this document of contract, should also be considered as conveyed (as a result of this declaration of transfer — *A. P.*).

A34, 6—9:

Ut anī guft kū pat markaržān ēvar pursišn-nāmak ōh kunišn. Apāk (7) anī apar Aβyātkār hampaččēn ēv ī pat-ič muhr ī Veh-Šāhpuhr ī magupatān magupat (8) būt ăvišt pat-ič gōβišn (ī) magupatān magupat mart ēv pursišn-nāmak pat-iš ut pat (9) sar pātifrās kartan apāyītan rāδ nipišt.

A34, 9—10:

Ut anī guft kū pat yazdān-(10)dušmanīh ut xvatāy-dušmanīh ut ahramōγīh pursišn-nāmak ōh kunišn.

A34, 10—13:

Apāk anī apar (11) hampačēn ham mart ⟨rāδ⟩ pat gōβišn ī magupatān magupat nipišt kū yazdān-dušmānīh ut xvatāy-(12)dušmanīh[+] ut mihrōdružīh ut ahramōγīh ut družīh ut anāst-gōβišnīh (rāδ) aβyātkār (13) kart (apāyēt) u-š ōy vināს rāδ pursišn-nāmak pat-iš kunišn[+].

A34, 13—16:

Ut anī guft kū mart kē (14) pat markaržān pursišn-nāmak pat-iš kunišn ka pat pursišn-nāmak vināskārtar (15) paytāk būt ⟨rāδ⟩ vinās-ič ī nē markaržān nipišt ⟨an⟩ āhōk nēst. Apāk anī apar (16) aβyātkar yumāy vinās ī markaržān anī-č vinās rāδ pat ān aδvēnak nipišt ēstēt.

A34, 17—**35**, 3:

Ut anī guft kū pat vinās kē pursišn-nāmak pat-iš kunišn āšnākīh-ič ī šahr (1) ut dusrav[īh pat s]ar andar vičōδišn dārišn čē pat-ič pursišn-nāmak ī hač pēš ōrōn kart (2) ōγōn nipišt kū mērak dusrav ut andar šahr vatmartīhā raft ēstēt (3) dusravīh-ič čim ī kartan apāyistan ī pursišn-nāmak rāδ frāč patigīrēnd.

A35, 4—5:

Apāk anī pat vas šahr ut gyāk nūn-ič pat pursišn-nāmak nipēsēnd kū mērak (5) pat kartan ī ān vinās pātram dusrav.

A35, 5—6:

Ut anī guft kū druvistīh ī 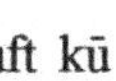 (?) ut dāt ī (6) šahr rāδ vināhišn-ič pātifrās ut ōkārišn kunišn.

A34, 6—9:

It is also said that a record of the trial (or: "interrogation") must be drawn up ("made") for the sake of the trustworthiness / authenticity (of the decisions, sentences) in cases of capital offences. Furthermore, in one of the copies of the *Aβyātkār* ["*Memorandum*"] sealed with the seal of Veh-Šāhpuhr the *magupatān-magupat*, some one has written, from the words of the *magupatān-magupat*, regarding the indispensability of drawing up a record of the trial / interrogation in such a case ("as regards this") and of joining it to (the document containing the sentence of) the punishment.

A34, 9—10:

And another (thing) has been said: (that) a record of the trial (or: "of the interrogation") should be drawn up ("made") in (cases) of evil intention against the gods, and of evil intention (malice, hostility) against (one's) master, and in (matters of) heresy.

A34, 10—13:

And besides other (things), in the copy (of the *Memorandum of Veh-Šāhpuhr*; *cf. supra* **A34**, 6—9 — *A. P.*), this man has written from the words of the *magupatān-magupat* (Veh-Šāhpuhr), that a memorandum (must) be drawn up (= kept; a record drawn up — *A. P.*) in (cases) of evil intention / hostility toward the gods or (one's) master, (or those) of breach of contract, of heresy, falsehood or slander. And (so) a record of the trial / interrogation should be drawn up as regards these offences.

A34, 13—16:

And this is said: that a man — concerning whose accusation on a capital charge a record of interrogation / trial has been drawn up — is not guilty of the fact that he has been shown to be a greater criminal according to the record of trial interrogation, but his offence has not been specified ("written down") as a capital one (in the verdict). Moreover the same is also written in the *Memorandum* (*of Veh-Šāhpuhr*) about other crimes as well as about cases dealing with capital offences.

A34, 17—**35**, 3:

It is also said, that the reputation (enjoyed by the accused) in the *šahr* and (any) evil rumour (concerning him) should be included in the investigation (= taken into consideration — *A. P.*) at a criminal (trial) requiring the drawing up of a record of interrogation for it is also written in the record(s) of interrogation drawn up from ancient times to the present that: "(this) man has a bad reputation in the city / *šahr* and passes for an evil man". Similarly a bad reputation is taken as a basis ("cause") for the necessity of drawing up a record of the trial / interrogation.

A35, 4—5:

Besides other (things), in many cities, *šahr*s, localities (the following) is still written down in records of interrogation / trial: "(this) man has a bad reputation in the neighbourhood as (the one who) committed this crime".

A35, 5—6:

It is also said, that for the sake of security ... (*cf. infra* **A35**, 9—11) and of the law / justice of the realm, as well as (because of) the damage (inflicted) [86], (a man ?) should be subjected to punishment and exile (or "isolation", lit.: "removal" — *A. P.*).

A35, 6—9:

Apāk anī guft kū (7) zan kē šōy pat aṯvadāt ut daštānmāh vičārtan vināskār ka duž (8) kunēt duž nē zan bē šōy bavēt. Ut pas ka-š gīrēnd aδvēn (ī) šahr (9) rāδ bē drōšišn.

A35, 9—11:

Ut apāk anī guft kū mart ōy ī pat markaržān varōmand (10) kart ēstēt ka-č-iš avināsīh dānist (Ms.: dānēt) aδak-ič-iš [illegible] (?) ī šahr rāδ vāč hač-iš (11) nē gīrišn ut avi-š ⟨avi-š⟩ nē dahišn.

A35, 11—12:

Ut anī guft kū andar dūtak zāt ān čē (12) čakar frazand bavēt.

A35, 12—13:

Apāk anī pat vas gyāk pat nipišt ut ăvašt ī dastaβarān (13) patigīrēnd frazand ī čakarīhā nipišt ēstāt.

A35, 13—14:

Ut apāk anī vas ōstaβarān (14) guft kū pat kartak andar dūtak zāt pat frazand dāšt.

A35, 14—16:

Ut apāk anī apar (15) handarz ī ham Veh-Šāhpuhr pat gōβišn ī Veh-Šāhpuhr nipišt ēstēt kū ān ī stūrīh ī (16) nām šīrēnvar rāδ man frazand ut aβγātak bavēnd ēn čiš ōγōn hēβ kunēnd.

A35, 16—**36**, 3:

Ut anī (17) guft kū Mihr-Narsēh ī vazurg framātār ātaxš 2 rāδ guft kū-m pat (1) sardārīh ēvak mērak ut ēvak mērak dastaβar kart Mahraspand ī rat būt [vičī]r kart kū (2) ātaxš+ sardārīh pat patvand ī avēšān mart nē ravēt. Ut Yuvān-Yam guft (3) kū pat patvand bē ravēt.

A36, 3—6:

Apāk anī apar (h)andarz ī Āturpāt ī Zartuštān (4) ⟨būt⟩ ī magupatān magupat būt ⟨ī⟩ pat gōβišn ī Āturpat ⟨ī⟩ ātaxš+ rāδ nipišt (5) kū hač frazandān ī man ōy pātimār/dastaβar kē mart pahlom hāt (Ms.: [illegible] = [illegible]). Ut anī Pērōž ⟨ī⟩ guft (6) kū ōy ēvak bavēt.

A35, 6—9:

Besides other (things) it is said, that if a wife — whose husband is accused of an *at̠vadāt* (offence) and of (the offence) of sexual relations with a woman during her menstruation — commits a theft, then the thief is (= is considered to be) not the wife but the husband. And furthermore, when he is seized, he should be subject to branding in accordance with ("for, for the sake of") the custom of the *šahr*.

A35, 9—11:

And together with this it is said, that a man for whom an ordeal trial is ordained (on the accusation) of (his) having committed a capital offence, may not perform the prayer ritual and should not be allowed to participate in the *Drōn-yašt* ritual, because of the custom/regulations (?) (in force in) the *šahr*, even in the case where his innocence is known.

A35, 11—12:

It is also said that the one "born in the family" (is) a *čakar*-son.

A35, 12—13:

Together with that, the designation "*čakar*-son" figures ("was written down") in many places in sealed (documents) accepted by persons (in positions) of authority (or: "official persons") [87].

A35, 13—14:

And also many authorities have said that, in accordance with the regulation (or: "in judicial procedure" — *A. P.*), (the one) "born in the family" is equated with son.

A35, 14—16:

And besides other (things) it is written in the *Testament* of Veh-Šāhpuhr, word for word as Veh-Šāhpuhr said it: "let him who for the sake of greater service to my name (= lineage — *A. P.*) shall become my child and grandchild do this thing (*i. e.*. a disposition made in the will — *A. P.*) in this manner".

A35, 16—**36**, 3:

And it is also said, that the *vazurg-framātār* Mihr-Narsēh declared as regards two Fires (=Fire-temples): "I have made a disposition regarding the appointment of one man as trustee over one (Fire-temple), and another (man) over the other". Mahraspand, the *rat*, rendered [a decision] according to which the trusteeship over a Fire-temple should not be transmitted (by inheritance) to the descendants of these two persons. But Yuvān-Yam has said that (the trusteeship) should pass to the descendants [88].

A36, 3—6:

Together with this, from the words of Āturpāt ī Zartuštān, (this) is written about a Fire-temple in the will of (the same) Āturpāt ī Zartuštān, who was the *magupatān magupat*: "the one of my sons who proves to be the most worthy (= pious) man (must be) designated as trustee". And Pērōž has also said that he is one alone (= only one of the sons becomes trustee — *A. P.*).

A36, 6—12:

Apāk anī guft kū Āturpāt ī Martbūtān (ī magupatān magupat) būt pat (7) ruvān ī Āturpāt ātaxš nišāst ut ātaxš pat sardārīh ī ōy kē Dātxvaš ī ham (8) Āturpāt xvah ut zan būt dāštan guft^{+} (ut) dāštan rāδ framān dāt (9) ut pat ān dastaβarīh ātaxš nišāst ut ⟨Dātxvaš⟩ ān ātaxš frāč hač Dātxvaš (10) Farraxvyān ut frāč hač Farraxvyān anī mart dāštan rāδ guft. Ut pat muhr ī Rōšn-Ōhrmizd (ī) (11) ātur ī Ērān-Xvarreh-Xusrav ⟨ī⟩ čašān būt GT'k ǎvašt ut framān-ič ī Āturpāt (12) pat 'wšk'n (Ms.: [illegible]) ō GT'k burt.

A36, 12—16:

Apāk anī guft kū xvāstak ī-šān kart kū (13) ōy kē Farraxv xvēš būt gōβēt xvēš ut Farraxv tā 10 sāl mart 1 ut pas hač (14) 10 sāl mart 1 xvēš būt (rāδ) guft ōγōn dārišn čiγōn xvēš būt rāδ gōβišn (15) guft. Būt kē guft kū tā 10 sāl ut pas-ič hač 10 sāl avēšān mart pat (16) ākanēn dārišn.

A36, 16—**37**, 1:

Apāk (17) anī apar (h)andarz ī ham Veh-Šāhpuhr pat dāt ī dastkart pat gōβišn ī ham Veh-Šāhpuhr(1) nipišt kū hač anšahrīk ī-š andar mānēnd ham(m)is ōγōn hēβ bavēt.

A37, 1—15:

Ut anī guft (2) kū apar ōy baγ Husrav ī Kavātān mart-ē(v) Dandān (? Ms.: KK') nām būt mart-ē(v) Āturtōxm (3) nām būt pat zamīk hāvand pat uzdēs-čār dāšt čiγōn pat^{+} (Ms.: šn) framān ut dastaβarīh ī (4) magupatān uzdēs hač-iš kand (ut) ātur(r)ōk-ē(v) pat-iš nišāst ka ān ātur(r)ōk-ē(v) (5) apāč ō dīvān ī kartakān kāmist kart hač a-pat-ziyān ī Dandān ut Āturtōxm ān (6) zamīk hač ān ātur(r)ōk-ē(v) (ham(m)is ān Dandān) ut ān Āturtōxm u-šān frazandān aβγātakān dāštan rāδ framān (dāt). (7) Dandān ut Āturtōxm ān ātur(r)ōk pat Varahrānīh ō dātgāh nišāst ut ān ātaxš (8) pat sardārīh tā Dandān ut Āturtōxm žīvandak būt Dandān ut Āturtōxm dāšt ut vitart (9) Dandān ut Āturtōxm Burzak ī Artaxšahr-Xvarreh magupat būt pat ēn kū pat framān (10) dastaβarīh ān ātaxš pat sardārīh ⟨ān (ī) Dandān nišāst⟩ hamaδvēn frazandān ut aβγātak (11) duxtdāt-ič dārišn vičīr (ut) Vātayār vičīr kart Dāt-Farraxv ī Dāt-Ōhrmizd (1) mōγān (12) (h)andarzpat būt pat ēn kū hakar avēšān kē ān ātaxš nišāst

A36, 6—12:

Together with this it is said, that Āturpāt ī Martbūtān (who) was ... (the title — *magupatān magupat* — has been left out by the copyist — *A. P.*) established a Fire (= Fire-temple/altar) "for the soul" of Āturpāt (= the *magupatān-magupat* Āturpāt ī Zartuštān; *cf. supra* **A36**, 3, *et infra* **A38**, 10 — A.P,), and he declared and gave the order of transfer of this Fire to the trusteeship of Dātxvaš the sister and wife of the (above)mentioned Āturpāt ī Zartuštān. And the Fire was established according to this disposition, and he made a declaration regarding the transfer of this Fire to Farraxvyān after Dātxvaš ('death) and to another person after Farraxvyan. And the testamentary document was sealed with the seal of Rōšn-Ōhrmizd who was the superior (or: "supervisor") of the Ērān-Xvarreh-Xusrav Fire-temple, and the disposition of Āturpāt regarding *'wšk'n* (= the foundation "for the soul" — *A. P.*) was also included ("brought") into the testamentary document.

A36, 12—16:

Together with that, it is said that as regards a thing — of which it has been declared that it shall belong ("belongs") to the person of whom Farraxv will say that it is his (= the one whom Farraxv designates as the empowered holder of the title to it — *A. P.*), and (of which) Farraxv declares that it shall belong to one man until ten years have elapsed and to another man after the ten years have passed — it shall be held in the same order as he made the declaration regarding the possession (of this thing). But some have said that these two men should hold (this thing) jointly as well before as after the passage of ten years.

A36, 16—**37**, 1:

In the *Testament* of the same Veh-Šāhpuhr (this is also) written from the words of the above-mentioned Veh-Šāhpuhr, alongside other things concerning the transfer of a *dastkart*: "let it be conveyed in this manner together with the slaves living/dwelling in it (= in the *dastkart*)!".

A37, 1—15:

It is also said, (that) under (our) late sovereign Xusrav son on Kavāt, one man named Dandān (or: "Kakā") and another named Āturtōxm held equal (lots) of land under an idol-shrine, when the temple of the idols was dug up from that place ("from there") by the order and with the sanction of the *magupat*s, and a Fire-altar was set up there instead. When it was desired to transfer this Fire-altar to the supervision of the department of pious foundations, it was ordered that this land (together) with this altar should be conveyed to the trusteeship of (this Dandān) and this Āturtōxm and their sons and grandsons — so that Dandān and Āturtōxm should not suffer any loss because of this. Dandān and Āturtōxm set up this altar in the temple of the Varahrān Fire. And as long as Dandān and Āturtōxm were alive, Dandān and Āturtōxm kept this Fire under their trusteeship. But after the death of Dandān and Āturtōxm, Burzak, the *magupat* of Artaxšahr-Xvarreh (rendered) a decision regarding (the fact that) through the title (given by) this order, (their) sons, grand-sons, and (their) successors, born from an *epikleros*-daughter, should hold this Fire as trustees in the same manner (or: "fully, entirely", or: "on the same basis") and Vātayār drew up the document. Dāt-Farraxv son of Dāt-Ōhrmizd, the *(h)andarzpat* of the Magi (rendered the decisardārīh ī (13) ān ātaxš rāδ čiš framān nē dāt ān ī Dandān nišāst hamē(v) hač frazandān (14) ut aβyātakān ī Dandān ut ān ī Āturtōxm nišāst hamē(v) hač frazandān (ut) aβyātakān (ī) Āturtōxm (15) ān ī meh (ut) veh dārišn ut nāmak kart ut ǎvašt.

A37, 15—**38**, 4:

Apāk anī guft kū xvāstak ī (16) framān būt pat āzātīh ut xvēšīh ō mart dāt(an) ān mart u-šān frazandān (17) aβyātakān pat āzātīh ut xvēšīh dāštan ut xvēš rāδ varz ut āpātānīh apar(1) kartan (pātixšāy) ut ān mart hamaδvēn ān xvāstak pat yutākīh ī hač frazandān dāštan ut bē (2) dātan ōγōn pātixšāy čiγōn apārīk-ič xvāstak ut būt asrōš kē andar patkārt⁺ (3) kū xvāstak ī pat ān aδvēnak pat apasēk ī pitarān apāč nē kunišn čē ō-č (4) frazandān dāt ēstēt bē pat kartak pat apasēk ī pitaran (apāč) ōh⁺ kart.

A38, 4—6:

Ut anī guft (5) kū ka gōβēt kū-m xvāstak sāl ēvak pat Fravartīkān xrīt ō duxt (6) dāt ān ī pat panǰak ī Ahunavait gāh xrīt pus xvēš.

A38, 6—12:

Apāk anī ham (7) aβyātkār hampaččēn ī pat-ič muhr (ī) magupatān magupat pat gōβišn (ī) magupatān magupat (8) nipišt kū hakar Yazdkart andar *satō.zim-* ī dahom pat pañǰāhak ī pēš būt (9) xvatāyīh-ič ōy baγ Anōšakruvān pitarān amāh frahist ut ān ī andar ān *satō.zim-* būt. (10) Ut hakar pat panǰāhak ī pas būt Hudāt-ič ut Farnbaγ ut Āturbōžēt (ut) Āturpāt ī Zartuštān (11) andar ān *satō.zim-* pat pātixšāyīh ēstāt hend ka ōγōn čiγōn nipišt (12) ēstēt panǰāhak ī pēš ān guft bavēt ī aptom uzīt⁺.

A38, 12—16:

Anī guft (13) kū ōy ī yātūk xvāstak ī-š hast ka-šān yātūkīh ōst pat rat ēstēt (14) ut ka-šān marnǰēnišn kart ō ōy kē marnǰēnišn andar kart ut ka-š vikāyīh (15) apar dahēnd ut vinās andar kē kart pat nāmčišt nē paytāk ō vikāyān ap(p)ār (16) ut zandīkīh (ōγōn čiγōn) yātūkīh.

sion) that if the persons who established this Fire made no disposition as to the trusteeship of this Fire, then that which was established by Dandān [89] should be always (or: "invariably") under the trusteeship of (one) of Dandān's sons and descendants, and that which was established by Āturtōxm should be always (under the trusteeship) (of one) of the children and descendants of Āturtōxm, and specifically of the one who is the eldest and most pious of them; and he drew up and sealed the documents.

A37, 15—**38**, 4:

Together with that, it is said (as regards) a plot of land concerning which a disposition was made for its transfer to a person as an hereditary and personal share, that this person and his children and descendants (= sons and grandsons) (are entitled to hold (it) on the basis of a personal inheritance title [90], and to work (it) and build (on it) for themselves. And this man is entitled to possess this plot ("thing") separately from his sons, and to alienate ("convey") it in the same manner (= under the same conditions) as (he is entitled to dispose — *A. P.*) of the rest of (his) possessions (having the same title, *i. e.*. that of an inheritance fund — *A. P.*). But an unduteous ("disobedient") one disputed this in court (and asserted) that the plot of land (received) on such a basis (or: "of this type" — *A. P.*) might not be taken away and returned (to the royal treasury; *cf. supra* **A27**, 13—**28**, 3 — *A. P.*) for (failure to pay) an indebtedness inherited from the father (lit.: "against the fathers' liabilities"), since it (= the plot) was also conveyed to the sons. However, according to judicial norms (or: "according to the court judgement"), (the possession) was taken (from him) for (failure to pay) an inherited debt.

A38, 4—6:

It is also said, that if he declares: "I have conveyed to (my) daughter the thing that I bought a year (ago) in the (five days of) Fravartīkān", then that (thing) which was bought in the five days of *Ahunavait gāh* must belong ("belongs") to (his) son.

A38, 6—12:

Beside other (things) it is written from the words of the *magupatān magupat* in the same copy of the *Memorandum* sealed with the seal of the *magupatān magupat*, that if Yazdkart was (= lived) in the first half ("fifty years") of the tenth century ("hundred winters"), we learn in this manner about the reigns of the ancestors ("fathers") of his late majesty Anōšakruvān, and about those who were (= lived) in that century ("hundred winters"). But if he (= Yazdkart II, 439—457 A.D. — *A. P.*) was in the second half ("fifty years") (of the century), then (it will follow) that Hudāt and Farnbaγ and Āturbōžēt (and) Āturpāt ī Zartuštān also held the power in that century. If it is as it was written there, then the first fifty years are presumed to be those (fifty years) which elapsed last.

A38, 12—16:

(And) another (thing) is said: all the property possessed by a sorcerer shall go to the *rat* if it is firmly established that he is a sorcerer, but if he (= the sorcerer) has brought material harm ("destruction"), then (his property shall go) to (the person) to whom he brought harm ("destruction"); and if evidence is given concerning him (= the sorcerer), but it is not possible to establish exactly to whom in particular he brought harm, then (the property of the sorcerer) is seized for the benefit of the witnesses. Heretics are treated in the same manner as sorcerers.

A38, 16—**39**, 1:

Apāk anī hač dip ī pātixšāy-kart ut xvēškārīh-nāmak ī (17) kārframān ī šahrīhā (frēstāt/visēh kart) paytāk kū zandīkīh ut zandīk rōδišnīh rāδ xvāstak (I) ⟨xvāstak⟩ [ō] šāhīkān (apāč)? kart.

A39, 1—3:

Ut anī guft kū ātaxš ka apar stūrīh nišānēt (2) šāyēt ut ka ōh nišānēt u-š xvāstak pat stūrīh dahēt stūrīh nē pat (3) raft dārišn.

A39, 3—7:

Apāk anī guft kū pat GT'k ī Dāt-Gušnasp ī Šahr ⟨ī⟩(4)-Zāpalakān kart ut pat muhr ī Veh-Šāhpuhr (ī) magupatān magupat ǎvašt pat gōβišn ī (5) Dāt-Gušnasp ⟨ī⟩ ōγōn nipišt kū-m ātaxš 1 pat Varahrānīh ō dātgāh (6) nišāst ut ēn xvāstak pat stūrīh ī man ut xvēšīh ī ātaxš dāštan ō ātaxš (7) dāt.

A39, 7—8:

Apāk anī Mahraspand (ī) rat būt (guft kū) mart kē kart kū-m pat dūtak ī xvēš (8) ātaxš 1 pat Varahrānīh ō dātgāh nišāst stūr gumārtan.

A39, 8—11:

Ut anī guft (9) kū āturān bandak (ī) āzātīh ī pat mart rāδ pat āturān bandakīh ⟨ī⟩ hač šāhīkān bē dāt (10) pat vināskārīh ī xvēš dehpatān ō ōstān ōh kart ut hač ōstān ō yut (11) ātaxš ōh dāt.

A39, 11—17:

Apāk anī (guft kū) ka ōy baγ Vahrām šāhān šāh Yazdkartān Mihr(12)Narseh ī vazurg framātār pat bandakīh (ō) ātaxš ī Artvahišt ut ātaxš ī Aβzōn-(13)Artaxšahr dāt čand sāl pat ān dāt pat āturān dāšt ut pas pat framān ī (14) ōy baγ Yazdkart šāhān šāh ī Vahrāmān ut nām ī vināskārīh apāč ō ōstān (15) kart (ut) čand sāl pat ōstān dāšt ut pas ōy baγ Pērōž šāhān šāh pat ham(16)pursakīh ī Martbūt (ī) magupatān magupat būt ut apārīk dastaβarān ī mat ēstāt (17) hend pat bandakīh nē ō ham ātaxš ⟨ī⟩ bē ō ātaxš ī Ōhrmizd-Pērōž dāt.

A38, 16—**39**, 1:

Besides other (things) it appears from the mandating document and from the administrative letter / *The Book regarding the Duties of Officials* which (was / were sent out) to the *šahrs*, that property is confiscated for the royal treasury for the practice of Manichaeanism / heresy and for the dissemination of Manichaeanism / heresy.

A39, 1—3.

And another (thing) is said, that if anyone establishes a Fire with the funds of a *stūr*-foundation (lit.: "on a *stūr*ship"), then (it) is permissible. And if he (= the *stūr*) founds (a Fire-temple / altar) and transfers to it (= the Fire) the property which he holds as a *stūr*-possession, then the *stūr*ship should not be considered to have lost its force (lit.: "gone away").

A39, 3—7:

Together with this it is said, that in the testament left by Dāt-Gušnasp (from the family / lineage) of Šahr-Zāpalakān and sealed with the seal of the *magupatān-magupat*, Veh-Šāhpuhr, (the following) is written from the words of Dāt-Gušnasp: "I have founded one Fire and placed (it) in (the temple) of the Varahrān Fire, and I have conveyed to the Fire this thing (= property) as a possession which is the foundation of my *stūr*ship and belongs to the Fire".

A39, 7—8:

Besides this, Mahraspand, who was a *rat*, (said that) a *stūr* (should be) appointed for a man who has declared (the following) in his will: "I have founded a Fire for my family and placed (it) in the temple of the Varahrān Fire".

A39, 8—11:

It is also said that: for the commission of a crime a *hierodulos* — who is made free (lit.: "is given into freedom") by the royal treasury as regards other (private) persons (= who has the status of a freeman before men — *A. P.*) but a slave as regards Fire-(temples) — is formally transferred ("assigned, appointed") by the rulers to the royal *ōstān* (to perform his labour service as a punishment there — *A. P.*) and from the *ōstān* he is transferred to another Fire-temple.

A39, 11—17:

It is also said, that when (our) late sovereign Vahrām, King of Kings son of Yazdkart, conveyed the *vazurg-framātār* Mihr-Narsēh as a slave (= a *hierodulos*; lit. "into slavery" — *A. P.*) to the Artvahišt Fire-temple and the Aβzōn-Artaxšahr Fire-temple, then,. in accordance with this transfer he (= Mihr-Narsēh) stayed ("was kept") at the (above)mentioned Fire temples for several years; then, at the order of his late majesty Yazdkart, King of Kings son of Vahrām, he was taken to the *ōstān* for a crime / an offence, and he was in the *ōstān* during the course of several years (*cf. supra* **A39**, 8—11, *et infra* **A40**, 1—3, **A40**, 3—6 — *A. P.*); and subsequently he was conveyed into slavery by his late majesty Pērōz, King of Kings, with the consent of the *magupatān-magupat* Martbūt and other authorities who were present [lit.: "who appeared" (evidently at the royal council that settled the question of Mihr-Narsēh) — *A. P.*], but not to the same Fire temple, but to the Ōhrmizd-Pērōz Fire-temple.

A40, 1—3:

Ut anī guft (kū ka gōβēt) kū-m āturān bandakīh [vinās]īh(?) ī pat pit ut šōy rāδ⁺ (Ms.: L'-nē) vindāt ka xvat (2) avinās aδak-ič pat vināskārīh ī pit ut šōy pat framān ī dehpatān ō ōstān (ōh)?(3) kart.

A40, 3—6:

Apāk anī Mihr-Narseh⁺ hač zan ut rahīk ham(m)is pat āturvaxšīh ut bandakī[h] (4) ut paristārīh [91] bē dāt (...) vināskārīh ī zan ut rahīk čiš nē nimūt ⟨ut⟩ zan-ič ut rahī[k] (5) ō ōstān kart ēn dātastān apāk vičīr ī pat-ič ⟨bē⟩ Dandān ut Āturtōxm ham moγān⁺ (6) (h)andarzpat kart (ut)? hačapar nipišt ēstēt nikerītan.

A40, 6—9:

Ut anī guft kū ka gōβēt kū-m (7) xvāstak pat stūrīh ō zan ī dūtak stūr dāt būt kē guft kū dāt bē (8) nē bavēt ut būt kē guft kū stūrīh nēst ut xvāstak pat xvēšīh ⟨ī⟩ bē ō dūtak (9) rasēt.

A40, 9—11:

Apāk anī hač e(v)-kart ōrōn pat dīvān ī magupat⁺ (ī) Artaxšahr-Xvarreh kart (10) dāštan kū ka zan ut frazand ī čakar rāδ gōβēt kū-m pat pātixšāyīhā zanīh (11) ut pātixšāyīhā frazandīh patigrift⁺ ān gōβišn pat kār nē dārišn.

A40, 11—14:

Ut apāk anī (12) Pusānveh ī Burzātur Farnbaγān guft kū ka zan ut [f]razand ī čakar pat pātixšāy zanīh (13) ut pātixšāy frazandīh dātastān ōγōn čiγōn kas pat pusīh⁺ ut duxtīh patigrift⁺ hē (14) ut zan xvāstak ⟨ī⟩ ka pātixšāyīhā hē apar mānēt ut avi-š rasēt.

A40, 15—16:

Ut apāk anī apar vas nipišt ut ăvašt dastaβarān kart [...] nipišt kū-m pat pusīh (16) patigrift⁺.

A40, 16—17:

Ut anī guft kū (ka) apāk zan ī stūr pašt kunēt kū-m ēn (17) xvāstak ō tō frazandān ōγōn dāt kū ō dūtak kē tō pat-iš stūr hēh...

A40, 1—3:

It is also said, that if she declares (the following) "I have obtained the *hierodu-late* (= the status of a *hierodulē*) as a consequence of [an offence]? committed by (my) father and husband", then even if she herself is innocent, (she) is formally transferred ("assigned") to the *ōstān* by the rulers because of the offence of (her) father or husband.

A40, 3—6:

And again (the following). Mihr-Narsēh together with (his) wife and slave were conveyed (to a temple) for their respective performance of the duties of *āturvaxš* [92], slave and *hierodulē*. ... (And even though) nothing pointed to any offence of the wife or the slave, both the wife and slave were also sent to the *ōstān* (= the royal domain / the royal household).

This decision should be examined together with the decision taken by the already mentioned *handarzpat* of the Magi with regard to Dandān and Āturtōxm (and) concerning which it was written above (*cf. supra* **A37**, 1—15) [93].

A40, 6—9:

It has also been said, that if he declares: "I have conveyed a thing as a *stūr*-possession ('for *stūr*ship') to the woman who is a family's *stūr*", certain (authorities) emitted the opinion that (in this) case the transfer does not take place (= is not valid — *A. P.*), whereas some have said that conveyance on the basis of *stūr*ship (lit.: "the *stūr*ship") cannot take place and that the thing shall go to the family as its own possession [94].

A40, 9—11:

And also hereupon in the chancellery of the *magupat* of Artaxšahr-Xvarreh, it has been decreed to take into account (lit.: "have, hold"), that if (anyone) declares as regards a wife and child from a *čakar*-marriage: "I have received (her / him) as a *pātixšāy*-wife and as *pātixšāy*-children", then such a decision should not be considered to have legal force [95].

A40, 11—14:

Besides that, Pusānveh ī Burzatūr Farnbaγān has said, that when (a question of the taking) a wife or child from a *čakar*-mariage as a *pātixšāy*-wife and *pātixšāy*-children (is examined), then this question is resolved in accordance (with the existing general rules) for the adoption of a son or daughter. And the wife, if she becomes a *pātixšāy* one, shall inherit (her husband's) estate and it must go to her.

A40, 15—16:

Together with that, in many documents / writings sealed with a seal, authorities have established [...] wrote / written: "I adopted".

A40, 16—17:

It is also said, that (if) anyone makes (the following agreement with a woman who is a family's *stūr*: "I shall convey this thing to your children in such a way that the family of which you are the *stūr*, ...". (The text breaks off here — *A. P.*).

NOTES TO THE TEXT

1. This article supports the fact that the terms *bandak* and *anšahrīk* were not synonymous when used in combination with the word *ātaxš*, "Fire(-temple)". The expression *ātaxš bandak* or *bandak ī ātaxš* had the technical sence of "*hierodulos*", whereas *anšahrīk ī ātaxš* merely designated a temple-slave, *i. e.* a slave belonging to a temple.

2. *I. e.*, the heirs of the late head of household and the co-heirs of his son and successor.

3. *I. e.*, the successor does not have the right to claim from his co-heirs who are not successors a participation in the settlement of the debts of the *de cuius* corresponding to their share of the inheritance.

3a. Lit. "what (= the part of the debt from which) they (= the judges — *A. P.*) release (these persons) is the same as (that) from which they release (in the case of) warrantors".

4. The annulment of a warranty-contract by the creditor after the expiration of the time limit set for the discharge of the original debt could entail the cancellation of the debt or come as the result of its settlement by the debtor.

5. The political term, *dahyupat* (*dhywpt*. Av. *daiŋhəuš daiŋhupaiti*) meaning 'ruler, supreme secular power' was an archaism for the period of the *Law-Book*. Like the article itself, it is undoubtedly borrowed from the Pahlavi commentary on one of the legal *nasks* of the *Avesta*.

6. The plaintiff apparently brings the thing to court in token of his protest against the form of compensation for the debt or for a portion thereof.

7. The reference here is to suits dealing with very small amounts or with minor misdemeanors.

8. The various shades of meaning of the term *dastaβar* must be taken into account for an understanding of lines 7—8 of this article. In the first instance, Farraxv's rôle in the case is seen as that of the person disposing of the thing (= selling it), and as such, the one summoned to confirm Mihrēn's title before the court. In the second instance, however, his participation in the case is that of an agent (= mandatary) having sold a thing conveyed to him for such a purpose and obliged to respond to a suit brought by the buyer. As a defendant (or as one of the litigants in general), Farraxv was not obliged to appear in person at the place where the

case was being tried; he could pass this obligation to his "legal representative", *yātagōβ*. Vide *infra*, **6**, 6—9.

9. The word "disposer" found in the ms. is probably a *lapsus calami* on the part of the scribe.

10. The presumable substitution of *dstwbl* for *d'twbl* in the ms.by the copyist is by no means extraordinary and is easily explicable here because of the great graphic similarity of the two words, as well as the prevalence of the first term in the text of this article and of the entire chapter. The article can, however, also be understood without the proposed rectification. The alternate translation of this article would then be: "If an agent (= a mandatory, or: the latter's *mandator*, a person having disposed of a thing and defending in court the respondent's title to it — *A. P.*) demands — concerning the thing regarding which he (is appearing in court) as the disposer — the summoning of a court session with the participation of the disposer (= the giver of the mandate or other disposers, *i. e.*, the former legal possessors from whom he received the thing and who are capable of confirming his right to dispose thereof — *A. P.*); then (such) a session must be arranged ('given')".

11. The correction of ms. *psym'l* "respondent" into *pyšym'l*, "plaintiff" seemed advisable for the sake of a more coherent translation.

12. It is considered as the estate of the father, not as that of the adopted son, and is, therefore, liable to descend — via *stūr*ship — to the father's personal successor.

13. The beginning of this article coincides with the article **69**, 10—12.

14. *Cf.* the Avestic formula *pasu vīra*, Umbr. *viro pequo*, Lat. *pecudesque virosque*. See, H. Lüders, "Eine arische Anschauung über den Vertragsbruch", *SPAW*, XXVI (1917), pp. 366—368; E. Benveniste, *Le Vocabulaire des institutions indo-européennes*, I (Paris, 1969), pp. 41—52.

15. The *bona adventicia* are intended here.

16. The content of this article coincides with that of article **31**, 15—**32**, 1. The reference here is to a suit brought by a third party demanding the settlement of a debt of the late head of household.

17. After a woman or a minor has been endowed, through an agreement, with the legal capacity of acquisition, they become the acquirers of transfers conveyed to them from outside and not the head of household.

18. The Avestan phrase *yō hē pasčaēta*, having the conventional sense of "auxiliary or substitute succession; the charge of creating a successorship for a man who died sonless, *stūr*ship", forms here a part of the attributive syntagma and is given in the ms. in both the Avestan script and in the Pahlavi transcription.

19. The situation considered here is presumbaly one in which the *stūr* instituted by the father is removed from the *stūr*ship by a court decision because of some circumstance or misdemeanor and a new *stūr* must be appointed for the dead man.

20. In other words, when a daughter assumes the *epikler*ate for her father, her marriage "with full rights" [= *pātixšāyīh*]must be transformed into a marriage *sine manu mariti*.

21. Lit. "a guardian must be appointed for the son's family". This means that the point of departure for the calculation of the degrees of kinship in the selection of a candidate and the appointment of a guardian on the basis of agnatic calling must be the son who died after having come of age.

22. Inasmuch as the Fire-altar was already in existence at the time of the offence committed by its endower, the latter's disposition was not liable to annulment — an existing Fire-altar could not be destroyed. The only possible step was the alteration of the clause concerned with the trusteeship in the deed of endowment.

23. The share of the endower is intended here; *i. e.*, the excess revenue from the foundation which customarily went to the endower/trustee and his family. The institution of a Fire-altar was always accompanied by the conveyance of a property "for the soul". *Cf.* **51**, 2—6.

24. Property conveyed by the giver before committing an offence is not taken away from the new possessor to pay the fine imposed upon the giver for his offence. If, however, the offender willed an estate to someone, and the recipient has not yet entered into the rights of possession, then the sum needed to cover the fine, etc. shall be subtracted from the willed property. *Cf.* **30**, 17—**31**, 2; **31**, 2—3.

25. According to article **106**, 9—11, a slave (evidently a Zoroastrian) could be subjected to the ordeal (= to testify under oath) in a case regarding his revendication of his freedom.

26. What is intended here is the original loan agreement secured with a pledge, which remains in force, and not the subsequent agreement with Farraxv.

27. The copy of the document setting down the terms of the loan transaction held by the creditor was equivalent to a promissory note and consequently had to be returned to the debtor just before the settlement of the debt.

28. A *dastkart* is obviously intended here. The case under consideration is the pledge of a landed estate together with its inventory which included the slave. *Cf.* **38**, 13—17.

29. The equivalent of the price of the slave who remained pledged had to be conveyed to the debtor-pledger having settled his debt as a guaranty that the slave would be returned to him.

30. *I. e.* after the expiration of the time limit for the return of the loan, if the loan-contract stipulated a time-limit, or after the refusal to satisfy the demand of the creditor that the debt be settled, if the time-limit was set by the wish of the creditor (= until his demand of a settlement) rather than by contract.

31. As security for a debt contracted by the creditor with a third party.

32. Lit. "from among the kinsmen of Farraxv by birth from a daughter"; *cf.* also the term *duxtdāt* = Gk. θυγατριδοῦς = Skt. *putrikāputra*, "a successor-son through an *epikleros*".

33. The necessity of appointing a *stūr* for Farraxv who had a son and a grandson from that son might arise in one of the three following cases: 1) Farraxv's only son Pusak died before his father, then his own son might have to take on his grandfather's succession; 2) although he already had a legal successor, Farraxv instituted a supplementary succession for himself (*stūr ī kartak*) but did not desig-

nate the *stūr*, in such a case his agnatic group had to appoint a *stūr* for him; 3) Farraxv instituted a *stūr*ship for himself and designated the *stūr*, but this *stūr* died without producing a successor, in such a case his agnatic group had to appoint a *stūr* for Farraxv. In all cases of the appointment of a *stūr*, the choice fell on the dead man's nearest kinsman, a practice noted in this article as well.

34. This is a case where the grandfather on the mother's side has no direct successor. In such a case his granddaughter through a daughter may be called to assume his succession (*i. e.* to the *epiklerate*) and she would receive her mother's share (= her mother's daughter's-share in her father's estate) which would thus return to the family of her mother's father.

35. Should the eldest sister marry, the grandfather's *epikler*ate shall be assigned to the younger sister (= the next in order of seniority).

36. The first formula ("after my death") is invalid on formal grounds: the transfer of the *stūr*ship after death took place only by court decision or through agnatic designation. The transfer by a *natural stūr* (in this case, by the mistress of the house) could take place only "in case of death".

37. A man having assumed the *stūr*ship in the line of *natural* (*būtak*) calling (*e. g.*, a brother, a son or grandson of the dead man) had the right to dispose of the *stūr*-endowment in accordance with the regime of an estate acquired as an inheritance-share; *i. e.*, he could appropriate the entire revenue (or interest) derived from it, obviously minus the amount needed for working and restoration expenses. A female "natural" *stūr*, as well as a *stūr* (of either sex) of another type (either "instituted", *kartak*, or "designated", *gumārtak*) could possess such an endowment only on the basis of a *stūr*'s-possession with the right of appropriating merely a given share of the revenue (or interest) — one corresponding to the reglementary payment for *stūr*ship — from the estate. Everything left from the revenue after the subtraction of the payment and the working expenses was evidently added to the "principal" of the endowment: the permissible forms of disposal of this share by the *stūr*-possessor were contributions to religious charities and pious foundations (Fire-altars, foundations "for the soul") usually dedicated to "the soul and posthumous cult" of the person for whom the *stūr*ship had been instituted. Indeed even the principal or at least a portion thereof, could be disposed of for such purposes.

38. The case under consideration is one where all other possibilities in the circle of the dead man's nearest agnates have been exhausted or when the dead man in his own lifetime appointed as *stūr* his *čakar*-wife who had already assured the suc-cession of her husband from a *pātixšāyīh*-marriage.

39. The number 70 in the ms. may be an error. Alternately, this phrase should be taken conventionally as setting the age limit for the appointment of a *čakar*-widow to the *stūr*ship of her *čakar*-husband and her performance of this function.

40. The case intended here is one where the remainder of the escheated estate (or of the instituted *stūr*-endowment) after the settlement of the debts contracted by the dead man is insufficient for the institution of a *stūr*ship (*i. e.*, it is less than 60 *drahms*/*satērs*?).

41. According to the interpretation attributed to Veh-Ōhrmizd, minors who became *stūrs* would remain such unless they refuse the *stūr*ship upon coming of age.

42. "Profit" or "increment" is to be taken apparently as the entire amount of revenue or increment from the estate conveyed to the instituted Fire-altar. *Cf.* also **27**, 9—12.

43. Consequently, the daughter and the son receive equally.

44. A son born to the mistress of the house after the division of the inheritance of the late head of household has taken place and after her daughter has married and consequently received her share of her father's estate, shall receive his mother's share and not his sister's share.

45. *I. e.*, if one thing consists of two definite parts with two legal titles, then, if one part is destroyed, what remains is one (= a whole or entire) thing with a single legal title.

46. The copyist's interpolation ⟨Vahuman⟩ enclosed here in pointed brackets results possibly from his mechanical association of the word  (= hmNKSY' = *hamxvāstak*) with the outwardly similar 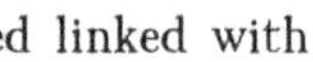 (= *hampursakīh*) which in Pahlavi religious texts is severally attested linked with *Vahuman* when rendering verbal forms of Av. *fras-* and Av. *frasā-* (fem.) used with *Vohu Manah-*. See more particularly the Pahlavi commentary on **Y**.44, 8; 44, 13; 45, 6; 47, 3; 49, 2.

47. A possible though less satisfactory translation (of lines 14—15) would be. "Except for the one (of the co-heirs) who is endowed by the (late) head of household more than the others ('preferentially')...".

48. It is likewise possible to read *ō bavet* (= *avi bavaiti*) in line 3 which should then be translated. "...accept, then they will receive it as inheritance".

49. The *status quo ante* shall be reinstated inasmuch as the receiver infringed the condition of the agreement by which the thing was conveyed to him without the right of transferring it to another person.

50. The text of this article may be corrupt. The incomprehensible word 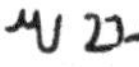 is also found in article **108**, 6—8. From this point the translation of the article is hypothetical.

51. Specifically, if the transfer for adoption was made with the utterance of a formula presupposing the complete loss by the one adopted of a place in the family of his natural father.

52. The promise to bring to court the principal litigant — in this case the plaintiff who gave his mandate to the representative — might be provoked by the indispensability to authenticate the title of the legal representative if he did not have with him the document confirming his mandate. See also **77**, 12—14.

53. The text enclosed in parentheses is a variant of the formula for the appointment of a legal representative.

53a. In its eschatological sense.

54. Evidently for the older one.

55. Specifically, as a result of the fact that the woman's second husband died while still a minor and she thereby continued to remain under the guardianship of his father: her first husband.

56. *Cf.* the *Rivāyat ī Ēmēt ī Ašavahištān*, B. T. Anklesaria ed. (Bombay, 1962), XIII, 17.

57. The refusal of the creditor to accept the estate of the debtor (who is evidently dead, here) carries with it the liquidation of the latter's indebtedness.

58. What is being considered is the conveyance by the creditor (A) to a third person (C) of the right to claim for his own profit the interest loan which A. lent

to another person, the debtor (B). As a result of this transfer, C becomes B's creditor.

59. *I. e.*, the epithet "defender of the interests of the destitute", *yātakgōβ ī driyōšān* (*cf. infra* the "Glossary" *s. v. driyōšān*) appeared on the official seal of the *magupat* of Pārs instead of his title.

60. The number 1000 may be an interpolation by the copyist.

61. Another possible variant of the translation of **1**, 7 in the ms. is "and that the investigation of these (affairs, *i. e.*, of legal affairs in which slaves are involved) should be excluded from (the procedure established) by this edict (of the magupat Burzak)". *Cf.* also *supra* **92**, 6—10.

62. The text breaks off here. On the free margin of the page there is a note in Persian dated in the 1006th year of the era of Yazdkart (= 1637 A.D.) which gives the information concerning the exchange of this manuscript by its possessor, the daughter of Asfandyār Nōširvān for a manuscript containing the *Yašts* and the *Visparad*. The exchange was made with her brother Rustam Nōširvān Bamānyār who also paid her one thousand dinars. *Cf. MHD* I, p. xii, 98 *et supra* "Introduction", p. 9.

63. *I. e.* Ōhrmizd IV (A.D. 579—590).

64. The alteration by a party of its testimony to the court could not be imputed as a legal offence liable to a punishment — a fine, if the truthfulness of the last testimony was incontrovertible (*cf.* **102**, 11—12). Some attention may also be paid to the fact that in the case cited, the proven title to the thing, cited by the litigant in his second testimony presupposes his holding of a fundamental real right (personal property), and not a derivative (possession of a pledge) which he claimed in his first testimony.

65. The case referred to here is one in which the co-partner or warrantor refuses to pay and the matter is taken to court.

66. The reference here is to the case of the death of a childless man having left no available estate, or in any case not enough for the institution for him of a *stūr*-succession.

67. Through a will or through a transfer with a stipulated date of entry into effect.

68. The manuscript has "to Farraxv" which makes no sense from a legal point of view and contradicts the general context of this article. The substitution of names was evidently suggested to the copyist by the refrence to the death of Mihrēn in the preceding line.

69. That is to say until the time when the relinquishment of the thing valued at 60 (*drahms/satērs*?) to Mihrēn comes into effect and a *stūr*ship which will acquire the dead man's income may be established.

70. *I. e.*, she betrays her husband by living with other men.

71. If while she is the *stūr* of her late husband she refuses to live with his agnate.

72. If the declaration regarding the conveyance to the second person takes place within the time-limit for the rejection of the first transfer.

73. The words enclosed here in pointed brackets may be a later interpolation.

74. In the interpretation of the expression *dāt pašt — xvaš* as the two halves of the formula pronounced by both parties at the conclusion of an oral declaration — after which it goes into effect, and in the corresponding correction of the ms. NPŠH = *xvēš* into *xvaš*. I have followed Chr.Bartholomae, "Zum sasanidischen Recht", I, *SbHAW* (1918, Abt. 5), pp 13—20.

75. The heterogram YK(= Q)TLWN- = *ōzatan* (Iran. **gan-*) "to kill" in the ms. is probably used to render the homonymous verb *ōzatan* (**zām-*) "to condemn". *Cf. infra* "Glossary", *s. v. ōzatan*.

76. If the word *vičīr* has the sense of "document" here, the following variant translation is possible. "The drawing up by the same judge of a later (= antedated) document instead of an improperly drawn up document regarding a judicial decision is to be considered invalid".

77. This article contains a typical example of formalistic analysis for the sake of which the expression *Asaβār-nipēk* "*List of Horsemen*" (*Cf.* **A16**, 11—14; **A16**, 14—**17**, 1) is split into two seemingly independent elements. An analogous case in found in *DkM*, 695, 11—19.

78. This article derives from the separation of the title to the land (= soil) on the one hand and to the vineyard and the trees planted on this plot — on the other, as well as from the separation of the title to the vineyard from the title to the remaining economic elements included within the complex of the *dastkart*.

79. The original text has *čē* (lit. "since, inasmuch as, because"), a conjunction that introduces a phrase through which the author attempts to clarify what led him to note the equivalence of the given (= third) formula to the two others cited above. The beginning of this phrase might be translated: "(and the equivalence of the last method of expression to the preceding two is noted here/should be noted), because when he formulates (his declaration with the word) 'or', there are people who argue...".

80. With *yāt-gēhan cf.* Av. *yātəm gaēθanąm*, *Fr ī oīm*, 4f. This article is entirely borrowed from a legal *nask* of the *Avesta* as witnessed by the content and by the archaic social terms found in it. In particular, the term, *dehpat*, has here its ancient meaning of "ruler, sovereign". The translation of the end of the article is puzzling.

81. The translation of this article is hypothetical.

82. The ms. has 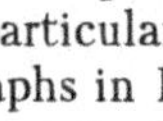, which in my opinion may be interpreted as PWT-*š*, where PWT is the corruption of the heterogram *TPWT < *ṬBWT('). Mute and voiced consonants, particularly *p*/*b* (*pē*/*bēth*) were often confused in the renderings of Aramaic heterographs in Pahlavi (*e. g.*, ṢPWN/ṢBWN = *hēr*, GB'/KP' = *kapīč*, GWBNT'/GWPT' = *panīr*, ḤNDB'/HNDP' = *kāšnīk*, GB(B)H/GPH = *pušt*). One should also note Aram. *ṭēth*/*thāw bēth* > Pahl. *pē* in the heterogram TWP' < < *TWTB' (*yāmak*). The restorable form *ṬBWT(') corresponds to Aram. **ṭabbūθā*, "seal", *cf.* Akkad. *ṭabbū*, Hebr. *ṭabba'at*. For the dropping of the initial, *cf.* Pahl. ML' (= *šāhīkān*) < *HML'. The heterogram may be read as *muhr* (the normal, historical spelling of the word, is *mwdr*) or as *muhrak*, which had acquired the sense of "a document", *cf.* Arm. *murhak* (<*muhrak*) "a document", specifically "a document authenticating a title". Such an interpretation is entirely consonant

with the contest; *cf.* the expression *muhr patigriftan* (**A30**, 3—5), *nipišt ut avašt ī dastaβarān patigīrēnd* (**A35**, 12—13) attested present in contexts similar to this one.

83. In other words, the principal contractor can be pronounced insolvent only if his warrantor is likewise insolvent.

84. *Cf.* the "Corpus iuris der persischen Erzbischofs Jesubocht", E. Sachau ed., *Syrische Rechtsbücher*, III (Berlin, 1914), VI, 1, § 7.

85. In other words, the term "document" should be taken as indicating the unity of the written text and of the seal.

86. The reading is hypothetical. The ms. has *wn'dšn* (with the *-d-* rendering the pronounced *-y-/-h-*?) instead of the usual historical orthography *wn'sšn*.

87. The discussion apparently concerns which of the formulae, "born into the family" or "*čakar*-son" is preferable for an official document. *Cf. supra* **A35**, 11—12, *et infra* **A35**, 13—14.

88. What is intended are the relatives and descendants of the persons designated as trustees by the institutor of the foundation, in this case the successors and kinsmen of the trustees appointed by Mihr-Narsēh.

89. What is intended is the property which each of the two founders gave the common endowment for the Fire, specifically the corresponding plots of land and other possible dedications.

90. That is to say as a possession which may be included in a transmission fund and which shall go to the principal holder's own successors.

91. The ms has *knskyh*, a corruption of the heterogram KNŠK(yh) at the foundation of which lies the word *kanīžak* "a maiden", "a maidservant", given in Aramaic/Parthian orthography and serving in Pahlavi writing as the heterogram of the word *paristār* "maidservant" (*FiP* XIII); in the present text a "*hierodule*".

92. A person obliged to watch over the Fire in a Zoroastrian Fire-temple. As it is seen from the context, Mihr-Narsēh as a *hierodulos* bore the duties of *āturvaxš* in the temple, whereas his wife was a *hierodule* in the same temple, and his slave — a slave (evidently serving them).

93. The final phrase gives the impression of having been accidentally included in this article, whose content in no way echoes the case of Dandān and Āturtōxm (**A37**, 1—15). It presumably ended an article omitted by one of the copyists of the text.

94. The basis for this case and its solution is that a woman who has already assumed a *stūr*ship is not entitled to take upon herself a second *stūr*ship. Therefore, either the transfer of the thing to her for a second *stūr*ship is invalid, or the transfer remains in force but alters its nature of a transfer intended for the institution of a *stūr*ship; and the thing conveyed to the woman is included in the family estate (= family property) of the family of which the woman already is *stūr*. A man as against a woman could be burdened with the *stūr*ship of several persons at the same time.

95. The taking of a *čakar*-wife as a *patixšāy*-wife, as well as the adoption of her child from (her) *čakar*-husband, could take place only if her eldest son came of age, and if — having become the successor of her (late) *pātixšāy*-husband and his own mother's guardian — he sanctioned this action. *Cf.* the next article.

GLOSSARY

A

abar: "bearing no fruit; bringing no income/revenue". — **34**, 4; *cf. bar.*

abaxt: "undivided" — **53**, 16; **54**, 1, 4, 5, 16; **94**, 17; **95**, 3; **96**, 11; **A20**, 14. — See *baxtan, baxtīk, baxtikīh.*

aβγātak ('wb'tk'): "posterity, descendants". — **96**, 15; **101**, 10, 11; **A16**, 12, 13, 16, 17; **A 35**, 16; **A37**, 6, 10, 14, 17. — P. Ps. *'wb't = ā(v)vāt* "generation, family", Jud.-Pers. *'w'd* (*āvād < avvāt < *aβγāt < *abi-gāta-*, MacKenzie, *BSOAS*, XXXI (1968), 251.

abōδīh: "unconscious state". Term designating the unconscious state of a delinquent at the moment when he commited an act of physical violence (struck "a blow"). — **10**, 10. Antonym Av. *baoδō.varšta-*, *AirWb.*, 920.

aβurtan, aβar-: "bring". — *Passim*; *apāč āβurtan* "to take away; remove from; withdraw from transfer; annul". — **4**, 6—7; **30**, 8, 11—13; **31**, 1—2, 5—17; **32**, 17; **49**, 15; **101**, 3.

aβyātkar: "document, memorial". — **A34**, 7, 12, 16; **A38**, 7.

aβzāyišn: "increase; growth (of trees)". — **39**, I. — See *aβzūtan.*

aβzōn: "increase; growth; profit". — **40**, 16, 17; **85**, 13, 15; **86**, 1. — See *aβzūtan.*

aβzūtan, aβzāy: "increase, augment, grow (of prices)". — **54**, 14; **85**, 14, 15, 17; **86**, 1; **66**, 12, 16. — Iran. **abi-gav-*, OP *abi-ǰāvaya-*, NP *afzūdan.*

adahišnīh: "non-transfer, absence of transfer". — **A21**, 14. — *Cf. adāt, dāt, dātan.*

adastaβar: "unentitled, unempowered" — *Cf. dastaβar.*

adāt (būtan): "non transferred" (regarding the revocation of a transfer or declaring it invalid. — **A9**, 15. — See *dāt, dātan.*

ādehīk: "fellow-citizen, member of a community". — **44**, 2 — Corresponding to Av. *ā.dahyav-*; *AirWb.*, 320; *cf.* also *DkM*, VIII, 707, 21—22.

aδenišn: "entry; bringing in". — **98**, 4. — Iran. **adi + ayana-*? *Cf.* MMP *'dyn-* "bring, lead".

aδvēnak: "mode/variety". — *Passim.* — *Cf.* in particular *aδvēnak ī dāt, aδvēnak ī xvēšīh, aδvēnak ī dāšt(an).*

aδvēn (būtan): "to be proper, appropriate; due". — **A22**, 7, 9, 12, 15, 16. — Iran. **abi-daina-* "custom, norm"; Parth. *aβδēn* > Arm. *awrēn* "custom, norm, law", *awrinak* "example, model", NP *āyīn* [Henning, *TPS* (1944, 110].
For constructions with the copulative verb, *cf.* the Arm. calque *awrēn ē*, etc. "to be due (by right, by custom); be proper", and *'bdyny YHWt* in the Parthian version of the inscription of Šāhpuhr i (*ŠKZ*, 19).

aframān: "invalid, ἄκυρος". — **28**, 13; **96**, 7; **A18**, 5; **A23**, 17.

agraβ: "an unpledged thing, one free from hypothec". *agraβ kartan*: "to redeem a pledge, release from hypothec". — **38**, 13; **40**, 4. — *Cf. graβ, graβīh, graβakān.*

āgraβ: "subject to seizure (for the settlement of a debt)". — **89**, 9. — Iran. **ā+grab-*; Av. *ā-grab-* "to take"; to claim as a fine, as a punishment" (*Nīr.*, 54). *Cf.* next entry.

āgraβīh: "seizure (in settlement of debts)". — **29**, 12; **62**, 15.

aγdēn: "infidel, heterodox"; *aγdēnīh* "non-Zoroastrian faith" — **1**, 13, 16; **44**, 7; **60**, 16, 17.

ahambatīkīh: "lack/absence of hostility". — **79**, 8.

āhang: "order, mode (of arrangement); rule". — **13**, 13; **35**, 1. — NP *āhang* "plan, sketch; manner, mode; harmony"; *cf.* Arm. *ahang* "order, disposition (of troops)". See also *s. v. frahaxtišnīh.*

āhanǰišn: "raising/increase", lit. "pulling out, raising" (regarding the deliberate increase of the seriousness of an offence). — **A14**, 17.

āhōk: "guilt". — **A34**, 15. — NP (*ShN, VR*) *āhō* "vice, sin, fault; disapproval, reprobation"; Arm. (< MP) *ahok* "fault; damage, shortcoming; reprobation; accusation".

ahramōγīh: "heresy". A category of offence — **A34**, 10, 12.

ahravdāt: "religious beneficience and act of piety; foundation for pious purposes". — **31**, 2; **34**, 14; **36**, 1; **60**, 1; **61**, 14; **71**, 8, 14, 17; **72**, 2; **A1**,1. *Cf.* also *s. v. ruvān.*

Ahunavait gāh, panǰak ī Ahunavait gāh: "the five days of the Gāthā *ahunavaitī*" (this corresponds to the five intercalary days of the year, the holiest in the sixth *gāhānbār*, the *Fravartīkān*, of which the celebration began five days before the end of the lunar year. The first intercalary day bore the name of the Gāthā *ahunavaitī*, the first in the Yasna). — **A38**, 6. *Cf.* also *s. v. Fravartīkān.*

ākanēn, pat ākanēn: "jointly"; this designates the relationship of co-partnership and correal (joint) responsibility. (Antonym *yut-yut, pat yutākīh*). — *Passim.*

ākāsīh: "knowledge, information"; *hač ākāsīh ī* "with the knowledge of". — *Passim.*

a-mān: "a minor, not mature, not of age". — **51**, 12 — Possibly a derivative of Ir. **mā-* < I-E **meH₂-* "rechtzeitig sein"; *cf.* Lat *mātūrus* "rechtzeitig" > "reif"; "vor der Zeit" > "zu früh", "zur Unzeit", Hitt. *mehur* "rechtzeitig sein"(see Eichner, *MSS* 31 [1972], 53—100, esp. p. 89, n. 28). For Iranian *cf.* LW in Arm. *parmani* "a youth (having reached the age of consecration into the life of the community)". The text of **51**, 6—12 having many gaps, one cannot be sure of this interpretation.

āmār: "taken into consideration". — **8**, 11; **23**, 13; **48**, 10; **56**, 11; **59**, 6; **A5**, 3.

āmatan, āy-: "to come". Technical usages: 1) *mat ēstātan* "to appear (in court or in any other office)", also "to appear within the stipulated time limit (for the settlement of a debt)", *cf. e. g.* **41**, 3, 4; **53**, 17; **A39**, 16. 2) "to come to (through transmission or transfer), to pass into the possession of"; *xvāstak ī pas mat*; *pas mat dārišn* = "*bona adventicia*"; *apāč āmatan* "to be returned, revert to" (of a thing), *e. g.* **6**, 3; **7**, 2; **8**, 4; **9**, 16, 17; **10**, 5; **14**, 6; **30**, 15; **31**, 16; **34**, 16; **35**, 1, 6; **105**, 16; **108**, 7; **A11**, 4, 10.

amrāv / armāv: "date; date-palm". — **40**, 15. — OP **hamrāva-* / **armāvaka-* (various spellings in the Persepolis Fortification Texts), NP *xurmā*. *Cf.* Arm. *armaw* "date", *armaweni* "date-palm" (Hübschmann, *AG* I, 111).

Anaγrān (rōč): "the day *Anaγrān*". — **71**, 9; **108**, 6.

ānāftān, ānām: "to remove" (from office). — **75**, 16. — Iran. **ā-* + *nă̄m-*, **ānāmaya-*; Andreas-Barr, *P. Ps.*, *s. v.*; Henning, *Verbum*, 190; Benveniste, *BSOAS*, XXX (1967), 505—511.

anandarz: "intestate". — **27**, 16; **44**, 9; **47**, 3; **90**, 3.

anāsān-tan: "unhealthy, sick". — **8**, 11.

anast-gōβišnīh: "slander, falsehood" (offence). — **A34**, 12.

anāstīh: "spoiling, destruction; falsification" (of a seal). — **99**, 2.

anattān: "insolvent", *anattānīh* "insolvency". — **39**, 3; **56**, 6; **57**, 9; **58**, 17; **59**, 1, 3—5, 7; **60**, 8; **A13**, 17; **A32**, 4—6. — *Cf. attān*.

anayār: "failure to give aid". (The failure to give aid / assistance is listed as a serious offence). — **A15**, 10.

anbas(s)ān: "accuser, plaintiff; opponent, adversary"; *anbas(s)ān ah- / būtan* "to accuse, bring an action (against s.-o.), sue; to object, dispute, contradict"; *A. hač B. anbas(s)ān* "A. brings an action against B.". — **8**, 9, 12; **74**, 10; **84**, 1; **101**, 2, 4, 7; **102**, 4, 17. — *Cf.* MMP *'mbs'n* 1) "calumniator"; 2) "legal action". — Iran. **ham-pati-sāna-* (from **sā-* "say, declare", if OP *ϑā-* = Iran. **sa-*, but see C. Haebler, *Sprache*, XIII, 1967, 83f.) or rather **ham-pati-sa(n)hana-* (from **sa(n)h-* "*id.*") > MP **hampat*ⁱ*sān* > *(h)ambas(s)ān* > *anbas(s)ān*. *Cf.* Arm. *ambastan* "accuser, plaintiff; calumniator; accusation, legal action; calumny" with metathesis from an earlier **ambatsan* < M. Med. / Parth. **ambatisān*. See my *Materialy*, 107—113. See also the next entry.

anbas(s)ānīk: "contradicting". — **A11**, 10.

andāčak: "proof, example". — **55**, 14; **83**, 13. — Iran. **hamtač-* (?); MMP *hnd'č-*, P. Ps. *'nd'č-*, *'nd'xty* "to measure, plan, calculate; to judge", NP *andāza* "measure, proportion". For the sense "proof", *cf.* Arm. (Vth C.) *andačem*, *ə ndacěm* "to investigate; to prove, demonstrate".

andarz: see (*h*)*andarz*.

anēr: "non-Zoroastrian". — **38**, 2; **44**, 7.

ānītan, ānay: "to bring, lead; to bring forward/produce a witness or a document". — 77, 14, 16; **91**, 2; **A26**, 1.

***anītar**: "alien, stranger", — **71**, 7. — The reading *'nytr* of the spelling  may be interpreted as *anītar* "alien, stranger" < Iran. **anyatara-*, comparative of *anya-* "other; alien", or as the adjective from the adverb *anyăt*. For this formulation *cf.* Iran. **abitara-*, Av. *aiwitara-* "alien, foreign", Arm. *awtar* "foreign, foreigner". *Cf.* also Gk. ἀλλότριος "alien, foreign" alongside Skt. *anyatra* "in another place". For the use of the restored word in the context *hač kust ī anītarān* "*via* strangers, outside the line of agnatic calling" *cf.* *hač kust ī xvēšāvandān/nabānazdištān* "*via* agnates; according to agnatic calling".The word seems to be a *hapax*. Morover, the spelling being doubtful because of a blot in the ms. (see Modi's note in the facsimile ed., p. 13, *infra*), both the reading and the explanation proposed here are conjectural. One could perhaps analyze the spelling as a Pahlavi rendering of Av. *aiwitara-* 'alien' (AirWb., 90), *cf.* Arm. (from Parth.) *awtar* 'alien'.

anšahrīk: "slave; slave-woman". — **1**, 2, 4, 6—11, 13, 14, 16, 17; **7**, 5; **11**, 17; **12**, 4, 7; **18**, 10; **20**, 8, 9; **31**, 16, 17; **33**, 11; **38**, 13,15, 16; **39**, 2—5, 7—9; **85**, 1; **48**, 14; **54**, 12; **58**, 16; **64**, 12—14; **69**, 3, 4; **94**, 6, 8, 10—13; **96**, 14,15; **97**, 3, 5; **98**, 5; **101**, 15; **105**, 16;**107**, 10, 11; **108**, 9; **A2**, 11, 13, 16, 17; **A3**, 6, 8—11, 13; **A5**, 2, 10; **A11**, 12, 14; **A18**, 3; **A37**, 1. — Lit. "foreigner"; *cf.* Arm. loan word *anašxarhik* "foreigner, stranger" from MMed. **an-axšahrīk*. *Cf.* also *bandak*, *paristār(īh)*, *rahīk*, *tan*, *vēsak/vešak*.

anšahrīkīh: "slavery". — **11**, 17; **33**, 13; **A31**, 16.

'nw'n (?): "smart money". — **30**, 8; **31**, 1; **71**, 8, 13, 14, 17; **72**, 1; **A12**, 17; **A13**, 8. — The spelling is 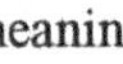. The reading is not known but the meaning "smart money" can be established with considerable security. The word is used together with *tāvān* "fine" and is formally opposed to it.

āp: "water" (for irrigation, for mills). — **33**, 10; **38**, 6; **85**, 14, 17; **105**, 11; **106**, 12—15; **107**, 1, 2.

apakandan, apakan-: "to throw". — **A13**, 11, 13.

apakanišnīh in **karp apakanišnīh**: "disfigurement"; one of the categories of offences of physical violence. — **A14**, 16. — < **apa* + *kan-*; *cf.* Arm. *apakan*, *apakanem* "damage; bring damage, destroy, disorder/unsettle"; see Bailey, *TPS* (1956), 105.

apām: "loan, debt"; *apām bē dātan* "to give a loan"; *apām statan* "to take a loan, borrow"; *apām hištan* "to discharge from a debt"; *apām xvāstan* "to demand the return of a loan or the settlement of a debt". — **2**, 1, 2, 6, 7, 14; **13**, 14; **15**, 15; **29**,13, 15; **30**, 2, 9, 14, 16; **31**, 2, 13, 14; **38**, 7; **40**, 5, 10—12; **85**, 2; **49**, 11—14; **50**, 3, 4; **53**, 4, 6; **55**, 11, 13, 17; **56**, 9; **57**, 5, 7; **59**, 2; **60**, 9; **61**, 6, 8, 12; **63**, 2; **67**, 3; **68**, 1; **71**, 2; **76**, 13—16; **88**, 9, 12; **99**, 14; **105**, 13, 14; **109**, 7, 8; **A1**, 17; **A13**, 1; **A30**, 10, 17. — Parth. *'b'myh* (Henning, *List*, 80), NP (*ā*)*vām* "loan, debt". There is no satisfactory etymology for this word (*cf. ZsR* 1, 43). See also H.W.Bailey, "Sad-Dharma-Puṇḍarīka-Sūtra. The Summary in Khotan Saka", The Australian University of Asian Studies. *Occasional Papers*, 10 (Canberra, 1971), 27, § 16(7), and the next entry.

apāmdān: "loan, debt"; *vičīr ī apāmdān* "loan contract". — **3**, 3; **40**, 8, 9; **89**, 8; **78**, 17; **100**, 3; **102**, 1; **107**, 3. — *Cf. apām.*

aparmānd: 1) "succession, inheritance; inheritance as a transmitted fund including both the estate acquired on the basis of personal inheritance and the estate acquired as a *stūr*-possession". Consequently two varieties of inheritance are mentioned: *aparmānd ī pat stūrīh* (*stūr*-inheritance) and *aparmānd ī pat xvēšīh* (inheritance on the basis of a personal heir acquiring the estate as a personal share); opposed to this is *xvāstak ī handōxt* or *handōžišn* (*q. v.*); *aparmānd dastaβarīh* "testamentary disposition regarding inheritance"; *pus ī aparmānd* "son-successor", *aparmānd burtan* "to bear (the obligation), of succession, to be called to the succession" (concerning an *epikleros* daughter); 2) "successor; heir (masc. and fem.)", *aparmānd būtan* "to become a successor". — **2**, 4; **21**, 6, 17; **22**, 3, 7, 8; **24**, 8, 9; **26**, 3; **59**, 12; **61**, 4, 5; **62**, 3, 8, 12; **69**, 12, 15; **70**, 3, 4, 11; **88**, 10; **90**, 1, 16; **94**, 8, 9; **96**, 4, 7; **A2**, 3; **A7**, 7. — This term is widely attested outside the *Law-Book*, see Zaehner, *JRAS* (1940), 35—42. For the etymology (*apar* + *mānd*) and the semantic content see also *apar māndan*, ²*āzātīh*, ²*zātan*, *apar zātan* and my *Obščestvo*, 195—218.

aparmat: "decision, disposition". — **49**, 16, 17; **103**, 9; **A12**, 11.

***apasēk** ('**psyk**'): "liability, debt". Seems to denote more particularly the liabilities connected with the emphyteutic lease of an estate on the crown-or temple land. *'psyk ī pitarān* "liability/debt inherited from one's father". — **A38**, 3, 4. — From Iran. **upa* + *saik*-; *cf.* Parth. *'wpsyk, ptsyk* (Nysa); see, Périkhanian, *REArm*, VI (1969), 2; *idem*, *VDI* (1973/1), 14; *idem*, *Obščestvo*, 160, 334; Livshits, *Acta Antiqua Hung.*, XXV, 183—184.
The OP term **patiϑaika-*, *patiϑaičana-* corresponding to the Parth. *ptsyk* (**pati* + *saik*-) and designating a variety of yearly regular payments is transmitted through the Elamite form *battišekaš*, *battišezana-* (Gershevitch *apud* Hallock, *Tablets*, p. 16 and Nos. 259, 1953, 1954, 2006; Hinz, *Lentz Festschrift*, 37). See also the next entry.

***apasēkōmand** (*'psyk'wmnd*): "burdened with liabilities/debts/rent (regarding an emphyteutic tenure)". *xvāstak ī dārišn pat *apasēkōmand būt*; *xvēšīh* (*q. v.*) *ī apasēkōmand*. — **A27**, 15, 16. — See **apasēk*.

apaspārtan: see *apispārtan*.

apastāk: "direction, instruction, prescription". — **48**,15. — *Cf. Apastāk*, "*Avesta*" = "directions/injunctions (of Zoroaster)", Sogd. *'pšty-* "to order, to prescribe", *'pšt'w'nh* "order, injunction"; see Henning, *BSOAS* XI/4 (1946), 725.

āpātān: "built up, cultivated"; *āpātānīh*. "building, cultivation". — **86**, 3; **A37**, 17.

apātixšāyīhā: "illegally, unlawfully". — **5**, 9; **6**, 3; **11**, 13; **12**, 14; **13**, 17; **14**, 3; **16**, 13; **73**, 7, 8; **107**, 13. — See *pātixšāy*, *pātixšāyīh*, *pātixšāyīhā*.

apatvand: "without relatives", — **70**, 14. The reading is not certain.

a-pat-ziyān: see, *ziyān*; *cf. apēziyān kartan / būtan*.

apāyistan, apāy-: "to be necessary, required", *andar* (*nē*) *apāyēt*. "(not) necessary, (not) required" (one of the formulae for the acceptance or rejection of a transfer); *cf.* also *kāmistan, kāmak, dōšītan, sahistan*). — **12**, 5; **17**, 7, 9; **19**, 9, 11, 16; **26**, 13; **41**, 7; **44**, 6; **109**, 10; **A3**, 2, 3, 5; **A4**, 7; **A11**, 13, 14, 17; **A12**, 1; **A16**, 4 — Iran. **upa* + *ī*-; NP *bāyad*. *Cf.* Arm. *pēt, pēt-k'* *et. al.* (from early MI **upēt* < **upa* + *ita*).

apaytāk (būtan): "not to be officially declared" (*e. g.* of value, price). — **39**, 17. — See, *paytāk kartan, paytākēnītan*.

apēč: "clean, pure". — **80**, 17. — MMP *'byčg*, NP *wēža* "clean".

apēdastaβar, apēdastaβarīhā: "without rightful sanction, in an unentitled manner". — **24**, 7; **56**, 8; **A31**, 7. — See *dastaβar*.

apēsaxvan būtan: "to renounce, disavow", *apēsaxvanīh* "renunciation, recantation". — **64**, 5—7; **89**, 6, 9; **99**, 13, 14.

apēziyān kartan: "to compensate / idemnify for losses", *apēziyān būtan* "to receive compensation for losses". — **1**, 12; **2**, 15, 16. — See *ziyān*.

apēziyānīh: "compensation, indemnity for losses". — **85**, 10. — See *apēziyān, ziyān*.

apispārtan, apispār- (*xvastak, graβ*): "to convey; hand over, entrust"(a thing, a pledge, a security); *apač apispārtan* "to return, restitute". — **11**, 1, 5—7, 9, 10, 13, 15, 16; **12**, 5—7, 9,15; **14**, 8; **15**, 5, 7, 13, 16; **18**, 3; **29**, 16, 17; **30**, 3, 9; **39**, 6, 7; **49**, 17; **50**, 4; **54**, 15; **57**, 13, 14; **58**, 2, 3, 5—7, 9, 10, 14, 16; **67**, 15, 17; **68**, 1, 16; **72**, 4, 11, 12; **73**, 10; **89**, 1,3; **102**, 5, 8; **107**, 6, 7; **A1**, 17; **A4**, 3—4; **A7**, 12—13; **A8**, 2; **A9**,4—5; **A13**, 2; **A26**, 6; **A30**, 9; **A31**, 15.— From **apa* / *upa* + *spār*-; MMP and Parth. *'bysp'r-*, NP *supurdan*, Khwaresm. *b'sp'ryd-*. *Cf.* Arm. LW *apsparem* (< **apisparem*) "to convey / transfer, entrust".

ap(p)ār: "taking away, tearing away, removal", *ap(p)ārīh* "removal"; *hač A ap(p)ār* "to take away from A"; *ō A ap(p)ār* "to take away for the benefit of A". — **22**, 17; **24**, 10; **28**, 16; **29**, 5; **35**, 8; **38**, 10; **89**, 4; **97**, 16; **98**, 1, 11; **102**, 3, 12; **104**, 5, 7,8; **106**, 13; **107**, 1, 2; **A38**, 15. — Iran. **apa* + *bar*-; see ZSR IV, 15; V, 4, 8; Henning, *Verbum*, 175.

ap(p)arakīhā: "by brigandage, by force". — **102**, 6. — *Cf. ap(p)ur, ap(p)urtan*.

ap(p)ur: "robbery, brigandage"; as a term of criminal law distinct from "theft". — **9**, 14; **A15**, 3, 6. — *Cf.* Arm. *apuṙ* "robbery" < MI *ap(p)urr* < **apa* + *bṛna* — See next entry.

ap(p)urtan, ap(p)ar-: "to rob; to seize forcibly", as opposed to *dužītan* "to steal". — **9**, 13; **11**, 8; **80**, 12; **A30**, 8. — Iran. **apa* + *bar*-, Henning, *Verbum*, 175; MMP *'pr*.

apurnāy: "minor, not yet of age". — **41**, 7; **48**, 3; **51**, 16; **52**, 5, 15; **69**, 17; **89**, 15; **110**, 15; **A23**, 1—3. — Antonym *purnāy* (*q. v.*).

apurnāyak: "a minor". — **4**, 2, 3; **17**, 8; **19**, 9—11, 16; **20**, 2, 3, 5, 13, 15, 16; **26**, 8; **27**, 14, 15, 17; **28**, 10, 17; **30**, 11, 13; **31**, 5; **32**, 15; **33**, 3; **41**, 8, 9; **43**, 17; **44**, 7; **48**, 11; **49**, 7; **50**, 17; **52**, 2, 6—8; **53**, 2; **54**, 12; **58**, 16; **67**, 6, 7, 9; **69**, 12; 16; **70**, 12; **73**, 9, 10; **87**, 4, 11; **88**, 8; **107**, 6, 7; **A13**, 5, 6.

apurnāyīh, apurnāyakīh: "minority, minor age". — **4**, 3; **19**, 10, 11, 14; **20**, 3, 13; **43**, 17; **50**, 14; **52**, 2; 77, 2; **87**, 5, 11; **90**, 3; **110**, 16; **A5**, 11, 4. — Antonym, *purnāyīh*.

āpustan: "pregnant", *āpustanīh*: "pregnancy". — **80**, 1.

āpvarīh: "aqueduct". — **106**, 15, 16. — Iran. **āp-* + *bara-*.

armēšt: "crippled, invalid". — **53**, 2. — Av. *armaēštā-* "motionless", *AirWb.*, 197; for the etymology see Bailey, *Prolexis*, 203; *cf.* Narten, IIJ, 10, 4 (1968), 239—250.

Artvahišt: "day of the month in the Zoroastrian calendar" — **35**, 14; **A13**, 7.

arž: "value/cost; price", *arž ī šahr* "market price", lit. "the price (of a thing) in a (given) *šahr*", "local price"; *apač arž* "fall in value, fall in price; mark-down"; *pat arž dātan* "to sell". — **12**, 7; **17**, 17; **18**, 2, 5; **30**, 7; **37**, 1, 2; **43**, 12, 13; **53**,11, 12; **54**, 11—15, 17; **55**, 1, 4, 6—8; **61**, 13; **66**, 6—9, 11; **68**,10, 13, 15; 77, 8; **79**, 15; **96**, 17; **110**, 12; **A9**, 7; **A26**, 17; **A27**, 13.

aržistan/aržītan, arž-: "to cost, to be worth". — **12**, 7; **17**, 17; **18**, 2, 5; **54**, 7, 9, 12, 13; **66**, 6—9, 11; **67**, 5; **68**, 2, 4, 7, 10, 11, 13, 15; **88**, 5; **94**, 15; **110**, 12.

asaβār: "horseman". — 77, 6, 8.

asaβār-nipēk: "List of Horsemen". — **A16**, 11, 13, 15—16; **A17**, 1; **A19**, 2—5.

asardār: "without guardian". — **29**, 2. — See *sardār*, *sardārīh*.

asīm: "silver". — **17**, 16; **18**, 1—5.

asīmēn: "of silver, silver" — **104**, 9, 11, 12, 14.

asp: "steed, horse". — **72**, 4, 5.

āspōžišn: "thrusting; pressing" (?). — **A14**, 17. — Perhaps Iran. **ā* + *spuǰ-*, *cf.* MP *spuxtan*, *spōž-*. "to push, to push out; push over; step on, press on; crush, destroy", Arm. *spužem*. "to put off, delay", NP *sipōxtan*, *sipōz-* "to pierce through, thrust into, insert".

āsravan: "priest" (learned term for a representative of the priestly estate). — **A27**, 7 — Av. *āθravan-*.

ast, ast-ē(v): "portion, share". — **2**, 7; **19**, 5; **34**, 10; **50**, 5; **55**, 5, 6; **75**, 6; **104**, 2; **A21**, 2—4. — Iran. **ans-*. *asta-*, Skt. *áṁśaḥ* "part, portion", Av. *ąsa-*, Parth. *ast.* (Nysa), Sogd. Mugh *(γypδ)'st* "(own) share", *i. e.* "the personal share (of a daughter) in her father's estate. —*A. P.*)".

āstūtan, āstāv-: "to approve". — 7, 3; **78**, 8. — Iran. *ā*+*stāv-*.

āsyāp: "mill" — **105**, 11; **106**, 12, 14, 15.

***asūn**: "small, scant" (of income). — **15**, 17. — Iran. **a-sūna-*, root **sav*; *cf.* Skt. *suná-* (n.) "Erfolg. Wohlergehen, Gedeihen", Av. *sava-* "Nutzen, Vorteil", *a-sūna-* **Y**. **28**, 10. Both the reading and the interpretation are hypothetical. The spelling is 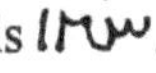.

āšnāk: "known, identified"; *āšnākīh* "identification", *āšnāk guftan, tan āšnāk kartan* "to identify" (regarding the authentification of a seal on a document and the establishement of the identity of persons participating in a lawsuit); *tan āšnākīh, āšnākīh ī tan* "the establishment of the identity of a participant in a lawsuit by a court official". — **76**, 2; **80**, 1; **A26**, 5; **A29**, 13—14; **A30**, 2, 4; **A31**, 5; **A32**, 1; **A34**, 17.

Aštāt: name of one of the liturgies in the Zoroastrian ritual. — **35**, 17; **36**, 1. — Av. *Arštāt-*, *Air. Wb.*, 205.

[1]**atarsakāy**. "misconduct; disobedience" (of a wife; a category of offence). — **A3**, 15, 17; **A4**, 3, 13; **A5**, 17; **A6**, 4. — *Cf. tarsakāy, tarsakāyīh.*

[2]**atarsakāy**: "(judicial document regarding) the bad conduct (of a wife)". — **A3**, 16; **A6**, 6; **A7**, 12.

atarsakāyīh: "misconduct, disobedience (primarily of a wife)"; a category of offence. — **A4**, 12, 16; **A5**, 1, 5, 6; **A6**, 2—3; **A7**, 15; **A8**, 1. — *Cf.* [1]*atarsakāy.*

ātarvaxšīh; see *āturvaxšīh.*

ātaxš (more correctly *ātaš* < *ātarš* with an instrusive graphic *-x-*)"holy Fire; Fire-(temple)"; *ātaxš nišāstan* "to institute a Fire temple/altar"; *ātaxš sardārīh* "trusteeship over a privately instituted Fire altar or temple"; *(h)ēr ī ātaxš* "temple treasury; temple fund, properties", *ātaxš ī Varahrān* (*q. v.*). — **1**, 7—9; **24**, 13; **25**, 8, 16, 17; **26**, 1, 13, 14; **27**, 5, 9, 15; **28**, 5, 14; **29**, 7; **34**, 1; **45**, 15; **46**, 2—4; **50**, 3, 4; **51**, 4; **78**, 12, 13; **93**, 4; **95**, 16, 17; **103**, 5; **110**, 3, 4, 7; **A14**, 1; **A16**, 4, 8; **A26**, 13; **A27**, 1, 3; **A35**, 17; **A36**, 2, 4, 7, 9; **A37**, 7, 10, 12, 13; **A39**, 1, 5, 6, 8, 11—13, 17. — See also, *ātur, āturōk.*

atēn: "entrance, entry". — **A27**, 1. — MMP *'dyn* "entrance" < **ati* + *ayana-*, Bartholomae, *MiMund.* I, 31—32.

atōžišnīh: "non-payment". — **3**, 6. — See *tōžišn, tōžišnīh, tōxtan.*

attān: "solvent", *attānīh* "solvency". — **12**, 6; **56**, 2, 10; **57**, 6; **58**, 17; **59**, 1,5; **A15**, 7. — From Iran. **ati-* + *tāvana-* "able" > "able to pay/solvent" according to Bartholomae, *ZsR*, III, 53, note. The synonym, *tuvānīk* is formed from the same root **tav*. "to be powerful, to be able".

ātur: "Fire-temple". — **50**, 3, 4; **101**, 9—11; **A39**, 9. — See also *ātaxš, ātur(r)ōk/ātarōk.*

Ātur: "(the month) Ātur". — **35**, 13; **37**, 14; **A18**, 13.

āturān bandak: see, *bandak.*

āturgān: "Fire altar". — **110**, 4.

ātur(r)ōk/āturōk/ātarōk: "Fire-altar"; *ātur(r)ōk ō dātgāh pat Varahrānīh nišāstan* "to institute a Fire-altar; to set up an altar (in a Varahrān Fire-temple)". — **26**, 17; **27**, 6,8; **31**, 9—11; **94**, 3; **A37**, 4, 6, 7. — The spelling *'twrlwk'* (constant in the ms. of the Lawbook) suggests the reading *ātur(r)ōk* < **ātr̥-* + *rauk(a)-* "(the place of) the blazing of the (sacred) Fire", as it has been proposed in the Russian edition. This explanation seems to be supported by Arm. *patroyk* "wick" < Parth. *patrōk* < **patirauk(a)* — and especially so, by Arm. *atrušan* "Zoroastrian altar of the sacred Fire", a synonym analysed as MI **āturōšăn* < Iran. **ātr̥-aušăna-* lit. "(the place of) the blazing of the Fire" by Benveniste see *JA* (1964), 45—58. For the formation *cf.* also Av. *ātrə.saoka-* (*Vd.* **8**, 81—85; *AirWb.*, 319) "Feuerbrand" translated as *ātaxš ī sōzak* in the Pahlavi *Vīdēvdāt* and glossed (**8**, **81**) with *ātur(r)ōk* However the reading *āturōk* / *ātarōk* > *ādarōg* lit. "little fire" (see Boyce, *BSOAS*, XXXI [1968], 52—68, 270—289; MacKenzie, *Pahl. Dict.*, 5) cannot be discarded. The presence of the diminutive suffix *-ōk* in a term designating the deified Fire, an object of worship, could have been brought about by the worshippers' desire to win the favour of the divinity.

āturvaxšīh, ātarvaxšīh: "the function of a junior priest whose duty was to watch over the maintenance of the sacred Fire in a Zoroastrian temple". — **A40**, 3 — Av. *ātrəvaxš-*, *ātravaxš*, *Air. Wb.* 318—319.

atuvānīk: "incapable (in a legal sense); insolvent"; *atuvānīkīh* "incapacity; insolvency". — **58**, 6, 8; **71**, 8; **72**, 11. — See, *tuvānīk, tuvānīkīh.'*

at̲vadāt: 1) "offence consisting in the driving out of the house and abandoning without means of subsistance a wife or any person in wardship"; 2) "utterly destitute or helpless state"; 3) "a specific level of offence". — **33**, 7, 15; **A15**, 1; **A35**, 7. — Av. *aδwaδātay-* < **advan* + *dāti-* (*Nīr.* 9; *Air. Wb.*, 61), lit. "put out, set forth on the road, on the way" (for the purpose of driving out of the community). See Bartholomae, *IF*, XII (1901), 118—122. For the formation and the semantic content *cf.* Arm. *panduxt* "exile, alien" < Iran. **pantaduxta-* (Périkhanian, *REArm*, VI (1969), 1—14) and NP *rāh-dāde* "exile" in the Pers. version of the tale of Bilauhar and Būdāsaf; see Henning, *A Locust's Leg*, 103—104.

ăvaštak kartan: "to seal". — **A12**, 15. — See *ăvaštan*.

ăvaštan / ăvištan, *ăvart- (heterogr. ḤTYMWN-): "to seal"; *nipišt ut ăvašt* "document". — **2**, 1; **9**, 7; **16**, 15; **20**, 13; **30**, 16, 17; **31**, 10, 12; **38**, 7; **64**, 3; **77**, 5; **78**, 6, 15; **99**, 2, 4, 5; **100**, 6, 10, 15; **107**, 3; **110**, 6; **A5**, 14; **A6**, 14; **A10**, 11, 12; **A12**, 14, 16; **A13**, 7, 8; **A15**, 9; **A16**, 12, 13, 16; **A17**, 1; **A19**, 3—5; **A27**, 7, 17; **A28**, 9; **A30**, 5, 7; **A35**, 12; **A36**, 11; **A37**, 15; **A39**, 4; **A40**, 15. — MMP *'wyšt*. The Parthian (Nysa) composite *mwdrwrt* (= *mwhrvart*) "setting a seal" points to the etymology **ava* / *ā*+*vr̥t*: **varsta-* > *varšta*. Iran. **ava-varsta-* is attested in the Khot.-Sak. *vūlsta* "to roll down", (Bailey, *Prolexis*, 332). The origin of the word is evidently due not so much to the practice of rolling up documents into scrolls before sealing as to the widespread earlier use of cylinder seals that were rolled out on clay to obtain an impression. A different etymology (**abi* + *pašta-*, root *pas* "to bind, tie up") has been proposed by Henning, *BSOAS* (1946), 725 and Bailey, *Prolexis*. 186—187. See also *ăvaštak kartan, ăvišt*.

avāvarīkān(īh): "unauthentic, invalid". — **74**, 2. — *Cf.* *vāvarīkān(īh)*.

avikāy: "unwitnessed". — **91**, 3. — *Cf.* *vikāy, vikāyīh*.

avinās: "innocent, not guilty". — **72**, 12; **101**, 6. — *Cf.* *vinās*.

avināsih, **avinās**: "innocence, guiltlessness". — **53**, 14; **58**, 7; **98**, 11; **A35**, 10; **A40**, 1, 2. — *Cf. vinās, vināskār(īh), vināhišn.*

ǎvišt: "document" (lit. "sealed"). — **A9**, 10; **A10**, 8—11. — See *ǎvaštan.*

axunsand: "opposed to; disagreeing with" (a judicial decision). — **89**, 16. — *Cf. xunsand(īh), xvastūk(īh).*

axunsandīh: "disagreement" (with a judicial decision); *axunandīh kartan* "to declare one's disagreement, dissatisfaction with a judicial decision" (for the purpose of appealing it). — **3**, 7; **43**, 3; **93**, 9; **A26**, 5. — *Cf. xunsand(īh), xvastūk(īh).*

āxēzītan: "to gush" (of a spring). — **85**, 4.

āyazišn: "religious worship; ritual purposes". — **34**, 4. — Iran. *ā+yaz*: The word is spelled *'yč(=z)šn* and most scholars read it *izišn* or *ēzišn* (from an earlier *yazišn*). But since the term is clearly of NW origin and belongs to the traditional priestly vocabulary, it seems preferable to assume that the spelling *'yčšn* stands for a prefixed formation of which we have an example recorded in the Parthian documents from Nysa, where an *āyazan nanēstānakān* (*'yzny nnystnkn*) "temple of Nanē" is mentioned. (See Diakonoff and Livshits, *Documents.* No. 1682). Iran. *āyazana-* is likewise attested in OP *āyadana-* (*Bh.* 1, 14).

ayōγēn / ayuγēn: see under *Avestisms, s. v. *ayaoγaēnī-/ *ayuγaēnī-.*

āzāt: 1) "member of a noble family, nobleman". (*Cf.* Arm. loan word *azat* a) "agnate"; b) "nobleman"); 2) "free; freedman". — **1**, 7, 12; **39**, 3; **69**, 6; **A31**, 16. — Iran. *āzāta-<ā+zan-* "to be born", lit. "born in the family; agnate"; whence come the two basic meanings of this social term: "member of a family, of a community", "person having civic rights, citizen" (as against non-citizen and slave) and "member of a noble family, nobleman". See also *āzāt-hišt*, *[1]āzātīh*, *āzāt kartan.*

āzāt-hišt: "manumission, manumission document". — **A31**, 17. — See, *āzāt.*

[1]**āzātīh**: "freedom; civic legal status (as opposed to slavery)". — **106**, 10; **A39**, 9 — See *āzāt.*

[2]**āzātīh**: "inheritance, patrimony"; *pat āzātīh ut xvēšīh* "into (one's) personal inherited possession" (a variety of real rights; it designates a possession passing on through inheritance to the personal successors of the owner). — **A37**, 16, 17. — Arm. *azatut'iwn* "inheritance, inherited fund, succession". For the etymology, from Iran. *ā+zā-*: *zāta-* (= Skt. *hā-*, *jahāti*) "to leave, to abandon; to separate (oneself) from, to (be) freed from", see Perikhanian REArm., V (1968), 9—16. The following examples may be added to those mentioned there: *ŠGV*, XIII, 1—2: *nipēk ī-š āzāt xvānēnd* "the text that they (= Jews) describe as having come down through transmission / tradition" (what is intended is the Torah). *ŠGV*, XIV, 80: *āzāt dastaβar* "a rabbi", lit. "a person competent in (the texts of the Jewish) tradition". *Šahr. ī Erān.*: ... *u-š dašt ī Tāčīk pat xvēšīh ut āzātīh bē ō Buxt-Xusrav ī Tāčīk-šāh dāt patvand dārišn ī xvēš rāδ* "... and he conveyed the Arabian plain as a personal inherited possession to Buxt-Xusrav, the king of the Arabs, so that his descendants should (also) possess (it)". With *xvēšīh ut āzātīh*, *cf.* the Arm. calque attested in V . c. texts. *sephakan azatut'iwn* "personal share

(of a son or daughter) in the father's estate; personal inherited possession". See also [2]*zātan* and my *Obščestvo*, 223—225, 348. *Cf. aparmānd, vāspuhrakān, xvēšīh.*

āzāt kartan: 1) "to free (a slave), manumit"; 2) "to release from payment; to release from a debt". — **1**, 6; **20**, 8; **31**, 16—17; **39**, 3; **48**, 14; **69**, 4—5; **83**, 6; **101**, 13; **103**, 5, 6; **A2**, 16. — See *āzāt.*

B

baγ: "lord". — **78**, 2; **100**, 11; **A37**, 2; **A38**, 9; **A39**, 11, 14, 15. — Iran. **baga-* "god". See Bartholomae, *MiMund.*, III, 6—10; Bailey, *BSOAS*, XIV/3 (1952), 420—423.

bāγ: "measure of punishment or amount of the fine set for an offence of a given degree". — **A15**, 2,3. — Av. **bāγa-*, lit. "portion, share". See also *tasubāγ.*

baγaspān: technical term designating one of the varieties of marriage *sine manu mariti*. See **xvasrāyōnīh.* — **21**, 9. — Probably from Iran. **bagaspāna-*, *cf.* Sogd. *βγ'nyšp, bγ'nypš, βγ'npš* (*βaγānīpš/βaγānīšp*) " bridegroom", lit. "Baga-son", "son by the Baga-rites". For the Sogdian term see M. Schwartz, *AoF* I (1974), 259—260. See also *infra bagaspāndāt.*

baγaspāndāt: "child born from a *baγaspān* marriage", *q. v.* — **41**, 10. — For this formation *cf. čakardāt, duxtdāt.*

bahr — "share, portion"; *bahr ī ēvakīh* "ordinary share" (of inheritance), *bahr ī dō(v)īh* "double share". — *Passim.* — See also *bahr ī pusīh, b. ī duxtīh, b. ī zanīh/katak-bānūkīh, b. ī stūrīh, bahr ut xvēšīh, bahrak.*

bahr ī duxtīh: "a daughter's share in her father's estate". — **44**, 10—13; **51**, 15; **52**, 10. — *Cf. vāspuhrakān.*

bahr ī māt: "a mother's share in her father's estate". — **41**, 3. — *Cf. supra.*

bahr ī pus/pusīh: "a son's share in his father's estate". — **51**, 13; **52**, 10; **62**, 5; **90**, 17. — *Cf.* also *bahr ut xvēšīh, vāspuhrakān.*

bahr ī stūrīh/bahr pat stūrīh: "a *stūr*'s portion, a *stūr*-foundation; the share of the dead man's estate acquired — as a *stūr*-possession — by the one called to secure his succession (= the *stūr*)". — **44**, 10, 12. See *stūr, stūrīh, aparmānd.*

bahr ī zanīh/bahr ī katak-bānūk(īh): "a widow's share in her late husband's estate". — **44**, 12, 13; **51**, 13; **52**, 11, 12.

bahr ut xvēšīh: "a (son or daughter's) personal share in the father's estate". — **44**, 8—9. — *Cf. bahr ī pusīh, bahr ī duxtīh, xvēšīh, vāspuhrakān, aparmānd.*

bahrak: "portion, share". — **11**, 12. — See also *bahrak kartan, bahrak ōšmurt.*

bahrak kartan: "to apportion, to divide". — **65**, 12, 14.

bahrak ōšmurt: "estimated/figured in ideal shares". — **65**, 8, 9.

bandak: "slave". In specific constructions with *ātaxš*, *ātur*, this word also takes on the technical sense of "*hierodulos*". — **1**, 7—10; **33**, 11; **101**, 9—14, 16; **103**, 9; **106**, 2, 4, 10; **A2**, 1; **A39**, 9. — See also, *bandakīh*, *anšahrīk*, *paristārīh*, *rahīk*, *tan*, *vēsak / vēšak*.

bandakīh: "slavery"; "*hierodulic* status" in constructions with *ātaxš*, *ātur(ān)* — (see also *paristārīh* for this meaning). — **1**, 1, 2, 9; **101**, 9, 11; **103**, 5; **A39**, 9, 17; **A40**, 1, 3. — See, *bandak*, *šāhān šāh bandakīh*.

bar: "fruit, harvest; revenue"; as against *bun* "basis, principal". *Bar ut vaxt* "revenue and interest"; *bar burtan* "to take, to acquire the fruits / the revenue, to be the usufructuary". — **9**, 15; **12**, 13; **34**, 2, 7, 8, 10, 11; **35**, 9; **38**, 3—5; **39**, 10, 11; **40**, 3, 4; **48**, 2; **49**, 14, 15; **53**, 14; **54**, 8—10; **102**, 14; **103**, 13; **105**, 15; **A8**, 5, 9, 11; **A30**, 16. — *Cf.* *barōmand*, *bar-xvēš*, *bar-xvart*, *vaxt*.

[1]**bār**: see *hark ut bār*.

[2]**bār**: "once, at once, at a time". — **73**, 1; **91**, 17; **92**, 9, 11—13, 15, 16; **97**, 1.

barōmand: "bearing fruit, bringing revenue". — **34**, 2; **39**, 2.

barvar: "able to bear children" (of a woman). — **49**, 2, 3. — *Cf.* Afgh. *brālba*, *blārba*: "pregnant" < **bārbara-* (Morgenstierne, *EVP*, 15).

bar-xvart: "usufruct". — **A7**, 8. — For the formation *cf.* Sogd. *ptrq'n-xw'r* "heir". (See Bailey, *ZP*, 73; Henning, *BSOAS*, XI/4 (1946), 716). *Cf.* *bar-xvēš*.

bar-xvēš: "possessor of the revenue, usufructuary". — **37**, 14—15; **90**, 9. — *Cf.* *bun-xvēš*, *bar-xvart*.

bastan, **band-**: "to bind; to arrest". — **A15**, 11.

bavandak: "sufficient; entire, full". — *Bavandak*, *pat bavandak* "entirely, fully"; *bavandak būtan* "elapse, be fulfilled" (as regards time); *var bavandak* "an oath / ordeal is sufficient (in the legal sense)". — **14**, 5, 7; **22**, 8; **30**, 6; **54**, 8; **58**, 2; **60**, 11, 12, 15; **72**, 15; **101**, 15; **A23**, 7—9. — *Cf.* the Arm. loan-words, *bovandak* "full, whole; fully, entirely; sufficient, suficiently"; *bovandakem* "to include, comprise; to complete,finish"; *bovandakim* "be fulfilled, be completed; be sufficient".

baxšitan, **baxš-**: "to allot, to convey". — **38**, 6.

baxškarīh(?): "gift" — **107**, 14. — Neither the reading nor the interpretation are certain.

baxt: "fate", *pat baxt šutan* "to die". *E. g.* **105**, 2—3; **109**, 14.

baxtan, **baxš-**: "to divide, apportion, distribute". — **A28**, 4.

baxtīkīh: "division of an inheritance"; *baxtīk kartan* "to divide an inheritance". — **22**, 13; **23**, 6, 7; **47**, 6; **51**, 3; **52**, 4, 15; **53**, 1, 2; **90**, 15; **96**, 12.

bāzūk masā ut sēnak masā (Ms.: **b'z'y ms'd, synwk ms'd**): "Learned" term borrowed from the *Avesta* and having acquired the meaning of "a measure, a norm (established by custom)" in Pahlavi texts. In the present case, it designates the amount of pay-rations alloted to an "appointed" guardian; this norm was equal to the minimal amount required for the maintenance of one person. — **27**, 2. — Av. **bāzu.masah-*, *sraoni.masah-*; the Pahl. rendering *sēnak* "breast" (NP *sīna*) presumably a corruption of the original *srēnak*, is also registered in this formula which literally signifies "the size of/as large as an arm, the size of a hip"; see, *AirWb.*, 956, 1633. It is, however, also possible to presume the existence of a parallel formula: "the size of an arm, the size of a breast".

bēšahrīk: "alien, foreigner, from another town". — **A28**, 8. — *Cf. šahrīk.*

bizišk: "physician". — **108**, 8. — NP *pizišk*, Arm. (from Parth.) *bžišk*. In the manuscript this word is represented by the heterogram 'SY', *cf.* the Akkadism in Syriac, *'âsiâ* "physician". To the best of my knowledge this heterogram is recorded here for the first time.

^{1}**bōxtan, bōxtītan, bōž-**: 1) "to free; to cancel/dissolve"; 2) "to be acquitted, to win a case"; in this sense it is opposed to *ēraxtan* and to ^{2}*ōzatan*. — **14**, 16; **83**, 11, 16; **92**, 13; **102**, 2, 6; **A15**, 16. — Iran. ^{1}**bug-* "to free, to save; dissolve, cancel, loosen", Av. *baog- baoxtār- et. al.*; *cf.* also Arm. *bužem*: "to heal; save; free (from)".

^{2}**bōxtan, bōž-**: "to make use of, to use".— **95**, 10.— Iran. ^{2}**bug-* "to be useful, to serve; to make use of; enjoy"; *cf.* Skt. *bhuǰ-*, *bhunākti*, Arm. (from MI) **boxšnem* in *əmboxšnem* "to make use of, enjoy", see, Benveniste, *Titres*, 108—115. *Cf.* ^{2}*bōžišn*.

^{1}**bōžišn**: "decision (in a legal case)". — **40**, 3; **49**, 10, 12; **74**, 3; **76**, 8; **83**, 1; **106**, 10; **A12**, 3, 16; **A13**, 3. — Iran. **bug-*, see ^{1}*bōxtan*.

^{2}**bōžišn**: "use; right/title to use, usufruct". — **A33**, 10, 11 — Iran. ^{2}**bug-*, see, ^{2}*bōxtan*.

brāt: "brother"; *brāt ī hambāy*; see *hambāy*; *dātastān brāt*, see *dātastān*.

^{1}**brīn**: "part, portion". — **3**, 3.

^{2}**brīn**: "excluding, except"; *bar brīn*: "excluding the revenue, except for the revenue". — **102**, 14.

^{3}**brīn**: "established, limitted by agreement; stipulated"; *brīn zamān*: "set, stipulated time-limit". — **2**, 9, 10, 13.

brītan, brīn-: 1) "to cut off, to detach, to separate"; 2) "to determine, delimit"; 3) "to decree, create, establish"; *sar brītan*. "to decapitate"; *pargār* (var. *pursišn-nāmak, saxvan-nāmak*) *brītan*. "to prepare (a document regarding) a judicial decision", "to draw up the records, court records/documents". — **14**, 17; **73**, 12; **74**, 1; **78**, 11; **A26**, 14; **A27**, 2. — Iran. **brāy-*, NP *buridan*; with *pargār/saxvan-nāmak britān*, *cf.* Khwar. *xṣwmt* in the locution, *mpxyt'h 'y xṣwmyt- δ'r* "he decided (lit. 'cut') the litigation" (MacKenzie, *Khwar. Gl.*, I, 548).

bun: "base, basis, foundation". Specifically , 1) "the principal" of a thing as against the revenue brought by the thing, *bar*; 2) "the principal person", "the principal or original possessor/owner" (*cf. bun-xvēš*); "the principal contractor" (as against his warrantor), *cf. mātak, mātakvar*); "the principal litigant" (as against his legal representative); 3) "the principal taxes and payments into the royal treasury (as against various charges likewise paid to the treasury; 4) "the principal residence". *Cf.* also the following technical expressions: *apāč ō bun matan*, *apāč ō bun šutan / āβurtan* (regarding the return of a thing to its original or principal possessor, regarding the return to the *status quo ante*). — **17**, 13; **19**, 5; **20**, 4; **25**, 10, 12—13; **34**, 3; **35**, 5; **40**, 4; **41**, 15; **53**, 15; **56**, 7; **64**, 17; **72**, 9—10; **102**, 15; **105**, 15; **A2**, 9; **A27**, 1; **A31**, 5. — Iran **bŭna-*.

bun-dārīh: "repository / treasury of foundations". — **79**, 10.

bun-xvēš: "principal owner"; the person holding the basic right (= title) to a thing as against the person endowed with the derivative right to the same thing, the temporary possessor, the usufructuary, *etc.* — **37**, 14; **39**, 12, 14, 15; **A15**, 3; **A30**, 16. — See also, *bunxvēšīh*; *cf. bar-xvēš, bar-xvart.*

bunxvēšīh: "the basic real right, the basic title to a thing". This term is opposed to *dārišn* "the fact of possession" as well as to the secondary, temporary title. — **12**, 15.

burtān, bar: "to carry; to carry away". — *Passim.* — *Cf.* the following special usages: *dužītan ut burtan* "to abduct", see **A26**, 4, 8; *andar ... burtan* "to relate to ...", see, **A3**, 89; *andar ō ... burtan* (regarding the bringing by the wife of a dowry, thing, or revenue to her husband; regarding the master's acquisition of a thing conveyed to his slave), see, **101**, 14; **A1**, 8, 10, 12; **A2**, 15; **A3**, 13; *apāč ō ... burtan* (regarding the obligation of a slave to give to his master a revenue conveyed to himself), see, **A2**, 2.

būtak: "natural". Designation, depending on the variety of order of calling, given to a guardian or *stūr*. — **26**, 6, 11; **28**, 4; **47**, 13; **69**, 8; **90**, 12; — See, *būtakīh*; *cf. gumārtak*, *⁴kartak* (antonyms).

būtakīh: "natural calling". The calling (to *stūr*ship, guardianship, trusteeship) *via* the kinship within a family and dependent upon the degree of this kinship. *Būtakīhā*, *hač kust ī būtakīh* "*via* the line of natural calling". — **47**, 2, 13; **49**, 5, 6; **69**, 8. — See *būtak*. Antonyms *kartakīhā*, *gumārtakīhā*.

Č

čāh: "a well". — **19**, 2.

čak: "document". — **73**, 17; **74**, 3, 7; **A26**, 1; **A28**, 8. — NP *čak* "document".

čakar, čakarīh: "levirate marriage", — **3**, 11; **28**, 7. Concerning the etymology of this term (as formed on the reduplication of the root **kar-* "to make", *cf.* NP *čākar* "servant, maidservant", Osset. *caγar* "slave") and its technical meaning, see Bartholomae, *SRb*, 7—8; *ZsR* I, 31—33; Perikhanian, *Henning Mem. Vol.*, 353—357. A different analysis (Pahl. *čkl* = MP **čaγr* < Av. **čaγrā̆-* "giving, providing", an *-r-* extension of Iran. **čag-*) has been proposed by Klingenschmitt, *MSS* (1971), 123—125. See also *infra.*

apurnāyak, duxt, frazand, pus ī čakar / čakarīhā: "son or daughter born from a person's levirate marriage with the widow of his agnate , and consequently not one of his own successors and heirs" (as against his children born from a *pātixšāyīh* marriage). — **27**, 14; **28**, 9, **32**, 3, 15, 17; **41**, 6; **42**, 12; **48**, 3; **A24**, 1—8; **A35**, 12, 13; **A40**, 10, 12. — Antonyms *duxt, frazand, pus ī pātixšāyīhā* (*q. v.*).

pit ī čakar / čakarīhā: "*čakar*-father". The natural father of the person and the *čakar*-husband of his mother,as against his legal father, that is the (late) first husband of his mother with whom she had entered into a marriage with full rights. — **32**, 15, 17; **48**, 5. — *Cf. pit ī pātixšāyīhā.*

zan ī čakar / čakarīhā: "*čakar*-wife". A widow having entered into a levirate marriage with an agnate of her late husband. Together with an *epikleros*-daughter (see **ayōγēn* / *ayūγaēnī*-), this is one of the varieties of "natural *stūr*ship", *stūr ī būtak* (*q. v.*). — **28**, 9; **32**, 17; **49**, 2; **A4**, 14, 16; **A5**, 3, 11; **A8**, 1; **A40**, 10, 12. — Antonym *zan ī pātixšyīhā, pātixšāy zanīh.*

čakardāt: "born from a *čakar*-marriage; *duxt* / *pus ī čakardāt.* — **A14**, 10. — For the composition *cf. baγaspāndāt, duxtdāt.*

čambar: "hoop, circlet, diadem". In this case the hoop is worn around the wizard's neck. — **A15**, 15, 17. — NP *čanbar* "hoop, rim"; *cf.* Arm. *čambar* 1) "diadem", 2) "military camp", a meaning derived from the usual circular lay out of the tents in a military encampment.

čanār / čandāl: "plane-tree", — **39**, 1; **40**, 15; — NP *čanār* "plane-tree". The spelling *čnd'l* also permits the reading *čandal, cf.* NP *čandăl* "sandal tree".

čāšān: "teacher, preceptor, superior". A temple function / office. — **A36**, 11. — Iran. **čăšan*-, *cf.* Av. *čašan*- derived from the root *kas*-, *čaxš*- "to see, teach, instruct"; *cf.* Osset. fæʒæxsyn "to give instruction, edify", Abaev, *HEDO*, 1, 430.

čašmakāy: "eyewitness, witness". — **78**, 5, 6. — Synonym *vikāy*. For the etymology *cf. tarsakāy.*

čāštak: "teaching, precept". Name of the commentaries to the *Avesta* as against ^{2}*kartak* — norms of jurisdiction both official and traditional (= based on practice) — **22**, 5; **26**, 6; **52**, 3; **98**, 5; **A3**, 6; **A13**, 7. — See also *čāštan*, ^{2}*dastaβar.*

čāštan, čāš-: "to teach, instruct, interpret" (regarding the commentary to the *Avesta*). — **26**, 10; **106**, 17; **A10**, 6. — *Cf. čāštak.*

čiš: "thing". — **16**, 5, 10. — *Cf. xvāstak, (h)ēr.*

D

dar: "gate" (as part of a building complex). — **15**, 1.

dār ut draxt: "plantation of trees". — **106**, 14, 16.

^{1}**dārišn**: "possession". This term is used both in the concrete sense of "estate", "thing possessed" and in the following abstract meanings: 1) "the factual possession of a thing; the fact of possession"; 2) "the legal possession of a thing", according to whatever title, on the basis of real right of any type; *cf. xvēšīh. Dārišn bē kartan* "to transfer the possession (= the real right) to another person; to alienate";

dārišn (ī) pat apasēkōmand (*q. v.*) "a possession burdened with liabilities; *dārišn ī ōzītak/uzītak* (?) "possession of an escheated (?) estate/property"; *dārišn ī pat vidāšt* (?); *pat mat dārišn* "future possession" = *bona adventicia*". — **10**, 1, 6, 13; **12**, 15; **14**, 14, 16; **15**, 15, 17; **31**, 1, 3; **32**, 10; **39**, 9, 15; **55**, 13; **57**, 14; **84**, 13-15; **89**, 1; **91**, 3; **95**, 8—10; **105**, 16; **108**, 6—7; **A26**, 3, 10, 11; **A27**, 15, 16. - See, *dāštan*, *aδvēnak ī dašt*, *xvēšīh*.

[2]**dārišn**: "maintenance; expenditure for maintenance"; *dārišn ī pat zēndān* "keeping in prison".— **19**, 16; **30**, 10; **A13**, 13; **A28**, 11. — See also *xvarišn ut dārišn*.

dart: 1) "pain"; 2) "premeditated inflicting of physical pain"; one of the forms of offences of the *žahm* category. — **91**, 16; **A14**, 16.

[1]**dastaβar**: 1) "an entitled, plenipotentiary person; a person competent/entitled to give this or that disposition, a disposer (as a position/office, *cf. e. g.*, *tasūk ī Xūnāpakān pat m... dastaβar*, **100**, 15), trustee (over a foundation for the soul), and in particular, "a person having disposed of a title", "a *mandator*, the giver of a mandate" 2) "an empowered, entitled person; a legal representative (= the representative of a litigating party in a case/trial); a *mandatary*"; 3) see, [2]*dastaβar*. — **5**, 3, 5, 11—17; **6**, 6, 9—11; **7**, 3, 6—8, 12—19; **8**, 2—5, 9—11, 14; **10**, 2, 6; **13**, 10, 11; **22**, 2; **48**, 6; **95**, 12; **96**, 2; **100**, 15; **A14**, 1; **A15**, 8; **A17**, 6, 10; **A33**, 11; **A35**, 12; **A36**, 5; **A39**, 16; **A40**, 15. — Iran. **dastaβara-*, where *dasta-* is probably not "hand" despite this widespread interpretation, but is rather formed on **danh-* "to be able/capable, entitled, gifted, competent", as was already pointed out by Bailey, *ZP*, 160; *TPS* (1945), 8-9; *cf.* Skt. *daṁs-*, Av. [3]*dahma-* 1) "learned, competent"; 2) "a member of a civic-religious community who is of age and in possession of full legal capacity". Av. *dąstvā-* "teaching, dogma", Parth. *dast* "capable", *dast ah-* "to be capable", (Andreas-Henning, *MiM*, III, Gloss. *s. v.*), MMP *dastan* "capable, empowered", Buddh-Sogd. *δstβ'r* "*s-* "s'emparer souverainement, saisir par voie d'autorité", Buddh.-Sogd. *δstβ'r(y)* "by means of, through, with the help of, by force of" in the expression *čnn δrm'yk δstβ'ry* (Benveniste, *JA* (1955), 315—316), *Cf.* with this etymology, Christ-Sogd. *myn'βr* "authoritative, powerful" (< **manya-* + *bara-* "possessing/endowed with authority, power", Henning, *BSOAS*, XII (1948), 309; Benveniste, *Et. oss.*, 53, Osset. *minævar* "mediator intercessor" (alongside Osset. *miniuæg* "capacity"); see also *s. v. dastkart*. For the meaning of this term see Bartholomae, *ZsR*, IV, 52-54 (the meaning "judge" which is not attested in the *Law-Book* or in other texts of the Sasanian period or reflecting a Sasanian tradition should be excluded. It was derived by Bartholomae on the basis of incorrect translations of a series of passages of the *Law-Book* where the term appears in all the given contexts with the sense of "representative of one of the parties at a trial"). It is also important to note the heterographic rendering of this term [illegible] : [illegible] = PQDW(N), PQYDN/W, which should be taken as the original heterogram of the word *dastaβar* (see *e. g.*, **100**, 15; **A36**, 5). *Cf.* Late Babyl. *paqdu*, which is used

in the cuneiform documents of Aršama to designate a person named Bel-supe-muhur who is presented in these documents as Aršama's "agent" for the lease of cattle and the "plenipotentiary administrator" of his estate. (See Driver, *Aram. Doc.*, 44—52), and Aram. *pqyd'* "(fully) empowered" — according to the context of the letters edited by Driver, *e. g.*, "Letter IV", in which Aršama refers to Psamšek as *pqyd' zyly* "my plenipotentiary", and "Letter X", in which Hatuvasti is called *pqyd Wrwhy, i. e.* "the plenipotentiary of (prince) *Wrwhy*", as against his likewise mentioned name-sake who was "the plenipotentiary" (*pqyd' zyly*) of Aršama. The same heterogram — PQDWN — is used for the MP term *dastaβar* "trustee (over a foundation for the soul)" in the "Inscription of Kartīr", see Perikhanian, *REArm*, V (1968) 22—23. In Pahlavi cursive this heterogram fused with that of the word *pātimār* "sentence, punishment" (*PWQDN', Aram. *puqdānā* "disposition", *cf.* also Aram. *pwqdn'* having the specialized meaning of "emprisonment" in the Nippur texts, Montgomery, *Aram. Incant.*, 299). — *Cf.* [2]*dastaβar, dastaβarīh, pātixšāy kartan.*

[2]**dastaβar**: "authority, competent person, commentator of the Avestan *nasks*". — **6**, 6; **13**, 16; **21**, 1; **28**, 9; **55**, 1; **76**, 6; **88**, 7; **93**, 16; **95**, 6; **A28**, 12. — See [1]*dastaβar*; *cf.* *čāštak, ōstaβar.*

dastaβarīh: 1) "competence, title"; 2) "empowerment, authorization, mandate"; 3) "legal representation". *Pat dastaβarīh andar ēstātan* "to appear as an empowered person (= as the representative of one of the parties at a trial or as disposer)". — **5**, 7, 17; **6**, 1, 11, 12; **7**, 4; **8**, 9, 16, 17; **10**, 1, 3, 4, 6; **23**, 1, 7, 8; **37**, 16; **48**, 2; **84**, 13, 17; **86**, 6; **100**, 4; **103**, 1; **A5**, 15; **A6**, 15; **A7**, 2, 7; **A8**, 6; **A17**, 5, 8, 12, 13; **A30**, 11; **A36**, 9; **A37**, 3, 10. — See, *dastaβar*; *cf.* the synonyms, *ōstaβarīh, pātixšāyīh.*

dastaβarīhā: "competently, in a legally authorized manner. — **49**, 14; **88**, 2; **A17**, 16; **A18**, 1.

dastīk: 1) "disposition" (?); 2) "possessions, things which are actually at the conveyor's disposal (as against the *bona adventicia* and things lent to a third party)". — **77**, 3; **105**, 12. — The second of the meanings indicated suits well the context in **105**, 12—14, whereas the damaged state of **77**, 1—3 does not allow to establish with any degree of certainty the meaning of the term here.

dastkarīh: "(agricultural) tasks". — **37**, 14.

dastkart: "*dastkart*; landed estate, plot; estate (as a complex thing)". — **18**, 6, 7, 9, 11, 14—16; **38**, 13, 15, 17; **39**, 2; **51**, 7—8; **105**, 5, 6; **A8**, 14, 15; **A9**, 6, 7; **A18**, 2, 3, 5; **A20**, 11, 13; **A34**, 4; **A36**, 17. — NP *dastgird*, Arm. (from Parth.) *dastakert*, Aram. (Babylonian Talmud) *dsqrt'*. From Iran. **dasta-* + *kṛta-*, which is usually analyzed as "hand-made", see *e. g.* Geiger, *WZKM*, 42 (1935), 123—128. This interpretation is doubtful on semantic grounds (*cf.* Skt. *hastakṛta-* "hand made") although the association of the first element of this term with the word *dast* "hand" is very early (= popular etymology), *cf.* the synonym-calque in Class. Arm. *jeṙakert*, as well as the heterography, *YDHkrt*. It seems to me preferable to analyze the original form, **dasta-kṛta-* as "(a possession/person), made (from **kar-* 'to make') or proclaimed (through an official public declaration, **kar-* 'proclaim, declare') authorized/rightful/empowered/competent" (*cf. dastaβar*), because such an interpretation is more suited to the series of meanings of this term in Iranian and Classical Armenian texts in which this word is attested as applied not only to the possession of land but also to persons. In such a case, the more common meaning. "plot of land; estate; domain" would go back to the ancient custom of periodic reapportioning of the land-holding of the community during which the rightful possession of a particular plot was officially secured to a particular clan or family through a proclamation/declaration at the assembly of the community or clan. The same initial sense of "endowment with rights, power" emerges from the uses of this term when it designates the foundation (by the king) of a city, fortress or settlement together with the conferring of a particular legal status. Thus for example, Buzandaran (IV, xiii) refers to the city of Aršakawan founded by Aršak II as his *dastakert*; Movsēs Xorenac'i (II, 90) designates the city of Drasxanakert as the great *dastakert* of (king) Artašēs"; the word is used here with the sense of "the (royal) foundation", and not "the creation of the (king's) hands", as Sarkisian has interpreted it (in the *Hellenistic Near East*, 97—101); *cf.* also the designation of the city-fortress Kangdez in Pahlavi texts as "the *dastkart* of Syāvaxš". The use of this term as applied to persons in the inscription of Šāhpuhr I (KZ) is particularly important for its etymology. In this inscription Dēnak Queen of Mēšān is designated as "Šāhpuhr's *dastkart*". [(MP) *Dynky ZY myš'n MLKT' dstklt Šḥpwḥry*; (Gk.) Δηνακης βασιλίσσης Μησῶν δαστικιρτ Σαπωρ]. *i. e.* as "a person empowered by Šāhpuhr (= her late husband, the king of Mēšan, or Šāhpuhr I himself) to hold the regency or some other office, *cf. kartak* in the expression *stūr ī kartak, sardār ī kartak*. In the same inscription, Šāhpuhr I calls himself "the *dastkart* of the gods" ("the gods have made us their *dastkart*") and expresses his wish that the gods might also make his successors their *dastkart*. Šāhpuhr is proclaiming thereby that his title to the kingship is derived from the gods, he is as it were "the gods' annointed", and he expresses the hope that the gods will honour his personal successors in the same way. An analogous meaning for the same term may be noted in the text of Ełišē (V century A.D.) where the word is found in the prayers addressed to God by the participants in the rebellion against the Sasanian overlordship who had been deported to Iran and were awaiting execution. Ełišē (VIII, 23): *znoragiwt dastakerts k'o barexōs aṙnemk' vasn anjanc' meroc'*, "we make this newly manifested *dastakert* of thine our mediator". Here as well as in the passages cited below the text alludes to the *magupat* of Aparšahr converted to Christianity owing to a miraculous vision; the story of this conversion precedes the prayers. The translation of both passages given in the Russian edition of the *Law-Book* is inexact. *Cf.* also Ełiše (VIII, 65): *Lur inj, Tēr, ... ew ənkal zogi im i žołovs surb zorakanin k'o, or erewec'aw norakert dastakertin k'oy*, "Hear me, Lord, ... and receive my soul within the ranks of thy holy host which appeared to that newly manifested *dastakert* of thine". In both prayers this outstanding convert is described as the Lord's appointee, as a person empowered by God himself as a missionary of the Christian faith. It is unlikely that the term with which we are concerned can be translated "création, créature" < "made by hand", as this is done by Maricq (*Class. et Or.*, 56—57, n. 2). Such an interpretation of this term would rob it of any expressiveness and meaning in all the contexts of the indicated passages of the KZ or of Ełišē. Everything living or not was considered to be "God's creation" by the praying Christians in the works of Ełišē, and although a Zoroastrian's idea of the creation was not exactly the same, King Šāhpuhr would have had little ground for stressing in his inscription that he had been "created by the gods", since this was true of all humans in a Zoroastrian's eyes. A most interesting usage of this term in the sense of "institution, foundation" (referring specifically to foundations *piae causae*) is to be found in the Armenian Canons of the Covenant of Ałuēn (488 A.D.). Thus , Canon xix reads, "*Ark' azatk' orč'ap' iwreanc' dastakertk' en, zerec' aranc' episkoposi mi išxesc'en hanel ew aṙnel* "Let no nobleman remove or appoint a priest without the permission of a bishop on the grounds that (the monasteries/churches/hospices) presided over by the given person were their (own) institutions (*i. e.* were founded by themselves or by their fathers as endowments 'for the soul', Arm. *hogec'aturk'*. — *A. P.*)". This canon was directed against old social and legal norms and practices, more particularly against those which reflected the legal régime of the Iranian *pat ruvān* foundations introduced into Ałbania during the epoch preceding that country's Christianization.

dastvarz: "household articles". — **29**, 14. — *Cf.* NP *dastvārz* "artisan", *dastvarzī* "handicraft; artisanal".

dašt: "field". — **85**, 9, 10.

dāštan, **dār-**: "to hold; have, possess; to maintain; to have under one's guardianship"; *pat graβīh dāštan* "to hold (a thing) as security/as a pledge"; *pat xvap dāštan/dārišn* "to consider as lawful"; *xvāstak pat xvēšīh ī M. dāštan* "to consider a thing as M.'s lawful possession/holding"; *frāč dāštan* "to put off, to delay"; see also, *xvarišn ut dārišn*. — **5**, 9; **6**, 4; **18**, 12, 16; **19**, 3; **24**, 12—14, 16, 17; **25**, 2, 3, 5, 6, 17; **26**, 7, 17; **27**, 4, 13; **29**, 4, 10, 11; **32**, 6, 7; **34**, 5, 9, 13, 16; **35**, 3, 4; **36**, 8; **37**, 12, 17; **38**, 2; **39**, 5; **40**, 6, 8, 10, 12; **44**, 4; **45**, 2, 10; **46**, 6, 8, 10, 12, 16; **47**, 8; **50**, 1—2, 8—11; **53**, 6, 7; **66**, 16, 17; **74**, 2; **A16**, 9, 10; **A17**, 2, 3; **A36**, 8, 10; **A37**, 3, 6, 11, 15, 17; **A38**, 1. — *Cf. dārišn, dāštārīh.*

daštānmāh vičārtan: "(the offence of) having sexual relations with a woman during her menstrual period". — **A35**, 17.

dāštārīh: 1) "maintenance"; 2) "the pay-rations allotted to the trustee over a foundation for the soul", (lit. "maintenance"). — **27**, 10, 11; **31**, 10; **51**, 5.

[1]**dāt**: "law, justice". — **A35**, 5. — *Cf. dātastān.*

[2]**dāt**: "the transfer (of a thing), *traditio*". The formal opposite of *andarz, ōzīt/uzīt* (*q. v.*); *dāt pat sar bavēt* (regarding a transfer in accordance with the latest testamentary disposition); *dāt paytāk kartan* "to make a declaration of transfer". — **17**, 1; **30**, 10, 12; **31**, 6, 8; **90**, 4; **95**, 1; **A9**, 8; **A27**, 13; **A28**, 1. — *Cf. dātan, adahišnīh, adāt, rāt.*

[3]**dāt**: "age". — **26**, 16; **28**, 6; **29**, 8; **48**, 3; **87**, 16.

dātaβar: "judge"; *dātaβar ī kas* "junior/lower judge"; *dātaβar ī mas* "senior judge"; *dātaβar ī pasēmār/pēšēmārān* "judge of the respondent/of the plaintiff"; **3**, 3, 7, 8; **5**, 6; 7, 11; **8**, 10; **14**, 10, 11, 14, 16; **40**, 1; **43**, 15; **49**, 16, 17; **54**, 1, 2; **71**, 9, 16; **73**, 2, 14; **75**, 6, 8; **77**, 11; **86**, 5, 13, 14; **91**, 10 15; **92**, 3; **93**, 3, 6, 10; **94**, 3; **99**, 10, 17; **100**, 5, 12; **110**, 5, 6, 14; **A12**, 11—13, 15; **A13**, 14—16; **A14**, 6; **A15**, 5; **A25**, 16; **A26**, 7, 10, 11, 14; **A27**, 9; **A28**, 9; **A29**, 8, 11; **A30**, 2. — Iran. **dātabara-*, NP *dāvar*; loan word in Bibl. Aram. *dtbry'* (Dan. 3, 3).

dātaβarīh: "a judge's jurisdiction". — **99**, 10.

dātan, **bē dātan**, **dah-**: "to convey, to give/present, to accomplish the transfer of a thing (with all due formalities)". — *Passim*. — *Cf.* also the following usages: *apāč dātan* "to return (a debt/loan); to compensate for losses", **38**, 8; **39**, 13—14; **86**, 1; **102**, 1; **110**, 13—14; *bē dātan* "to give (in marriage)", **83**, 7; **A14**, 12—13; *bē ō pēš dātan/ō pēš dātan* "to transfer further, to another person; to transfer in one's turn", **25**, 12; **26**, 6, 9 (*cf. ō pēš apispārtan*). — *Cf.* [2]*dāt*.

[1]**dātastān**: 1) "law, right, justice"; 2) "court, legal process", see [2]*dātastān*; 3) "judicial affair, legal case and its resolution", also "case" in a broader sense, "*causa*", see, [3]*dātastān*. For the first meaning ("law"), *cf. xvat-dātastān* "*ipso iure*" (?), see **31**, 12; see also below, the terms *dātastān brāt*, *dātastān pus*, *dātastān duxt*, *dātastān xvah*. — Iran. **dāta-* "law", Av. *dāta-*, NP *dādestān*, Arm. (from Parth.) *dat*, *datastan* and their derivations.

[2]**dātastān**: "court, legal process"; *dātastān dātan/kartan* "to assign to/arrange for legal process, a court session/hearing"; *dātastān rāδēnītan* "to conduct a case; to participate in a trial as one of the parties"; *dātastān pat var* "trial by ordeal"; *dātastān sar ah-/būtan* "to be terminated (of a case/trial)"; *pat dātastān andar ēstatān* "to be present at a trial, to participate in it". — **5**, 13; **6**, 5, 10—12; **7**, 10; **8**, 16—17; **9**, 10, 12; **11**, 11, 12; **12**, 5; **14**, 1, 10; **16**, 8, 15, 16; **32**, 5, 9; **36**, 5; **73**, 13; **74**, 11, 13, 14; **75**, 3, 4, 6, 10, 11; **76**, 3, 6, 7, 9; **77**, 15—16; **78**, 1; **84**, 3, 15; **90**, 6; **91**, 1, 6; **93**, 17; **94**, 2; **107**, 12; **A15**, 8; **A16**, 2; **A26**, 1, 2; **A29**, 8; **A30**, 8, 11; **A31**, 17; **A32**, 1, 7—10, 13. — See also *rāδēnišn*.

[3]**dātastān**: "cause, legal case and its resolution, court decision, judgement", likewise "case" in a broader sense, "*causa*". — **9**, 3—5; **10**, 7; **12**, 16; **13**, 9; **15**, 14; **21**, 12; **28**, 4; **39**, 2; **42**, 17; **46**, 1; **48**, 4, **57**, 5; **61**, 1; 77, 4; **78**, 12; **86**, 15; **87**, 6; **90**, 11; **95**, 6; **104**, 7; **A1**, 5; **A5**, 9; **A11**, 18; **A16**, 7.

dātastān brāt, **dātastān brātārīh**: "legal brother, brother 'according to law'". — **28**, 7; **42**, 8, 16, 17; **71**, 6. — The one who is the "legal" son and heir (see, *dātastān pus*) of the person's father (likewise "legal"). See the commentary *s. v. dātastān duxt*.

dātastān duxt: "legal daughter; daughter 'according to law'". — **42**, 9—11, 13,14. — Synonym of *duxt ī pātixšāyīhā* (*q. v.*) but more inclusive: this term designates both person's daughter-heiress born from a marriage with full rights (*pātixšāyīh*), and the daughter-heiress born to him, by his *stūr* (see *stūr*) of any type (see also *duxtdāt*, *dūtak-zāt*). Corresponding to this designation is the category of "children according to law" (*bĕnajâ bə-namusâ*) in the classification of

Išō'bōxt (IV, 1—4) which underwent a Christian redaction and where the "children according to law" are opposed to "natural (*i. e.* blood)" and "adopted" children. *Cf.* also *dātastān brāt, dātastān pus, dātastān xvah.*

dātastān pus/pusīh: "legal son, son 'according to law'". — **28**, 7; **42**, 14; **71**, 6. — The successor of the person: both a son born from a marriage with full rights (*pātixšāyīh*) and a successor acquired through a *stūr*. This term unites in a single group the terms. *pus ī pātixšāyīhā, duxtdāt, stūrīk pus, dūtak-zāt.* See also the commentary *s. v. dātastān duxt.*

dātastān xvah: "legal sister, sister 'according to law'". — **42**, 9. — "the legal daughter" (see *dātastān duxt*) of the person's (likewise "legal") father; *cf. dātastān brāt, dātastān pus.*

dātgāh: "a proper, prescribed place". Specifically the place in a Zoroastrian temple designated for the setting up of the Fire-altar; "Fire-temple". *Cf.* the expression *ātaxš/ātur-(r)ōk pat Varahrānīh ō dātgāh nišāstan* (regarding the setting up of an instituted Fire-altar in a great temple of the Varahrān-fire). — **27**, 1, 7; **110**, 8; **A33**, 7; **A39**, 5, 8. — Iran **dātya gāθu-, cf.* Av. *dāityō.gātav-.*

dātīhā: "in a legally prescribed fashion, lawfully ". — **101**, 6.

daxšak: "sign, mark". — **A15**, 11; **A20**, 6.

deh: "village". — **78**, 14; **A29**, 13.

dehkān: in the expression *dehkān ī šāhān šāh* "subject of the King of Kings, citizen". — **1**, 1. — *Cf.* the synonym *šāhān šāh bandak.*

dehpat: "ruler, dahyupat". — **3**, 1; **A27**, 5, 7; **A39**, 10; **A40**, 2. — Av. *daiŋhupaiti-*, MMP *dhybyd*, Arm. (from Parth.) *dehpet, dehapet* (Hb., *AG*, 1, 139).

dēn: "religion". — **26**, 16.

dēnīk (?): see *var ī dēnīk.*

dēmān: "hearing (by a judge)/(court) hearing; judicial office". — **73**, 14; *cf.* also, **A9**, 3. — Iran **daiman-* (**day-* "to see"), *cf.* Parth. *andēmān* "opposite, before the eyes of", Arm. (from Parth.) *yandiman* "opposite/in front of", MP *(h)andēmānkar handēmān, handēmānēnītan*; see Bartholomae, *Air.Wb.*, 159; *ZsR* IV, 16-17; Hübschmann, *AG*, 1, 140-141.

***dēp**: "meeting, encounter"? — **A14**, 1. — *Cf.* Parth. *dyb, dybg* "happiness, luck, fate", Arm. (from Parth.) *dēp, dēp-k'* "meeting occasion/chance", *dēp, dipan* "favourable"; *dipīm, handipim* "to collide with/run into, meet, coincide", Iran. *daip-*; see Benveniste, *TPS* (1945) 72.

dip: "document"; *dip ī patixšāy-kart* "mandating document/mandate". — **84**, 2; **100**, 12—14; **102**, 15, 16; **103**, 3, 4; **110**, 9, 10; **A7**, 3; **A14**, 6; **A26**, 5; **A28**, 2, 3; **A29**, 15, 16; **A30**, 1; **A38**, 16.

dipīr: "scribe, secretary". — **78**, 4.

dipīrīh: "document". — **8**, 17; **A16**, 16.

dīvān: "chancellery, department, bureau". — **65**, 9; **A27**, 2; **A37**, 5; **A40**, 9. — Iran, **dipi+pāna-* "repository/archive of documents and letters"; see Henning, *BSOAS*, XIII/3 (1951), 644 n. 7. See also below.

dīvān ī kartak(ān): "department/chancellery of pious foundations". — **A27**, 2; **A37**, 5. — *Cf. kltk'n* (= *kartakān*) with the sense of "foundation for the soul" in *KKZ*,, 2, together with *kltk'n ZY yzd'n* (*ibid.*, 11, 1, 4, 6, 8, 9, 10, 15) which is also attested in *ŠKZ* with the Greek translation (11. 68, 19) χρεία καὶ θρησκεία τῶν θεῶν. *Cf.* also MMP *ruvānēn kirdagān* (M74 V13). See Perikhanian, *VDI* (1973/1), 3—24; *Obščestvo*, 160—176.

dīvān ī magupat ī Artaxšahr-Xvarreh: "the chancellery of the *magupat* of Artaxšahr-Xvarreh". — **A40**, 9.

dīvān ī ōstāndārīh: "department for the administration of the royal domain/lands; chancellery of the *ōstāndār*". — **65**, 9. — See, *ōstāndār*.

dīvānpān: "head of the chancellery, archivist". — **A26**, 6.

dō-kasīh: "conjunct persons, association of two persons"; *pat rāh ī dō-kasīh* **"**on the condition of the presence of two persons; *via* 'two people'**"**. — **69**, 9, 12. — *Cf. ēv-kasīh. Cf.* also Aram. (Bab. Talm.) *tndw* (= MP *tan dō*) "*ambo, coniunctim*" [Telegdi, *JA* (1933), 224].

dōšītan, dōš-: "to approve"; *kāmak dōšītan* "to express one's approval/agreement of a disposition (of the conveyor) regarding the transfer of a thing". — **55**, 5; **66**, 2, 4, 8, 10; **67**, 12; **68**, 14, 16. — Iran. **zauš-*, OP *dauš-*, Av. *zaoš-*, see Bartholomae, *ZsR* III, 22—26; Benveniste, *Titres*, 117—119. *Cf. kāmak, kāmistan, patigriftan, sahišn, sahistan.*

dō-vartān: "two-fold, twice"; *dō-vartān avaštan* "to seal twice" — **110**, 6.

drahm: "*drahm* (monetary unit); money". — **1**, 15; **12**, 7, 9; **37**, 15, 16; **38**, 9, 11; **39**, 5, 6, 9, 13, 16; **85**, 3, 5; **54**, 9; **59**, 12; **68**, 5; **79**, 3; **81**, 5, 6, 10, 12—14; **88**, 10; **89**, 4, 6, 7, 10, 14; **104**, 6, 7; **109**, 4, 5; **A16**, 1, 2, 4; **A18**, 13—15; **A19**, 14, 15, 17; **A20**, 1—4.

drang: "period, time"; *fražām drang* "the final period" (in the eschatological sense). — **79**, 10.

draxt: "tree". — **39**, 2; **40**, 13. — See also, *dār ut draxt.*

driγōšān yātakgōβīh: "advocacy, defense of the interests of the destitute". The legend on the official seal of the *magupat* of Pārs. — **93**, 8. — This title goes back to the Avestan tradition, *cf.* Av. *θrāyō.driγav-* (*Air. Wb.*, 805) and the designation of Zarathuštra as the "pastor-protector (*vāstar-*) of the deprived (*driγu-*)", *Y.* 27, 13; see Bartholomae, *MirMund*, II, 16-24; de Menasce, *Mélanges Massé*, 282—287; Lommel, *Pratidānam* (1969), 127—133; Bailey, *Studies in Indo-Asian Art and Culture* 11, 16—19; Shaked, *Monum. H. S. Nyberg* 11, 213—216. A legend containing this title (*Sthly dlgwš'n y'tkgwby W d'twbly*) is found on a seal impression from Qaṣr Abu Naṣr, see Henning, *Asia Major*, II/1 (1951), 144; *Mitteliranisch*, 46. The title is attested in its Armenian form *ǰatagov amenaym zrkeloc'* "the advocate/protector of all the deprived" as a characteristic of the IVth C. kat'ołikos Nersēs I; see Buzandaran, IV, 3.

droɣ: "lie". — **91**, 2.

droɣ-čāš: "a preacher of false doctrine". — **A15**, 10.

Drōn: "*Drōn*", name of a liturgical service. — **35**, 14, 15. — Av. *draonah-*, *Air Wb.*, 769—770.

drōš: "stamp, brand"; *drōš ī šahr* "brand of the *šahr*; *drōš kartan* = *drōšītan* (*q. v.*) — **1**, 14; **3**, 5; **73**, 1; **A15**, 2.

drōšītan, **drōš-**: "subject to branding, to brand". — **A35**, 8. — Iran. **drauš-*, Av. *draoša-*, *draošišvant*, *društa-*; MP *drōš*, *drōšm* "brand"; Arm. *drošm* "brand, mark made by burning or cutting", and its derivatives, see Bailey, *BSOS*, VI/3 (1931), 594—595.

druvist: "whole, intact, preserved" (of a thing); *druvist dāštan* "to preserve intact (a thing deposited), to keep as a deposit". — **6**, 13—14; **31**, 15; **64**, 11—14; **91**, 15; **104**, 2. — Bartholomae, *ZsR* I, 22—25; V, 43.

druvistak: "rightful, fair". — **A26**, 11.

druž šikastan: "to crush the demon (lit. 'the lie')"; designation of the action taken against a sorcerer. — **A26**, 9.

družīh: "lie". Variety of offence. — **A34**, 12. — Iran. **drauga*, Av. *draoga-*, *et al.*, *cf.* Arm. *druž* "perfidy; falsification", *družan*, *držem* "to deceive, betray, break a contract, bring damage" (Hb., *AG*, 146).

dusrav: "having a bad reputation, of ill-repute". — **A15**, 15; **A35**, 2, 5. — Iran **duš-sravah-*, Av. *dǝ̄uš.sravah-*, Arm. *dsrov*, *dsrovem*, Hb., *AG*, 146. See also next entry.

dusravīh: "bad reputation, ill-repute". — **78**, 10; **A35**, 1, 3.

duškartan, ***duškār-**/***duškun-** "to perform evil deeds, to harm" (of a sorcerer). — **A15**, 16. — *Cf.* Av. *duš.kǝrǝt-*, *Air Wb.*, 752.

dušman: "enemy, foe". — **103**, 8, 10.

dušnīrmat: "with damage, at a loss; disadvantage, lack of profit/revenue". — **A33**, 8. — See *nīrmat*.

dušpātixšāy: "impermissible, unlawful, illegal, arbitrary". — **A30**, 7.

dūtak: "family"; *(h)ēr ī dūtak*: "family estate/property". — **13**, 14; **14**, 7, 8; **15**, 3—6, 8, 9, 11, 13, 17; **16**, 1—5, 10, 12, 14; **19**, 12; **20**, 6, 13; **22**, 6; **23**, 17; **24**, 1; **25**, 11—15; **26**, 1, 3, 4, 8, 11, 12; **27**, 1, 4, 14, 15, 17; **28**, 1, 12, 15; **29**, 2; **41**, 3; **42**, 16; **43**, 9, 11; **46**, 17; **48**, 10, 11; **51**, 3, 6, 14, 16; **52**, 6, 8, 10—12, 15; **63**, 3; **67**, 7; **69**, 9, 10; **71**, 4; **75**, 14; **82**, 2, 3; **83**, 1, 2; **90**, 11; **94**, 11, 14; **96**, 1; **107**, 4; **109**, 8; **110**, 2; **A5**, 13; **A7**, 10; **A11**, 7, 9; **A13**, 5, 6; **A20**, 11; **A31**, 12; **A35**, 11, 14; **A39**, 7; **A40**, 8, 17.

dūtak sardār, see *sardār*.

dūtak stūr, **dūtak stūrih**: see *stūr*, *stūrīh*.

dūtak-zāt, also **andar dūtak-zāt**: "a successor acquired through *stūr*ship", lit. "born into the family (of the man whose *stūr*ship was assumed by the child's mother —

A. P.)". — **42**, 5, 14; **110**, 2; **A20**, 11; **A35**, 11, 14.— *Cf. duxtdāt, dātastān pus / duxt, stūrīh.*

duxt, **duxtak**: "daughter". — *Passim.* — See *duxt ī pātixšāyīhā, duxt ī čakarīhā, dātastān duxt.*

duxtakānīh: "adoption as a daughter; adopted daughter"; *pat duxtakānīh bē dātan / patigriftan* "give for adoption as a daughter / adopt as a daughter". — **33**, 6; **50**, 17; **69**, 1, 2; **70**, 2. — *Cf. duxtīh.*

duxtdāt: "a son and successor born to an *epikleros*-daughter (= *ayōγēn / ayuγēn, q. v.*)". — **41**, 3, 6, 13; **110**, 3; **A37**, 11. — Iran. **dugda-dāta-*, *cf.* Gk. θυγατριδοῦς. *Cf. čakardāt, dutak-zāt, dātastān pus / duxt, stūrīh (stūrīk pus).*

duxtīh: "daughterhood"; *pat duxtīh patigriftan*: "to adopt as a daughter". — **A40**, 13.

duž: "thief; theft". — **1**, 14; **37**, 5; **73**, 9; **A15**, 2, 9; **A27**, 11; **A28**, 13, 15, 17; **A29**, 1—5; **A35**, 8. — See also *duž kartan, dužītan.*

dužītan, **duž-**: "to carry off, to abduct; to steal". — **38**, 10; **73**, 3, 5, 8, 10; **A26**, 4, 8. — *Cf. ap(p)urtan.*

duž kartan: "to steal". — **73**, 3, 5; **A35**, 7—8. Synonym of *dužītan.*

E

ē: "time, period". — *Passim.* — Iran. **āyav*; *cf.* Av. *āyav-* "time, period of time, age", *Air Wb.*, 333.

ēhrpat: "*hērpat*, priestly calling". — **5**, 13. — Av. *aēθra-pati-*, *Air Wb.*, 20.

ēmōčan: in the expression, *pat ēmōčan*, lit. "for outfit, equipment"; technical term designating the allotment given by the royal treasury in conditional possession for life to a horseman — 77, 6, 8. — Iran. **adi-maučana-* derived from **adi + mauk-*, *cf.* MP *patmōčan* "clothing, vestments". Arm. *patmučan.*

ērangīh: "guilt, imputation of guilt, condemnation / sentence to a measure of punishment". — **3**, 5; 7, 9; **8**, 15; **9**, 9, 10. — See *ēraxtan, ēranǰēnītan, handraxtan.*

ēraxtan / ēraǰēnītan, **ēranǰ-**: "to declare, recognize as guilty, to condem / convict, to sentence (to pay a fine or to any form of punishment); *ēraxtītan* "to be guilty, condemned / covicted, sentenced". In opposition to *bōxtan (q. v.)*. — **7**, 9; **8**, 7; **9**, 2, 3, 4, 8, 15; **10**, 2, 6, 9, 11; **11**, 2, 4, 7, 9, 15; **77**, 10, 12; **83**, 11, 16; **84**, 14; **97**, 15; **102**, 8, 11, 12; **A13**, 10, 15, 16. — Spelling, *'ylnč-*: *'ylxt.* This verb and its derivations is frequently attested with the meanings indicated in other Pahlavi texts as well, as often as the antithesis of *bōxtan* "to free from guilt, release from a debt; acquit", *Cf.* also Jud.-Pers. *ēraxteh* "godless", *ēraxtegī* "sin, offence; godlessness", see de Lagarde, *Pers. Stud.*, 71. In the translations of Neryosangh, *bōxt ut ēraxt* are rendered in Skt. as *śuddham aśuddhamca, ērang = aśuddhaḥ.* Bartholomae [*IF*, XII (1901) 111—114; *SRb*, 23—25; *ZsR* IV, 8], while correctly interpreting the word as "*für schuldig erklären, condemnare*", suggests its derivation from Iran. *adi + rik- "linquere". Although this etymology may seem possible on semantic grounds (cf. Lat. delinquere, delictum: "to let escape; to make a mistake; to commit an offence") it is not acceptable for formal reasons: in the given word the root vowel is -a- and not -i- (Bartholomae gave too great an importance to the Paz. transcription ərəxt, parallel to ēraxt, and to the isolated cases of the spelling 'ylyxt which evidently arose from the plene 'yl'xt). Subsequently the Pahlavi and Judæo-Persian forms were compared, without any great certainty, by Henning with the verb 'yrnz-, ʿyrxt "to fight, struggle (?)" of the MMP texts, which he derived from adi + ranǰ-, cf. NP ranǰ "suffering/travail, toil" (Verbum, 199, 217). However, the semantic content of the Pahlavi forms is incompatible with their derivation from this root, ranǰ-, with which the MP 'yrnz, ʿyrxt may likewise not be related. Anyhow, whatever the etymology of MP ēraxtan "to fight", ēraxtār "fighter, warrior" [I should suggest a connection with Iran. *ark-/rak- "to offer a resistance; to defend"; on this root see my article in Studia Iranica 17/2 (1988), 131—140], one must keep these words distinct from those under discussion here. Moreover, the Manichaean contexts do not exclude the possibility of the interpretation "to accuse, condemn". Far more interesting is Henning's indication (l. c.) of F.Andreas' comparison of bōxt — ēraxt in the Pahlavi texts with Parth. bōxt — andraxt. Parth. 'ndrnj-/'ndrynj-: 'ndrxt of the Manichaean texts means "to acknowledge guilty, condemn, sentence" (likewise in Andreas' and Henning's translations), cf. e. g. g138—144 (A—H, MiM 111, 873) cw'gwn kd pt tl'zwg rzwr pdhynj'h bwxtg'n 'wd 'ndrxtg'n "like a judge weigh on a scale the acquitted (= innocents) and the condemned (= guilty)!"; m22—23 (ibid., 884) bwj'd bwtg'n 'ndrxtg'n 'ndrynj'd "the acquitted are freed, the guilty condemned/acknowledged as guilty", cf. also 'ndrxtgyft "Verurteilung, condemnation, sentence" as opposed to bwxtgyft "acquittal, release from accusation" (g162). Its exact correspondence in Pahlavi is handraxtan "to sentence, condemn, compel by law" (vide infra s. v.), in Manichaean MP texts — 'ndrxt̠ [M2 RI, 25—26: srxšynyd w 'ndrxt 'w qyš'n "he (= Addai) inflicted destruction on (?) and condemned/declared sinful the dogmas"; Henning's translation (MiM II, 302; Verbum, 199) is "he fettered ('fesselte') the dogmas"]; cf. also MMP 'wdrnz- "to condem", the form with the preverb ava- (Henning, BSOAS, XI/3 (1945), 485). Not only are the Pahl. ēranǰ-: ēraxt, ērang(īh) synonymous with the word given above, but they are formed on the common root *drang-, compounded in this case with the preverb adi- (*adi + drang- > MP *ēhrang/ǰ- > ērang/ǰ/z-, with the regular development of the historical intervocalic -dr- > -hr- and with the equally regular subsequent dropping of the -h- after the long vowel (ē- < adi-) and before r in the MP form), Moreover, in opposition to the opinion expressed (see Ghilain, 51; Bailey, JRAS (1955), 14—15; and Emmerick, SGS, 141) the root *drang restored in words having the meaning "to establish guilt. condemn, sentence", cannot be identified for semantic reasons with Iran. *drang- "to make firm; to hold", nor with Iran. *tr̥(n)k- "to press", as it was suggested by Henning (BSOS, X/i (1939), 101 n. 3). Iran. *dra(n)g-: draxta- with the basic meaning "to owe, be indebted" should apparently be related to I.-E. *dl̥gh- attested in western Indo-European dialects, Goth. dulgas "debt", dulga-haitja "creditor", OIrish dligim "I deserve, I claim", *dliged* "debt, obligation", OSl. *dlŭgŭ*, Rus. *dolg* 1) "debt"; 2) "tribute". The proposed connexion entails neither semantic nor other difficulties. The semantic development "debt → guilt, sin, culpability, offence", "debt → compensation, fine, punishment (debt as the atonement for an offence, a compensation)", "debt → responsibility", "to owe, be guilty", "to declare liable, guilty; to condemn, sentence" is well known (see *e. g.* Schrader—Nehring, *Reallexicon* II, *s. v. Schulden, Verbrechen*). This root unquestionably appears likewise in Av. *suptiδarənga-*, a compound whose meaning ("who has a liability on his shoulders") was correctly established by Gershevitch (*Mithra*, 266—267). The Avestan term designates an agnate, a representative of a blood-kinship group all of whose members in the legal sense were "co-possessors, partners" and were bound together by a joint responsibility. Another Iranian term **ādranga-* (< **ā+ drang-*), Aram. *'drng* has the same meaning in the document Kraeling 11, 9. Here the obligation to answer for the debts of the dead man is laid not only on his successors, but also on his *'drng*, evidently his agnates (or partners) held to be jointly responsible for a debt and for an offence (in other Aramaic documents *hngyt* = *hangaiθa-*, *hnbg'* = *hambāga-* "co-partner, partner" are mentioned in analogous contexts). *Cf.* also MP *drang* "guilt, responsibility" [*e. g. DkM* 723, 14—16. *Apar čandīh ī drang ī dātaβar pat ākās kū pēšēmar zūr-xvāh pasēmār drōγ-xvastūk* "Concerning the degree of guilt / responsibility of the judge if aware that the plaintiff is malicious (and that) the defendant has agreed to (= accepted) an injust decision of the court"]. See also *ērangīh, handraxtan*.

ēstātan, **ēst-**: "to stand, to be, to stay". — *Passim*. — With prepositions. *andar ēstātan* "to remain, to abide", *pat hamēmārīh andar ēstātan* "to be present at (= to participate in) a trial", **70**, 5, 9; **A15**, 10; *apāč ēstātan* "to renounce; desist, deviate", — **35**, 15; **37**, 6, 9; **82**, 13, 14; **A12**, 1; *apāč ō...ēstātan* "to hold to ...; withhold, to hold back", **104**, 4; **A18**, 11—12; *apar ēstātan* "to support", **A12**, 4—5, 7; *bē ēstātan* "to be outside; be put outside": **64**, 4—5; *bē ēstātan* (*hač*) "to diverge (from), withdraw" — **27**, 13 — Iran. **adi + stā-*.

ēvāč: "formula, formulation". — **A16**, 17. — Iran. **adi-vāčah-*.

ēvar: "authentic, trustworthy, competent". — **3**, 3; **12**, 15; **32**, 4, 9, 10; **75**, 8; **77**, 12; **83**, 3; **86**, 14, 15; **93**, 1, 3; **102**, 10; **A16**, 5; **A26**, 4, 5, 7, 9, 11, 14, 16; **A27**, 4, 5, 13; **A28**, 3, 5, 7, 10—12; **A29**, 7, 9, 11, 13, 14, 16; **A34**, 6; — Iran. **adi + var-* "to chose; to decide; to believe". *Cf. vāvarīkan*. Antithesis [1]*varōmand, avāvarīkan*. See also next entry.

ēvarīh: "authenticity, truth; validity (in the legal sense); competence"; *pat ēvarīh kār hač-iš kartan* "to consider it (= the seal) valid, authentic"; *ō ēvarīh vartītan / vaštan* "to give authentic testimony after an initially false or inexact one". — **5**, 15; **8**, 16; **9**, 1—3; **13**, 3; **14**, 14; **75**, 8; **86**, 14; **91**, 5, 8; **99**, 2, 3, 8; **102**, 11; **107**, 9; **108**, 7; **A10**, 12; **A13**, 9; **A25**, 15; **A27**, 6; **A28**, 10, 12. — *Cf. ēvar, vāvarīkānīh*.

F

frahaxtišnīh: "education, instruction, knowledge". — **79**, 16. — Parth. *frhynj-* "to give an education, to instruct"; MP *frahang*, NP *frahang* "method, knowledge, education, good manners", *frahangī* "teacher", *et al*; Arm. (from. Parth.) *hrahang* "instruction, teaching, training, schooling"; *cf.* also MP *āhang* (*q. v.*) "rule order, arrangement, Arm. *ahang*. As it was already admitted by Bartholomae, *Air Wb.*, 1745, this may derive from Iran **hang-*: *haxta-*, *cf.* Av. *haxta-* "regular, lawful, educated, competent", *anahaxta* "irregular, incompetent", Sogd. *'γt'w.* "judge", Osset. *æγdau* "rule, norm, custom" *et al.* (on this root see Benveniste, *Et. oss.*, 51—53), and not from **θang-* "to draw, to pull", as it has usually been assumed (see *e. g.* Salemann, *Mittelpersisch*, 302; Nyberg, *Hb.*, II, 70; Ghilain, 51).

frahistan: "to learn, to receive information". — **A38**, 9. — From **fraδist* < **fradišta* (SW transit. *-št-* > *-st-*), **fra + dais*, Av. *fra- daēs-*; see Nyberg, *Hb.*, II, 70; *cf.* Henning, *Verbum*, 180.

[1]**framān**: "order, disposition; royal edict; court order, judicial decision; testament/will". — **3**, 1; **26**, 15; **27**, 13; **29**, 10; **32**, 3; **34**, 10, 12; **35**, 15; **41**, 16; **44**, 4, 17; **45**, 10, 12; **46**, 6; **47**, 17; **76**, 16; **83**, 2; **93**, 6, 11; **96**, 2; **105**, 8—10; **A14**, 11; **A16**, 15; **A27**, 5, 7; **A36**, 8, 11; **A37**, 3, 6, 9, 13, 16; **A39**, 13; **A40**, 2.

[2]**framān**: "*framān*"; name of a degree of guilt/delinquency. — **A8**, 1. — Av. **framă-na-* (?). This term is also attested in the *ŠnŠ* (I,1), in the paragraph derived from the Pahlavi commentary on the *Vīdēvdāt*, and in the Persian *Rivāyats* (*Riv. Horm. Fram*; 288—289) where it designates the first and lowest degree of misdemeanor — and correspondingly of guilt — in the *žahm* group (*q. v.*), that includes various acts of physical violence. A possible meaning for Av. **framăna-* is "threat (of the use of physical violence)"; *cf.* the Latin derivatives from the same I.-E. root, *mĭnor* "to step forward; to threaten"; *minatio* "a threat"; *minax*, *minator* 1) "stepping forward" 2) "threatening"; *cf.* also Lat. *promineo*.

framān būtan: "to obey, be under the power of". — **A5**, 4.

framātan/framūtan, framāy-: "to dispose, order"; *kār framūtan* regarding the legal act of disposal, *cf.* Av. [5]*kār*. — **55**, 11, 16; **65**, 9; **A5**, 7; **A25**, 10.

fraškart: "(the final) renovation (of the word)"; *tā fraškart* "forever/eternally" (of a transfer). — **A2**, 14. — See next entry.

fraškartīk: "eternal, eternally"; regarding the transfer of a thing into someone's possession, — **62**, 5; **A1**, 1.

fravartak: "document" (of title). — **93**, 3. — MMP *prwrdg* "a letter", Sogd. *prw'rt* "a scroll, book", Arm. *hrovartak* "official letter; title document", Aram. (Talm.) *prwrtq'* "edict". See *s. v. nāmak* for the synonyms.

Fravartīkān: "(the five days of) *Fravartīkān*". The reference is to the first five day period of the *Gāhānbār Fravartīkān*, which corresponds to the terminal five days of the lunar year. — **A38**, 5. — See also *s. v. Ahunavait gāh*.

Fravartīn: "*Fravartīn*"; the first month of the Zoroastrian calendar. — **35**, 10.

frazand: "child, son, offspring". — *Passim*. — See, *frazand ī čakar(īhā)*, *frazand ī pātixšāyīhā*.

fražām: "time-limit". — **35**, 11.

frēžvan; see [1]*parēžvan*.

frōxtan, **frōš-**: "to sell"; *frōxt ut dāt* "alienation"; *frōxtan ut dātan* "to alienate". — **1**, 13, 16; **5**, 6; **6**, 7, 13; **7**, 15; **31**, 13; **32**, 3; **33**, 9, 14, 15, 17; **35**, 5; **38**, 12, 13; **85**, 1; **64**, 11; **70**, 1; **74**, 13; **96**, 14, 15; **105**, 17; **A8**, 12, 13; **A11**, 17; **A22**, 9, 10, 12—17.

G

gām: "step"; *andar 3 gām* "at a distance of three steps/paces". — **A26**, 3. — According to an ancient custom attested in the *Avesta*, the litigants were separated from each other and from the judges during the trial by a distance of "three steps"; see *Fr. ī oīm*, 27, *s. v. arəθavanō*, Reichelt, *WZ*, 15 (1901), 125; *cf.* also Av. *θri.gāmya-*, *Air Wb.*, 806.

ganǰ: "treasury". — **A27**, 10—12.

garzišn: "complaint, appeal". — **86**, 5.

garzītan: "to complain, appeal"; *garzītan ī must* (*q. v.*). — **A26**, 4.

gāt: 1) "sexual cohabitation"; 2) "a marriage *sine manu mariti*"; 3) "adultery" (the offence of); *tan pat gāt dātan* "to enter into sexual cohabitation or into a marriage *sine manu mariti*". — **36**, 15, 16; **73**, 7, 8; **77**, 3; **A15**, 4; **A31**, 7—8. — *Cf. gātan, gātār.*

gātan, **gay-**: 1) "to enter into sexual cohabitation"; 2) "to enter into a marriage *sine manu mariti*"; 3) "to commit adultery". — **10**, 8; **12**, 8; **36**, 6, 7, 17; **73**, 8; 83, 7; **A14**, 4. — *Cf. gāt*, [1,2]*gātār*.

[1]**gātār**: 1) "sexual intercourse"; 2) "a marriage *sine manu mariti*"; 3) "(the offence of) adultery". — **24**, 8, 9; **33**, 1; **83**, 8; **A13**, 5; **A14**, 3.

[2]**gātār**: 1) "cohabitor"; 2) "husband (without full rights)"; as against *šōy*. — **A4**, 10; **A14**, 3, 5.

gāv: "cow, bull". — **102**, 4—6, 9; **A19**, 10.

gavākīh: "growth". — **79**, 12. — Iran. **gav-* "to increase to grow".

gēhān: "property". — **98**, 1. — Iran. **gaiθā(nām)*; Av. *gaēθā-* "property", specifically, "the property belonging to agnates", *haδō.gaēθā-* "co-owner, co-proprietor" = Pahl. *hamgēhān* [*Air. Wb.*, 476—478; Perikhanian, *VDI* (1968/3), 36—37]. OP *gaiθa-*, Afgh. *γēlē* "herd" (Morgenstierne, *EVP*, 25), Aram. (Targ.) *gyt'* "property; cattle" (Telegdi, *JA* (1935), 237).

gil: "clay"; here "seal". — **A34**, 2.

***gitāk**; see *GT'k*.

gizīr: "policeman, guard". — **A26**, 4, 8. — Spelling *gčyr'n*. *Cf.* Syr. *gəzîrâi̯ê* "police" (Hoffmann, *Auszüge*, 62, No. 542; Nöldeke, *ZDMG*, 35 (1881), 233), NP *gizīr* "elder; tax collector"; New Arm. *gzir*; see Hübschmann, *Pers. St.*, 272.

gōβ: "declaration; court testimony; court session; trial"; *ō gōβ šutan* "to go to a court session, a trial. — **71**, 11; **73**, 15—17; **74**, 2; **75**, 7. — See also *gōβišn*, *gōβišnīh*, *guftan*.

gōβišn, gōβišnīh: official statement or declaration; pronouncement of a specific formula". — **2**, 11; **54**, 15; **55**, 5, 6; **60**, 8; **63**, 8, 10, 14, 15; **64**, 6, 12, 14; **73**, 4, 6; **77**, 15; **95**, 14; **100**, 13; **106**, 6; **A9**, 7; **A28**, 7; **A33**, 6; **A40**, 11. — *Cf. gōβ*.

gōβišnīh dātan: "to issue a judicial statement or formula". — **86**, 7.

gōhrak: "property; wealth, capital". — **A29**, 6.

gōspand: "small cattle, sheep". — **12**, 9—12; **104**, 6; **A12**, 6.

gōš-vālāδ: "up to the ear"; as regards the depth of a channel. — **85**, 8. — Traditional measure of height and depth; *cf.* Av. *gaošō.bərəz-*, *Air Wb.*, 486.

gōšvār: "earring". — **A15**, 16, 17.

graβ, graβīh: "pledge, hypothec; *antichresis*-security", likewise "a mortgaged or hypothecated thing, one pledged"; *graβ apispārtan* "to transfer a pledge"; *graβ kartan* "to pledge"; *pat graβ bē nihātan* "to pledge"; *pat graβ dāštan* "to hold (a thing) as security"; *(pat) graβ griftan/patigriftan* "to take, receive (as a) security"; *hač graβīh hištan* "to release from pledge/mortgage" (of the action performed by the creditor). — **7**, 17; **11**, 1, 6, 9, 15; **12**, 6, 9, 13; **14**, 13; **15**, 6, 7; **31**, 13; **34**, 15; **37**, 12—17; **38**, 2, 9, 12, 14, 17; **39**, 1, 2, 5, 12, 14, 17; **40**, 1, 4, 13, 16, 17; **74**, 17; 77, 13; **85**, 2—4; **86**, 2, 13; **89**, 4—6; **99**, 17; **100**, 4; **102**, 1, 10; **104**, 3, 5; **A8**, 6; **A9**, 4; **A30**, 14. — NP *giraw* "pledge, security", Arm. (from Parth.) *graw* "pledge, hypothec". See also *agraβ*, *graβakān*, *graβakāndār*.

graβakān, graβakānīh: "pledge, security", primarily "a thing held as a pledge/security". Defined as one of the varieties of real right to a thing (*aδvēnak ī xvēšīh*). As a derivative real right arising from a contract and limited by the latter's conditions, a creditor's title to the pledged thing is opposed to the fundamental (*pat xvēšīh*) title to it held be the original (principal) owner, a title transmissible to the original owner's personal heirs and seccessors. *Graβakān andar nihātan* "to repledge the security to another (= third) person". — **37**, 11; **38**, 3, 7, 9, 13; **39**, 4, 6, 10; **40**, 3, 5—7, 9, 10, 12; **67**, 5; **83**, 4; **85**, 5; **89**, 4, 7; **104**, 4, 5. — NP *girau̯gān*; Arm. (from Parth.) *grawakan*. See also, *graβ*, *graβakāndār*.

graβakāndār: "creditor, security-holder". — **37**, 11, 13; **38**, 16; **39**, 4, 5, 7, 8, 11, 13—17; **40**, 13—14, 15; **89**, 3; **104**, 4; **A30**, 16. — See above, *graβ*, *graβakān*.

griftan, gīr-: "to take". — *Passim*.

griftār kartan: "to seize" (against an unsettled debt). — **58**, 11.

griftārōmand: "subject to arrest". — **A30**, 5.

GT'k = *gităk: "will/testament, document". — **110**, 5; **A36**, 11, 12; **A39**, 4. — A word apparently borrowed by Iranian from Aramaic chancellery practice in the Achaemened period (*cf.* Akkad. *giṭṭu* "a tablet, letter of receipt", Syr. *geṭṭâ* "testament", late Heb. *geṭ* "document, certificate of marriage or divorce") with the accretion of the Iranian suffix *-ak*(*a*), and transmitted through Iranian (= Parthian) to Armenian, **gitak* > **gtak* > *ktak* "testament (with the unvoicing of the first consonant through assimilation); *cf.* also the derivatives, *Hin/Nor Ktakaran*: "Old/New Testament", *ktakem* "to bequeath". This term is also attested in epigraphy (*cf.* Naqš-ī Rajab, 1.26) with the spelling *gtky* which may be considered (together with the one above) equally as a direct rendering of the Iranian form *gitāk* and as a heterogram (Aram. GT') with an Iranian complement. See Nyberg, *MO* (1937), 80 n. 2, Szemerényi, *Henning Mem. Vol.*, p. 420 and Schwartz, *ZDMG*, 120/2 (1970) where in addition to these forms Khwarezmian *γyck* is joined to the evidence.

guftan: "to declare, to make an official declaration; to testify at a trial". — *Passim* — *Cf.* gōβ, *gōβišn*, ²*kartan*, *paytākēnītan*.

guharēn: 1) "exchange"; 2) "compensation for losses". *Guharēn ī rāst* "equal/equivalent exchange"; *guharēn kartan* "to make an exchange". — **37**, 2, 3, 5—8, 9; **54**, 9; **A12**, 4. — See next entry.

guharīk, guharīkān: 1) "equivalent, equal value"; 2) "exchange"; *Guharīk kartan* "to exchange"; *hač kār guharīk kartan* "to depose/remove from office, relieve of one's function"; *pat guharīkānīh* "in exchange". — **7**, 16, 17; **8**, 1; **32**, 14; **33**, 1, 5, 6; **39**, 4, 7, 17; **40**, 1, 17; **53**, 5, 8; **58**, 10; **86**, 7, 11; **102**, 4, 13; **A12**, 13—14; **A15**, 3; **A26**, 17. — NP *guharī* "exchange; compensation, restitution", *guharīdan* "to exchange, compensate". For this term and its etymology (*guharīk* < **guahrīk* < **vyarθya-*, Iran. **vi* + *arθya-*, *cf.* Av. ²*arəθa-*, *vyarəθya-*); see Pagliaro, *RSO*, XV (1935), 303—315. *Cf.* the etymology subsequently proposed by him [*RSO*, XXII (1947), 60-61] *guhar-* < **guγar-* < **vigar-*, **vi* + *gar-* "to take in exchange, exchange, compensate/make restitution", which seems more convincing to me. *Cf.* from the same root, **gar-* "to take", (papyr.) Aram. *'bygrn'* = **abigarana-* "fine, compensation, restitution"; for the development of Iran. *-g-* > late MP *-h-* in an intervocalic position, *cf.* **Bagastāna-* > *Bahistun*. On the other hand, despite the difference in shades of meaning and areas of use, Henning (*apud* Boyce, *Hymn-Cycles*, Gloss., *s. v. whyrd*) may be right in postulating a link between NP *guharīdan/guhurīdan* "to exchange, to barter" and MMP *whwr-*, *whwryd* (= **vihurīd*, p.p.p.), *whwrydn*, inf. "to change, be changed, confused", MParth. *whyrd* "confused, disturbed", Pahl. *vihirišn*, *vihirīh* "change", *yatak-vihirīh* "transformation, transfiguration" (DKM 161, 10; 420, 17). Bailey proposed (*ZP*, 82—83) a derivation from *vi-kar-* (via **vikīr-*), which cannot be accepted. Henning (*BSOAS* X, 2, 1940, 509) derived all these forms from Iran. **vi-far-*. His reconstruction seems to be supported by Saka verbal forms *āphar-* (**ā-far-*)/*āphär-* (**ā-fṛya-*) "to disturb/be disturbed", *haphar-* (**fra-far-*)/*haphär-* (**fra-fṛya-*) "to be distracted", *phir-* (**fṛya-*) "to be disturbed" (see Emmerick, *SGS*, 8—9, 90), if only the Saka verbs and the group of Pahl. *vihir-* etc. are etymologically related, of which I doubt for phonological reasons: an Iran. **vi-far-/fṛya-* would not give MP or Parth. *vihar/vihir-*. To the evidence of Western Middle Iranian languages may be added Arm. *veher* "vaccilating; unsturdy; fearing, frightened" with its derivatives attested from the Vth C. on and doubtlessly borrowed from Parthian. A semantic development from "vaccillate" to "reciprocate, alternate, (ex)change, interchange" and from "interchangeable" to "equivalent" seems natural to me. — See also *guharēn*, **guhartan*.

***guhartan**: "to make an exchange". — **A12**, 5. — This word has been restored by me in the text. *Cf. guharīk, guharēn.*

gumārtak, **gumārtākīhā**: "appointed; by appointment", designation, depending upon the form of calling, given to a guardian or *stūr* (in these cases the appointment came from the agnatic group of the late head of household); *cf.* the antithesis *būtak, kartak*; *dātastān gumārtakīhā* "through judicial decision". — **26**, 3; **27**, 2; **29**, 1; **44**, 2; **46**, 12; **49**, 6; **90**, 12; **A15**, 8—9. — See also, *gumārtan*.

gumārtan, **gumār-**: "to appoint"; *apāč gumārtan* "to reappoint". — **3**, 5; **16**, 1, 16, 17; **20**, 1; **21**, 12; **23**, 3; **26**, 2, 3, 5, 9; **27**, 6, 14; **28**, 17; **29**, 3; **41**, 2, 8, 9; **42**, 2, 3, 5—9, 13; **43**, 4, 5, 7, 12, 13, 15; **44**, 3, 8; **46**, 4, 7, 11; **47**, 4; **48**, 7, 9, 13, 15, 16; **49**, 8; **50**, 3, 6; **51**, 12; **60**, 17; **70**, 2; **75**, 2, 3, 5, 8; **76**, 1; **78**, 16; **81**, 2, 3, 5, 7, 9, 13, 14, 16; **83**, 1; **87**, 11, 14, 16; **88**, 3, 4, 13, 14; **94**, 2; **97**, 12—14; **106**, 11; **109**, 4, 7, 11, 13; **110**, 3; **A13**, 7; **A14**, 7—12; **A26**, 12; **A31**, 5, 7, 8, 10—12; **A33**, 7; **A39**, 8. — Iran. **vi* + *mār-*.

gumaštan: in the construction *apāč gumaštan* "to deduct". — **23**, 12. — *Cf.* Arm. *gumarem* "to sum up, perform the addition, to collect", likewise "to gather into a unit, into one place", *gumar* "sum".

gurtakīh: "captivity". — **79**, 13. — Pahl. (Psalter) *wldky* "prisoner; slave", *wldkyḥy* "captivity; slavery, bondage"; *AZ*, 12, *vartak* (*wltk*); *KKZ*, *wltky* "military booty"; MMP *wrdk*, NP *barda*. *Cf.* Av. ^{2}*varəta*, *Air Wb.*, 1368.

gyāk: "locality"; *šahr ut gyāk*. — **A35**, 4.

H

hačašmānd: "delay, default; delay of a trial because of the default at the court session by one of the litigating parties; contumacy". — A trial by contumacy usually occurred through the fault of the respondent; *hačašmānd hač pasēmār* "contumacy through the non-appearance/default of the respondent". — **3**, 7; **7**, 13, 15; **10**, 12, 13, 15, 17; **11**, 1, 3—5, 8, 14, 17; **14**, 12, 17; **15**, 5, 6; **73**, 12, 17; **75**, 12; 77, 12; **98**, 15, 16; **A9**, 4; **A13**, 17; **A15**, 1; **A26**, 1; **A30**, 14; **A32**, 2. — Compound from MP *hač-iš* + *mānd* (*mān-* "to leave behind, to remain"). An incorrect interpretation of this term identifying it with the interdictum of Roman law is given by Pagliaro, *RSO*, XXIV (1949), 120—135. See Perikhanian, *Mem. de Menasce*, 305—318.

hamaδvēn: 1) "same, identical; in the same way, on the same basis"; 2) full, entire; fully, entirely, wholly". — **30**, 1, 6; **35**, 12; **41**, 13; **53**, 5; **55**, 3, 12; **69**, 5; **82**, 9; **101**, 14; **107**, 16; **A20**, 15; **A21**, 5; **A23**, 6; **A30**, 11; **A37**, 10; **A38**, 1. — MIr. *ham* + *aβδēn* (< **abidayana-*); P.Psal. *ḥ'm'dwyn* "all, *sämtlich*". *Cf.* Arm. *hamawrēn* "full, entire; fully, entirely, wholly".

hamahl: "partner, co-partner". — **63**, 5. — Sogd. *"m'rδ-* co-partner, partner", NP *hamāl* From Iran. **hămarəθa-* (Skt. *samartha-*); Bartholomae, *Zum Air Wb.*, 118; *MiMund* I, 5, 28—30; Henning, *BSOAS*, XI/4 (1946), 726.

hamākdēn: "full ritual; liturgical service with full rites". — **109**, 14. — MMP *h'm'gdyn* (Salemann, *Man. St.* 21, 81). *Cf.* Arm. (Ełišē) *hamakden*, see Hubschmann, *AG*, 1, 177.

hamāpēr: "building having an economic purpose (storehouse?)". — **19**, 1, 2. — MMP, Parth. *ḥ'm'byr*. "*Bau?*", "storehouse" (corresponds to the Gk. οἰκοδομή in *The Shepherd of Hermas*, 12, 4); see Salemann, *Man. St.*, 81, 145; Bartholomae, *ZsR* III, 49; Boyce, *Mél. Morgenstierne*, 36.

hamărkar: "financial official, *hamărkar*". — **93**, 5; **A27**, 3, 13; **A28**, 3, 5. — Iran. **hmărakara-*; Parth. (inscrip.) *'ḥmrkr*, Aram. *ḥmrkr*, Syr. *'hmr'gr*, Arm. *hamarakar*. See also Greenfield, *Henning Mem. Vol.*, 180—186.

hambāγ: "co-partner, co-heir, partner"; *brāt ī hambāγ* "a brother co-heir; *cf.* also *hambāγ ī zēnīk / dēnīk* (?) whose meaning is not clear, **23**, 15; **24**, 2. — **1**, 17; **2**, 3, 6; **4**, 4; **22**, 4; **23**, 12, 14, 15; **24**, 2; **26**, 11; **28**, 8; **51**, 17; **52**, 4, 5, 8, 9; **59**, 14, 15; **62**, 17; **83**, 6; **85**, 7; **86**, 5, 6, 12, 15—17; **88**, 8, 12, 15; **90**, 10; **102**, 13; **104**, 16; **106**, 5; **A6**, 15; **A13**, 3. — Iran. **hama* + *bāga-* "holder of a common share, co-possessor"; Aram. (papyri) *hnbg'* "co-partner, partner"; NP *anbāγ* "concubine". *Cf.* next entry.

hambāγīh: "joint-partnership, partnership". — **4**, 7—9; **22**, 6; **23**, 4, 6, 8, 10; **52**, 7; **55**, 10; **88**, 10, 12, 13, 16, 17; **A5**, 16; **A6**, 2; **A13**, 13.

hambarakān: 1) adj. "common, joint"; 2) adv. "jointly, together". — **19**, 6; **78**, 12; **85**, 8. — From **ham* + *bar-*, *cf.* Av. *ham-bərətī-* "gathering", Khot.-Saka *haṃbar-* "to compose", *et al.*

hambasān; see ambas(s)ān.

hambăstan, hambāh-; see, *hanbăstan*.

hamčašmānīh: "presence; stay in front of someone's eyes"; *pat hamčašmānīh ī M* "in the presence of M, before M's eyes". — **A10**, 5.

hamdātastān būtan: "to be in agreement with, be unanimous". — *Passim.*

hamdātastānīh: "agreement, unanimity". — *Passim.*

hamdūtak: "member of the same family". — **29**, 9, 11.

hamēmāl: see *hamēmār*.

hamēmār: "litigant"; *hamēmārīh* "trial, litigation"; *hamēmar būtan / kartan* "to bring action against, to litigate, to sue"; *hamēmārīh kartan* "to conduct / organize a case/trial (as regards the judge)". — **5**, 6, 10; **6**, 8; **11**, 8; **12**, 17; **13**, 1, 6; **15**, 4, 8, 14; **16**, 2; **38**, 1—11; **74**, 11; **75**, 3; **84**, 1; **86**, 14; **91**, 8, 9; **99**, 11; **107**, 10; **A12**, 13; **A15**, 9; **A25**, 16; **A27**, 7, 9; **A30**, 17; **A32**, 6, 8; **A33**, 13. — *Cf.* Arm. (IXth C. documents) *hamimał* "litigant", *hamimał kal* "to dispute, sue", Judaeo-Pers. *hamĕmāl*. The suggestion of Bartholomae (*ZsR* I, 21; 11, 49-50), as to the relation of the element *-mār* in the words *hamēmār* ("litigant"), *pēšēmār* ("plaintiff"), *pesēmār* ("respondent") with NP *mār* "calculation", Pahl. *mārīk* (<*mahr*<*manθra-*) "word", and the interpretation of these terms as having the literal significance of "speaking together", "speaking before, first", "speaking after" are hardly felicitous. Still less convincing is Nyberg (*Hb.*, 11, 95, 172, 185) who agrees with Bartholomae as regards the analysis of the terms *pēšēmār* ("*der zuerst das Wort hat*"), and *pasēmār*, but separates from them the term *hamēmār*/*hamēmal*, which in his opinion continues OP **ham* + *adi* + *marδa-* (Iran. **marz-* "to touch"). All three terms may possibly have as a base MIr. **hamahr*/**hamahl* "litigant, litigating < Iran. **hamarθa-* (*arθ-*>*-ahr-*/*-ahl-*, with a subsequent loss of the aspirate and a substitute lengthening of the vowel), *cf.* Av. [1]*arəθa-* "litigation, quarrel; thing", [2]*arəθa-* "plaintiff", *arəθavan-* "respondent", *arəθra-* "suit, litigation", Av. *hamarəθa-* "opponent, enemy, antagonist" (*cf.* Skt. *artham* "striving, urge, demand, goal, thing", *samṛti* "quarrel, conflict, struggle/fight"). On this form (**hamahr/l*>**hamār/l*) with prefixal *ham-*/*pēš-*/*pas-*) were apparently composed the terms *hamēmār/l*, *pēšēmār/l*, *pasēmār/l* (with an internal contraction, *pēšᵉhamār/l*>*pēšĕmār*). *Cf.* the rendering of the last two MP terms in the Syrian translation of the *Law-Book* of Īšō'bōxt by means of Syr. *be'ldînâ qadmâịâ*, *be'ldînâ 'aḫrâịâ*.

hamešak-sōz: "eternally burning" (as regards a variety of altar or Fire-temple). — **95**, 16, 17; **96**, 1, 2.

ham-mat: "uterine" (brother or sister)". — **87**, 16.

hammuhrīh: "certification/establishment (by the judges) of the authenticity of the seal on a document presented to the court". — **A26**, 3.

hamnāmīh: "certification/establishment (by the judges) of the authenticity of one's name/identity". — **A26**, 3; **A28**, 12, 16; **A29**, 9.

hampaččēn: "copy, copy of a document". — **93**, 3; **A28**, 7; **A30**, 7, 8; **A32**, 11; **A33**, 17; **A34**, 7, 11; **A38**, 7. — Iran. **pati-čagnya-* "copy"; *cf.* MSogd. *p'tcγnyy* "answer"; see Benveniste, *JA*, CCXXV (1934), 180—183; MP *paččēn*, Hebr. *paθšeγen*, Bibl. Aram. *paršeγen* "copy", Syr. *paršaγnâ*, Arm. (from Parth.) *patčēn* "copy, example (Hübschmann, *AG*, I, 224).

hampāyandān: "co-warrantor". — **2**, 1; **56**, 1, 3, 9, 10; **57**, 6; **59**, 4. — *Cf.* next entry; see *pāyandān*.

hampāyandānīh: "co-warrannty". — **55**, 10. *Cf. pāyandānīh*.

ham-pit: "consanguinous (brother/sister)". — **87**, 16.

hampursakīh: "interrogation/inquest; consultation, council, agreement". — **78**, 5; **A39**, 15—16. — *Cf.* Khwar. *'nbš-* "to counsel < **ham* + *pṛsa-*, Mackenzie, *Khwar. Gl.*, IV, 529.

hamtanīh: "establishment (by the judge) of the authenticity (= identification) of the persons participating in a trial". — **A26**, 2; **A28**, 12—13; **A29**, 11.

hamtōžišn būtan: "to be jointly liable for payment; to have a joint debt". — **59**, 5.

hamvaxš: "revenue, interest". — **51**, 2, 4 (?). — The text is poorly preserved and the reading doubtful.

hamvindišn, hamvindišnīh: "joint possession of the revenue". — **23**, 12; **A1**, 3—5, 12; — *Cf. vindišn*.

hamvināsīh: "identification of an offence". — **A28**, 12; **A29**, 3.

hamxvāstak: "person bound by a solidary responsibility, joint-debtor, *correus*". — **1**, 17; **53**, 4; **55**, 13; **86**, 5, 9—11. — Iran. **ham+xvăz-* (OP *xvăd-*) "to wish; to seek".

hanbăstan, hanbāh-: "to demolish (of a house); to cast, pull down, (trees); *hanbāhišn* "felling, casting down". — **39**, 1; **40**, 15; **86**, 8. — Iran. **ham+pad-*, MacKenzie, *Zarth. Mad. Cent.*, 131.

hanbārtan, apač hanbārtan, hanbār-: "to fill; make up, compensate, indemnify (loss, damage)". — **28**, 17; **29**, 1. — Iran. *ham+pār-* "to fill".

[1]**(h)andarz**: "testament". — **30**, 11, 13; **31**, 8; **64**, 4, 8; **94**, 16; **105**, 11, 12, 14; **110**, 1; **A9**, 10; **A10**, 8, 9; **A35**, 15; **A36**, 3, 17. — Iran. *ham+darz-* (**darz-* "to fasten, hold, tie") "precept, instruction, commandment". *Cf.* Aram. (papyr.) *hndrz* "notification", MMP; Parth. *'ndrz* "commandment" (*cf.* also the title *(h)andarzpat*), Np *andarz* "precept, instruction, testament", Arm. (from Parth.) *andarj* "testament", *(h)anderjapat* "(title)". *cf. anandarz.*

[2]**handarz**: "clothing/vestments, equipment/outfit". — **29**, 14. — Iran.**ham+darz-*, **darz-* "to fasten, to tie, to sew together". *Cf.* Arm. (from Parth.), *handerj* "clothing, outfit", *handerjem* "I outfit/equip, prepare, arrange".

[3]**handarz**: "jointly, together with". — **37**, 1. The context is unclear and the interpretation hypothetical. For the given meaning and usage *cf.* Arm. (from Parth.) *handerj* "together with" (a pre- and postposition used with the noun in the instrumental case). Iran **ham+darz-* "to fasten, to tie".

handōxt: "accumulated"; *handōxt ī xvēš* "personally accumulated/acquired property (as against inherited property, *aparmānd*)"; *cf.* Gk. τὸ αὐτόκτητον, τὰ ἐπικτητά as against τὰ πατρῷα, τὰ παππῷα. — **81**, 12; **88**, 15. — *Cf. handōžišn, handōxtan.*

handōxtan, handōž-: "to accumulate, to amass". — **60**, 15; **88**, 9, 10, 11; **A2**, 3, 6. — *Cf.* NP *toxtan* "to collect, to acquire", Osset. *ænt'ūxyn*: *ænt'yxt* "to draw together, to drag" (Abaev, *HED*, I, 167—168). See also preceding entry.

handōžišn: (wealth) amassed, personally acquired (as against that which is inherited)". — **103**, 11, 12; **A2**, 4, 5 — *Cf.* preceding entry.

handraxtan, handranj-: "convict, sentence, condemn". — **A27**, 2. — *Cf. ērang, ēraxtan/ēranjēnītan.*

hangām: "time, time-limit; circumstance". — **71**, 16; **75**, 3; **78**, 10; **84**, 9.

hangartan: "to be put down to the account, to be included into the account; to be taken into consideration". — **A15**, 1. — *Cf. hangārtan.*

hangārtan, **hangār-**: "reckon as/count for, consider; count, take into account". — **61**, 15, 16; **62**, 1; 77, 6; **A13**, 4; **A27**, 2; **A28**, 5. — Iran. **ham + kăr*, Av. *[2]kar-*; *cf.* Av. *hankərəti-*, NP *angārdan*, Arm. (from Parth.) *angarem* "take into consideration, to count/reckon", Hübschmann, *AG*, I, 97—8); *cf.* also Arm. *hančar* "reason, knowledge".

hangōšītak: "collateral (as regards kinship). — **41**, 6. — For the etymology (< **ham + kauš-*) see, Nyberg, *Hb.*, 11, 102; Benveniste, *TPS* (1945), 73—74.

hanǰāftan, **hanǰām-**: "to resolve, exhaust, complete". — **87**, 10. — MMP *hnz'm-*: *hnz'ft*, Parth. *hnj'm-*: *hnjft*, *hnjpt* "to complete, fulfill" (Henning, *Verbum*, 190—191; Ghilain, 72—73).

(h)anǰaman: "assembly, gathering (of witnesses) at a trial; trial. — **78**, 5.

hark ut bār: "taxes and charges/dues". — **34**, 2; **40**, 5, 6, 7, 8 (bis), 10 (bis), 12, 13, — For the MP *hark/*harāk* (>*harāg*> Arab. *xarāǰ*), see Bartholomae, *MiMund.*, I, 10—16; Henning, *Mitteliranisch*, 41; Benveniste, *JA* (1959), 125—126; for the meaning see also MMP *ḥrq bwrdn* "to pay taxes", Arm. (from OP or Parth.) *hark* 1) "tribute, dues, taxes; 2) "service (particularly labour-service), obligation/duty"; 3) "need, requirement, obligation". Iran. **bāra/i-* "tribute, tax" is attested as *ba-a-ri* in Babylonian documents dated 399 B.C.; see Dandamaev, *Slavery*, 317.

hāvand: "equal; equivalent" (as regards a thing, a security). — **11**, 1, 6, 7, 15; **26**, 16, 17; **A37**, 3.

(h)ēr: "thing, property, treasury"; *(h)ēr ī dūtak* "family property, estate", *(h)ēr ī ātaxš/ataxšān* "temple treasury (or 'temple estate')", *hēr ī šāhīkān* "royal treasury, fisc". — **15**, 11; **30**, 7; **32**, 13, 15, 16; **34**, 1; **44**, 6; **91**, 4, 11; **95**, 17; **96**, 1; **103**, 7—10; **107**, 4, 11; **A27**, 1, 3; **A28**, 2, 3. — According to Andreas [see Lentz, *ZII*, IV (1925), 292; Nyberg, *Hb.*, II, 106], from **ēhr* < **arθ(i)ya-*, *cf.* Av. *[1]arəθa-* "thing"; according to Bailey (*TPS* (1960), 84—85, but *cf. Prolexis*, 415), from Iran. **arya- cf.* Skt. *aryáḥ* "thing, wealth", MMP *xyr*, *x'yr* "thing, material, matter", NP *xīr*, Parth. *'yr* (= *ēr/īr*), Arm. (from Parth.) *ir* "thing", see Benveniste, *REArm.*, I (1964), 11—12.

[1]**hilišn**: "divorce". — **87**, 9. — See also *hilišn/hišt-nāmak, hišt, hištan.*

[2]**hilišn**: "discharge; release from debt". — **50**, 4. *Cf. hištan.*

hilišn/hišt-nāmak: "divorce document". — **87**, 10.

hišt: "divorce". — **4**, 9, 11, 17; **87**, 9.

hištan, **hil-**: 1) "to free/release (from slavery, prison, debt, etc.), discharge from a debt, release from pledge (action performed by the creditor); dissolve a marriage, divorce; yield, leave; allow, permit; remove"; *hač graβīh hištan* "to release from pledge (action performed by the creditor); *hač kartak hištan* "to free from judicial procedure; remove from judicial inquest"; *hač rāδēnišn hištan* "to remove, to free from the conduct of a case"; *sardārīh pat gātār bē hilišn* "the guardianship is transferred (= should be yieded) to the husband", *stūrīh pat ham mart bē hilišn* "the *stūr*ship should be left to that man"; 2) to resolve a legal case, to judge; see ²*hištan*. — **2**, 1, 5, 8—13; **3**, 9, 10, 12, 13, 15; **4**, 1, 6; **8**, 15, 16; **9**, 10; **13**, 5; **21**, 6, 9, 11, 14; **25**, 9; **37**, 13; **38**, 9; **39**, 9; **40**, 2, 4; **85**, 4; **43**, 3; **49**, 4, 5; **58**, 12, 14; **59**, 8; **73**, 2; **75**, 6; **85**, 13, 16; **87**, 4, 7—10; **89**, 6, 9; **90**, 6; **95**, 1,7, 8; **104**, 3, 7, 17; **105**, 17; **109**, 8; **A3**, 1; **A7**, 17; **A13**, 2—3; **A14**, 3; **A15**, 17; **A31**, 15; **A32**, 11. — Iran. **hṛz-* "to release / let go", "loosen". *Cf.* ¹*bōxtan*, ¹˒²*bōžišn*, *vičartan*.

²**hištan**, **hil-**: "to resolve a legal case, to judge". — **97**, 7; **A26**, 14; **A27**, 2. — See ¹*hištan*.

hudēn: "a Zoroastrian". — **1**, 11, 14. — Antonym *aγdēn*.

hudēnīh: "Zoroastrian religion, affiliation with Zoroastrianism". — **1**, 10, 12. — *Cf.* *aγdēnīh*.

huyōδ: "fighting for a just cause". — **80**, 4. — Iran. **hu* + *yauda-*; it is also possible to interpret this term as the Persian form of Iran. **hu* + *yauza-* "having striving for the good", Iran. **yauz-* "to seek", *cf.* Av. *yaoxšti-* (with an intrusive *-x-*), Arm. yuzem "to search, seek", *yoyz* "striving, urge, dream".

K

kahas: "canal, channel"; with the verbs *kandan*, *rāδēnītan*. — **18**, 12, 16; **85**, 7, 8, 10, 11, 16; **86**, 2, 3, 8; **106**, 14, 15. — The spelling is *kts*, MMP *khs* (Henning, *List*, 84, 91).

kāmak: "will, testamentary disposition"; *kāmak guftan* "to express one's will (specifically, in transfers)"; *kāmak dōšītan* "to express one's agreement / acceptance of the conveyor's disposition", *cf.* *sahistan*. — **28**, 10; **54**, 4; **55**, 5; **67**, 16; **68**, 14; **A33**, 17. — *Cf.* *kāmistan*.

kāmistan, **kām-**: "to wish / desire; declare one's will (in an official, legally-binding manner)". — **6**, 14; **28**, 10; **85**, 6; **56**, 1, 2, 4, 11; **59**, 13; **66**, 3; **68**, 13; **101**, 4; **A1**, 12; **A7**, 1, 9. — See Bartholomae, *ZsR* III. *Cf.* *guftan*, *kartan*, *paytāk kartan*, *paytākēnītan*.

kamistih in **pat kamistīh**: "minimum" (opposite of *pat vēšistīh*). — **A32**, 14.

kandan, **kan-**: "to dig; incise, engrave (a seal); destroy; upset; revoke, abolish, make void, cancel". — **48**, 17; **85**, 9, 11, 12, 14; **93**, 7, 9; **94**, 4; **97**, 14, 15; **A31**, 10; **A37**, 4.

kanīžak: "girl, maiden". — **87**, 12.

¹**kār**: "work, affair; working off (= discharge by labour); function, office"; *pat kār ō apaspārišn* "(to be) handed over for working off"; *kār rāδēnītan* "to carry on, conduct a case / trial (= to participate in it as one of the litigating parties)"; *hač kār guharīk kartan* "to remove from office". *Cf.* also the expressions *pat kār apāyēt* "it is indispensable"; *kār nēst* "it is not necessary / needed". — **21**, 8; **39**, 6; **A10**, 12; **A12**, 13—14; **A25**, 17; **A26**, 1, 16; **A32**, 4.

^{2}kār: "(to have) legal action, force, be legally binding, be valid"; *pat kār nē darišn* "to hold as invalid, to consider unlawful". — **23**, 16; **31**, 3; **55**, 11, 16; **59**, 3; **75**, 4; **95**, 15; **105**, 10; **107**, 9; **A40**, 11. — *kār nēst* "invalid, devoid of legal force". — **4**, 17; **6**, 12; **16**, 17; **28**, 3; **43**, 8; **54**, 15; **63**, 8; **87**, 9; **90**, 4; **A12**, 3.

^{3}kār: "people, others". — **A4**, 13, 14. — Iran. **kāra-*, OP *kāra-* "people-host".

kardar: "court or yard in front of a house" (?). — **19**, 1. — Salemann (*Man. St.*, 145) compared this form (*kldl*) of the *Law-Book* with NP *kardar* "a hilly or rocky plot; a valley, a ravine, gorge".

kārdār: "an official, a functionary". — **A25**, 15. — *Cf.* the Armenian calque *gorcakal* "an official at the Arsacid court"; see, Perikhanian, *VDI* (1968/3), 42—45.

kār-framān: "an official, a functionary; an overseer, steward. *Cf.* also *muhr ī pat kār-framān dāštan* (see *muhr*), *nāmak ī kār-framān* (see *nāmak*). — **48**, 8; **78**, 2—3; **A27**, 7. This term is attested with the meanings given outside the *Law-Book* as well; from it is derived the Arab-Pers. *qahramān* by way of the Median form *karhraman taken over into Aramaic (*qhrmn'*); see Henning, *Mitteliranisch*, 49, n. 2.

kār-vindišn: "revenue, income, earning". — **24**, 10; **33**, 2—5; **62**, 14—15; **A2**, 14, 15. — *Cf. vindišn.*

karp: "physical appearance"; *karp apakanišnīh* "disfigurement (a variety of offence)". — **A14**, 16. — Av. *kəhərpa-*, MP *kyrb* "form", Arm. *kerp* "form, appearance, figure, shape" (with numerous derivatives).

karp: "declaration". — See *^{2}kartan.*

^{1}kartak: "religious rites, ritual; foundation for religuous purposes". See *dīvān ī kartak(ān)*, *ruvān.*

^{2}kartak: "norms governing judicial practice"; in particular the norms and regulations introduced into judicial practice through official decrees (royal edicts, encyclical letters of the high priests and through accumulated secular usage, as against the norms reflected in the *čāštak*s (the commentaries on the legal *nask*s of the *Avesta*) which were the traditional basis of the legislation. This term is formally opposed to the terms *čāštak*, *^{2}dastaβarān* (*q. v.*). *Hač kartak hištan* "to remove from judicial procedure; to release from the necessity of undergoing legal process"; *ō kartak kartan* "to subject to judicial procedure; to resolve a suit through trial"; *pat kartak* "according to the norms of judicial practice"; *pat kartak matan* "to appear at a trial". — **4**, 10, 12; **8**, 12; **23**, 15; **24**, 2—3; **30**, 9; **31**, 5, 7; **36**, 5; **42**, 5; **52**, 4; **55**, 2, 8; **61**, 17; **65**, 17; **75**, 10; **93**, 1; **97**, 17; **98**, 3; **102**, 12—13; **A11**, 8; **A12**, 10; **A13**, 1, 2, 7—12, 14, 17; **A15**, 14; **A16**, 1, 4; **A26**, 7; **A32**, 4; **A35**, 14; **A38**, 4. — Iran. **kṛta-/kṛti-* "action, activity" (*^{1}kar-*); *cf.* Pagliaro, *RSO*, XXIII (1948), 52—68.

^{3}kartak: "instituted". Designation given to a guardian or *stūr* who received his title to the guardianship or *stūr*ship through an official declaration of the will of the late head of household (publicly stated or set down in a testament or other document) made during his lifetime. Antitheses: *būtak*, *gumārtak* (*q. v.*). — **21**, 11, 13; **26**,

9, 11; **41**, 15; **43**, 16; **46**, 12; **82**, 4; **87**, 15; **90**, 9, 12. — Iran. **kṛtaka-*, from **kar-* "to do, to make" or from **kar-* "to declare, proclaim" (see [2]*kartan*).

[4]**kartak**: "piece" (as regards a plot of land). — **55**, 7. — Iran. **kart-* "to cut".

kartakīhā in **dātastān kartakīhā**: "according to the norms customary in judicial procedure" (?). — **41**, 2. — The text is fragmentary and the interpretation hypothetical.

[1]**kartan, kun-**: "to make, to do". — *Passim.* — Construed with prepositions and prepositional particles *apāč kartan* "to return; to return to the *status quo ante*, reinstate, rebuild (a channel, a house); to extract; to retain/hold back, exact, recover, take away, seize (as a forfeit)". — **33**, 5; **65**, 10, 11; **67**, 5—6; **68**, 5; 77, 7; **86**, 8; **99**, 15, 17; **106**, 16; **A5**, 15; **A13**, 12; **A18**, 6—7; **A25**, 9; **A26**, 12, 17; **A27**, 12; **A30**, 16; **A33**, 2; **A37**, 5; **A38**, 3, 4; **A39**, 11, 14. — *bē kartan* "to take away, withdraw, remove, exact; pay in full; alienate, transfer ownership rights to another person"; *tāvān bē kartan* "to settle/pay a penalty, a fine"; *dārišn bē ō M. kunišn* "to transfer the possession to M." (or "to adjudge the possession to M."); *cf.* also (**84**, 13) *u-š dārišn bē ō man kart* following after *bē ō man dāt* as an indication of the official transfer of the real right. The context, the absence of the preposition *hač* which is indispensable for a series of cases, and the presence of the phonetic spelling BR' *kwnšn*, BR' *krt'* (see *e. g.* **15**, 15; **16**, 1, 14) in identical contexts makes the variant reading *bē grīftan* of the verbal heterogram unlikely. *Cf.* also *DkM* VIII, 7, 17, 18—19; *Apar nē pātixšāyīh ī mart dānakīh ī andar patkār rāδ pēš hač ēvarīh (ī) ōy ī adānak xvāstak bē kart* "Concerning the impermissibility (= unlawfulness) of a man's taking away of a (disputed) thing on the basis of his knowledge of the judicial process (= of the outcome of the trial — *A. P.*) before the person who is not informed (of the decision of the court) has received an official ('authentic') notification (regarding the outcome of the case"). — 7,17; **8**, 1; **11**, 12; **14**, 11, 16; **15**, 11, 15; **16**, 1, 14; **31**, 1, 3; **32**, 7, 8, 10; **84**, 13; **97**, 16; **98**, 16; **102**, 6, 9. — *frāč kartan* "to suspend from, to take away"; a possible reading is *frāč grīftan/gīrišn* — **82**, 9. — *ōh kartan* "to appoint, to dispose (through an official declaration; *cf.* [2]*kartan*). — **A39**, 11; **A40**, 2—3, 5.

[2]**kartan**, ***kun-/kar-**: "to declare, to proclaim officially, to enunciate; to designate, establish by means of a declaration". This verb is very widely attested in the *Law-Book* as a synonym of *guftan, gōβišn guftan/kartan, paytākēnītan, paytāk kartan* (*q. v.*); *axonsandīh kartan* "to declare one's dissatisfaction/disagreement with the decision of a court" (**3**, 7); *dātaβarān aparmat kart* "the judges have rendered/proclaimed (their) decision" (**49**, 16—17); *mat ut kart ēstātan* "to appear (in court) and declare" (**53**, 17). — See *e. g.*, **8**, 3—10; **13**, 14; **28**, 13; **30**, 4, 5; **31**, 4, 6; **34**, 12; **35**, 17; **39**, 17; **41**, 16; **89**, 17; **90**, 2. — Iran. **kar-* "to speak solemnly, to proclaim" (*cf.* Skt. *carkṛti-* "*id.*" *kīrtíh* "mention, glory, praise", *kārúh* "poet"; Gk. κῆρυξ, κᾶρυξ "herald"), Av. [2]*kar-*, [2]*kərəta-* "solemn commemoration/mention, proclamation", [3]*kərəti-* "solemn proclamation, notification, news", *ā-kərəti-* "news"; likewise in the compounds *yasnō.kərəti-* lit. "the solemn mention/utterance of the word *yasna-*" (the name of the prayer begin-

ning with the words *yeŋhē hātąm*), *xšaθrō. kərəta-* "the solemn (three-fold) proclamation of the stanza beginning with the word *xšaθrəmča* in the *Yaθā ahū vairyō* prayer". (*Air Wb.*, 310, 448. 466, 547, 1273). Arm. (from Parth.) *čar* "solemn speech, discourse, sermon, praise". *Cf.* ³*kartak*.

kartār: "skilful, masterly, experienced, competent". — **26**, 16. — *Cf.* Arm. (from Parth.) *čartar* "skilful, clever; masterly, experienced", see Benveniste, *Et. oss.*, 9.

kašišn: "stretching (of a wound)"? — **A14**, 17.

katak: "house (as an economic complex); lodging / housing (in particular for the sacred Fire); *katak ut mān* "*id*". — **19**; 1, 7; **110**, 8, 10.

katak-bānūk: "mistress of the house". — **13**, 5—9; **14**, 7; **15**, 11, 12; **16**, 5—8, 10, 14, 16; **26**, 3; **43**, 13; **51**, 7, 9, 11, 13, 14, 16; **52**, 3, 9, 12—16; **62**, 8, 16; **63**, 1, 4; **67**, 12; **75**, 12—14; **81**, 17; **82**, 1—3; **87**, 13; **88**, 7, 8, 10—15; **90**, 2, 3, 9—11, 13, 16, 17; **94**, 13, 14; **107**, 3, 8; **A13**, 5, 6; **A15**, 8, 12; **A31**, 6—8. — *Cf. bahr ī zanīh / katak-bānūkīh, katak-xvatāy.*

katak-xvatāy: "head of household, *paterfamilias*". — **13**, 4, 10, 11; **20**, 7; **26**, 5, 9; **28**, 1; **29**, 8; **31**, 16; **39**, 17; **41**, 1; **42**, 14; **44**, 15; **45**, 7, 12, 17; **46**, 1; **51**, 2; **59**, 15; **61**, 3; **64**, 2; **82**, 2, 4; **88**, 7, 8, 14; **94**, 14; **95**, 1, 3—4; **110**, 2; **A20**, 9. — On this term see Bartholomae, *MiMund.*, III, esp. pp. 33—40.

kem nē ... rasēt: "no less; none the less; likewise". — **4**, 4; **22**, 9; **35**, 16; **44**, 10, 11; **87**, 5—6. — *kem* < **kambyah.*

kirpak: "virtue" (religious). — **35**, 12.

kōδpān (?): "head of a quarter / neighbourhood, highway"? — **A29**, 6. — *Cf. DkM*, VIII, 733, 10. *Apar ānītan ī mazdesn(ān)* **kōδpān* (*ut*) *xvēškārīh ī* * *kōδpān*. According to West [SBE, XXXVII (1892), 92] this term has the sense of "street keeper", and its first component is to be identified with NP *kuy, ku* "quarter, highway, street".

kurt: "Kurd". — **9**, 8, 11.

kust: "side, line of calling"; *hač kust ī nabānazdištīh / xvēšāvandān* "on the agnatic side; *via* agnatic calling"; *hač kust ī būtakīh* "*via* 'natural' caling". Synonym *pat rāh ī* (*q. v.*) — **47**, 13, 14; **69**, 7—9; **71**, 5—7.

kustak: "border, province". — **A31**, 4.

M

magupat: "*magupat*, priest". — **93**, 4, 5, 7, 8, 10; **95**, 16; **98**, 2, 13; **99**, 7; **100**, 4, 5, 9, 10, 12—14; **110**, 14; **A12**, 12, 13; **A14**, 11; **A18**, 16, 17; **A26**, 12, 13, 15, 16; **A37**, 4, 9; **A40**, 9. — Iran. **magupat-*; Arm. loanword. *mogpet, movpet*; see Hüschmann, *AG*, I, 195.

magupatān magupat: "chief *magupat*, high priest". — **55**, 12; **A10**, 13; **A27**, 4, 5; **A28**, 6—7; **A34**, 7, 8, 11; **A36**, 4; **A38**, 7; **A39**, 16.

magupatīh: "duty, office of the magupat, *magupat*ship". — **93**, 7; **97**, 5; **98**, 2.

mān: "house, lodging" — **110**, 8—10. — *Cf. katak, xānak.*

mānak (?): "judicial office, department" (?) — **78**, 3; **110**, 14, 15. — The reading and interpretation are hypothetical.

mānăkan / mānēkān: "the spirits of the hearth, *manes*". — **80**, 9.

māndan, mān-: (transit.) "to leave; to leave as an inheritance, bequeath"; (intrans.) "to remain". — **4**, 14; **20**, 7; **25**, 10; **102**, 9. — *apar māndan, apar ō māndan* "to inherit (a thing, a status); to become the succesor"; *cf. aparmānd, apar* [2]*zātan*. — **21**, 8, 11—12, 16; **22**, 6, 7, 10—12; **23**, 4—6, 9, 14, 16, 17; **24**, 4, 6, 7; **41**, 14; **42**, 12, 15; **44**, 10 ,14; **81**, 17; **87**, 3, 15; **90** ,1; **95**, 11; **97**, 8, 10; **A40**, 14. — *apar māndan* "to retain, hold back".— **106**, 15. — *frāč māndan* "to go to, fall to the lot of"; *apar frāč māndan* "to obtain / receive by transmission, inherit". — **27**, 2—3; **88**, 13.

mānišn: "dwelling"; **pat mānišn** "for habitation". — **19**, 2.

mar: "count, account; calculation, computation; registration"; *marīhā* "according to calculation"; *arž marīhā* "corresponding to the value"; *bahr mar / marīhā* "according to shares, allotted"; *ō mar kartan* "to take into account; enter into the register of accounts, to register". — **55**, 8; **60**, 2; **63**, 5; **65**, 11; **85**, 3; **104**, 3, 4, 17; **A33**, 17.

markaržān: "the accused / guilty on a capital charge; a capital offence". — **14**, 17; **24**, 5; **29**, 2; **31**, 2; **82**, 14; **92**, 4—6; **97**, 8, 9, 13, 15, 17; **98**, 13, 15, 17; **A16**, 2, 3; **A28**, 13, 15, 17; **A29**, 1, 3—5, 12; **A34**, 6, 14—16; **A35**, 9. — Lit. "deserving the death penalty".

marnǰēnišn: "destruction, material damage". — **A38**, 14.

mart ī šahr: "citizen, fellow-citizen". — **14**, 7; **51**, 7—8; **60**, 3, 6, 7; **61**, 9, 11; **62**, 4; **70**, 3, 17. — *Cf. šahrīk, zan ī šahr.*

masrūk⁺: "beard". — **A14**, 16. — Iran. **masru-ka, cf.* Skt. *śmáśru-* < **smaśru-*, I-E. **smok̂ru-* "beard".

[1]**mātak**: 1) "value, stock, money"; 2) "principal (sum), principal debt (as against the interest)". — **61**, 2; **67**, 14, 15; **68**, 1, 17; **71**, 13, 14, 17; **86**, 13; **89**, 11; **104**, 2, 5; **A15**, 1—3. — *Cf.* [2]*mātak.*

[2]**mātak**: "principal person, principal litigant as distinguished from his legal representative, the giver of the mandate (mandator) as against the agent / mandatary". — 7, 3, 17; **8**, 1, 11. — *Cf.* [1]*mātak, mātakvar, bun,* [1]*dastaβar.*

mātakdān: "book". — **79**, 5, 6. — Arm. *matean* < MIr *matiyān* < *mātakdān*, Henning, *BSOAS*, XVI/3 (1952), 511 n. 3.

[1]**mātakvar**: "the principal person, the principal contractor (as distinguished from his warrantor), the principal litigant (as opposed to a legal representative)". — **57**, 2, 6, 9; **75**, 15; **76**, 1, 9; **77**, 14, 16(?); **A32**, 5. — See Bartholomae, *ZsR* IV, 23. *Cf.* [2]*mātakvar, mātak, bun,* [1]*dastaβar.*

[2]**mātakvar**: "original copy of a document, original"; as opposed to *hampaččēn* "copy". — **77**, 14, 16; **A33**, 16.

mātīk: "text (?). — **79**, 9.

mērak: "husband"; often found paired with [2]*ziyānak* (*q. v.*) — **3**, 14; **45**, 7; **50**, 8—10; **52**, 11; **55**, 6; **63**, 12, 16, 17; **68**, 15, 17; **82**, 15; **83**, 2; **93**, 14, 15; **94**, 12; **100**, 13, 14; **A5**, 14; **A14**. 7—9; **A29**, 10, 15; **A30**, 1; **A31**, 4; **A35**, 2, 4. — Iran. **maryaka-*. See Bartholomae, *ZsR* IV, 6, 50—52; Benveniste, *TPS* (1945), 44; Bailey, *Roc. Or.* (1957), 66; Gershevitch, *Mithra*, 152—153.

mih (ēstātan): "object, oppose". — **54**, 8; **58**, 2; **65**, 8; **76**, 8; **86**, 9, 16; **100**, 2. — Iran. **miθa-* (= Skt. *mitháḥ* "opposed", *cf.* *mithū* "wrongly, falsely", *méthati* "to be hostile"), Av. *miθō* (= Skt. *mithū*), *miθah-* (*Air Wb.*, 1182), OP *miθah-* "evil".

mihrdružīh: "breach of contract" (offence). — **A34**, 12. — Av. *miθrō.drujim* "breaker of contract"; *cf.* Parth. *druxtmihr* (Henning, *List*, 82), Arm. (from Parth.) *uxtadruž* "oath-breaker".

miyān: "middle"; *apāč ō miyān āβurtan* "to present again, anew (as regards testimony at a trial)"; *apāč ō miyān matan* "to present (oneself) again (in court)"; *hač miyān bē āβurtan* "to destroy, to withdraw from circulation (as regards the destruction of a thing)"; *pat miyān* "at the expense of", "with the means of"; *pat miyān būtan* "to be in use"; *pat miyān kartan* "provide for, maintain". — **31**, 10—11; **32**, 13, 14; **55**, 3; **78**, 9; **99**, 5; **A13**, 10.

mizd: "pay". — **8**, 12; **34**, 3; **85**, 10; **A27**, 17. — *Cf.* *rōčīk*.

moγān (h)andarzpat: "*handarzpat* of the Magi" (title). **57**, 12; **59**, 10; **98**, 3; **A15**, 14—15; **A37**, 11—12; **A40**, 6. — Arm. *movan anderjapet, movan handerjapet, mogacʻ anderjapet*; Syr. *muγ(ân) andarzbaδ* (Hübschmann, *AG*, I, 99, 195).

muγ: "date-palm". — **102**, 14; **103**, 13; **A2**, 5.

muhr: "seal"; *muhr ī ēvar/vičurt* "valid, authentic seal"; *muhr ī pat kār-framān dāštan* "official seal"; *muhr apar nihātan* "to affix a seal, to seal"; *muhr patigriftan* "to acknowledge the authenticity of the seal on a document (= to admit the document as legally valid)". — **32**, 4; **73**, 12; **76**, 2; **93**, 5, 7, 8, 12, 13; **99**, 1, 3, 4, 6; **100**, 6, 10, 13—15; **103**, 4; **106**, 11; **A12**, 14—16; **A18**, 15, 17; **A19**, 1, 5, 6, 8; **A26**, 5; **A30**, 4; **A34**, 7; **A36**, 10; **A38**, 7; **A39**, 4. — Iran (OMed.?) **mudra-* (> Skt. *mudrā́-*) "seal"; see Junker, *IF*, 35 (1915), 273; Mayrhofer, *Etym. Wb.* II, 653—654 (with bibliography). *Cf.* *muhrak, muhr-brīt, muhr-dāt, muhr-vēxt.*

muhrak/muhr: see **A29**, 7—9 and note 82.

muhr-brīt: "(document) with a cut seal (= an opened, unsealed document)". — **102**, 16; **103**, 3. — *Cf.* *muhr-vēxt, višāt.*

muhr-dāt: "(document) concerning a functionary's return of his seal of office upon his removal from office". — **A12**, 14, 16.

muhr-vēxt: "(document) whose seal has been removed (= an opened, unsealed document)". — **102**, 15; **103**, 3. — *Cf.* *muhr-brīt, višāt.*

must: "complaint"; *garzītan ī must* "appeal" (*cf.* also *Mustaβar-nāmak* "*The Book of Appeals*", **A5**, 11). — **A26**, 4. — Iran. **musti-*, from the root **mud-* "to complain, to beg for alms"; *cf.* MP (inscrip.) *mwsty* "an act violence and injustice", (Pahl.) *mustkar* "offender; offended", *mōδak*, NP *mūye* "complaint", Sogd. *mwδ* "begging", Arm. (from Parth.) *moyr* "begging, alms"; *muram* "to beg for alms"; see Nyberg, *Hb.* II, 152; Henning, *Asia Major*, IV/1 (1954), 101—102; but *cf.* Benveniste, *REArm.*, I (1964), 5.

N

nabānazdišt, -īh: "agnate", — **22**, 11; **28**, 1; **45**, 10, 12, 13, 16; **81**, 10, 15; **87**, 12. — Av. *nabānazdišta-*, *AirWb.*, 1040; Perikhanian, VDI (1968/3), 28—52, *Obščestvo*, 50—79. *Cf. patvand, tōxmak, xvēš, xvēšāvand.*

nahang: "province". — **78**, 3, 13. — The historical spelling is *nsng*. *Cf.* Arm. *nahang* "province".

nakīrā(k): "to contest, deny, reject" (in construction with *ah-/bav-*). — **6**, 4, 12; **8**, 2, 8; **13**, 14; **16**, 15, 17; 77, 10; **83**, 10, 11; **84**, 1; **95**, 8; **102**, 2, 7; **107**, 7. — On this term representing an Accadism in Aramaic and Iranian, see my *Materialy*, 115—122. Antonym: *xvastūk*. See next entry.

nakīrā(k)īh: — "denial; contesting in court" (said of the respondent). — **3**, 6; **16**, 17; 77, 10; **99**, 4; **102**, 2, 13.

nām kartan: "to mention, to indicate in an agreement, in a declaration; to stipulate". — **71**, 11, 13, 14, 17.

nāmak: "letter, document"; *nāmak kartan/pas(s)āxtan* "to draw up a document"; *nāmak pas(s)āč* "the drawing up of documents"; *xvēškārīh nāmak ī kār-framān* "*Letter concerning the obligations of magistrates/officials*". — **78**, 12; **93**, 12, 14, 17; **99**, 1, 3; **100**, 9; **110**, 13; **A3**, 8, 9, 11, 12; **A15**, 17—**A16**, 1, 4; **A18**, 16, 17; **A19**, 1, 7, 8; **A26**, 6; **A27**, 17; **A28**, 1; **A31**, 9, 10; **A34**, 3; **A37**, 15; **A38**, 16—17. — *Cf. avišt, dip, dipīrih, čak, fravartak, hampačēn, GT'k, hilišn/hišt-nāmak, mātakdān,* [2]*mātakvar, pătixšāy-kart, pursišn-nāmak, saxvan-nāmak, uzdāt-nāmak, vičīr, yazišn-nāmak.*

nāmak-niδān: "archive". — **78**, 12—13. — *Nāmak + niδān* < **nidāna-* (Skt. *nidhāna-* "repository, treasury"), MMP *ny'n* "treasury, treasure". For the formation *cf.* OP *ganza-nidāna-* (in the Elamite transcription); see Benveniste, *JA* (1954), 307.

nāmak-pas(s)āč: "ordeal-letter". Document containing the court decision appointing an ordeal procedure, and specifying its form, for the litigant; see also *var.* — **78**, 10, 16.

nām-burzišn: "elevation of the name" = continuity and prosperity of one's clan/family. — **80**, 10.

nāmčišt, nāmčištīk: "definite, precisely indicated". — **18**, 3; **34**, 6, 8; **36**, 6; **38**, 14; **39**, 12; **45**, 7; **47**, 6; **73**, 3; **77**, 13; **78**, 10; **89**, 12; **92**, 7, 9; **94**, 5; **95**, 6. —Iran.

**nāman-* "name" + **čišta-*, *cf.* Av. *²kaēš-*, *čiš-* "to determine, fix (by a religious or a magic force); confer, indicate, recognize, avow". For this radical see J. Narten, "*Mon. Nyberg*" II (1975), 81—92. *Cf.* Arm. *čišt* "exact, correct, true" *et al.*

narīh ut mātakīh: lit. "being a male or a female"; the indication (in a judicial document) of the sex of the participants in a trial and of the witnesses. — **A26**, 2; **A30**, 1—2.

nasā⟨k⟩-nikān: "one who has corpses buried" (a variety of offence)". — **A15**, 11. — Av. **nasu. nikāna-*, *cf.* Av. *zəme.nikan-*; see Benveniste, *A Locust's Leg*, 39—43.

nasā⟨k⟩-pāk: "one who cremates corpses"; a person guilty of the offence of cremating corpses. — **A15**, 11. — Av. *nasu.pāka-*, *Air Wb.*, 1059. *Cf. nasā⟨k⟩-nikān.*

nayīhītan, ***nayīh-**: "to transfer". — **110**, 10.

nērōk: "physical force". — **8**, 12.

niδān; see *nāmak-niδān.*

nihātak: "endowment, foundation (dedicatory)". — **29**, 10; **34**, 1, 7, 8. — See Bartholomae, *MiMund.*, II, 8—12. *Cf.* Skt. *ukṣayanidhi-*, the designation of the *nibandha-* "rent" given to a temple as an *utsarga*-foundation, the Indian counterpart of Iranian foundations "for the soul".

nihātan, **nih-**: "to put, to place"; *pat graβ nihātan* "to pawn, pledge, mortgage"; *apar nihātan*: "allot, institute a foundation (for specific purpose)"; *muhr apar nihātan* "to affix a seal"; *sāk/nisāk apar nihātan*: "assess/impose a tax"; (*graβakān*) *andar nihātan* "to hypothecate, pledge (regarding re-pledging)". — **29**; 10; **34**, 1, 7, 8; **35**, 10, 16; **37**, 12; **100**, 13; **104**, 5; **A27**, 12.

nikerišn: "judicial investigation/inquest". — **78**, 6, 7. — *Cf. nikerītan.*

nikerītan/niker-: "investigate, to look into, examine, consider". — **7**, 2; **9**, 11; **15**, 1; **20**, 1, 4; **25**, 11; **28**, 9; **35**, 9; **64**, 2; **67**, 13; **68**, 12; **69**, 6; **70**, 16; **72**, 13; **87**, 10; **95**, 4; **104**, 8; **A2**, 5; **A40**, 6. — Iran. **ni- karya-*, **kar-* "to think"; NP *nigarīdan*; *cf. uskārtan.*

nimūtan, **nimāy-**: "to show, testify, give evidence (at a trial)". — **A15**, 1; **A40**, 4.

nipēk: "document". — **110**, 13. — From OP *dipi-*, see Henning, *BSOS*, X/4 (1942), 949 n. 4; *cf.* Bartholomae, *MiMund.* IV, 30, n. 2. See also *s. v. asaβār-nipēk.*

nipišt: "receipt, voucher". — **7**, 10.

nipištak: "document". — **92**, 4, 6; **97**, 6, 7; **98**, 2; **A15**, 12.

nipištan/nipēs-: "to write". — *Passim.*

nīrmat: "advantage, profit; recompense". *nīrmattar* "more profitable, more advantageous". — **19**, 16; **29**, 9, 11; **37**, 4; **41**, 9; **45**, 8; **59**, 14; **66**, 13, 14; **67**, 11; **73**, 4, 6; **A13**, 17. — Iran. **nĭ+r̥+mati-*, **ar-* "to acquire, attain, reach, etc.", see Bartholomae, *ZsR* V, 44; Bailey, *BSOS*, IX (1937—1939), 230.

niruzd, **niruzdīh**: "deprived, destitute, poor; destitution, poverty". — **101**, 6. — Av. *niuruzda-* (*Air Wb.*, 1085), Skt. *niruddha-*.

nisāk/sāk: "tax"; *nisāk/sāk apar nihātan* "to assess/impose a tax, to tax". — **A26**, 13, 17. — See Pagliaro, *RSO*, XV (1935), 305. This may be a distorted writing of the word *sāk* (*q. v.*).

[1]**nišān**: "sign, mark". — **A26**, 9, 10. — NP *nišān*: "sign"; *cf.* also Arm. (from Parth.) *niš*, *nšan* "sign", Syr. *nišâ* (Hübschmann, *AG*, I, 204). For the etymology see Gershevitch, *Iran and Islam. V. Minorsky vol.* (1971), 272—279 = *Philologia Iranica* (1985), 242—249.

[2]**nišān**: see *var ī pāδ nišān*.

nišāstan, nišān- (ātaxš, ātur(r)ōk n.): "to institute, establish, set-up (a Fire-altar or temple)"; *apāč nišāstan* "to rebuild, re-install, set-up again". — **26**, 14—15; **27**, 1, 7, 9—11, 16; **29**, 7; **31**, 10; **45**, 15; **46**, 3, 4; **78**, 14; **94**, 4, 6; **110**, 7; **A36**, 7, 9; **A37**, 4, 7, 10, 12, 14; **A39**, 1, 2, 6, 8.

nītan, nay-: "to conduct (a family's affairs); to abduct (a girl)"; *stūrīh nītan = stūrīh kartan*. — **36**, 5; **46**, 17; **96**, 10.

niyāpēt: "suits, is proper for, is fitting". **2**, 3; **11**, 12; **85**, 3; **86**, 7, 17. — The spelling is *nyd'pyt'*; *cf.* MMP, Parth., *ny'bg* "suitable, fitting", *ny ny'bg* "*non decet*", Henning, *A List*, 86. Iran. **ni + āp-*, root **ăp-* "to reach, to attain"; Av. *ap-* "to attain, to gain possession of; to be fitting, proper, suitable" (*cf.* Skt. *āpnóti* "to attain", *āptáḥ* "fitting, suitable"; Lat. *aptus*).

***nizūtan**; see *vizūtan*.

nižāδ/*vižāδ: "claim(?); appeal(?); in the construction *pat nižāδ/*vižāδ hištan*. — **A26**, 14; **A27**, 2.— Iran. **ni + ǰad-* "to ask, to request", *cf.* MMP *nyz'y* "request", *nyz'y-* "to implore" (Henning, *Verbum*, 188). The reading and interpretation given are hypothetical.

O

ō bavēt (būtan, bav-): "goes to, comes to, is allotted to, falls to the lot of". — *E. g.* **4**, 5, 10; **27**, 2, 4. — *Cf.* Av. *avi bavaiti* (*Yt.* 8, 14; *Air Wb.*, 931—932); Bartholomae, *MiMund.* II, 6; Nyberg, *Hb.* II, 41.

Ōhrmizd (xvatāy): "*Ōhrmizd* (the god)". — **35**, 17; **79**, 3.

Ōhrmizd: "*Ōhrmizd* (the day of the month)". — **35**, 13, 17; **57**, 14, 16; **72**, 3, 5; **A18**, 13; **A19**, 14; **A28**, 13—15.

ōkārišn: "removal, alienation, banishment". — **A35**, 6. — The given meaning of the verb *ōkārtan* is established beyond doubt by its use in other Pahlavi texts; in the Sanskrit translation of the *ŠGV*, *ōkārēnd* (Paz. *hugārand*, *ŠGV*, 11, 138) is rendered by Skt. *apaharanti*. (See Bailey, *ZP*, 202, n. 3).

ōst: "firmly established; undoubted, unquestionable". — **A38**, 13. - Iran. **ava + stā-*.

ōstaβar: 1) "an empowered, entitled, trustworthy person"; 2) "a commentator of the *Avesta*". This is a synonym of [1,2]*dastaβar* (*q. v.*); in its second meaning *ōstaβar* is formally opposed to ²*kartak*. — **75**, 14; **87**, 14; **A15**, 14; **A35**, 13. — MMP *'wystw'r* "an entitled/empowered representative of a family (= of an agnatic group)". Iran. **ava-stā-bara-*/**abi-hišta-bara-*; see Henning, *Verbum*, 194—195, 224—225; Nyberg, *Hb.*, II, 186. *Cf. ōst, ōstaβarīh, ōstaβartar*.

ōstaβarīh: "empowerment, title, etc.". Synonym of *dastaβarīh* (*q. v.*). — **26**, 14.

ōstaβartar: "trustworthier, more rightful". — **110**, 9.

ōstān: "royal domain". — **A39**, 10, 14, 15; **A40**, 2, 5. — *Cf.* MMP *'wyst'm* "province", Arm. *ostan* "royal domain", *ostanik* "class of conditional holders of large landed complexes within the royal domain possession of which had become hereditary". *Cf. infra ōstāndār, ōstāndārīh.*

ōstāndār: "*ōstāndār*". Official heading the department administering the royal domain. — **A27**, 12, 16. — NP *istāndār*; *cf.* Aram. (Bab. Talm.) *'ystndr'*. *Cf. ōstān, ōstāndārīh.*

ōstāndārīh; see *dīvān ī ōstāndārīh.*

ōstāt: "mentor, teacher, master". Here a form of address to a spiritual personage. — **57**, 5, 11. — MMP *'wyst'd*, NP *ustād, ōstād* "master". *Cf. ōstaβar.*

ōstīkānīh: "*ostīkān*ate" (office, function). — **100**, 8. — Arm. *ostikan*, Hübschmann, *AG*, I, 215.

ōšmurtan, ōšmăr-: "to count". — **65**, 9.

¹**ōzatan, ōzan-**: "to kill". — **92**, 3; **97**, 4, 5.

²**ōzatan, ōzam-**: "to condemn". — **A13**, 11. — The ms. has *YK(=Q)ṬLWN-t*, the usual heterogram for ¹*ōzatan* "to strike, to kill" of which the meaning contradicts the context. It seems therefore preferable to see here its homonym *ōzatan*, **ōzam-* representing Iran. **ava+zam-*: *ză̄ta-*; *cf.* Sogd. *'wz'm-*, *'wzty* "to condemn, to sentence" on which see Henning, *BBB* 65, n. 1; Gershevitch, *GMS*, § 584. *Cf.* also **A13**, 13—15 where the antonym *hištan* "to acquit" is used in a similar but opposite context. The present entry corrects my previous attempt (*Sudeb.*, *s. v.*) to connect ²*ōzatan* with Iran. **zāy-* "to leave behind, abandon *etc.*"

ōzīt/uzīt: "left behind, abandoned, escheated" (?) — **A28**, 1. — The spelling is *'wčyt'*. Possibly from Iran. **ava/us+zīta-*, root **zā(y)-*, Av. *zāy-* (*Air Wb.*, 1688), *cf.* Skt. *jáhāti, ujjháti* (Mayrhofer, *Etym. Wb.*, I, 100, 426) "to leave behind, to abandon". The translation and interpretation of this word are hypothetical. See also the next entry.

ōzītak/uzītak: "abandoned, escheated" (?). Of a possession (*dārišn ī ōzītak/uzītak*). — **A26**, 11. — *Cf.* the preceding entry.

P

pāδ; see, *var ī pāδ nišān.*

panǰāhak "fifty years, fifty-year period" — **A38**, 8, 10, 12.

pardaxtan, **pardāč-**: "to remain over". — **34**, 3, 7, 8. — Parth. (KZ) *prtšyWd* (Henning, *Mitteliranisch*, 66). The alternative reading is *par(r)ēxtan* (*q. v.*).

[1]**parēžvān/frēžvan**: "obligatory, due". — **92**, 2, 5. — Iran. **pari/fra+raiǰa-* (root **raig*, *cf.* Lat. *obligāre*) + *pāna-*, see Bartholomae *ZAirWb.*, 52, note; MacKenzie, *Henning Mem.* Vol., 268.

[2]**parēžvān**: "court magistrate directing an inquest". — **A27**, 9, 10; **A30**, 3, 5. — Compound from *parēž/frēz* "obligation, duty, function" + *pān*; see the preceding entry.

***pargār**: "sentence, conviction"; *pargār-nāmak* "document containing the judicial decision, sentence"; *pargār brītan* "to draw up a document containing the court decision" (see *brītan*). — **78**, 4, 7; **92**, 2; **A26**, 14; **A27**, 2 — The spelling is *plg(<k?)'l*. The meaning given is deduced from the contexts. The reading **fragār* (< **fra+kāra-*, *cf.* Skt. *pra+kār-* "to appoint, to institute") is likewise possible.

paristārīh: "status of *hierodule*, sacred-slavery" (of a woman). — **A40**, 4.

parmātan, **parmāy-**: "to determine; to measure". — **A15**, 12, 14. — Iran. **pari+mā-*; *cf.* Arm. *parmayem* "to determine, measure", Hübschmann, *AG*, I, 228.

par(r)ēxtan, **par(r)ēč-**: "to remain over". — **34**, 3, 7, 8; **60**, 15. — Iran. **pari/pa+raik-*; Bartholomae, *MiMund.*, II, 11, 38—40; Benveniste, *Et. oss.*, 99, 101—102. *Cf. pardaxtan.*

parvartan, **parvar-**: "to maintain, foster", *parvarišn* "maintenance, fostering care" (synonym *xvarišn ut darišn*, *q. v.*). — **31**, 5; **33**, 4, 5; **36**, 9.

parvartār: "foster-father, nurse". — **33**, 4; **A4**, 10, 11.

pās: "guard, watch post". — **A26**, 4, 8. — Iran. **pāϑra-*, OP **pās̯sa-*, NP *pās*; *cf.* Arm. (from Parth.) *parh*, *pah* "guard, *et al*", Hübschmann, *AG*, I, 217.

pasēmār/pasēmāl: "respondent, defendant; *pasēmār šutan* "to appear in court as respondent". — **2**, 9, 10; **3**, 4, 7; **5**, 4, 9, 10, 15; **73**, 11—16; **74**, 1, 2, 4—6, 9—11; **75**, 5, 7, 9; **76**, 2, 14, 15; **77**, 9, 11, 12, 16, 17; **83**, 3, 9, 11, 14, 15; **84**, 6—9, 11—13; **90**, 4, 5, 7; **93**, 9, 11; **95**, 11; **99**, 4, 6; **100**, 14; **101**, 17; **102**, 2—8; **107**, 10—13; **A13**, 16; **A16**, 5; **A27**, 11; **A30**, 17; **A31**, 1, 2; **A32**, 7, 10. — See *hamēmār*. *Cf. pēšēmār.*

pasēmārīh: "participation in a case as respondent, the responding party at a trial, the defence". — **44**, 6; **73**, 17. — See the preceding entry.

pas(s)andārīh: designation of a variety of real rights. — **83**, 4. — This word may be composed from MP *pas(s)and* (< **pati+sanda-*) + *dār(īh)*.

pas(s)andītan, **pas(s)sand-**: "to be pleased with, to approve". One of the terms designating the second stage in the transfer of a real right: the acceptance of the declaration of conveyor's intention and the choice of the object. — **66**, 3. — *Cf. andar apāyistan*, *dōšītan*, *kāmak dōšītan*, *patigriftan*, *sahistan*, *sahišn guftan*.

pas(s)āxtan, **pas(s)āč-**: "to accomplish, perform, to make; to arrange the ordeal ceremony" — **33**, 13; **100**, 9.

pas(s)axv: "the responding declaration, the defence (in court)"; *passaxv guftan*: "to appear as respondent" (*cf. saxvan*). — **7**, 10; **A26**, 4. — *Cf.* Arm. *patasxani* in the sense of "defence; ἀπολογία".

paš(a)dātakān / pas(ā)dātakān: "dowry; paraphernalia". Attested linked with *vāspuhrakān* (*q. v.*) in composite *paš(a)dātakān ut vāspuhrakān ī zan*. — **4**, 11; **43**, 2; **101**, 14; **106**, 8; **A2**, 8, 10. — The word occurs also — likewise linked with *vāspuhrakān* — in Pahl. Vd. XIV, 15 where both terms serve to render Av. *nāməni-* "share, part" (Iran. **nam-*, I-E. **nem-* "to divide"; *cf.* Gk. νέμω "*id.*", medially "to obtain / enjoy as one's share"). The Pahlavi word (attested with various spellings: pyšyk'n / ps'k'n / ps'yg'n / pyš'k'n, all of them corruptions of Late MP **pasāyēgān / pasāyγān / pasēyān* < OP **pasădātakāna-*) continues Iran. **pas-ča-dāt(a)-*, lit. "after-gift", OP **pasă-dāt(a)-* enlarged with adjectival *-akāna-*. Both Arm. (from Parth.) *paštatakan* < **pašdatakan* "dowry, wedding gift" (Bible, Xorenac'i) and Aram. *psšdt* "paraphernalia" (Papyri Kraeling 10, 9; 12, 10) corroborate this etymology. See Périkhanian, *REArm.*, XX (1986—1987), 47—53. See also *s. v. vāspuhrakān, bahr ī duxtīh*.

pašt: "agreement, contract"; *pašt kartan / dātan* "to make an agreement". — **6**, 13; **17**, 3, 4; **21**, 2; **42**, 11; **53**, 11; **71**, 8, 10; **93**, 12; **A7**, 6; **A10**, 17; **A11**, 4, 5, 8; **A18**, 11; **A40**, 16. — Iran. **pašti-*, root **pas-*, *cf.* Lat. *pactio*. See Bartholomae. *MiMund*, II, 3—15; *ZsR* I, 7—22; III, 5—6. *Cf. paštak, patmān, vičīr*.

paštak: "agreement; wager"; *paštak būtan*: "to make a legal wager". — **10**, 14.

pātan, pāy-: "to wait, await; to delay, defer, put off". — **71**, 10, 12; **A25**, 17.

pātifrās: "punishment". — **A34**, 9; **A35**, 6. — Iran. **pātifrāsa-*; *cf.* OP *a-p(a)rsam* "to punish", *(h)u-frašta-* "well punished", MP *p'dypr'h*, NP **pādafrāh*, Arm. (from Parth.) *patuhas* < **paturhas* "punishment" [see Benveniste, *TPS* (1945), 74]. For Iran. **frăs-* "to punish" < "to strike", Skt. *plakṣṇóti*, see Burrow, "*Pratidhānam*", 247.

patigriftan, patigīr-: "to receive, to accept". In particular, "to accept (a thing)", *patigīrišn* "acceptance", as the designation of the second stage in the transfer of real rights (see the synonyms *s. v. pas(s)andītan*); *pat duxtīh / frazandīh / pusīh patigriftan* "to adopt"; *pat patixšāy zanīh patigriftan* "to take a woman into *pātixšāyīh* marriage; to transfer a *čakar*-wife to the status of a *pātixšay* wife"; *yātakgōβ patigriftan* "the admission (of someone) by the court to participate in a trial as legal representative upon the certification of his mandate"; *muhr patigriftan*, see, *muhr*; *var patigriftan* "to receive the taking of an oath; to admit someone to the ordeal". — **16**, 10, 11; **17**, 8, 12, 15; **19**, 17; **20**, 4; **28**, 13; **39**, 9; **75**, 8, 10; **77**, 14; **102**, 1; **106**, 2, 3; **A3**, 4, 5; **A8**, 10; **A23**, 10; **A40**, 10—13.

patigriftak: "adopted". See below.

duxt ī patigriftak: "adopted daughter". — **69**, 12. — *Cf. duxtakānīh*.

frazand / pus ī patigriftak: "adopted son". — **16**, 3; **26**, 11, 12; **28**, 8; **29**, 7—9; **42**, 1—3, 10, 11; **69**, 10, 12—14; **70**, 12, 14, 16; **71**, 3, 4; **110**, 15. — *Cf. pusakānīh*.

pit ī patigriftak: "adopter, adoptive father" (as against *pit ī čakar, pit ī patixšāyīha*). — **69**, 14—16; **70**, 3; **71**, 4, 5.

pātīmār: "disposition; judicial decision, sentence". — **A15**, 7; **A26**, 16; **A28**, 4. — Iran. **patya + māra-/pati + ā+ māra-*; *cf.* Khot.-Saka *patämara* "report" (Bailey, *Prolexis*, 156—157). Heterogram PK(= Q)DWN; see *s. v. dastaβar*.

pātīrān: "counteraction, abbrogation, revocation; retention, restraint; delay"; (*bar/xvāstak*) *pātīrān kartan* "to retain, keep back, exact"; *pātīmār pātīrān* "the revoking/delay of a court decision"; *pātīrān saxtan ī dāstastān* "to obstruct/delay a trial", *cf.* also *rāδēnišn ī saxvan pātīrān*; *pātīrān ī var* "delay/revoking of the ordeal procedure". — **77**, 17—**78**; 1; **A8**, 9, 11; **A26**, 7, 16; **A27**, 8. — Iran. **pāti + arāna-*, **[1]ar-* "to move", *cf.* Av. *paityārəna-* "*contrarius*", *et al.* It is unlikely that it is formed on the root **pā(y)-* "to keep, to take care of" as suggested by Bartholomae (see *ZsR* II, 31—34). *Cf.* next entry.

pātīrānēnītan, pātīrānēn-. "to retain, restrain, impede; to refrain from". — **46**, 13—14; **A9**, 2; **A14**, 12, 13; **A20**, 5. — Denominative verb from *pātīrān* (*q. v.*).

patīt: *pat patīt būtan* "to expiate one's guilt, to bear the punishment". — **98**, 17. — Av. *paitita-*, *paititay-*, *Air Wb.* 829.

pātixšāy: "competently, lawful, authorized"; *pātixšāy ah-* "to be competent, to be entitled". — Iran. **pati + xšāy-*.

pātixšāyīh: "competence, right, (legal) title". Synonym of *dastaβarīh*. — **3**, 11; **76**, 12. — *Cf. dastaβarīh, dastaβārīha, ōstaβarīh*. See below.

pātixšāy/pātixšāyīhā frazandīh; see *duxt, pus, frazand ī pātixšāyīhā*.

duxt/pus/frazand ī pātixšāyīhā: "daughter/son from a marriage *cum manu mariti*" (the antithesis of *duxt/pus ī čakar, čakardāt, baγaspān, q. v.*); *pat pātixšāyīhā frazandīh patigriftan* (as regards the adoption of a *čakar*-son by his *čakar*-father (= by the *čakar*-husband of his mother). — **2**, 4; **3**, 11; **26**, 11; **28**, 8; **29**, 7; **31**, 9; **33**, 9; **36**, 17; **41**, 3; **46**, 1; **82**, 15; **100**, 17; **A24**, 1—8; **A40**, 10, 11, 13. — See also *dātastān brāt, dātastān duxt, dātastān pus, dātastān xvah*.

pit ī pātixšāyīhā: "legitimate father; *pātixšāy*-husband of the person's mother", as against *pit ī čakar* (*q. v.*). This term designates also the person's own father as against the adopter, *pit ī patigriftak*. — **41**, 3—4; **70**, 13, 15; **101**, 1; **110**, 16, 17.

šōy ī pātixšāyīhā: "a woman's legitimate husband with whom she has entered into *pātixšāyīh* (= *cum manu mariti*) marriage". — **A1**, 6. — *Cf. zan ī pātixšāyīhā*.

zan ī pātixšāyīhā: "legitimate wife; woman who is her husband's wife in a *cum manu mariti* wedlock", as against *baγaspān, zan ī čākar, xvāsrāy-* (*q. v.*). — **33**, 9; **36**, 2, 16—17; **44**, 4; **49**, 3; **64**, 2; **70**, 6, 10; **82**, 9, 15; **90**, 14; **101**, 5; **103**, 2; **A1**, 3; **A4**, 14, 17; **A5**, 10, 15; **A6**, 6, 14; **A7**, 13; **A40**, 4, 12, 14.

pātixšāy zanīh: "legitimate wedlock (= *cum manu mariti*)". — See *pātixšāy* et sqq.

pātixšāy-kart: "mandate, mandating document"; *dip ī pātixšāy-kart* (*q. v.*). — **76**, 5; **A38**, 16.

pātixšāy kartan: "to empower, entitle". — *E. g.* **3**, 10, 16; **17**, 10, 11—12, 13, 15; **37**, 16; **74**, 13—15; **76**, 5, 10—12; **103**, 11; **A1**, 7; **A2**, 1, 2; **A3**, 7, 12, 14; **A4**, 3; **A7**, 1, 12. — *Cf. pātixšāy-kart*.

pātixšāyōmand: "rightful, entitled". — **82**, 13; **A30**, 4.

patkār: "responding declaration, statement (in court); trial". — **25**, 11; **91**, 14; **A5**, 9. — MMP *phyk''r*, NP *paykār*; Arm. *payk'ar* "dispute", *payk'arim* "to dispute" (Hübschmann, *AG*, I, 220).

patkārišn: 1) "trial; litigation"; 2) "matter of controversy, a controversial circumstance". — **5**, 8; **53**, 16; **86**, 4, 9, 10, 13, 16.

patkārtan, patkār: "to answer, to object (in court); to litigate; to contend, controvert"; *apar / andar patkārtan* "to contend for, dispute about, controvert". — **7**, 4, 5; **8**, 5; **9**, 17; **70**, 5; **13**, 8; **14**, 9; **16**, 13; **22**, 15; **32**, 5; **64**, 9; **67**, 7; **77**, 13, 14, 17; **83**, 3, 5, 10; **85**, 14; **93**, 1, 3; **95**, 7; **102**, 6, 10; **106**, 10; **A6**, 11; **A17**, 4—6, 8, 9, 11—13; **A18**, 3, 5, 7; **A22**, 2, 3, 5, 9, 11; **A24**, 13; **A27**, 16; **A31**, 2, 13, 16; **A38**, 2.

patmān: "agreement, treaty; condition"; *patmān kartan* "to make an agreement"; **4**, 4; **6**, 15, 16; **20**, 11; **29**, 15; **30**, 8; **38**, 14; **39**, 13; **40**, 5; **54**, 6, 9, 11; **55**, 17; **56**, 15; **58**, 4; **59**, 2; **64**, 11; **67**, 3, 13; **68**, 1; **71**, 8; **89**, 12; **90**, 14; **108**, 9; **A1**, 3; **A7**, 14; **A10**, 13; **A19**, 16; **A22**, 3, 7; **A24**, 5, 16; **A25**, 1, 9; **A33**, 7. — NP *paymān* "agreement, contract"; Arm. (from MP) *payman* "condition, contract; definition; limit; measure", *paymanem* "to make an agreement, engage oneself" (Hübschmann, *AG*, I, 220). *Cf. pašt.*

patmūtan, patmāy-: "to measure". — **105**, 4.

pātram: "surrounding people, milieu; people". — **A15**, 15; **A35**, 5. — Iran. **pă-ti + rama-*; *cf.* MP *ram, ramak* "herd, flock; crowd, people", Parth. *ram.*, NP *ram(a)*, Arm. (from Parth.) *eram, eramak* "flock, herd; crowd"; (from MP) *ṙam, ṙamik* "commoner, plebeian", *et al.* (See Hübschmann, *AG*, I, 147, 233).

pātrōč: "daily allowance, daily provisions, rations". — **93**, 11. — MMP *pādrōzag*, M. Parth. *pādrōžag* (*p'drwcg*) "day by day, dayly"; see Salemann, *Man.* IV, 46; see also Henning (*BBB*, 81) who compares this word with Sogd. *pṯmyδyy* "daily", abandoning his former (*Verbum*, 230) revision of Salemann's interpretation. The comparison with Arm, *patručak* and *awrapahik* in *Sudeb.*, Gloss., *s. v.* is erroneous.

patvand: "relation, family, kinsman, kinship". — **24**, 15; **25**, 1, 7, 16; **26**, 1; **27**, 15; **28**, 15; **29**, 5; **35**, 6, 8; **41**, 3, 4; **42**, 15; **49**, 7; **A33**, 6; **A36**, 3.

pāyakīhā: "gradually". — **79**, 13.

pāyandān: "warrantor". — **2**, 8, 9, 11; **56**, 5, 6, 17; **57**, 2, 6, 8, 9; **59**, 3, 6; **102**, 13; **A32**, 5. — NP *pāyandān* "warrantor". See also *hampāyandān, hampāyandānīh, pāyandānīh.*

pāyandānīh: "warranty" also "warrantors (collectively)". — **2**, 12; **55**, 10; **56**, 6, 16; **57**, 15; **89**, 2.

paytāk: "obvious, evident"; *paytāk būtan* "to be, to become clear". — *Passim.* — See next entry.

paytāk kartan / paytākēnītan, paytākēn-: "to reveal; to declare". This verb indicates an official declaration both at a trial and at the performance of some legal action;

cf. e. g. patigīrišn paytākēnītan regarding the official acceptance by the receiving party of the declaration of intention of the conveyor during the act of transfer. Similarly *paytāk guftan*. — **12**, 12; **13**, 3; **15**, 15—17; **17**, 8, 15; **18**, 3; **19**, 17; **20**, 1, 4; **24**, 12, 14, 17; **25**, 1—4, 6; **27**, 12; **29**, 4, 9—10; **32**, 6; **34**, 1, 3—6, 8, 9, 12, 13; **35**, 2, 3, 4; **41**, 6, 17; **42**, 4; **44**, 16, 17; **45**, 2, 5, 7, 9, 14, 16; **46**, 5—6; **47**, 6, 8; **53**, 14; **57**, 7; **68**, 16; **105**, 6; **106**, 3; **A3**, 5, 6; **A6**, 1; **A8**, 10; **A19**, 17; **A20**, 1; **A27**, 13; **A30**, 8; **A31**, 3; **A33**, 8. — *Cf. gōβišn, guftan, ²kartan.*

paz(z)āftan, ***paz(z)ām-**: "to pay, redeem". — **54**, 8. — Iran. **pati + zăm-*, root **zam-* "to pay"; *cf.* Av. *zəmanā-* "payment", Afgh. *zamnə*, Sogd. (Mugh) *z'mn'k* "payment". On this root see Schwartz, "*Monumentum Nyberg*", II. (1975), 196—207.

pēšak: "estate (social)"; *pēšak ī as̱rawanān* "priestly estate. — **A27**, 6. — See also next entry.

pēšak sardār: "head of a social estate". — **2**, 17—**3**, 1.

pēšēmār: "plaintiff". — **3**, 3; **5**, 9, 10; **53**, 17; **59**, 13; **73**, 11, 15, 16; **74**, 3—6, 8, 9; **75**, 5, 7, 9; **76**, 1, 3, 4, 8; **77**, 11, 13, 15, 17; **83**, 3, 5, 8, 10—13, 15—17; **84**, 2, 4, 5, 7, 8, 10, 11, 15; **90**, 4, 6; **95**, 11; **100**, 13; **101**, 7; **102**, 2, 3, 4, 5, 6, 9; **107**, 9, 12, 14; **A13**, 15, 16; **A16**, 5; **A28**, 9; **A29**, 7; **A30**, 17; **A32**, 12. — For the etymology see *hamēmār. Cf. pēšēmārīh, pāsēmār, pāsēmārīh.*

pēšēmārīh: "prosecution; prosecuting party". — **44**, 6; **A28**, 8, 10; **A33**, 4, 12, 14.

pēš-tōžišnīh / paštōžišnīh⁺: "the settlement of the debt of a head of household or relinquisher by his heir or by persons having acquired his estate". — **29**, 12; **30**, 17; **31**, 3. — The interpretation suggested by Pagliaro (*RSO* XV (1935), 286) "advance payment". "*pagamento in anticipo*" is not acceptable since in all cases where this term is used (as well as in all the articles of this chapter of the *Law-Book*) the subject under discussion is that of death-settlements (as well as death-claims, see *āgraβīh*) of the dead man's estate. For the formation, see Parth. *p'šn'm* "memory, commemoration" (lit. "after-name"), MP, NP *pašiman*, *pižman* "repentance", Osset. *fæsmon*, Sogd. *pyšn'm'k* "surname", *pyšn'myk* "copy", *et al.*

pit, pitar: "father". — *Passim*. — See also *s. v. čakar, patigriftak, pātixšāyīhā.*

pitarān: "ancestors, forefathers" (on the paternal side). — See *apām ī pitarān, apasēk ī pitarān, xvāstak ī pitarān.*

purnāy: "of age". — **27**, 17; **32**, 12, 15; **36**, 8, 9; **41**, 7; **48**, 4; **51**, 16; **52**, 4—6; **56**, 13, 14; **67**, 9; **89**, 16; **107**, 7; **A20**, 7; **A22**, 17; **A23**, 2, 4, 5; **A32**, 9, 15. — Iran. **pr̥nā- + āyav-*, NP *burna*. Antonym *apurnāy, rētak* (*q. v.*). See also *purnāyīh.*

purnāyīh: "majority, full age", — **14**, 9; **15**, 13; **19**, 9; **26**, 2, 4; **50**, 14—16; **67**, 10; **105**, 7; **A4**, 17; **A5**, 4; **A23**, 6; **A32**, 17.

pursišn: "inquiry". — **43**, 7.

pursišn-nāmak: "court record". *p.-n. kartan / rāδēnītan* "to draw up; to keep the record of court procedure". — **78**, 4—5, 7, 14, 15; **98**, 4; **100**, 7, 11; **A13**, 13; **A15**, 6; **A16**, 6; **A34**, 6, 8, 10, 13, 14, 17; **A35**, 1, 3, 4. — *Cf.* Arm. (Vth C., Ełišē) *p'ursiš* "court procedure, trial".

pusak: "son; *pusakīh*: "sonship" (*cf. duxtak*). — **105**, 6, 8, 9; **A18**, 3, 4; **A19**, 7.

pusakānīh: "adoption, adopted sons (collective)". — **33**, 6; **41**, 4; **50**, 17; **70**, 1. — *Cf. patigriftak.*

R

rāδēnītan, **rāδēn-**: "to lead, to conduct; to prepare, to make"; "to submit oneself"; *dātastān rāδēnītan* "to conduct a case (of the judge); grant one's participation at a trial, participate in it (of a respondent who does not default, and of a legal representative who is accepted by the judge — after the verification of his mandate — to participate in the trial and carries out his functions)"; *kahas rāδēnītan* "to dig out a canal"; *saxvan-nāmak rāδēnitan* "to draw up the record of a court case"; *var rāδēnītan* "to undergo the ordeal" (= to give oneself up to the ordeal procedure; let oneself be subjected to the ordeal; *cf. pas(s)āxtan*) — *Passim* — Iran. **rād-*, Skt. *rādh-* "to prepare, make ready; to arrange; to grant, to submit oneself; to care etc.". *Cf.* also the next entry.

rāδēnišn: 1) "the conduct of a case, a court trial"; 2) "the regulation, putting in order, payment in full, settlement (of a debt)". *Rāδēnišn kartan* "to conduct a case against someone"; *hač rāδēnisn hištan* "to remove from participation in a case"; *rāδēnišn ī var* (*q. v.*) "the undergoing of the ordeal"; *'nw'n* (?) *pat rāδēnišn xvāstan* "to demand the payment of smart money". — **59**, 7—9, **75**, 6, 17; **A13**, 8; **A15**, 6; **A31**, 5; **A32**, 9, 11, 13. — *Cf. rāδēnītan.*

raftan, **rav-**: "to go"; *frač raftan* "to die". — *Passim* — With the sense of "to go to, to come to someone (of a thing, guardianship, *stūr*ship)" *apāč ō būn* (*q. v.*) *ravēt*; (*stūrīh*) *pat raft dārišn* "(the *stūr*ship) is to be considered as having gone to that man". — **25**, 1, 8; **27**, 1; **28**, 15; **29**, 5; **35**, 6, 8; **A31**, 14; **A36**, 2, 3; **A39**, 2—3.

[1]**rāh**: "road, way". — **19**, 7; **57**, 4; **106**, 17; **107**, 1, 2. — See also next entry.

[2]**rāh**: "through, by means of, by way of" (= Rus. *путём*, Lat. *viā*); *rāh ō* ... "the right of regression to ...; the right to claim"; *rāh pat xvēšīh* "to enter into/assume the real rights"; *pat rāh ī* ... "on the basis of, by way of, through"; *pat rāh ī nabānazdištīh* "*via* kinship line; through agnatic calling"; *pat rāh ī ēv/dō-kasīh* "alone"/"two people jointly" (of the right of acquisition or calling); *pat* ... *rāh* "by means of, by way of, through"; *pat hanǰaman ut pat hampursakīh rāh* "though, by means of the assembling (the witnesses) and an inquiry/inquest". — **1**, 15; **20**, 4; **21**, 2; **23**, 12; **31**, 14; **45**, 12; **56**, 5—6, 17; **57**, 2, 6; **59**, 3; **60**, 9, 12, 15, 17; **61**, 14; **62**, 9, 12, 15; **71**, 5; **78**, 5; **80**, 9, 13, 16; **81**, 10, 15; **88**, 13; **A6**, 9. 10.

rahīk: "a slave". — **A40**, 3, 4. — NP *rahī*: "servant". According to Salemann, *Mittelpersisch*, § 22b and Bailey, *BSOS*, VII (1933), 71, hypothetically from **raθyaka-* "a chariot-servant"; however, it seems preferable to derive it from Iran. **rǎθ-* "to tie, bind, to fasten together" (Av. *rāθ-*; *rāθman-* "attached, adherent to", _Air Wb._, 1521—1523) with the primary meaning of the word being "tied", _cf._ _bandak_ "slave" < "tied". The spelling _lsyk_ is pseudo-historical.

ramak: "commoners, plebeians". **92**, 10.— _Cf._ _pātram._

rasītan, ras-: "to reach, to attain; to go to". — _Passim_ — _apāč rasītan_ 1) "to receive back; to receive a compensation": **59**, 14—16; **63**, 1; **86**, 10; **102**, 13-14; **104**, 7; **A6**, 13; **A10**, 10; 2) "to be returned" (in particular, of the return of a thing to the conveyor): **19**, 15; **50**, 13; 72, 7—8; **110**, 17; **A1**, 10, 11, 16; **A5**, 17—**A6**, 1, 3—5; 3) "to lack; to be in deficit": **32**, 14.

[1]**rāst** (adj.): "equal, equivalent (of an exchange), fair, equitable, just". — **31**, 6; **37**, 3, 8; **82**, 11; **A5**, 9; **A31**, 10.

[2]**rāst, rāstīhā** (adv.): "equally". — **55**, 11, 17; **96**, 5, 8; **105**, 4; **A10**, 8; **A21**, 5.

rāstīh: "fairness, equity, justice". — **91**, 10.

rat: "_rat_" (spiritual master). — **1**, 14; **13**, 4; **38**, 10; **78**, 2; **89**, 4; **98**, 13; **103**, 9; **A12**, 11; **A18**, 15, 17; **A26**, 17; **A28**, 3; **A36**, 1; **A38**, 13; **A39**, 7. — Av. [2]_ratav-_, _Air Wb._, 1498—1502; Arm. _ṙat._

rāt: 1) "gift, transfer". 2) "giver, donor, conveyer"; _mart ī rāt_ "donor, giver". — **32**, 3; **53**, 15; **54**, 4; **A11**, 2; **A19**, 13; **A25**, 7; **A34**, 1 — Iran. *_rāti-_ (*_rā-_ "to give; to be generous") Av. _rāiti-_ "gift; generosity"; _cf._ Skt. _rātiḥ_ 1) _fem._ "gift"; 2) _masc._ "giver, donor". _Cf._ also MP _rāt_ "generous", NP _rād_, Arm. _aṙat_ "generous, abundant, plentiful (Hübschmann, _AG_, I, 107).

ravāk: "fugitive, runaway". — **A13**, 10.

raxt: "sick". — **108**, 8. — Iran. *_raxta-_, root *_rang-_ "diminish, decrease, suffer damage, wear out (the same root with _-s-_ extension in Skt. _rákṣaḥ_ "damage", cf Av. _raš-_, _rašah-_); _cf._ Afgh. _rangai_ "thin, shallow" (Morgenstierne, _EVP_, 63). Av. _rənǰyō_, MSogd. _rynč'k_ "small" (Henning, _BSOAS_, XI/3 (1945), 482; Gershevitch, _Mithra_, 215), Khot.-Saka _ārraṃǰ-_ (< *_ā-ranǰaya-_) "to press; decrease, diminish", _pāramj-_ (< *_pati-ranǰaya-_) "to decrease, diminish", _pāraṃgga_ "the decrease" (Emmerick, _SGS_, 10, 81; Bailey, _Prolexis_, 181—182). A second possibility is Iran. *_rang-_ "to be weary, suffer", _cf._ MP _ranǰ_ "suffering"; "toil", _et al._ _Cf._ NP _raxta_ "wounded, sick". However, the given reading and interpretation are hypothetical, the text of the article not being clear to me here.

raz: "vineyard". — **A20**, 12—14.

[1]**rēš**: 1) "damage, loss"; 2) "wound". — **105**, 17; **A14**, 15. — Iran. *_raiša-_ "damage, wound", Iran. *_raiš-_ "to cause / suffer damage". Skt. _reṣáyati, riṣyati_ "_id._", _reṣa-_ "damage". See also [2]_rēš._

[2]**rēš**: "offence of the intentional infliction of physical damage / harm". — **A14**, 16; **A15**, 3. — Av. [2]_raēša-_, _Air Wb._, 1486.

rētak: "boy, youth (minor)". — **87**, 12; **103**, 7, 8; **A22**, 17; **A23**, 1—6; **A32**, 15, 16. — _Cf._ _apurnāy, apurnāyak._

rištakīh: "sickness; mutilation". — **33**, 14. — Formed from Iran. *_rišta-_ (*_raiš-_).

rōčak: "day, twenty four hours". — **71**, 10, 11.

rōčīk: "allowance, rations, pay-rations, maintenance"; *rōčīk ī zan ut frazand* "maintenance". — **34**, 3; **97**, 16. — NP *rōzī*, Arm. (from MP) *ṙočik* "pay; daily ration, maintenance", Hübschmann, *AG*, I, 234.

[1]**rōčkār**: "work days (of a slave)". — **12**, 4. — See [2]*rōčkār*.

[2]**rōčkār**: "(daily) allowance". — **86**, 5. — *Cf.* *pātrōč*.

rōčpānak: "window". — **19**, 1.

rōtastāk: "*rōtastāk*". — **78**, 3. — For the etymology, see Bailey, *Stud. on. V. Pisani*, 93. NP *rustā*; Arab.-Pers. *rustāq*; *cf.* Arm. *ṙotastak*. For other administrative-territorial units see *s. v. deh, nahang, šahr, tasūk*.

rŭnišnīh: "tearing out, plucking"; *vars rūnišnīh* "tearing out of hair", a form of offence of the *žahm* category. — **A14**, 16. — See, *rūtan*.

rūtan, **rŭn-**: "to deflower". — **73**, 9. — Iran. **rŭ(n)*-: *rūta-* "to pull out, tear out", see Geiger, *A Locust's Leg*, 70—75.

ruvān: "soul"; *xvāstak ruvān rāδ/pat ruvān bē dātan/paytāk kartan* "to institute a foundation for the soul'". — **24**, 12, 14, 17; **25**, 3, 6; **26**, 1; **27**, 12; **29**, 3, 9; **34**, 1—6, 8, 9, 12—15; **35**, 2, 7, 10, 13, 16; **45**, 16; **46**, 5, 8; **71**, 1, 2; **A21**, 3; **A36**, 7. — See Perikhanian, *VDI* (1973/1), 3—24 (with bibliography); *Obščestvo*, 160—176. See also *ahravdāt, dīvān ī kartakān*, [1]*kartak*.

S

sahišn guftan/paytākēnītan: see, *sahistan*.

sahistan, **sah-**: "seem/consider suitable, valid, approve"; *sahišn guftan/paytākēnītan* "to declare one's approval/acceptance of the declaration of intention of the conveyor as regards the conveyance of a thing". Synonym of *dōšītan* (*q. v.*). — **29**, 14; **34**, 5; **44**, 3; **46**, 3; **54**, 13; **66**, 2, 10—13, 15—17; **67**, 1, 2, 4, 7, 8, 11; **68**, 1—3, 7—9, 11, 15, 17; **A3**, 4; **A6**, 14; **A32**, 14; **A33**, 2, 8, 9. — Iran, **sa(n)d-*.

sahmān: "border, frontier"; the meanings: "regulation, definition, order" are likewise possible. — **79**, 15. — Arm. (from Parth. *sahman* "border, frontier; definition, regulation, dogma". NP *sāmān*: "border; order". Iran, **sahman-*, root **să(n)h-* (See *s. v. saxvan*); *cf.* Skt. *śasman-*.

sāk/*nisāk: "tax, duty, tribute"; *hangartan ut statan ī sāk* "the assessement and collection of tax"; *sāk apar nihātan* "to tax". — **A26**, 13, 17; **A27**, 12; **A28**, 5. — The reading is not certain because of variant and corrupt (?) spellings ([illegible], [illegible], [illegible]). *Cf.* Arm. *sak* "tax, tribute"; NP *sāv*, *sā*.

[1]**sar**: "summit; end"; *pat sar būtan* "to come to an end, to be completed/concluded"; *dātastan sar* "the conclusion of a legal case". — **10**, 13—14, 16—17; **11**, 3, 14, 17; **12**, 1, 3, 6, 9; **16**, 9; **A9**, 8.

[2]**sar**: "union, connexion"; *pat sar* "together"; *pat sar dāštan* "to include, to hold together"; *pat sar kartan* "to join, unite". — **A34**, 8—9; **A35**, 1. — Iran. **sar-* "to

unite, to join". Av. [1]*sar-*, [2]*sar-* (*Air Wb.*, 1563—1564); *cf.* Parth. *pd... sar* "together with", Henning, *List*, 87. In **A34**, 8, *sar* is given in the ms with the help of the heterogram LYŠH for its homonym [1]*sar* "head, summit".

sarāy: "hall". — **19**, 1. — Iran. **srāda-*, NP *sarāy*. Jud.-Pers. *sr'h*; Arm. (from Parth.) *srah*, *srahak* "αὐλή: στόα", Hübschmann, *AG*, I, 241.

sardār: "guardian, tutor, trustee"; *ātaxš sardār / sardār ī ātaxš* "trustee of a Fire temple/altar". — **1**, 4, 5; **3**, 10, 16; **4**, 10; **13**, 5—9; **14**, 7; **15**, 4, 5, 10, 12; **16**, 2, 6—8, 11, 13, 15—17; **19**, 8; **22**, 4, 5, 10, 12; **23**, 7, 9; **25**, 12; **26**, 2, 3, 5, 6, 9, 11; **27**, 2, 6; **28**, 1, 4, 17; **29**, 5, 9; **33**, 16; **34**, 3; **36**, 3, 4, 6; **44**, 6; **46**, 9; **48**, 3—5, 7, 9, 16; **49**, 8; **67**, 7; **75**, 12—14; **89**, 17; **94**, 4, 6; **103**, 7; **107**, 3, 8; **A13**, 6, 7; **A14**, 3, 10; **A31**, 6, 8; **A32**, 9—2. Np. *sālār*, (Vth C.) Arm. *salar*. See also next entry.

sardārīh: "guardianship, trusteeship"; *ātaxš sardārīh* "trusteeship over a privately instituted sacred Fire". — **3**, 16; **4**, 15—17; **5**, 1; **19**, 13; **21**, 6, 7; **22**, 8, 9, 11, 14—16; **23**, 11, 15; **24**, 1, 8, 11, 13; **25**, 8, 10—17; **26**, 5, 6, 8, 12, 13, 15; **27**, 2, 3, 5, 8, 14, 17; **28**, 1, 2, 5, 10, 12—16; **29**, 1, 2, 6, 7, 11; **31**, 14; **33**, 6; **34**, 11; **35**, 8, 15; **44**, 5; **45**, 15, 17; **46**, 2; **48**, 17; **49**, 5, 7; **53**, 2; **67**, 7; **69**, 9; **71**, 6; **77**, 1; **87**, 6, 8—10; **110**, 15; **A13**, 2, 3.

sarṯak (= **sardak**): "variety", *hamsarṯak*. "same, of the same type". — **67**, 15, 16. — Av. *sarəδa-*; MMP *s'rg*, Jud.-Pers. *srdg* "variety".

sarv: "cypress". — **39**, 1; **40**, 14.

satēr: "*satēr*; monetary weight unit equivalent to 4 Sasanian *drahms*". — **73**, 7. — Spelling *styl*, Arab-Pers. *istēr*, *astēr*, Khwar. *'strk*, *'stryk* (Henning, *Mitteliranisch*, 53), Arm. *sater*. From Gk. στατήρ.

saxtak: "equipped, outfitted, provided for, settled". — **4**, 12.

saxvan: 1) "declaration, testimony, statement (of one of the parties) at a trial"; 2) "trial", *cf. gōβ*; 3) "disposition, injunction, order"; *rāδēnišn ī saxvan* "testimony at a trial; trial"; *saxvan pat kār rāδēnītan* "to testify at a trial; to participate in a case". — **12**, 16; **13**, 10; **25**, 10; **35**, 15; **73**, 15, 16; **74**, 3, 7; **75**, 11; **78**, 7; **91**, 4, 5, 7, 9; **A21**, 6, 8, 10, 12; **A26**, 3. 7. — Formed from Iran. **sa(n)h-* "to proclaim, establish, determine, indicate" (for the sense of the root see Benveniste, *Voc. I-E.*, 11, 143—148; Mayrhofer, *Etym. Wb.*, *s. v. śáṁsati*, *śāsti*). See next entry.

saxvan-nāmak: "record of a legal case, minutes"; *saxvan-nāmak kartan / brītan* (*q. v.*). "to draw up a court record/minutes of a trial"; *saxvan-nāmak rāδēnītan* 1) "to keep/draw up a record/minutes, 2) "to testify for the record"; 3) to participate in a trial". **4**, 8; **9**, 7, 8; **73**, 12—14; **74**, 1, 4, 9—11; **90**, 4; **102**, 15, 16; **103**, 3, 4; **A28**, 8; **A31**, 17. — *Cf. pursišn-nāmak.*

saxvan-vaštakīh; see *vaštak*, *vaštakīh*.

sažākīh: "fitness, suitability". — **71**, 6.

sažāktar: "more suitable". — *Passim*.

sažistan, **saž-**: "to be proper, to be fitting". — **A14**, 6.

sēnak masāδ; see, *bāzūk masāδ*.

sneh: "the weapon (of the crime)". — **A14**, 15. — Iran. **snaθya-*; Av. *snaiθiš-* "instrument for striking a blow", *Air Wb*. 1627—1628.

sōkand: "oath". — **13**, 9; **76**, 16. — Iran, **saukantavant-*, Av. *āpəm saokəntavaitīm* (*Vd*. 4, 54, 55) "sulphur water (ordeal)"; NP *sau̯gand* (*xurdan*). See Bartholomae, *ZsR* II, 10—18.

spurr būtan: "to be fulfilled, concluded, filled". — **85**, 12. — Iran. **us+pr̥na-*; Arm. *spaṙ*.

spurrīkīh (**ī sneh**): "completeness/perfection (of a weapon)", "the striking, destructive character (of a weapon)" — **A14**, 14. — Iran. **us+pr̥na-*, **par-* "be full". *Cf. uspurrīkīh ī sneh* in *DkM* 695, 21; 700, 2; 700, 1—4 and Arm. *spaṙazēnkʻ* "outfit of arms".

srāδ: "stake in a judicial wager (in particular in trials by default)". — **11**, 9, 14. — The spelling is (*sr'd*). Iran. **srāda-* "stake, wager, bet"; *cf.* the forms of compounds of this root with *dā-* "to put", Skt. *śraddhā-*<*śrad-dhā-*, Av. *zrazdā-*<**srazdā-*, Lat. *crēdō*<**crezdo* (*I-E*. **kred-dhē*; for the sense of "*gage, enjeu*" of *I-E*. **k̂red*, see Benveniste, *Voc. I-E*., 1, 171—179). See also Skt. (*R̥V*, *Maitr. Saṁh.*) *śrat kar-* "to guarantee (with a pledge), to pawn". On the Pahlavi term see Périkhanian. "*Mem. J. de Menasce*", 305—318.

[1]**Srōš**: "*Sraoša*" (a *yazata*). — **36**, 1.

[2]**Srōš**: "*Sraoša*" (day of the month). — **36**, 1.

staβr: "big, large, strong". — **86**, 12.

stahm: "an act of cruelty, of violence". *Cf.* žahm. — **1**, 5; **16**, 12. — Iran. **staxman-*, *cf.* Av. *staxra-* "strong, hard", *AirWb*., 1591; NP *sitam*.

stahmakīhā: "by force, forcibly". — **A30**, 7.

statan, stān-: "to receive"; *apam* (*bē*) *statan* "to receive as a loan"; *guharīk* (*bē*) *statan* "to receive the equivalence/a compensation"; *apač statan* "to receive back". — **9**, 14; **13**, 14; **28**, 11; **34**, 13—14; **38**, 11; **40**, 9, 11—13, 17; **49**, 9—10, 12; **57**, 5, 7; **59**, 2; **76**, 5, 10, 12, 14—16; **85**, 3; **A9**, 13, 16, 17; **A10**, 10; **A25**, 11.

stōr: "draught cattle". — **18**, 10.

stūn: "column, pillar; portico". — **19**, 1.

stūr: "*stūr*". Person (woman or man) upon whom is laid the obligation to provide a successor for a dead man who left no male issue. Depending on the line of calling, the following distinction were made. 1) a "natural" (*būtak*) *stūr* (in this category are found the *epikleros*-daughter of the deceased, and likewise the deceased man's widow who entered into a *čakar*-marriage with one of his agnates; see, **ayōγēn/ayuγen, čakar*); 2) an "instituted" (*kartak, q. v.*) *stūr*; and 3) an "appointed" (*gumārtak, q. v.*) *stūr*. *Stūr kartan* "to institute, establish as a *stūr*;

rāδēnišn ī stūr "the appointing as *stūr*"; *stūr āδvēn* "like a *stūr*", "on a *stūr*ship basis" (?). The meaning of the terms *tan stūr* and *zēnīk/dēnīk stūr* (see **46**, 14—15; **48**, 11) is not quite clear. The latter, however, may be brought into relation with M. Parth. *zyn'yy* "entrusted things", *hwzynyy*, Pahl. *zēn* "watching, care" (*cf.* Av. *zaēnah-* "Wachsamkeit *etc.*"), B. Sogd. *zynyh* (*VJ.* 1205, 1210), Kh.-Saka *ysīnī(ya)*, *ysīnīta* "entrusted" (on these words see Henning, *BBB*, 89; Bailey, *Prolexis*, 295) and signify lit. "entrusted *stūr*", which will correspond to *stūr ī kartak*. If so, *tan stūr* may be just another designation of the *stūr ī būtak*. — **3**, 15; **15**, 9; **16**, 12; **20**, 1; **21**, 11—13; 16; **23**, 3; **24**, 3; **26**, 9, 11; **41**, 2, 11, 13; **42**, 13; **43**, 9—11, 13, 15, 16; **44**, 8, 14; **46**, 4, 11, 12, 14, 15; **47**, 4; **48**, 5, 7, 9—11, 15, 16; **49**, 17; **50**, 3, 6, 8, 10; **51**, 12; **60**, 17; **70**, 1, 6; **81**, 5, 7—9, 13, 14, 16; **82**, 4, 10; **87**, 11; **88**, 2, 4, 13, 14; **90**, 9, 12; **94**, 11; **97**, 9, 10, 12; **100**, 17; **109**, 4, 5, 7, 10, 13; **A5**, 12, 13; **A14**, 7, 8, 10; **A27**, 17; **A31**, 3; **A33**, 17; **A39**, 8; **A40**, 7, 16, 17. — Av. **stūiri-*, *cf.* acc. sing. *stūirīm* (< **stūirya-*?) in the Avestan fragment preserved in the Pahlavi *Rivāyat Purs. Āturfarnbaγ*, 75, 4. On this term and institution see, Perikhanian, *Henning Mem. Vol.*, 351—357; *Obščestvo*, 177—195; Klingenschmitt, *MSS*, 29 (1971), 136—142. See also *stūr-škand*, *stūrīh*.

stūr-škand: "a person not fulfilling his/her *stūr*-duties"; lit. "the destroyer of the *stūr*ship". The neglect of a dead man's *stūr*ship was considered to be a capital offence. — **A15**, 11. — *Cf.* Av. *stūirīm* +*upasčindayōiṯ* [*Purs. Āturfarnbaγ*, 75, 4; Klingenschmitt, *MSS*, 29 (1971), 136]. See also *stūr*, *stūrīh*.

stūrīh: "*stūr*ship". This term designates both the status or function of a *stūr* (*q. v.*) and one of the two forms of acquiring and holding an inherited estate (see *aparmānd*). In this second sense, *stūrīh* — *stūr*-possession — is opposed to *xvēšīh* (*q. v.*), the prossession of a personal-share of the estate. A *stūr*-posession is likewise in antithesis to the holding of a foundation "for the soul" (see *ruvān*). *Stūrīh kartan/nītan* "to bear/fulfil the functions of a *stūr*". — **4**, 3; **9**, 13; **21**, 7, 11, 16, 17; **22**, 2, 6; **33**, 6; **36**, 6, 10, 13, 14; **41**, 4—8; 15—17; **42**, 2, 3—6, 15; **43**, 1, 5, 6, 10, 13, 14, 16; **44**, 2, 4, 6, 16; **45**, 1—3, 5, 6, 9, 11—13, 17; **46**, 2, 5, 7—9, 13, 15; **47**, 8, 12—16; **48**, 2, 3, 6, 11—13, 17; **49**, 3, 9, 16; **50**, 1, 5—12, 14, 17; **52**, 2; **62**, 2, 8, 11; **69**, 6, 9; **70**, 14; **71**, 5, 6; **81**, 5, 11, 16; **82**, 5, 6, 8, 9, 12, 13, 15—17; **87**, 5, 11, 13—16; **88**, 3, 5, 6; **90**, 3, 8, 10, 11, 13; **96**, 4—6, 8—12; **97**, 12—14; **100**, 1, 2; **101**, 2; **103**, 1; **105**, 5; **109**, 10; **A8**, 6; **A14**, 8, 9; **A15**, 8, 13; **A17**, 1—4, 17; **A18**, 1, 2; **A21**, 3; **A26**, 12; **A31**, 10, 11, 13—15; **A35**, 15; **A39**, 1, 2, 6; **A40**, 8.

sūtōmand: "advantageous, beneficial".

syāh ut spētīh: lit. "blackness and whiteness" (of the hair) — designation serving as an indication of the age and appearance of a participant in a case, in court documents. — **A26**, 2.

Š

šāhān šāh: "King of Kings. — **30**, 14; **63**, 2; **100**, 11; **A14**, 11; **A39**, 11, 14, 15.

šāhān šāh bandak: "subject of the King of Kings". One of the designations of civic status; opposed to slavery. — **1**, 1; **20**, 9; **31**, 17. — OP *bandaka* — "(a king's) subject", see Widengren, *Festschr. Leo Brandt*, 523. *Cf. Dd* LVI, 2: *mart-ē(v) vehdēn ī āzāt ī šāhān šāh bandak* "a man of Zoroastrian faith, a citizen with full rights and subject of the King of Kings". The opposition between *bandak* "slave" and *šāhān-šāh bandak* "citizen, subject of the King of Kings" is also found in the Pahlavi *Ēhrpatistān* (ed. Sanjana, fol. 16). *Cf.* also the classical Armenian translation of this term in the text of Eznik (IV, 12), *ark'ayic' ark'ayi caṙay*.

šāhīkān: "treasury, royal fise". — **65**, 10; **77**, 7; **A27**, 3, 13—15; **A28**, 2, 4; **A39**, 1, 9.

šahr: "*šahr* (country, district, city)"; *šahrīhā* "throughout the *šahrs*". — **48**, 7, 8; **100**, 5; **A34**, 17; **A35**, 2, 4, 6, 8, 10; **A38**, 17. — see also *arž ī šahr, mart/zan ī šahr*.

Šahrevar (rōč): "the day *Šahrevar*". — **A29**, 11.

šahrīk: "city-dweller, citizen". — **78**, 5, 6.

šapak: "24 hour day". — **A12**, 1, 2, 4—7.

šāyēt (šāyistan): "it is allowable", it is lawful". — *Passim*.

šētak: "just, righteous, correct". — **79**, 8. — *Cf.* Arm. *šitak* "correct, straight".

šnāsakīh: "knowledge". — **79**, 15; **80**, 5, 8.

šnōm: see *šnūm*.

šnūm: "propitiation, gratification". — **35**, 17; **36**, 1. — Av. *xšnūman-*, *xšnaoma-*, *Air Wb.*, 557, 560. *Cf.* Arm. *šnum, šum, šnom*. Hüschmann, *AG*, I, 214.

šōn: "order, mode of action". — **11**, 12; **31**, 1; **55**, 14; **58**, 17 — Iran. **čyavana-/*šyavana-*, see Bailey, *BSOS*, VI (1934), 947; Pagliaro, *RSO*, XXII (1947), 62.

šōy: "husband"; *pat šōy bē dātan* "to give in marriage". — *Passim*.

šōy kartan: "to marry, take a husband". — **3**, 11, 17; **21**, 10, 11, 13, 15; **22**, 1—2; **24**, 4—6; **25**, 6; **30**, 14; **32**, 12; **41**, 12, 14; **51**, 14, 15; **62**, 14; **63**, 1, 4. — *Cf. zan kartan* "to marry, take a wife". The reading *kartan* (and not *griftan*) is confirmed by examples of phonetic spelling (**3**, 11, 17; **21**, 13, 15; **24**, 4—6).

šutan, šav-: "to set out, to go to". — *Passim*. — *andar ō (kas) šutan* (of a thing) "to go to (someone)"; see *e. g.* **101**, 16; **A11**, 2. — *bē šutan* "to be conveyed, alienated (of a thing)"; see *e. g.* **60**, 10, 13, 14, 16. — *frač šutan, pat baxt šutan* "to die"; see *e. g.* **61**, 3; **66**, 16; **67**, 6; **70**, 12.

T

[1]**tan**: "body, self" — *Passim*. — *tan pat zanīh dātan* "to enter into a marriage (of *sine manu* type) without the handing over of the bride by the guardian"; *tan pat gāt dātan* "to enter into sexual cohabitation or a marriage *sine manu mariti* (of a woman). — **A31**, 7—8; *tan pat āšnāk guftan* "to identify". — **A26**, 5, 6.

[2]**tan**: "slave"; *pat tan patigriftan* "to receive as a slave". — **57**, 13, 15, 17; **58**, 1—3, 7, 9, 11, 15; **72**, 12; **89**, 2, 3; **A13**, 11, 12. — *Cf.* [1]*tan*. For the sense "slave", *cf.* Gk. σῶμα.

tarsāk: "Christian". — **1**, 10. MMP *trs'g*, NP *tarsā*.

tarsakāy: "well-behaved, obedient". *Cf.* the antithesis *atarsakāy*, *atarsakāyīh* "the offence of disobedience by a wife". — **33**, 9; **A6**, 1. — The spellings (in the *Law-Book* and in other tests) are *tlsk'd(y)* / *tlsk'y* = *tarsakāy*; *tlsk'dyh*, *tlsk'dyyh* = *tarsakāyīh*; likewise *tlsk'syh* (< *tlsk'dyyh*, *cf.* the spellings *gwk's*, *gwk'syh* < *gwk'dy*, *gwk'dyyh* = *vikāy*, *vikāyīh*), whence the spelling *'tlsk 'YŠ* = *atarsak kas* "a person ignorant of fear", as the result of a secondary analysis by the scribe (*e. g.* **A3**, 15, 17; **A5**, 17). The term is evidently composed of Iran. **tr̥sa-* + *kāy-*, *cf.* Skt. *cāyati* "to perceive, apprehend; to fear, respect", *cāyamānāh*, *cāyúḥ* "*Ehrfurcht bezeugend*", Mayrhofer, *Etym. Wb.*, I, 383), Church-Slav. *čajati*. *Cf.* also *čašmakāy*.

tarsakāyīh: "good behaviour, obedience"; *tarsakāyīhā* "in a well-bahaved manner, piously". — **A5**, 13; **A7**, 5—6. See *tarsakāy*, *cf.* *atarsakāy*, *atarsakāyīh*.

***task** / ***tasak**+: "rent, lease"; **tas(a)k*+ *vičārtan* "to pay rent", *pat* **tas(a)k*+ *dāštan* "to lease; to hold as leased property"; *xvāstak ī* **tas(a)k*+ "a leased thing"; *xvāstak pat* **tas(a)k*+ *patigriftan* "to receive (accept) a thing as a leasehold". — **72**, 13—16; **A25**, 8—11; **A33**, 1, 2. — The spelling is *t'lhk*. The meaning "rent, lease" fits every context. Consequently it seems possible to relate the given word with Aram. *tasqâ* / *ṭasqâ*, an Iranian term in the *Babylonian Talmud* which likewise has the sense of "rent, lease" as was demonstrated by I. Hahn (*Acta Antiqua Accademiae Hungaricae*, VII, 1959, pp. 149—150). Arab. *ṭasq*, derived from Aramaic, had the same meaning of "rent", *cf.* also Syr. (Bar Bahlūl) *ṭasqâ* "tributum". Th. Nöldeke (*ZA* 23, 1907, 147) linked these forms with Gk. τάξις. Still this derivation is met with a semantic difficulty: alongside with its usual meaning "arrangement, order", the Greek word meant "assessement", as in τάξις τοῦ φόρου "assessement of tribute" (once in Xenophon's *Respublica Atheniensium* 3, 5), likewise: "list, register", "account" (Roman Egypt) and is not attested as a designation of "rent, lease" or "taxation" in any written document of either the Hellenistic or the Roman periods. One must look therefore for a different explanation. Possibly one can posit **čás̮sak(a)-* "quarter", an innovation of the Late Achaemenian period replacing — as a noun — the older **čas̮sušuva-* "(one) fourth" attested in Elam. *ṣa-iš-šu-iš-maš*, *ṣa-šu-iš-ma* [pronounced *čašuš(u)u̯a*; see K. Hoffmann, "*Aufsätze*", I, 183], *cf.* Av. *čaθrušva-*. The development Late OP **čás̮sak(a)-* > MP *task* is regular, the shift *č-* > *t-* as a result of

dissimilation is well attested in MMP *tis* : MP *čiš* "thing", MMP *tasom* "fourth" *tasūk/tasōk* "district" (Arab. *ṭassūǰ*, Syr. *ṭasûγâ*) *et al.* (see P. Tedesco, *MO* XV, 1923, 209—211; *Language*, XXI, 1945, 128—141). As for the spelling *t'/hk* in the present manuscript, it can easily be explained palaeographically as a slight distortion of the original **tsk* found in an earlier copy. The reading **tāk* (< Iran. **tavāka-/*tahaka-*) or **tahak* (< OP **taθaka-*) is much less likely since these models provide no useful associations.
In the light of this explanation, the original (*i. e.* Achaemenian) amount of the rent must have been a fixed portion — one fourth — of the average income from the leased estate.

tasubāγ: "measure of punishment equvalent to 4 *bāγ*s (*q. v.*)". — **A15**, 3. — From OP **čas͜subāga-*; Iran. **čaθrubāga-*.

tasūk: "*tasūk*, district". — **100**, 6, 15. — Arab.-Pers. *tasūǰ*.

tāšt: "definite". — **5**, 10; **13**, 15. — From **tāšta-* "cut off", see Bailey, *BSOS*, VII/2 (1934), 280—281.

tāvān, tāvānīh: "fine". — **1**, 5; **6**, 16, 17; **9**, 6; **11**, 9, 10, 14; **36**, 17; **71**, 8, 10, 11, 13; **72**, 4, 5; **73**, 7, 8; 77, 3; **102**, 8; **A14**, 4; **A15**, 4; **A17**, 5, 7, 9, 10, 12, 13; **A28**, 2, 3. — NP *tāvān* "fine".

tāvānōmand: "obliged to pay a fine".

tāyak: "time, once"; *pat ēv tāyak* "at once, at one time, simultaneously". — **40**, 11; **81**, 4, 11. — Iran. **tāva-ka-* "piece, bit, time", *cf.* NP *tāy*; *cf.* also MP *tāk* "piece, unit".

Tīr: "*Tīr* (name of a month)". — **35**, 10; **37**, 14.

tōxmak: "kinship, relationship (agnatic)". — **42**, 15 — Iran. **tauxman-*, — MMP *twhmg*; NP *tuhma*, Arm. *tohm*. *Cf. nabānazdišt*.

tōxtan, tōž-: "to pay off, settle one's debts". — **30**, 1, 3, 4, 17; **31**, 15; **60**, 2, 6, 16; **62**, 15; **63**, 5; **69**, 15; **76**, 4, 5; **89**, 9; **107**, 4; **A1**, 16, 17; **A25**, 12. — Iran. **tug-* (Skt. *tóhati* "to cause damage, suffering"), Sogd. *tw'z-*, *twy'z* "to pay off, to pay", NP toxtan "to pay off", Arm. (from Parth.) *toyž*, *tugan* "restitution for a loss; fine damage, expenses"; *tužem*, *tuganem* "to oblige to pay, to make restitution; to fine, punish, *tužim*, *tuganim*"; "to compensate; to pay; to suffer damage". See also *tōžišn*, *tōžišnōmand*.

tōžišn: "financial obligation; payment"; *tōžišn ī pitarān* "inheritance debts"; *tōžišn xvāstan* "to claim a debt, demand payment"; *ō tōžišn matan/rasītan* "to be due, to be liable for payment"; *xvāstak-tōžišn būtan* "to be liable for payment (of debts; see, **60**, 2, 6—7). — **2**, 4, 5, 8, 10, 12; **3**, 5; **6**, 17; **13**, 1, 4, 10, 11; **14**, 8, 9, 11; **15**, 2, 4, 8, 9, 10, 12; **16**, 1, 4; **29**, 13, 15; **30**, 6, 7, 9, 15, 16; **56**, 10; 57, 9; **59**, 7, 12; 13, 15; **60**, 2, 6—7, 11, 13—15; **61**, 2; **63**, 2, 3; **71**, 2; **72**, 5; **78**, 1; **86**, 15; **99**, 15, 16; **102**, 13; **107**, 17; **109**, 15; **A13**, 1; **A14**, 14, 16; **A17**, 7, 10, 13; **A32**, 6. — See *tōxtan*.

tōžišnōmand: "liable for payment". — **68**, 17; **76**, 17; **83**, 6.

tuvān: "capable, entitled". — **2**, 6, 16; **6**, 11. — For synonyms see *s. v. patixšāyīh*. See also next entry.

tuvānīk: "capable, entitled, solvent"; *ō tuvānīkīh rasītan* "to become solvent" (here). *Cf. attān*. — **8**, 13; **57**, 9; **58**, 7, 8; **59**, 8; **72**, 12.

U

urvar: "plant, vegetation". — **33**, 10.

uskārtan, uskār-: "to investigate". — **2**, 13; **17**, 14; **37**, 10; **41**, 14; **43**, 1; **44**, 1; **51**, 2; **64**, 15; **67**, 9; **87**, 12; **A31**, 2. — NP *sigālidan* "to reflect on, ponder, to plan, contemplate", Jud.-Pers. *'wsk'rd* "to take counsel, to discuss". — Iran. **us + kar-, cf. hangārtan*.

uštōmand: "good, blessed". — **79**, 12. — The spelling is *'wšt'wmnd*; adj. from Av. *uštă-* "blessing, fortune (*cf.* also *uštatāt-*, *uštă.barati-*, *Air Wb.*, 417, 418).

uzdāt-nāmak: "a judicial document on the setting of the ordeal". *Cf. nāmak-pas(s)āč*. — **78**, 14. — Iran. **us + dāta- / dāti-*. *Cf.* Av. *uzdā-*: *uzdāta-* "to establish, set up, designate, arrange (a religious ceremony; a procedure)".

uzdehīkīh: "alien status, status of a foreigner; sojourn in a foreign land". — **48**, 7, 9. — Av. *uzdahyav-* "*peregrinus*". — *cf. ādehīk*.

uzdēs: "idol". — **94**, 4; **A37**, 4.

uzdēs-čār: "idol-shrine, heathen temple". — **A37**, 3. — See also next entry.

uzdēs-katak: "house of idols, idol-shrine". — **94**, 4.

uzēnak: "expenses, costs". — **6**, 9; **30**, 7; **33**, 12; **34**, 2, 6; **86**, 1, 2, 6, 9, 12, 13; **93**, 11; **107**, 4; **A15**, 17; **A16**, 4. — *Cf. uzītan*.

uzīt, uzītak; see *ōzīt, ōzītak*.

uzītan, uzīh-; 1) "to lapse, expire" (of a time-limit, term); 2) "to die"; 3) "to spend, to use up". — **23**, 3; **24**, 14; **38**, 15; **89**, 1, 2; **A38**, 12. — Iran. **uz + aya-*; MMP *'wzyd, 'wzyh-*; *cf.* also *uzēnak* (< **uzayanaka-* "exit, going out; out come; out lay, expense"), NP *hazīna* "expenses"; see Bartholomae, *MiMund.* I, 30—47.

V

vāč in the technical expressions: *vāč dātan* "to admit to participate in the *drōn yašt* ritual, or in the prayer ritual before a meal"; *vāč griftan* "to perform a prayer, to pray", *cf. e. g. PNīr*, 39—49, 112—115; *ŠnŠ* 3, 21b; *PVd*, 16, 11(23). — **A35**, 10. — MP *vāč griftan* corresponds to Jud.-Pers. *b'j st'nyh* (= *bāǰ stānīh*). "saying grace"; see MacKenzie, *BSOAS*, XXXI/2 (1968), 251, also Boyce and Kotwal, *BSOAS*, XXXIV/1 (1971), 56—73.

vāčak: "question; formula; instruction". — **17**, 14; **59**, 9; **A11**, 15; **A12**, 10.

vahāk: "price"; *pat vahāk dātan / frōxtan*: "to sell"; *vahāk aržistan* "to cost, be worth". — **1**, 11, 13; **17**, 7; **18**, 2, 5; **40**, 17; **54**, 7, 12; **55**, 4; **66**, 6, 7, 11; **67**, 5; **68**, 2, 4, 7, 10, 13, 15; **70**, 1; **94**, 15; **103**, 8, 10; **104**, 7; **A8**, 12; **A9**, 6; **A26**, 17; **A27**, 14. — MMP *wh'g* "purchase, price", NP *bahā*.

Vahuman: "*Vahuman* (day of the month)". — **35**, 14; **57**, 14, 16; **A28**, 13—15.

vālāδ: "dignity, position" (<"height"); *katak-xvatāyīhā vālāδ* "dignity (= height of position) of the *paterfamilias*". — **42**, 15. — Formed on **vard-* "to grow", Av. *varəd-*, NP *bālīdan*.

vanī: "annulled; vanished, perished"; *vanībūt ēstatān* "to perish, to disappear". — **80**, 13; **99**, 5. — MMP *wnybwt̠* "annihilated", *wnywdyẖ* "destruction, annihilation", see Henning, *List*, 89.

[1]**var**: "ordeal, oath"; *var datān* "to grant / prescribe the ordeal"; *var varzītan* "to perform, undergo the ordeal; to take an oath"; *rāδēnišn ī var* "the undergoing / arrangement of the ordeal procedure"; *dātastān pat var mat* "the trial has reached the stage of the ordeal-court". — **6**, 5; **13**, 1—3, 5—10, 12, 15; **14**, 1—7, 10, 11, 16; **74**, 16; **76**, 6—8; **78**, 16; **A12**, 11; **A13**, 17; **A19**, 5; **A23**, 7—10, 14; **A27**, 8; **A28**, 7; **A32**, 7. — Av. [2]*varah-* "ordeal", root *var-* "to proclaim solemnly", *cf.* MP(*Dk*) *varastān* "ordeal-court, place of oath and of ordeal", Orm. *war* "oath", Yidgha *wor* "oath" *et al.*, see Bartholomae, *ZsR* II, 5—36; Bailey, *TPS* (1954), 141—142; *Prolexis*, 78, 311. See below the terms designating varieties of the ordeal, and also *var sardār*, [2]*varōmand, varzītan*. *Cf.* also *pas*(*s*)*āč-nāmak, sōkand, uzdāt-nāmak xvārastān, zūr-xvart.*

[2]**var**: "side"; here "litigating party". — **A13**, 17. — *Cf.* NP *var* "side".

var ī dēnīk (?): a form of ordeal; *cf.* *dēnīk* (?) *var*, *DkM* 894, 2. — **13**, 1.

var ī pat nāmak-pas(s)āč: the ordeal whose form is indicated in the court document prescribing an ordeal. — **78**, 16.

var ī pāδ nišān (?): "ordeal with bound feet (?)". — **13**, 2—3; **14**, 3. — The spelling is RGLH *w / nš'n*; the second word may be **nišāna-*, the participle formed on *-na-* from **ni* + *ha*(*y*)- "to tie together, bind". *Cf.* the description in the (long version) of the *Saugand-nāma* of the ordeal procedure during which the feet of the subject being tried were bound with the sacred string usually used for tying the branches of the *barsom*. (see *Pers. Riv. Horm. Fram.*, 47—48).

var ī pat sōkand: "ordeal with sulphur water". — **13**, 9; **78**, 16. — See *sōkand*.

Varahrān (ātaxš ī V.), Varahrānīh: "(temple of) the *Varahrān*-fire". — **26**, 17; **27**, 1, 7; **51**, 3; **78**, 12; **94**, 5; **110**, 7; **A39**, 5, 8.

varg (?): *xvāstak ī varg* (?). — **A4**, 2. — The reading of the word (*w / nlg*) is hypothetical, the meaning unknown.

[1]**varōmand**: "questionable, doubtful, to be verified"; antithesis of *ēvar, vāvarīkān* (*q. v.*). — **12**, 15; **32**, 7; **A16**, 6.

[2]**varōmand**: "subject to the ordeal"; *varōmand kartan* "to subject to undergo the ordeal". — **8**, 17; **33**, 12; **78**, 9; **92**, 2, 9, 10, 15, 16; **97**, 3, 6, 13; **106**, 10; **A15**, 16, 17; **A35**, 9. — See [1]*var*.

vars: "hair". — **A14**, 16.

var-sardār: "head of the ordeal"; the person (usually a *rat*) who conducted the ordeal procedure in a special ordeal court (see *xvārastān*). — **A27**, 7. — See also Pahl. *Yasna* **34**, 4; **43**, 4; **47**, 6.

vartēnītan, vartēn-: "to turn, to change; to alter; to revoke"; in particular "to alter the testimony given at a trial"; — **9**, 15; **10**, 1, 2, 6; **A1**, 5; **A10**, 9; **A15**, 15. — Iran. **vart-*, NP *gardānīdan*; Arm. *vert* "turn, circle". See also, *vartītan, vaštak, vaštakīh, vaštan*.

vartītan, vart-: "to turn, to change". — **9**, 1—3; **102**, 11. — *Cf. vartēnītan*.

varz: "cultivation (of the soil)". — **86**, 4; **A37**, 17. — NP *varz, barz* "agricultural work".

(var) varzitan, varz-: "to carry out the ordeal procedure, to undergo the ordeal (of whatever type)"; *varzišnīh*, verbal noun. — **6**, 6; **13**, 2, 3, 5, 8, 12, 13, 15; **14**, 2, 4, 6; **76**, 7; **A19**, 5; **A23**, 7—10, 14; **A27**, 8.

vāspuhrakān: "a (son/daughter's) share in the father's estate; dowry". — **4**, 11; **32**, 17; **101**, 14; **106**, 8; **A2**, 9, 11. — Lit. "belonging to 'the family's son' (**vis-puθra-*)" as a personal share in the father's inheritance → "inherited"; *cf.* Arm. (from Parth.) *sephakan* "inherited; personal/own (share of a son/daughter in the father's estate)". A daughter's share in her father's estate formed her dowry, hence the use of this term for "dowry" in both MP (see also *PVd.*, XIV, 15) and classical Armenian texts. For a detailed analysis of the origin and meaning of this term (with bibliography), see Périkhanian, *REArm*, V (1968), 16—23; *Obščestvo*, 218—223. *Cf. āzātīh, xvēšīh*.

vastrak: "clothing", *xvārišn ut vastrak* "maintenance". — **36**, 9; **A7**, 10, **A13**, 4.

vaštan, vart-: "to turn, to take back; to revoke a transfer, to rescind a disposition". — **101**, 4; **110**, 1. — NP *gaštan*, root **vṛt-*, see also *vartēnītan*.

vaštakīh, vaštak saxvanīh: "alteration of testimony, the making of contradictory statements at a trial by one of the litigants"; *vaštak būtan* "to alter one's statement/testimony". If the final statement was not the truth, an alteration of testimony was considered to be a judicial offence. — **8**, 6—8, 15; **9**, 1, 4, 6—8; **10**, 9; **102**, 11; **A26**, 2. — See *vartēnītan, vaštan*.

vaštīh: "sickness". — **A13**, 4. — *Cf. raxt, vēmārīh*.

vat-āhang: "ill-intentioned, malicious". — **A15**, 10. *Cf. vatxvāh*.

vatmartīhā raftan: "to be considered an evil man, to be of ill-repute". — **A35**, 2.

vatxvāh: "ill-intentioned; malice". Offence consisting in a slanderous accusation brought against the respondent by the plaintiff. This is also mentioned in the *Dēnkart* (see *e. g. DkM*, 550, 20—21). — **83**, 11, 16; **A32**, 11.

vāvarīkān: "trustworthy" (also "juridically valid/authentic" as regards a seal or document); *vāvarīkānīh* "trustworthiness, authenticity". — **93**, 12, 13; **99**, 1. — Parth. *w'wr, w'wryft* "belief", Arm. *vawer, vawerakan* "true, valid, authentic, authorized", *cf.* also MMP *w'wrydn* "to believe". *Cf.* Av. ²*var-* and the stems *vavar-, vāur-*. See Henning, *Verbum*, 195.

vaxš: "percentage, interest". — **30**, 8; **31**, 1; **53**, 4, 6; **89**, 10; **104**, 1, 3; **A8**, 6; **A12**, 17; **A30**, 17; **A31**, 1. — Av. *vaxša-* "increase, interest", *AirWb.*, 1339; *cf.* also MP *vaxšakar* "usurer", Arm. *vaxš* "interest", *vašxaṙu* "usurer". *Cf. vaxt.*

vaxt: "increase, profit"; *bar ut vaxt* "revenue and profit/increase. — **35**, 10; **72**, 14, 17; **96**, 17. — See *vaxtan.*

vaxtan, vaxš-: "to give an increase, to bring profit/revenue". — **72**, 16. — Iran. **aug-*/**vag-* "to grow, increase"; *vaxš-* < **vag-* + *-s-*.

veh: "(more) virtuous, (more) pious", *vehīh*: "(religious) virtue, piety". — **26**, 16. — Iran. *vahyah-*, *AirWb.*, 1405; MMP *why, wyh*, Arm. (from Parth.) *veh.*

vehdātastāntar: "having the preferential right/the legal advantage". — **6**, 5; **13**, 7; **14**, 10, 12, 15—17. — *Cf.* Lat. *optimo iure, optima lege. Cf.* also *xvat-dātastān.*

vēhdēn: "a Zoroastrian". — **61**, 1. — *Cf. hudēn, aγdēn.*

veh vehān; the meaning is unclear. — **65**, 17.

vēmārīh: "sickness". — **109**, 16, 17; **110**, 1. — For the etymology (Iran. **amayavā-bara-* "affliction-bearer") see Gershevitch, *Unvala Mem. Vol.* 93—94. — Synonyms: *raxt, vaštīh.*

vēšak: "slave; servant, menial; household slave" (?); *vēšak ut ramak varōmand nē kunišn*: "a slave/menial and common man should not be subjected to the ordeal". — **92**, 10. — The spelling is *wyšk* (*wysk* in the facsimile, but see Modi's correction). Iran. **vaisya-ka-*, lit. "belonging to the family", from Iran. *vis-* "family, clan"; the palatalisation of *-si̯-* > *-š-* in the present form points to its Middle-Median origin. *Cf.* Khot.-Saka *bīsa-* "house servant" (Bailey, *Prolexis*, 249—250). As a semantic parallel *cf.* OP **garda-* "slave", Arm. *gerdastanik* "houseservant, menial; member of the household". *Cf.* also Gk. (Gortyna) Ϝοικεύς, Attic οἰκέτης "house servant; slave", οἰκεῖος, Ion. οἰκήϊος "of the house, familiar, kinsman".

vēšistīh: *pat vēšistīh* "maximum". — **A32**, 14, 16; **A33**, 4, 5. — *Cf. kamistīh.*

vēxtan: "to redeem, to release from pledge" (from the basic meaning of "to separate" > "to free, release"); *apāč vēxtan* "*id*". — **37**, 14—16; **39**, 16. — Iran. **vaik-* "to separate, sort out, to differentiate", Av. *vaēk-*, NP *bēxtan* "to sift". *Cf.* the Arm., loan-word *věč* "quarrel" *vičem* "quarrel" (from the basic meaning. "to separate; to differ (in opinion from one another)"; for the semantic development, *cf.* French *différend* "quarrel, dispute". See, however, a different explanation offered by Bailey, *Khotan Saka Dict.*, 280.

vičār: "decision, investigation, solution"; *pat vičār daštan* "to take up for investigation in order to render a decision". — **93**, 10. — See *vičārtan.*

vičārtan, **vičār-**: 1) "to pay up, to settle a debt, to compensate/reimburse for a loss"; 2) "to release (from pledge)"; 3) "to resolve (a legal case); to render a decision". — **2**, 7; **3**, 3, 4; **8**, 15; **9**, 9, 10; **11**, 16; **13**, 10, 11; **28**, 17; **29**, 3; **30**, 15; **35**, 8; **37**, 15, 17; **38**, 2, 11, 15; **39**, 4—6, 12, 16; **40**, 7, 11; **85**, 3, 5; **53**, 4, 5, 7—10; **54**, 6; **56**, 2, 4, 7, 8, 10; **57**, 5; **61**, 7, 12; **63**, 3, 5; **67**, 4; **72**, 15; **74**, 8; **77**, 17; **83**, 10, 15, 16; **86**, 17; **89**, 14; **93**, 1, 2; **99**, 16; **102**, 13; **104**, 1, 2; **A15**, 5; **A25**, 2—5, 9—11; **A30**, 17; **A31**, 1. — MP *wyč'r-*, *wyč'rd* "to decide", Buddh. Sogd. *wyc'rt*, Chr. Sogd. *wycrt* "exactly, distinctly", Jud.-Pers. *bz'rd*, NP *guzārdan* "to interpret, explain; to fulfil; to pay". Usually analyzed as the compound **vi + čārya-*, root **čar-*, Av. *⁵kar-*, Skt. *cárati* "to be in movement, abide, be occupied with" (see *e. g.* Salemann, *Mitterlpersisch*, 229, Henning, *Verbum*, 192); *cf.* Skt. *vicarati* "to separate; to go from place to place; to stray from the path"; but in the causative "to move (mentally) in different directions, to reflect, to decide" (*cf.* the analogous shade of meaning in Lat. *versare*), Av. *vičarəna-* "a separation of the ways, a bifurcation" (*AirWb.*, 1437). Although Lat. *versare*, which is close in meaning to Iran. *vičār-* was also used to designate the banking operation of the transfer of funds, *cf.* Lat *pecuniam versare* (*cf.* also Lat. *versura* "exchange; loan") and the figurative Russian "им не разойтись" (= "they will not equalize the bill, will not settle their accounts"), such an analysis can only be applied with considerable strain to the rich semantic context of the MP verb. This fact seemingly led Nyberg (*Hb.*, Gloss. *s. v. vičārišn*) to propose an alternate analysis (*vi + ²kar-* "*gedenken*") which is, however, less satisfactory than the preceding one (Nyberg derived it exclusively from the meaning "to decide"). I believe that it is possible to suggest here the contamination of two homonymous bases. On the basis of the semantic content of the MP verb, it is more convincing to suppose the compounding of the preverb *vi-* with **čar-* "to detach, to separate", *cf.* Iran. **čarman-* "hide, skin", Av. *čarman-*, Skt. *carman-*. As we know, Gk. κρῖνω "to separate, to sift; to sort out, discern; to judge, decide; to decree; to interpret", κρίσις "judicial investigation; judicial decision, sentence; interpretation", κρίτης "judge", Lat. *cĕrno* (< *crĭ-nō*), *decerno* "to detach, separate, sift; to decide, resolve", *certus* (< **crĭ-tos*) "resolved, determined, certain, trustworthy", *decretum* (a secondary formation on the base *crevi*) "decision, decree" are all formed on the same I-E root. For the semantic development "to detach, separate, resolve/solve" > "to pay; to settle a debt; to release from pledge", *cf.* Gk. λύω "to separate, loosen, untie; to release; to resolve", λύσις "loosening, resolution; dissolution; release; ransom", λύτρον "ransom money, ransom; atonement", Lat. *luere* "to pay; to atone"; *solvere* (< *se-luere*) "to resolve; to pay"; *absolvere* "to unbind; to remit (sins)/absolve; to conclude", *solutio* "solution; pay", *absolutio* "payment; atonement"; MP *vēxtan* (**vaik-*) "to separate, sift; to release from pledge, redeem", MP *hištan* "to release, dissolve; to release from pledge; to resolve a legal case"; *Cf.* also *vičārišn* "remission of sins; release" *vičār* "explanation", *vičārtan* "to separate, differentiate; to explain" which are all cited in other Pahlavi texts. The meaning of the Parth. loan words in Arm. *včar* "payment; compensation; conclusion; ending"; *včarem* "to conclude; to pay, redeem, settle one's accounts, compensate; to release; to untie" (see Hübschmann, *AG*, I, 248) are also instructive. *Cf.* *vičurt*.

[1]**vičīr**: "decision"; in particular, "judicial decision", "resolution of a legal case"; *vičīr xvāstan* "to bring suit in court". — **2**, 17; **3**, 1—3, 5—7; **4**, 9; **7**, 8, 15; **10**, 14, 17; **11**, 3, 4, 14, 17; **12**, 2, 8; **14**, 11, 14, 16; **54**, 2; **57**, 12; **59**, 10; **65**, 4; **70**, 12; **74**, 1; **75**, 12; **78**, 3; **83**, 12, 16; **84**, 4; **90**, 7; **91**, 10; **93**, 9, 10; **99**, 17; **100**, 5; **107**, 6, 7; **A5**, 12, 15; **A14**, 5; **A15**, 4, 5; **A26**, 5; **A30**, 14, 15; **A32**, 12; **A36**, 1; **A37**, 11; **A40**, 15. — Iran. **vi-čī-ra-*, root **čay-* "to put in a particular order; to choose"; *cf.* Av. *vī-čidyāi* "to distinguish" / "to choose", *vī-čira-*, *Air Wb.*, 1437—1438; Arm. *včiṙ* "judicial decision; end" (Hübschmann, *AG*, I, 248). See also *vičīrkart*.

[2]**vičīr**: 1) "agreement, contract"; 2) "document (contractual or judicial)"; *vičīr kartan ut avaštan* "to draw up and seal a contractual document"; *vičīr ī apāmdān* "a loan-agreement; a contractual document regarding a loan". — **2**, 1; **18**, 12, 14; **20**, 13; **30**, 16, 17; **31**, 10—12; **32**, 5—10; **38**, 7, 8; **64**, 2; **78**, 17; **100**, 3; **107**, 3, 6, 7; **A6**, 14; **A14**, 5; **A26**, 6; **A28**, 7; **A33**, 10, 15; **A34**, 2, 4, 5. — See [1]*vičīr*, *vičīrkart*.

vičīrkart: "a judicial sentence; document regarding a judicial decision". — **A15**, 14; **A16**, 5. — See [1—2]*vičīr*.

vičōδišn: "inquest, investigation". — **A13**, 14; **A35**, 1. — See *vičustan*.

vičurt: "valid, authentic". — **32**, 4. — Iran. **vi* + *čar-* "to detach, to separate", *cf.* Lat. *certus* "definite, certain, trustworthy, authentic". See *s. v. vičārtan*.

vičustan, vičōδ-: "to investigate; to make an investigation, hold an inquest". — **A13**, 14. — Jud.-Pers. *bzwb-*, NP *pižōhīdan* "to investigate".

viδānmānīh: "nomadism, nomadizing". — **99**, 9—12. — Lit. "tent-dwelling"; Iran. **vidāna-* "tent". *Cf.* Parth. *wd'n* "tent", *wd'nm'n* "nomad", MMP *wy'n*, NP (Asadī) *giyān*, Arm. (from Parth.) *vran* "tent".

***vidāštan, *vidār-**: "to separate, to divide; to distribute". — **110**, 4; **A28**, 4. — Iran. **vi* + *dār*, *cf.* Av. *vīδār-* "to divide, to distribute, to grant", M. Sogd *wδyr-* "disjoin, hold apart, sort out", see, Gershevitch, *Mithra*, 182; *cf.* also Skt. *vi-dhṛti-* "division, separation". For the meaning, "to transfer elsewhere" (see 110, 4), *cf.* Av. *vīδārayat̰* "*hinwegbringen über ... zu*" (*Vd.* 2: *yahmat̰ hača puθrō haōm urvānəm činvat̰.pərətūm vīδārayat̰*), *Air Wb.*, 692.

vikāy: "witness". — **7**, 7; **76**, 2; **91**, 12; **92**, 4, 5; **98**, 4; **106**, 10; **107**, 11, 14; **108**, 7; **A10**, 13; **A15**, 5; **A25**, 16; **A29**, 7, 8; **A38**, 15. — Iran. **vi-kāya-*; MMP *gwg'y* "witness", NP *guvāh*, Arm. (from Parth.) *vkay*. See also next entry.

vikāy-druž: "false-witness". — **91**, 11.

vikāyīh: "witness' statement; testimony". — **73**, 4, 6; **93**, 13; **98**, 2; **A14**, 13; **A29**, 9, 12; **A38**, 14.

vimāyītan / vimītan, vimāy-: "to diminish, to suffer damage". — **9**, 7. — Iran. **vi* + *may-* (Skt. *mināti* "*minuere*; to cause damage"); *cf.* Av. *vī-mītay-* / *vīmaiti-* "damage, destruction", *vīmītō.dantan-* "with damaged (= decayed) teeth" (*AirWb.*, 1450—1451).

vināhišn: "injury, offence". — **A35**, 6. — See *vinās*.

vinās: "damage, harm; offence, crime; guilt". — **1**, 5; **16**, 12; **29**, 6; **33**, 12; **73**, 1; **78**, 10; **89**, 4, 5; **92**, 5, 6; **98**, 5; **104**, 8; **A26**, 2; **A34**, 13, 15—17; **A35**, 5; **A38**, 15. — Iran. **vi + nas-* "to disappear, to perish"; MMP *wn'h*, NP *gunāh* "sin", Arm. (from Parth.) *vnas* "damage, loss, harm; offence; fault, guilt" (Hübschmann, *AG*, I, 248—249). *Cf.* also *āhōk*, *rēš*, *vināskārīh*, *ziyān*.

vināskār: offender, criminal". — **78**, 8, 9; **A15**, 4; **A34**, 14; **A35**, 7. — MMP *wn'hg'r* "sinner"; Arm. (from Parth.) *vnasakar* "harmer; delinquent".

vināskārīh: "offence, crime; fault". — **7**, 13, 16; **14**, 13; **33**, 1, 3; **78**, 7; **107**, 5; **A13**, 14; **A39**, 10, 14; **A40**, 2, 4.

vindātan, **vind-**: "to acquire". — **62**, 10; **80**, 15; **A4**, 5; **A40**, 1. — Iran. **vid-*, Av. ^{2}*vaēd-*, *vind-* "to find, obtain, acquire" (*Air Wb.*, 1318—1320). See also *vindišn*, *vindišnōmand*.

vindišn: "revenue; acquisition". — **7**, 4; **36**, 15, 17; **52**, 6; **101**, 12, 15; **103**, 11, 12; **A1**, 2, 5, 7—9, 11, 13, 15—17; **A2**, 1, 2, 4, 9, 11—17; **A3**, 1, 14; **A4**, 1, 3, 11; **A7**, 12; **A10**, 17. — See *vindātan*. *Cf.* also *hamvindišn*, *kār-vindišn*, *vindišnōmand*, *yut-vindišn*.

vindišnōmand: "endowed with revenue / income". — **A1**, 4.

virāδišn: "ordering, arranging". — **86**, 3. — *Cf. virāstan*.

***virāδkar** ?: "watcher, arranger of order" (?). This term is found in the expression **virāδkar bastār* "binder of the arranger of order" (?) which designates a type of delinquent. The suggested reading and interpretation are hypothetical. — **A15**, 10.

virāstan, **virāδ-**: "to arrange"; of a document "to formulate". — **A16**, 16. — Iran. **vi + rād-* "to establish in order" / "to arrange, to prepare".

virōpišn: "sweep, dispersal"; *hač pās virōpišn ī gizīrān* "the sweeping, dispersal of the guards from their post" — **A26**, 4, 8. — Iran. **vi + raup-* "to sweep off"; *cf.* Khot.-Saka *burūvāni* (< **vi-raup-*) "to be destroyed, swept away"; Parth. *pdrwb-* "to chase away, put to flight".

visēh kartan: "to send away; to revoke, annul". — **75**, 8; **93**, 10; **A38**, 17. — Iran. **vi + said-*, Av. *saēd-*: "to tear apart, to cleave"; *cf.* Parth. *wsyd kyrdn* "to send off; to dispatch; cancel / dissolve", NP *gusē kardan* "to send, dispatch", *gusistan* "to tear (oneself) apart, to disconnect; to revoke, annul (a court decision)".

Visprat: name of a religious service. — **35**, 13—15.

višāt: "opened, open" (of a document whose seal has been removed). — **102**, 16; **103**, 4. — Iran. **vi + hā(y)- / hyā-* "to tie together" (Skt. *vi-ṣyati* "to open, to untie"); Parth. *wyšah-*, *wyš'd* "to open; to release, to free", NP *gušādan* "to open". For the etymology see in particular Szemerényi, "*Die Sprache*", 12/2, 1966, 217; Mayrhofer, *Etym. Wb.*, III, 549—550.

višuftan, **višōβ-**: "to be cancelled, to be dissolved, broken" (of contractual relations). — **37**, 13. — Iran. **vi + xšaub-* "to go into motion; be excited, be stirred".

vitartan, **vitīr-**: "to die". — *Passim*.

vitīrišnīh: "death"; *pat vitīrišnīh* "in case of death". — **43**, 13—14, 16.

vizand: "harm, damage". — **46**, 3; **53**, 14; **72**, 17. — MMP *wzynd*, NP *guzand*.

vizāyītan, vizāy-: "to deprive". — **10**, 13—15, 17; **11**, 1, 3, 4; **A33**, 4, 10, 13. — Bartholomae (*SRb.*, 18; *WZKM*, XXIX, 17, 20; *ZsR* III, 51—55) read this verb as *vīžāstan, vīžāy-* (< *vī + ǰād- "to ask") comparing it with Lat. *obrogare* (*legem*). "to cancel, annul" [this was accepted by Pagliaro, see *RSO*, XXIV (1949), 125—129]. But in his translations of articles from the *Law-Book*, Bartholomae gave to the MP verb the sense "*stören* (to disturb, hinder; to upset)", which cannot be derived from the etymological analysis proposed by him. Whatever the etymology of the MP verb, its comparison with Lat. *obrogare* is unacceptable because the Latin verb has a specific origin: it arose as the antithesis of the Roman *rogatio*, the special act of request of the presentation of the draft of a law for the approval of the senate, and it is not attested outside of this specific context. As for the meaning "to disturb", it cannot be reconciled with the root **ǰad-* nor with the contexts and their grammatical constructions (*u-m pasēmār hač dārišn / hač-iš vizāyēt*; *u-m pasēmār hač pat xvēšīh dāštan vizāyēt*; *tō hač ēn xvāstak / hač-iš nē vizāyom; tā dātastān sar bavēt ma vizāy*). The meaning "to deprive" suits all the contexts; the meaning "to remove from (the possession of a thing") may likewise be substituted. On this basis the MP form *vīzāy-* may be derived from Iran. **vī̆* + *zāy-*, *cf.* Skt. *jáhāti* "to (be) deprive(d), to leave, to abandon, to separate (oneself) from" (I-E **ĝhē-*, *ĝhēi-*), and specifically from the causative stem **vī* - *zāyaya-* with the transitive sense of "to deprive, bar from, sever". *Cf.* Parth. *wzyh-*, *wyz'd* "to abandon", Parth. *zys-* "to renounce" (inchoative), Gk.* χάζω (κεκᾰδήσω, κεκᾰδών) "to deprive", χῆρος "deprived, emptied; widowed, orphaned". This explanation which was already suggested by me in *REArm.*, V (1968), 10—11, is not, however, the only one possible. The given verbal form may equally be derived from **ǰay-* / **ǰya-*, Skt. **ji-* / *jyā-*, *cf. jinā́ti, jáyati* (= Av. *ǰayai*, *Air Wb.*, 605), *jī́yate, jītá-* "to take by force, overpower; suppress, jam, injure" (I-E. **gu̯eiə-*), especially from the palatalized variant (**zāy-* / **zyā-*) of this root in Iranian for which (as well as for the Skt. *jinā́ti*) the meaning "to take away" and "to deprive someone of something" is attested. *Cf. e. g.* Av. *zināt̰* in *Y* 11, 5: *yō mąm tat̰ draonō zināt̰ vā trəfyāt̰ vā apa vā yāsāiti* "whoever shall deprive me of this share (of the animal sacrifice), (whether he) steal (it) or take it away...". [Here "to steal" and "to take away" are specifications of the broader verb "to deprive"; this formulation in the Avestan text is in complete agreement with Ancient Iranian law which made a rigorous difference between theft, as the seizure of another man's property by stealth, through deceit, and robbery, as forcible seizure taking place openly). OP *dinā-*, *dīta-* "to take away", MSogd. *zyn-*, *zyt-* "to take away, to deprive", Khot.-Saka *ysän-*, *ysäta-* "to take away by force" (Bailey, *Prolexis*, 292—293; Emmerick, *SGS*, 112), Balōčī *zin-*, *zita* "to seize, to tear out, to take away by force" may also be pointed out. See also Burrow, *JAOS*, 79/4 (1959), 255—260. *Cf. vizītan.*

vizītan, vizīn-: "to bring a loss, to cause damage". — **A28**, 4. — Iran. **vi* + *zyā-* "to cause damage", Av. *zyā*, OP *diyā-*; for the compound with *vi-* *cf.* Arm. *vzean*, *vzenak* "loss, fine" < Parth. **viziyān*, Iran. **vizyāna-*.

vizūtan, **vizāy-**: "to diminish, decrease" — **A15**, 6; **A16**, 6. — Iran. **vi-ǰāvaya-*, Iran. **gav-* "to grow, to increase"/"to lessen decrease", *cf.* Parth. *wyg'w* "diminution", *prg'w-* "be insufficient".

***vižaδ**; see *nižāδ*.

X

xān, **xānak**: "house, family"; *xān ut xvāstak* "farmstead, estate"; *andar xānak ī pitarān zāt*, *cf. andar dūtak zāt* — **19**, 2, 7; **24**, 3; **33**, 10; **41**, 13; **44**, 8; **86**, 2—4, 8; **110**, 10; **A30**, 8.

xānīk: "spring, source". — **85**, 4.

xar: "donkey". —**102**, 3, 4, 6, 8; **A19**, 10.

xonsand / xunsand būtan: "to be satisfied, to declare one's satisfaction with a court decision", *xonsandīh* "satisfaction; declaration of the litigating parties of their satisfaction". — **2**, 17; **3**, 1, 2, 4, 5, 12; **4**, 2, 13; **36**, 3, 4; **40**, 16; **49**, 16; **56**, 17; **58**, 14; **69**, 5; **75**, 5, 6; **87**, 4; **89**, 16; **90**, 8; **95**, 1; **A4**, 7, 9; **A26**, 5. — Iran. **hu / hva + ni-sanda-*; MMP *hwnsnd* "satisfied, pleased", Sogd. *xwsndy'* "satisfaction", NP *xorsand*. Synonyms: *xvastūk*, *xvastūkīh*; antonyms: *nakīrā(k)*, *axunsand*, *axunsandīh*, *mih*.

Xordat (**roč**): "the day *Xordat*". — **A23**, 8.

xrītakīh: "purchase. — **102**, 10. — *Cf. xrītan*, *xrītarīh*, *frōxtan*.

xrītan, **xrīn-**: "to buy"; *apāč xrītan* "to redeem", *pat vahāk xrītan* "to buy". — **7**, 5, 6; **38**, 2; **103**, 8, 10; **106**, 2; **109**, 5, 6; **A8**, 17; **A9**, 6; **A26**, 17; **A27**, 12; **A38**, 5, 6.

xrītārīh: "purchase; purchased". — **6**, 8.

xūn: "blood; bloodshed". Variety of offence of the *žahm* group. — **A14**, 16.

xunsand; see *xonsand*.

xvah: "sister". — **A31**, 12—15.

xvāhišn: "demand, claim, suit, action". — **3**, 5; **21**, 7, 8; **43**, 2, 5, 6; **49**, 16; **58**, 11; **101**, 6; **A14**, 5; **A16**, 17; **A33**, 15. — *Cf. xvāstan*, *xvāstārīh*.

xvap: "good, lawful, valid"; *pat xvap dāštan* "to consider valid, lawful". This term is part of the formula of verbal agreements; *cf. xvaš*. — **4**, 6; **15**, 14; **16**, 8; **22**, 2; **28**, 14; **35**, 1, 3; **36**, 4; **43**, 7, 15, 16; **47**, 11; **51**, 10; **57**, 16; **63**, 5, 8; **64**, 2; **66**, 13; **68**, 11; **75**, 1, 8, 13, 14; **78**, 2; **93**, 1; **94**, 14; **106**, 10; **A14**, 6; **A18**, 7.

xvārastān: "ordeal-court". — **8**, 15, 17; **57**, 3; **65**, 4; **A12**, 12. — Iran. **xvāra + stāna-* "place of oath-taking"; **xvāra-* is formed on the root **xvăr-* "to swear" (I.-E. **su̯er-*, *cf.* Engl. *swear*, Germ, *schwören*, *Schwur*), see Bartholomae, *ZsR* IV, 38—42. For Iran. **xvar-* "to swear" *cf.* also *zūr-xvart* "false oath" (*q. v.*). Iran. **ka-xvarda-/*ka-xvardī-* "sorcerer/sorceress", found in Av. *ka-*

xvarəδa-, *ka-xvarəiδī-* and in Arm. (from Parth.) *kaxard* "sorcerer / sorceress", may contain a base of this root with *-d-/-dh-* extension as the second element of the compound; in this case, the compound designates the person uttering evil conjurations. *Cf.* however, other explanations "how black!" (Bartholomae, *Air Wb.* 462) and "what a shouter / howler!" (Schwartz, *Henn. Mem. Vol.*, 389—391). This root can unquestionably be identified in Osset. *ard xæryn* "to swear an oath". The Ossetic expression cannot be compared with NP *sau̯gand xordan* (*cf.* Abaew, *HEDO*, I, 60—61) and cannot mean "to eat an oath". Nor did the Persian idiom ever have such a meaning: its literal sense is "to swallow / drink sulphur (water)" and it describes the sulphur-water ordeal which was one variety only of oath-taking. Primarily, MP *sōkand* (> NP *sau̯gand*) meant "sulphur" (Iran. **saukant-*, Av. *saokənta-*, *cf.* *āpəm saokəntavaitīm*, *V.* 4, 54, 58; *AirWb.*, 1550), the meaning "oath" having arisen secondarily from this specific usage; whereas in Oss. *ard xæryn* the verb continuing Iran. **hvar-* is construed with *ard* 'oath' < **arta-* "fittness; what fits", also "order; truth; right". Here the meaning "oath" has developed from the basic "fitted / right word" (see Bailey, *ZP*, XXX) and a comparison with Skt. *r̥tám am(i)-* "to swear an oath" [Skt. *am(i)-*: Gk. ὄμνυμι] suggests itself. On Skt. *am(i)-* and its derivatives (*e. g.* *samāmá-* "contractual oath") as well as on *r̥tám* with *vad-*, *brū-*, *kr̥-* "to swear an oath" and *ánr̥tam* "perjury" (used with *sap-* and *kr̥-*) see K. Hoffmann, "*Aufsätze*", I, 288—305. *Cf.* also Lat. *iurare* "to swear", *iusiurandum* "oath". [According to Benveniste (*Vocabulaire*, I, 166) *r̥tám amīṣva* means "jure par le *r̥ta*!" (= "en prenant pour garant le *r̥ta*"). Such an interpretation, however, seems less convincing, *r̥tam* functioning rather as the direct object of the verb in this phraseological unit]. One has good reasons to believe that the ancient Iranian verb **hvar-* "to swear" survives in Oss. *ard xæryn*. — See also *var*.

xvarišn: "maintenance, support"; likewise; *xvarišn ut darišn* (*q. v.*), *xvarišn ut vastrak* (*q. v.*), *parvarišn* (*q. v.*) *ut xvarišn ut vastrak*. — **30**, 10; **32**, 11—13; **33**, 2, 12; **36**, 9; **A7**, 9. — See Bartholomae, *ZsR* V, 6—8. See also *Fr. ī oīm*, XXV, 6. With *xvarišn ut vastrak cf.* Arm. *ročikk' ew handerjagink'* "rations and outfitting / clothes-money".

xvārtar: "heavier, more severe" (of a blow). — **92**, 1; **97**, 2.

***xvas̱rāyōnīh**: form of marriage *sine manu mariti*, synonym of **baγaspān* (*q. v.*). — **41**, 10. — The spelling 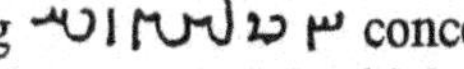 conceals a learned word borrowed from the Avesta (missing in the extant text) which is attested also outside the Lawbook (Fr. *ī oīm* 2f; *Riv. Em. Ašav.* XLIII; *Riv. Āturfarn.* III). As to its reading and interpretation several suggestions have been already made, none of them conclusive. J. de Menasce [*RHR*, 162 (1962), 75, 81—82] read tentatively *a-nisrāyēn*, from Av. *ni-srāy-* (*AirWb.*, 1638) interpreting the word in the sense of "le fait de n'être pas conjoint", which is hardly defendable. The hypothesis of Klingenschmitt [*MSS*, 29 (1971), 168] restoring Av. **xvasaraēnī-* < **xvăsar(a)-* "eigene Mut habend" seems unacceptable if only because of the absence in Iranian of **sara-* with the meaning of "guardianship". In MP *sardār* cited by Klingenschmitt the first member of the compound is **săra(h)-* "head, summit" and the word means lit. "who keeps the summit, the upper rank, the top position" > "chief, commander", whence its ordinary (and primary) use for "military chief, commander", the sense of "guardian" being a secondary one (in *pātixšāyīh* marriage a father or a husband, apart from presiding over the cult and other family activities, had the power over the women and the minors and thus functioned as the family's "head" or "chief"). Besides, K's reconstruction leaves unaccountable the length of the vowel (*-ā-*) in the syllable preceding the suffixation. Proceeding from the gloss in Fr. *ī oīm* 2f where the term is explained as *duxt-ē(v) kē šōy xvat kunēt*, as well as from the resemblance between this type of marriage and the Indian *svayaṁvara*, I explained the word as a formation on the base **srăy-* 1) "to lean, to rely upon; 2) to trust, to entrust" (in Pahlavi translation of the Avesta verbal derivatives of *srăy-* are often rendered by *apaspārtan* "to convey"). The reading proposed was *xw'sl(=r)'yn'* or *xwsl'ywn* "(a girl) conveying/entrusting herself (into marriage)". See *Henning Mem Vol.*, 350—351. The difficulty here is that for * *srăy-* the meaning "to entrust" is attested in medial forms only (*cf.* also Skt. *śrayaṇa-*), whereas the spelling points to a long vowel in the radical. My next proposal was to see here a compound with **srād-* "stake in a wager, gage": *xwsl'dyn'* < Av. **xvăsrāδaēnī-* "engaging herself" = "conveying herself (in marriage)". Still this reconstruction is likewise vulnerable on formal (= morphological) grounds. I now think it safer to transliterate the word as *xws̱l'ywn*, with |*-s-*| standing for Av. *-ϑ-* (which is normal in Pahlavi, *cf.* *'s̱lwn'* = *āϑravan-*, *'ys̱lp'ytyš*= *aēϑrapaitiš* etc.). The Avestan original might be restored as **xvăϑrāyaonī-*, that is *xvă-* compounded with a feminine noun **ϑrāyaonī-* of which the masc. form *ϑrāyavan-* "having/carrying the (divine) protection", an epithet of *āϑravan-*, is attested (see Yt **5**, 86; **14**, 56). The radical is Iran. **ϑrā(y)-*, Skt. *trayate* "to protect, to take care of". It is well represented in the Avesta, *e. g.* *ϑrātar-* "protector guardian" : (fem.) *ϑrāϑrī-* (= Skt. *trātr̥-* : *trātrī-*), *ϑrātī-* "protection", *ϑrāyō.drīγu-* "who takes care of the poor". As to the formation, *cf.* Skt. *maghavan-* : (fem.) *maghonī-*, Av. *magavan-*, *myazdavan-* *arəϑavan-* etc. The proper sense of Av. **xvăϑrāyaonī-*, Pahl. *xvăs̱rāyōn*, that of "taking care of herself", "acting as her own guardian", does not seem unsuitable. Note that in a Pers. Rivāyat (Bartholomae, *Zend-Handschriften*, 131) the *xvăs̱rāyōn*-wife is described as *xud sālār zan*. On this type of marriage see my Obščestvo, 106—111.

xvāstak: "thing, property, *res*" (in certain contexts this term may also signify "money"); *xān ut xvāstak* "house and estate", *xvāstak ī rasēt* "*bona adventicia*", as against *xvāstak ī mat* "present possessions"; *xvāstak ī apāmdān* (*q. v.*) "debt"; *xvāstak ī ruvān* "foundation/endowed estate 'for the soul'"; *xvāstak ī varōmandīh* "questionable property" (= property the title to which is not clear). — *Passim*. — *Cf.* *čiš*, *(h)ēr*, *gēhān*.

xvāstakdar: "heir" (but not necessarily the successor of the *de cuius*). — **2**, 5; **25**, 4, 5; **29**, 16; **58**, 15; **60**, 8, 9, 16; **61**, 4, 6, 10, 11; **66**, 4, 13, 14, 16, 17; **67**, 11; 77, 8; **99**, 15; **A1**, 15; **A13**, 6; **A32**, 6—7; **A33**, 1, 11, 12, 15. — Arm. (from MP) *xostakdar* "heir" (in a broad sense).

xvāstakdārīh: 1) "inheritance; inherited possession/estate"; 2) "status of heir; the heirs (collectively)". — **59**, 11, 17; **60**, 5—7, 10, 12, 14; **61**, 2, 8, 10, 11, 15; **62**, 4, 6, 7, 13; **69**, 14.

xvāstan, **xvāh-**: "to claim, to request; to sue; to call to"; *apāč xvāstan* "to demand reimbursement" (of a regression). — **2**, 3, 6, 16; **6**, 14; **11**, 1; **15**, 3, 4, 9—11; **16**, 1, 6, 7, 13; **23**, 13; **30**, 2; **38**, 8; **39**, 13, 15; **40**, 1, 6; **85**, 6; **41**, 4, 15; **42**, 12; **43**, 2—4; **44**, 2; **49**, 3, 7; **53**, 5, 8, 9, 13; **54**, 16, 17; **55**, 12; **56**, 1, 3—5, 11, 12; **57**, 9; **58**, 1, 4, 5, 10; 13, 14; **59**, 13—16; **60**, 11, 13, 14; **62**, 16, 17; **63**, 3; **68**, 5; **75**, 12; **76**, 5, 10, 12, 13; **77**, 9; **86**, 7, 14, 17; **87**, 14; **88**, 3; **90**, 7; **102**, 7; **A9**, 4; **A12**, 8, 9; **A13**, 8, 9; **A26**, 12; **A30**, 11; **A32**, 1, 12; **A33**, 14. — Iran. **xvāz- Cf.* Arm. (from Parth.) *dataxaz* "plaintiff, accuser" (Iran. **dāta-+xvāza-*). *Cf.* also *xvāhišn*, *xvāstārīh*.

xvāstārīh: "a claim, demand". — **53**, 5, 10; **54**, 1.

xvastūk: "agreeing; confessing". — **14**, 8, 10; **15**, 12; **16**, 11, 15, 16; **77**, 11; **92**, 5; **A31**, 1. — Iran **hu/hvă-stu(v)-aka-*, MacKenzie, *BSOAS*, XXXI/2 (1968), 253. Arm. *xostuk* "avowing, confessing; vouching for, warranting", NP *xostū* (legal) "having confessed (to a crime)".

xvastūkīh: "agreement; confession, avowal; warranty". — **16**, 11, 15; **77**, 9; **107**, 3, 5, 8; **A26**, 3; **A28**, 5.

xvaš: "good, it is good". Formula pronounced by one of the parties in confirmation of a verbal agreement; *cf. xvap*. — **A10**, 17; **A11**, 4, 5, 8. — See *ZsR* I, 15—20.

[1]**xvatāy**: "master (of a slave)" — **1**, 4, 5, 16; **33**, 13; **39**, 3, 4; **97**, 4; **98**, 6; **101**, 9, 16; **106**, 1—3; **A2**, 2; **A3**, 13; **A31**, 16; **A32**, 1. — Iran. **xva-tāvan-*, Nom. Sg. **xva-tāvā*, *cf.* Sogd. *xwt'w*.

[2]**xvatāy**: "the god Ōhrmizd". — **35**, 17. — See preceding entry.

xvatāy-dušmānīh: "evil intent, hostility toward one's master". An offence. — **A34**, 10, 12.

xvatāyīh: "reign". — **1**, 2; **A38**, 9.

xvēš: "own". When applied to things, it designates any lawful possession of a thing irrespective of the type of title to it, held by the person. Therefore the designation *xvēš* "own" could represent both the most characteristic and widespread type of real right in antiquity — a personally inherited possession on the basis of one's personal share in the father's estate, and the holding of a temporary title to a thing — even an altogether precarious one such as, for instance, that of a mandatary over a thing entrusted to him by the giver of the mandate. The following usages can also be noted in the *Law-Book*: *ān ī xvēš* "a relative, kinsman"; *xvēš būtan* "to belong (on any legal basis)"; *xvēš dāštan* "to own by right"; *xvēš kartan ī kār ut kirpak* "the fulfilment of a duty of religious virtue"; *xvēš pat-iš kartan* "to declare the transfer of a thing into ownership; to transfer the title to a thing". — *e. g.* **1**, 10; **5**, 9, 10, 12, 15, 17; **6**, 1, 3, 4, 6; **9**, 3, 4; **10**, 12, 14, 16, 17; **11**, 2; **17**, 2, 3—5; **33**, 15; **47**, 10—11; **110**, 6—7. — Iran. **xvaipaθya-*, Av. *xvaē-paiθya-*, OP *(h)uvaipašiya-* "own, personal"; *cf.* also *(h)uvaipašiyam kar-* "*proprium facere*; to make one's own", in a predicative construction. See Benveniste, *Problèmes*, I, 301—307. *Cf. xvēšīh*.

xvēšāvand: "agnate, relative"; *xvēšāvandīh* "relations, kinsfolk". — **22**, 12; **44**, 2; **87**, 12, 13; **88**, 3; **89**, 1; **94**, 5; **A6**, 13; **A30**, 9. — *cf. nabānazdišt*.

xvēšīh: "belonging of a thing to the person", "real rights" in general (on whatever legal basis), whence *aδvēnak ī xvēšīh* = *aδvēnak ī dāšt* "variety of real right". In this sense of a lawful possession of the thing by the person the term is opposed to *de facto* possession" (*dārišn*). But the term appears most frequently as the designation of one of the two varieties of lawful holding of inherited property (see *aparmānd, āzātīh, vāspuhrakān*) — possession on the basis of one's personal title as against *stūr*-possession (see *stūr, stūrīh*). It was also used to designate any acquisiton of property (likewise by transfer) as the personal share of the acquirer with right of transmission to his personal successors, *pat āzātīh ut xvēšīh dāštan* "to hold (a thing) on the basis of a personal and inherited title (*i. e.* to be passed on to one's successors) *pat vāspuhrakān xvēšīh* (*DkM* 748, 14—15), *cf.* Arm, *sephakan azatut'iwn*. In its special sense of "personal inherited holding", *xvēšīh* is opposed both to *stūr*-possession and to any other variety of real right. — **2**, 2; **5**, 4, 10, 15, 16; **7**, 1; **9**, 15; **10**, 7, 17; **11**, 4, 10, 15; **17**, 6, 16; **18**, 2, 5; **19**, 3; **20**, 4, 14, 17; **21**, 1, 17; **30**, 14; **38**, 17; **41**, 13, 17; **44**, 9, 17; **45**, 4, 5; **46**, 3; **47**, 13, 14; **48**, 14, 16; **50**, 2; **51**, 16; **52**, 2; **55**, 4; **60**, 4; **61**, 13, 14; **62**, 7, 8; **63**, 2; **66**, 6, 16; **67**, 5; **68**, 2, 7; **69**, 8; **76**, 11—14; **82**, 7; **83**, 5; **85**, 16; **89**, 13; **90**, 16; **91**, 4; **94**, 13—15; **95**, 4; **96**, 8; **101**, 4; **103**, 13; **A4**, 8, 9; **A5**, 16; **A6**, 13; **A8**, 7, 13; **A17**, 17; **A18**, 1, 2; **A21**, 3; **A24**, 9—12; **A25**, 16; **A27**, 16; **A29**, 7; **A37**, 16, 17; **A39**, 6; **A40**, 8. — *Cf.* *xvēš*. On the legal value of *xvēš, xvēšīh* see "Obščestvo", 129—142.

xvēškār: "duty"; *čiš ī xvēškār*, lit. "an obligation thing" = a thing confirming and guaranteeing the debt obligation of the mandator or the right of regression by the mandatary. — **38**, 1.

xvēškārīh: "obligation, function". — **80**, 6; **A26**, 15, 16; **A38**, 16.

Y

yām: 1) "vessel"; 2) "pledge-deposit". — **102**, 2. — For the second meaning *cf.* *Išō'b.*, VII, §§ 1—3 where *mânâ* "vessel" is given as a pledged object. A vessel was a symbol of moveable property (hence convenient for deposit) as against immoveable wealth. *Cf.* also *yāmdār* "pledge-holder" (? see, *e. g.* *DkM* 716, 17), *yāmdārīh* "pledge-deposit" (*q. v.*). *Cf.* also Arm. (Bible) *yanawt' aṙnum* "to borrow" lit. "to take as a vessel, an utensil; to take on the basis of a vessel, an utensil"), *yanawt' tam* "to give as a loan". See also ²*yāmak, yamdārīh*.

¹**yāmak**: "clothing". — **73**, 10.

²**yāmak**: 1) "vessel"; 2) "deposit"; in particular "pledge-deposit" (presented in court). — **A26**, 4, 8; **A27**, 11; **A30**, 12, 13. — See, *yām*.

yāmdārīh: "pledge-deposit" (?). — **83**, 4. — See, *yām*.

Yašt: name of the liturgy. — **35**, 13, 14; **36**, 1.

yaštan, yaz-: "to perform a religious ritual"; *hamākdēn yaštan* "to perform a religious service with full rites". — **35**, 14, 16; **36**, 1; **109**, 14, 15. — Arm. (from Parth.)

yazem, *yašt* (Hübschmann, *AG*, I, 197—198); *cf.* also Arm. *hamakden* (Ełišē V c.). *Cf. yazīhītan*, *yazišn*.

yātakgōβ (= **yātagōβ**): "advocate, legal representative"; formally opposed to [1]*mātakvar* "the principal litigant"; *yātakgōβ gumārtan/kartan* "to appoint as representative"; *yātakgōβ patigriftan* "to admit a litigant's representative to participation in a case" (the admission was authorized by the judges after the verification of his mandate). — **16**, 11; **74**, 16, 17; **75**, 1—11, 13, 15, 17; **76**, 1, 9; **77**, 12, 15; **78**, 1, 16, 17; **93**, 16; **94**, 2; **106**, 11; **A29**, 7, 8; **A32**, 1; **A33**, 6. — Iran. **yātagauba*-, **yāta*- "share, part; *causa*", Bartholomae, *ZsR* IV 55—57. Arm. (from MP) *ǰatagov* (see *s. v. driyōšān*) "advocate, representative". For the formation *cf.* the MP synonym, *yātavāč*, *DkM* 700, 6—9. *Cf.* also [1]*dastaβar*, *yātakgōβānak*, *yātakgōβīh*.

yātakgōβānak: "relating to (legal) representation"; adjective from *yātakgōβ*. — **74**, 12.

yātakgōβīh: "(legal) representation"; *pat yātakgōβīh patigriftan*: "to admit as representative for participation in a case". — **75**, 16; **76**, 2, 3; **93**, 8, 15, 17; **94**, 1; **A29**, 9. — See *yātakgōβ*.

yāt-gēhān = Av. **yātəm gaēθanąm**: ("property-share"); see, *Vd.* 19, 29; *Āfrīn.*, 3, 11; *Fr. ī oīm*, 4f. — **A27**, 7.

yātūk: "sorcerer, sorceress". — **78**, 10; **A15**, 11, 15; **A38**, 13. — MMP *ǰ'dwg*, NP *ǰādū*. See next entry.

yātūkīh: "sorcery", "sorcerers (collectively)". — **78**, 10; **A15**, 11, 15; **A38**, 13.

yāvētānak, **yāvētānīk**: "forever"; as regards the transfer of property. Opposed to *tā žīwandakīh* "for life". — **19**, 3; **28**, 11; **80**, 15.

yazdān-dušmānīh: "hostility, evil-intent toward the gods" (offence). — **A34**, 9, 11. — *Cf. xvatāy-dušmānīh*.

yazīhītan: "to be performed" (of religious ritual). — **35**, 14. — see *yaštan*.

yazišn: "religious ritual, performance of religious rituals, liturgy". — **29**, 10; **34**, 1, 3, 6, 8, 9, 15; **35**, 2, 7, 10—12, 16; **A27**, 8. — *Cf. āyazišn*.

yazišn-nāmak: "document concerning the ordeal/oath". — **A13**, 7; **A27**, 8.

yōy: "irrigation channel". — **19**, 6.

yumāy: "jointly, together". — **65**, 2, 6, 7, 10; **70**, 7. — Synonym: *ākanēn*.

yutākīh: "separation"; *pat yutākīh* "separately". — *Passim*.

yut-dātastān, **yut-dātastānīh**: "disagreement in opinions, judgements". — **20**, 10; **32**, 1; **A11**, 16; **A15**, 7.

yut-kāmak: "disagreement". — **67**, 12.

yut-vindišn: "possession of a separate revenue/income". — **A1**, 12. — *Cf. hamvindišn*, *vindišn*.

yut-yut: "separately, apart". — *Passim*. — Antonym: *ākanēn*.

Z

zahakīh: "direct succession *via* kinship", — **60**, 17.

[1]**zamān**: "time, term, limit"; *andar zamān* "at once"; *brin zamān / dāt zamān* "a set time-limit / term". — *Passim.*

[2]**zamān**: "court session, *terminus*"; *zamān ī ō dastaβar* "court session with the participation of the (entitled) person who disposed of the disputed thing and is able to confirm the title of the respondent"; *zamān ī ō ēvarīh* "(supplementary) court-session (arranged) to demonstrate the authenticity of the testimony of one of the litigating parties (usually at its demand *cf. zamān ī ō dastaβar*)"; *zamān kartan* "to appoint, arrange a court-session"; *zamān xvāstan / dātan* "to demand/assign, arrange a court-session". — **3**, 8; **5**, 5, 11—16; **6**, 10; **7**, 6; **8**, 10, 11; **84**, 7, 9; **A12**, 12; **A13**, 16; **A15**, 7—8; **A25**, 17. — Bartholomae, *ZsR* IV, 29, 52—53.

zamīč: "land, plot of land". — **37**, 13.

zamīk: "land". — **19**, 5—7; **33**, 10, **38**, 5; **55**, 7; **85**, 4, 8, 9; **105**, 10; **106**, 12; **A20**, 12, 14; **A30**, 16; **A37**, 3, 6.

zan: "woman, wife". — *Passim.*

zan ī šahr: "female-citizen; country / townswoman". — **82**, 11, 14. — *Cf. mart ī šahr.*

zan kartan: "to take a wife, to marry". — **26**, 3; **44**, 13. — *Cf. šōy kartan.*

zandīkīh: "Manichaeanism; heresy". — **A38**, 16, 17. — Arm. (Eznik, Ełišē, V Century) *zandik* "Manichaean".

zandīk-rōδišnīh: "spread, propagation of Manichaeanism or of heretical teachings". Offence. — **A38**, 17.

zanīh: "marriage"; *hač zanīh hištan* "to dissolve a marriage, to divorce"; *ō zanīh matan* "to enter into a marriage" (of a woman); *pat zanīh andar šutan* "to enter into a marriage" (of a woman); tan *ōlpat zanīh datān* "to enter into a marriage *sine manu*" (of a woman); *pātixšāyīhā zanīh* (see *pātixšāyīh*). — **3**, 9, 12, 15; **4**, 1, 2, 11—16; **5**, 1; **10**, 9; **12**, 3, 8; **21**, 6; **22**, 7; **23**, 3; **25**, 9; **36**, 3, 4, 12, 14, 15; **42**, 10; **44**, 11; **48**, 6; **50**, 11—12; **83**, 13—15; **84**, 4; **87**, 4, 7, 8, 17; **89**, 17; **95**, 7; **106**, 8; **A1**, 2; **A2**, 8, 10; **A18**, 9, 11, 12; **A20**, 9, 10; **A24**, 14, 15; **A40**, 10, 12.

zarr: "gold". — **17**, 16, 17; **18**, 4, 5.

zarrēn: "golden; gold". — **104**, 9, 11, 12, 14.

[1]**zatan, zan-**: "to strike a blow; to commit an act of physical violence. — **10**, 10; **91**, 17; **92**, 7, 8, 11—15. — Iran. **gan-*.

[2]***zatan, *zam-**; see [2]*ōzatan.*

[1]**zātan, zāy-**: "to be born". — *Passim.* — Iran. **zan-*.

[2]**zātan, zāy-**: "to inherit"; *apar zātan* "*id.*". — **51**, 13; **52**, 12, 16; **90**, 13, 14, 17. — In the manuscript this verb is given by means of the heterogram for its homonym *zātan* "to be born". Iran. **zā(y)-*. *zāta- / zīta*, Skt. *jáhāti* (I.-E. **ĝhē-*, *ĝhēi-*) "to

deprive, be deprived; to leave, abandon, separate (oneself)". As regards the meaning "to inherit", the following may be pointed to: Lat. *heres* "heir" (**ĝhēro* + *ē- do- "das verwaiste Gut an sich nehmend*", Pokorny, 418—419) beside Gk. χήρā "orphan, widow", χηρωστής "collateral heir"; for a semantic parallel *cf.* the derivations from the I-E. synonym **orbh-* "to be deprived": Goth. *arbi* "inheritance", Germ. *Erbe* "heir", *erben* "to inherit" beside Gk. ὀρφανός "deprived, empty, deserted, orphaned", Arm. *orb* "orphan", Lat. *orbus* "deprived, orphan" (see in particular, Benveniste, *Vocabulaire*, I, 83—85). *Cf.* the Iranian derivations from the root **zā(y)-*, Arm. (from Parth.) *zat* "except, separately" (*cf.* Gk. χωρίς "except for, separately") *zatakan* "separating, separate, released/free", *zatem, zatanem, zatnum* "to separate, to release/free", MP *āzātīh* (*q. v.*), Arm. *azatut'iwn* "inheritance" (Iran. **ā*+*zāta-*), NP (prop. n.) *Bāyazīd*, lit. "successor", Arm. *payazat* "successor, heir", *payazatem* "to inherit, to succeed to", *payazatut'iwn* "succession", Osset. *bajzäddag* "successor, descendant", alongside *bazzajyn* "to remain" (Iran. **upāya-zāta-/zīta-*, *cf.* Germ. Nachlass), MP *vizāyītan* "to deprive" (*q. v.*) *et al.* [see Périkhanian, *REArm.*, V (1968), 9—16]. With *apar zātan* "to inherit", *cf.* also *apar māndan* "to inherit", *aparmānd* "inheritance" (*q. v.*).

zēndān: "prison"; *ō zēndān kartan* "to emprison". — **73**, 2; **A13**, 13, 15; **A28**, 11, 14, 16, 17; **A29**, 1, 3—5. See also *zēndānīk, zēndānpān*.

zēndānīk: "prisoner". — **A13**, 9, 10.

zēndānpān: "warden, governor of a prison". — **A13**, 9, 11; **A26**, 6; **A28**, 11, 12, 15; **A29**, 2, 5.

zēnīk / dēnīk. See *stūr, hambāy*.

ziyān: "damage, harm"; *a-pat-ziyān* = *apēziyān* (*q. v.*) — **28**, 16, 17; **29**, 1, 3; **35**, 7; **39**, 11; **74**, 5, 8; **A28**, 2, 3; **A30**, 16; **A31**, 11; **A37**, 6. — Iran. **zyānā-/zyānī-* (**zyā-* "to harm"), Av. *zyānā-*, NP *ziyān*. See also next entry. *Cf. vinās*.

ziyānak: "damage harm"; *pat ziyānak*: "causing losses; in detriment". — **102**, 5.

zūr-vikāy: "false-witness". — **A15**, 10. — *Cf. vikāy-druž*.

zūr-xvart: "false-oath". Offence. — **27**, 6. — Iran. **zūrah* + *xvarta/i-*, root *xvar-* "to swear", see *s. v. xvārastān*. For the composition *cf.* Av. *zūrō.jata-*, *zurō.bərəta-* (*AirWb.*, 1698), Arm. (from Parth.) *zrpart* "slander, slanderer", *zrpartem*, "to slander" = Iran. **zūrah* + *pr̥tu-* "false accusation; slander".

zyānak: "woman, wife"; paired with *mērak* (*q. v.*), — **4**, 5, 15; **32**, 5, 6; **44**, 5; **45**, 6, 8; **50**, 8—11; **64**, 4, 5; **65**, 13; **87**, 8; **95**, 8; **103**, 11, 12; **A5**, 13, 14; **A6**, 4, 5. — See Bartholomae, *SRb.*, 16.

Ž

žahm: "a blow"; legal term serving as the general designation for all forms and grades of acts of physical violence (*cf.* πληγαί in Ancient Greek law). — **1**, 5; **10**, 10; **16**, 12; **30**, 12; **36**, 17; **92**, 17; **97**, 1, 2; **A14**, 13—17. — Parth. *jxm* "wound"), Iran. **jaθman-*; *cf.* [1]*zatan*.

INDEXES

A) *Rare and Unidentified Spellings*

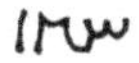 — **asūn*. See Glossary, *s. v.*

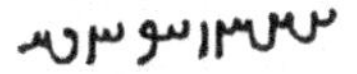 — (= *āšnavākānīh*)? — **79**, 12.

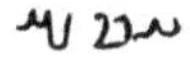 — 'SY' = *bizišk* (*q. v.*).

 — ? — **67**, 16, 17.

 — ? — **91**, 16.

 — **anītar* (see "Glossary").

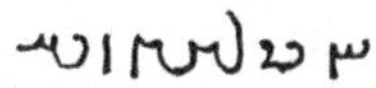 — **xvāsrāyōnīh* (see "Glossary").

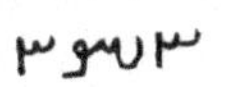 — *'wšk'n*. — **A36**, 12.

 — ? — **A35**, 5, 10.

 — see *'nw'n* (?).

 — *āpvarīh* (*q. v.*)

 — *aparmat* (*q. v.*)

 — ? — **75**, 6, 7.

 — see *dastīk* (?).

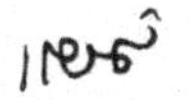 — ? — "dam" (?). — **106**, 13.

 — **srāδ* (*q. v.*).

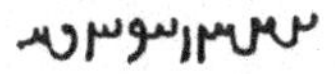 — ? — "satisfaction" (?); "compensation" (?). — **105**, 17.

 — **vidāštan* (*q. v.*).

 — ? —. — **75**, 3.

 — ? —. — **80**, 12.

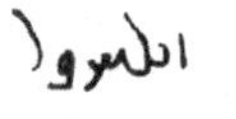 — see *virāδkar* (?).

 — ? —. — **37**, 1.

 — see *nisāk, sāk*.

 — *varγ* (?). — **A4**, 2.

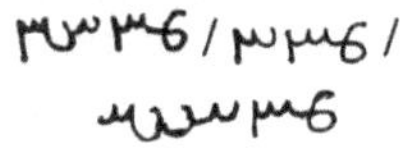 — see *mānak* (?).

 — ? — **103**, 2.

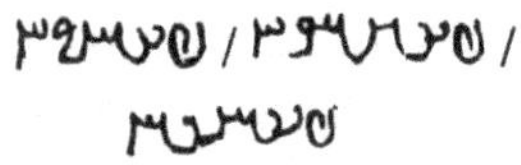 = *Paš(a)dātakān/pas(a)dātakān*. — See Glossary, *s. v.*

 — **1**, 15.

 = PWT-š; PWT < TPWT < *ṬPWT('). Aram. *ṭabbûθâ* "seal" (*cf.* Ak. *ṭabbû*) = MP *muhr/muhrak* (?); see note 82.

 — see **pargār*.

 — see Glossary, *s. v. tas(a)k*.

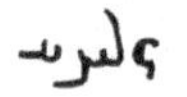 = ṢLYB' "cross"?! — **79**, 12.

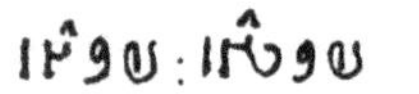 — see *s. v. dastaβar*.

B) *Avestisms:*

aδwadāti-: see Glossary, *s. v. at̲vadat*.

ayaoγaēnī-** /ayŭ̄γaēnī-**, Pahl. : "*epikleros* (daughter/sister)"; *ayaoγaēn-īh/ayŭ̄γaēn-īh* "epiklerate". Variety of *stūr* succession (see *stūr, stūrīh*). — **21**, 4, 10; **22**, 10, 12, 16; **23**, 1, 3, 4, 5, 9, 13, 14, 16; **24**, 1, 4, 5, 7; **49**, 2; **69**, 12; **87**, 3; **90**, 1. — I abandon my previous reading [*'*ynwkk'yn'* = Av. **aēnō.kaēnā-*, lit. "redeemer, expiator (of her father's sin of dying *a-puθra-*, sonless)" offered in *Henning Mem. Vol.*, 351—353. A reading which is by far more plausible (Pahl. *'*ywkk̲'yn'* = Av. **ayaoγaēnī-/ayŭ̄γaēnī-* with Pahl. -*k̲*- = Av. -*γ*-) has been proposed by Klingenschmitt [see *MSS*, 29 (1971), 168] who cites Skt. *ayugū́ḥ* (lit. "not bound") attested in *Gobhilagṛhyasūtra* (3, 5) and interpreted in *Karmapradīpa* 3, 9[4]) as "her mother's only child". There seems to be no formal obstacle for connecting these terms and the Sanskrit word likewise holds good semantically when explained as "the one not bound (with the ties of a wedlock *cum manu mariti*", "not to be bound/not bound (in an ordinary way to

C) *Texts Cited in the Law-Book:*

D) *Fire-Temples:*

E) *Offices and Institutions:*

F) *List of Persons:*

G) *Toponyms:*

ABBREVIATIONS

Abaev, *HEDO I* — V. I. Abaev, *Istoriko-etimologičeskij slovar' osetinskogo jazyka I*, Moskva—Leningrad, 1968.

Acta Antiqua Hung. — *Acta Antiqua Accademiae Scientiarum Hungaricae.*

AO — *Acta Orientalia.*

Āfr. — *Āfrīnakān.*

AION — *Annali dell'Istituto Orientale di Napoli,* sezione linguistica.

AirWb. — Chr. Bartholomae, *Altiranisches Wörterbuch*, Strassburg, 1904. [Reprint: Berlin, 1961].

A Locust's Leg — *A Locust's Leg. Studies in honour of S. H. Taqizadeh.* [W. B. Henning, E. Yarshater, edd.], London, 1962.

AM — *Asia Major.*

AMI — *Archaeologische Mitteilungen aus Iran.*

Andreas—Henning, MiM, I—III — F. C. Andreas, W. B. Henning, *Mitteliranische Manichaica aus Chinesisch-Turkestan*, I—III, *SPAW*, 1932, X, 173—222; *ibid.*, 1933, VII, 292—363; *ibid.*, 1934, XXVII, 846—912.

AoF — *Altorientalische Forschungen.*

AZ — *Aβyātkār ī Zarērān.*

Bailey, *Dict. of Kh. Saka* — H. W. Bailey, *Dictionary of Khotan Saka*, Cambridge, 1979.

Bailey, *Prolexis* — H. W. Bailey, *Indo-Scythian Studies. Prolexis to the Book of Zambasta*, Cambridge, 1967.

Bailey, *ZP* — H. W. Bailey, *Zoroastrian Problems in the Ninth Century Books*, Oxford, 1943. [2nd ed.: Oxford, 1971].

Bartholomae *Mir Mund.* I—IV	— Chr. Bartholomae, *Zur Kenntnis der mitteliranischen Mundarten*, *SHAW*, 1916—1925.
Bartholomae, *SRb.*	— Chr.Bartholomae, *Über ein sasanidisches Rechtsbuch*, *SHAW*, 1910, 11 Abhandl.
Bartholomae, *ZAirWb.*	— Chr. Bartholomae, *Zum altiranischen Wörterbuch*, Strassburg, 1906.
Bartholomae, *ZSR*, *I—V*	— Chr. Bartholomae, *Zum sasanidischen Recht*, I—V, *SHAW*, 1918—1923.
Bd.	— *The Bundahišn.* T. D. Anklesaria (ed.). Bombay, 1908.
Benveniste, *Et. oss.*	— E. Benveniste, *Etudes sur la langue ossète*, Paris, 1959.
Benveniste, *Problèmes*	— E. Benveniste, *Problèmes de linguistique générale*, Paris, 1966.
Benveniste, *Titres*	— E. Benveniste, *Titres et noms propres en iranien ancien*, Paris, 1966.
Benveniste, *Vocabulaire*, I—II	— E. Benveniste, *Le vocabulaire des institutions indo-européennes*, I—II, Paris, 1969.
Boyce, *Hymn-cycles*	— M. Boyce, *The Manichaean Hymn-cycles in Parthian*, Oxford, 1954.
BSL	— *Bulletin de la Société linguistique de Paris.*
BSO(A)S	— *Bulletin of the British School of Oriental (and African) Studies.*
CHI	— *The Cambridge History of Iran.*
CII	— *Corpus Inscriptionum Iranicarum.*
Darmesteter *ZA*	— J. Darmesteter, *Le Zend-Avesta*, Paris, 1892.
Dd.	— *Dātastān ī dēnīk.*
Diakonoff, Livshits, *Documents*	— I. M. Diakonoff and V. A. Livshits, *Parthian Economic Documents from Nisa*, Texts, CII, Part II, vol. II, London, *s. a.*
DkM	— *Dēnkart* [D. M. Madan, ed.], Bombay, 1911.
Driver, *Aram. Doc.*	— G. R. Driver, *New Aramaic Documents of the Fifth Century B. C.*, Oxford, 1953.
Emmerick, *SGS*	— R. E. Emmerick, *Saka Grammatical Studies*, Oxford, 1968 ["London Oriental Series", vol. 20].
Fr. ī oīm	— *Frahang ī oīm.*
Fr. ī P.	— *Frahang ī Pahlavīk.*

Gersh. *GMS* — I. Gershevitch. *A Grammar of Manichaean Sogdian*, Oxford, 1954 [Reprint: 1964]

Gersh., *Mithra* — I. Gerschevitch, *The Avestan Hymn to Mithra*, Cambridge, 1959.

Ghilain, *Essai* — A. Ghilain, *Essai sur la langue parthe*, Louvain, 1939.

Hallock, *Tablets* — R. T. Hallock, *Persepolis Fortifications Tablets*, Chicago, 1969.

Hansen, *BST* — O. Hansen, *Berliner soghdische Texte*, Mainz, 1954.

Henning, *BBB* — W. B. Henning, *Ein manichäisches Bett-und Beichtbuch*, "Abhandlungen der Preussischen Akademie der Wissenschaften", 1936, no. 10.

Henning, *List* — W. B. Henning, *A List of Middle Persian and Parthian Words*, BSOS, IX, 1 (1937), 79—92.

Henning Mem. Vol. — *W. B. Henning Memorial Volume*. [Ed. by M. Boyce and I. Gershevitch]. London, 1970.

Henning, *Mitteliranisch* — W. B. Henning, *Mitteliranisch*, "Handbuch der Orientalistik" hrsg. von B. Spuler, I, Abt., IV, 1, Leiden, 1958, 20—129.

Henning, *Sogdica* — W. B. Henning, *Sogdica*, London, 1940.

Henning, *Verbum* — W. B. Henning, *Das Verbum des Mittelpersischen der Turfanfragmente*, ZII, IX (1933), 158—253.

Hoffmann, *Aufsätze* — K. Hoffmann, *Aufsätze zur Indoiranistik*, I—II, Wiesbaden, 1975, 1976.

Hübschmann, *AG* — H. Hübschmann, *Armenische Grammatik I, 1. Die persischen und arabischen Lehnwörter im Altarmenischen*, Leipzig, 1895.

Hübschmann, *Pers. St.* — H. Hübschmann, *Persische Studien*, Strassburg, 1895.

IF — *Indogermanische Forschungen*. Zeitschrift für Indogermanistik und allgemeine Sprachwissenschaft.

IIJ — *Indo-Iranian Journal*.

Išō'b. — *Išō'bōxt. Corpus juris der persischen Erzbischofs Jesubocht* hrsg. von Ed. Sachau. Syrische Rechtsbücher, Bd. III, Berlin, 1914.

JAOS — *Journal of the American Oriental Society*.

JRAS — *Journal of the Royal Asiatic Society*. London.

Kellens, *Noms-racines* — J. Kellens, *Les noms-racines de l'Avesta*, Wiesbaden, 1974.

KiZ (*Kartīr*) — *Ka'be-yi Zardušt. Kartīr's Inscription*.

KiZ (*Šāhpuhr*) — *Ka'be-yi Zardušt. Šāhpuhr's Inscription*.

Kraeling, *Papyri* — E. G. Kraeling, *The Brooklyn Museum Aramaic Papyri*, New Haven, 1953.

KZ — *Zeitschrift für vergleichende Sprachforschung* hrsg. von A. Kuhn.

Lagarde, *Armen. Stud.* — P. de Lagarde, *Armenische Studien*, Göttingen, 1877.

Lagarde, *Pers. Stud.* — P de Lagarde, *Persische Studien*, Leipzig, 1886.

Lentz Festschr. — *Festschrift für W. Lentz*, Göttingen, 1970.

MacKenzie, *Pahl Dict.* — D. N. MacKenzie, *A Concise Pahlavi Dictionary*, Oxford, 1971.

MacKenzie, *Khwar Gloss. I—IV* — D. N. MacKenzie, *The Khwarezmian Glossary, I—IV*, *BSOAS*, XXXIII, 3 (1970), 540—547; XXXIV, 1 (1971), 74—89; XXXIV, 2 (1971), 314—328; XXXIV, 3 (1971), 521—535.

Materialy — A. G. Perixanjan, *Materialy k etimologičeskomu slovarju drevnearmjanskogo jazyka*, Erevan, 1994.

Mayrhofer, *KEWAI* — M. Mayrhofer, *Kurzgefaßtes etymologisches Wörterbuch des Altindischen*, I—III, Heidelberg, 1956—1979.

Mayrhofer, *Onom. P.* — M. Mayrhofer, *Onomastica Persepolitana. Das altiranische Namengut der Persepolis-Täfelchen*, Wien, 1973.

Mélanges Massé — *Mélanges d'orientalisme offerts à Henri Massé*, Téhéran, 1963.

Mél. Morgenstierne — *Indo-Iranica. Mélanges présentés à G. Morgenstierne*. [G. Redard, ed.], Wiesbaden, 1964.

Mém. de Menasce — *Mémorial Jean de Menasce*. [Ph. Gignoux and A. Tafazzoli, edd.]. Louvain, 1974.

MO — *Le Monde Oriental*. Uppsala.

Montgomery, *Aram. Incant. Texts* — J. A. Montgomery, *Aramaic Incantation Texts from Nippur*, Philadelphia, 1913.

Monum. Nyberg II — *Monumentum H. S. Nyberg*, vol. II, "Acta Iranica", 4, Leiden—Téhéran—Liège, 1975.

Morgenstierne, *EVP* — G. Morgenstierne, *An Etymological Vocabulary of Pashto*, Oslo, 1927.

Morgenstierne, *IIFL* — G. Morgenstierne, *Indo-Iranian Frontier Languages, I—IV*, Oslo—Bergen—Tromsö, 1929—1973.

MSL — *Mémoires de la Société de linguistique de Paris*.

MSS — *Münchener Studien zur Sprachwissenschaft*.

Nöldeke, *Tabarī* — Th. Nöldeke, *Geschichte der Perser und Araber zur Zeit der Sasaniden*, Leyden, 1879.

Nyberg, *Hb.*	— H. S. Nyberg, *Hilfsbuch des Pehlevi*, II, Uppsala, 1931.
Nyberg, *Manual*	— H. S. Nyberg, *A Manual of Pahlavi*, *II*, Wiesbaden, 1974.
Nīr.	— A. Waag, *Nīrangistān, der Awestatraktat über die rituellen Vorschriften*, Leipzig, 1941.
NTS	— *Norsk Tidsskrift for Sprogvidenskap*. Oslo.
Obščestvo	— A. G. Perixanjan, *Obščestvo i pravo Irana v parfjanskij i sasanidskij periody*, Moscow, 1983.
P.Ps.	— F. C. Andreas, K. Barr, *Bruchstücke einer Pehlevi-Übersetzung der Psalmen*, SPAW, 1933, 91—150.
Phil. Iranica	— I. Gershevitch, *Philologia Iranica*. [N. Sims-Williams ed.]. Wiesbaden, 1985.
Pok(orny)	— J. Pokorny, *Indogermanisches etymologisches Wörterbuch*, Bern—München, 1959.
"*Pratidānam*"	— *Pratidānam. Studies presented to F. B. J. Kuiper*, The Hague—Paris, 1968.
Purs. Āturfarnbaγ	— *The Pahlavi Rivāyat of Āturfarnbaγ and Farnbaγ-Srōš*, ed. by B. T. Anklesaria, Bombay, 1969.
P. Vd.	— *Pahlavi Vīdēvdāt.*
P.Y.	— *Pahlavi Yasna.*
P.Yt.	— *Pahlavi Yašt.*
REArm.	— *Revue des Etudes Arméniennes.*
Riv. Dd.	— *The Pahlavi Rivāyat accompanying the Dādistān ī dēnīk*, ed. by B. N. Dhabhar, Bombay, 1913.
Riv. Em. Ašav.	— *Rivāyat ī Ēmēt ī Ašavahištān*. [B. T. Anklesaria, ed.]. Bombay, 1962.
Riv. Horm. Fram.	— *The Persian Rivāyats of Hormazyar Framarz and others*, transl. with introduction and notes by B. N. Dhabhar, Bombay, 1932.
Roc. Orient.	— *Rocznik Orjentalistyczny* (Krakow).
RSO	— *Rivista degli Studi Orientali.*
R̥V	— *R̥gveda.*
Salemann, *Man. St.*	— C. Salemann, *Manichaeische Studien I*, "Zapiski Imp. Akademii Nauk", St. Petersburg, 1908.
Salemann, *Mittelpers.*	— C. Salemann, *Mitttelpersisch*, "Grundriss der iranischen Philologie", hrsg. von W. Geiger und E. Kuhn, Bd. I, Lief. 3, Strassburg, 1901.

SBE	— *The Sacred Books of the East.* [F. Max Müller, ed.].
SHAW	— *Sitzungsberichte der Heidelberger Akademie der Wissenschaften.*
SPAW	— *Sitzungsberichte der preußischen Akademie der Wissenschaften.* Phil.-hist. Klasse. Berlin.
SWAW	— *Sitzungsberichte der österreichischen Akademie der Wissenschaften in Wien.*
Šahr. ī Ērānš.	— *Šahristānīhā ī Ērānšahr.*
ŠGV	— *Škand gumānīk vičār.* Ed. J.-P. de Menasce, Fribourg, 1945.
ŠnŠ	— *Šāyast nē-šāyast.* Ed. J. C. Tavadia, Hamburg, 1930.
Schrader—Nehring, *Reallexicon*	— O. Schrader—A. Nehring, *Reallexicon der indogermanischen Altertumskunde*, Berlin, 1917—1929.
TPS	— *Transactions of the Philological Society.* London.
Unvala Mem. Vol.	— *Dr. J. M. Unvala Memorial Volume*, Bombay, 1964.
Vd.	— *Vīdēvdāt.*
VDI	— *Vestnik Drevnej Istorii.*
WZKM	— *Wiener Zeitschrift für die Kunde des Morgenlandes.*
Y.	— *Yasna.*
Yt.	— *Yašt.*
Zarth. Mad. Cent.	— *Sir J. J. Zarthoshti Madressa Centenary Volume*, Bombay, 1967.
ZDMG	— *Zeitschrift der deutschen morgenländischen Gesellschaft.*
ZII	— *Zeitschrift für Indologie und Iranistik.*

BIBLIOGRAPHY

Abajev, V. I., *Istoriko-etimologičeskij slovar' osetinskogo jazyka*. Vols. I—IV. Moscow—Leningrad, 1958—1989.

Andreas, F. C., Barr, K., "Bruchstücke einer Pehlevi-Übersetzung der Psalmen". — *SPAW* (1933), pp. 91—150.

Andreas, F. C., Henning, W. B. (edd. and transl.), "Mitteliranische Manichaica aus Chinesisch-Turkestan", I—III. — *SPAW* (1932/10), pp. 175—222; (1933/7), pp. 294—362; (1934/27), pp. 848—912.

Anklesaria, B. T. (ed.), *Rivāyat-î Hêmît-î Ašavahištān*. Vol. I. — Pahlavi Text. Bombay, 1962.

The Pahlavi Rivāyat of Āturfarnbag and Farnbag-Srōš. I—II. Bombay, 1969.

Anklesaria, T. D., *The Social Code of the Parsees in Sassanian Times or the Mâdigân-î-hazâr Dâdistân, part II.* Bombay, 1912.

Back, M., *Die sassanidischen Staatsinschriften*. — *Acta Iranica* 18. Leiden—Téhéran—Liège, 1978.

Bailey, H. W., "To the Žāmasp-nāmak, I—II". — *BSOS*, VI (1930—32), pp. 55—85, 581—600.

"Iranian Studies, I" — *BSOS*, VI (1930—32), pp. 945—955.

"Iranian Studies, II" — *BSOS*, VI/1 (1933), pp. 69—86.

"Iranian Studies, III" — *BSOS*, VII/2 (1934), pp. 275—298.

Review of W. B. Henning, "Ein manichäisches Bet-und Beichtbuch". — *BSOS*, IX (1937—39), pp. 229—231.

Zoroastrian Problems in the Ninth-Century Books. Oxford, 1943. Reprint: Oxford, 1971.

"Asica". — *TPS* (1945), pp. 1—38.

"Kusanica". — *BSOAS*, XIV/3 (1952), pp. 420—434.

"Analecta Indoscythica II". — *JRAS* (1954), pp. 26—34.

"Buddhist Sanscrit". — *JRAS* (1955), pp. 13—24.

"Armeno-Indoiranica". — *TPS* (1956), pp. 88—126.

"A Problem of the Indo-Iranian Vocabulary". — *Roc. Or.*, XXI (1957), pp. 59—69.

"Indagatio Indo-Iranica". — *TPS* (1960), pp. 62—86.

Indo-Scythian Studies. Prolexis to the Book of Zambasta. Cambridge, 1967.
Iranian *rōpānak.* — *Studi V. Pisani.* Brescia, 1969, pp. 91—96.
Sad-Dharma-Puṇḍarīka-Sūtra. — *"Occasional Paper"* 10, Canberra, 1971.
Dictionary of Khotan Saka. Cambridge—London—New York—Melbourne, 1979.

Bartholomae, Chr., *Altiranisches Wörterbuch.* Strassburg, 1904. Reprint: Berlin, 1961.
Zum altiranischen Wörterbuch. Strassburg, 1906.
"Über ein sasanidisches Rechtsbuch". — *Sb. HAW* (1910).
"Zur Kenntnis der Mitteliranischen Mundarten, I—VI". — *Sb. HAW* (1916—1925).
"Mitteliranische Studien I—VI". — *WZKM* 25 (1911), pp. 245—262; 389—409; 27 (1913), pp. 19—24; 347—374; 29 (1915), pp. 1—47; 30 (1917—1918), pp. 1—36.
Die Zendhandschriften der K. Hof-und Staatsbibliothek in München. München, 1915.
"Zum sasanidischen Recht. I—V". — *Sb. HAW* (1918—1923).
Die Frau im sasanidischen Recht. Hiedelberg, 1924.

Benveniste, E., "Les classes sociales dans la tradition avestique". — *JA*, CCXXI (1932), pp. 117—134.
"Termes et noms achéménides en araméen". — *JA*, CCXXV (1934), pp. 177—193.
"Traditions indo-iraniennes sur les classes sociales". — *JA*, CXXX (1938), pp. 529—549.
"Etudes iraniennes". — *TPS* (1945), pp. 39—78.
"Eléments perses en araméen d'Egypte". — *JA*, CCXLII (1954), pp. 297—310.
"Etudes sur quelques textes sogdiens chrétiens. I". — *JA*, CCXLIII (1955), pp. 297—337.
Etudes sur la langue ossète. Paris, 1959.
"Sur la terminologie iranienne du sacrifice". — *JA*, CCLII (1964), pp. 45—58.
"Coutumes funéraires de l'Arachosie ancienne" — *A Locust's Leg*, pp. 39—43.
"Eléments parthes en arménien". — *REArm.*, n. s. I (1964), pp. 1—39.
Titres et noms propres en iranien ancien. Paris, 1966.
Problèmes de linguistique générale. Paris, 1966.
"Le verbe iranien *nam-* en sogdien". — *BSOAS*, XXX (1967), pp. 505—511.
Le vocabulaire des institutions indo-européennes. 2 vols. Paris, 1969.
"Que signifie Vidēvdāt?" — *Henning Mem. Vol.*, pp. 37—42.

Boyce, M., *The Manichaean Hymn-Cycles in Parthian.* Oxford, 1954.
"On the Sacred Fires of the Zoroastrians". — *BSOAS*, XXXI (1968), pp. 52—68.
"The Pious Foundations of the Zoroastrians". — *BSOAS*, XXXI (1968), pp. 270—289.

"On the Zoroastrian Temple Cult of Fire". — *JAOS* 95 (1975), pp. 454—465.
A Word-List of Manichaean Middle Persian and Parthian. Leiden, 1977.

Cameron, G. G., *Persepolis Treasury Tablets*. Chicago, 1948.

Cowley, A. C., *Aramaic Papyri of the Fifth Century B.C.* Oxford, 1923.

Dandamaev, M. A., *Rabstvo v Vavilonii*. Moscow, 1974.

Darmesteter, J., "Le Hvaētvadatha". — *RHR*, 24 (1891), pp. 366—375.
Le Zend-Avesta. I—III. Paris, 1892.

Dhabhar, B. N. (ed.), *The Epistles of Mânûšchihar*. Bombay, 1912.
The Pahlavi Rivāyat accompanying the Dādistān ī Dīnīk. Bombay, 1913.
Pahlavi *dastakart*. — *Modi Mem. Vol.* Bombay, 1930, pp. 37—44.
The Persian Rivāyats of Hormazyār Framarz and others. Bombay, 1932.
Pahlavi Yasna and Visperad. — *Pahlavi Text Series*. Bombay, 1949.

Diakonoff, I. M. and Livshits, V. A., *Parthian Economic Documents from Nisa. Texts*. — *CII*, Part II, vol. II. London, *s.a.*

Dresden, M. J. (ed.), *Dēnkard. A Pahlavi Text*. Facsimile of the MS. B of the K. R. Cama Oriental Institute Bombay. Wiesbaden, 1966.

Driver, G., *Aramaic Documents of the Fifth Century B.C.* Oxford, 1954.

Ełišē, *Vasn Vardanay ew Hayocʻ paterazmin* (E. Ter-Minasean, ed.). Erevan, 1957.

Emmerick, R. E., *Saka Grammatical Studies*. Oxford, 1968.

Eznik, *Ełc ałandocʻ*. Venice, 1926.

Garsoïan, N., "Sur le titre de protecteur des pauvres". — *REArm.*, n. s. XV (1981), pp. 21—32.

Geiger, B., "Mittelpersische Wörter und Sachen". — *WZKM*, XLII (1935), pp. 114—128.
"Indo-Iranian rŭ-, *lŭ*- 'to pluck'". — *A Locust's Leg*, pp. 70—75.

Geldner, K. F., *Avesta, the Sacred Books of the Parsis*, 3 vols. Stuttgart, 1889—96.

Gershevitch, I., *A Grammar of Manichaean Sogdian*. Oxford, 1954. Reprint: Oxford, 1964.
The Avestan Hymn to Mithra. Cambridge, 1959. Reprint: Cambridge, 1967.
"Etymological Notes on Persian *mih*, *naxčīr*, *bēgāne* and *bīmār*". — *Dr. J. M. Unvala Memorial Volume*. Bombay, 1964, pp. 89—94.

Ghilain, A., *Essai sur la langue parthe*. Louvain, 1939.

Gignoux, Ph., "Les bulles sassanides de Qasr-i Abu Nasr". — *Mém. de Menasce*, pp. 169—187.

Hansen, O., *Berliner Soghdische Texte*. I, Berlin, 1941; II, Wiesbaden, 1955.

Hallock, R. T., *Persepolis Fortification Tablets*. Chicago, 1969.

Henning, W. B., "Das Verbum des Mittelpersischen der Turfanfragmente". — *ZII*, IX (1933), pp. 158—253.
Ein manichäisches Bet-und Beichtbuch. Berlin, 1936.

"A List of Middle Persian and Parthian Words". — *BSOS*, IX/1 (1937), pp. 79—92.
"Sogdian Loan-words in New Persian". — *BSOS*, X/1 (1940), pp. 93—106.
Sogdica. London, 1940.
"Sogdian Tales". — *BSOAS*, XI/3 (1945), pp. 465—487.
"The Sogdian Texts of Paris". — *BSOAS*, XI/4 (1946), pp. 713—740.
"A Sogdian Fragment of the Manichaean Cosmology". — *BSOAS*, XII (1948), pp. 306—318.
"A Pahlavi Poem". — *BSOAS*, XIII (1951), pp. 641—648.
"A Farewell to the Khagan of the Aq-Aqatärān". — *BSOAS*, XIV/3 (1952), pp. 502—520.
"The Inscription of Fīrūzābād". — *Asia Major*, IV/1 (1954), pp. 98—102.
"Notes on the Great Inscription of Šāpūr I". — *Jackson Memorial Vol.* Bombay, 1954., pp. 40—54.
"Mitteliranisch". — *Handbuch der Orientalistik.* Spuler, B. ed., I Abt. IV/1. Leyden, 1958. Pp. 20—129.
"Persian Poetical Manuscript from the Time of Rūdakī". — *A Locust's Leg*, pp. 89—104.
"The Survival of an Ancient Term". — *Indo-Iranica, Mél. G. Morgenstierne.* Wiesbaden, 1964, pp. 95—97.
"A Sogdian God". — *BSOAS*, 28 (1965), pp. 242—254.

Hoffmann, G. (ed.), *Auszüge aus syrischen Akten persischer Märtyrer*. Leipzig, 1880.

Hübschmann, H., *Armenische Grammatik*, I. Leipzig, 1895.
Persische Studien. Straßburg, 1895.

Humbach, H., *Die Gathas des Zarathustra*. 2 vols. Heidelberg, 1959.

Jamasp, H. (ed.),*Vendidâd. Avesta text with Pahlavi Translation.* I—II. Bombay, 1907.

Jamaspasa, K. M. and Humbach H. (eds. and trsls.), *Pursišnīhā. A Zoroastrian Catechism.* I—II. Wiesbaden, 1971.

Jamasp-Asana, J. M. (ed.), *The Pahlavi Texts Contained in the Codex MK...* I—II. Bombay, 1897—1913).

Junker, H. F., *The Frahang i Pahlavīk*. Heidelberg, 1911.
"Zu skr. *mudrā*". — *IF*, XXXV (1915), pp. 273—288.
Das Frahang ī Pahlavīk in zeichengemäßer Anordnung. Leipzig, 1955.

Kellens, J., *Les noms-racines de l'Avesta*. Wiesbaden, 1974.

Klingenschmitt, G., "Die Erbtochter im zoroastrischen Recht nach dem Mādiyān ē hazār dādistān". — *MSS*, XXI (1967), pp. 59—70.
"Neue Avesta-Fragmente". — *MSS*, XXIX (1971), pp. 111—174.

Kraeling, E. G., *The Brooklyn Museum Atamaic Papyri*. New Haven, 1953.

Lagarde, P. de, *Armenische Studien*. Göttingen, 1877.
Persische Studien. Leipzig, 1886.

Lentz, W.,"Die nordiranischen Elemente in der neupersischen Literatursprache bei Firdosi". — *ZII*, IV (1926), pp. 251—316.

Livshits, V. A., "New Parthian Documents from South Turkmenistan". — *Acta Antiqua Hung.*, XXV (1977), pp. 157—185.

Lommel, H., "Awestisch *drigu*, *vāstra* und Verwandtes". — *Pratidānam*. The Hague, 1969, pp. 127—133.

Lüders, H., "Eine arische Anschauung über den Vertragsbruch". — *SPAW*, XXVI (1917), pp. 366—372.

Lukonin, V. G., "Political, Social and Administrative Institutions, Taxes and Trade". — *CHI* 3/2. Cambridge, 1983. Pp. 681—746.

MacKenzie, D. N., "'Sheep' and 'show': two Pahlavi ideograns". — *Acta Orientalia*, 30 (1966), pp. 151—157.

"An Early Jewish-Persian Argument". — *BSOAS*, XXXI (1968), pp. 249—269.

"A Zoroastrian Master of Ceremonies". — *Henning Mem. Vol.*, pp. 264—271.

"The Khwarezmian Glossary", I—IV. — *BSOAS*, XXXIII/3 (1970), pp. 540—559; XXXIV/1 (1971), pp/ 74—90; XXXIV/2 (1971), pp. 314—330; XXXIV/3 (1971), pp. 521—537.

A Concise Pahlavi Dictionary. Oxford, 1971.

MacKenzie, D. N. and Perikhanian A. G., "The Model Marriage Contract in Pahlavi". — *K. R. Cama Oriental Institute Golden Jubilee Volume*. Bombay, 1969, pp. 103—112.

Macuch, M., *Das sasanidische Rechtsbuch "Mātakdān ī hazār dātistān"*. Teil II. Wiesbaden, 1981.

Rechtskasuistik und Gerichtspraxis zu Beginn des siebenten Jahrhunderts in Iran. Wiesbaden, 1993.

Madan, D. M. (ed.), *The Complete Text of the Pahlavi Dinkard*. 2 vols. Bombay, 1911.

Maricq, A., "*Res gestae divi Saporis*", *Classica et Orientalia*. Paris, 1965, pp. 37—101.

Markwart, J. (ed. and transl.), *A Catalogue of the Provincial Capitals of Ērānšahr*. Rome, 1931.

Mayrhofer, M., *Kurzgefasstes etymologisches Wörterbuch des Altindischen*. 3 vols. Heidelberg, 1956—1979.

Onomastica Persepolitana. Das altiranische Namengut der Persepolis-Täfelchen. Wien, 1973.

Menasce J.-P. de, *Une apologétique mazdéenne du IXe siècle. Škand gumānīk vičār. La solution décisive des doutes*. Fribourg, 1945.

Une encyclopédie mazdéenne le Dēnkart. — *Bibliothèque de l'École des Hautes Études*, section des sciences religieuses, LXIX. Paris, 1958.

"Le Rivāyat d'Ēmēt ī Ašavahištān". — *RHR*, 162 (1962), pp. 69—88.

"Le protecteur des pauvres dans l'Iran sassanide". — *Mélanges Massé*. Téhéran, 1963. Pp. 282—287.

Feux et fondations pieuses dans le droit sassanide. Paris, 1964.

"Some Pahlavi Words in the Original and in the Syriac Translation of Išōbōxt's Corpus Juris". — *Dr. J. M. Unvala Mem. Vol.* Bombay, 1964. pp. 6—11. [Reprint: *Studia Iranica*, 3 (1985), pp. 119—124].
"Les données géographiques dans le Mātigān i Hazār Dātistān". — *Mélanges Morgenstierne* (1964), pp. 149—154.
"Textes pehlevis sur les qanats". — *Acta Orientalia* 30 (1966), pp. 167—175. [Reprint: *Studia Iranica*, 3 (1985), pp. 145—154].
"Formules juridiques et syntaxe pehlevie". — *Bulletin of the Iranian Culture Foundation*, I (1969), pp. 11—20. [Reprint: *Studia Iranica*, 3 (1985), pp. 109—119].

Modi, J. J., *Mâdigân-i-Hazār Dâdîstân. A Photozincographed Facsimile of a Ms. belonging to the M. L. H. Hâtariâ Library in the Zarthoshti Anjuman Âtashbeharâm.* Poona, 1901.
The Religious Ceremonies and Customs of the Parsees. Bombay, 1937.

Montgomery, J. A., *Aramaic Incantation Texts from Nippur.* Philadelphia, 1913.

Morgenstierne, G., *An Etymological Vocabulary of Pashto.* Oslo, 1927.
Indo-Iranian Frontier Languages, I—IV. Oslo—Bergen—Tromsö, 1929—1973.
Movsēs Xorenac'i, Patmut'iwn Hayoc'. Tiflis, 1913.

Nöldeke, Th., *Geschichte der Perser und Araber zur Zeit der Sasaniden.* Leiden, 1879.
Review of Prym, E. and Socin, A., "Der neu-aramäische Dialekt des Ṭûr 'Abdîn". — *ZDMC*, XXXV (1881), pp. 218—235.

Nyberg, H. S., *Hilfsbuch des Pehlevi*, II. Uppsala, 1931.
"Contribution à la flexion verbale iranienne". — *MO*, XXI (1937), pp. 63—86.
A Manual of Pahlavi, II. Wiesbaden, 1974.

Pagliaro, A., "L'anticresi nel diritto sasanidico". — *RSO*, XV (1935), pp. 275—315.
"Note di lessicografia pahlavica". — *RSO*, XXII (1974), pp. 60—73.
"Note di lessicografia pahlavica, VIII: *pat kartak*, una formula della terminologia giuridica del *MhD*". — *RSO*, XXIII (1948), pp. 52—68.
"Aspetti del diritto Sāsānidico: *hačašmānd 'interdictum'*". — *RSO*, XXIV (1949), pp. 120—130.
"Notes on Pahlavi Lexicography". — *Jackson Mem. Vol.* Bombay, 1954, pp. 72—83.

P'awstos Buzand, *Patmut'iwn Hayoc'.* Venice, 1933.

Périkhanian, A. G., "Agnatičeskije gruppy v drevnem Irane". — *VDI* (1968/3), pp. 28—52.
"Notes sur le lexique iranien et arménien". — *REArm.*, n. s.V (1968), pp. 9—23.
"Sur arm. *panduxt*". — *REArm.*, n. s. VI (1969), pp. 1—14.
"On Some Pahlavi Legal Terms". — *Henning Mem. Vol.* London, 1970. Pp. 349—357.
"Častnye celevye fondy v drevnem Irane i problema proisxoždenija vakfa". — *VDI* (1973/1), pp. 3—24.

Sasanidskij sudebnik: "Kniga tysjači sudebnyx rešenij" (Mātakdān î hazār dātastān). Erevan, 1973.
"Ordalija i kljatva v sudoproizvodstve do-islamskogo Irana". — *Peredneaziatskij Sbornik*, III. Moskva, 1979, pp. 182—192.
Obščestvo i pravo Irana v parfjanskij i sasanidskij periody. Moscow, 1983.
"Iranian Society and Law". — *CHI*, 3/2. Cambridge, 1983. Pp.627—680.
"Un terme pour la 'dot' en iranien et en arménien". — *REArm.*, XX (1986—1987), pp. 47—53.
"'Protivnik (v sudebnom processe)' i 'vrag' v iranskom i v armjanskom". — *Materialy*. Erevan, 1994, pp. 107—125.

Pokorny, J., *Indogermanisches etymologisches Wörterbuch*. Bern—München, 1959.

Reichelt, H., *Der Frahang ī oīm I—II*. Wien, 1900—1901.
"Aramäische Inschriften aus Kappadocien". — *WZKM* (1901), pp. 51—56.

Sachau, E. (ed. and transl.), *Corpus juris des persischen Erzbischofs Jesubocht. Erbrecht oder Canones des persischen Erzbischofs Simeon. Erbrecht des Patriarchen Mâr Abhâ*. Berlin, 1914.

Salemann, C., "Mittelpersisch" — *Grundriss der iranischen Philologie*, I/3. Strassburg, 1901, pp. 249—332.
Manichaeische Studien I. St.-Pétersbourg, 1908.

Sarkissian, G. H., "Les deux significations du terme *dastakert* dans les sources arméniennes". — *REArm.*, n. s.V (1968), pp. 43—50.

Schrader, O. and Nehring, A., *Reallexicon der indogermanischen Altertumskunde*. 2 vols. Berlin, 1917—1929.

Schwartz, M., "Miscellanea Iranica". — *Henning Mem. Vol.*, pp. 385—394.
"On the Vocabulary of the Khwarezmian *Muqaddimatu l-'Adab*". — *ZDMG*, 120/2 (1971), pp. 288—304.
"Scatology and Eschatology in Zoroaster". — *Acta Iranica*, II sér. XI.Leiden, 1985, pp. 473—496.

Shaked, Sh., "Some Legal and Administrative Terms of the Sasanian Period". — *Monum. Nyberg* (1975), pp. 213—225.

Tavadia, J. C. (ed.), *Šāyast-nē-šāyast. A Pahlavi Text on religious customs*. Hamburg, 1930.

Telegdi, S., "Essai sur la phonétique des emprunts iraniens en araméen talmudique". — *JA*, CCXXVI (1935), pp. 177—256.

Unvâlâ, M. R. (ed.), *Dârâb Hormazyâr's Rivāyat*. I—II. Bombay, 1922.

Waag, A., *Nīrangistān, der Avestatraktat über die rituellen Vorschriften*. Leipzig, 1941.

Widengren, G., "Über einige Probleme in der altpersischen Geschichte". — *Festschrift für Leo Brandt zum 60 Geburtstag*, Meixner, J. and Kegel, G. edd. Köln, 1968, pp. 517—533.

Wolff, F., *Avesta. Die Heiligen Bücher der Parsen*. Straßburg, 1910.

Zaehner, R. C., "Aparmänd". — *JRAS* (1940), pp. 35—45.

About Mazda Publishers

Since its establishment in 1980, Mazda Publishers has built a strong reputation for excellence in both scholarly and trade publishing. The company has consistently produced high-quality texts, reference materials, literary works, and general interest books aimed at both researchers and the general public. Mazda's diverse catalog spans a wide array of subjects, including art and architecture, politics, religion, history, language, and culture.

At the heart of Mazda Publishers' mission lies the study of what we refer to as the Iranicas—an academic exploration of the many facets of Iranian civilization throughout history. This includes not only the political, social, and cultural dimensions of the Iranian world, but also the broader influence of Iranian elements across regions and time periods. While modern Iran is central to this focus, Mazda Publishers also explores the enduring legacy of Iranian civilization in areas beyond its contemporary borders—reaching from ancient China to the Mediterranean shores. This broad approach is essential due to the inclusive and eclectic nature of Iranian civilization.

In line with this vision, Mazda Publishers has produced works on a variety of subjects, including the history and cultures of Armenia, Tajikistan, Afghanistan, and the countries surrounding the Persian Gulf. The publishing house has also explored themes in Islamic studies, Zoroastrianism, Jewish history, the Kurdish people, Ottoman Turkey, Mughal India, and Egypt, among others. This ongoing commitment to expanding the scope of Iranian studies ensures that Mazda will continue to produce vital and diverse scholarship for years to come.

About the Publisher

Dr. A. K. Jabbari, the founder of Mazda Publishers, is a distinguished figure in the field of Iranian studies. Holding a B.S. and M.S. in Aerospace Engineering from Pennsylvania State University, as well as a Ph.D. in Economics from Washington University in St. Louis, Dr. Jabbari has significantly contributed to the dissemination of scholarly works on Iran and Persian culture.

Through Mazda Publishers, Dr. Jabbari has played a pivotal role in expanding the availability of academic resources on a range of topics related to Iran and its historical and cultural spheres. The publishing house has produced numerous books on Persian literature, history, art, philosophy, and linguistics, becoming an invaluable resource for scholars, researchers, and enthusiasts alike. Under Dr. Jabbari's leadership, Mazda Publishers has earned a reputation as a respected and trusted source in the field of Iranian studies.

For more informaion please visit www.mazdapublishers.com